Alex Lewis
Andrew Abbate
Tom Pacyk

Microsoft® Lync
Server 2010

UNLEASHED

D1511579

 800 East 96th Street, Indianapolis, Indiana 46240 USA

Microsoft® Lync Server 2010 Unleashed

ISBN-13: 978-0-672-33034-6
ISBN-10: 0-672-33034-2

The Library of Congress Cataloging-in-Publication data is on file.

Printed in the United States of America

Second Printing July 2011

Trademarks

All terms mentioned in this book that are known to be trademarks or service marks have been appropriately capitalized. Sams Publishing cannot attest to the accuracy of this information. Use of a term in this book should not be regarded as affecting the validity of any trademark or service mark.

Warning and Disclaimer

Every effort has been made to make this book as complete and as accurate as possible, but no warranty or fitness is implied. The information provided is on an "as is" basis. The authors and the publisher shall have neither liability nor responsibility to any person or entity with respect to any loss or damages arising from the information contained in this book.

Bulk Sales

Sams Publishing offers excellent discounts on this book when ordered in quantity for bulk purchases or special sales. For more information, please contact

U.S. Corporate and Government Sales
1-800-382-3419
corpsales@pearsontechgroup.com

For sales outside of the U.S., please contact

International Sales
international@pearsoned.com

Associate Publisher
Greg Wiegand

Acquisitions Editor
Loretta Yates

Development Editor
Sondra Scott

Managing Editor
Kristy Hart

Project Editor
Jovana San Nicolas-Shirley

Copy Editor
Ginny Munroe

Indexer
Lisa Stumpf

Proofreader
Mike Henry

Technical Editor
Jeff Guillet

Publishing Coordinator
Cindy Teeters

Cover Designer
Gary Adair

Compositor
Nonie Ratcliff

Contributing Writers
Chris Amaris
Mitch Steiner
Marshall Harrison

Contents at a Glance

Table of Contents

About the Authors

Alex Lewis has a mixed background in telecommunications, IT, and consulting with more than 15 years experience. Alex has worked with a wide range of environments from small organizations to large enterprises requiring complex or custom communications solutions. Alex is a strong believer in the power of business and technology alignment using technological solutions to reduce costs and drive revenue. Including titles on Active Directory and Exchange, this is the seventh book that Alex has participated in writing. He currently is a principal consultant at Convergent Computing in Oakland, California and leads its Unified Communications practice. He loves a challenge and brings a wealth of experience to each new engagement.

Andrew Abbate is a 17-year veteran of consulting and IT and has a wealth of practical knowledge about communications, collaboration, and security. Andrew has helped some of the largest and most complex environments in North America improve their capability to quickly and securely communicate and collaborate with internal and external resources. In addition to his Lync and OCS background, Andrew has written several other books covering topics such as Exchange, Active Directory, and information security. Andrew currently enjoys the position of principal consultant and partner at Convergent Computing where he continues to consult with both large and small clients to help improve their IT practices.

Tom Pacyk, MCITP, MCSE, is a senior systems engineer specializing in Lync, OCS, and Exchange projects while working at ExtraTeam in the Bay Area, CA. Tom began his career as a systems administrator and has moved into working as a consultant for the last five years where he designs and implements collaboration solutions for large and small customers. His work began with the original Exchange 2000 instant messaging service and he has been involved with implementations of every version of the product since then and now with Lync Server 2010. Outside of work, Tom runs a blog related to Microsoft Lync and Exchange topics.

Dedication

*This book is dedicated to my best friend who kept me company through all the late nights,
my pug, Pugsley. Thank you for the companionship and warm nuzzles
encouraging me to keep writing way too late into the night.
If only I could teach you to write for me, that would be a trick!*
—Alex Lewis

*I dedicate this book to my niece Nora. Seeing the joy you've brought to your family
reminds me that I need to keep life in perspective and focus on the truly important things.*
—Andrew Abbate

*I dedicate this book to my fiancée, Elizabeth, for putting up with the endless late nights
and lost weekends of writing with an incredible amount of patience.
Thank you so much for your support the entire time.*
—Tom Pacyk

Acknowledgments

Alex Lewis: First, thank you to the Lync team at Microsoft, including Miru Gunarajah and the whole Dr. Rez team. You've done a great job with the product and thanks for giving us an opportunity to play with it a bit earlier than everyone else! Next, of course, thank you to the team at Sams including Loretta Yates, Jovana Shirley, and development editor extraordinaire Sondra Scott. Without them, the book wouldn't exist or likely be readable. To my coauthors Andrew and Tom, thank you for joining me in this endeavor and thank you for all the troubleshooting help and guidance you give me on a regular basis.

To all my friends, thank you for putting up with the late nights and all the times I couldn't join you for a night out. The next round's on me. And to Kate, you've been a great friend and brought me take-out or pizza more times than I can count so that I could continue working uninterrupted. I owe you big time!

Andrew Abbate: As always, it's a real trick to try to make sure one thanks all the people that make these books possible. I'll start off with thanking the great folks at Sams who make these books possible and who perform the impressive task of taking the materials we produce and turning it into an impressively polished book. I'd like to thank my coauthors Alex and Tom, for helping to keep me on track and making this book as painless as possible.

Last and certainly not least, I'd like to thanks my friends for being supportive and accepting of the fact that I disappear for months on end when I start one of these projects. Thanks for always being there.

Tom Pacyk: Writing a book for the first time seemed like such a great idea when the opportunity presented itself, but once the writing began I found myself beginning to think otherwise. The process had its ups and downs, but it's a great feeling now that it's been completed, and I'm very proud of the work we've compiled here.

Thanks so much to the Sams team for putting it all together, and to my co-authors, Alex and Andrew, for their assistance and tremendous efforts on this book.

I'd also like to thank John Weber for giving me a kick in the right direction when I started my consulting career. I don't know if I would have reached this point without his mentoring and advice back when I started out Portland, OR. His infamous line, "Let's not confuse the issue with facts," continues to be one of my all-time favorite quotes.

Lastly, I'd like to thank my parents, family, and friends for all their support over the years and all their assistance in my career. I couldn't have done this without their help.

We Want to Hear from You!

As the reader of this book, *you* are our most important critic and commentator. We value your opinion and want to know what we're doing right, what we could do better, what areas you'd like to see us publish in, and any other words of wisdom you're willing to pass our way.

You can email or write me directly to let me know what you did or didn't like about this book—as well as what we can do to make our books stronger.

Please note that I cannot help you with technical problems related to the topic of this book, and that due to the high volume of mail I receive, I might not be able to reply to every message.

When you write, please be sure to include this book's title and author as well as your name and phone or email address. I will carefully review your comments and share them with the author and editors who worked on the book.

Email: feedback@samspublishing.com

Mail: Greg Wiegand
        Associate Publisher
        Sams Publishing
        800 East 96th Street
        Indianapolis, IN 46240 USA

Reader Services

Visit our website and register this book at informit.com/register for convenient access to any updates, downloads, or errata that might be available for this book.

Introduction

The authors of this book have been working with Communications Server since the Live Communications Server 2003 days. I remember when it launched on December 29, 2003. Back then, Windows Messenger 5.0 was the main client used and the terminology was completely different. However, even then, TLS communication was supported, although most IT departments went with the more familiar TCP option instead. Needless to say, a lot has changed through the years. Most people I work with don't realize that Lync Server is a fifth-generation product! It is even older if you count the Exchange Instant Messenger Service that was included in Exchange Server 2000, which was pulled out to build the first version of Live Communications Server.

In the beginning, Live Communications Server 2003 was only an IM server. With Lync Server, it has evolved into many more things, including

- ▶ Web and audio conferencing server

- ▶ Unified Communications (UC) integration across many other platforms, such as Office, SharePoint, and Exchange

- ▶ Soft phone

- ▶ Video conferencing system

- ▶ PBX replacement

Back in 2003, IM was perceived as a novelty. No one used it to conduct business or even imagined it as a gateway to multimodal communications. Starting with Office Communications Server 2007 R2 and continuing with Lync Server, Microsoft introduced the concept of Communications Enabled Business Processes (CEBP).

> **NOTE**
>
> It seems every vendor and analyst defines CEBP in a different way. However, for this book, we stick with a more generic definition. CEBP adds a communications medium to a business process with the intent of streamlining and automating the process or with the intent of reducing human latency through real-time communications.

Chronology of Lync Server

Let's go through some history and chronology to better understand why and how Communication Server 2010 came to be.

- ▶ **Microsoft Exchange Server 2000 Instant Messenger Service**—It's hard to believe so few people, even Exchange administrators, have heard of the Exchange 2000 IM service. However, it is not hard to believe that even fewer deployed it. It was a rudimentary service with little integration to Exchange or other Microsoft Server products. Later versions utilized special engines, whereas the Exchange 2000 IM service leveraged an in-house middleware platform called Exchange Interprocess Communication (EXIPC) to translate between IIS 5 and Exchange. The solution was essentially composed of two types of servers: home servers and routing servers.

Home servers handled IM communications similarly to a front end in Lync Server. However, there was little Active Directory integration. That's where routing servers came in. If two users were homed to different home servers, they would need to jump through a bunch of hoops to talk with each other. The routing server acted as a bridge connecting any two home servers. It was a basic solution, especially at a time when public IM providers such as Yahoo! and AOL offered significantly more in terms of functionality.

▶ **Live Communications Server 2003**—Instant messaging functions were taken out of Exchange and given their own platforms with the 2003 wave of Microsoft Server products. It was code named Greenwich and initially called Office Real-Time Communications Server 2003 before being renamed Live Communications Server 2003 just prior to release. It wasn't long before it was better known by its three-letter acronym LCS 2003. LCS 2003 was the first version to support certificates and offer TLS-encrypted communications as the recommended method. LCS 2003 was also the first version to support enterprise archival of IM communications, although it was rarely implemented because the compliance regulations in effect today simply didn't exist or include IM conversations in 2003.

▶ **Live Communications Server 2005**—Live Communications Server 2005, or LCS 2005 as it's more commonly known, was the first widely deployed version of the Microsoft real-time communications platform. It was code named Vienna. Although one might argue that LCS 2005 was Microsoft's first attempt at a unified communications platform, few organizations deployed functions beyond IM and presence. LCS 2005 added new functions including a more advanced presence engine that would change a user's presence status based on information from a user's Exchange calendar and remote access through the access proxy role. LCS 2005 SP1 added the capability to communicate with Office Communications Server 2007 users and a number of other features. In today's Microsoft nomenclature, it would likely be called Live Communications Server 2005 R2.

▶ **Office Communications Server 2007**—Code named RTC12, this is when the creative codenames went the way of the dodo bird. Commonly known as OCS 2007, the platform made huge jump in terms of functionality and acceptance. OCS 2007 added the following functions:

  ▶ **On-Premise Web Conferencing**—The ROI from bringing web conferencing in-house almost always justified the cost of implementing OCS, and thus, it became an important feature. However, voice conferencing was PC-only or needed to be hosted through a third-party provider.

- ▶ **Multiparty IM**—It might seem insignificant to add more than one person to an IM conversation, but it became an important market differentiator compared to products such as IBM SameTime and Cisco CUPS.

- ▶ **Enhanced presence**—Also known as "rich presence," it enabled users to expose additional information beyond the red, green, and yellow gumdrop that was standard at the time. This information included name, title, and detailed calendar information. It also included a multitiered access mechanism called levels of access to display different amounts of personal information to different tiers of users.

- ▶ **Improved federation**—Open federation and widespread adoption of OCS 2007 changed the landscape of intercompany communication. E-mail became secondary for partner communication as users could see real time availability data and collaborate immediately removing the latency inherent to asynchronous methods of communication.

- ▶ **Enterprise Voice**—It's simply not possible to call your solution a Unified Communications solution without the inclusion of a voice platform. Although it was basic, it was a proactive step in the right direction because almost every other UC vendor would also roll out a combined IM, meeting, and voice platform around the same time or soon after.

▶ **Office Communications Server 2007 R2**—When combined with Exchange Unified Messaging, this was the first version that could realistically be considered a PBX replacement, although it still lacked many traditional PBX features. Code named Wave 13 or W13, OCS 2007 R2 added a bunch of collaboration and voice features as noted in the following:

- ▶ **Call Delegation**—Also known as the boss-secretary function, this enabled delegates to answer a call for another user. The primary user also notified the delegate answered the call. This function was designed to be used with the Communicator Attendant Console. Much like with delegates in Exchange, the assistant could be given the rights to do almost everything for the manager yet make it appear that the manager was doing the work. A full call delegation feature list includes call screening for audio, video, or IM; joining a voice conference on behalf of the manager; checking voicemail for the manager; initiating a person-to-person call on behalf of the manager; initiating conference calls on behalf of the manager; and transferring calls to the manager.

- ▶ **Team Call**—A simple workflow that enabled call forwarding to multiple people. The call could be forwarded to specific people in sequence or in parallel. This was often used for out-of-office or out-to-lunch functions.

- ▶ **Group Chat**—A separate server role that also required a separate client from Communicator. It allowed persistent chat similar to IRC.

▶ **Desktop sharing**—This included desktop sharing from the Communicator client and with anonymous users through the Communicator Web Access service.

▶ **Audio conferencing**—Much like web conferencing in OCS 2007, this is another great ROI story. Third-party audio conferencing services can be expensive; tens of thousands of dollars per month can be saved by bringing it in-house. Many companies deployed OCS 2007 R2 strictly for this functionality; everything else was just a bonus.

▶ **Response Group Service**—This is Microsoft's version of a simple IVR workflow. It's often used for small call centers or IT help desks.

▶ **SIP trunking**—SIP trunking is still new but seeing a growth in adoption. Essentially, it enables OCS 2007 R2 to connect to a SIP trunking provider that handles all outbound call routing. Although the process can be a little complex to set up initially, it greatly eases call routing topology because everything goes to the cloud service provider.

▶ **Improved codecs**—Improved codecs for voice and video enable better voice quality and more tolerance for nonideal networks. They also enable HD-quality video between clients over reasonable network links.

How This Book Is Organized

Everything you'll want to know about new features for Lync Server is included in Chapters 1–4. These chapters describe new features and benefits.

You will find that the improvements Microsoft has made to Lync Server are not only evolutionary, but they represent a major step forward for UC. Lync Server solidifies Microsoft's role as market leader in the UC field.

CAUTION

This book covers all aspects of Lync Server. However, the book does assume you have at least a cursory knowledge of the basics of Active Directory, DNS, and the associated infrastructures of each.

This book is organized into nine parts, each one made up of several chapters focusing on a different core area of Lync Server.

▶ **Part I, "Overview"**—This part provides an introduction to Lync Server not only from the perspective of a general technology overview, but also to note what is truly new in Lync Server and what has compelled organizations we've worked with to implement it during the beta phase.

▶ **Part II, "Microsoft Lync Server 2010 Server Roles"**—This part provides an in-depth discussion of all the Lync Server roles including a general overview, the installation process, configuration, administration, troubleshooting, and best practices. Each role is examined in detail with step-by-step installation instructions and valuable screenshots.

▶ **Part III, "External Dependencies"**—Lync Server leverages many other technologies including Active Directory, DNS, certificates, and SQL Server. It also has specific prerequisites and requirements around network latency, bandwidth, and firewall and reverse proxies for external access and federation. Lync Server relies heavily on Active Directory for integration to other Microsoft Server components such as Microsoft Exchange and Microsoft SharePoint.

▶ **Part IV, "Administration and Management"**—This part covers common administration tasks and the Communications Server Management Shell, which is the heart of all administration tasks. It moves on to discuss monitoring Lync Server through Microsoft Systems Center Operations Manager and the backup and restore processes for all the Communications Server roles.

▶ **Part V, "Migrating from Older Versions"**—This part reviews the process of upgrading from Office Communications Server 2007 and 2007 R2. It also explains how to upgrade from Live Communications Server. A green field deployment is easy; migrating users, response groups, and dial plans from previous versions of Communications Server can cause headaches. A solid, tested migration strategy is important for minimizing downtime and ensuring a successful migration. The bad news is there is only one way to do it. The good news is that it is explained in great detail in Part V.

▶ **Part VI, "Voice"**—Microsoft has heavily invested in making Lync Server a voice-focused platform. There are huge improvements from previous platforms. Lync Server now supports branch office survivability, e911, and improved conferencing. This part covers PBX integration, enterprise voice, and audio conferencing. With these improvements, Communications Server is ready to be a full PBX replacement. It can even work as a call center solution integrated with solutions from Aspect for larger deployments, Altigen for smaller deployments, and a host of other partners.

▶ **Part VII, "Integration with Other Applications"**—Lync Server has unique communications and collaboration features when integrated with other applications. Presence can be brought into a SharePoint page or Exchange Outlook Web Application. The Exchange Unified Messaging server completes the Microsoft UC solution. However, Microsoft didn't stop there. There is also an open API called Unified Communications Managed API (UCMA) for developers to create their applications and extensions that plug into the UC ecosystem.

▶ **Part VIII, "Clients"**—From a user's perspective, the solution *is* the client. That's all a user sees. The Communicator 2010 client is designed to be easier to use with more information in the main page and not hidden in menus and submenus. For example, the dial pad is front and center for all Communicator conversations.

In addition to soft clients, this part also has a chapter on UC endpoints including headsets, webcams, and handset phones. Due to popular demand, many new types of endpoints are available for Lync Server, including a true conference room phone, which fills a major gap for previous versions.

▶ **Part IX, "Planning for Deployment"**—Every good deployment starts with a good plan. This part can help you build a plan for your organization. It covers the new virtualization policy that enables all roles to be virtualized, designing a nonvoice deployment, designing edge architecture, and planning for a voice deployment. Although Communications Server expertise is required, many other skill sets are also important to plan a successful deployment. Communications Server touches many other areas including PBX/telecommunications, Active Directory, Exchange, and the enterprise network. Although bringing in an expert is always a good strategy, this part educates you with the basics for planning your deployment.

The real-world experience we have working with Lync Server, our combined experience with the platform since its beginnings, and our field experience deploying Communications Server enable us to present this information to you. We made the mistakes, found the workarounds, and simply know what works and how to make things work. We know you will find this book valuable with the planning and deployment of your Lync Server infrastructure.

PART I

Overview

IN THIS PART

What Is Microsoft Lync Server?

Lync Server is the latest incarnation of a product line dating back to 2000. Microsoft has made a substantial commitment to providing a single integrated communications suite that enables users to communicate with each other more easily. Lync Server represents a fundamental shift in how telephony is handled. Lync Server attempts to remove telephony from dedicated systems such as Private Branch Exchanges (PBX) and places them in a software-based infrastructure that can more easily adapt to changing needs and so they can be extended to provide new functionality as technologies change.

Picture a world in which users are no longer tied to a single device for their communication endpoint. They can choose to use a traditional style desk phone, a headset attached to a laptop, or a mobile device to place and receive calls. Not only do they have these choices, but these choices also don't need to be static. Rather than being assigned a phone and a phone number, a user can log into any supported phone with his own identity and that phone becomes his phone. Calls to users are routed to this device or other devices that they have requested and ring at the same time. Rich presence information in the system enables a user to know whether another user is available even before picking up the phone to call the user.

Lync Server attempts to enable users to alter their forms of communications seamlessly as the situation demands without having to make drastic changes. For example, Andrew might have a question for Sean. Andrew looks at his Lync Server client and sees that Sean is listed as available. As such, Andrew sends Sean an Instant Message via Communications Server asking him whether he has a moment for a question. Sean replies, "Yes." After a few messages, Sean determines that Andrew's question is a little complicated to handle over IM and suggests they speak by phone. Andrew is able to convert the IM to a point-to-point voice chat with a single click. Now Andrew and Sean are able to speak directly. After a few minutes, Andrew determines that he still doesn't quite understand what Sean is explaining and asks whether Sean could show him what he means. At this point, Andrew converts the call to a video conference with application sharing. Sean is able to draw out his explanation via his favorite application and explains it as he goes by simply talking.

In this scenario, everything can be accomplished by two people on beaches over laptops. Lync Server doesn't require participants to reserve video conferencing resources ahead of time, to schedule conferences, or even to use specific hardware. Through these functions, Lync Server is able to make the world a much smaller place by enabling users to dynamically control their own communications and to be available almost anywhere at most any time.

Lync Server at a High Level

Lync Server is an integrated suite of communications tools that enable point-to-point or point-to-multipoint communications across various mediums. Lync Server enables simple instant messaging between two or more users for simple text-based communications. Lync Server also enables voice chat between clients. This voice chat is entirely IP-based and simple to configure. This enables end users on the same network to communicate between each other. This functionality can be extended beyond simple point-to-point conversations. Through the use of media gateways or a PBX, one can effectively convert an IP conversation on one side to a traditional phone call on the other. This is an example of Voice over IP. By transcoding through a gateway, a VoIP endpoint can talk to a traditional Public Switched Telephone Network to allow communications to a non-VoIP endpoint.

Lync Server also enables more complex methods of conferencing such as audio/video conferencing. Lync Server enables users to use anything from a simple web cam to a dedicated video conferencing system. Users on both sides of the conference can see each other. In large A/V conferences, Lync Server enables one to separate the voice and video into two different mediums to allow for higher numbers of participants.

An extension of the video conferencing is the capability to share applications with other participants. One participant can share an application or even an entire desktop, granting other users control so that they can interactively work on the same document or presentation.

Earlier versions of Communications Server introduced the concept of presence where one can view the status of their contacts in real time. This presence has been extended into other applications such as Microsoft Office, Outlook, and SharePoint. Presence enables you to quickly determine whether another user is available before going through the effort of trying to contact that person. You can literally look at a document created by a coworker that is stored in SharePoint and based on the information showing the document owner, that coworker can also see the status of that document owner and contact that document owner with a single click. This click can start an IM conversation or a voice call. It doesn't matter where the document owner is because the call can either ring a desk phone, a mobile device, or a laptop, assuming the coworker is logged into Communicator.

Instant Messaging

Instant Messaging (IM) is the oldest function available in Lync Server. This is the now-ubiquitous function of being able to see that a contact is online and to send him or her a simple text-based message. Lync Server takes this IM capability to a whole new level. Lync Server continues to support Public IM Connectivity (PIC) with AOL, MSN, and Yahoo! IM, but it is now easier than ever to federate with other Communications Server environments.

Federation effectively sets up a connection between multiple implementations of Communications Server that enable both sides to selectively share presence information with one another. This is especially useful for partner relationships where it's necessary for the partners to quickly contact one another. One can receive an e-mail from a partner or have a question, and rather than launch into a series of back-and-forth e-mail messages, the partners can simply fire IMs back and forth.

> **NOTE**
>
> Although this might seem like a small distinction in methods of communications, groups that manage e-mail systems are quite happy when users are able to offload communications to methods such as IM. No e-mail administrator likes to find out that 15% of all the data stored in mail systems is "Where do you want to go for lunch?" conversations.

Client-to-Client Chat

Client-to-client chat in Lync Server is easy to configure and support because it doesn't need to integrate into any other systems. Much like IM, a point-to-point conversation is created, and in this case, the input and output is audio rather than text. As one might suspect, this requires more bandwidth and is sensitive to network latency, but is generally a fairly low resource requirement. For example, Lync Server couple with the G.729 Codec utilizes only 8 Kbps for a conversation. Because these client-to-client chats go across a data network only, it is easy to allow these to cross one's wide area network (WAN) or even the Internet.

> **TIP**
>
> Because the encoding and decoding are handled entirely by the Communicator client, there is no need for special media gateways. Those aren't needed until one talks from Communicator to a traditional Public Switched Telephone Network (PSTN).

Audio/Video Conferencing

A popular feature of Lync Server continues to be audio/video (A/V) conferencing. This feature enables face-to-face communications between compatible systems. Although Communicator -based video conferencing is well supported, it is up to the Lync Server administrator to ensure that cross-platform video conferencing is supported.

CAUTION

Although most A/V conferencing systems agree on at least one common codec and protocol, this isn't guaranteed to be the case in all situations. If one is considering a proprietary video conferencing setup in a location, it is important to work with the vendor to ensure its compatibility with Lync Server first before purchasing it.

Enterprise Voice

The big focus in Lync Server is in the area of Enterprise Voice. This is to say that Lync Server intends to be the entire voice system. Between soft clients running on desktops and laptops to standalone desk phones to receptionist call routing consoles to conference room phones, Lync Server is capable of providing the functionalities needed to maintain a full phone system.

Lync Server is able to bridge internal Lync Server calls to external phone systems through PSTN gateways and other forms of transcoding. Based on Session Initiation Protocol (SIP), Lync Server is able to interoperate with many other existing voice systems.

An interesting coexistence option offered with Lync Server is the concept of remote call control. Although this capability is not emphasized in Lync Server, it can allow the Communicator client to place calls via an existing PBX or IP-PBX phone. This enables companies to more easily integrate Lync Server into an existing telephony infrastructure while older components are eventually retired in favor of Lync Server–based functionality.

PBX Replacement

Lync Server provides all the functionality currently provided by a traditional PBX system. This includes the familiar concepts of call routing, call parking, call transfer, conferencing, single-purpose phones, and so on. Lync Server is able to integrate with most PBX solutions through the use of gateways and mediation servers. Similarly, it can replace existing PBX systems either through attrition or via a green field replacement.

Historically the big roadblock to Communications Server replacing a traditional PBX was in the area of equivalent functionality. Features such as call parking, where an attendant can receive a call and then transfer it to a pool of public phones by tying it to an extension, didn't exist (for example, "Bob, pick up on line 4"). Another big gap was in the area of 911 services, where the abstracted nature of VoIP made it difficult to determine where a caller was physically when he dialed another line.

By tracking location specific information from both the client and the network, Lync Server can work around this limitation. Lync Server actually tracks significantly more information than a traditional PBX. This enables useful features such as placing a "subject" line into a call. Imagine that instead of simple caller ID information displaying on your phone, it actually said, "Incoming call from Bob: Discuss potential destinations for lunch." This enables users to better prioritize their time by knowing the purpose of a call ahead of time.

Presence

Presence has been around since Live Communications Server 2005. Presence provides an additional level of information around contacts in Communications Server-aware applications. At a simple level, Presence tells a Lync Server user that another Lync Server user is online. More specifically, it tells whether they are busy, in a call, away from the desk, or do not wish to be disturbed.

Although it might seem minor, knowing you aren't going to get in touch with someone if you call can be useful. Actually, it can be useful both ways. Many times, a person won't bother to call another person if he knows the other person will not answer. Other times, someone might want to intentionally call someone who isn't available so that they can avoid a lengthy conversation and simply leave a quick message instead. This is a wonderful use of Presence data.

Potential Presence statuses include

- ▶ Unknown
- ▶ Offline
- ▶ Available
- ▶ Away
- ▶ Busy
- ▶ Do Not Disturb

Other applications can also process Presence information. One of the more interesting examples is how a Windows Mobile phone and Microsoft Exchange can interact with Lync Server and Presence. In addition to the Communicator client, Presence information can also be determined by viewing a user's free/busy data in Exchange. So, while Fred might be logged into Communicator 14, Lync Server might know that based on his calendar, Fred is in a meeting from 4 pm until 5 pm and shows him as Busy in his Presence information.

Toll Bypass

A popular use of VoIP systems such as Lync Server is the capability to bypass some long-distance toll charges through the use of call routing. For example, if a company has an office in San Francisco and an office in New York and these two locations are on a common WAN call between the sites, which are routed internally via Lync Server and VoIP, the call is effectively free because the data network is already paid for.

If, on the other hand, a user in San Francisco needs to call an external user in New Jersey, there are two ways to handle this call. Either the VoIP call from San Francisco would immediately go out the PSTN gateway to the long-distance provider, or, the call could first route through the New York office and then out of the PSTN gateway.

Why would one want to route the call in this manner? Most likely, the charges for New York to call New Jersey are lower than the charges for San Francisco to call New Jersey. Through the use of dialing plans and call routing, a Lync Server administrator can set up rules about how various calls are routed. These rules are typically done by area code so that the number of rules is somewhat manageable.

Lync Server Related Acronyms

This book introduces a lot of new concepts and tends to utilize a lot of acronyms. Therefore, it's useful to familiarize yourself with the following acronyms to absorb the information in the upcoming chapters more quickly.

▶ **Call Admission Control (CAC)**—A method of preventing oversubscription of VoIP networks. Unlike QoS tools, CAC is call-aware and acts as a preventive congestion control by attempting to route calls across other media before making a determination to block a call rather than impacting the quality of existing calls.

▶ **Call Detail Records (CDR)**—A record produced by a phone system containing details of calls that have passed through it. They track information such as the number of the calling party, the number of the called party, the time of call initiation, the duration of the call, the route by which the call was routed, and any fault condition encountered. These records might be used for cross billing, for tracking of an employee's usage of the system, or for monitoring system uptime and issues.

▶ **Client Access License (CAL)**—A software license that entitles a user to access specific systems or specific features in a system. Usually these come in two flavors: Standard and Enterprise.

▶ **Common Intermediate Format (CIF)**—A format used to standardize the vertical and horizontal resolutions in video signals, often in video conferencing systems.

▶ **Communicator Web Access (CWA)**—The browser-based Communicator client provided by Lync Server.

▶ **Direct Inward Dialing (DID)**—A service offered by telephone companies wherein one or more trunk links is provided to a customer for connection to the customer's PBX. Incoming calls are routed to internal destination numbers at the PBX. This enables a company to have significantly more internal lines than it does external lines.

▶ **Dual-tone multi-frequency (DTMF)**—A method for providing telecommunication signaling over analog telephones lines in the voice frequency band. DTMF is also referred to as *Touch Tone*. This technology enables users to initiate events in the phone system by simply pressing a button on a keypad.

▶ **Extensible Markup Language (XML)**—A set of rules for encoding documents in a machine-readable format. The goal of XML is to be a simple and open standard for representing arbitrary data structures, most often in web services.

▶ **Extensible Messaging and Presence Protocol (XMPP)**—An open, XML-based protocol designed to provide near real-time extensible IM and presence information. It has since expanded into VoIP and file transfer signaling.

▶ **Hardware Load Balancing (HLB)**—A method of distributing a workload across multiple computers to optimize resource utilization, increase throughput, and provide a level of redundancy through the use of an external hardware device.

▶ **IM**—A form of real-time, direct, text-based communication between multiple parties. IM is sometimes referred to as *online chat*.

▶ **Interactive Voice Response (IVR)**—A technology that enables a system to detect voice and dual-tone multifrequency inputs. IVR is often used in telecommunications for automated decision trees. This technology powers concepts such as "press 1 for English" when providing for call routing.

▶ **Mean Opinion Score (MOS)**—In multimedia, MOS provides a numerical indication of the perceived quality of a call after compression and/or transmissions. MOS is expressed as a single number ranging from 1 to 5 where 1 is the lowest perceived audio quality and 5 is the highest perceived audio quality.

▶ **Network Address Translation (NAT)**—A method of modifying network address information when packets pass through a traffic routing device. This effectively remaps a packet from one IP space to another. NAT is common in home usage where multiple computers with a private IP addressing site behind a router or firewall that holds a publically routable address. NAT maps a port back to the initiating internal host and reroutes responses back to the originating host.

▶ **Network Load Balancing (NLB)**—A method of distributing a workload across multiple computers to optimize resource utilization, increase throughput, and provide a level of redundancy through the use of software running in the operating system.

▶ **Personal Identification Number (PIN)**—A secret numeric password shared between a user and a system that is used to authenticate the user to the system.

▶ **PSTN**—The network of the world's public circuit-switched telephone networks. The first company to provide PSTN services was Bell Telephone.

▶ **Plain Old Telephone Service (POTS)**—Another term for a PSTN.

▶ **Private Branch Exchange (PBX)**—A telephone system that serves a particular business or office as opposed to a common carrier or a system for the general public. This is what traditionally provides voice services to companies that are connected to the local exchange to provide external connectivity for telephone calls.

▶ **Quality of Experience (QoE)**—A subjective measure of a customer's experiences with a vendor or service.

▶ **Quality of Service (QoS)**—A mechanism to control resource reservation in a system; typically, it is a method to prioritize various traffic types to ensure a minimum level of performance for a particular type of traffic.

▶ **Real Time Protocol (RTP)**—A standardized packet format for delivering audio and video over the Internet. RTP's claim to fame is the capability to deal with large amounts of packet loss before the impact on the call becomes noticeable.

▶ **Remote Call Control (RCC)**—A method of utilizing a phone resource on one system with a resource on another. Typically, in the context of Lync Server, this is the capability to use a Communicator client to place a call through a desk phone that is controlled by a PBX rather than by Lync Server.

▶ **SIP**—An Internet Engineering Task Force (IETF) defined protocol used for controlling multimedia communications sessions. The goal of SIP is to provide a common signaling and call setup protocol for IP-based communications.

▶ **SIP for Instant Messaging and Presence Leveraging Extensions (SIMPLE)**—An open standard protocol suite that provides for the registration of presence information and the receipt of presence status notifications.

▶ **Survivable Branch Appliance (SBA)**—A combination of Registrar, Mediation Server, and PSTN gateway that is designed to maintain most voice services for a site that has lost connectivity to the main Lync Server site.

▶ **Role Based Access Control (RBAC)**—An approach to restricting system access to authorized users by granting the rights based on the role served by the user. This normally results in granular permissions with an eye toward granting the minimum level of rights needed to perform a task.

▶ **Transmission Control Protocol (TCP)**—Generally considered one of the core protocols of the Internet. TCP is a protocol that provides reliable ordered delivery of a stream of packets from one device to another. TCP has the reliability advantage of performing an acknowledgement of receipt of a packet back to the sender. This acknowledgement, however, comes at a performance price and ultimately limits the scalability of TCP.

▶ **Uniform Resource Identifier (URI)**—A string of characters used to identify a name or a resource on the Internet. This allows interaction with representations of the resource over a network, often the Internet, using various protocols.

▶ **User Datagram Protocol (UDP)**—Another method of delivering a stream of packets from one device to another. UDP does not attempt to order or verify delivery of packets, nor does it need to first initiate a conversation with a destination host via a handshake. This behavior makes it faster and more scalable than TCP, but ultimately, it is less reliable.

▶ **Virtual Private Network (VPN)**—A method of passing packets across a public network in a secured and authenticated manner. VPNs enables users to access their private corporate networks through connections to the public Internet.

▶ **Voice over IP (VoIP)**—A generic term for transmission technologies that deliver voice communications over IP-based networks. Also referred to as *IP Telephony* or *Internet Telephony*.

Versions and Licensing

Lync Server, much like OCS 2007, comes in two flavors: Standard Edition and Enterprise Edition. The two versions give companies the option to create relatively simple or fairly complex topologies based on their needs and budgets. Features between the two are fairly similar, with Enterprise focusing on providing high availability and disaster recovery options that aren't available in the Standard Edition. Similarly, Enterprise Edition requires the higher-end components; for example, a dedicated SQL server is needed rather than a local SQL Express, which is what Standard requires.

Standard Edition

The Standard Edition of Lync Server provides a relatively easy way to deploy telephony features into a network. Its relatively low cost of entry is based on the fact that it's meant to run everything on a single server with the potential for adding an edge server if one needs to support external connectivity.

Standard Edition utilizes a local SQL express database to store information and it isn't eligible for any of the high-availability functions offered by Enterprise Edition. Standard Edition is meant to handle relatively low user loads because its all-in-one nature results in it being less scalable in terms of performance. At the same time, this all-in-one nature makes it easy to deploy and eaiser to troubleshoot than its more advanced cousin, Enterprise Edition.

A typical Standard Edition deployment would contain a single front-end server, a PSTN gateway, and potentially an edge server to service external users. This configuration is sufficient to provide voice and video services to an internal network of users and can still provide services such as public IM connectivity, A/V conferencing, and so on.

NOTE

It is important to note that Standard Edition doesn't allow for high availability, so if this is meant to be a PBX replacement, you should strongly consider stepping up to the Enterprise Edition to provide higher uptime.

TIP

Although Lync Server Standard Edition is typically used in smaller deployments, it is perfectly acceptable to deploy both versions into the same architecture. You can mix and match Enterprise and Standard editions if you need to place different levels of service and cost into different locations.

When planning for a Standard Edition installation, be aware of the following necessary components:

- Windows 2008 x64 SP2 or R2
- .NET Framework 3.5 with SP1 or later
- Microsoft Visual C++ 2008 Redistributable
- Windows PowerShell 2.0
- Microsoft SQL Server 2008 Native Client
- Microsoft Silverlight 4
- Windows Media Format
- Message Queueing Services
- Directory Service Integration
- Active Directory Management Tools
- IIS 7.0 or 7.5

There are also several specific role services needed by Lync Server for IIS that need to be installed before the installation of Lync Server, including

- Static Content
- Default Document
- Directory Browsing
- HTTP Errors
- HTTP Redirection
- ASP.NET

- ▶ .NET Extensibility

- ▶ Internet Server API (ISAPI) Extensions

- ▶ ISAPI Filters

- ▶ HTTP Logging

- ▶ Logging Tools

- ▶ Tracing

- ▶ Anonymous, Basic, and Windows Authentication enabled

- ▶ Request Filtering

- ▶ Static Content Compression

- ▶ IIS Management Console and Scripts and Tools

Enterprise Edition

Enterprise Edition of Lync Server provides much higher availability and scalability than the Standard Edition. Enterprise Edition separates many of the roles that Standard combines and in many cases, it replaces components with higher-performing versions. For example, where Standard Edition can use only a local SQL Express database, Enterprise Edition requires full SQL (preferably 64-bit) and needs that SQL instance to be hosted on another system. This improves scalability by not only using a more robust database, but by isolating the database load from other systems.

Enterprise Edition is able to take advantage of SQL clusters for providing high availability for back-end data. Similarly, it is able to deploy its services into pools and spread the client load across the members of those pools. This provides for protection against a system failure and it provides a method to scale the performance of the system for large deployments.

TIP

Deploying SQL clusters into pools is critical because many Lync Server implementations utilize a somewhat centralized deployment of systems and depends on the WAN for connectivity to this central site. In this type of topology, localized services are often supplemented with a survivable branch appliance. This topic is described in detail in Chapter 11, "SQL."

When planning for an Enterprise Edition installation, be aware of the following necessary components:

- ▶ Windows 2008 x64 SP2 or R2

- ▶ .NET Framework 3.5 with SP1 or later

- ▶ Microsoft Visual C++ 2008 Redistributable

- Windows PowerShell 2.0
- Microsoft SQL Server 2008 Native Client
- Microsoft Silverlight 4
- Windows Media Format
- Message Queueing Services
- Directory Service Integration
- Active Directory Management Tools
- IIS 7.0 or 7.5

There are also several specific role services needed by Lync Server for IIS that need to be installed before the installation of Lync Server itself, including

- Static Content
- Default Document
- Directory Browsing
- HTTP Errors
- HTTP Redirection
- ASP.NET
- .NET Extensibility
- ISAPI Extensions
- ISAPI Filters
- HTTP Logging
- Logging Tools
- Tracing
- Anonymous, Basic, and Windows Authentication enabled
- Request Filtering
- Static Content Compression
- IIS Management Console and Scripts and Tools

Client and Server Licensing

As many administrators are already aware, Microsoft licensing can be a challenge to decipher. Microsoft offers licensing in the form of two suites:

- Core Client Access License (CAL) Suite
- Enterprise CAL Suite

The Core CAL Suite is equivalent to the following licenses: Windows Server CAL, Microsoft Exchange Server Standard CAL, Microsoft SharePoint Server Standard CAL, and Microsoft System Center Configuration Manager Client Management License.

The Enterprise CAL Suite is equivalent to the following licenses:

- ▶ The components of the Core CAL Suite listed previously
- ▶ The components of the Microsoft Forefront Protection Suite
- ▶ Microsoft Forefront Unified Access Gateway CAL
- ▶ Microsoft Exchange Server Enterprise CAL
- ▶ Microsoft SharePoint Server Enterprise CAL
- ▶ Microsoft Office Communications Server Standard CAL
- ▶ Microsoft Office Communications Server Enterprise CAL
- ▶ Windows Rights Management Services CAL
- ▶ The System Center Client Management Suite (composed of the Microsoft System Center Operations Manager Client Management License, Microsoft System Center Service Manager Client Management License, and System Center Data Protection Manager Client Management License)

For Volume Licensing, Lync Server falls under the Enterprise CAL Suite. However, access to the voice workload is licensed through its own Office Communications Server Voice Client Access License (CS Voice CAL). Customers have the option to license the Lync Server Enterprise CAL and the Lync Server Voice CAL either separately or together.

CAUTION

Keep in mind that the CS Voice CAL is not included in the Enterprise CAL Suite. This is a change from the way that Communication Server 2007 R2 was licensed and should not be overlooked.

Integration with Other Microsoft Applications

One of the greatest strengths of a Microsoft product is that it is guaranteed to integrate with other Microsoft applications. Not only does it integrate in the sense that applications work with each other, Microsoft actually hooks the Lync Server technologies into other applications. This means that rich presence information can be shared with other applications and that one doesn't necessarily have to switch to the Communicator client to interact with other users on the system. Not only do these integration points give other applications access to Lync Server, but in some cases, it also gives Lync Server access to information stored in other systems such as SharePoint or Exchange.

Integration with Exchange

Probably the coolest of the new integrations with Exchange is that Exchange 2010 Outlook Web App (OWA) now has Presence and IM integration built in. This provides useful features such as

▶ Presence for internal and federated Lync Server contacts

▶ The capability to start and maintain chat sessions directly from OWA

▶ Lync Server contact list integration, including adding and removing contacts and groups

▶ The capability to control the presence state from OWA

Lync Server also integrates into the meeting creation process, enabling you to create a voice and/or video conference at the time of the meeting creation. This gives users a one-stop shop to service meeting needs.

Lync Server also integrates with the Unified Messaging role in Exchange that enables Lync Server to use Exchange as the storage for voice mail messages.

Integration with SharePoint

Lync Server has taken an interesting approach to its integration with SharePoint. Like older versions of Communications Server, Lync Server displays Presence information anywhere a contact is shown in SharePoint and enables users to start an IM or audio conference with a click on the Presence icon.

What's new is that Lync Server can read information from SharePoint to allow users totally new functionality. Probably the best example of this is the concept of a skills-based search. A Communicator user can search a company for "anyone who knows Exchange" as an example, and then Lync Server looks at data stored in SharePoint about users and identifies those who list that particular skill. It returns a list of users who do have that skill.

This type of bidirectional integration opens up a whole world of possibilities for making it easier for users to connect with each other in a productive manner. Imagine being a new employee and having the option to ask Lync Server to show you a list of people in HR who deal with vacation requests and that are currently online and not busy. This is better than looking at a company intranet, searching for the HR pages, digging through documents to see who handles vacation requests, looking up the numbers, and then trying each of them until you finally get through to someone.

Integration with Office

Lync Server also integrates with some functions in Office 2010, including Backstage, a mechanism in Office 2010 that enables an unlimited number of people to concurrently edit a common document. Lync Server provides Presence information about other people working in the document, providing quick and easy IM collaboration between editors of the document.

The Competition

Lync Server obviously isn't the only game in town when it comes to integrated IM, A/V conferencing, and enterprise voice capabilities. Lync Server has its work cut out for it to keep up with or pass the competition. Other players in this space include

- ▶ Cisco CUCM, Cisco CUPS, and Cisco Unity
- ▶ IBM SameTime
- ▶ Avaya Aura
- ▶ Siemens Open Scape

Although many of these companies offer similar functionality, none achieve the level of integration with Microsoft applications and infrastructure services than Lync Server does.

Summary

As we've seen in this chapter, Microsoft Lync Server 2010 is the latest incarnation of Microsoft's communications suite and offers IM, conferencing and VoIP functionality. In this version, all the functions that were previously different clients have been consolidated into a single easy to use client that supports all of the available functionality. Microsoft Lync Server 2010 can be used for anything from a simple IM platform to a full PBX replacement to a distributed Voice over IP implementation with support for localized backup services. Microsoft Lync Server 2010 enables users to simplify their communications and expand the ways in which they can collaborate.

What Is New in Microsoft Lync Server?

Lync Server improves on previous versions of Communications Server in many areas and introduces several new technologies that enable Lync Server to better support companies in their quest for a completely integrated communications suite. Technologies ranging from branch office and data center resiliency to emergency 911 support for Voice over IP (VoIP) to improved interoperability with existing PBXs all position Lync Server to serve as a one-stop shop for environments seeking to upgrade their communications suite.

This chapter highlights the technologies new to Lync Server. It also highlights improvements to technologies that were introduced in OCS 2007 and OCS 2007 R2 to provide insight into how Lync Server can best be utilized in one's infrastructure.

Introducing New Management Tools

Lync Server introduces several new management tools and alters the way that administrators interact with Lync Server. In the past, Communications Server administrators used MMC-based interfaces, whereas now Lync Server offers a new management interface, a new management shell, a web-based interface, and even offers role-based access control features for delegating access in these new tools.

Lync Server Role-Based Access Control Features

Taking a page from the Exchange 2010 book, Communications Server has similarly adopted a role-based access control approach. This is something that administrators have clamoring for across Microsoft technologies and Lync Server delivers. Lync Server RBAC allows an administrator to add users to predefined administrative roles, of which there are 11 predefined roles that should cover most common administrative scenarios. Gone are the days when a help desk tech had to have the rights to modify a topology just to have rights to enable Communications Server for a new user. With RBAC in Lync Server, administrators can follow a least privilege model and grant someone only the rights they need to do their job and no more. Each role is tied to specific cmdlets in the Server Shell that the role is allowed to perform.

Web-Based Management Tools

Another technology, first seen in Exchange 2010 that is also in Lync Server is the web-based management tool known as the Lync Server Control Panel. This replaces the MMC-based management interfaces of OCS 2007 and OCS 2007 R2.

The real benefit of this web-based interface is that it enables a Lync Server administrator to manage the system from almost anywhere, without the need to install specialized software on a workstation. This is especially useful from a software management standpoint because you no longer need to worry about which systems might have outdated management interfaces installed on them.

The web-based interface operates by calling the Management Shell cmdlets to affect changes in the system. These calls are first passed through the RBAC restrictions to ensure that users are able to perform only the tasks that they have been delegated.

The Lync Server Control Panel requires Microsoft Silverlight 4.0 and supports the following browsers:

▶ Internet Explorer 7.0

▶ Internet Explorer 8.0

▶ Firefox 3.0

Lync Server Management Shell

A continued trend with newer Microsoft technologies is the adoption of PowerShell as the primary management and administration interface. This continues to be the case with Lync Server. The Communications Server Management Shell introduces a slew of Communications Server-specific cmdlets to enable administrators to perform management and administration tasks. Administrators can master the management shell that makes automation of bulk events simple and fast, greatly reducing the errors associated with repetitive manual tasks.

Central Management Store

Although not specifically part of the new server administration tools for Lync Server, it is nonetheless useful to understand that the information modified by the management tools is now stored in a different way. Although attributes such as a user's SIP URI or a phone number is still stored in Active Directory, items such as server configurations or the services are now stored in a Central Management Store. This store, not surprisingly, runs on the Central Management Server, and it's typically collocated on one front-end pool or on a Standard Edition server.

The move to this Central Management Store allows Microsoft to better store the data needed to set up, operate, maintain, and administer a Communications Server deployment. By storing this data in a schematized format, it is able to add a layer of validation of the data to ensure consistency of the configuration information.

Easier Maintenance Through Server Draining

Lync Server implements a feature that is likely familiar to many administrators who have managed Windows-based network load balancing in the past. This feature is called *server draining*. The idea with server draining is that an administrator can take a server offline to do maintenance on it and it stops taking new connections or calls. Assuming at least one other server exists in the pool, the end users do not suffer any loss of service. When the existing connections on the draining server are ended, the system can truly go offline and any necessary maintenance can begin.

Based on this approach, a Lync Server administrator can potentially perform regular maintenance on pooled components during the business day, so long as the pool is designed to support the load while one node is offline. This is typically referred to as an "n+1" configuration where "n" is the number of systems needed to support a given user load.

Monitoring Server Features

Readers who previously managed OCS 2007 or OCS 2007 R2 are likely aware that the Monitoring Server features are not up to par with the rest of the product. Lync Server addresses many of the legacy issues and greatly improves on the functionality. Some of the new features include

► **Rich reporting**—The Monitoring Server role now uses SQL Server Reporting Services to provide useful information about media quality, call reliability, and system usage. Administrators can access a custom dashboard view that presents each of these reports in a single interface.

► **Updated database schema**—The Quality-of-Experience (QoE) and Call Detail Records (CDR) databases have been updated to include new diagnostic and usage data. This results in schema updates for both.

► **New management features**—All administration and management tasks associated with the Monitoring Server role are now integrated into the Communications Server Management Shell.

▶ **Optimized Infrastructure**—The Monitoring Server infrastructure has been updated to improve reliability and maintainability compared to previous versions.

Archiving Server Features

Lync Server offers several changes that enhance the archival of IM and meeting content, especially for compliance purposes. Some of these changes include

▶ **Consolidation of IM and meeting content archiving**—In past versions of Communications Server, IM and web conference content were managed separately. As such, the archival of each was also stored separately. In Lync Server, the policy settings around archiving for IM and meetings are combined for easier administration. Similarly, the core archive store contains both IM and web conferencing content together.

▶ **Searchable transcripts**—Lync Server offers a new cmdlet that creates a searchable transcript of archived content. This transcript includes links to files that were shared, attendee entries and exits, and IM content.

▶ **Per-user settings for conferences**—In Lync Server, per-user archive settings work for all types of conferences. As such, if a given user's activity is archived, IM and meeting content in all types of conferences is archived. It is no longer necessary to configure this behavior in multiple places for a single user.

▶ **New policy settings**—Lync Server includes a new policy setting that enables you to disable features that do not support archiving, such as annotation, application sharing, or peer-to-peer file transfers. This prevents situations in which an archived user can participate in activities that are not actually archived.

Topology Changes

Lync Server introduces a change in topology requirements from previous versions of Communications Server that must be taken into account when designing a Lync Server implementation. The introduction of Communications Server Sites, the separation of the Audio/Video (A/V) conferencing role from the Front End role, the modifications to the Director role, and the integration of the Mediation role noticeably affect how Lync Server is deployed compared to OCS 2007 or OCS 2007 R2.

Communications Server Sites

In Lync Server terms, a Communications Server Site is a set of well-connected computers on a network that contains one or more Lync Server components. In this context, *well connected* means a high-speed, low-latency network such as a local area network (LAN) or two or more networks connected by high-speed fiber optics.

2

> **TIP**
>
> Although many readers might recognize this description as being essentially the same as an Active Directory site or an Exchange site, it is important to distinguish that a Communications Server Site does not necessarily map directly to AD sites, based on the requirement of containing one or more Lync Server components.

Each Communications Server Site is defined as either a central site or a branch office site. A central site must contain at least one front-end pool or Standard Edition server. Branch sites will often contain only a survivable branch appliance, which is a concept introduced in this chapter and covered in more detail in Chapter 18, "Enterprise Voice."

A/V Conferencing Server Role

Unlike OCS 2007 and OCS 2007 R2, Lync Server allows the A/V Conferencing Server functionality to be separated from the Front End Server role. This new server role is referred to as the *A/V Conferencing Server*. By separating this role from the Front End Server, one is able to noticeably improve scalability and performance for A/V conferencing.

> **TIP**
>
> As a rule of thumb, it is a good idea to separate off this role for sites with more than 10,000 users and to form an A/V Conferencing pool.

Other Topology Changes

Some other topology changes within Lync Server include changes to the Director role. In OCS 2007 and OCS 2007 R2, the Director was usually collocated with the Front End Server and required additional configuration steps to act as the Director. In Lync Server, the Director role is a unique server role. If a server is deployed as a Director, it cannot home users. It instead acts as a next-hop server for edge servers and connection requests.

Also new to Lync Server for the Director role is that it no longer requires a separate back-end database running SQL. Instead, the Director will utilize a locally installed version of SQL Server Express. This SQL Server Express component will install automatically when you deploy a Director.

Lync Server now allows the Mediation Server role to be collocated with the Front End Server role, no longer requiring a dedicated Mediation Server in sites where transcoding is needed.

> **TIP**
>
> With Lync Server, collocating the Mediation Server role with the Front use using Direct SIP or SIP trunking.

Also new for small deployments is the capability to collocate the Archiving Server role and the Monitoring Server role with the Front End Server role. This is especially helpful for small deployments that might have a hard time justifying dedicated hardware for the Archiving and Monitoring roles.

New Enterprise Voice Features

Lync Server focuses on improving existing enterprise voice features and introducing new features. Feedback from OCS 2007 and OCS 2007 R2 implementations has pushed Microsoft to make improvements in the areas that caused the most pain for administrators. Lync Server addresses site resiliency and overall scalability in a number of ways. Features in Lync Server make it clear that Microsoft takes enterprise voice seriously and intends to be a market leader in this area.

Branch Office and Data Center Resiliency

OCS 2007 and OCS 2007 R2 shipped with a somewhat limited set of features to provide for continued services in the case of a system failure. Depending on the configuration, a failure of a local OCS server might have resulted in a loss of voice services for a branch office. A failure in a centrally deployed model might have resulted in clients losing all functionalities. Lync Server introduces several technologies and options that can result in only a small loss of noncritical services in the case of a branch or central failure.

Chapter 19, "Audio Conferencing," covers this functionality in greater detail. However, the following sections provide a summary of the options available and their implications in the case of a failure. Lync Server offers Data Center Disaster Resiliency in two potential options described as follows.

Option 1: Implement Single Lync Server Split Across Two Data Centers

In this configuration, both pools operate as one logical system. Front-end loads are shared across data centers and the SQL back-end is geographically clustered. This configuration depends on relatively low latency across the WAN. The net result of this configuration is that in the case of a disaster, clients connect to the other data center.

> **CAUTION**
>
> When a disaster happens, most features are still available, although some are not. The available and nonavailable features are summarized in the following list. The following features are available after a primary site failure:
>
> ▶ PSTN inbound/outbound
>
> ▶ Intrasite calls and intersite calls
>
> ▶ Hold, retrieve, transfer
>
> ▶ Authentication and authorization
>
> ▶ Two-party intrasite IM and A/V
>
> ▶ Call detail records

- ▶ Call forwarding, SimulRing, Boss-Admin, team-call
- ▶ Conferencing AA (through PSTN)
- ▶ Remote user, inbound PSTN calls
- ▶ Conferencing (IM, A/V, and web)
- ▶ Presence and DND-based routing
- ▶ Updating call forwarding settings

The following features are not available after a primary site failure:

- ▶ Response Group Service
- ▶ Voicemail deposit (redirect to Exchange UM in the data center)
- ▶ Voicemail Retrieve (through PSTN)

Option 2 – Implement Primary and Secondary Lync Server Deployments in Two Data Centers
In this scenario, the two pools operate as separate systems. Clients identify primary and secondary SIP registrars through SRV records stored in DNS. If the primary connection is unavailable, the client connects to the secondary connection.

This scenario depends on data replication for full features. It also enables clients to automatically fail over and fail back based on availability of the SIP registrars.

> **CAUTION**
>
> Compared to Option 1, there are more services that become unavailable in the failover scenario. However, Option 2 isn't as dependent on WAN latency and might be the only option for some environments. The following lists summarize the available and unavailable features

The following features are available after a primary site failure:

- ▶ PSTN inbound/outbound
- ▶ Intrasite calls and intersite calls
- ▶ Hold, retrieve, transfer
- ▶ Authentication and authorization
- ▶ Two-party intrasite IM and A/V
- ▶ Call Detail Records

The following features are not available after a primary site failure:

- ▶ Call forwarding, SimulRing, Boss-Admin, team-call
- ▶ Conferencing AA (through PSTN)
- ▶ Remote user, inbound PSTN calls
- ▶ Conferencing (IM, A/V, and web)
- ▶ Presence and DND-based routing
- ▶ Updating call forwarding settings
- ▶ Response Group Service
- ▶ Voicemail deposit (redirect to Exchange UM in the data center)
- ▶ Voicemail Retrieve (through PSTN)

Call Admission Control

Call admission control (CAC) is, at a high level, a mechanism that is designed to protect a network from becoming overloaded by voice and video traffic. Simply put, CAC prevents users from establishing calls that result in a degradation of quality for the existing calls.

> **NOTE**
>
> CAC should not be confused with Quality of Service (QoS), although the net results can be similar. QoS focuses on prioritizing certain types of traffic or traffic between a specific source and destination to guarantee certain levels of quality. Although this might be layered into a Communications Server design to ensure that a particular number of calls or video streams can be maintained, CAC is capable of tracking calls and not just tracking packets. QoS allows more calls to be initiated and they compete with each other for resources. This can result in dropped packets that are perceived as "clipping" by voice users. Rather than allow this situation to occur, CAC has the option of rerouting new calls through the PSTN or it can offload the media portion of a call over the Internet. This gives Communications Server administrators increased flexibility to deal with call spikes rather than simply let the oversubscribed sessions fail.

CAC also provides reports on redirected and blocked calls. This helps administrators better tune their systems to properly handle their call load. In general, blocking a call is preferable to impacting call quality, but redirecting a call to another route (Internet or PSTN) is preferable to blocking a call in the first place.

Although Chapter 19, goes into more detail, the process generally works like this when calling from Lync to Lync:

In a normal call, the following occurs:

1. Penny initiates a call to Sheldon.
2. Sheldon's Lync receives a call notification.
3. Sheldon's Lync checks the CAC policy to see whether the call can be established.
4. If so, Sheldon's Lync accepts the call.
5. The call is established, and audio flows across the WAN.

If the CAC policy denies the connection, the following occurs:

1. Penny initiates a call to Sheldon.
2. Sheldon's Lync receives a call notification.
3. Sheldon's Lync checks the CAC policy to see whether the call can be established.
4. The call is not allowed to be established over the WAN because it would negatively affect existing calls.
5. The call is accepted, but the audio path is redirected to the Internet.

If the CAC policy denies the connection and the call cannot be routed over the Internet, the following occurs:

1. Penny initiates a call to Sheldon.
2. Sheldon's Lync receives a call notification.
3. Sheldon's Lync checks the CAC policy to see whether the call can be established.
4. The call is not allowed to be established over either the WAN or the Internet.
5. The call is rerouted to the PSTN.
6. Call audio flows across the PSTN.

As you can see, CAC enables administrators to create a multitiered approach to how their calls flow where the WAN can failover to the Internet and/or the PSTN should the call load become too high for only the WAN to handle. At the same time, it prevents situations in which existing calls suffer from degraded quality. CAC provides the following:

▶ Fully configurable locations, topology, links, and limits

▶ Preferred interlocation routes for voice and video

▶ Policy rules by link and media type

▶ Dynamic enforcement

▶ Full path assessment at session initiation

▶ Reroute or fail of call if session exceeds limits (voice can be rerouted to PSTN)

▶ The capability to use different links for voice and video if desired (for example, a WAN link for voice and direct video over Internet)

E911 Support

In the early days of VoIP, one of the biggest challenges was providing useful 911 services. Although it was easy to reach 911, the problem was that through the virtualization of the phone services, it was difficult to determine where a call originated. In the case of an emergency where a user was able to dial 911 but not speak, it was almost impossible for emergency services to determine where the person was to send help. This functionality has been addressed through the concept of E911.

In E911, emergency signaling and location information is conveyed from the client through SIP trunks to a third-party partner for Public Safety Answering Point (PSAP) routing. In the case of E911 with Lync Server, this no longer requires Pseudo ANIs (P-ANI).

Lync Server adds Location Information Server (LIS) to the Lync Server web components. This enables one to base location on subnet, switch, port, or Wi-Fi AP, and those locations are updated on each client registration or network change. The way the process works is as follows:

1. A map of network elements and locations is created in LIS.
2. LIS addresses are validated with the Master Street Address Guide.

3. A Premise-connected client acquires LIS URI, emergency dial strings, and configuration settings, and sends a Location Request with IP, MAC, and Basic Service Set Identifier (BSSID) address to LIS during registrations or network changes.

4. LIS returns a civic address to the client based on a network address lookup in the database.

911 Routing works through the following process:

1. The client initiates a 911 call and includes the location and E.164 number in SIP Invite.

2. Lync matches the 911 number pattern and routes to the SIP trunk connecting to E-911 SP.

3. The E-911 router references the civic address to route the call to the correct PSAP.

4. The service provider optionally conferences in an on-premises security person to the call.

5. PSAP can call back using an E.164 number.

When a client is in the office, his location is retrieved automatically from LIS. If the client is outside a controlled environment, the client might prompt the user for location based on a policy created by the administrator. A user can select location information from previously entered locations. If no location information is available for a user, E911 services are not available.

Mediation Server Bypass

In Lync Server, the flow of media traffic can be configured to potentially bypass the Mediation Server. The advantage of doing this is that service quality improves by reducing unnecessary transcoding, packet loss, and latency when the Mediation server can be skipped.

This functionality can also potentially reduce bandwidth used in cases in which a Mediation Server and a PSTN gateway (or PBX) are at different sites. By bypassing media processing by the Mediation Server, call scalability can be improved because one simply doesn't tie up resources that aren't needed.

Mediation Server and Gateway Topologies

In previous versions of Communications Server, it was necessary to maintain a one-to-one ratio of Mediation Servers to gateways. In Lync Server, a single Mediation Server can now control multiple gateways. An additional enhancement is that a Mediation Server can now be deployed as a pool to prevent a single point of failure for a service. This pool can be a standalone pool or it can collocate with an Enterprise Front End pool or the Registrar. This enables an administrator to save hardware by collocating and potentially providing fault tolerance for the Mediation Server or even to improve scalability of the Mediation Server role by providing a load-balanced pool.

Call Translation Rules

All versions of Communications Server require dial strings to be normalized to the E.164 format. This is necessary for performing reverse number lookups (RNL). Often, downstream components such as PBXs, SIP trunks, or gateways require numbers in local dialing formation. It is sometimes necessary to modify downstream components or even reroute calls to accept the E.164 dial string.

Lync Server enables administrators to create rules that assist in manipulating the Request URI prior to handing it off to the gateway. For example, a rule might remove +44 from a dial string and replace it with 0144 to allow a gateway to handle the call properly.

New Call Management Features

Lync Server makes it more feasible than ever to replace an existing PBX with a full Communications Server architecture. In addition to scaling up the back end, Microsoft has created many improvements that deal with the day-to-day needs to end users and call attendants. Receptionists and help desks greatly appreciate some of the newly introduced call management features and the improvements to existing ones.

Call Parking and Other PBX Features

Call parking is the capability to place a call on hold from one endpoint and then retrieve the call from a different endpoint. This is useful in locations where a large number of people share a relatively small number of phones.

Imagine a situation in which a reception person receives a call for a given employee and is able to park the call on an "extension" and announce to the employee that a call is waiting on that particular extension. Administrators can control behavior such as how long a call can be parked before it returns to the original target. For example, a receptionist might park a call and announce it on a specific extension and after two minutes, if the call is picked up, it rings the receptionist so that he or she is aware that the call wasn't picked up by the person who the caller was trying to reach.

Call park and retrieval features include

- ▶ Simple park experience
- ▶ Parking in a parking lot or orbit assigned
- ▶ Retrieve from analog and common area phones
- ▶ Unretrieved calls return to user
- ▶ IT admin management of orbit and park time

Some other traditional call features that are available in R2, but improved in Lync Server include

▶ Dial by name, number, and search

▶ Rollover, hold, and retrieve

▶ Simul-ring, forward, and redirect

▶ Transfer (blind, safe, and consultative)

▶ Conferencing (ad-hoc and scheduled)

Call features that are exclusive to Lync Server include

▶ Reverse number lookup

▶ Manage calls for others (admin)

▶ Music on hold

▶ Endpoint transfer (for example, to mobile)

▶ Malicious call trace

▶ Calling party name display

▶ Call park and retrieval

▶ Private line (incoming calls)

▶ Visual access to voice mail

▶ Ringer cut off and distinctive ring

▶ Response group agent anonymity

Response Group Features

Response groups are a way to allow multiple endpoints to receive a call to a single entity. A classic example of this is a help desk phone number where the goal is to ring multiple phones until a member of the group answers it. Response group features are enhanced in Lync Server and include the following features:

▶ **Anonymous call handling**—When a response group is configured, members can accept calls and initiate calls on behalf of the response group in an anonymous fashion. In this manner, callers cannot directly call a response group member unless that member has given the caller a direct number. Members of a response group can see a call is anonymous and can add IM or video to the call without giving out her true identity.

▶ **Attendant routing method**—This new routing method enables all signed-in members of a response group to receive calls to the response group regardless of their current presence. This routing method also enables the attendant user to see all calls that are queued for a given routing group and to choose to answer a call out of order if she thinks it's necessary. When a call to a response group is answered, the attendant no longer sees the call.

▶ **Integrated manageability**—Lync Server integrates response group management with server management. This is to say that response group management tasks are covered by Communications Server Management Shell cmdlets and many of the management tasks are also available in the Lync Server Control Panel.

▶ **Web services**—Lync Server provides a robust web service for response groups that allows the creation of customized agent consoles. One can utilize this web service to access information about agents, group memberships, agent sign-in statuses, call statuses, and the response groups that support anonymous calls. By leveraging this functionality along with the RBAC functionality of Lync Server, one can create useful (though limited) interfaces into managing and maintaining response groups.

Announcement Application

The Announcement Application in Lync Server enables an administrator to configure how a phone call is handled if a dialed number is valid but not assigned to a user or common area. Options include transferring these types of calls to a predetermined destination or to play a recorded message or both. This avoids the situation in which a caller misdials and simply hears a busy tone, resulting in a confused caller.

Integrated Mediation Server

Previous versions of Communications Server required the integration of dedicated mediation servers to provide signaling and media translation between the Enterprise Voice infrastructure and a Basic Media gateway. Previous versions provided various functions such as

▶ Translating SIP over TCP to SIP over mutual TLS

▶ Encrypting and decrypting SRTP on the Communications Server

▶ Translating media (G.711) on the gateway to RT Audio on CS

▶ Connecting external clients to internal Interactive Connectivity Establishment (ICE) for media traversal of NAT and firewalls

▶ Acting as an intermediary for call flows that aren't supported by a gateway, such as remote worker calls on an Enterprise Voice client

Lync Server now integrates the Mediation Server to provide for these functions, which results in fewer systems to deploy and manage. By integrating the Mediation Server, deployment is easier for environments that use a basic media gateway as opposed to an advanced media gateway.

CAUTION

Keep in mind that the Mediation Server cannot coexist with Lync Web Access, SE Server, Edge Server, or Enterprise Edition Front End Server. Although the topology builder will not allow you to make this mistake, it is better to catch it while you are still designing your solution.

New Presence Features

Lync Server introduces a few new features that enhance the existing presence functionality. These new presence features are summarized in the following sections.

Privacy Controls

The first new feature is enhanced privacy controls. This feature gives users more choices in how they make their information available to others. Privacy controls include options such as whether or not a user displays location information. They also provide the ability to show only presence information to people who are on their contact list. Privacy controls can also be a useful security feature for companies that deploy Lync Server with open federation. This can help prevent user-based information from getting to the wrong people.

Display Photos of Contacts

Another new feature is the capability to show photographs of contacts in the contact list. This can be surprisingly helpful when one gets a call from an unfamiliar name in the company. Most users have an easier time recognizing faces than they do names when it is a coworker they don't know well.

Display Message Waiting Indicator

Lync Server introduces a new class of phones that run the Microsoft Lync Phone Edition, which enables these phones to display a message waiting indicator. This functionality is provided by the Exchange UM features in Exchange 2010 and requires integration with Exchange 2010 to work correctly.

New Conferencing Features

One of the strengths of previous versions of Communications Server was the conferencing features, which covered audio/video (A/V) conferencing, dial-in conferencing, and application sharing. Lync Server continues to provide improvements in this area as companies come to depend on these features more and more. The following sections explain.

Web Conferencing and A/V Conferencing Features

Lync Server made many improvements to web conferencing and A/V conferencing through both frontend and backend changes. Some of these improvements include

- **Downloadable meeting client**—Lync Server introduces the Microsoft Lync Attendee. This new downloadable client enables users who lack the full Microsoft Lync client to attend a meeting to which they have been invited. When the invitee first attempts to join the meeting, he is prompted to download the Microsoft Lync Attendee. This client enables the invitee to join the meeting, but it does not contain any functionality for IM, Presence, or Meeting Scheduling. The Attendee persists on the user's computer so that he does not have to download it again the next time he joins a Lync Server meeting.

- **Single meeting client**—Microsoft Lync is now the only client needed for all Lync Server meetings. This covers both scheduled meetings and ad-hoc meetings.

- **Meeting admission policy and controls**—In older versions of Communication Server, after a user sent an invitation to a meeting, the authorization types could not be altered if they had been set incorrectly. In the new client included in Lync Server, an organizer can alter the authorization types even if the meeting has already started. This can noticeably reduce the number of calls to the help desk in situations where a meeting is set up incorrectly.

- **Meeting types**—Lync Server users are now able to create templates for their meeting types that enable them to predefine who is allowed to attach to a meeting. This is useful for executive assistants or administrators to regularly set up meetings for other people. By building templates based on the invitee list, it is much faster and less prone to error to set up a meeting with the correct permissions.

- **Simple URL**—Conference join links now start with http://, which makes them much friendlier to send via e-mail and results in an easy click to launch web clients. This functionality enables administrators to create easy-to-remember links to find meetings based on a fully qualified domain name and a short friendly word. For example, users at CompanyABC.com might use https://cs.companyabc.com/Meeting for their simple meeting URLs and something such as https://cs.companyabc.com/Meeting/123456 to link to a specific meeting.

Dial-In Conferencing Features

Lync Server also provides many improvements to the dial-in conferencing features, including

- **The Lobby**—If a dial-in user is required to authenticate and does not, he no longer needs to disconnect and retry. Users in this situation are now transferred to The Lobby. This gives the organizer of the call the ability to either accept or reject callers who do not authenticate. If callers stay in The Lobby past a configurable time, they are timed out and disconnected.

- **Recorded names for anonymous callers**—Users who are not authenticated are now prompted to record their names. This enables the organizer of the conference to determine who is on the call. That said, the name recorded is whatever the caller chooses to say.

▶ **Access to DTMF commands during a call**—Lync Server dial-in conferences now give callers access to dual-tone multifrequency (DTMF) commands. The means the user can press buttons on the phone to make stuff happen. Specifically, options such as muting callers, locking or unlocking the conference, controlling entry and exit announcements, playing a private roll call, and so on can be accessed via the keypad on the phone.

Application-Sharing Features

A small but useful upgrade to the application-sharing functions of Lync Server is that users can now choose to share a single application with other participants rather than be required to share their entire desktop the way they were in OCS 2007 or OCS 2007 R2. Although this may seem minor, users who have had an embarrassing e-mail "toast" or IM arrive while sharing a desktop will be happy to see this option.

DNS Load Balancing

A new and highly useful feature in Lync Server is the capability to implement load balancing via DNS. This enables an administrator to create multiple SRV (service) records. By manipulating the priority associated with them, administrators can enable clients to balance their SIP and Media traffic across multiple servers. This effectively lifts the old restriction where one was allowed only a single _sipinternaltls._tcp record per domain.

In older versions of Communications Server where there was a distributed implementation, an expansive Global Server Load Balancer was required to allow various regions to connect to a local director to log in. Although this might be of less concern to companies that have deployed regionally with multiple subdomains, it is useful for companies that have consolidated to a single AD domain and accompanying DNS domain.

> **NOTE**
>
> It is important to note that DNS load balancing does not replace the need for hardware load balancing to balance server pools. However, the configuration of said load balancers is primarily for HTTP traffic.

Survivable Branch Appliances

Although not necessarily a feature of Lync Server itself, a concept that is now possible via Lync Server is that of a Survivable Branch Appliance (SBA). Several vendors have announced appliances that run Lync Server. These appliances allow for simplified implementation of dial plans and offer localized services with the capability for a centralized data center to take over in the case of a localized failure of the appliance. The appliances integrate a PSTN gateway, Mediation Server, and Registrar. Built in various formats by companies like Audiocodes, Dialogic, Ferrari, HP, and NET, these devices provide many services such as the capability to hand control of local calls back and forth between the appliance and a remote data center, enabling one to serve as a backup for the other for branch user calls.

When configured in this manner, the following services are available in the event of a WAN outage:

- ▶ PSTN and other voice services

- ▶ Hold, retrieve, transfer

- ▶ Authentication and authorization

- ▶ Call forward, simul-ring, boss-admin, team-call, and do-not-disturb routing

- ▶ Call detail records

- ▶ Intrasite IM and A/V

- ▶ PSTN audio conferencing

The following services are unavailable in a WAN outage:

- ▶ IM/V/W conferencing

- ▶ Presence

- ▶ Update call forwarding setting

- ▶ Response group service

Operating System Support

An often missed change in many new Microsoft products is the shift to 64-bit computing. Lync Server is no exception to this trend because it is available only in a 64-bit edition. This means, of course, that the servers on which Lync Server are hosts must have processors that support a 64-bit architecture. The operating system must also be 64-bit.

The client, however, does not have the same requirements. The Lync client for Lync Server can be run as either a 64-bit or 32-bit application with no change in available features. As such, the following operating systems are supported for Lync Server:

- ▶ Windows 2008 SP2 x64 Standard

- ▶ Windows 2008 SP2 x64 Enterprise

- ▶ Windows 2008 SP2 x64 Data Center

- ▶ Windows 2008 R2 x64 Standard

- ▶ Windows 2008 R2 x64 Enterprise

- ▶ Windows 2008 R2 x64 Data Center

New Lync Client Features

Lync Server comes with an updated client that accesses all of the improved functionality of Lync Server. This client comes in several flavors including Lync "14," Lync Attendant "14," and Lync Phone Edition. As one might guess from the names, these cover the typical computer user, the "receptionist," and hardware phones, respectively. Improvements to the clients are significant enough that they are introduced in the following sections.

Client Appearance

The new Lync client comes with an updated appearance and updated functionality. The new unified UI lists contacts, recent conversations, missed calls, and even the latest updates from your contacts. It also supports customization of the view of contacts to enable users to alter the appearances of their interfaces. Items such as contacts and missed calls now appear in a tabbed list. Updates from your contacts show up in the Activity Feed. These updates are primarily implemented to promote a more social aspect to collaboration.

The "Me" Area

At the top of the new Lync client is a view into how other users see you. One can quickly and easily update one's statuses and other information in this area. Information managed via the "Me" area can also include things such as adding a photo from SharePoint to use on your Lync contact card or updating location information that can be used by services like E911 to locate you physically.

Enhanced Contacts

Interacting with one's contacts is better than ever in Lync "14." Users can customize their displays of their contacts based on availability, groups, or level of privacy. They can also choose whether to display photos and start meetings or conversations from the Contacts by simply pointing to the contact. Even editing contacts is available in Lync "14."

With integration to SharePoint, Lync users can now perform keyboard searches when looking for contacts. Information such as a title or a specific skill can be used to search for other users. This makes it easier than ever to find the right person when you need assistance.

Imagine running into a problem with PowerShell and being able to search in your company for users who know PowerShell. You can search a person out, see whether that person is available, and launch right into IM to ask a question. By populating the new expanded contact card, you can show and search more information about people in the rest of the organization.

Privacy Relationships

Users now have more control over what information they share with other users. For example, a user can set his presence to be visible to contacts in his contact list, but not to anyone else. This type of functionality can be applied to various groups and even to trusted domains outside your organization.

Integration with Office and Windows 7

For users of Office 2007 or higher, many Lync functions become available in other applications. By consolidating to a single unified contact store, it is no longer necessary to maintain contacts in multiple applications. Functionality works both ways for applications. For example, you can start an IM conversation from within Microsoft Word and share the application or you can send an Outlook message directly from Lync "14." With this new release, Microsoft leverages its capability to integrate all of its application suites.

Whiteboarding and Application Sharing

In previous versions of Communications Server, users in conferences only had the option of sharing their entire desktop. In Lync Server with Lync "14," those options expand to application sharing, Office PowerPoint presentations, whiteboard and annotation tools, and meeting recording and playback.

Lync Server goes a step further with PowerPoint and utilized DHTML to present PowerPoint files to participants without requiring them to download a rich client. Participants can even view and save files that are uploaded to meetings in their original file format.

Improved Meeting Join Experience

When updating the meeting join process for Lync Server, the goal was for it to take two seconds or less to join a meeting. Lync Server even includes metrics to measure the achieved join performance. This enables Lync Server administrators to better handle users whose perception of a join is that it is slow.

Creating and scheduling meetings is easier than ever with the new client. Simpler URLs make it much easier to browse for a meeting, and policy-based meeting creation makes it easy for users to create meetings that allow the usual suspects to join. The new client even enables meeting creators to modify authentication settings on a meeting after the meeting has started. In older versions of Communications Server, not only was it impossible to alter access control on a meeting in progress, but it also wasn't possible to alter it on an invite that had already been sent.

Conferencing Attendant and Scheduling

Organizers of meetings in Lync Server now have the ability to change the language of an invitation to English. It's now possible to schedule an online meeting even when Lync Server is not available. Mobile phone users enjoy a single click of an invitation to join audio conferences.

PSTN Dial-In Conferencing Improvements

Lync Server has noticeably reduced the number of messages that a user must respond to when joining a call. Rather than disconnect a caller if no one is available to accept a call, they now wait in the lobby until an organizer decides whether he wants to add the caller to the conference. Callers are also now notified if a call is being recorded.

Video Improvements

Lync now includes the following video conference support:

▶ Panoramic video

▶ Multipoint video

▶ Subscription video

▶ VGA

▶ High definition video

Manager/Admin Improvements

Lync has added support for delegate features. This means that a delegate no longer has to switch between Lync and an Attendant console to access the features they need. Lync also now supports the capability for one delegate to support multiple managers. Because they no longer have to use an Attendant console to manage other accounts, they now have access to the collaboration tools such as application sharing and file sharing that are not supported by the Attendant console.

Lync includes a new contact group called "People I manage calls for," which makes it simpler to pass information along when they become available again.

Improved Phone Experience

The new Lync client provides more PBX-like functions and productivity features. For example, the client UI now includes a tally of the number of voice mail messages and missed calls for the user. A new Phone tab offers a list of the voice mails and call logs and even gives the user an on-screen dial pad.

Support for a new generation of Lync Server–compliant phones gives users greater choices in endpoints and supports a much greater number of conference-style phones. The party continues to grow in terms of available hardware for Lync Server and includes many phones that are reasonably priced compared to previous generation offerings.

Summary

As we've seen in this chapter, Microsoft Lync Server 2010 adds a fair amount of new functionality that addresses perceived weaknesses in the previous generation products. By providing enhanced PBX and Enterprise Voice functionality along with concepts like the Survivable Branch Appliance, Microsoft has gone a long way in making Lync Server 2010 a very viable choice to run an entire voice system.

New topology options offered by Microsoft Lync Server 2010 give administrators added flexibility in designing an infrastructure that can meet their needs. Added support for clients beyond just Windows and just Internet Explorer make it that much easier to support a heterogeneous environment. By understanding these new features and taking advantage of them, administrators are well situated to build useful and resilient implementations to keep their end users happy.

Feature Overview of Microsoft Lync Server

Lync Server is difficult to summarize in a single phrase, but it can be considered a secure, flexible, and extensible collaboration platform. From many people's perspective, it is simply considered Microsoft's instant messaging (IM) product since its inception. However, Lync Server has transformed into a complete Unified Communications (UC) solution for a business that encompasses presence, IM, web conferencing, audio/video (A/V) conferencing, and complete voice over IP (VoIP) services.

This chapter is a high-level overview of what Lync Server provides to an organization. Its features can be deployed together or in pieces, as determined by business requirements. This flexibility is exactly what makes the product so compelling and beneficial to organizations.

Presence

Presence is the core feature of Lync Server and drives or enhances almost every other feature. In its simplest form, *presence* is defined as the combination of a person's availability and willingness to communicate at any given time. This presence is published to colleagues and peers. It is what allows others to determine an appropriate time to contact a user and what communication modality makes the most sense at that time. A user has complete control over his presence state, which means he can choose when to appear available or unavailable to peers.

Without presence information, users tend to fall back on other communication methods such as sending e-mail messages that say, "Are you free?" or "Do you have time to talk now?" With presence information at their disposal, users have no need to send these types of messages. With a quick glance, users can see a contact's presence and make a determination about when it's appropriate to initiate a conversation. These conversations are not necessarily IM-based; they can be in the form of an IM, a phone call, or a video conference. However, the appropriate time and modality of communication are driven by the presence information. For instance, a user whose presence is currently Busy most likely isn't going to be receptive to a phone conversation, but might be willing to communicate through IM for a short period of time.

Enhanced Presence

Many presence engines have only a few presence states, such as Available or Away. These provide some insight into availability, but traditionally require manual user management and offer little control over what information is actually published.

The presence engine Microsoft has developed behind Lync Server is referred to as Enhanced Presence, which is a combination of a numerous presence states, access levels, interruption management, automated updates, application integration, location information, and multiple points of presence (MPOP). These features interconnect to provide a prolific amount of presence information that is simply not possible in many other systems.

Presence States

Lync Server presence consists of a presence icon and a status text string. A number of colors are associated with each presence class that operate on a similar scale as a stoplight from green to red. Although each of these colors provide a good indicator of presence, they are paired with a textual representation of the user's presence when published, providing even more insight to the current status. Some colors can take on separate text strings depending on the user's availability. For instance, the color red is displayed when a user manually sets her presence to Busy, but red can also be associated with the In a Call, In a Conference, and In a Meeting presence states. These are unique presence states, but indicate a similar level of willingness to communicate at that moment. The core availability classes are listed in Table 3.1.

TABLE 3.1   Microsoft Lync Server Presence States

Presence Color	Presence Text String
Green	Available
Yellow	Away
	Out of Office
Red	Busy
	In a Call
	In a Conference
Dark Red	Do Not Disturb
	Urgent Interruptions Only
Empty Color	Offline

Access Levels and Privacy Relationships

Privacy relationships are the component of enhanced presence used to control the amount of information visible to contacts. In prior iterations of Communications Server, these were referred to as *access levels*, but they are now called *privacy relationships* in Lync Server. Instead of publishing the same presence to all subscribers, a user can control the flow of information based on differing privacy relationships assigned to contacts.

The enhanced presence model publishes more than just a user's presence name; it also includes e-mail address, title, company, address, working hours, and a multitude of other attributes.

NOTE

A user might not want to expose all of this information to a user, so privacy relationships can be used to distribute only the necessary information to subscribers. A user can also adjust the relationship for each contact individually, giving the user complete control and flexibility for managing the information provided to contacts.

The privacy relationships available in Lync Server are

- ▶ **Friends & Family**—Shares all contact information except for meeting subject and meeting location. This level is intended for personal contacts.

- ▶ **Workgroup**—Shares all contact information except for nonwork phone numbers. Contacts assigned to this relationship level can interrupt the user when his status is Do Not Disturb.

- ▶ **Colleagues**—Shares all contact information except for nonwork phone numbers, meeting subject, and meeting location. This is the default relationship assigned to contacts in the organization.

- ▶ **External Contacts**—Shares all information except for phone numbers, meeting subject, and meeting location.

- ▶ **Blocked Contacts**—Shows only the user's name and e-mail address. Contacts assigned to this relationship cannot reach the user through Lync endpoints.

Table 3.2 details what information is available to end users assigned to each privacy relationship.

TABLE 3.2   Information Shared Based on Privacy Relationship

Information	Blocked	External	Colleagues	Workgroup	Friends & Family
Offline Presence	X				
Presence State		X	X	X	X
Display Name	X	X	X	X	X
E-mail Address	X	X	X	X	X
Title		X	X	X	X
Work Phone			X	X	X
Mobile Phone				X	X
Home Phone					X
Other Phone					X
Company		X	X	X	X
Office			X	X	X
Work Address			X	X	X
SharePoint Site			X	X	X
Meeting Location				X	
Meeting Subject				X	
Free/Busy			X	X	X
Working Hours			X	X	X
Endpoint Location				X	X
Note			X	X	X
Last Active				X	X

Interruption Management

Access levels control interruption management because they determine whether a contact can initiate a conversation with the user at a particular time. For example, a contact assigned to the Company access level cannot interrupt with a phone call or IM message when the user's presence is set to Do Not Disturb, but someone assigned to the Team access level sees the status as Urgent Interruptions Only. This provides a visual cue to the team members that the user doesn't want to be disturbed, but can be interrupted for a critical issue. When a conversation is initiated, the receiver sees a pop-up notification called the *toast* in the lower-right corner of her screen.

TIP

Enhanced presence doesn't only help to suspend toast pop-ups or phone calls. Endpoints have the option to suspend audio sounds when a user's status is Busy or Do Not Disturb. And as an added bonus, they have the capability to pause Windows Media Player audio when an incoming audio or video call is detected. Although automatically pausing a media player might seem trivial, the value of not having to bring Windows Media Player to the foreground and fumble for a Pause button or Mute button before answering the phone call is significant. This speaks to the seamlessness of Lync Server and the productivity gains it can provide to end users.

Automated Status Updates

Presence is a great indicator of a user's willingness to communicate, but if left to the users to manually manage, it tends to be inaccurate. A user cannot always remember to change his presence to Busy when walking into a meeting or back to Available when returning to his desk, so Lync Server leverages a user's calendar and manages these kinds of updates on his behalf. If a user has an appointment on the calendar, his presence automatically changes to Busy during the appointment and then goes back to Available when the appointment concludes.

Endpoints also differentiate between personal calendar entries considered appointments and meetings where multiple attendees exist. In the previous example, if the calendar entry is a meeting instead of appointment, the status changes to In a Meeting instead of Busy, indicating the user is most likely in the company of others and probably engaged in conversation.

This calendar integration can be performed from Microsoft Office Outlook if installed, or if the user's mailbox is hosted by a Microsoft Exchange Server 2007 or later, endpoints can use Exchange Web Services to log in and pull the calendar data directly from the mailbox using Lync Server credentials.

In addition to the calendar integration, Lync Server keeps track of a user's activity at an endpoint and can automatically mark an endpoint as Inactive or Away after a period of time. This ensures that if a user has walked away from an endpoint without changing his presence, subscribers can see the last presence state with an Inactive designation as part of the status. Even though the user is still signed in, subscribers can tell they probably won't get a response when trying to initiate a conversation.

NOTE

The integration points mentioned previously provide a way to keep presence information up-to-date automatically. However, the user has the option to manually override her presence to any state.

Multiple Points of Presence

Lync Server presence has the added flexibility of being read from multiple endpoints simultaneously. This enables a user to be signed in at multiple locations or endpoints that publish presence independently. The server then aggregates these endpoints and forms a single presence class that is published to subscribers.

For instance, a user can be signed in to Lync on a desktop, again on a roaming laptop, at home on a Mac, and also on a mobile device. Each of these endpoints publishes presence independently, and the server then forms the user's presence appropriately.

Having multiple clients signed in is generally considered a problem because how does a user know which endpoint to send a message to? Without multiple points of presence (MPOP), there is a problem. However, when a user sends another user a message, the Lync Server determines which endpoint is currently most active for that user. For example, a user might be Away at three of the four endpoints, so the server sends the message only to the endpoint where the user is Available.

If the server is unable to determine which state is most active, it sends the message to the endpoint it determines most likely active and waits to see if the user acknowledges the toast at any location. If the user opens the toast at an endpoint, the server removes the message from the other endpoints. If an endpoint doesn't acknowledge the message, the server leaves the message at only one location—the most likely endpoint.

MPOP might not be perfect at all times, but it does enable a user to publish presence from multiple locations and still receive conversations at the most likely endpoint.

Extensible Presence

The built-in presence states provide an excellent array of options for users, but the Lync Server platform is extensible, and businesses can build on these choices using custom presence states. These custom presence states enable the user to select one of the standard presence classes and colors, but to customize the text displayed with the status. Although a subscriber might still see a green icon synonymous with availability, the user's presence can read Catching Up On E-mail, which gives subscribers an additional piece of information to consider before initiating a conversation.

Some applications use the extensibility features to provide more information about an endpoint's capabilities. Mobile clients generally append a Mobile indicator to the presence status. This gives subscribers information that the user might be slow to respond because he is likely without a full keyboard or computer. Subscribers are aware they won't likely be able to have a lengthy conversation, but that they can have a quick or short conversation. This designation might also give users an idea that calling the user's mobile at that time is probably the quickest way to initiate a conversation.

Application Integration

Another component of Enhanced Presence is the automatic availability of presence in other Microsoft products. This means that although a Lync client runs in the background, users are able to see presence for those contacts in Outlook right next to their names.

This presence can be seen directly in the context of the mail message, so there is no need to switch between applications to view a user's presence. Right from the e-mail message or contact card, the user can see the presence and initiate an IM, e-mail, or phone conversation with only one or two clicks of the mouse.

Lync Server can also integrate with Microsoft Exchange Server 2010 Outlook Web App to provide presence and IM capabilities directly within the Outlook Web App interface. This allows users to see presence information within the context of e-mail either from the full Outlook client or while using a web browser.

The same rich presence information is also available in Microsoft Office SharePoint where users can view presence in the context of documents and files. The contact card displayed in other applications is the same card and interface displayed within Lync, ensuring users have a consistent view of contacts and presence across any application.

With Lync any kind of telephone number displayed on a web page in Internet Explorer suddenly becomes a hyperlink and can be clicked to initiate a phone call. All of these integration points are not overwhelming by themselves, but collectively create an improved end-user experience unique from any other product.

NOTE

The presence integration discussed previously is provided out-of-the-box with applications such as Outlook and SharePoint. However, presence can also be extended to other applications through the use of the published APIs. Companies can use these APIs to integrate presence into any existing applications or workflows of their own. Microsoft provides a software development kit with tools and documentation of the APIs to help businesses develop Lync and application integration.

Location

Another component of presence is the concept of publishing a user's physical location, which can be as vague as whether they are in the office or at home, or as exact as being in a particular floor of a building. Administrators can configure a Location Information Service (LIS) to integrate with Lync Server, which allows Lync Server endpoints to automatically identify what physical location they are connecting from and then publish that information with the user's presence. If the Location Information Service cannot identify the user's location, they will be prompted to enter one and the endpoint will retain that information if the user returns to that location at any time so a user never has enter a location twice.

TIP

A user always has the option to block the publication of location if necessary.

Instant Messaging

Along with presence, collaboration through the use of IMs has been a part of Lync Server since the beginning. Although IMs are a simple mode of communication, they can be an excellent way to conduct a conversation in a quick manner without needing to resort to e-mail or a phone call.

In Lync Server, IM is not unlike IM conversations that use other providers, but the main advantage to IM with Lync Server instead of a public solution is that all the messaging is encrypted through TLS connections to the servers and an organization has complete control over how the system is used. This means that a rogue user on your network can't start a packet sniffer application and read messages sent between two other users.

> **NOTE**
>
> Although it might be an acceptable compromise on an internal network, this security in signaling extends to remote access scenarios too, ensuring conversations that take place across the Internet are also encrypted.

The Lync Server endpoints support the same kind of features found in many other IM clients, such as rich text, emoticons, and saving messages. The end user and security features enable an organization to standardize on a single messaging client such as Lync instead of multiple clients and services. Figure 3.1 shows the new Lync interface, which should be familiar to any user who has used other IM products.

FIGURE 3.1   The Lync Interface

3

> **NOTE**
>
> A long-standing issue with many IM applications is that users think the conversation is not captured unless conducted through e-mail. Through integration with Microsoft Office Outlook, IM conversations can be saved automatically to the user's Microsoft Exchange mailbox. These conversations are then searchable in the same way that e-mail messages are, so users can reference them at any time.

Web Conferencing

Lync Server gives users the ability to create or join virtual meetings referred to as *web conferences*, including attendees from inside the organization or guest users without an account in the Lync Server environment. In prior versions of Lync Server, the web conferencing experience was separated into the Live Meeting client. However, in Lync Server, the web conferencing experience has been unified and is now conducted through the same Lync client instead of through a required, separate download and installation of Live Meeting. Many of the same features from the previous release exist, and some additional capabilities have been added. These new capabilities include

- ▶ **Desktop Sharing**—Enables users to share an entire desktop or just a single monitor when multiple monitors are connected. When users select a specific monitor to share, the edges of the screen glow to give a visual clue of which monitor is about to be presented.

- ▶ **Application Sharing**—Users can share only a specific application that runs on the desktop. Attendees see only the application shared by the presenter instead of an entire desktop or monitor.

- ▶ **Presentation**—Upload and share a PowerPoint presentation. Rather than share PowerPoint through the application-sharing feature, this option can be used to give a better experience for attendees. It has transitions and slide change controls for the presenter.

- ▶ **Polls**—Presenters can conduct a questionnaire with responses attendees can select by clicking the options. The poll tallies the results for the presenter to see or for all attendees to see.

- ▶ **Whiteboard**—The whiteboard in Lync Server has greatly improved and is now reminiscent of Microsoft Office OneNote where text blocks can be inserted or moved easily and images can be inserted and dragged around the screen. Whiteboard sessions can be shared among multiple presenters and saved later for reference.

Web conferencing attendees have a number of different client options for joining meetings; these offer varying degrees of functionality. They are

- ▶ **Lync**—The full client can be used to join a conference or act as a presenter. This is the most complete end-user experience and has no restrictions.

- ▶ **Lync Attendee**—This application is a subset of the Lync application and offers full web and A/V conferencing capabilities, but can be used only for joining a meeting.

NOTE

Lync Attendee is a free download that is available to any user, even if she does not belong to the organization. However, it does require installing the client.

▶ **Lync Web App**—This web application is a third option for joining web conferences. Lync Web App is a browser-based Silverlight application that requires no installation other than the Silverlight prerequisite. Participants can access Lync Web App through the meeting link that can be used by anonymous, external participants or by authenticated users who want to sign in. Lync Web App does not offer any audio or video capabilities, but users can provide a phone number for the conferencing server to call them in to the meeting. Any user with a browser and Silverlight can join a meeting this way regardless of operating system or platform.

Audio and Video Conferencing

Organizations can leverage Lync Server to provide audio and video (A/V) conferencing services to their users without deploying additional clients or software. Deploying A/V conferencing enables users to perform peer-to-peer or multiparty conferences using high-fidelity audio and video conducted across the IP network. Users have a consistent experience because they can make and receive A/V calls through the same Lync client used for presence, IM, and web conferencing. Although A/V conferencing is sometimes linked to Enterprise Voice features, it can be deployed separately from any kind of telephony integration.

NOTE

It is important to note that although the term A/V is used, video is not a required component of these conversations. Users can conduct audio-only conversations using the Lync endpoint instead of a traditional phone call. These audio conversations are performed at a higher level of audio quality than a traditional PSTN call and are not be subject to any long distance or international charges like a regular call.

With video conversations, peer-to-peer endpoints can negotiate to use high-definition video quality, and in a multiparty scenario where the server hosts the conference, VGA quality video can be provided.

Organizations have a wide variety of webcams to select what is compatible with Lync Server and Microsoft provides a continuously updated list of certified devices. In Lync Server, video endpoints such as the Microsoft RoundTable or Polycom CX5000 can be used in Lync to provide a full 360-degree panoramic view of the room.

Lastly, Lync Server video endpoints can be integrated with video conferencing systems from vendors such as HP, Polycom, and Tandberg.

Dial-In Conferencing

In addition to web or A/V conferencing, Lync Server can act as a conferencing bridge service for users. This enables individuals to schedule or launch an audio conference using a mix of Lync Server users and endpoints with users dialing in to a conference using traditional phone lines. Local numbers can be provided by region or organizations can provide a toll-free number associated to one or many regions to external participants.

> **TIP**
>
> Instead of purchasing a third party on the premise or hosted, subscription-based audio conferencing service, Lync Server can be used to give each user in the organization a unique conference bridge through the existing infrastructure.

The dial-in conferencing service can be used as a standalone system or in conjunction with the web conferencing components of Lync Server to enable users to bridge PSTN audio with any web conference being conducted.

> **TIP**
>
> There isn't a dependency to deploy web conferencing or dial-in conferencing one before the other, but they offer the most beneficial feature set when deployed together.

Dial-in conferencing also has no dependency on Enterprise Voice services for users, meaning users do not need to be enabled for Enterprise Voice to use the audio conferencing service. A user can be enabled simply for IM and presence, but also to schedule and join dial-in conferences through the Lync client or PSTN. Enterprise Voice users can also use the conferencing service, but being enabled for Enterprise Voice does not provide additional audio conferencing features from a user perspective.

The Lync Server conference bridge has a number of added benefits over a traditional conferencing service:

Permissions

Users can adjust the permissions for each conference to control specific types of attendees from participating. This gives end users the option to prevent meetings from being forwarded or from being accessed by anonymous participants on a per-meeting basis.

Flexible Conference IDs

When enabled for Lync Server, users are assigned a static, unique conference ID that is used for all of their meetings. A user's conference ID is persistent by default, but if a user has back-to-back meetings, it is beneficial to schedule the second meeting with a unique ID.

End users can do this easily when creating a conference and it helps to prevent attendees from the second meeting joining the first meeting if it runs to the end of the time slot.

Lobby

The Lync Server lobby feature can be considered a type of waiting room where meeting attendees can be held before the meeting begins. As a presenter, the meeting can be configured to automatically admit all attendees from the lobby, admit only authenticated corporate users from the lobby, admit only authenticated corporate users invited specifically by the organizer, or to admit no user from the lobby without manual acceptance. Attendees are allowed to join the meeting, but when held in the lobby, they are unable to hear the presenter or other users. The meeting organizer has the ability to allow or not allow attendees waiting in the lobby to attend the meeting.

As the organizer, participants are listed in the visual roster. Authenticated users show a display name and users joining from the PSTN can display the phone number they dialed in from. Lync Attendee or Lync Web App users have the ability to enter a display name, which is shown in the roster, too.

Announcements

Typical conferencing services prompt a user to record his name, business name, or possibly location when dialing in to a meeting from the PSTN, and then the user can play that recorded greeting as he enters or leaves the conference. In Lync Server, where a visual roster is available to all participants, the need for this service is greatly diminished and can actually become a distraction to the actual meeting as attendees enter and leave.

Organizers can enable or disable the announcement service per-meeting basis, and it is actually disabled by default. Attendees who dial in from a PSTN telephone and want to hear a roster might use dual-tone multi-frequency (DTMF) tones to request a roll call, which is played only to the attendee. Additionally, the conferencing service aggregates announcements when batches of users enter or leave at the same time and make an announcement such as "Eight users are leaving" instead of announcing each user individually.

Languages

Administrators can define regions, and dial-in numbers for the regions can be associated with specific language support. If multiple languages are associated with the region, users are presented with the option to select a language when joining via the PSTN. This enables users who speak different primary languages to participate in a single audio conference and hear menu or announcement recordings conducted in their selected language.

Enterprise Voice

Enabling a user for Enterprise Voice in Lync Server is a matter of associating a telephone number with the user's account, merging a user's audio conversations with the many functions Lync Server already provides. When telephony integration is in place, any calls to the user's telephone number ring at any Lync Server endpoints the user is signed into, and a user can place calls to the PSTN from a Lync Server endpoint.

Enterprise Voice users have a flexibility not found in most traditional PBX systems because the user has control over many functions that typically require a PBX administrator to configure such as forwarding and simultaneous ringing. Enterprise Voice users also see visual call controls when in a call where they can mute, transfer, or end calls all with the click of a button, which can be an improvement over traditional key sequences on a phone to perform the same operations.

NOTE

An Enterprise Voice user has a wide array of endpoint choices from vendors that Microsoft has certified to use with Lync such as USB and Bluetooth handsets or headsets. These devices, which are designed to be plug and play, require no drivers and provide a high-quality experience to the end user. Some vendors also provide standalone IP phones that can log in to Lync Server directly through the Lync Phone Edition application.

Voice services are a large component of Lync Server and include some of the features mentioned in the following sections.

Call Forwarding

Call forwarding settings are available to Enterprise Voice users, which gives some flexibility not found in traditional PBX systems. Enterprise Voice users can control exactly what actions occur when an incoming phone call is received, such as ringing for a specified amount of time before being forwarded to an alternate number or to voice mail.

When an incoming call is received, users can have it ring their work number, mobile number, home number, or simultaneously ring a combination of any of them. Furthermore, if the user doesn't answer any of these options, the call can be forwarded after a user-specified timeout either to voice mail such as Microsoft Exchange Unified Messaging or until it rings an additional number.

Endpoints automatically use phone numbers published to Active Directory as options for the users, but individuals can add additional mobile or home phone numbers if necessary.

TIP

If a user works remotely—even for just a day—at a phone number not published in Active Directory, the user can configure Lync Server to forward calls to or simultaneously ring that number. These settings can also be configured based on working hours defined in Microsoft Office Outlook so that forwarding or simultaneous ringing occurs only during business hours.

The flexibility is the key component here because each user can configure settings individually to meet his own needs, and unlike a traditional PBX, the changes require no effort from the administrator because the controls are part of Lync. Figure 3.2 displays just how easy it is for users to configure call forwarding settings.

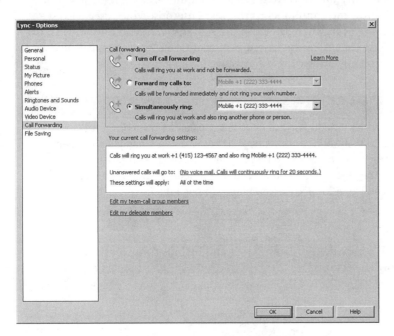

FIGURE 3.2   Enterprise Voice Call Forwarding Settings

Team Call

An Enterprise Voice user has the ability to define a team-call group in her Lync client, which is a list of contacts who can answer calls on behalf of the user. When an incoming phone call is received for the individual, any users in the team call group can also receive the incoming call notification, but with an indication of who the caller originally attempted to contact.

TIP

Enterprise Voice users can configure their team-call groups in call forwarding settings the same way as managing call forwarding. This allows Enterprise Voice users to enable or disable the team-call feature as necessary.

Delegation

Being enabled for Enterprise Voice enables users to define delegates to answer calls on their behalf, but the delegate functionality is slightly different from team-call. In the situation of a delegate and a boss, the boss might elect for calls to ring only the delegate first, allowing delegates to screen calls on behalf of the boss and transfer users if necessary.

> **TIP**
>
> Delegate functionality is best provided through the Attendant Console client, which is designed specifically for these types of scenarios. It offers delegates an interface more focused on call answering, transfers, and taking notes about callers, which can be useful for delegate or front desk reception users.

Delegates have the option to use a blind or consultative transfer to send the caller to a boss. In a blind transfer, the caller is sent directly to the boss without notification, whereas in a consultative transfer, the delegate first calls the boss to check whether he wants to accept the call or not accept it. Only if the boss desires to accept the call does the delegate transfer the caller.

Delegates can also perform safe transfers where they remain on the line with the caller and principal to ensure the two parties are connected before removing themselves from the conversation. A key advantage of Enterprise Voice delegation is that these options are performed using a graphical user interface, and users have no need to memorize phone keys and codes to perform these types of transfers.

Response Groups

Response Groups are a feature that Lync Server provides to manage and direct inbound callers to agents. Workflows can be defined where callers are prompted for specific questions and then directed to a queue of agents who consist of Enterprise Voice users. The callers' responses to any questions are converted from speech to text and displayed to the agent when receiving the call.

Additionally, Response Group agents appear as anonymous to the caller. Administrators can define multiple workflows, queues, and algorithms for routing callers to the correct agents. Agents can also participate formally or informally, meaning they can either manually sign out of a Response Group or they can be automatically included in a group that receives calls any time they are signed in to Lync Server.

Call Park

Call park features allow a Lync Server Enterprise Voice user to answer a call at one endpoint and then put the user on hold, or park the call temporarily. The user can then pick up that same call at some other location or endpoint by calling the phone number used to park the call.

Private Lines

An Enterprise Voice user can have a private telephone number hidden from address lists and contacts in addition to the primary telephone number, which is published to users. This additional line can be configured to ring with a different sound to differentiate calls to the private line from the regular number.

SIP Trunking

The concept of SIP trunking is a feature that has been supported in Communications Server since OCS 2007 R2. SIP trunking enables Lync Server to connect either to another IP-based PBX using SIP or to an Internet Telephony Service Provider (ITSP).

SIP trunking is generally used when integrating Lync Server directly with an existing IP-PBX from vendors such as Cisco or Avaya without the need for a media gateway device. Alternatively, it can be used to provide telephony service to Lync Server without the need for traditional PBX, media gateway, or wiring. Instead, an ITSP provides SIP trunking services across the Internet to allow Lync Server to make and receive phone calls using purely VoIP without a traditional phone infrastructure, as depicted in Figure 3.3.

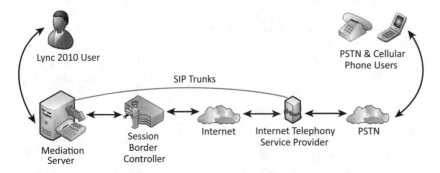

FIGURE 3.3   Lync Server SIP Trunking with an Internet Telephony Service Provider

E911

Enhanced 911 features are now provided in Enterprise Voice so that users can dial 911 and have that call connected to an emergency routing service. Through the use of the location information discussed previously, the routing service is automatically provided with the endpoint location when dialed.

> **NOTE**
>
> It is important to note that Lync Server does not provide E911 capabilities, but can provide location information to an E911 routing service on behalf of the endpoints.

Remote Access

One of the strongest advantages of Lync Server is that it offers users a completely seamless and consistent user experience regardless of location. Users who travel and use a hotel's public Wi-Fi have access to the same features as users in an office that uses the corporate network. This consistent experience is provided without a VPN connection or manual client configuration changes by the user, which allows all features to work from any location.

A Lync Server endpoint is aware whether it connects internally or externally by means of service records (SRV) in DNS, so users don't need to make any changes to their client configurations depending on their locations. When a user is remote, the signaling is performed over the standard HTTPS port 443, so it is secure and accessible from almost any remote network.

This feature is similar in function to the Outlook Anywhere feature, which has existed for Outlook users since Exchange 2003. Just as users have come to expect Outlook to function identically whether inside or outside the office, a remote user has full access to the Lync Server feature set. They can view presence, exchange IMs, host or attend web conferences, share desktops, or perform A/V conversations. This even extends to Enterprise Voice users who can make and receive phone calls with their office numbers from anywhere in the world across the Internet.

Federation

Federation is a feature that enables organizations that have deployed Lync Server to communicate easily and securely across the public Internet. As long as both organizations have deployed an Access Edge server, federation can be used to view presence and exchange IMs.

Organizations can also use federation to participate in web conferences with each other or have audio and video conversations with one another. Similar to the way e-mail has become a standard means of communication, federation for rich collaboration capabilities has emerged as a standard way to conduct business across organizations.

> **NOTE**
>
> Federation is not limited to organizations with only Lync Server, but can also be used with IBM SameTime or Cisco Unified Presence Server for organizations that have not deployed Lync Server.

Public IM Connectivity

A special type of federation called Public IM Connectivity (PIC) enables MCS users to communicate with contacts using the various public IM networks. Although many organizations have deployed previous versions of a Communications Server and support federation, there are still needs to communicate with public IM contacts at times.

Lync Server supports the following public IM providers:

- AOL
- Yahoo!
- MSN

Additionally, federation to Google Talk users can be provisioned through the XMPP Gateway Server role. PIC connectivity provides presence and peer-to-peer IM for all providers, but in Lync Server, peer-to-peer A/V conversations can also be used with Windows Live contacts. Figure 3.4 shows how a Lync server infrastructure can communicate both with federated partners and the public IM networks across the Internet.

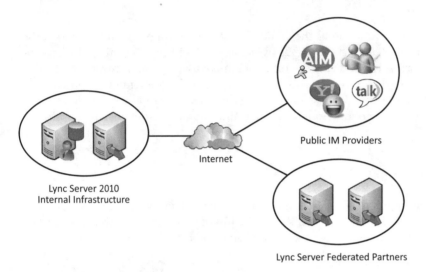

Public IM Providers

Internet

Lync Server 2010
Internal Infrastructure

Lync Server Federated Partners

FIGURE 3.4   Lync Server Federation and Public IM Connectivity

Archiving

For organizations that have archiving or compliance needs, Lync Server provides the Archiving Server role, which can capture IM traffic. All archiving data is saved to a Microsoft SQL Server database and is separate from the database used for all user services and contact lists.

Archiving can be enabled at the pool level to capture traffic for all users or it can be enabled on a per-user basis if archiving needs to done for only a select group of users. If an organization has no need to capture internal traffic, archiving can also be configured to log only federated traffic.

> **TIP**
>
> In the event of an archiving server failure, the administrator has the option to shut down the pool and user services to ensure the organization meets compliance regulations.

Monitoring

A key factor in determining the success of an audio and video deployment is insight into how the system performs for the end users. Lync Server provides out-of-the-box monitoring capabilities with the Monitoring Server role. When deployed, endpoints submit reports when completing an audio or video call, which are then stored in SQL databases dedicated to call records and monitoring data.

There are two types of reports collected. One report is referred to as *call detail records (CDR)* and it contains information about when the call occurred and what endpoints were involved. The other is a quality of experience (QoE) report that contains comprehensive data, including Mean Opinion Scores (MOS) of various components, which indicates the call quality in both directions. These reports also identify which subnet the endpoints used so that administrators can quickly isolate any issues to a specific device or network segment.

NOTE

A SQL Server Report Pack is bundled with the installation media so that administrators have immediate access to rich reports about how the system is used.

Lync Server also supports synthetic transactions that are PowerShell cmdlets an administrator can run, which simulate actions taken by users against the server. Examples of these transactions are a user signing in, two users sending IM messages to each other, or a test audio call between two endpoints. These synthetic transactions can be used to test user functionality systemwide on a recurring basis or in conjunction with the Microsoft System Center Operations Manager management pack for Lync Server, which includes support for the transactions.

Summary

All the features discussed in this chapter are compelling reasons to use Lync Server as an organization's UC solution, but users have come to expect a certain degree of reliability with communications, especially with a phone system. In Lync Server, all the features can be made redundant and resilient to a single server or site failures so that users can continue to operate in the event of a malfunction.

The methods of providing high availability and disaster recovery for each server role vary and are outlined later, but steps have been taken to ensure users can always hear a dialtone when they pick up a phone. Some key advancements include allowing a Mediation Server role to use multiple gateways, users receiving primary and backup pool information when signing in, and endpoints that don't depend on Active Directory during a network failure. These types of changes have made Lync Server a highly reliable, end-to-end UC solution for an organization.

Benefits of Microsoft Lync Server 2010

Overview of Unified Communications

Since the first time a call was placed to a phone that did not answer, users of communications devices needed unified communications (UC). However, ask 1,000 IT professionals what UC means, and you'll likely get close to that number of answers. This is due to that fact that unlike Voice over IP (VoIP), where there is a tangible description of what a technology is or does, UC is s bit more difficult to qualify. Is it collaboration? Is it the capability to see someone's presence? Is it instant messaging? Is it all of these in a single client? The answer is yes... and no. Without realizing it, as we attempt to collaborate on a more granular and contextual level, we have been unifying our communications slowly and steadily for years.

The truth is that UC more closely defines how humans interact in person. For example, how did you communicate with someone who was having a conversation on a mobile phone? Without thinking about it, you updated his presence to busy in a call. If it wasn't important, you would probably just wait. However, if you really needed to communicate with someone, you would most likely make eye contact, and, if he signaled to you that he could accept communication from you, you would either use a gesture or speak to him.

This is nearly the same way you communicate when using a UC solution. Utilizing tools such as instant messaging, presence, voice, video, and screen sharing, you are able to interact with others in near real-time, using a familiar interface to provide the same clues and info you get when you interact with someone face to face.

Software-Powered Communication

As computer-processing power has dramatically increased (compare even a low-end work-station of today to the high-end workstations of less than a decade ago), the communications industry has realized that software-powered communication servers allow for dramatic changes in the way both enterprises and consumers interact with one another.

No matter how you define UC, the desire to reduce the latency in user-to-user communication should be a primary goal of any UC strategy. For example, how many times have you been involved in an email thread that stretched out over days or weeks due to time zones or some other reason that could have been solved with a quick, real-time audio conference call?

Enabling users to communicate in the method that best suits their needs at any particular moment, while relaying their willingness and availability to communicate, goes a long way towards reducing the human latency inherent in attempts at collaboration and communications today.

Brief History of UC

Before Voice over IP (VoIP), voice calls were sent over a dedicated network. Each call passed through a dedicated circuit and was switched from one point to the other, hence the term *circuit-switched*. Although this guaranteed a quality connection, it required dedicated processing power and physical connectivity. For example, the wire that went from your home telephone to the central office (CO) connected you to a physical port on the CO telephone switch. The processor of the CO switch had to constantly monitor each port to determine whether a particular phone (port) made a request to dial a number or access a feature, such as call forwarding.

With a telephone connected to a dedicated network, either the public switched telephone network (PSTN) or an enterprise class private branch exchange (PBX) network, it was difficult for outside influences to affect the quality of a connected call. Although having this separate network held numerous advantages, most notably quality and reliability, individual PBX or CO switches used proprietary protocols limiting interoperability and feature expansion. It also meant, for example, that if you wanted to access your PBX voicemail box from your email client, you were subject to the whim of the PBX voicemail vendor's decision as to what you could and couldn't do and what standards were supported.

Using LANs and Packet-Switched Networks

As more and more communications began using LANs and packet-switched networks (the Internet is just a huge packet-switched network), the voice networks were forced to open up and connect to other networks. Unified messaging was probably the first mainstream attempt at UC. Accessing voicemail from your email client and unifying your inbox gave users the potential of true UC. In fact, some traditional phone vendors still consider unified voice messaging the equivalent to UC. Of course, anyone who has shared a desktop with a single click, made a call without dialing a phone number, or created a conference using only the mouse certainly knows that is not the case.

The capability to leverage a database of phone numbers to make calls using the phone was also an early attempt at UC. Anyone who attempted to deploy this type of integration, even as recently as a decade ago, knows that it's not for the faint of heart and was generally implemented only in narrow cases, such as when a huge database of contacts were dialed by large calling centers. The average enterprise had neither the expertise nor the time and money to implement such a system.

VoIP Becomes Mainstream

When VoIP finally became mainstream, again, the promise of truly UC was presented to the enterprise community. In theory, now that the voice packets were riding the same network as the data packets, how difficult could it be to unify them? A lot harder than it looked.

Although VoIP brought the capability to easily perform day-to-day administrative tasks such as moves, adds, and changes, little was done to unify the communications. Users' identities were still synced from, and stored outside of, the VoIP PBX, voicemail systems still use proprietary interfaces, and now the quality of the voice call was subject to influences outside of the PBX administrator's hands. It seemed that, aside from adding complexity to the building of a communications system, VoIP didn't add that much value overall.

As a new technology, most of the effort in deploying VoIP was put into the actual engineering and the proper deployment of the technology, not in the leveraging of the endless possibilities that existed. In addition, VoIP was initially positioned as a replacement end state for the traditional TDM infrastructure. Enterprises that saw cost savings over dedicated point-to-point (T1) links saw value in VoIP-compatible PBXs, but just replacing the line cord that went into the desktop phone with an Ethernet patch cord didn't alter the user experience much.

Users still had to remember phone numbers, dial a multitude of phone numbers to reach someone, leave and retrieve voicemail messages using the handset, check multiple voicemail inboxes, and so on. Communications were unified simply because they were using a VoIP-based communications system.

To truly unify communications, begin with a central repository of user attributes at the core of your strategy. This repository should be easily updated, secure, and extensible so that as new features are created, the required attributes can be easily added. If an enterprise has deployed a Windows server infrastructure, it already has a repository in place: Active Directory.

Unlike other solutions, Microsoft's UC architecture directly uses Active Directory and does not rely on a separate data feed for synchronization. Unlike previous versions, Lync Server now utilizes a Central Management Store (CMS) for all settings and configuration details. This store is replicated to all servers so that servers are now survivable.

Benefits for Lync Server Users

UC solution begins with the end-user experience. Lync Server's newly designed Communicator client provides a concise, seamless, and logical view to enable users easy access to all communications modalities.

Contacts

Lync Server provides many new, yet familiar, ways to interact, learn about, and communicate with colleagues. The clear view of many data streams enables the user to choose the proper modality to communicate with another user.

Users can save time when locating resources because they can search for others using keywords as well as names. Even with incomplete information, users can locate and communicate with others.

Lync Server also leverages the concept of social networks. Live contact cards, photos, and spoken names enable users to recognize and discover more about the people in their social network that matter to them most.

Users can save time and be more granular when searching, thanks to SharePoint skill search with address book service web queries (ABS-WQ). By simply placing a mouse over a contact, the hover card provides a consistent view of vital user data across all Office products, including Lync Server, enabling users to be more productive and save time by not switching applications as often.

Users that are part of a large enterprise might be overwhelmed by team-level or corporatewide changes by having users' photos and their spoken name populating the OCS contact list. In this way, users can become familiar with their evolving social network. Users can become better corporate citizens by learning how a new colleague's name is pronounced prior to meeting or speaking with him or her. You can now quickly see updates from all your contacts in a single concise view, called the Activity Feed.

Contact management is simpler thanks to the unified contact store. Lync Server now utilizes Exchange 2010 for its contact list, so users save time by not having to manage contacts in both Lync Server and Exchange. When the Outlook Social connector is deployed, users can search across their entire social network, such as Facebook from within Communicator.

Users now have easy access to the history of their communication with a particular contact, enabling them to easily determine the context of a conversation and eliminate the need to catch up on a conversation, for example, when usually just a simple IM can answer a question. Similarly, when starting new conversations, a user can easily provide context to a session to further streamline communications.

Managing Communications

Although there are many ways to initiate a call to a contact, users that are transitioning to Lync Server from traditional PBXs will benefit from having an easily accessible dialpad. In the previous version of OCS, the dialpad existed but was not easy to find.

Lync Server users migrating from simple instant messaging and presence on previous versions of OCS to Enterprise Voice on Lync Server will benefit from being able to conduct communications using any modality from a familiar, consistent interface.

When coupled with exchange unified messaging, users can now have a simple-to-view visual representation of each voicemail message. Lync Server users save time by easily managing voicemails within Communicator.

Panoramic Mode

Lync Server clients can leverage the panoramic video of roundtable devices, allowing for a more comfortable face-to-face video experience. This emulates a telepresence environment that integrates well with commodity desktop hardware.

Activity Feed

Users of common current social networks (Twitter, LinkedIn, Facebook, and so on) will immediately recognize and be comfortable with the new activity feed in the Lync Server Communicator client. With a simple glance, you can receive updates (notes) and pictures from those in your social network.

Privacy and Presence Enhancements

Executive users benefit most from the new privacy enhancements in Lync Server. By adding enhanced privacy to a pool, users added to a contact list appear as offline until granted permission by the added contact to see their presence updates. This is valuable, for example, to create ethical walls between departments or divisions. Even if this setting is applied to a pool, users can opt out, enabling all others to see their presence.

Audio and Video to MSN PIC Contacts

Although public instant messaging communication (PIC) has always been a benefit of OCS, Lync Server takes the PIC story a bit further by enabling one-to-one audio and video exclusively to PIC contacts that are homed to the MSN service. This change enables corporate users with a strong MSN presence outside of work to reduce the need to run a separate client on their corporate workstation, yet maintain a robust communications experience.

Enterprise Voice Benefits

Perhaps some of the most tangible, new, and exciting benefits of Lync Server are those related to the Enterprise Voice set of features. With the new release, Lync Server competes with the voice features provided by traditional PBXs. In fact, at VoiceCon 2010, Lync Server won the Voice RFP competition competing against the major PBX manufacturers.

Mediation Server Role Collocation

In prior versions of OCS, the Mediation Server was a dedicated role and required a one-one relationship between the server and the gateway. OCS configuration enabled only a single, next-hop configuration from the Mediation Server to the media gateway (PBX, PSTN, and so on). Although certain gateway manufacturers were able to load-balance calls from the gateway to OCS, OCS was limited to only the single next hop. In Lync Server, the mediation role now runs on the Front End Server as a service. This concept of mediation server collocation provides tangible benefits from a topology, administrative, and user perspective.

With Lync Server, each Front End Server can have its own mediation service, enabling pools to route to gateways instead of the mediation servers. This enables multiple mediation servers to route to the same gateway or multiple gateways to route to a single mediation service.

This capability provides tremendous flexibility to design engineers and enterprises with a large number of PBX/PSTN trunks at a single site or many smaller sites. In previous versions of OCS, these scenarios required a mediation server at each location. In addition to a tangible reduction in servers, this topology change provides greater resiliency, more flexible routing choices, and more options for media flow.

Media Bypass

One of original roles of the mediation server was to transcode between RealTime audio (RTAudio) and G.711 to integrate with standards-based media gateways and PBXs. With Lync Server, calls can be sent using G.711 directly to a supported gateway or PBX. Although low bandwidth signaling (SIP) still traverses the mediation service role, higher bandwidth media (RTP) flows directly from a Lync Server endpoint to the GW/PBX, bypassing the Mediation Server role.

This change provides several benefits, including

- ▶ Removes a potential single point of failure that a mediation server introduced

- ▶ Reduces the overall server footprint of OCS

- ▶ Reduces the number of hops a media stream takes

In addition, in scenarios where a branch appliance is deployed, calls from PBX users at a branch to Lync Server users at the same branch, media now remains at the branch. Prior to Lync Server, an extra mediation server at the branch was required to enable similar call flow.

Optional Dedicated A/V Conferencing Role

In scenarios that require heavy conferencing resources, or MCUs, the A/V Conferencing role can be split off from the Front End Server role. Multiple A/V servers can be placed in a pool and this A/V pool can be designated as the conferencing resource for many other pools. This topology offers a distinct advantage enabling conference-centric enterprises the capability to provide a highly available conferencing resource to the users, but also keeping this resource-intensive application isolated from the day-to-day IM presence and telephony services. Additionally, this enables an enterprise to virtualize basic telephony services while providing physical hardware for A/V services.

Site Survivability

For Lync Server to better compete with other enterprise-grade telephony platforms, resiliency and survivability needed to be addressed. New, additional options for Lync Server topology, along with the introduction of new hardware and server roles, coupled with the support of new DNS options, provide Lync Server architects the ability to craft deployments that are highly available and able to survive failures at various points in the enterprise. This enables Lync Server to continue to provide vital telephony services to Lync Server users.

Survivable Branch Appliance

With the registrar role moved to the Front End Servers and possessing its own SQL express database, pools now have reduced requirements on the back-end SQL database. A survivable branch appliance (SBA) can be set up for branch users as their primary registrar with the pool as their backup registrar.

Lync Server branch users still get their user services from the Front End pool, usually located in a central datacenter. However, in the event of a pool failure, because the branch appliance is aware of the branch user registrations, users at the branch will experience only a loss of user services and still be able to access the PSTN because routing is running on the SBA. Unlike some traditional PBX branch scenarios, Lync Server users benefit from this topology change by not having to re-register to the SBA during a failure.

Supporting DNS Load Balancing

By supporting DNS load balancing (DNS-LB), enterprises that deploy Lync Server can benefit greatly thanks to simplified hardware load-balancing (HLB) configurations. In enterprise HA deployments, HLB are still required for certain traffic, notably HTTP and HTTPS. However, because these are the protocols that are commonly run through load-balanced configurations, their deployment is simpler than in previous versions when SIP traffic also passed through HLBs.

> **NOTE**
>
> The use of DNS-LB allows for simpler server shutdown through draining. This is a benefit that any support engineer who has ever had to take a server out of service can greatly appreciate! In an N+1 scenario, where a subset of the servers in a pool can support the entire enterprise, it is possible to remove a server during normal business hours.

With Lync Server, SBAs are now managed from the CMS database, which provides tremendous savings in the deployment and management of remote locations. Help desks and ISVs can prestage a branch appliance prior to shipping to a remote site. Once onsite, a technician can complete installation. This ease of deployment can be repeated for an unlimited number of sites, greatly reducing the workload of domain and enterprise administrators.

Another topology benefit is a new role, known as a *branch office server* that can support approximately 1000 users. The new role enables enterprises the flexibility to standardize their deployments across many branches of varying sizes, without sacrificing reliability, providing highly available PSTN connectivity.

In OCS 2007 R2, a common topology was to have dedicated pools at regional datacenters. With this new backup registrar capability, these same deployments can provide an available telephony solution by simply designating an alternative pool from another datacenter as the backup registrar. This feature is known as *data center resiliency* and provides a limited set of features, including PSTN access, to users whose primary datacenter is unavailable.

When datacenters are connected through low latency (<15ms rtd) WAN links, a single pool can be spread across multiple datacenters. In this configuration, an enterprise provides the entire robust set of Lync Server features out of either datacenter. This configuration is known as *metropolitan data center resiliency*.

Call Admission Control and DiffServ

Although RTAudio is a flexible payload codec, many larger enterprises believe that Lync Server should support call admission control, or CAC, as well. Already a fixture in many VoIP communications servers, call admission control is now configurable in Lync Server. With Lync Server, network managers can control the amount of bandwidth voice and video calls consume on a given link. By configuring the bandwidth policy service to control a specific site, calls can be rejected or rerouted to the PSTN when sufficient bandwidth is not available to complete the call. This ensures quality audio or video sessions. Enterprises can garner tremendous benefit from planning their CAC strategy prior to deployment.

Lync Server users benefit from its capability to leverage the concept of differential services code points (Diffserv—or DSCP) for audio and video traffic. By separating port ranges for audio and video, Lync Server enables network administrators to provide different per-hop behaviors (for example, EF or expedited forwarding) for these streams. This enables latency sensitive traffic to route ahead of web or other non-real-time traffic. Windows 7 and Vista desktops can leverage Windows-based QoS. This enables them to be provisioned to apply DSCP markings to packets based exclusively on application and port ranges.

By combining CAC, DSCP, and Windows-based QoS policies, network administrators can rely on Lync Server to adhere to the policies they create and deploy on their network to enable all packets to arrive as required and ensure a quality user experience.

E911

Primarily developed for North America, enhanced 911 (E911) allows for additional information to be presented to the public service answering point (PSAP) that enables emergency personnel to obtain details about the specific location of an emergency call. These additional attributes are a building number, mailstop, cubicle number, or any other specific attribute that can save precious seconds in an emergency situation.

Because VoIP is mobile, simply relying on a telephone number is not suitable for IP communications. The new location information service (LIS) role in Lync Server enables network identifiers such as switch ports, subnets, and wireless BSSID information to be matched up with location information and transmitted to the PSAP when setting up a 911 call. In addition to regulatory compliance benefits, e911 allows for a safer telephony environment. With Lync Server's E911 service, end users trust that calls made to a 911 service will provide the vital details to emergency personnel.

Location can be set through the policy or manually. Visual indication of the current location is presented directly in the Lync Server client. E911 can also be configured to enable other onsite users to be automatically conferenced into an emergency call, enabling corporate first responders to be aware of 911 calls as they happen, which coordinates with police, fire, and other emergency services as they arrive.

Malicious Call Trace

When a Lync Server user receives a call that she deems is harassing or threatening, she can flag it in the call database. By alerting system administrators of this fact, they can quickly determine the source of the call and trace it back to its origin for evaluation by security personnel.

Caller ID Controls

Lync Server allows for a user's caller ID to be modified dynamically based on the destination of the call—internal or external. This enables an enterprise to maintain full reverse name lookup to the corporate directory for internal calls, but provide a uniform departmental or location number to be presented when making external calls. This is used in certain situations such as outbound call centers, support desks, or any other situation where it is necessary to block caller ID digits to external parties. This can be set at a user level or by policy.

Anonymous Agents

Lync Server response group agents can be placed in anonymous groups. This feature enables help desk personnel to participate in a response group without providing a name and number to internal users.

Prior to Lync Server, users calling a response group saw the agent they were connected to in their Communicator client and frequently then bypassed the response group on subsequent calls, defeating the purpose of the group by failing to leverage the available pool of agents. Lync Server response groups in anonymous mode are suitable for use in scenarios where the agent's number needs to be kept private.

On-Net and Off-Net Voice Routing

For an enterprise to benefit from a large geographically dispersed voice network with many PSTN egress points, the capability to route calls through these points is crucial.

However, when the points are located in different cities or countries, each point can require different dialing formats, prefixes, or other access codes. This can add tremendous complexity to a corporate dialing plan. Fortunately, Lync Server provides central alternative routes and number-formatting changes to manipulate the dialed number prior to routing to a PBX or the PSTN.

Media Gateway Certification

Beginning with OCS 2007, Microsoft developed the open interoperability program (OIP) for PBX and gateway vendors to enable enterprises to determine whether a particular piece of hardware or software version is certified to work with OCS. Beginning with Lync Server, audio quality and performance testing is included in OIP certification. This enables systems engineers to design a solution that will perform properly for all communication modalities.

Client-Side Benefits

Lync Server takes huge strides to improve the client experience. Based on hours of user testing, the Microsoft team released an improved client in terms of functionality and usability.

Pre-Call and In-Call Quality Feedback

Lync Server users can determine, in advance, what kind of call quality to expect on a given call based on real-time feedback from within Communicator. Familiar bars icons, such as on a cell phone, tell users at a glance how their network is performing during a call. This provides, for example, a user currently connected through a public Wi-Fi network the knowledge that the available bandwidth might not provide a quality experience, enabling him or her to consider other options for the call.

With location services, Lync Server has the capability to determine whether multiple users are joining a conference call from the same physical location or a location that can cause poor conditions, including feedback. During a call, Lync Server alerts users, through a pop-up, that they might be causing call quality issues and suggests actions to resolve the problem, such as going on mute.

Lync Server users who need to confirm the quality of a call prior to initiating it can make a test call to an audio test service. This functionality is built into the client and provides users who deploy a new audio device or roam to an unknown network a chance to test their call by calling the test service, recording a short sentence, and playing the message back.

Private Lines

Lync Server users can have a private line for incoming calls. This enables calls from important business contacts and family members to be easily identified and receive priority handing. Calls to a user's private number are uniquely identified on the incoming toast and with a distinct ring. Calls to private lines override DND and other redirection settings to ensure that they always route to the user.

> **TIP**
>
> This feature benefits users who provide their private line to an important caller such as a priority customer or family member because they know the incoming call will always ring through to their endpoint.

Call Parking

Have you ever placed a call on hold and picked it up somewhere else, but didn't transfer it because you knew you couldn't get to the other phone in time? Well, that is a situation for which Call Park was invented. Now users can park a call in an orbit number and go to another client to retrieve it. By combining Call Park with a third-party overhead paging system, an attendant can answer a call, park it, and page the requested person. Enterprises that have mobile internal users, such as shop floor or manufacturing employees, have been using park-and-page for many years. Now Lync Server users can enjoy the same feature.

Common Area Phones

When considering a PBX replacement, not every existing phone location can have a PC. Hallways, lobbies, and transient worker areas are locations that can benefit from the concept of common use phones. The expense of providing a Tanjay-type device and the access control requirements (domain account, and password or fingerprint) made OCS 2007 R2 ill-suited for this task.

With Lync Server, endpoint devices are available that provide simple calling features by being plugged in and provisioned by an administrator. These phones retrieve parked calls and make internal calls without users signing in to Lync Server.

On recovering from a power failure or being unplugged, common-use phones automatically reregister with the registrar. Calling rules for default behavior can be set using the same management tools that other CS users are managed. Common-use phones have their own domain accounts in Lync Server.

Hot Desking

For transient areas, common use phones can be logged in to with a standard user's account, enabling the user to make and receive calls wherever logged in. By using a PIN code or pairing the phone with a PC, transient workers can have all the benefits of a fully functional Lync Server endpoint wherever they need it. By signing into a phone designated as a hot-desking location, a Lync Server user gets a contact list, recent calls, and other contact-related information where he or she signs in. Hot-desking phones revert back to their common-use configurations based on a configurable timeout, allowing for a touchless user experience. Hot-desking options are easily managed by group policy settings similar to all other CS users.

Collaboration Benefits

In concert with Microsoft Office 2010 and Sharepoint 2010, Lync Server is the lynchpin to a successful enterprise collaboration strategy.

Improved Web Conferencing Experience

Possibly the most significant change to, and benefit of, the new collaboration tools in Lync Server is the deprecation of the live meeting client. Lync Server users can join and manage live meetings through their Communicator client. Help desk personnel no longer need to explain which client to use for what kind of call. Simple, tight integration of scheduling and managing conferences provides a huge confidence boost even for inexperienced users. With just a few clicks, users can schedule, manage, and provide content for a meeting. Conference invitees, who do not use Lync Server, can join Lync Server web conferences by using a new lightweight client, the Lync Server Attendee online client.

Administrators looking to provide limited communicator web access to non-Windows or remote users in OCS deployed Communicator web access (CWA). CWA was a dedicated server role in OCS. In Lync Server, this role is deprecated and replaced with the Communicator web app, which is a service running on the Front End Server.

This topology change benefits to administrators and users alike. Administratively speaking, eliminating this server role offers a reduced overall Lync Server server footprint and simplifies management responsibilities. Lync Server users accessing CWA can share their desktops, and manage inbound and outbound calls no matter what OS they used to access the CW application.

In previous versions of OCS, only Windows users could share their desktops; users could not receive calls. By bringing these additional options to the CWA experience, non-Windows Lync Server users are provided with an improved experience.

Lobby Experience

With Lync Server, after joining a conference, it is possible to apply a new experience to attendees that enhances the meeting join experience. This is known as the *lobby*. When a nonpresenter joins a meeting that has not started, she is placed in the lobby until the presenter joins. In addition, the lobby mode can be used during a call to avoid the disturbance of people entering and exiting a conference. The presenter can control when lobby users are admitted to the conference. This enables a presenter to maintain control of a meeting, especially one with several attendees.

Multiple Language Support

Users at multinational enterprises benefit from this new Lync Server feature. Each Lync Server site can have its own language for meeting prompts. When users join a meeting, they hear prompts in the language of their site, regardless of the site of the organizer.

Simplified Join Experience

If you have ever had a difficult time getting users to connect a live meeting and were confused by the obfuscated meeting URI in previous versions, fear not. The new simplified meeting URIs make the meeting-join experience quicker and more reliable. System administrators can set a simple URL (for example, HTTP://meet.contoso.com) that will be used by all meetings. This simple URL cleans up the body of the default Outlook message so that even those unfamiliar with joining a live meeting can join easily.

Visual Conference Calls

Sometimes, a simple audio conference is all that is required for quick collaboration. If users frequently attend audio-only meetings in Lync Server, they will be presented with a familiar, clear, and concise listing of users who join their conference. Users can manage their audio conferences with confidence, using the same interface from which they make individual calls.

Mute All, DTMF, and Roll Call

Users conducting large conferences benefit from the mute all option. Using the simple, familiar Communicator interface, a meeting organizer can mute attendees to gain control of a meeting or conduct a press conference-type meeting.

Meeting participants can control their meeting status using the dialpad. This also enables mobile users to have full control over their meeting experience.

When conducting larger meetings, Lync Server meeting organizers can obtain an audio roll call of meeting participants. The recorded name or text-to-speech spoken name is played to only the organizer, enabling administrators to keep track of meeting participants.

Meeting Content Control

Collaboration power users can skip ahead in uploaded content shared in meetings. If you have ever been in a meeting where the presenter spent too much time on content you already knew about, you will appreciate this feature. A simple mouse click returns you to the content currently being shared.

Join from PBX

Users who are not Enterprise Voice–enabled can still participate in meetings with Lync Server Communicator. Users who have their extension homed to their corporate PBX phone can click the simple meet URL in a meeting invite. Communicator can be configured to call the meeting participants at their PBX number. This enables non-Enterprise Voice users to enjoy the benefits of Lync Server's advanced UC features as well.

Management and Administration Benefits

Lync Server joins with the current Microsoft platforms by including functions such as roles-based administrative access and clear virtualization support.

Central Management Store

From a topology perspective, the most significant change in Lync Server from its predecessors is its most significant benefit as well. The CMS is a centralized database of all Lync Server settings, which is replicated to all servers in a deployment, including edge servers. The Lync Server topology benefits of this change are quite significant on many levels.

The centralized management store

- ▶ Reduces Lync Server's reliance on Active Directory domain services replication to remote locations.

- ▶ Enables an edge server to be configured as part of the main deployment, significantly reducing configuration errors.

- ▶ Is automatically replicated to each server (and through HTTPS to edge servers) automatically whenever configuration changes are made to a topology. This ensures that nonprimary survivable servers are able to take over their designated roles when required, while being aware of newly added servers or roles.

- ▶ Enables a branch office server or appliance to continue to process calls even if its link to the pool is lost.

Administration Tools

Administrators familiar with previous versions of OCS undoubtedly know the Installation Wizard and Microsoft management console (MMC) snap-in that is used to administer OCS. Beginning with Lync Server, these tools are deprecated and have been replaced with a more flexible and robust toolset. Deployment engineers, system architects, and those responsible for the day-to day-upkeep of Lync Server benefit greatly from these new tools. Designing even complex OCS deployments is much simpler thanks to the new Topology Builder client.

> **NOTE**
>
> Topology Builder is an application that enables an architect to design and validate a complete deployment. The output of Topology Builder, the topology document, is then published to the CMS and replicated throughout the environment automatically.

By offloading the design and detailed configuration of Lync Server from the deployment of the actual server roles, Lync Server engineers can focus their efforts on the design process, not the Installation Wizards. Additionally, errors such as FQDN typos are eliminated because topology documents must be validated before they can be published to the CMS. The Topology Builder methodology provides an accurate and complete deployment strategy, one that results in shorter deployment times and fewer errors.

After your topology is published and activated, there is still much work to do. Luckily, you have the Communications server control panel (CSCP). CSCP is a Silverlight-based user interface that is supported by all major browsers. Lync Server administrators can manage their deployments from any machine on the corporate network without having to download software. Online help is available from within CSCP and enables novice administrators to perform most common tasks with just a few mouse clicks.

For tasks not available in CSCP, or for bulk user operations, PowerShell cmdlets are available for every option and setting within Lync Server. Windows administrators have been able to leverage the nearly limitless capabilities of PowerShell for many types of system management, including WMI and COM operations, since its introduction in 2006. This capability allows for script-based operations, third-party extensions, and alternative management interfaces.

With these new tools available in Lync Server, Microsoft provides the framework to enable system administrators the ability to manage Lync Server effectively, and in a manner that suits their abilities and preferences.

Roles-Based Access Controls

Microsoft Exchange 2010 administrators will recognize Roles-Based Access Controls (RBAC) as the standard for controlling systems access. Lync Server provides standard, predefined roles that are applied to users to determine who, what, and where they can add, view, and change Lync Server data. When logging into CSCP, a user's RBAC rules are applied as well. RBAC ensures that administrators are not given access to more data than they require to complete their assigned tasks.

With the further expansion of Lync Server features into the telephony realm, RBAC plays an important role in Lync Server administration, giving the telephony group the ability to modify users' phone numbers, but not any other Lync Server attributes. With RBAC controls, system administrators can be sure that their data is safe and in the proper hands.

Virtualization Support

Lync Server supports virtualization for all roles, within specific guidelines. This represents a tremendous benefit, enabling Lync Server to leverage the virtualization infrastructure already present in most enterprises. Supporting Hyper-V R2 and VMware, many Lync Server scenarios are supported. Certain restrictions apply, such as branch servers and live migration of VMs, but overall, VM support represents a significant enhancement to Lync Server.

Monitoring Benefits

For Lync Server to become the platform of choice for enterprise-class UC, it must provide a robust monitoring solution. Lync Server provides a multitude of call health indicators that provide details, such as MOS scores and best and worst performing endpoints. This level of granularity enables administrators and help desk personnel to resolve issues quickly. When paired with Microsoft System Center Operations Manager (SCOM), administrators can set up alerts that are linked back to a CDR record for easy tracking. The monitoring tools provide a clear and concise view into the health of a Lync Server deployment.

To provide ongoing, consistent monitoring, Lync Server combined with SCOM can perform scheduled synthetic transactions. This enables monitoring personnel the ability to find problems before users do and proactively solve them.

Summary

With improvements at nearly all levels of the product, from the design, deployment, feature set, management, and survivability to the end-user experience, Lync Server promises to excel in all areas when compared to current market UC solutions, legacy phone systems, and branch office solutions.

Wherever the software-powered communications revolution takes UC, Microsoft's communications server products will lead the way in innovation and completeness of vision. With each evolutionary step, it gets better and better.

PART II

Microsoft Lync Server 2010 Server Roles

IN THIS PART

Microsoft Lync Server 2010 Front End

Overview

Microsoft Lync Server has a number of different server roles. These can be combined different ways to produce a myriad of architectural options. Even the collocation of services for a given role can be split for added flexibility.

The Front End role in Lync Server is significantly changed from previous versions. Three significant architectural changes are related to the Front End Server role.

▶ The Office Communications Server 2007 R2 Mediation Server role is now collocated on the front end as a best practice for all architectures. The exception is a direct SIP connectivity to a PBX or a SIP trunking provider.

▶ The A/V Conferencing role can now be broken into a dedicated pool. This is recommended for large deployments with more than 10,000 users.

▶ The Director role is no longer simply a front end pool with no users assigned to it. It has been separated out to a unique role and is discussed further in Chapter 9, "Director."

As in previous versions of Communications Server, a single Front End or multiple Front End Servers are organized into logical pools. A Standard Edition server exists as the only server in a pool, whereas multiple Enterprise Edition servers can exist in a pool to provide redundancy and scalability. HTTP traffic should still be load balanced by a hardware load balancer; however, other OCS services are now load balanced via DNS. This architecture moves complex traffic,

SIP, and media off of hardware load balancers traditionally designed solely for HTTP traffic, and it simplifies the overall design.

This chapter highlights the full lifecycle of the Front End Server role. Because the Front End Server is deployed first, this chapter also reviews the steps necessary to prepare Active Directory. Then it moves on to the installation of the Standard and Enterprise Editions of the Front End Server role, followed by configuration and administration. Finally, the chapter concludes with troubleshooting and best practices.

Active Directory Preparation

Lync Server leverages Active Directory more than any previous version of Communications Server. This results in tight integration across the Microsoft stack, including Microsoft Exchange and Microsoft SharePoint Server. However, first Active Directory must be prepared before installation can begin. All the Active Directory preparation steps can be performed either in the Deployment Wizard GUI or the Lync Server Management Shell, a customized version of PowerShell. This chapter reviews both methods.

The first step is to ensure that your Active Directory environment meets the minimum requirements for Lync Server. The requirements are outlined here:

▶ All domain controllers in the forest where Lync Server is deployed must be Windows Server 2003 SP2 or higher.

▶ All domains where you deploy Lync Server must have a functional level of Windows 2003 native or higher.

▶ The functional level for the forest must be Windows 2003 native or higher.

After the Active Directory prerequisites have been met, the next step is to extend the Active Directory schema to support Lync Server. The schema preparation process adds new classes and attributes to Active Directory that are required for Lync Server. This process must be run as a user that is a member of the Domain Admins and Schema Admins groups.

> **NOTE**
>
> To run the preparation steps from another domain member server other than the Schema Master, ensure that the remote registry service runs and the appropriate registry key is set on the Schema Master. In addition, the Active Directory Remote Server Administration Tools (AD DS) feature must be installed on the server where the preparation steps will run.

Figure 5.1 displays the Lync Server preparation steps main page.

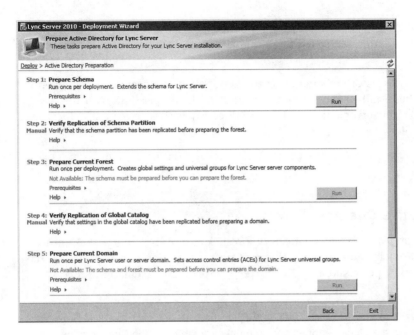

FIGURE 5.1   Lync Server Deployment Wizard

To extend the Active Directory schema using the Lync Server Deployment Wizard, follow the steps that follow:

1. From the Lync Server installation media, run Setup.exe.

2. For **Step 1: Prep Schema**, click **Run**.

3. At the Prepare Schema screen, click **Next**. You can see the Management Shell command that is executed, as shown in Figure 5.2.

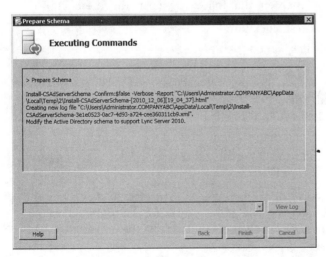

FIGURE 5.2   Schema Prep Command

4. Ensure the process is successful, and then click **Finish** to close the window.

5. Ensure the information replicated to all domain controllers before continuing to the next step.

To prepare the Active Directory schema using the Lync Server Management Shell, open the shell and run the Install-CSADServerSchema cmdlet. The proper syntax for the command is Install-CsAdServerSchema –LDF <full directory path where the LDF files are located>. For example:

```
Install-CsAdServerSchema –LDF "C:\Program Files\Microsoft Lync Server\
➥Deployment\Setup"
```

Prepare the Active Directory Forest

The next step is to prepare the Active Directory forest. A user of the Enterprise Admins group for the root domain must run this process. Forest preparation creates global objects and sets the appropriate permissions and groups to complete the installation process.

> **NOTE**
>
> In a new deployment, the global settings are automatically stored in the Configuration partition. If you are upgrading from an older version of Communications Server, you might still store the settings in the System container as was standard during previous versions of the installation. However, although it is not a requirement, it is recommended that the global settings container be moved from the System partition to the Configuration partition as part of the Lync Server installation process.

The Deployment Wizard should still be open from the last step. If not, run setup.exe and it picks up where you left off. Follow the steps that follow to prepare the forest:

1. For **Step 3: Prepare Current Forest,** click **Run**.

2. At the **Prepare Forest** screen, click **Next**.

3. Specify the location where the OCS universal security groups are created. By default, this is the local domain, but you can also select the FQDN for the domain where you want the groups to be created. Then click **Next**. You can see the management shell command that is executed, as shown in Figure 5.3.

4. Ensure the process is successful and then click **Finish** to close the window.

5. Ensure the information replicates to all domain controllers before continuing to the next step.

To prepare the Active Directory forest using the Lync Server management shell, open the shell and run the Enable-CsAdForest cmdlet. The proper syntax for the command is Enable-CsAdForest –GroupDomain <FQDN of the domain to create the universal groups>. For example:

```
Enable-CsAdForest –GroupDomain companyabc.com
```

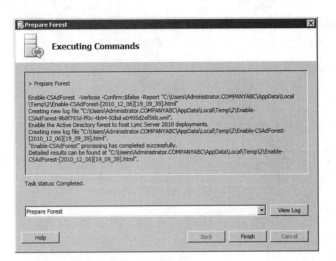

FIGURE 5.3   Prepare Forest Command

The final step is to prepare the Active Directory domain or domains. You need to run this in every domain where you plan to deploy Lync Server. This step adds the necessary ACEs (access control entries) to universal groups. Like the two previous steps, this can be done through the Lync Server Deployment Wizard or the Lync Server management shell.

Using the Deployment Wizard, perform the following steps.

1. For **Step 5: Prepare Current Domain**, click **Run**.
2. At the **Prepare Domain** screen, click **Next**. You can see the management shell command that is executed, as shown in Figure 5.4.
3. Ensure the process is successful, and then click **Finish** to close the window.
4. Ensure the information replicates to all domain controllers before continuing to the next step.

To prepare an Active Directory domain using the Lync Server management shell, open the shell and run the Enable-CsAdDomain cmdlet. The proper syntax for the command is Enable-CsAdDomain –Domain <current domain FQDN> -GroupDomain <FQDN of the domain where the Universal groups were created>. For example:

```
Enable-CsAdDomain –Domain companyabc.com –GroupDomain companyabc.com
```

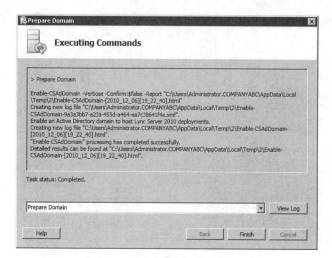

FIGURE 5.4   Prepare Domain Command

Active Directory Administration Groups

Following is a list of Active Directory Administration groups created by the preparation processes. They are referenced throughout the book and it is good to be familiar with them.

The service groups are

- **RTCHSUniversalServices**—Includes service accounts used to run the Front End Server and allows servers read/write access to Lync Server global settings and Active Directory user objects

- **RTCComponentUniversalServices**—Includes service accounts used to run conferencing servers, web services, the Mediation Server, the Archiving Server, and the Monitoring Server

- **RTCProxyUniversalServices**—Includes service accounts used to run Lync Server Edge Servers

The administration groups are

- **RTCUniversalServerAdmins**—Allows members to manage server and pool settings

- **RTCUniversalUserAdmins**—Allows members to manage user settings and move users from one server or pool to another

- **RTCUniversalReadOnlyAdmins**—Allows members to read server, pool, and user settings

Infrastructure groups include

- **RTCUniversalGlobalWriteGroup**—Grants write access to global setting objects for Lync Server.

▶ **RTCUniversalGlobalReadOnlyGroup**—Grants read-only access to global setting objects for Lync Server.

▶ **RTCUniversalUserReadOnlyGroup**—Grants read-only access to Lync Server user settings.

▶ **RTCUniversalServerReadOnlyGroup**—Grants read-only access to Lync Server settings. This group does not have access to pool-level settings; it can access only settings specific to an individual server.

Forest preparation then adds service and administration groups to the appropriate infrastructure groups, as follows:

▶ RTCUniversalServerAdmins is added to RTCUniversalGlobalReadOnlyGroup, RTCUniversalGlobalWriteGroup, RTCUniversalServerReadOnlyGroup, and RTCUniversalUserReadOnlyGroup.

▶ RTCUniversalUserAdmins is added as a member of RTCUniversalGlobalReadOnlyGroup, RTCUniversalServerReadOnlyGroup, and RTCUniversalUserReadOnlyGroup.

▶ RTCHSUniversalServices, RTCComponentUniversalServices, and RTCUniversalReadOnlyAdmins are added as members of RTCUniversalGlobalReadOnlyGroup, RTCUniversalServerReadOnlyGroup, and RTCUniversalUserReadOnlyGroup.

Forest preparation also creates the following role-based access control (RBAC) groups:

▶ CSAdministrator

▶ CSArchivingAdministrator

▶ CSBranchOfficeTechnician

▶ CSHelpDesk

▶ CSLocationAdministrator

▶ CSResponseGroupAdministrator

▶ CSRoleAdministrator

▶ CSServerAdministrator

▶ CSUserAdministrator

▶ CSViewOnlyAdministrator

▶ CSVoiceAdministrator

Installation

This section outlines the steps for installing the Standard and Enterprise Editions of Lync Server. The Standard Edition is generally used for small deployments, whereas the

Enterprise Edition offers significant benefits for redundancy and a scalability. The largest difference between the Standard Edition and Enterprise Edition of Lync Server is that the Standard Edition uses SQL Server Express, previously known as MSDE, whereas the Enterprise Edition uses a full version of SQL Server 2005 or 2008.

Lync Server Topology Builder

After preparing Active Directory, the next step is to install the Lync Server Topology Builder. This tool is new and powerful. With a single tool it enables an administrator to design and validate a Lync Server topology, and then publish it to Active Directory. This process greatly simplifies deployments compared to previous versions of Communications Server.

Installation of the Topology Builder comes with some prerequisites and requirements. First, the administrator must be a member of the Domain Admins account in Active Directory. The right to install the Topology Builder can be delegated, but only by a user who is a member of both the Domain Admins and RTCUniversalServerAdmin groups. The other requirements and prerequisites are outlined in the following list:

▶ 64-bit edition of the following:

  ▶ Windows Server 2008 R2

  ▶ Windows Server 2008 SP2 or later

  ▶ Windows 7

  ▶ Windows Vista SP2 or later

▶ Net Framework 3.5 SP1 or a later service pack.

▶ Microsoft Visual C++ 2008 Redistributable x64 9.0.30729.4148. The Deployment Wizard automatically installs this package if it is not already installed.

▶ Windows PowerShell 2.0. This is already installed for Windows 7 and Windows Server 2008 R2. For Windows Server 2008, it must be downloaded separately (Microsoft KB968930).

CAUTION

Note that the previous versions of PowerShell must be uninstalled prior to installing PowerShell 2.0.

▶ Message Queueing (MSMQ) services. Be sure to also install Directory Services integration during the "Features" Installation Wizard.

▶ Backward Compatibility Pack for SQL Server 2005 v. 8.05.2312. Although this is not technically required to install Topology Builder, it is required to run the Install-CsDatabase cmdlets. These cmdlets are sometimes called by Topology Builder, depending on the chosen topology, and this should also be considered a prerequisite. This installation package can be found on the installation media in the \Setup\amd64 directory as SQLServer2005_BC.msi.

After the prerequisites are installed, the actual installation of the Topology Builder tool can begin. To install Topology Builder, follow these steps:

1. Run **setup.exe** from the installation media. It is located at \setup\amd64\setup.exe.

2. If the installer prompts you to install the Microsoft Visual C++ 2008 Redistributable, click **yes** and follow the Installation Wizard.

3. Click **Install Topology Builder** in the right column menu of the Deployment Wizard.

4. After installation is complete, there is a check mark next to the Install Topology Builder link, which is grayed out, as shown in Figure 5.5.

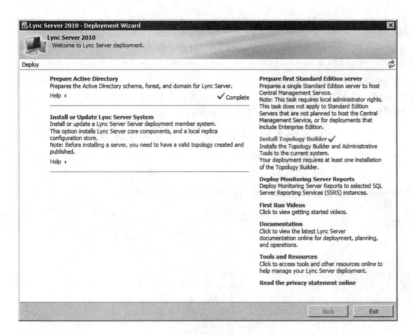

FIGURE 5.5   Completed Topology Builder Installation

The Topology Builder tool functions differ depending on your choice of Standard Edition or Enterprise Edition deployment. The process is outlined in each respective section that follows.

Standard Edition Installation

As noted previously, Lync Server Standard Edition is designed for smaller deployments. Standard Edition deployments can have only one server per pool and use SQL Server 2008 Express on the same server as the front end. This results in limited scalability and no redundancy. For this reason, Standard Edition is recommended only for small deployments or where high availability is not a requirement.

The first step for any Standard Edition deployment is to prepare the server as a Central Management Store and prepare the database.

1. From the main Deployment Wizard screen, in the right pane, click **Prepare the first Standard Edition Server**.

2. Click **Next** at the first screen.

3. The window displays the actions performed to prepare the server as the first Standard Edition server, including the setup of the Central Management Store. This process takes a few minutes to complete.

4. When it's done, ensure it completed successfully and then click **Finish**.

The next step is to define the topology with Topology Builder.

Topology Builder for Standard Edition Deployments

Lync Server uses the published topology to process traffic and maintain overall topology information. To ensure the topology is valid, it is recommended you run Topology Builder before your initial deployment and publish an updated topology after each topological change. This example shows a Standard Edition topology. Remember, if you change the topology later, it should be republished to ensure consistency.

When you first launch Lync Server Topology Builder, you see a partially blank MMC screen, as shown in Figure 5.6. Compare that to the detailed result at the end of this example.

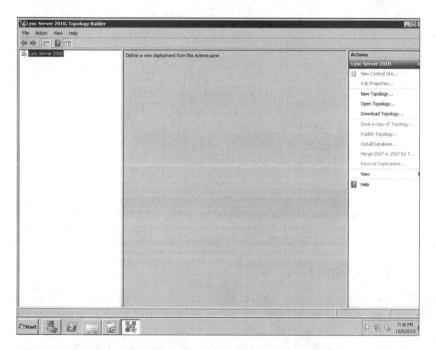

FIGURE 5.6   Topology Builder without a Defined Topology

To begin using Topology Builder, follow the steps that follow:

1. In the right side of the Action pane, click **New.**

2. Define the default SIP domain. In many deployments, this is simply your domain name, as shown in Figure 5.7. In more complex deployments, additional SIP domains might be added by clicking the **Add** button. When you are done defining SIP domains, click **OK.**

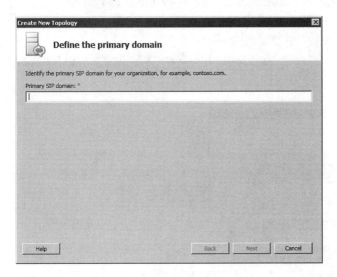

FIGURE 5.7   Define Default SIP Domain

3. The Next window will ask you to define the first site name as shown in Figure 5.8.

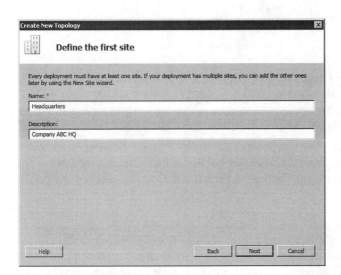

FIGURE 5.8   Define Site

NOTE

Note that Lync Server sites have no relationship to Active Directory sites. They are completely separate and unique to Lync Server.

4. The next window prompts the Administrator for the geographic location of the first site. Click **Finish** to complete the wizard.

5. This brings up the Define Front End Pool wizard.

6. Define the pool FQDN and select the radio button for Standard Edition, and then click **Next** as shown in Figure 5.9.

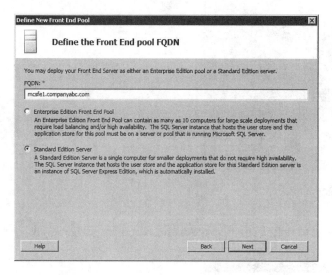

FIGURE 5.9   Define Front End Pool

7. Choose the appropriate workloads for your deployment, and then click **Next**. Choose the proper collocation options and click **Next**. Choose whether other server roles such as Archiving and Monitoring should be associated with this pool and click **Next**.

8. Define the database to be used by the pool, as shown in Figure 5.10. For a Standard Edition deployment, the SQL box is grayed out because a local instance of SQL Express is always used. Click **Next**. Then define the file share to be used by the pool and click **Next**.

NOTE

Note that you need to manually create the share on the front end before progressing past step 8. After the share is created, Lync Server assigns the appropriate permissions.

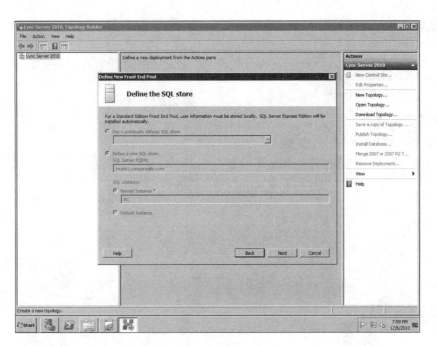

FIGURE 5.10   Define SQL Instance and File Share for Front End Pool

9. When you are ready, click **Next**.

10. Specify the Web Services URL and click **Next**. Specify the PSTN Gateway as shown in Figure 5.11 and click **Finish**.

This completes the initial topology definition. However, there are additional steps to complete a fully functional topology. The next step is to define easy-to-remember URLs for common Lync Server functions.

1. From the main Topology Builder page where Lync Server 2010 is highlighted, expand **Simple URLs** in the main pane, as shown in Figure 5.12, and then click **Properties** in the right pane.

2. Enter easy-to-remember URLs, as shown in Figure 5.13.

NOTE

The following three examples are all valid for Lync Server simple URLs:

▶ https://<function>.<domain _fqdn>: https://dialin.companyabc.com

▶ https://<sip_domain>/<function>: https://companyabc.com/dialin

▶ https://<External_WebPool_FQDN>/<function>: https://cs2010.companyabc.com/dialin

Note that these are the only allowed syntaxes.

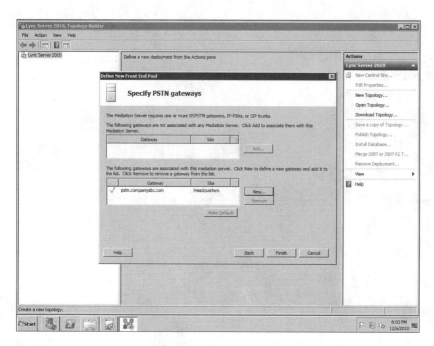

FIGURE 5.11   Enterprise Voice Topology

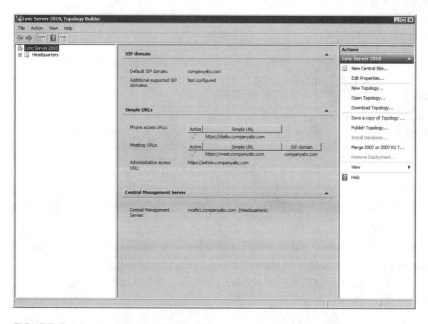

FIGURE 5.12   Expand the Simple URLs

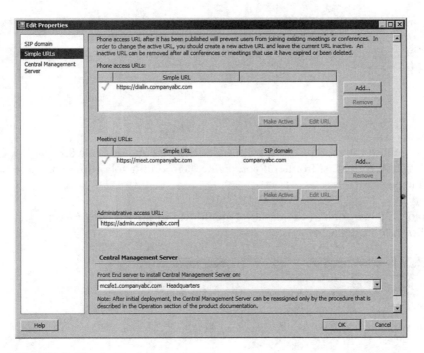

FIGURE 5.13   Configured Simple URLs

Port information, such as https://dialin.companyabc.com:443, is invalid. If you choose the first option, the FQDNs need to be included as SANs on your certificates. If you choose the second or third option, note that the following virtual directory names are reserved and cannot be used as part of a simple URL:

- ▶ ABS
- ▶ Conf
- ▶ LocationInformation
- ▶ RequestHandler
- ▶ AutoUpdate
- ▶ cscp
- ▶ OCSPowerShell
- ▶ RGSClients
- ▶ CertProv
- ▶ GetHealth
- ▶ ReachWeb
- ▶ RGSConfig

▶ CollabContent

▶ GroupExpansion

▶ RequestHandlerExt

▶ WebTicket

Publish the Topology

The final step is to publish the topology to the Central Management Store. In a Standard Edition deployment, this is the first front end you define. Perform the following steps to publish your topology:

1. In the Topology Builder tool, in the top-level menu item in the left pane, select Lync Server, as shown in Figure 5.14.

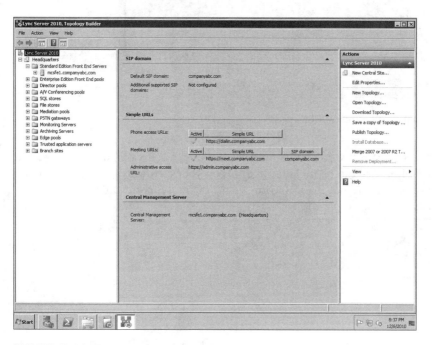

FIGURE 5.14   Top Level of Topology Builder

2. In the right pane, select **Publish Topology**.

3. At the opening screen, click **Next.**

4. Ensure that correct Central Management Store is selected, and then click **Next**. This starts the publishing process and overwrites any existing topologies.

5. The **Publish Topology** window displays the actions being performed. Ensure it says "Succeeded" at the bottom when it is finished, as shown in Figure 5.15, and then click **Finish.**

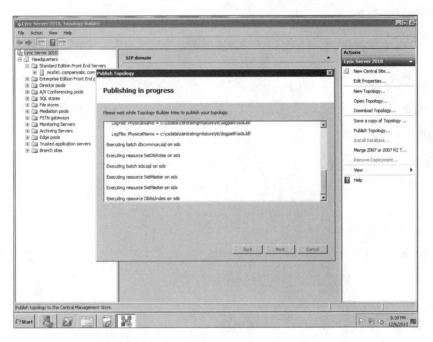

FIGURE 5.15   Successfully Published Topology

Installing the Front End Role

It is important to note that if you jumped to this section before completing the previous steps, you need to go back. Preparing the server for the first Standard Edition server and building a valid topology in the Topology Builder tool are both prerequisites to installing the Front End role. This is a different process from Office Communications Server 2007 and 2007 R2, and it involves more steps.

> **TIP**
>
> Administrators new to Lync Server are advised to review the new features, requirements, and prequisites before beginning the installation process.

The following prerequisites are required to install the Standard Edition Front End role:

- ▶ IIS with the following options:

    - ▶ Static Content

    - ▶ Default Document

    - ▶ Directory Browsing

    - ▶ HTTP Errors

- ▶ HTTP Redirection

- ▶ ASP.NET

- ▶ .NET Extensibility

- ▶ Internet Server API (ISAPI) Extensions

- ▶ ISAPI Filters

- ▶ HTTP Logging

- ▶ Logging Tools

- ▶ Request Monitor

- ▶ Tracing

- ▶ Basic Authentication

- ▶ Windows Authentication

- ▶ Request Filtering

- ▶ Static Content Compression

- ▶ IIS Management Console

- ▶ IIS Management Scripts and Tools

- ▶ Message Queueing with Directory Service Integration

After you've completed the steps outlined previously, the server is ready to install the Front End role. In the main Lync Server Deployment Wizard screen, click **Install or Update Lync Server System** from the main pane. Follow the steps that follow to complete the installation process:

1. Click **Run** to Install the local configuration store and follow the wizard.

2. For **Step 2: Setup or Remove Lync Server Components**, click **Run**.

3. The next screen shows the actions being performed, as shown in Figure 5.16. This process takes a few minutes to complete.

4. After the task completes, click **Finish,** and you are brought back to the Deployment Wizard.

5. Review **Step 3: Request, Install or Assign Certificates** and click **Run**. This deployment requires a total of four certificates, so you need to run this step eight times: four times to request certificates and four times to assign them.

6. Because this is a new deployment, choose **Create a new certificate.**

7. At the next screen, choose **Default** as shown in Figure 5.17, and then click **Request.**

8. Assuming you are using an internal CA, choose **Send the request immediately to an online certificate authority** and click **Next**. This is the default option.

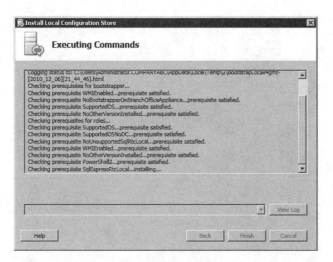

FIGURE 5.16   Installing the Front End Role

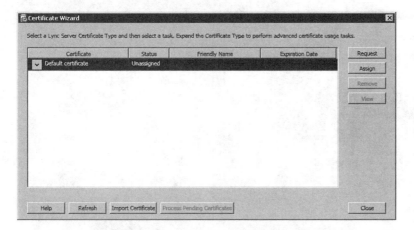

FIGURE 5.17   Request the Default Certificate

9. Select the appropriate CA for your environment from the drop-down list, choose a friendly name and key length, enable **Mark the certificate's private key as exportable** as shown in Figure 5.18, and then click **Next**.

10. Enter your Organization Name and Organizational Unit, and then click **Next**.

11. Select your country from the drop-down menu, and then enter your state/province and city/locality. Remember that full names must be entered, and abbreviations are not considered valid for certificate requests. When complete, click **Next**.

12. The Deployment Wizard automatically adds the SANs required based on the published topology. Unless you have special requirements, select the option to **Skip** and then click **Next**.

13. Review the information to ensure it is correct, and then click **Next**.

14. This screen shows the commands executed, as shown in Figure 5.19.

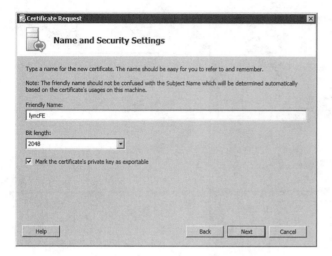

FIGURE 5.18   Certificate Request Settings

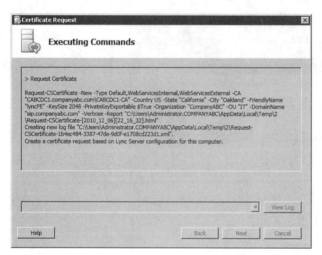

FIGURE 5.19   Certificate Request Process

15. Click **Next**.

16. Ensure the **Assign this certificate to Lync Server usages** box is checked and click **Finish**. Click **Next** through the wizard to assign the certificate. Figure 5.20 shows the actions taking place.

17. Ensure the process completes successfully, and then click **Finish**.

18. Click **Close** to close the wizard.

19. After the certificates have been assigned, there is a check mark by step 3 as shown in Figure 5.21. If there is not a check mark, check your process because you might have skipped a step.

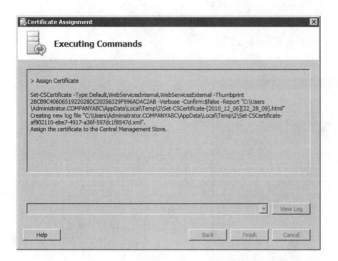

FIGURE 5.20   Choose the Default Certificate

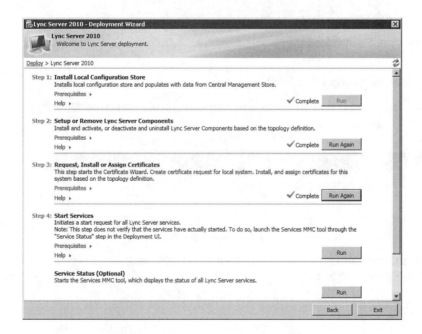

FIGURE 5.21   Certificate Process Completed

20. If the file store for the pool is located on this system, you need to reboot before continuing. After the reboot, restart the Deployment Wizard by launching Setup.exe.

21. Click **Install or Update Lync Server System**, and then click **Run** for Step 4: Start Services.

22. Click **Next**.

23. Ensure all services start, as shown in Figure 5.22.

FIGURE 5.22   All Services Started

24. Click **Exit** to leave the Deployment Wizard.

The Standard Edition front end is now installed and ready for further configuration using the Lync Server Control Panel.

> **NOTE**
>
> Note that the client autoconfiguration requirements are still the same.

The following DNS records are required for client autoconfiguration:

▶ SRV record of _sipinternaltls._tcp.<sip_Domain> for port 5061 pointing to the FQDN of your front end pool or Director

▶ Host (A) record of sipinternal.<sip_Domain> pointing to the IP address assigned to your front end pool or Director

▶ Host (A) record of sip.<sip_Domain> pointing to the IP address assigned to your front end pool or Director

Enterprise Edition Installation

Lync Server Enterprise Edition is designed for larger deployments or those that require high availability or redundancy. Enterprise Edition enables you to have multiple front end servers in a pool, and it scales to support larger user counts with an outboard SQL database.

Topology Builder for Enterprise Edition Deployments

Lync Server uses the published topology to process traffic and maintain overall topology information. It is especially important to ensure all information included in the Topology Builder is correct because it sets the initial configuration information for deployed server roles. To ensure the topology is valid, it is recommended you run the Topology Builder before your initial deployment and publish an updated topology after each topological change. This example shows a Enterprise Edition topology. Remember, if you change the topology later, republish it to ensure consistency.

When you first launch Lync Server Topology Builder, you see a partially blank MMC screen, as shown in Figure 5.23. Compare this to the detailed result at the end of this example.

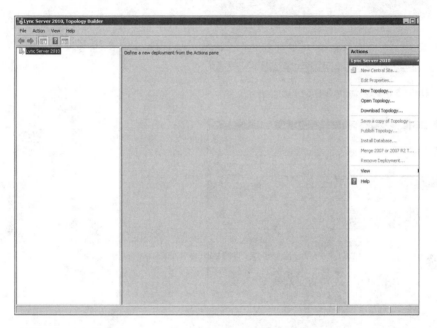

FIGURE 5.23   Topology Builder without a Defined Topology

To begin using Topology Builder, follow these steps:

1. On the right side of the Action pane, click **New**.

2. Define the default SIP domain. In many deployments, this is simply your domain name, as shown in Figure 5.24. In more complex deployments, additional SIP domains might be added by clicking the **Add** button. When you are done defining SIP domains, click **OK**.

3. On the right side of the Action pane, click **Define Site**. Enter the appropriate information, as shown in Figure 5.25, and then click **OK**.

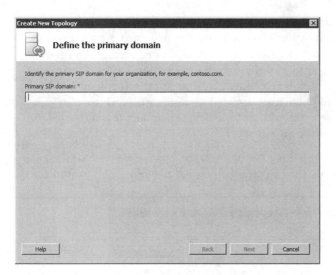

FIGURE 5.24   Define the Default SIP Domain

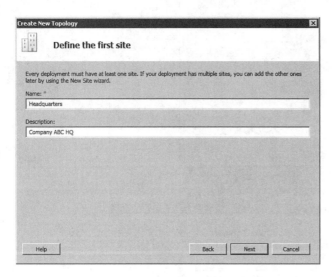

FIGURE 5.25   Define the Site

> **NOTE**
>
> Note that Lync Server sites have no relationship to Active Directory sites. They are completely separate and unique to Lync Server.

4. On the right side of the Action pane, click **Define Front End Pool**, and choose the radio button for the Enterprise Edition, and then click **Next**.

5. Define the pool FQDN, as shown in Figure 5.26. When you are done, click **Next**.

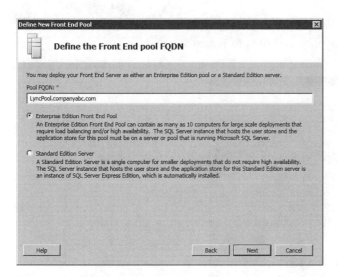

FIGURE 5.26   Define the Front End Pool

6. Define the Front End Server FQDNs and click **Next**.

7. Choose the appropriate workloads for your deployment, and then click **Next**. Associate the appropriate Archiving or Monitoring Servers for your pool and click **Next**.

8. Define the database and file share to be used by the pool, as shown in Figure 5.27. For an Enterprise deployment, SQL cannot be collocated on one of the front end servers. Also, you need to manually create the share on a server other than the front end before progressing past this step. After the share is created, Lync Server assigns the appropriate permissions. When you are ready, click **Next**.

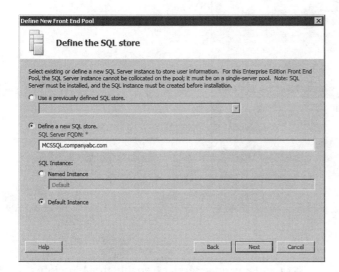

FIGURE 5.27   Define SQL Instance for Front End Pool

9. Specify the Web Services URL for the pool and click **Next**.

10. Define an A/V Conferencing pool as shown in Figure 5.28.

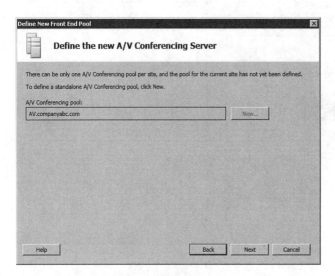

FIGURE 5.28   Conferencing Settings

11. If you deploy Enterprise Voice, define a PSTN gateway if required, as shown in Figure 5.29. Then click **Next**.

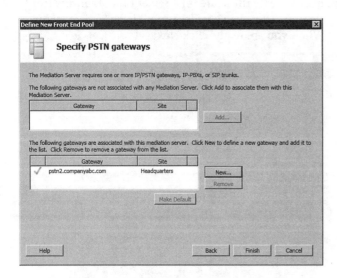

FIGURE 5.29   Specify Voice Gateway

12. If you plan to allow external access or add any edge services, enable the **Associate Edge Pool** box and select an Edge Server. When complete, click **Finish**.

This completes the initial topology definition. However, there are additional steps to complete a fully functional topology.

Configure Simple URLs

The next step is to define easy-to-remember URLs for common Lync Server functions.

1. From the main Topology Builder page where your site name is highlighted, expand **Simple URLs** in the main pane, as shown in Figure 5.30, and then click **Edit**.

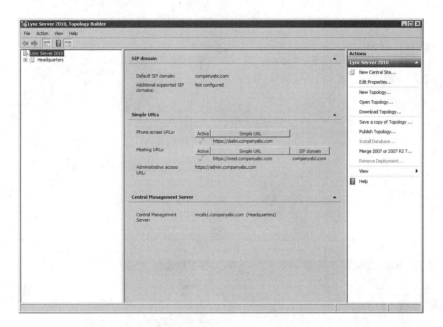

FIGURE 5.30   Expand the Simple URLs Item

2. Enter easy-to-remember URLs as shown in Figure 5.31.

> **NOTE**
>
> The following three examples are all valid for Lync Server simple URLs:
>
> ▶ https://<function>.<domain _fqdn>: *https://dialin.companyabc.com*
>
> ▶ https://<sip_domain>/<function>: https://companyabc.com/dialin
>
> ▶ https://<External_WebPool_FQDN>/<function>: https://cs2010.companyabc.com/dialin
>
> Note that these are the only allowed syntaxes.

Port information, such as https://dialin.companyabc.com:443 is invalid. If you choose the first option, all the FQDNs need to be included as SANs on your certificates. If you choose the second or third option, note that the following virtual directory names are reserved and cannot be used as part of a simple URL:

- ▶ ABS
- ▶ Conf
- ▶ LocationInformation
- ▶ RequestHandler
- ▶ AutoUpdate
- ▶ cscp
- ▶ OCSPowerShell
- ▶ RGSClients
- ▶ CertProv
- ▶ GetHealth
- ▶ ReachWeb
- ▶ RGSConfig
- ▶ CollabContent
- ▶ GroupExpansion
- ▶ RequestHandlerExt
- ▶ WebTicket

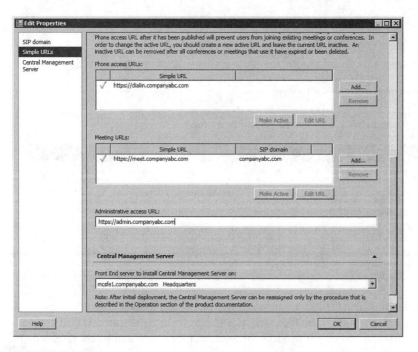

FIGURE 5.31   Configured Simple URLs

Publish the Topology

The final step is to publish the topology to the Central Management Store. Perform the following steps to publish your topology:

1. In the Topology Builder Tool, in the top-level menu item in the left pane, select Lync Server, as shown in Figure 5.32.

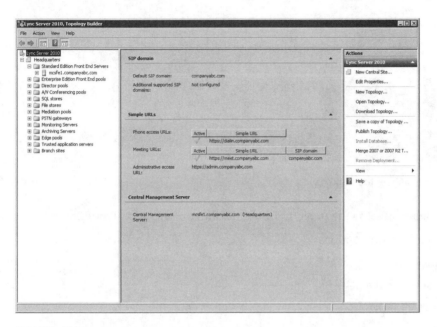

FIGURE 5.32   The Top Level of Topology Builder

2. Click **Publish Topology**.
3. In the opening screen, click **Next**.
4. Ensure that correct Central Management Store is selected, and then click **Next**. This starts the publishing process and overwrites any existing topologies.
5. Enable the **Create Other Databases** box. Ensure the account used for installation has permission to perform this function. Click **Next**.
6. The **Publish Topology** window displays the actions being performed as shown in Figure 5.33. Click **Finish**.

Installing the Front End Role

It is important to note that if you jumped to this section before completing the previous steps, you need to go back. Preparing the server for the first Enterprise Edition server and building a valid topology in the Topology Builder tool are prerequisites to installing the Front End role. This is a different process from Office Communications Server 2007 and 2007 R2, and it involves more steps. Administrators new to Lync Server are advised to review the new features, requirements, and prequisites before beginning the installation process.

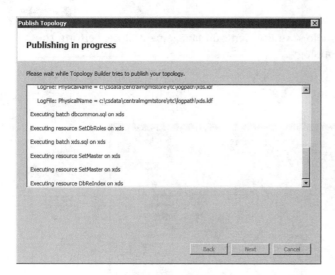

FIGURE 5.33   Publishing the Topology

The following prerequisites are required to install the Enterprise Edition Front End role:

▶ IIS with the following options:

    ▶ Static Content

    ▶ Default Document

    ▶ Directory Browsing

    ▶ HTTP Errors

    ▶ HTTP Redirection

    ▶ ASP.NET

    ▶ .NET Extensibility

    ▶ Internet Server API (ISAPI) Extensions

    ▶ ISAPI Filters

    ▶ HTTP Logging

    ▶ Logging Tools

    ▶ Request Monitor

    ▶ Tracing

    ▶ Basic Authentication

    ▶ Windows Authentication

    ▶ Request Filtering

    ▶ Static Content Compression

▶ IIS Management Console

▶ IIS Management Scripts and Tools

▶ Message Queueing with Directory Service Integration

After you've completed the steps outlined previously, the server is ready to install the Front End role. From the main Lync Server Deployment Wizard screen, click **Install or Update Lync Server System** from the main pane, and then click **Run** for Step 1: Install Local Configuration Store. Follow the steps that follow to complete the installation process:

1. For **Step 2: Setup or Remove Lync Server Components**, click **Run**.

2. As the screen that pops up, click **Next**.

3. The next screen shows the actions being performed, as shown in Figure 5.34. This process takes a few minutes to complete.

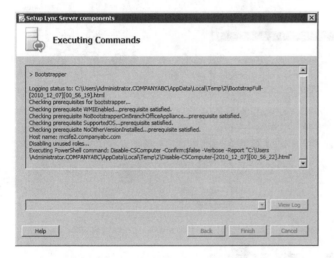

FIGURE 5.34   Installing the Front End Role

4. After the task completes, click **Finish** and you are brought back to the Deployment Wizard.

5. Review **Step 3: Request, Install or Assign Certificates** and click **Run**.

6. At the next screen, choose **Default**, as shown in Figure 5.35, and then click **Request**.

7. Assuming you are using an internal CA, choose **Send the request immediately to an online certificate authority**, and then click **Next**. This is the default option.

8. Select the appropriate CA for your environment from the drop-down list, choose a friendly name and key length, and enable the **Mark the certificate's private key as exportable** box as shown in Figure 5.36, and then click **Next**.

9. Enter your organization name and organizational unit, and then click **Next**.

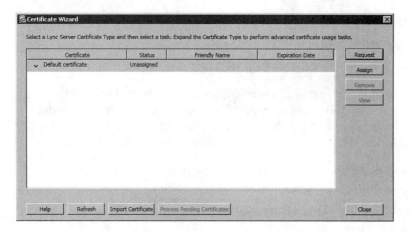

FIGURE 5.35   Request the Default Certificate

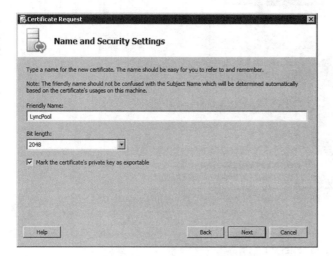

FIGURE 5.36   Certificate Request Settings

10. Select your country from the drop-down menu, and then enter your state/province and city/locality. Remember that full names must be entered, abbreviations are not considered valid for certificate requests. When complete, click **Next**.

11. The Deployment Wizard automatically adds the SANs required based on the published topology. Unless you have special requirements, select the option to **Skip**, and then click **Next**.

12. Review the information to ensure it is correct, and then click **Next**.

13. This screen shows the commands executed, as shown in Figure 5.37.

14. Click **Next**.

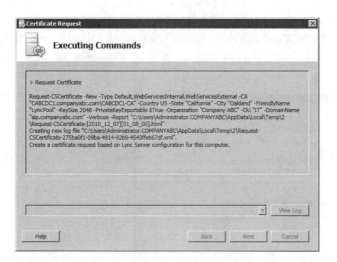

FIGURE 5.37   Certificate Request Process

15. Ensure **Assign this certificate for Lync Server certificate usages** is checked and click **Finish**.

16. On the first screen, click **Next**.

17. Review the certificate information and then click **Next.**

18. Figure 5.38 shows the actions to assign the certificate. When the actions are complete, click **Finish**.

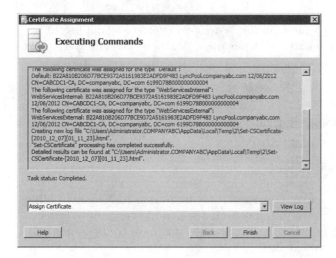

FIGURE 5.38   Assigning the Certificate

19. After all the certificates have been assigned, a check mark by Step 3 displays, as shown in Figure 5.39. If there is not a check mark, check the process because you likely skipped a step.

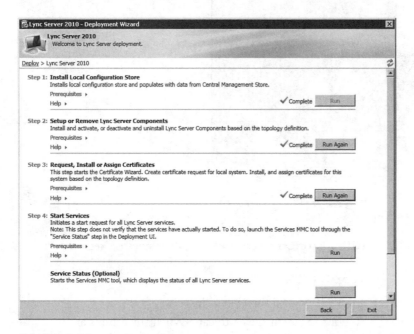

FIGURE 5.39   Certificate Process Completed

20. If the file store for the pool is located on this system, you need to reboot before continuing. After the reboot, restart the Deployment Wizard by launching Setup.exe.

21. Click Install or Update Lync Server System, and then click **Run** for Step 4: Start Services.

22. Click **Next**.

23. Ensure all services start, as shown in Figure 5.40.

24. Click **Exit** to leave the Deployment Wizard.

Configure Front End

The Standard Edition front end is now installed and ready for further configuration using the Lync Server Control Panel, as shown in Figure 5.41. The Lync Server Control Panel is the only GUI available to Lync administrators. It is assumed that most configuration will be done via the Lync Server Management Shell.

For Enterprise Edition deployments, you need to manually add an A record in DNS for the pool name of your front end pool. This is the FQDN that is used when you select **Lync Server Control Panel** from the Start menu.

FIGURE 5.40   All Services Started

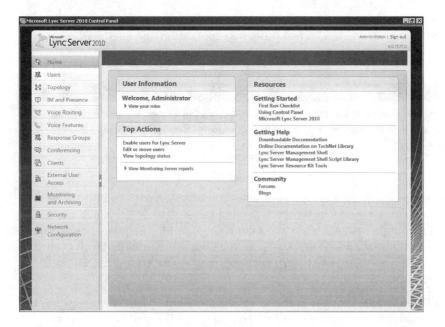

FIGURE 5.41   Lync Server Control Panel

Note that the client autoconfiguration requirements are still the same.

The following DNS records are required for client autoconfiguration:

▶ SRV record of _sipinternaltls._tcp.<sip_Domain> for port 5061 pointing to the FQDN of your front end pool or Director

▶ Host (A) record of sipinternal.<sip_Domain> pointing to the IP address assigned to your front end pool or Director

▶ Host (A) record of sip.<sip_Domain> pointing to the IP address assigned to your front end pool or Director

Configuration

The good news about Lync Server is that with the Topology Builder tool, much of the configuration is done automatically. Although both configuration and administration can be done from the Silverlight web GUI or the Lync Server management shell, the configuration section focuses on the former, whereas the administration section focuses on the latter to avoid duplication of concepts.

First, an introduction to the Lync Server Control Panel. This section reviews each of the tabs and options in the Silverlight Control Panel web application and cites management shell commands for functions that do not appear in the Control Panel.

> **CAUTION**
>
> Before opening the Control Panel for the first time, ensure the server is included in the list of trusted sites on the server or your client. Without this setting, the Control Panel fails to launch.

To launch the Control Panel on a Lync Server, select the Lync Server Control Panel link from the Start menu under the Microsoft Lync Server program group. To launch the Control Panel from another system, enter the Admin simple URL you entered during the initial installation or https://<poolFQDN>/cscp. In the sample environment, this is either https://admin.companyabc.com/ or https://Lyncpool.companyabc.com/cscp/. Either URL brings you to the Control Panel.

When you first log in, you're brought to the Control Panel home page. The navigation bar is on the left and includes options for Home, Users, Topology, IM and Presence, Voice Routing, Voice Features, Response Groups, Conferencing, Clients, External User Access, Monitoring and Archiving, and Security.

On the Home page, you can see a link to a quick start guide and other informational links in the center pane and shortcuts to common tasks in the right pane. This is certainly easier than hunting for them in the various other menus. The shortcuts include

- ▶ Add New User
- ▶ Configure Voice Routing Dial Plans
- ▶ Configure Voice Policy
- ▶ Configure Voice Routes
- ▶ Configure PIN Policy

As you can see, Microsoft has a strong focus on the voice functions of Lync Server.

The Users tab opens with a search bar. To find all users, simply leave the field blank and click the Search icon. All Communications Server–enabled users are returned, as shown in Figure 5.42. To enable a new user for Lync Server, click the **New** button and a wizard displays. Click **Add** under the **Select Domain Users** menu, and then type the name or names of users to be enabled. Choose a Front End pool and SIP URI generation method, and then assign telephony rules and user policies. Be sure to click the **Add** button at the top to save the user; otherwise, your changes are lost.

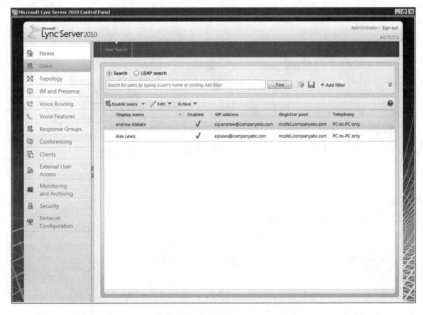

FIGURE 5.42   All Lync Server–Enabled Users

An administrator can also use the get-CsUser management shell cmdlet. With no arguments, the cmdlet returns all users. However, when run with the argument of a user's SIP address, the cmdlet returns detailed information about the account and configuration as shown in the following:

```
PS C:\Users\Administrator.COMPANYABC> get-CsUser alex@companyabc.com
Identity                           : CN=Alex Lewis,OU=CS Users,DC=companyabc,DC=
                                     com
OriginatorSid                      :
VoicePolicy                        :
ConferencingPolicy                 :
DialPlan                           :
LocationPolicy                     :
ClientPolicy                       :
ClientVersionPolicy                :
ArchivingPolicy                    :
PinPolicy                          :
ExternalAccessPolicy               :
HostedVoiceMail                    :
HostedVoicemailPolicy              :
HostingProvider                    : SRV:
RegistrarPool                      : lyncpool.companyabc.com
TargetRegistrarPool                :
CSEnabled                          : True
SipAddress                         : sip:alex@companyabc.com
LineURI                            :
LineServerURI                      :
EnterpriseVoiceEnabled             : False
TenantId                           : 00000000-0000-0000-0000-000000000000
HomeServer                         : CN=Lc Services,CN=Microsoft,CN=Headquarters
                                     :1,CN=Pools,CN=RTC Service,CN=Services,CN=C
                                     onfiguration,DC=companyabc,DC=com
TargetHomeServer                   :
PrivateLine                        :
IPPBXSoftPhoneRoutingEnabled       : False
RemoteCallControlTelephonyEnabled  : False
EnabledForRichPresence             : True
AudioVideoDisabled                 : False
DisplayName                        : Alex Lewis
SamAccountName                     : alex
UserPrincipalName                  : alex@companyabc.com
OriginatingServer                  : CABCDC1.companyabc.com
```

From the User Search menu, administrators can also save common searches for easy access later. This saves the search as a User Search Query file or .usf. The file can be loaded later by clicking the Open button and selecting the file. This can be especially helpful in multidomain environments.

The default Topology menu shows all servers in the Lync Server topology and their statuses. If there is an error, it shows to the right of the server name and the administrator can drill down by double-clicking the server name. There are also two other tabs at the top of the screen: Server Application and Trusted Application. The Server Application tab shows the services for each pool and their statuses. Under the Action menu, the administrator can choose to enable or disable services as required. The Trusted Application tab shows all trusted applications. This is the same as the get-CsTrustedApplication management shell cmdlet. By default, there are no trusted applications.

The IM and Presence tab can be a bit confusing. It actually controls the client file transfer filter and URL filter policies. These are similar to Office Communications Server 2007 R2 and function in a predictable manner. The file filter allows administrators to set file types that are blocked by file extension. Note that the tool doesn't do any deep inspection beyond file type suffix, so renaming a file to change the suffix works to circumvent it. The URL filter has three options: Allow URLs, Block URLs, and Send Warning. The warning option allows the administrator to configure a custom warning message.

Configure Voice Policy

The next four tabs—Voice Routing, Voice Features, Response Groups, and Conferencing—are covered in detail in the voice chapters included in Section 6, "Voice," later in this book. For this reason, this section offers only an overview of these tabs.

The Voice Routing tab has many options. The first one is Dial Plan. This is roughly equivalent to the location profile in Office Communications Server 2007 R2. It has options to configure normalization rules per dial plan. The Normalization Wizard successfully blends the best parts of the previous tools. It has the power and flexibility of raw regular expressions and the intuitive and logical interface of the Office Communications Server 2007 R2 Enterprise Voice Route Helper. This should go a long way toward helping administrators without traditional telephony backgrounds to create complex dial plans.

The Voice Policy option is something completely new. Although it has an associated usage policy, it also has a number of check boxes to enable or disable various calling features. The choices are

- ► Enable call forwarding
- ► Enable delegation
- ► Enable call transfer
- ► Enable call park
- ► Enable simultaneous ringing of phones
- ► Enable team call
- ► Enable PSTN reroute
- ► Enable bandwidth policy override
- ► Enable malicious call tracing

Many of these features require additional configuration that doesn't just involve simply checking a box. For example, orbits must be defined for call park to function correctly. This simply creates a policy to allow the functionality for users assigned to a specific voice policy.

The Route option focuses on policy-based routing. This allows logical call routing based on number patterns. This can be especially helpful in mixed Enterprise Voice and PBX scenarios or where Lync Server is used for conferencing but a PBX maintains enterprise call control. Note that a call follows the first applicable path, not all paths that match.

PSTN Usage, the next tab from the top bar, is essentially the combination of a route and a voice policy. When a usage is assigned only actions that fit, the voice policy is allowed, and then calls follow the appropriate route.

The next tab, Trunk Configuration, can apply to internal or external SIP trunk configuration. Proper configuration of the Trunk Configuration options allow interoperability with a wider scope of SIP trunks and SIP trunking providers.

The last tab under Voice Routing is Test Voice Routing. This allows an administrator to define and save test cases. This is especially helpful in rapidly changing or complex environments.

The Voice Features item on the left bar has two sections: Call Park and Unassigned Number. The Call Park section allows an administrator to define Call Park number ranges and assign them to a pool. The Unassigned Number section allows an administrator to define number ranges and an action where to redirect the call. In previous versions, the call simply disconnected, but in Lync Server, the call can be routed to Exchange UM or to the Announcement service for a front end pool. Multiple rules can be defined for different number ranges. This is helpful for multiple site deployments where using a local pool or one with a different language is valuable.

Response Groups have the same familiar pieces: Workflow, Queue, and Group definition fields. Existing Response Group workflows can also be imported from Office Communications Server 2007 R2.

Configure Conferencing Policy

The next tab in the left column is Conferencing. The Conferencing Policy Section allows configuration for data collaboration, application sharing, audio, video, PSTN, and recording options. Select the default global policy and click Edit to examine the options and default settings. The Meeting Configuration section allows administrators to define meeting settings such as PSTN caller bypass and who can be enabled as a presenter. The Dial-In Access Number section is much improved. It acts as a single screen for all dial-in conferencing numbers enterprisewide. Multiple numbers can be defined for different sites or pools. The final section is PIN Policy, which defines settings for PIN length, PIN expiration, and the maximum number of retries.

Configure Clients Tab

The Clients tab covers both Communicator clients and Communicator Phone Edition devices. This covers the following sections, client version policy, client version configuration, device update, test device, device log configuration, and device configuration. The client version filter allows explicit deny and allow for all types of clients. The client version configuration allows an administrator to define what happens for a client that doesn't fit one of the client version filters. The device update section allows administrators to upload .cab files to be deployed to Communication Phone Edition devices. The next section allows an administrator to define one or more test devices to test Communicator Phone Edition updates before they are widely deployed. The device log configuration is self-explanatory with options for defining log size and duration. The device configuration section allows administrators to define SIP security level, logging level, QoS settings, and device-locking settings.

Configure External Access Policy

The next tab is External User Access. The first section, External Access Policy, defines the access edge policy for communication with external users. The access edge configuration section controls settings for federation and remote user access. Next is the Federated Domains section. Administrators can explicitly allow or deny federated partners. If open federation is not enabled, all partners need to be defined in the allow list. The last section is for public IM providers. An administrator can enable each of the public IM providers separately. Note that a special client access license is required for some public IM federation.

The Monitoring and Archiving tab contains policy-based settings for CDR (Call Detail Recording) and QoE (Quality of Experience) information. It also contains global and policy-based archiving settings. These are explained in great detail in Chapters 7, "Microsoft Lync Server 2010 Monitoring," and 8, "Microsoft Lync Server 2010 Archiving."

The second-to-last tab in the Lync Server Control Panel is Security. The registrar section has options for Kerberos, NTLM, or certificate authentication. By default, all three are enabled. The web service section covers web service authentication methods. The options are PIN authentication, certificate authentication, and enabling certificate chain download. All are enabled by default.

The final tab is Network Configuration. This section includes various policy settings for voice configuration as related to the network. Specifically, this is the area where an administrator can configure Call Admission Control (CAC) and Media Bypass policies. Additionally, administrators can configure E911 and location-specific settings for users in the location policy.

Lync Server supports DNS load balancing for multiple server pools. This is a huge benefit because hardware load-balancing configuration for SIP traffic can be difficult and requires significant troubleshooting. Many load-balancer administrators don't understand the concept beyond balancing web traffic. Although DNS load balancing is used for SIP traffic in Lync Server, a hardware load balancer is still required for web services traffic, such as the address book service. DNS load balancing isn't exactly round robin DNS. A proper configuration using the Company ABC environment and assuming mcsfe1 and mcsfe2 are both Enterprise Edition servers in the same pool would be configured in DNS as shown in Table 5.1.

TABLE 5.1   Configuration of DNS Load Balancing

_sip._tls.companyabc.com	Cspool.companyabc.com
Mcsfe1.companyabc.com	192.168.1.172
Mcsfe2.companyabc.com	192.168.1.173
Cspool.companyabc.com	192.168.1.172
	192.168.1.173

When the client does an SRV record lookup as part of the automatic configuration process, the cspool.companyabc.com record is returned. From that, the DNS server returns the list of IPs assigned to cspool.companyabc.com (192.168.1.172 & 192.168.1.173). The client is programmed to choose an IP at random and register to that front end server. If the connection fails, the client tries the next random IP address in the list until it successfully registers or exhausts all the IP addresses returned by the DNS server.

Administration

This section reviews common administration tasks for Lync Server. As mentioned previously, the focus is primarily on the use of the PowerShell-based Management Shell. The most common administrative function is enabling a user for Lync Server. For example, to enable the user Rand Morimoto with the SIP address of rand@companyabc.com, you use the following command:

```
Enable-csUser -Identity "Rand Morimoto" -RegistrarPool
"cspool.companyabc.com" -SIPAddress "sip:rand@companyabc.com"
```

This example explicitly specifies the SIP address to be used. Lync Server can also automatically generate the address using the SIPAddressType parameter based on a number of options including first.last name (firstLastName), email address (emailaddress), UPN (userPrincipalName), and SAM account name (SAMAccountName). This is helpful when enabling a large number of users and when specifying the actual SIP address isn't practical. To enable a user with a SIP address that is his email address, use the following cmdlet syntax:

```
Enable-csuser -Identity <user Identity> -RegistrarPool <front end
pool FQDN> -SIPAddressType EmailAddress
```

Obviously, enabling a user can also be done in the Lync Server Control Panel. However, it's often faster to simply use the management shell.

Let's look at a more traditional PowerShell concept applied to Lync Server: the Get-CsUser and Get-CsAdUser cmdlets. On the surface, you might think these cmdlets are almost identical; however, that is not the case. They are actually different. The biggest difference is that Get-CsUser returns results only for Lync Server–enabled users. So, if users are currently enabled or the Identity parameter is specified to be a nonenabled user, the cmdlet won't return any data. Get-CsAdUser returns data for both enabled and nonenabled users.

That leads to the question, "Why not use Get-CsAdUser all the time?" The answer is the cmdlets return different information when used appropriately. Table 5.2 displays the attributes returned by each. As you can see, Get-CsAdUser returns general Active Directory information, whereas Get-CsUser returns Lync Server-specific information. There is a small bit of overlap, but only where Lync Server references a generic Active Directory field.

TABLE 5.2   Information Returned by Get-CsUser and Get-CsAdUser Cmdlets

Get-CsUser	Get-CsAdUser
	AddressListMembership
	AltSecurityIdentities
ArchivingPolicy	
	Assistant
AudioVideoDisabled	
	City
ClientPolicy	
ClientVersionPolicy	
	Company
ConferencingPolicy	
	CountryAbbreviation
	CountryCode
	CountryOrRegionDisplayName
CSEnabled	CSEnabled
	Department
	Description
DialPlan	
DisplayName	DisplayName
	DistinguishedName

5

TABLE 5.2   Information Returned by Get-CsUser and Get-CsAdUser Cmdlets

Get-CsUser	Get-CsAdUser
	EmployeeId
EnabledForRichPresence	
EnterpriseVoiceEnabled	
ExternalAccessPolicy	
	Fax
	FirstName
	Guid
	HomePhone
HomeServer	
HostedVoiceMail	
HostedVoicemailPolicy	
HostingProvider	
	Id
Identity	Identity
	Info
	Initials
IPPBXSoftPhoneRoutingEnabled	
	IPPhone
	IsValid
	LastName
LineServerURI	
LineURI	
LocationPolicy	
	Manager
	MiddleName
	MobilePhone
	Name
	ObjectCategory

TABLE 5.2   Information Returned by Get-CsUser and Get-CsAdUser Cmdlets

Get-CsUser	Get-CsAdUser
	ObjectCategoryCN
	ObjectClass
	ObjectState
	Office
	OriginatingServer
OriginatorSid	
	OtherFax
	OtherHomePhone
	OtherIPPhone
	OtherMobile
	OtherPager
	OtherTelephone
	Pager
	PasswordLastSet
	Phone
PinPolicy	
	PostalCode
	PostOfficeBox
	PreferredLanguage
PresencePolicy	
	PrimaryGroupId
PrivateLine	
	ProxyAddresses
RegistrarPool	
RemoteCallControlTelephonyEnabled	
SamAccountName	SamAccountName
	Sid
	SidHistory

5

TABLE 5.2   Information Returned by Get-CsUser and Get-CsAdUser Cmdlets

Get-CsUser	Get-CsAdUser
SipAddress	SipAddress
	StateOrProvince
	Street
	StreetAddress
TargetHomeServer	
TargetRegistrarPool	
TenantId	TenantId
	Title
	Url
	UserAccountControl
UserPrincipalName	UserPrincipalName
VoicePolicy	
	WebPage
	WhenChanged
	WhenCreated
	WindowsEmailAddress

There are many similar cmdlet relationships in the Management Shell. In fact, you can write a book to explain the various cmdlets, their syntaxes, and how to link them together to accomplish different tasks.

Troubleshooting

As with previous versions of Communications Server, there are two major gremlins with the Front End role: certificates and DNS. The new Deployment Wizard takes most of the guesswork out of certificate generation by automatically filling the SAN fields with the appropriate FQDNs for a given deployment. However, in more complex environments manual configuration might be necessary.

The added convenience of the Deployment Wizard doesn't lessen the importance of certificates. They are still core to all server and server-client communications. DNS, on the other hand, is not automated. For each pool created, the administrator needs to create an A record for each pool pointing to the load-balanced VIP for multiple-server pools or to the front end IP address for single-server pools.

The Lync Server event log is also a good place to check for errors. From the Start menu, select Administrative Tools, and then select Event Viewer. Expand the Applications and Services Logs item and select Lync Server. All events related to Lync Server functions reside here. Often, the error description is enough to identify the problem and make clear the resolution.

Best Practices

Following are the best practices from this chapter:

- ▶ Use DNS load balancing for SIP traffic. A hardware load balancer is still required for web services such as the address book service.

- ▶ Although the Lync Server Control Panel might seem more familiar at first, there are many functions that can only be accomplished in the Management Shell.

- ▶ Always install the SQL backward compatibility pack to ensure all cmdlets run correctly.

- ▶ For larger deployments, separate out conferencing services to a dedicated pool.

- ▶ Use the RBAC controls to delegate administration rights.

- ▶ Always publish a new topology before making changes or installing a new server role.

- ▶ Use the Get-CsUser cmdlet for Lync Server-specific information and the Get-CsAdUser cmdlet for general Active Directory information.

5

Microsoft Lync Server 2010 Edge

The Lync Server Edge Server enables remote access to the internal Lync Server infrastructure. In addition to providing feature parity for external or remote users, the Edge Server can also enhance a deployment by federating with partner organizations or public IM providers. These federation features help organizations use rich communication methods securely with each other across the Internet.

This chapter focuses on the Edge Server role installation and configuration. It covers how to deploy each of the Edge roles both in a standalone scenario and in a high-availability deployment where multiple Edge Servers are used.

This chapter also discusses why a reverse proxy server is required and shows how to use Microsoft Forefront Threat Management Gateway 2010 to publish external Lync Server services.

> ▶ For a more detailed discussion of planning for Edge Server sizing, networking, and firewall scenarios, see Chapter 27, "Planning for Deploying External Services."

Edge Overview

The Edge Server role in Lync Server comprises three separate subroles just as in previous versions of the product: Access Edge Server, Web Conferencing Edge Server, and A/V Edge Server role. Each role provides slightly different functionality and depending on the organization's requirements it might not be necessary to use all three services. With Lync Server 2010, all three roles are deployed together as opposed to individually like in previous product versions.

Unlike many of the internal roles, the Edge Server does not require database or file shares because it does not store data other than the Local Configuration Store replica from the Central Management Store. Because the Edge Server is designed to be deployed in a perimeter or DMZ network, it runs a limited set of services to make it as secure as possible. Edge Servers are also typically not joined to the internal Active Directory domain, but can be if necessary. The different Edge Server roles provide unique features, as shown in Figure 6.1. The reverse proxy server also provides some external services through the Front-End pool.

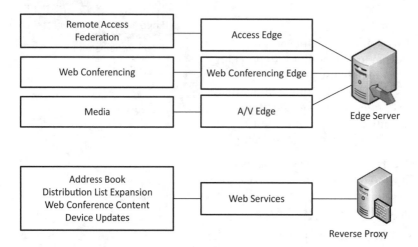

FIGURE 6.1   Lync Server External Access

Access Edge

The Access Edge role serves as the core of the Edge Server and is responsible for all of the signaling functionality. Without the Access Edge role deployed, the Web Conferencing Edge and A/V Edge roles cannot function. The Access Edge also serves a few distinct purposes including remote access, federation, and Public IM Connectivity.

Remote Access

One function of the Access Edge Server is to provide remote access capabilities to a Lync Server infrastructure. After an internal deployment of pools is complete, an Access Edge Server can be provisioned to enable users to sign in and use their endpoints across the Internet.

As long as the appropriate SRV records exist in DNS or the client is manually configured correctly, a user can travel in and out of the office without ever making a change to an endpoint. This enables users to have full access to their internal features regardless of location.

NOTE

Access Edge Server traffic is performed using port 443 over TCP, which is the standard for HTTPS traffic. Traffic is rarely blocked or interfered with by any kind of proxy or firewall software.

Federation

The Access Edge Server also provides the capability to federate with other organizations that have deployed Lync Server, meaning the two organizations can communicate with each other as if it were a single deployment.

Users have different feature sets available when using federation, depending on the version of Lync Server a partner has deployed. The feature set is the lowest common denominator between the two organizations. For example, if a partner runs Live Communications Server 2005, only IM and presence will be available. However, if a partner organization is running Office Communications Server 2007 R2, A/V and Desktop Sharing features can be used through federation. The largest feature set is available if both organizations are running Lync Server.

Access Edge Servers use certificates and mutual TLS (MTLS) to secure the SIP signaling used across the Internet with each other. This ensures that instant messaging and presence traffic is completely secure and never transmitted in plain text.

NOTE

Organizations generally procure a certificate from a public certificate authority so that partners trust their server by default. However, it is possible to exchange certificate chains with a partner to support additional certificate authorities.

Public IM Connectivity

A special form of federation is the capability to use Lync Server to communicate with contacts on the public IM networks, referred to as Public IM Connectivity (PIC). The AOL, Yahoo!, and MSN networks are the native Public IM Connectivity providers to Lync Server. To communicate with these contacts, users simply need to add the address to a contact list.

CAUTION

Although it is possible to federate with Google Talk contacts, this capability is not native to the Access Edge Server role. To federate with Google Talk, an organization must deploy the XMPP Gateway Server role, which was software introduced for Office Communications Server 2007 R2. There is no equivalent or updated product for Lync Server at this time.

Lync Server users can see presence and exchange instant messages with their contacts when Public IM Connectivity is provisioned. The conversations are limited to peer-to-peer, though, and they cannot include three or more participants as users are accustomed to within the organization or with federated contacts.

Audio and video support with the MSN or Windows Live networks is a new feature in Lync Server. The A/V conversations are performed using the same RTAudio and RTVideo codecs native to both platforms, but are also limited to two-party calls.

TIP

With Microsoft Xbox Kinect and Xbox Live service, it's possible to conduct a video conversation with an MSN user viewing a Lync Server user on his or her television at home or work, as shown in Figure 6.2. This functionality will be delivered in a future update to the Kinect software.

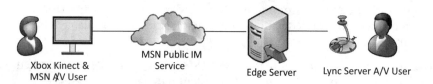

Xbox Kinect & MSN A/V User   MSN Public IM Service   Edge Server   Lync Server A/V User

FIGURE 6.2   Xbox Kinect Video Calls with Lync Server

As of this writing, only the Yahoo! network requires additional licensing, which is done on a per-user monthly subscription fee. As long as users have a Lync Server Standard CAL, the AOL and MSN Public IM Connectivity are provided at no extra cost.

Web Conferencing Edge

When joining a web conference, users first authenticate to the Access Edge Server before the client joins using the Web Conferencing Edge Server role. The Web Conferencing Edge Server enables remote users to participate in web conferences with internal users or other remote workers.

Organizations may also elect to enable anonymous or unauthenticated users to join web conferences with their own users. This functionality is similar to what many hosted web conferencing services offer. However, it is provided by the organization's own Lync Server infrastructure. Web conferencing uses Microsoft's Proprietary Shared Object Model (PSOM) protocol to facilitate the meetings and data. Like the Access Edge traffic, all Web Conferencing Edge traffic is conducted over HTTPS port 443, so it is secure and resilient to proxy servers.

A/V Edge

The A/V Edge role is responsible for providing audio and video media exchanges among internal, external, and federated contacts. The A/V Edge role uses the Interactive Connectivity Establishment (ICE), Simple Traversal Utilities for NAT (STUN), and Traversal

Using Relay NAT (TURN) methods to enable endpoints to communicate even if behind a NAT device.

When possible, endpoints attempt to use a peer-to-peer connection for media streams, but when an endpoint is behind a NAT device such as a home router, the A/V Edge role can act as a relay point between the endpoints to facilitate communication. The A/V Edge service uses a combination of HTTPS port 443 and UDP port 3478 to negotiate and provide the media stream.

To support media traffic between internal and external users, an additional service exists on the A/V Edge Server called the A/V Edge Authentication Service. This service is responsible for authenticating media requests from internal users to external contacts. When a user wants to initiate an external A/V conversation, she is provided with a temporary media token that she uses to authenticate to this service before media is allowed to flow.

Collocation

The Edge Server roles cannot be collocated with any other role in Lync Server. Although many of the other roles depend on access to Active Directory, Edge Servers are typically placed in a perimeter network and might not even be joined to the corporate domain for security reasons.

> **CAUTION**
>
> Although it is possible to join an Edge Server to the domain, this is not a recommended configuration because it will still not allow for the collocation of any other server roles.

In previous versions of Communications Server, it was possible to install only specific Edge roles. However, in Lync Server, the three roles are always installed together. This change cuts down on confusion of deployment models, which required knowing which Edge roles were safe to collocate together.

Reverse Proxy

In addition to the Edge Server roles that provide remote access, federation, web conferencing, and A/V conferencing, a reverse proxy is required to publish the web components services that don't run through an Edge Server.

> **TIP**
>
> Oftentimes, the reverse proxy component is overlooked or considered unnecessary. However, it is a critical step in deploying external access for users.

The reverse proxy provides remote access to the web components running on Front End Servers or Edge Servers. This includes the following features:

▶ Address Book

▶ Distribution Group Expansion

▶ Device Updates

▶ Web Conferencing Content (Whiteboards and PowerPoint File Uploads)

There are many vendors and types of reverse proxies, and almost any of them work with Lync Server because the publishing needs are fairly basic.

▶ Refer to Chapter 27 for more details about the reverse proxy requirements.

Edge Installation

The rest of this chapter focuses on the actual installation and configuration of the Edge Server. The next section discusses the Edge Server hardware, operating system, and software prerequisites.

Hardware Requirement

The Lync Server Edge Server processor requirements are as follows:

▶ Dual processor, quad-core 2.0 GHz or faster

▶ Four-way processor, dual-core 2.0 GHz or faster

CAUTION

Lync Server is only a 64-bit application and requires a 64-bit capable processor. This is generally not an issue with modern hardware, but be sure to verify that legacy hardware supports a 64-bit operating system before attempting to use it for an Edge Server.

The Lync Server Edge Server memory requirement is as follows:

▶ 12 GB RAM

The Lync Server Edge Server disk requirement is as follows:

▶ Local storage with at least 30 GB free space

The Lync Server Edge Server network requirement is as follows:

▶ Two 1 gigabit per second (Gbps) network adapters (recommended)

TIP

When teaming multiple network adapters, use them only for fault-tolerance. This means network adapters should be used for failover only and not be combined for greater throughput.

Operating System Requirements

The Lync Server Edge Server supports the following operating systems:

- ▶ Windows Server 2008, x64 Standard Edition with Service Pack 2
- ▶ Windows Server 2008, x64 Enterprise Edition with Service Pack 2
- ▶ Windows Server 2008, x64 Datacenter Edition with Service Pack 2
- ▶ Windows Server 2008 R2, Standard Edition
- ▶ Windows Server 2008 R2, Enterprise Edition
- ▶ Windows Server 2008 R2, Datacenter Edition

CAUTION

The Datacenter editions of Windows Server 2008, x64 with Service Pack 2 and Windows Server 2008 R2 are supported by Microsoft, but have not been fully tested for use with Lync Server.

The Windows Server Core, Web, and High Performance Computing editions for any operating system version are not supported for deployment.

Software Requirements

The Lync Server Edge Server requires the following components to be installed:

- ▶ .NET Framework 3.5
- ▶ Visual C++ 2008 Redistributable
- ▶ PowerShell 2.0
- ▶ Windows Installer 4.0
- ▶ WinRM 2.0
- ▶ BITS 4.0

Server Roles and Features

Unlike the other roles in Lync Server, the Edge Server has no requirements for server roles or features. All the required components are included within the Edge Server installation.

Configure Networking

After the required components are installed, it is important to get the Edge Server networking configuration completed. An Edge Server must have at least two network adapters: one for external traffic and one for communicating with internal servers or clients.

> **TIP**
>
> Make sure necessary routing statements are entered so that traffic for internal clients uses the correct adapter. As shown in Figure 6.3, only the external facing adapter should have a default gateway assigned to ensure consistent routing behavior.

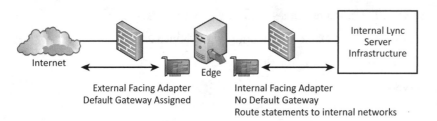

FIGURE 6.3   Edge Server Network Adapters

Create Edge Pool

After the server has been fully prepared for installation, the topology must be edited and published to reflect the new Edge Server pool. This involves editing the existing topology, if it exists, and then republishing the topology so that all other servers in the environment are aware of the new Edge Server pool.

Edit Topology

The next step in deploying an Edge Server is to edit the existing Lync Server topology. To edit the topology, perform the following steps:

> **TIP**
>
> If the Topology Builder is not already installed on the local computer or another computer in the environment, it can be installed from the Lync Server media.

1. Open the Lync Server Topology Builder.
2. When prompted to import an existing topology from Active Directory, click **OK**.
3. Expand the Site node where the Edge Server will deployed.
4. Right-click the **Edge pools** node, and select **New Edge Pool**.
5. Click **Next** to begin the wizard.
6. Enter the fully qualified name of the internal Edge Server pool in the Pool FQDN field.
7. Follow the appropriate following sections depending on whether a single Edge Server or pool of load-balanced Edge Servers will be deployed.

Deploying Standalone Edge Server

1. Select **Single computer pool**, and click **OK**.

2. If a single public IP address will be used for the Access Edge, Web Conferencing Edge, and A/V Edge services check the box **Use a single FQDN and IP address**. This requires using ports other than 443 for two of the services.

3. If federation is used, check the **Enable federation** box.

4. If the IP address used for the A/V Edge uses NAT, check the **The external IP address of this Edge pool is translated by NAT** box. Click **Next** when complete.

5. Under the SIP Access section, enter the external server FQDN and port. Typically, this is similar to sip.companyabc.com and port 443.

6. Under the **Web Conferencing** section, enter the external server FQDN and port. Typically, the name and port are similar to webconf.companyabc.com and port 443.

7. Under the **Audio/Video** section, enter the external server FQDN, IP address, and port. Typically, the name and port are similar to av.companyabc.com and port 443. Click **Next** when complete.

8. Enter an internal-facing IP address for the Edge Server pool and click **Next**.

9. Under the SIP Access section, enter the external IP address.

10. Under the **Web Conferencing** section, enter the external IP address.

11. Under the **Audio/Video** section, enter the external IP address and click **Next**.

12. If the A/V Edge IP address is translated by NAT enter the public IP address and click **Next**.

13. Select a next-hop pool to be used by the Edge Server pool and click **Next**. If a Director is deployed, that should be the next hop.

14. Place a checkmark next to any Front-End pools in the deployment that will use this Edge server pool for external web conferencing and A/V content. Click **Finish** to complete the wizard.

Deploying Load-Balanced Edge Server Pool

1. Select **Multiple computer pool** and click **OK**.

2. If a single public IP address will be used for the Access Edge, Web Conferencing Edge, and A/V Edge services on each server check the box **Use a single FQDN and IP address**. This requires using ports other than 443 for two of the services.

3. If federation is used, check the **Enable federation** box.

4. If the IP address used for the A/V Edge uses NAT, check the **The external IP address of this Edge pool is translated by NAT** box. Click **Next** when complete.

5. Under the SIP Access section, enter the external server FQDN and port. Typically, this is similar to sip.companyabc.com and port 443.

6. Under the **Web Conferencing** section, enter the external server FQDN and port. Typically, the name and port are similar to webconf.companyabc.com and port 443.

7. Under the **Audio/Video** section, enter the external server FQDN, IP address, and port. Typically, the name and port are similar to av.companyabc.com and port 443. Click **Next** when complete.

8. Click the **Add** button to define computers within the pool.

9. Enter the internal-facing IP address and internal FQDN of the server. Click **Next**.

10. Under the SIP Access section, enter the external IP address.

11. Under the **Web Conferencing** section, enter the external IP address.

12. Under the **Audio/Video** section, enter the external IP address and click **Next**.

13. If the A/V Edge IP address is translated by NAT enter the public IP address and click **Next**.

14. Repeat steps 8–13 for any additional Edge Server pool members and click **Next** when all nodes have been added.

15. Select a next-hop pool to be used by the Edge Server pool and click **Next**. If a Director is deployed, that should be the next hop.

16. Place a checkmark next to any Front-End pools in the deployment that will use this Edge server pool for external web conferencing and A/V content. Click **Finish** to complete the wizard.

Publish Topology

After the topology is modified to include the Edge Server pool, the configuration can be published. This step publishes the changes to the Central Management Store, and all existing Lync Server servers will update their local configuration stores to match.

1. Ensure that the Lync Server Topology Builder is open and contains the Edge Server pool recently added.

2. Click the top node of the management console, Lync Server.

3. Click the **Action** menu and select **Publish Topology**, or select Publish Topology from the Actions pane on the right side of the console.

4. Click **Next** to begin publishing the topology.

5. When the log indicates a successful update, click **Finish** to complete the wizard.

Install Server

At this point, the target server should be fully prepared and meet all prerequisites.

Export Topology

The process for installing a local configuration store on an Edge Server varies depending on whether an Edge Server is part of the Active Directory domain and can access the configuration store directly. Typically, the Edge Server is isolated and requires a few extra manual steps to read the topology. These steps involve exporting the entire topology to an XML file and copying it to the Edge Server.

1. Open the Lync Server Management Shell.

2. Run the following command:

   ```
   Export-CSConfiguration –FileName C:\Lync2010.zip
   ```

3. Copy the file to the Edge Server prior to beginning the installation.

Install Local Configuration Store

To install a server role in Lync Server, the target server must first have a local configuration store installed and populated with the topology information.

1. Insert the Lync Server media on the server to be used as an Edge Server and launch Setup.exe found in the Setup\amd64 folder.

2. Enter a location for the installation files to be cached and click **Install**.

3. Click **Install or Update Lync Server system.**

4. Under **Step 1: Install Local Configuration Store**, click **Run**.

5. Because the Edge Server is part of a workgroup and cannot access the Central Management Store, select **import from a file,** and then click **Browse**. If the Edge Server is part of the domain, it should be able to read the Central Management Store directly.

6. Select the .zip file copied earlier and then click Next.

7. Click **Finish** when the topology is imported successfully.

Install Lync Server Components

The following steps enable the server to read the topology information from the local configuration store, and then install the server roles matching its own FQDN.

1. Under **Step 2: Setup or Remove Lync Server Components**, click the **Run** button.

2. Select **Next** to begin the Edge Server installation published in the topology.

3. When prompted to install the Microsoft Network Service, click the **Install** button.

4. Click **Finish** when the installation completes.

Create Certificates

Like all other roles in Lync Server, the Edge Server communicates to other servers in the organization using Mutual Transport Layer Security (MTLS). The Edge Server requires a few certificates depending on the services published. At a minimum, the Edge Server always requires a certificate with its internal FQDN for communication to other servers.

▶ The subject name should contain the Edge pool's internal fully qualified domain name (FQDN).

The certificate used for Access Edge services should adhere to the following guidelines:

▶ The subject name should be the published address for Access Edge services.

▶ All supported SIP domains must be entered as a subject alternative name in the format sip.<SIP domain>.

The certificate used for Web Conferencing Edge services should adhere to the following guideline:

▶ The subject name should be the published address for Web Conferencing Edge services.

The certificate used for A/V Authentication service has no specific guidelines. The certificate is used only to generate encryption keys, but the name used by the wizard matches the internal Edge pool FQDN.

▶ See Chapter 27 for a more detailed explanation of certificate requirements.

> **NOTE**
>
> The Certificate Wizard in Lync Server automatically populates the subject name and required subject alternative names based on the published topology. This greatly simplifies certificate confusion created by prior versions. As long as the published topology is accurate, changing the certificate names or adding subject alternative names is unnecessary.

Use the following steps to request and assign the necessary certificates:

1. Under Step 3: Request, Install, or Assign Certificate, click the **Run** button.
2. Highlight the **Edge internal** option and click the **Request** button.
3. Click **Next** to begin the wizard.
4. Select to either **Send the request immediately to an online certification authority** or **Prepare the request now, but send it later (offline certificate request)** and click **Next**. Typically an Edge server will have to use the **Prepare the request now, but send it later** option.
5. Click the **Browse** button and select a file location for the certificate signing request (CSR) and click **Next**.
6. To use the standard WebServer template, click **Next** on the **Specify Alternate Certificate Template** page.
7. Enter a friendly name for the certificate such as **Lync Server Internal**.
8. Select a key bit length of 1024, 2048, or 4096.
9. If the certificate should be exportable, select the **Mark certificate private key as exportable** check box and click **Next**.
10. Enter an organization name, which is typically the name of the business.

11. Enter an organizational name, which is typically the name of a division or department, and click **Next**.

12. Select a country, enter a state or province, and enter a city or locality, and then click **Next**.

13. Click **Next** after reviewing the automatically populated subject and subject alternate names.

14. Do not add additional subject alternative names and press **Next**.

15. Click **Next** to complete the request, and then click **Finish** to complete the wizard.

After completing the wizard, run through it a one more time to generate a CSR for the External Edge certificate.

If the certificates are issued from an online certificate authority, they should be installed automatically. If an offline request is issued, the wizard must be re-run with the option to complete an offline request.

Assign Certificates

After creating the necessary certificates, the Edge Server services must have certificates assigned to them. This process binds each certificate to a specific Edge service. To assign a certificate, perform the following steps:

1. Under Step 3: Request, Install, or Assign Certificate, click the **Run** button.

2. Highlight **Edge internal** and click the **Assign** button.

3. Click the **Next** button to begin the wizard.

4. Select **Assign an existing certificate**, and then click **Next**.

5. Select the correct certificate for this usage. Certificates will not appear here unless they can be verified to a Trusted Root Certification Authority and have a private key associated. Press **Next**.

6. Verify that the certificate is selected, and then click Next.

7. Click **Finish** when the process is complete.

Repeat the previous steps for the External Edge services certificate.

Start Services

After the necessary certificates are requested and assigned, the Lync Server Edge Server services can be started.

1. Beneath Step 4: Start Services, and then click the **Run** button.

2. Click **Next** to start the Lync Server services.

3. Click **Finish** to complete the wizard.

At this point, the Edge Server installation is complete and functional.

Edge Configuration

Configuration of the Edge Servers is generally completed up front through the Topology Builder. If changes are required, the topology should be edited and then exported to the Edge Servers so that the installation routine can be re-run.

Edge Server Management Console

Administrators of Live Communications Server 2005 and Office Communications Server 2007 will notice that there is no longer a specialized Microsoft Management Console (MMC) snap-in for managing the Edge Server. Instead, all Edge Server configuration is done within the internal network and then replicated or exported to the Edge Servers.

This model creates a central point of management for the entire deployment so administrators don't have to manage each server individually. With the Topology Builder approach, each Edge Server pool member is configured identically, which reduces the risk of human error configuring one Edge Server slightly different from another and then having to troubleshoot why one media or signaling path is problematic.

Enabling Edge Server Features

To enable the Edge Servers to process remote access and federation requests, the Access Edge configuration must be updated to enable these features. Figure 6.4 shows a sample policy configuration. Use the following steps to enable Access Edge features to the Lync Server infrastructure:

1. Open the Lync Server Control Panel.
2. Select **External User Access** in the navigation pane.
3. Click **Access Edge Configuration**.
4. Highlight the **Global** policy, and then click **Edit** and then **Modify**.
5. Check the **Enable remote user access** box.
6. Check the **Enable federation** box.
7. If DNS SRV lookups are allowed to discover federated partners, check the **Enable partner domain discovery** box.
8. If an archiving disclaimer should be sent to federated contacts when initiating an IM conversation, check the **Send archiving disclaimer to federated partners** box.
9. If the web conferencing service enables anonymous external participants, check the **Enable anonymous access to conferences** box.
10. Click **Commit** to accept the changes.

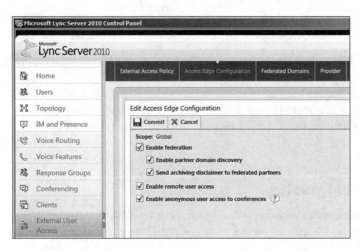

FIGURE 6.4   Access Edge Configuration

Alternatively, the Lync Server Management Shell also can be used to configure the following setting:

```
Set-CSAccessEdgeConfiguration –AllowOutsideusers $true –AllowFederatedUsers $true
–EnablePartnerDiscovery $true –EnableArchivingDisclaimer $true AllowAnonymousUsers
$true
```

There are some additional options available for Access Edge Server configuration that are not exposed in the Lync Server Control Panel. The following parameters can also be used as part of the Set-CSAccessEdgeConfiguration cmdlet to configure external access:

- ▶ **BeClearingHouse**—True or false value indicating whether the Access Edge Servers are directly connected to other organizations. A clearinghouse Access Edge Server can be used to support direct federation between multiple organizations. It can also be considered a federation gateway for multiple internal Lync Server deployments. Typically, this value is false.

- ▶ **DefaultRouteFQDN**—Used to override a default federation route. If it is required to proxy client connections through a specific server for federation, this parameter can be entered. This parameter must be used in conjunction with the UseDefaultRouting parameter.

- ▶ **UseDefaultRouting**—True or false value indicating whether the Access Edge Servers will use a manually entered default route FQDN. This value is false by default, which enables Access Edge Servers to use DNS SRV records for routing federation requests.

- ▶ **KeepCRLsUpToDateForPeers**—True or false value indicating whether the Access Edge Servers will periodically check whether a partner's certificate is still valid based on the CRL. This parameter is true by default.

▶ **MarkSourceVerifiableOnOutgoingMessages**—True or false value indicating whether the Access Edge Servers mark outgoing messages from a verified source. This enables partners to assign a higher level of trust to messages they receive from an organization marking messages as verifiable. This parameter is true by default.

▶ **OutgoingTLSCountForFederatedPartners**—Numeric value from 1 to 4 indicating the maximum number of connections that can be used for a federated partner. The default value is 4, but if connections should be more limited, this value can be reduced.

Managing A/V Edge Configuration

By default, an A/V Edge Server applies a global policy, which controls bandwidth limits for users and ports as well as the lifetime of media relay tokens. This setting is not exposed in the Lync Server Control Panel and must be managed with the Lync Server Management Shell.

First, use the Get-CsAVEdgeConfiguration cmdlet to view the Global defaults:

Identity:	Global
MaxTokenLifetime:	08:00:00
MaxBandwidthPerUserKb:	10000
MaxBandwidthPerPortKb:	3000

Unless there is a need to limit the values, leave the Global policy in place. To create a new A/V Edge configuration, which applies at the SF site level, use the following command. In this example, the MaxTokenLifetime is increased to 10 days, the bandwidth per user is decreased to 5000 KB, and maximum bandwidth per port is decreased to 2000 KB:

```
New-CsAVEdgeConfiguration "site:SF" -MaxTokenLifetime "10:00:00"
-MaxBandwidthPerUserKb 5000 -MaxBandwidthPerPortKb 2000
```

Introducing High Availability

Redundancy for Edge Servers requires just adding more Edge Servers to a pool. Like a Front End pool, up to ten servers can be defined in an Edge Server pool. Load balancing can either be done with DNS load balancing requests or by using a hardware load balancer.

DNS load balancing is done by entering multiple host records for the Edge Server pool name within DNS. When clients or servers attempt to reach a server that is unavailable, they will attempt to use an alternate server.

A hardware load balancer can still be used for Edge Servers in Lync Server, which adds greater load-balancing capabilities at the price of greater complexity. As in prior releases, the internal Access Edge and A/V Authentication Edge interfaces should be load-balanced, but the Web Conferencing Edge internal ports should not be load-balanced.

TIP

This method is best achieved using a single VIP for the internal-facing services. From an external perspective, all three services should be load balanced, but they should all use a separate VIP.

Adding Edge Servers to a Pool

Adding an additional Edge Server to a pool requires updating and publishing the topology to reflect the change. Use the following steps to add an additional pool member:

1. Expand the **Edge Servers** node.
2. Right-click the Edge Server pool name, and select **New Server**.
3. Enter the internal IP address and FQDN IP address of the Edge Server's internal interface. Click **Next**.
4. Enter the external IP addresses for the Edge Server's Access Edge, Web Conferencing Edge, and A/V Edge services. Click **OK**.
5. Click **OK** when complete.

Now, publish the topology again and proceed with the new Edge Server installation.

▶ To complete installation of the Edge Server, follow the steps defined in the "Install Server" section earlier in this chapter.

After installation, be sure to add the IP address to the pool in DNS so that clients can locate the new Edge Server.

Reverse Proxy

To support all the remote features available in Lync Server, a reverse proxy must be used to publish internal web services in addition to an Edge Server pool. The type of reverse proxy used is flexible because almost any kind of reverse proxy should be capable of handling the requirements. Microsoft recommends using either the Forefront Unified Access Gateway or Threat Management Gateway products for publishing Lync Server. Threat Management Gateway, or TMG, is the next generation of the Internet Security & Acceleration (ISA) Server product and Unified Access Gateway (UAG) builds on TMG with additional security and filtering capabilities. This section focuses on publishing the Lync Server Front End or Director pools using Forefront Threat Management Gateway 2010.

Reverse Proxy Installation

If a reverse proxy already exists in the organization, it can be used to also publish Lync Server web services. There is no requirement for a reverse proxy to be dedicated only to Lync Server, but if no reverse proxy exists, one should be deployed when an Edge Server is provisioned. The following section details how to use the Microsoft Forefront Threat Management Gateway 2010 as a reverse proxy for Lync Server.

Forefront Threat Management Gateway 2010 Prerequisites

This section discusses the hardware, operating system, and software requirements necessary for installing Forefront Threat Management Gateway.

Hardware Requirements   The Forefront Threat Management Gateway server processor requirement is as follows:

▶ 1.86 GHz dual processor or dual-core processor

CAUTION

Threat Management Gateway 2010 is only a 64-bit application and requires a 64-bit capable processor. This is generally not an issue with any modern hardware. However, verify that legacy hardware supports a 64-bit operating system before attempting to use it as a reverse proxy.

The Forefront Threat Management Gateway server memory requirement is as follows:

▶ 2 GB RAM (4 GB recommended)

The Forefront Threat Management Gateway disk requirement is as follows:

▶ Local storage with at least 2.5 GB free space

The Forefront Threat Management Gateway server network requirements are as follows:

▶ One network adapter for communication with the internal network

▶ An additional network adapter for each network connected to the Forefront TMG server

---

NOTE

Designing a high-availability solution for Threat Management Gateway is not discussed in detail here. However, this can be done with Windows Network Load Balancing or a hardware load balancer. Follow the documentation on TechNet to design a solution that matches and meets availability requirements for the Lync Server infrastructure.

Operating System Requirements   Forefront Threat Management Gateway supports the following operating systems:

▶ Windows Server 2008, x64 Standard Edition with Service Pack 2

▶ Windows Server 2008, x64 Enterprise Edition with Service Pack 2

▶ Windows Server 2008, x64 Datacenter Edition with Service Pack 2

▶ Windows Server 2008 R2, Standard Edition

▶ Windows Server 2008 R2, Enterprise Edition

▶ Windows Server 2008 R2, Datacenter Edition

The Windows Server Core, Web, and High Performance Computing editions for any operating system version are not supported for deployment.

Software Requirements The Forefront Threat Management Gateway server requires installation of the following components:

▶ .NET Framework 3.5, Service Pack 1

▶ Windows Web Services API

▶ Windows Update

▶ Windows Installer 4.0

Server Roles and Features

In addition to the operating system and software requirements listed previously, the Forefront Threat Management Gateway requires several Windows server roles, role services, and features to be installed. The following roles and features can either be preinstalled or installed automatically by the Forefront Threat Management Gateway preparation tool.

▶ Network Policy Server

▶ Routing and Remote Access Services

▶ Active Directory Lightweight Directory Services Tools

▶ Network Load Balancing Tools

▶ Windows PowerShell

Forefront Threat Management Gateway 2010 Installation

This section discusses installing a standalone Forefront Threat Management Gateway 2010 server to support the reverse proxy functionality required for external access. For detailed instructions on configuring an array of Threat Management Gateway servers or centralized management options, refer to TechNet.

1. Launch the Forefront Threat Management Gateway 2010 installation media.
2. If the required server roles and features have not applied, click **Run Preparation Tool**.
3. Click **Next** to begin the Preparation Wizard.
4. Select **I accept the terms of license agreements** and then click **Next**.
5. Select **Forefront TMG services and Management** and then click **Next**.

6. Select **Launch Forefront TMG Installation Wizard** and then click **Finish**.

7. Click **Next** to begin the installation.

8. Select **I accept the terms in the license agreement** and then click **Next**.

9. Enter a username, organization, and product serial number. Then click **Next**.

10. Enter an installation path and then click **Next**.

11. Click the **Add** button to begin entering internal network ranges.

12. Click **Add Adapter**, select the network adapter, and then click **OK**.

13. Verify the start and end addresses account for the internal network ranges of the Lync Server servers. Include additional ranges, and then click **OK** and **Next**.

14. Click **Next** and then **Install** to begin the installation.

15. Click **Finish** when the installation completes.

Reverse Proxy Configuration

After the Forefront Threat Management Gateway 2010 installation completes, the configuration of the reverse proxy rules can begin. The following sections describe how to create the components required to publish the Lync Server services.

Getting Started Wizard

After opening the Forefront TMG Console from the Start menu the first time, it presents the Getting Started Wizard. This wizard assists an administrator in configuring the initial setup tasks.

1. Click **Configure network settings**.

2. Click **Next** to begin the Network Setup Wizard.

3. Select **Edge firewall**, and then click **Next**.

4. In the Network adapter for the LAN selection box, choose the network adapter that faces the internal network.

TIP

When reverse proxy has multiple network adapters, only a single default gateway should be used, which is usually placed on the externally facing adapter. The internal-facing adapter should have an IP address and subnet mask assigned, but no default gateway. To reach the internal networks, add routing statements to the reverse proxy to direct traffic for those networks through the internal-facing adapter.

---

5. Verify the IP address and subnet mask configuration. Add required routes to internal networks, and click **Next**.

6. In the Network adapter connected to the Internet selection box, choose the external-facing adapter and click **Next**.

7. Click **Finish** to complete the Network Setup Wizard.

8. Click **Configure system settings**.

9. Click **Next** to begin the System Configuration Wizard.

10. Verify the computer name, domain membership, and primary DNS suffix. Click **Next**.

NOTE

To leverage the strongest form of Forefront Threat Management Gateway pre-authentication, Kerberos Constrained Delegation, it must be a member of the Active Directory domain.

---

11. Click **Finish** to complete the System Configuration Wizard.

12. Click **Define deployment options**.

13. Click **Next** to begin the Deployment Wizard.

14. Select a Microsoft Update option and click **Next**.

15. Select **Activate complementary license and enable NIS** in the Network Inspection System selection.

16. Select to enable Web Protection features if desired, and then click **Next**.

17. Configure the NIS Signature Update Settings to meet the organization requirements, and then click **Next**.

18. Select whether to participate in the Customer Experience Improvement Program and then click **Next**.

19. Select a participation level for Microsoft telemetry reporting and then click **Next**.

20. Click **Finish** to complete the Deployment Wizard.

21. Clear the **Run web access wizard** check box and then click **Close** to complete the initial configuration.

Install Certificates

Before creating rules or Forefront Threat Management Gateway rules the appropriate certificates should be installed on the server. The required subject name should match the external URL of the pool and include subject alternative names for simple URLs created for dial-in conferencing or meetings. If the Lync Server Certificate Wizard is used, the External Edge services certificate may already contain all the required names.

To present the certificate to external clients, the certificate must have the private key associated. If exporting certificates from other servers, include the private key. If the private key is not available for export, the certificate might need to be re-issued, but with the "private key is exportable" option.

Additionally, be sure the Forefront Threat Management Gateway has the root certificate of any internal certificate authorities used to issue certificates to internal Lync Server pools. For Threat Management Gateway to successfully publish internal pools, it must be able to access the HTTPS ports on the internal servers and trust the certificates presented for web services.

Create Web Listener

The first step in configuring any kind of HTTPS publishing in Threat Management Gateway is to create a web listener. *Web listeners* are objects that a web publishing rule uses to determine IP addresses and certificates to present to external clients. Web listeners can be created during the Web Publishing Wizard, but if changes are required, the entire wizard must be cancelled. For this reason, create the web listener object in advance of the rule configuration.

1. Open the Forefront TMG Console from the Start menu.
2. Expand the Forefront TMG (<Computer Name>) node and then click **Firewall Policy**.
3. In the far right pane, click the **Toolbox** link.
4. In the **Network Objects** section, right-click **Web Listeners** and select **New web listener**.
5. Enter a name for the Web Listener and click **Next**.
6. Select **Require SSL secured connections with clients** and click **Next**.
7. If the Threat Management Gateway publishes only a single public IP address, check the **External** box. If multiple IP addresses are bound to the server, click **Select IP addresses** and choose only the IP addresses used by the listener. Click **Next**.
8. Click the **Select certificate** button to choose the certificate that the web listener will present to external clients, as shown in Figure 6.5. Click **Select** and then **Next**.

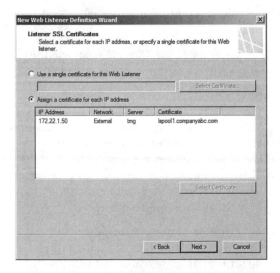

FIGURE 6.5   Certificate and IP Address Selection

9. In the **Select how clients will provide credentials to Forefront TMG** box, select **No authentication** and click **Next**.

NOTE

This selection does not necessarily mean anonymous access to Lync Server pools is allowed. It simply means the Forefront Threat Management Gateway is not responsible for pre-authenticating users. Instead, users are authenticated by the Front End pools before being allowed to access content.

---

10. Click **Next** because single sign on is not available with this type of authentication.
11. Click **Finish** to complete the wizard.

Publishing a Single Server Pool or Load Balancer

After the web listener is created, a web publishing rule can be created. The process for this rule creation differs slightly depending on whether the pool consists of only a single member, or whether the reverse proxy should publish the load balancer. In either of these cases, use the following steps. If the built-in load balancing features of Forefront Threat Management Gateway are used for external load balancing, follow the next section, "Publishing a Pool with Multiple Servers," to create the rule.

1. Right-click **Firewall Policy**, select **New**, and select **Web Publishing Rule**.
2. Name the rule descriptively and click **Next**.
3. Select **Allow** and then press **Next**.
4. Select **Publish a single web site or load balancer** and click **Next**.
5. Select **Use SSL to connect to the published Web server or server farm** and click **Next**.
6. Enter the internal site name and the fully qualified name of the internal pool and click **Next**.

TIP

Be sure the Threat Management Gateway server can resolve the name in DNS. If not, enter the IP address of the internal server or load balancer.

---

7. In the **Path** field, enter a /* to publish all internal paths behind the previously entered site name. Be sure to select the **Forward the original host header instead of the actual one specified in the Internal site name field on the previous page** check box. Click **Next**.

CAUTION

Forwarding the original host header was not important in OCS 2007, but is critical when using simple URLs for dial-in conferencing and meetings. If the original header is not forwarded, the Front End server can't tell whether the client requested meet.companyabc.com or lyncwebservices.companyabc.com. This can prevent external users from joining meetings.

8. In the **Accept requests for selection**, leave **This domain name** selected and enter the public FQDN of the external web services defined in the Topology Builder. Leave the Path field with the **/*** string, as shown in Figure 6.6, and then click **Next**.

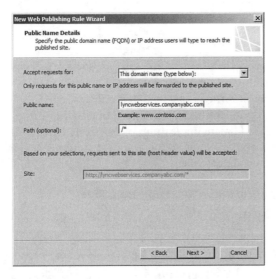

FIGURE 6.6   Public Name for Rule

9. In the **Web Listener** selection box, choose the web listener created in an earlier step, and then click **Next**.

10. In the **Authentication Delegation** method, select **No delegation, but client may authenticate directly**, and then click **Next**.

11. Leave the **All Users** set in the list and then click **Next**.

12. Click **Finish** to complete the rule.

Publishing a Pool with Multiple Servers

If the load-balancing capabilities of Threat Management Gateway are used to publish multiple Front End Servers in a pool, use the following steps:

1. Right-click the **Firewall Policy**, select **New**, and select **Web Publishing Rule**.
2. Name the rule descriptively and click **Next**.
3. Select **Allow** and click **Next**.
4. Select **Publish a server farm of load balanced Web servers** and click **Next**.
5. Select **Use SSL to connect to the published Web server or server farm** and click **Next**.
6. Enter the internal site name and the fully qualified name of the internal pool and click **Next**.
7. In the **Path** field, enter a /* to publish all internal paths behind the previously entered site name. Click **Next**.
8. Click **New** to create a new web server farm.
9. Name the web server farm and click **Next**.
10. Click the **Add** button and enter the name of a Front End Server or IP address if Threat Management Gateway cannot resolve internal DNS. Click **OK** and repeat for any additional Front End Servers in the pool.
11. Click **Next** after all servers are defined in the farm, as shown in Figure 6.7.

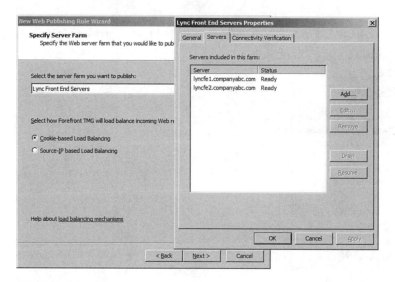

FIGURE 6.7   TMG Web Farm Definition

12. In the method used to monitor server farm connectivity, select **Establish a TCP connection** and enter port **4443**. Click **Next**.
13. Click **Finish** to complete the web farm creation.
14. Ensure **Cookie-based Load Balancing** is selected and then click **Next**.

15. In the **Accept requests for** selection, leave **This domain name** selected and enter the public FQDN of the external web services defined in the Topology Builder. Leave the Path field with the /* string and then click **Next**.

16. In the **Web Listener** selection box, choose the web listener created in an earlier step and click **Next**.

17. In the **Authentication Delegation** method, select **No delegation, but client may authenticate directly** and click **Next**.

18. Leave the **All Users** set in the list and click **Next**.

19. Click **Finish** to complete the rule.

Redirect SSL Bridging

When using the Web Server Publishing Wizard, there are some settings unavailable that need to be modified after creating the rule. Because the external web services run on an IIS website using port 4443, the following steps are required to redirect Threat Management Gateway rules to this port instead of 443.

1. Right-click the web site publishing rule just created and select **Properties**.

2. Click the **Bridging** tab.

3. In the **Redirect requests to SSL port**, change the 443 to **4443**, as shown in Figure 6.8.

4. Click the **Apply** button to save changes.

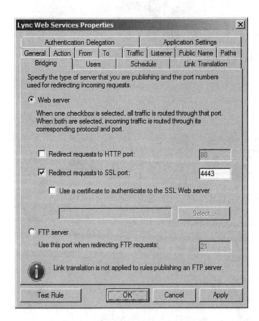

FIGURE 6.8   SSL Bridging Redirection

Listen for Additional Public Names

By default, the Threat Management Gateway only responds to requests for the public name entered during the Web Site Publishing Wizard. Because additional URLs can be used for dial-in conferencing or meetings, they must be added to the rule.

1. Right-click the web site publishing rule just created and select **Properties**.
2. Click the **Public Name** tab.
3. Use the **Add** button to enter any simple URLs published for dial-in conferencing or meetings.
4. Click the **Apply** button to save changes after all names have been added, as shown in Figure 6.9.

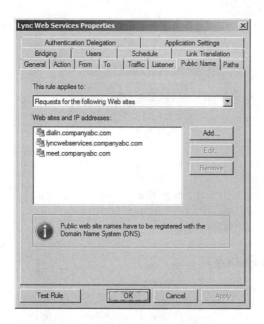

FIGURE 6.9   Additional Public Names

Test and Apply Rules

After creating and editing the rules, they can be applied to the Threat Management Gateway configuration, but should first be tested.

1. Right-click the web site publishing rule just created and select **Properties**.
2. Press the **Test Rule** button to check the published rule. Verify that the rule test returns a green check mark, as shown in Figure 6.10, and then click **OK**.

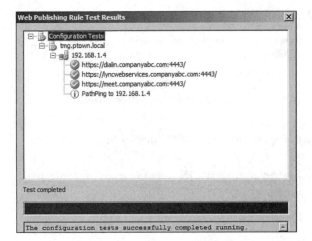

FIGURE 6.10   Test the Web Publishing Rule

3. Click **Apply** to submit the new rule and web listener.

4. Enter a description of the changes when prompted and click **Apply**.

5. Click **OK** when the configuration is applied.

Edge Server Administration

Administration of the Edge sever features is done either through the Lync Server Control
Panel or Lync Server Management Shell. Much of the administration is configuring
various external access and conferencing policies for the users.

Editing the Global External Access Policy

Even though the remote access services have been enabled on the Access Edge configuration, users must have their account enabled to use these features. This can be done at a
global level so that it applies to all users or it can be configured on a per-site or per-user
basis. The following steps show how to enable the features for all users in the organization.

1. Open the Lync Server Control Panel.

2. Select **External User Access** in the navigation pane.

3. Click **External Access Policy**.

4. Highlight the **Global** policy, click **Edit**, and click **Modify**.

5. Check the **Enable communications with remote users** box.

6. Check the **Enable communications with federated users** box.

7. Check the **Enable communications with public users** box.

8. Click **Commit** when complete. A sample configuration is shown in Figure 6.11.

FIGURE 6.11   Edit the Global External Access Policy

Alternatively, the Lync Server Management Shell can also be used to configure the following setting:

```
Set-CSExternalAccessPolicy Global –EnableOutsideAccess $true
–EnableFederationAccess $true
–EnablePublicCloudAccess $true –EnablePublicCloudAudioVideoAccess $true
```

TIP

The EnablePublicCloudAudioVideoAccess parameter in the previous example enables audio and video communication to the public IM providers. The only support provided for A/V at the time of this writing is the Windows Live and MSN network.

Creating a New External Access Policy

In some scenarios, it is best to enable these features only for a select group of users or sites. Instead of enabling remote access on the global policy, a new policy must be created and then assigned to a site or user accounts.

1. Open the Lync Server Control Panel.
2. Select **External User Access** in the navigation pane.
3. Click **Access Edge Policy**.
4. Click **New** and then select **Site policy** or **User policy** depending on what should be targeted.

NOTE

If a site policy is defined, all users associated with Front End pools in the site will automatically inherit the policy. This is used to automatically provision remote access features to some sites while not allowing it to others.

5. Select the **Enable communications with remote users** check box.

6. Select the **Enable communications with federated users** check box.

7. Select the **Enable communications with public users** check box.

8. Click **Commit** when complete.

Alternatively, the Lync Server Management Shell can be used to create the new policy:

```
New-CSExternalAccessPolicy "Allow all features" -EnableOutsideAccess $true
-EnableFederationAccess $true -EnablePublicCloudAccess $true
-EnablePublicCloudAudioVideoAccess $true
```

TIP

To create a policy with site scope using the Lync Server Management Shell, name the policy with a "site:" prefix followed by the site name. For instance, if a site called SF existed, the previous example policy should be named "Site:SF" to apply only to that site.

Assigning External Access Policies

After creating the new user policy, it must be assigned to a user account. If the external policy is created with a site scope, this step is not required.

1. Select **Users** in the navigation pane.

2. Search for a user, highlight the account, click **Modify**, and click **Assign polices**.

3. In the **Access Edge** policies section, select the new Remote Access policy, and click OK. An example of this configuration is shown in Figure 6.12.

The Lync Server Management Shell can also be used to assign a policy to a user:

```
Grant-CSExternalAccessPolicy <User's SIP Address> -PolicyName "Allow all features"
```

Managing Federation

After enabling user accounts for federation, administrators can manage the organizations they want to federate with through Lync Server. If partner discovery lookups are allowed on the Access Edge configuration, all domains are automatically allowed. Adding allowed domains can still be done to grant a higher level of trust to partners, but is not required. If partner discovery is not allowed, administrators must manually add all federated partners to the allow list.

FIGURE 6.12   Assign an External Access Policy

Blocking a federated domain can be used to prevent internal users from communicating with specific partners. This is used in situations where federation should be allowed globally, but blocked only to a few specific domain names. To allow or block a federated domain, use the following steps:

1. Open the Lync Server Control Panel.

2. Select **External User Access** in the navigation pane.

3. Click **Federated Domains**.

4. Click **New** and then select either Allowed Domain or Blocked Domain.

5. Enter the SIP domain name of the federated domain allowed or blocked as shown in Figure 6.13 and click **OK**.

CAUTION

When adding an allowed domain, the option exists to add the FQDN of the partner's Access Edge Server. This field is not required, but when done grants a higher level of trust to the domain by allowing more requests per second from the domain. Be careful when using this field because if a partner changes its FQDN later, the name will no longer be valid.

The Lync Server Management Shell can also be used to perform these tasks. To allow a new domain, use the following command. The only required parameter is the domain name, but a comment and partner's Access Edge Server FQDN can also be specified. In addition, the MarkForMonitoring parameter can be set to enable quality monitoring to this domain by a Monitoring Server role.

```
New-CSAllowedDomain –Domain <SIP Domain Name> -Comment <Comment string> -ProxyFQDN
<Partner Access Edge FQDN> -MarkForMonitoring <True¦False>
```

To block a domain from sending or receiving messages, use the following command:

```
New-CSBlockedDomain –Domain <SIP Domain Name>
```

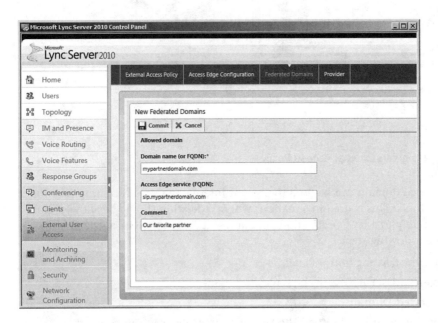

FIGURE 6.13   Adding an Allowed Domain for Federation

Managing Public IM Providers

Similar to managing federation, the Public IM providers can be allowed or blocked when configuring an Edge Server. By default, all three of the included providers are disabled and must be enabled before users can communicate with contacts in these domains.

The following additional options are available when dealing with the Public IM providers:

▶ **Allow communications only with users verified by this provider**—This is the default setting and means the Edge Server trusts the Public IM provider's determination of valid or invalid users trying to send messages to the Lync Server users.

▶ **Allow communications only with users on recipients' contact lists**—This setting limits communication only to users explicitly added to the contact list of a

Lync Server user. If a contact is not added and tries to initiate a conversation with an internal user, the message will be rejected by the Edge Server.

▶ **Allow all communications with this provider**—This setting enables all incoming communication from the provider regardless of whether the provider indicates the message should be trusted.

To manage access to the public networks, use the following steps:

1. Open the Lync Server Control Panel.
2. Select **External User Access** in the navigation pane.
3. Click **Provider**.
4. Highlight one of the providers, click **Edit**, and click **Modify**.
5. Check the **Enable communications with this provider** box to all access to the provider, and click **Commit**.
6. Repeat for enabling additional providers.

Figure 6.14 displays the default Public IM configuration for a Lync Server deployment.

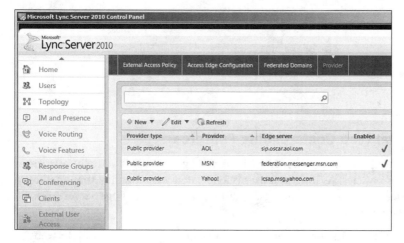

FIGURE 6.14   Configuring Public IM Providers

To perform these steps in the Lync Server Management Shell, use the following command:

```
Set-CSPublicProvider <Provider Name> -Enabled $true
```

To enable all three public IM providers in one step, use the following command:

```
Get-CSPublicProvider | Set-CSPublicProvider -Enabled $true
```

The status of the public IM providers can be viewed by running the Get-CSPublicProvider cmdlet.

```
Identity:              MSN

Name:                  MSN

ProxyFQDN:             federation.messenger.msn.c

VerificationLevel:     UseSourceVerification

Enabled:               True


Identity:'             Yahoo!

Name:                  Yahoo!

ProxyFQDN:             lcsap.msg.yahoo.com

VerificationLevel      UseSourceVerificatio

Enabled:               True


Identity:              AOL

Name:                  AOL

ProxyFQDN:             sip.oscar.aol.com

VerificationLevel      UseSourceVerificatio

Enabled:               True
```

Managing External Web Conferencing Features

Enable remote access to the web conferencing features of Lync Server is actually performed with the remote access policies. As long as a user is associated with a policy that enables remote access, the user has web conferencing capabilities through the Edge Server from the Global conferencing policy.

After deploying Edge services, the option exists to enable anonymous users to join web conferences hosted by the Lync Server infrastructure. Anonymous users are considered people who are not federated partners or users without a Lync Server enabled account. These users cannot authenticate with credentials, so they are considered anonymous to the pool users. Anonymous access to conferences can be enabled to allow authenticated, federated users, and anonymous users to all collaborate together.

To configure the external access rules and anonymous access, the conferencing policy must be edited.

1. Open the Lync Server Control Panel.
2. Select **Conferencing** in the navigation pane.
3. Highlight the Global policy, click **Edit**, and click **Modify**.

4. Ensure **Enable data collaboration** is enabled, which is key to conducting web conferences with a PowerPoint or whiteboard session.

5. Verify that the **Allow users to invite anonymous participants** check box is selected.

> **NOTE**
>
> The Allow users to dial out check box refers to PSTN Dial-In Conferencing and enables anonymous users to provide a phone number for the conferencing service to call them for audio collaboration. This topic is covered in more detail in Chapter 18, "Enterprise Voice."

6. If external users should be allowed to control shared applications or desktops, ensure that the **Allow external users to control shared applications** check box is checked. A sample configuration is displayed in Figure 6.15.

FIGURE 6.15   Editing Web Conferencing Policies

7. Click **Commit**.

To enable anonymous access and external sharing control for the Global policy through the Lync Server Management Shell, use the following command:

```
Set-CSConferencingPolicy Global –AllowAnonymousParticipantsInMeetings $true
–AllowExternalUserControl $true
```

NOTE

Selecting the Enable recording option in a meeting policy presents an additional check box, Allow external users to record meeting, which lets an administrator control whether only internal users may record a meeting.

If enabling anonymous access and external user control features must be limited to specific locations or user groups, an additional conferencing policy should be created. Like the External Access Policy, a site policy will automatically apply to an entire location, and user policies can be assigned to individual users.

Managing A/V Edge Features

After deploying an A/V Edge Server, users will be able to do peer-to-peer audio and video through the Edge Server without additional configuration. To support A/V conferencing features, the user must be associated with a conferencing policy that enables audio, video, and application sharing. The global policy can be edited to allow this or, as in the following example, a site policy can be created specifically for A/V conferencing and application-sharing features.

1. Open the Lync Server Control Panel.
2. Select **Conferencing** in the navigation pane.
3. Select **New** and select **Site Policy**.
4. Select a site to associate the policy to and click **OK**.
5. Specify a maximum meeting size for the conferences.
6. In the Audio/Video section, either select **Enable IP Audio/Video** or **Enable IP Audio** depending on requirements.
7. Select a maximum video resolution for conferencing of either **640x480 (VGA)** or **352x288 (CIF)**.
8. If the conferencing policy does not require data collaboration, select **None**, or if the policy should also allow web conferencing, leave **Enable data collaboration** selected.
9. To support application sharing, select the **Allow users to schedule meetings with application sharing** check box and then select **Enable application sharing for users** or **Enable application and desktop sharing for users**.
10. Click **Commit** to save the new policy.

Because a site policy was created, it should be automatically applied to users. To create a new policy, which can be assigned directly to users, the following Lync Server Management Shell command can be used.

```
New-CSConferencingPolicy "Allow AV and Desktop Sharing" -AllowExternalUserControl
➥$true
-AllowIPAudio $true -AllowIPVideo $true -MaxVideoConferenceResolution VGA
-AllowParticipantControl $true -AllowUserToScheduleMeetingsWithAppSharing $true
-EnableAppDesktopSharing Desktop -MaxMeetingSize 20
```

Assigning Conferencing Policies

After creating the new conferencing policy for users, it must be assigned. A site policy automatically applies to users and does not require this step.

1. Select **Users** in the navigation pane.

2. Search for a user, highlight the account, click **Modify**, and click **Assign polices**.

3. In the **Conferencing** policies section, select the new conferencing policy and click **OK**.

The Lync Server Management Shell can also be used to assign a conferencing policy to user.

```
Grant-CSConferencingPolicy <User's SIP Address> -PolicyName "Allow AV and Desktop
Sharing"
```

Edge Troubleshooting

Troubleshooting Edge Servers is necessary in the event that users are unable to sign in or some features become unavailable. This section discusses the key components of an Edge Server to check when issues arise. Common troubleshooting tools and tips are also provided, which should resolve many issues.

Firewall Ports

Connectivity to an Edge Server or reverse proxy can be limited by firewalls and tricky to troubleshoot because the connections generally cross a few network boundaries. See Chapter 12, "Firewall and Security Requirements," or Chapter 27 for detailed firewall information. Check firewalls between remote clients, Edge Servers, and internal servers. Also, check whether the Windows Firewall are blocking connections.

> ▶ For a more detailed explanation of firewall scenarios and requirements, see Chapter 27.

Routing

Any time a server has multiple network adapters, it can be problematic to make routing work correctly. Ensure that requests destined for the internal network are routed out the correct network adapter by using tools such as packet sniffers or traceroute. Packet capture tools have the capability to monitor a specific adapter, so it should be easy to determine whether traffic is flowing through an adapter.

Certificates

Incorrectly issued certificates are a potential issue with Edge Server configuration.

TIP

As a best practice, always use the built-in Certificate Wizards because they automatically generate the correct names for a server role. Only the Access Edge and Web Conferencing Edge certificates need to be issued by a public certificate authority. The internal Edge certificate and A/V Authentication certificates are used only by internal clients.

Follow the guidelines to rule out certificate issues.

▶ **Key Bit Length**—The certificate bit length must be 1024, 2048, or 4096 to be supported by Lync Server.

▶ **Template**—The template used to issue the certificate should be based on the web server template. If the Lync Server Certificate Wizard is used, the correct template will automatically be applied.

▶ **Private Key**—The server certificate must have the private key associated to be used by Lync Server. In situations where certificates are exported or copied between servers, export the private key with the certificate.

▶ **Certificate Chain**—The Edge Server must be able to verify each certificate up to a Trusted Root Certification Authority. Additionally, because the server presents the certificate to clients, it must contain each intermediate certificate in the certificate chain.

▶ **Certificate Store**—All certificates used by the Edge Server must be located in the Personal section of the local computer certificate store. A common mistake is to place certificates in the Personal section of the user account certificate store.

▶ **Certificate Trust**—Be sure that the clients and servers communicating with the Edge Server all contain a copy of the top-level certificate authority of the chain in their Trusted Root Certification Authority local computer store. When the certification authority is integrated with Active Directory, this is generally not an issue. When using an offline or nonintegrated certificate authority, install root certificates on clients and servers.

Additionally, each service has slightly different requirements for the subject and subject alternative names.

Edge Internal Certificate Names

The required name for an Access Edge Server certificate is as follows:

▶ **Subject Name**—Ensure the subject name matches the internal edge pool FQDN entered in the Topology Builder.

Access Edge Certificate Names

The required names for an Access Edge Server certificate are as follows:

- **Subject Name**—Ensure that the subject name matches the Access Edge FQDN entered in the Topology Builder.

- **Subject Alternative Names**—The SAN field must contain all supported SIP domains in the sip.<SIP Domain> format.

Web Conferencing Edge Certificate Names

The required name for a Web Conferencing Edge Server certificate is as follows:

- **Subject Name**—Ensure the subject name matches the Web Conferencing Edge FQDN entered in the Topology Builder.

A/V Authentication Certificate Names

The media relay certificate doesn't have any specific name requirements, but as a best practice use the following:

- **Subject Name**—Ensure the subject name matches the Edge Server's internal interface server or pool name.

Wildcard Certificates

Some organizations attempt to use wildcard certificates or a single certificate with subject alternative names that attempt to cover all possible names. There are certainly some cases where this configuration might work, but in the end the simplicity of following the actual name requirements tends to outweigh any small cost savings achieved by using fewer certificates. If attempting one of these configurations and experiencing issues, use the correct names to see whether it resolves the issue.

DNS Records

Successful sign-in to an Edge Server is heavily dependent on correctly configuring the DNS.

- The NSLookup tool can be used to verify that the necessary DNS records are in place as described in Chapter 10, "Dependent Services."

> **TIP**
>
> It is important to check that all necessary DNS records exist and resolve to the correct locations.

The following sample NSLookup sequence within a command prompt checks the host record of the pool:

```
nslookup
set type=a
lyncedgepool1.companyabc.com
```

A successful query returns a name and IP address. Verify that IP returned matches the IP addresses assigned to the Edge Servers or load balancer and that no extra, or surprise, IP addresses are returned.

To verify the SRV record required for automatic client sign-in externally the syntax is slightly different. The following is another sample NSLookup sequence:

```
nslookup
set type=srv
_sip._tls.companyabc.com
```

A successful query returns a priority, weight, port, and server hostname. Verify that the server name matches the Edge pool Access Edge FQDN and the correct port is returned.

Use the same steps to verify that the following services resolve correctly in public DNS:

- ▶ Access Edge FQDN

- ▶ Web Conferencing Edge FQDN

- ▶ A/V Edge FQDN

For internal DNS, verify that clients can resolve the following:

- ▶ Internal Edge Pool FQDN

TIP

Verify that the Edge Server can verify internal DNS names. It must be able to resolve the names of internal Lync Server servers to send and receive messages.

Logs

A good source of information when troubleshooting any server issue is the event logs. Lync Server creates a dedicated event log for informational activities, warnings, and errors within the standard Windows Server Event Viewer console. To view this event log, perform the following steps:

1. Click **Start**.
2. Type **eventvwr.msc** and click **Enter** to open the Event Viewer Microsoft Management Console.
3. Expand the Applications and Services Logs folder.
4. Click the **Lync Server** log.

5. Examine the log for warning or error events, which might provide additional insight into issues.

Lync Server Management Shell

The Lync Server Management Shell provides several cmdlets, which test various functions of a server. A useful cmdlet for verifying the overall health of a server is Test-CSComputer server, which verifies that all services are running, the local computer group membership is correctly populated with the necessary Lync Server Active Directory groups, and that the required Windows Firewall ports are open.

The Test-CSComputer cmdlet must be run from the local computer and uses the following syntax:

```
Test-CSComputer –Report "C:\Test-CSComputer Results.xml"
```

After running the cmdlet, open the generated XML file to view a detailed analysis of each check.

Telnet

Telnet is a simple method of checking whether a specific TCP port is available from a client machine. From a machine that has trouble contacting an Edge Server, use the following steps to verify connectivity to the Access Edge or Web Conferencing services:

> **TIP**
>
> The Telnet client is not installed by default in Windows Vista, Windows 7, Windows Server 2008, or Windows Server 2008 R2. On a desktop operating system, it must be installed by using the Turn Windows Features on or off option found in Programs and Features. On a server operating system, it can be installed through the Features section of Server Manager.

1. Open a command prompt.
2. Type the following command:

```
telnet <Access Edge FQDN> <443 or 5061>
```
If the window goes blank leaving a flashing cursor, the connection was successful and the port can be contacted without issue. If the connection fails, an error is returned. Check that the services are running on the Director and that no firewalls are blocking the traffic.

Services

Basic troubleshooting begins with making sure the Lync Server services are all running. When services are in a stopped state, users will notice many issues such as being unable to sign in or connect to the Edge Server. Verify that the following services are configured to start automatically and are running.

- ▶ Lync Server Access Edge

- ▶ Lync Server Audio/Video Authentication

- ▶ Lync Server Audio/Video Edge

- ▶ Lync Server Replica Replicator Agent

- ▶ Lync Server Web Conferencing Edge

Edge Server Best Practices

The following are best practices from this chapter:

- ▶ Use Edge Servers to provide secure remote access for Lync Server.

- ▶ Place the Edge Servers in a perimeter or DMZ network.

- ▶ Use DNS load-balancing or a hardware load balancer to provide high-availability for Edge Servers.

- ▶ Create external access policies with site level scopes to apply automatically to users.

- ▶ Plan to use a reverse proxy server to publish external web services.

- ▶ Use DNS SRV records for routing federation requests to reduce management overhead with federation.

- ▶ Use certificates from a public certificate authority for the Access Edge and Web Conferencing Edge roles so that they are trusted automatically by remote clients and federated partners.

- ▶ Use conferencing policies to control web conferencing and A/V capabilities.

Summary

The Edge Server is a big part of why Lync Server is such a compelling product. The fact that users can be inside or outside the office with complete access to the same features drives productivity and collaboration. With how the Edge services work regardless of location, users have no need to change their workflows whether they are in the office, at home, or traveling halfway around the world.

On the less glamorous side, the Edge Server is a safe and stable role designed to be a secure gateway to the Lync Server infrastructure. The granular external access and conferencing policies give administrators complete control over what features are deployed and who is allowed to use them.

The federation and public IM features enable an organization to extend the reach of their unified communications platform to partners or customers without additional products. Organizations considering Lync Server should include Edge services within the deployment to take full advantage of the features it offers.

9

Microsoft Lync Server 2010 Monitoring

Overview

Microsoft Lync Server has a number of different server roles. These can be combined in a number of ways to produce a myriad of architecture options. Even the collocation of services for a given role can be split out onto multiple servers for added flexibility.

The Monitoring role in Lync Server has evolved from previous versions. For those new to Lync Server, the Monitoring role collects and manages information from the Front End, Mediation, and other server roles, and it stores the information in a database that is separate from the one used by the front end. It leverages SQL Server Reporting Services to create reports related to call quality and metrics. These reports are often used for return on investment (ROI) justification. For example, if the legacy conferencing provider charged $1 per minute, and after moving conferencing to OCS, the current report showed 10,000 minutes of usage, the company saves $10,000 in conferencing costs for that month. I've found that most companies can achieve 100% ROI within one to three months after deployment, even in large, highly redundant deployments.

> **NOTE**
>
> As in previous versions, a single monitoring server can potentially monitor several pools of front end servers, depending on load and latency. It requires a separate SQL instance that is often a separate SQL server for scalability purposes from the front end pool.

This chapter highlights the full lifecycle of the Monitoring Server role. It starts with the installation of the Monitoring Server role and follows with the configuration and administration. Finally, the chapter concludes with troubleshooting and best practices.

Installation

This section outlines the steps for installing the Lync Server Monitoring Server role. The Monitoring Server role enables administrators to collect, trend, and review quantitative data related to audio calls, video calls, and instant messaging (IM) messages. The Monitoring Server leverages Microsoft Message Queuing technology to collect information and deposit it in the monitoring database. Then it leverages SQL Server Reporting Services to display a number of canned and custom reports.

By now, the Lync Server Topology Builder should already be installed. For a thorough review of the installation steps for the Topology Builder tool, see Chapter 5, "Microsoft Lync Server 2010 Front End." The first step in adding a Monitor Server to your Lync Server deployment is to add it in the Topology Builder tool.

Installing Microsoft SQL Server 2008 Reporting Services

The Lync Server Monitoring Server leverages Microsoft SQL Server Reporting Services to provide rich reports related to usage and the quality of experience data. This section assumes you already installed SQL and are familiar with the process. Small installations that chose to use the Enterprise Edition of Lync Server can use the same SQL Server as the front end pool; however, most larger deployments require a separate SQL Server, and in very large installations, a separate SQL Reporting Services Server is required. In the steps that follow, you walk through the installation process and post-installation steps for SQL Reporting Services.

During the SQL Server 2008 Installation Wizard, ensure the Reporting Services box is checked and then continue through the wizard.

TIP

Be sure to examine the scalability requirements for your environment to determine whether the Reporting Services role should be placed on the SQL Server or on a dedicated server.

The administrator must also decide where to install the Reporting Services database, either on an existing SQL Server or on the Reporting Services Server. In general, it is recommended you collocate the Reporting Services database on the Reporting Services Server. After the SQL Reporting Services role is installed, it needs to be configured before before the Monitoring Server can use it.

From the Start Menu, navigate to All programs, click Microsoft SQL Server 2008, and then click **Configuration tools**. Select **Reporting Services Configuration Manager**. Ensure the appropriate server and instance is selected and click **Connect**. Then follow these steps:

1. Select the **Server Account** button in the left column and set the appropriate report server service account.

2. Select the **Web Service URL** button. Review the settings. Usually the default settings are acceptable. However, if you want to use SSL, you need to pick the certificate to be used. A certificate can be requested from the IIS console.

3. Select the **Database** button. Ensure the proper database server is set. Ensure the correct credentials are set to access the database.

4. Select the **Report Manager URL** button. Select the virtual directory to be used to access reports. By default this is Reports.

Now the SQL Reporting Services Server is almost ready. After the Monitoring Server is installed, you need to deploy the Monitoring Server Report Pack to the SQL Reporting Server as reviewed in the following section.

Topology Builder for Microsoft Lync Server Monitoring Role

Lync Server uses the published topology to process traffic and maintain overall topology information. To ensure the topology is valid, it is recommended you run the Topology Builder before each topological change. This example shows the steps necessary to add a Monitoring Server to your Lync Server deployment. Remember, if you change the topology later, it should be republished to ensure consistency.

When you launch Lync Server Topology Builder, a pop-up message asks whether you want to download the existing topology. Click **OK** to continue.

To add a Monitoring Server in Topology Builder, follow these steps:

1. Expand your site in Topology Builder.

2. Select the **Monitoring** menu item, as shown in Figure 7.1.

3. On the right side, in the Action pane, click **New Monitoring Server**. Enter the appropriate information, as shown in Figure 7.2, and then click **Next** to finish the wizard.

NOTE

Note that Lync Server sites are not related to Active Directory sites. They are completely separate and unique to Lync Server.

4. Select the site name and choose **Publish**, as shown in Figure 7.3.

5. Click **Next** to publish the updated topology to the central management store, as shown in Figure 7.4.

6. Click **Finish** to return to the main Topology Builder screen.

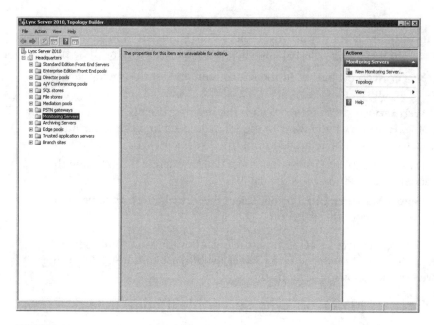

FIGURE 7.1   Monitoring Role Selected

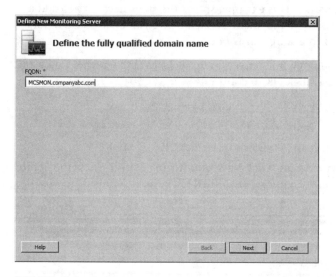

FIGURE 7.2   Define a Monitoring Server

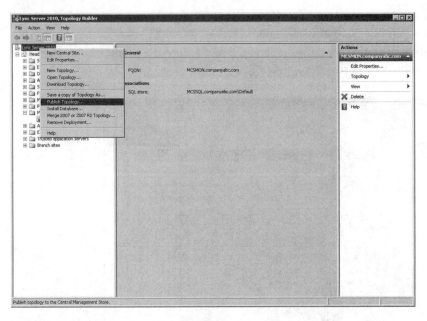

FIGURE 7.3   Choose the Publish Action

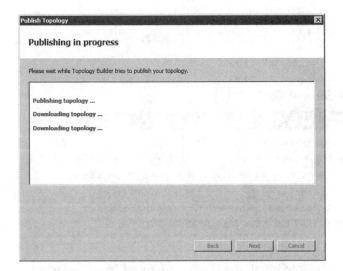

FIGURE 7.4   Publishing the Updated Topology

7. Expand the appropriate section, either Standard Edition front ends or Enterprise Edition front ends, and then select a pool.

8. In the main window, expand the General tab and ensure the Monitoring Server is assigned to the pool as shown in Figure 7.5.

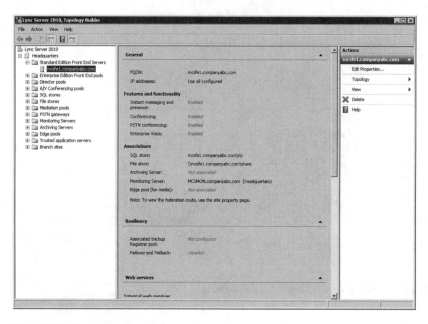

FIGURE 7.5   Monitoring Server Is Assigned to the Pool

Installing the Monitoring Server Role

CAUTION

It is important to note that if you jumped to this section before completing the previous steps, you need to go back. Building a valid topology in the Topology Builder tool is a prerequisite to installing the Monitoring Server role. This is a different process from Office Communications Server 2007 and 2007 R2, and it involves more steps. Administrators new to Lync Server are advised to review the new features, requirements, and prequisites before beginning the installation process.

The following prerequisites are required to install the Monitoring Server Front End role:

▶ IIS with the following options:

  ▶ Static Content

  ▶ Default Document

  ▶ Directory Browsing

  ▶ HTTP Errors

> ▶ HTTP Redirection

> ▶ ASP.NET

> ▶ NET Extensibility

> ▶ Internet Server API (ISAPI) Extensions

> ▶ ISAPI Filters

> ▶ HTTP Logging

> ▶ Logging Tools

> ▶ Request Monitor

> ▶ Tracing

> ▶ Basic Authentication

> ▶ Windows Authentication

> ▶ Request Filtering

> ▶ Static Content Compression

> ▶ IIS Management Console

> ▶ IIS Management Scripts and Tools

> ▶ Message Queueing with Directory Service Integration

After you've completed the steps outlined previously, the server is ready to install the Front End role. In the main Lync Server Deployment Wizard screen, click **Install or Update Lync Server System**.

1. Click **Run** for Install Local Configuration Store.

2. Leave the first option checked to retrieve configuration from the CMS, and then click **Next**. The window displays its progress, as shown in Figure 7.6.

3. For Step 2: Setup or Remove Lync Server Components, click **Run**.

4. At the screen that displays, click **Next**. A window displays, as shown in Figure 7.7.

5. When the process is complete, click **Finish**.

6. For Step 4: Start Services, click **Run**.

7. After the services start successfully, click **Exit** in the deployment wizard.

Configuration

The good news about Lync Server is that with the Topology Builder tool, much of the configuration is done automatically. Although both configuration and administration can be done from the Silverlight web GUI or the Lync Server management shell, the configuration section focuses on the former whereas the administration section focuses on the latter to avoid duplication of concepts.

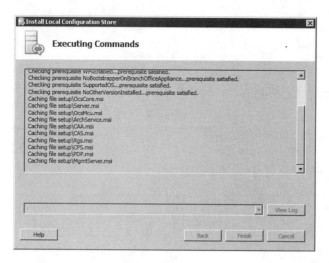

FIGURE 7.6   Installing the Local Configuration Store

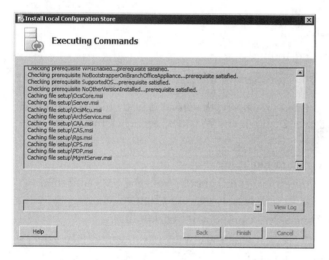

FIGURE 7.7   Installing the Monitoring Server Role

Open the Lync Server Control Panel. For reference, it can be found at the short URL you defined earlier, https://cspool.companyabc.com/admin in the sample environment or https://<pool_FQDN>/Cscp/. After the Lync Server Control Panel is open, click the Toplogy button in the left bar. Find the new Monitoring server in the list or search for it using the Search box at the top. Ensure the Service status has a check mark next to it, as shown in Figure 7.8. This indicates the monitoring service is running and responding.

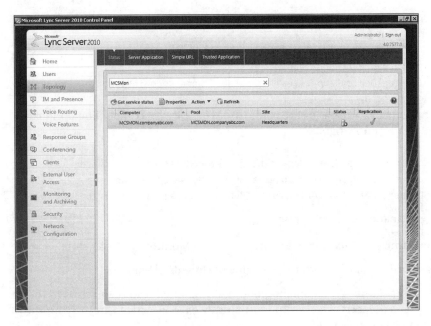

FIGURE 7.8   Examine Monitoring Service Status

Scrolling down in the left bar, click the Monitoring and Archiving button. This brings up the settings menus for the Monitoring and Achiving Server roles. By default, there is only one global policy. Select it, click **Edit**, and then click **Modify**. The available options are

▸ Name (this is the name of the policy)

▸ Enable monitoring of call detail recordings (CDR)

▸ Enable purging of call detail recordings (CDR)

▸ The options for duration to keep CDRs and error reports

Quality of Experience Data Menu

The next item at the top of the bar is the Quality of Experience (QoE) Data menu. Microsoft's approach to measuring the user experience is through QoE data, which provides qualitative and quantitative analysis of every call. New to Lync Server, it also provides some metrics around IM. This also comes with one policy by default. The only option determines whether to enable purging, and, if you do enable, it determines how long to keep QoE data. By default, this value is set to 60 days.

Deploy Monitoring Server Reports

The next step is to deploy the Monitoring Server reports to the SQL Reporting Server. This step can only be done using the Lync Server Management Shell. From one of the Lync Server servers, open the Lync Server Management Shell and run as administrator. Where D is the drive letter assigned to your CD/DVD drive, run the DeployReports.ps1 PowerShell script as follows:

```
C:\Program Files\Microsoft Lync Server
 2010\Deployment\Setup\DeployReports.ps1 –storedUserName <domain\user>
–storedPassword <password>
```

This is the most minimalist version of the command. The full syntax including optional items is outlined in the following:

```
DeployReports.ps1 –storedUserName <domain\user> –storedPassword <password>
–readOnlyGroupName <ReportReadOnlyGroupName> –reportServerSQLInstance
 <ReportServerSQLInstance> –monitoringServerIdentity <MonitoringServerID>
```

Following is an explanation of each option:

▶ **storedUserName**—The username used to access the Monitoring Server store.

▶ **storedPassword**—The password for the value of storedUserName.

▶ **readOnlyGroupName**—The domain group that is granted read-only access to the Monitoring Server reports. This group must already exist in Active Directory for the action to complete successfully.

▶ **reportServerSQLInstance**—The SQL instance that hosts SQL Reporting Services. If left blank, the script assumes it is the same server that holds the Monitoring Server databases.

▶ **monitoringServerIdentity**—This is used to specify the Monitoring Server in environments where more than one Monitoring Server exists. It is not needed in environments where only one Monitoring Server is deployed. The Monitoring Server identity can be found using the Get-CsService –MonitoringServer cmdlet.

When the script has run, ensure it finishes successfully, as shown in Figure 7.9.

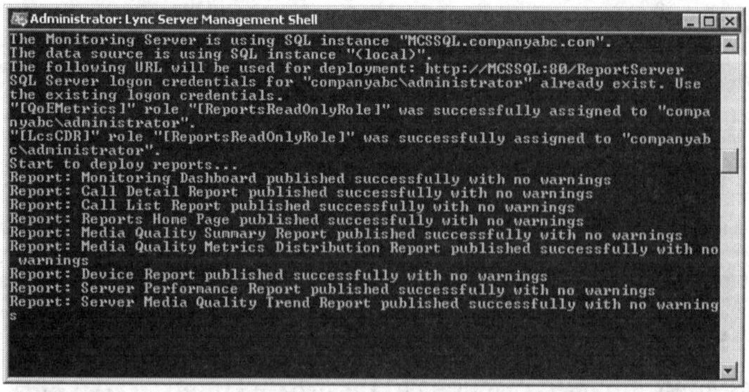

FIGURE 7.9   DeployReports.ps1 Script Completed Successfully

Run the get-CsService –MonitoringServer cmdlet and pay special attention to the ReportingURL field. This is the URL where you access the Lync Server reports. For the sample environment, it is http://mcssql.companyabc.com/ReportServer?%2fMCSReports% 2fMCS+Reports+Home+Page. The reports are covered in detail in the "Administration" section that follows.

Administration

This section reviews common administration tasks for the Lync Server Monitoring role. In general, there isn't much day-to-day administration of the Lync Server Monitoring Server role. Instead, this section focuses on the reports generated by the Monitoring Server.

Introduction to the Dashboard

The biggest change and welcome addition to the Monitoring Server reports page is the Dashboard. The Dashboard is broken up into four distinct areas or panes: System Usage, Per User Call Diagnostics, Call Reliability Diagnostics, and Media Quality Diagnostics. By default, the Dashboard shows this week and a six-week view. However, a monthly view is also available by clicking a link in the upper-right corner of the screen.

Table 7.1 shows System Usage, which is the first section. Although many of the fields are self-explanatory, they are useful for at-a-glance looks at the environment. For example, the total A/V Conference minutes item is great for back-of-the-napkin ROI on savings Lync Server provides overly outsourced conferencing services. Possibly even more importantly, it gives a snapshot of how your users use Lync Server. Are they using Communicator as a soft phone? Do they use application sharing? Has overall collaboration time increased since Lync Server was implemented? This report isn't the end-all for these answers, but it does provide an insightful view.

TABLE 7.1   The System Usage Section of the Dashboard

System Usage

Registration

Unique user logons	0	

Peer-to-Peer

Total sessions	0	
IM sessions	0	

TABLE 7.1   The System Usage Section of the Dashboard

System Usage

Registration

Audio sessions	0	
Video sessions	0	
Application sharing	0	
Total audio session minutes	0.00	
Avg. audio session minutes		

Conference

Total conferences	0	
IM conferences	0	
A/V conferences	0	
Web conferences	0	
Total organizers	0	
Total A/V conference minutes	0.00	
Avg. A/V conference minutes		
Total PSTN conferences	0	
Total PSTN participants	0	
Total PSTN participant minutes	0.00	

Table 7.2 shows the Per-User Call Diagnostics section. This is a great at-a-glance view of the overall health of your voice deployment. It also makes for great bragging rights in a well-planned deployment.

Table 7.3 shows the Call Reliability Diagnostics section, which provides a deeper view into the health of your UC deployment and a window into the end-user experience. This is something new to Lync Server and is a valuable resource to administrators.

TABLE 7.2   Per-User Call Diagnostic Section of the Dashboard

Per-User Call Diagnostics

Users with Call Failures

| Total users with call failures | 0 |
| Conference leaders with call failures | 0 |

Users with Poor Quality Calls

| Total users with poor quality calls | 0 |

TABLE 7.3   Call Reliability Diagnostics Section of the Dashboard

Call Reliability Diagnostics

Peer-to-Peer

Total failures	0
Overall failure rate	
IM failure rate	
Audio failure rate	

Conference

Total failures	0
Overall failure rate	
IM failure rate	
A/V failure rate	

Top Five Servers by Failed Sessions

No server has failure reported.

Table 7.4 shows the last section, which is Media Quality Diagnostics. This table gives information about the quality of calls in terms of total poor quality calls and percentage of poor quality calls compared to the total number of calls. It also offers the same metrics for conferences.

TABLE 7.4   Media Quality Diagnostics Section of the Dashboard

Media Quality Diagnostics

Peer-to-Peer

Total poor quality calls	0	
Poor quality call percentage		
PSTN calls with poor quality	0	

Conference

Total poor quality calls	0	
Poor quality call percentage		
PSTN calls with poor quality	0	

Top Worst Servers by Poor Quality Call Percentage

No server has media quality data based on current period.

From the main Monitoring Server reports page, Figure 7.10, there is a plethora of reports to review. The next section summarizes each report in the order it is presented on the main page. Also, following is a full list of the available reports. You can see that they are a deeper look at the snapshots presented in the Monitoring Server reporting dashboard.

- ▶ System Usage Reports
    - ▶ User Registration Report
    - ▶ Peer-to-peer Activity Summary Report
    - ▶ Conference Summary Report
    - ▶ PSTN Conference Summary Report
    - ▶ Response Group Service Usage Report
    - ▶ IP Phone Inventory Report

- ▶ Per-User Diagnostics Reports

  - ▶ User Activity Report

- ▶ Call Reliability Diagnostics Reports

  - ▶ Call Reliability Summary Report

  - ▶ Peer-to-Peer Activity Reliability Report

  - ▶ Conference Reliability Report

  - ▶ Top Failures Report

  - ▶ Failure Distribution Report

  - ▶ Media Quality Diagnostics Reports

  - ▶ Media Quality Summary Report

  - ▶ Server Performance Report

  - ▶ Location Report

  - ▶ Device Report

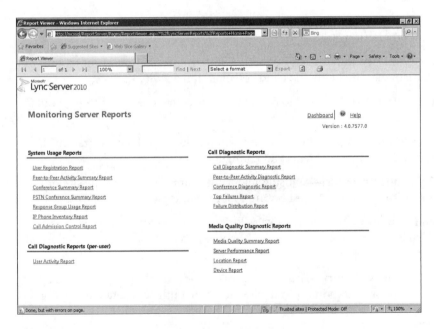

FIGURE 7.10   Monitoring Server Reports Main Page

The following list shows the reports available to an administrator from the main reports page.

▶ **User Registration Report**—Shows user registrations over time. This can be useful to determine peak login times and AD authentication requirements.

▶ **Peer-to-Peer Activity Summary Report**—Shows peer-to-peer activity including IMs, application sharing, and file transfers.

▶ **Conference Summary Report**—Measures conference metrics including Communicator conferences and PSTN conferences, the number of organizers, and the total conference minutes.

▶ **PSTN Conference Summary Report**—Contains data specific to PSTN conferences in Lync Server.

▶ **Response Group Service Usage Report**—Metrics for Response Groups including agent responses and the number of calls answered by the response group.

▶ **IP Phone Inventory Report**—Statistics about the number and type of IP phones in the Lync Server deployment. The report includes all Communicator Phone Edition devices.

▶ **User Activity Report**—This report reviews user-focused call failures for person-to-person calls and conferences. This report is useful for measuring the overall health of your conferencing deployment.

▶ **Call Reliability Summary Report**—A high-level view of failed calls, total call minutes, and other call metrics.

▶ **Peer-to-Peer Activity Reliability Report**—Contains information about failures in peer-to-peer activities, including IMs and collaboration activity.

▶ **Conference Reliability Report**—Reports on failures during IM, peer-to-peer calls, and PSTN conferences.

▶ **Top Failures Report**—A snapshot view of the top failures in the organization. This report can reveal systemic problems and configuration issues.

▶ **Failure Distribution Report**—Statistics about the failures related to the site or pool. This report is a great troubleshooting tool for finding error conditions.

▶ **Media Quality Summary Report**—Overall high-level view of media quality across the whole environment. This report should be referenced often to review the overall health of your voice deployment.

▶ **Server Performance Report**—This report breaks down media quality metrics by server. This is especially important in deployments that utilize separate mediation servers.

▶ **Location Report**—The Location Report reviews media quality statistics by location defined in Lync Server or by individual users.

▶ **Device Report**—Similar to the Location Report, the Device Report pivots media quality data by the type of device used when a failure is experienced.

Although some of the reports might initially seem similar, all of them examine the data from a different, unique angle. These reports are critical in proactively monitoring the health of your Lync Server environment. A wise administrator leverages these reports along with a monitoring platform such as Microsoft System Center Operations Manager.

Troubleshooting

The Monitoring Server role is straightforward, however there are a few things that commonly go wrong during deployment. This section covers the common issues and areas to check if you find your Monitoring Server deployment doesn't go smoothly.

Because there are a lot of server-to-server connections involved in a Monitoring Server deployment, the most obvious source of problems is ensuring proper permissions. Also, you must ensure that usernames and passwords are typed correctly. When in doubt, enter the usernames and passwords used for database access for the Monitoring Server and the Reporting Server. Also, ensure the accounts aren't subject to password expiration in Active Directory. There's no "d'oh" feeling like having a service account's password expire 30 or 90 days into your deployment.

> **TIP**
>
> If you've chosen to use SSL for your Reporting Services URLs, ensure the Common Name (CN) or Subject Name (SN) of the certificate matches the site name you've chosen. Note that this might not be the same as the FQDN of your server.

Ensure that the correct pool is assigned to send data to the Monitoring Server. A Monitoring Server can be deployed without a pool assignment, which means data is not collected for reporting.

The Lync Server event log is also a good place to check for errors. From the Start menu, select **Administrative Tools**, and then select **Event Viewer**. Expand the **Applications and Services Logs** item, and then select **Lync Server**. All events related to Lync Server functions reside here. Often, the error description is enough to identify the problem and determine the resolution.

Best Practices

The following are the best practices from this chapter:

- ▶ Leverage the Monitoring Server to keep a close eye on the overal and ongoing health of your deployment and to troubleshoot user experience quality issues.

- ▶ Although the Lync Server Control Panel might seem more familiar at first, there are several functions that can be accomplished only in the Management Shell; this includes deploying the Monitoring Server Report Pack.

▶ A single Monitoring Server can monitor up to three front end pools. However, in larger deployments, a dedicated Monitoring Server per pool might be required.

▶ For larger deployments, use a dedicated SQL Reporting Services Server.

▶ Before running the DeployReports.ps1 script, ensure the group you specify for Read Only access already exists in Active Directory.

▶ Always publish a new topology before making changes or before installing a new server role.

▶ Test your SQL Reporting Services deployment before loading the Monitoring Server Report Pack.

CHAPTER 8

Microsoft Lync Server 2010 Archiving

Overview

Microsoft Lync Server 2010 has several different server roles. These server roles can be combined in several ways to produce a myriad of architecture options. Even the collocation of services for a given role can be split for added flexibility.

The Archiving role in Lync Server 2010 primarily serves the purposes of legal compliance. That said, other companies might want to have a centrally searchable archive for other purposes because the Archive Server role is able to archive communications across both IM and meetings.

The Archiving role scales well with a single Archiving Server capable of handling up to 300,000 users. As such, it is common to collocate the Archiving role with the Monitoring role. The Archiving role supports redundancy and failover, so if it is a vital role—for example, if you have legal compliance issues that have prompted the installation of the Archiving role—strongly consider deploying the Archiving role as a pool.

The Archiving Server role can archive the following content:

▶ Peer-to-peer instant messages

▶ Multiparty instant messages

▶ Web conferences, including uploaded content and events (for example, join, leave, upload, and so on)

Content that cannot be archived includes

▸ Peer-to-peer file transfers

▸ Audio/video for peer-to-peer instant messages and web conferences

▸ Web conferencing annotations and polls

Organizations should decide prior to the implementation of the Archiving role how archiving will be configured. Decisions around site- and user-based archiving must be made. It is also critical to determine how archive data will be managed. The Archiving database was not meant to be a long term-retention solution and as such, Lync Server 2010 does not provide an e-discovery solution for archived data. This data should optimally be moved to other storage.

NOTE

Lync Server 2010 provides a session export tool in the form of the Export-CsArchivingData commandlet that can be used to export archived data and to create searchable transcripts of the archived data. This tool is discussed in more detail in the administration section of this chapter.

This chapter highlights the full lifecycle of the Archiving Server role. It starts with the installation of the Archiving Server role, followed by configuration and administration. Finally, the chapter concludes with troubleshooting and best practices.

From a perspective of supported topologies for Archiving Server, the Archiving Server can support either a single pool or multiple pools. This is to say, you can choose to create a unique archiving host for each individual Front End pool or a single Archiving Server can service all Front End pools (or Standard Edition pools). It is also possible to have multiple Archiving Servers attach to a single Archiving Database. This can prove helpful if you plan to pull archive data directly from the database.

The decision about how to configure the Archiving Server topology in terms of single versus multiple Archiving Servers is typically determined by the network that supports Lync Server 2010. If Front End Servers are a large distance from the Archive Server, there might be too much latency for the Archive Server to keep up properly, in which case a local Archive Server might be needed. Similarly, if there is not enough bandwidth to keep up with an archive across the WAN, it might be preferable to deploy a local Archive Server.

TIP

When deciding how to configure the Archiving Server topology, the obvious question might be, "How much bandwidth does my Archive Server need?" The answer depends on your archiving configuration, policy, and user load. The user load should be monitored during your pilot implementation to get a feel for how much load it will generate.

Installation

This section outlines the steps for installing the Lync Server 2010 Archiving Server role. The Archiving Server role enables administrators to archive IM and meeting content. The Archiving Server leverages Microsoft Message Queuing technology to collect information and deposit in the archiving database. Then it leverages PowerShell cmdlets to export and transcribe data.

By now, the Lync Server Topology Builder should already be installed. The first step in adding an Archiving Server to your Lync Server deployment is to add it in the Topology Builder tool, which is discussed in the following sections.

For a thorough review of the installation steps for the Topology Builder tool, see Chapter 5, "Microsoft Lync Server 2010 Front End."

Installing Microsoft SQL Server 2008

Archiving Server has the option to either point to a dedicated SQL server or it can be collocated with the back-end database, the Monitoring Server database, or the Response Group application database.

Detailed steps on the installation of SQL Server 2008 can be found in Chapter 11, "SQL."

Topology Builder for Lync Server 2010 Archiving Role

Lync Server 2010 uses the published topology to process traffic and to maintain overall topology information.

> **TIP**
>
> When deciding how to configure the Archiving Server topology, the obvious question might be, "How much bandwidth does my Archive Server need?" The answer depends on your archiving configuration, policy, and user load. The user load should be monitored during your pilot implementation to get a feel for how much load it will generate.

To ensure that the topology is valid, it is recommended that the Topology Builder run before each topological change.

The following example shows the steps necessary to add an Archiving server to your Lync Server deployment.

> **CAUTION**
>
> Remember, if you change the topology later, it should be republished to ensure consistency.

When you launch Lync Server 2010 Topology Builder, a pop-up message asks whether you want to import the existing topology. Click **Yes** to continue.

To add an Archiving server in Topology Builder, perform the following steps:

1. Expand your site in Topology Builder.
2. Select **Archiving Servers**, as shown in Figure 8.1.

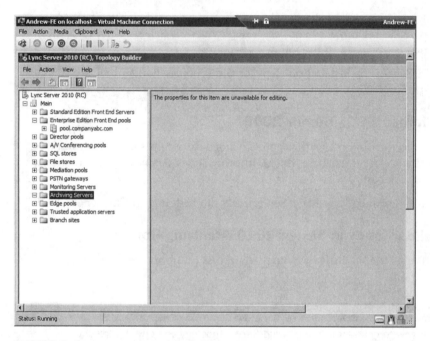

FIGURE 8.1   Archiving Role Selected

3. In the Action pane on the right, click **New Archiving Server**.
4. Enter the FQDN for the new Archiving Server, as shown in Figure 8.2, and click **Next**.
5. Choose the SQL store or define a new one. Click **Next**.
6. Choose the file store, either an existing or a new one. Click **Next**.
7. Associate the archive to a Front End pool by checking the box for the appropriate pool. Click **Finish**.
8. Select the site at the top of the Topology Builder, right-click, choose **Topology, and** then **Publish**, as shown in Figure 8.3.
9. In the screen that displays, select **Next**.
10. Ensure that the correct Central Management Store is chosen and click **Next**.

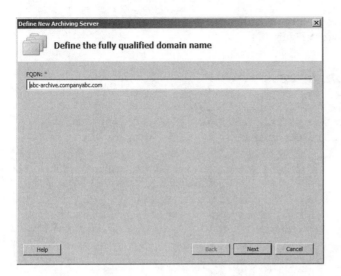

FIGURE 8.2   Defining the Archive Server

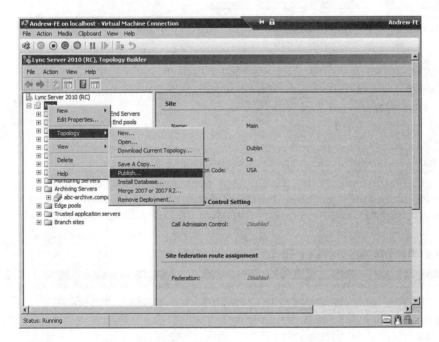

FIGURE 8.3   Choosing the Publish Action

11. Click **Next** one more time to begin publishing the updated topology to the Central Management Store, as shown in Figure 8.4.

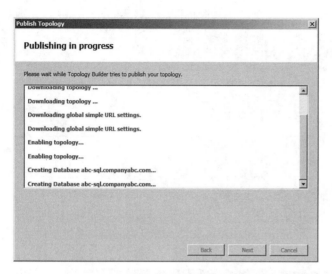

FIGURE 8.4   Publishing the Updated Topology

12. Click **Finish** to return to the main Topology Builder screen.

13. Expand the appropriate section, either Standard Edition front ends or Enterprise Edition front ends, and then select a pool.

14. Right-click and select **Edit Properties**.

15. Select the **Associate Archiving Server** check box and then select the Archiving Server FQDN you previously defined, as shown in Figure 8.5. Click **OK**.

16. Finally, republish the topology one more time by right-clicking the site name and choosing **Topology, and** then choose **Publish**. Click **Next** for the next three screens to publish the topology, and then click **Finish** when the task is completed.

Installing the Archiving Server Role

CAUTION

It is important to note that if you jumped to this section before completing the previous steps, you need to go back. Building a valid topology in the Topology Builder tool is a prerequisite to installing the Archiving Server role.

Installing the Archiving Server role in Lync Server 2010 is a different process than in Office Communications Server (OCS) 2007 and 2007 R2—it involves more steps. Administrators new to Lync Server 2010 are advised to review the new features, requirements, and prequisites before beginning the installation process.

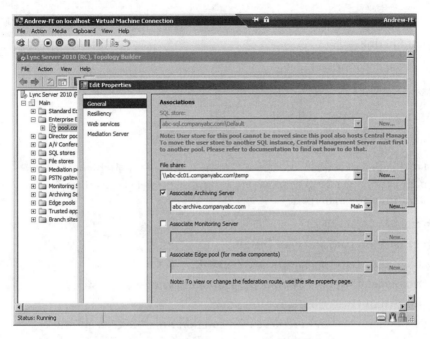

FIGURE 8.5   Associating Archiving Server to the Pool

The following prerequisites are required to install the Archiving Server Front End role:

- ▶ IIS with the following options:
    - ▶ Static content
    - ▶ Default document
    - ▶ Directory browsing
    - ▶ HTTP errors
    - ▶ HTTP redirection
    - ▶ ASP.NET
    - ▶ NET extensibility
    - ▶ Internet Server API (ISAPI) extensions
    - ▶ ISAPI filters
    - ▶ HTTP logging
    - ▶ Logging tools
    - ▶ Request monitor
    - ▶ Tracing
    - ▶ Basic authentication

▶ Windows authentication

▶ Request filtering

▶ Static Content Compression

▶ IIS Management Console

▶ IIS Management scripts and tools

▶ Message Queueing with Directory Service Integration

After you complete the previous steps, the server is ready to install the Archiving Server role. From the main Lync Server 2010 Deployment Wizard screen, click **Install or Update Lync Server System** from the main pane.

1. Run **Setup** from the setup files.

2. Choose an installation path and click **Install**.

3. Read and accept the license agreement and click **OK**.

4. From the Deployment Wizard, click **Install** or **Update Lync Server System**.

5. Click **Run for Install Local Configuration Store**.

6. Leave the first option checked to retrieve configuration from the CMS and click **Next**. The window shows its progress, as shown in Figure 8.6.

FIGURE 8.6   Installing the Local Configuration Store

7. For Step 2: Setup or Remove Lync Server Components, click **Run**.

8. In the pop-up screen, click **Next**. A window displays, as shown in Figure 8.7.

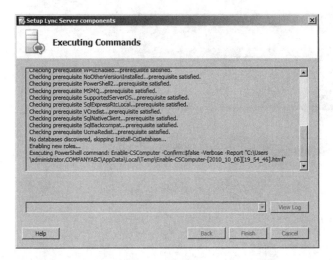

FIGURE 8.7   Installing the Archiving Server Role

9. When the process is complete, click **Finish**.

10. For Step 4: Start Services, click **Run**.

11. After the services start successfully, click **Exit** in the Deployment Wizard.

Configuration

With the Topology Builder tool, most of the configuration is done automatically. Although both configuration and administration can be done from the Silverlight web GUI or the Lync Server management shell, the configuration section focuses on the former and the administration section on the latter to avoid duplication of concepts.

Open the Lync Server Control Panel, which can be found at https://<pool_FQDN>/Cscp/.

> **NOTE**
>
> To access the interface, you must be a member of the RTCUniversalServerAdmins group. If the system you are accessing this web page from does not currently have Silverlight installed, Lync Server 2010 offers you a download link to install it.

After the Lync Server Control Panel is open, click the Topology button in the left bar. Find the new Archiving server in the list or search for it using the search box at the top. Ensure that there is a green check mark for Service Status, as shown in Figure 8.8. This indicates the archiving service is running and responding.

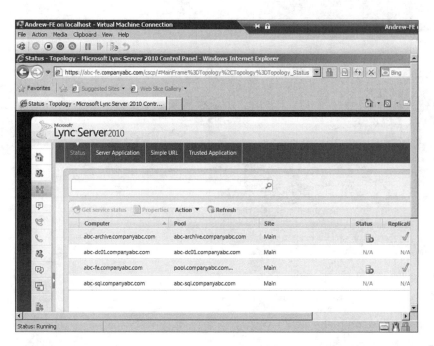

FIGURE 8.8   Examining Archiving Service Status

TIP

To modify archiving policies, the logged on user must be a member of the CSServerAdministrator group.

Scroll down in the left bar and click the Monitoring and Archiving button. This brings up the settings menus for the Monitoring and Achiving Server roles. Because Call Detail Recording and Quality of Experience Data are Monitoring functions, skip directly to the Archiving Policy tab. Here, you see the default Global Policy. Select it and click **Edit— Show Details**.

The available options are

▸ **Name**—The name of the policy

▸ **Description**—Your own notes to identify the policy

Along with two check boxes:

▸ Archive internal communications

▸ Archive external communications

By default, the check boxes for archiving internal and external communications are cleared. To enable archiving for these types of communications, check the boxes and click **Commit** in the upper area of the interface.

Archiving Configuration Tab

Now move to the Archiving Configuration tab. Again, you see the default Global Policy. Select it and click **Edit—Show Details**. The available options are

- **Name**—The name of the policy
- **Archiving settings**—Including three options in the drop-down list:
  - Disable archiving
  - Archive IM sessions
  - Archive IM and web conferencing sessions

Along with two check boxes:

- Block instant messaging (IM) or web conferencing sessions if archiving fails
- Enable purging of archiving data

If purging is enabled, there are two radio button options:

- Purge exported archiving data and stored archiving data after maximum duration (days)
- Purge exported archiving data only

If the "days" option is selected, the administrator has the option to define how many days the archived data is stored.

TIP

The capability to block IMs based on the archiving service is available only if IMs are archived.

If any changes in this policy are made, be sure to click **Commit** in the upper portion of the interface.

Create Site and User Policies

In addition to modifying the default Global policy, administrators have the ability to create additional policies.

1. From the Monitoring and Archiving window, click the **Archiving Policy** tab and click **New**.
2. Choose either a Site policy or a User policy.

TIP

A site policy can be associated with specific sites to allow their behaviors to be differ-ent from the default global policy. User policies are assigned directly to users and allow them to bypass the default global policy. This is useful when archiving is needed only for select users who are distributed across the environment.

3. For this example, choose **Site policy**. When prompted to select a site, choose it from the list and click **OK**.

4. Now, the policy is named after the site—this cannot be modified. Input a descrip-tion and choose whether internal and external communications will be archived. Click **Commit**.

For a user policy, repeat steps 1 and 2 but choose **User policy** and follow these steps:

1. Enter a name for the user policy.

2. Enter a description for the policy.

3. Choose whether or not internal and external communications will be archived. Click **Commit**.

This results in the creation of multiple policies that can be used to manage archiving.

TIP

The same process can be used to create additional archiving configurations, although those can be created only by site, not by user.

To apply a user-based Archiving Policy to a user, perform the following steps:

1. From the Lync Server 2010 Control Panel, click **Users** in the left pane.

2. Click **Find** in the search area to view the list of enabled users.

3. Double-click the user you want to modify.

4. Scroll down to Archiving Policy and choose the policy you want to apply from the drop-down list, as shown in Figure 8.9.

5. Click **Commit**.

NOTE

It is worth highlighting the Archiving Configuration option Block instant messaging (IM) or web conferencing sessions if archiving fails. This is what Microsoft refers to as *critical mode*. If archiving this content is deemed critical by an environment, usually due to regulatory compliance, this option prevents the possibility of unarchived IMs or web conferences from occuring.

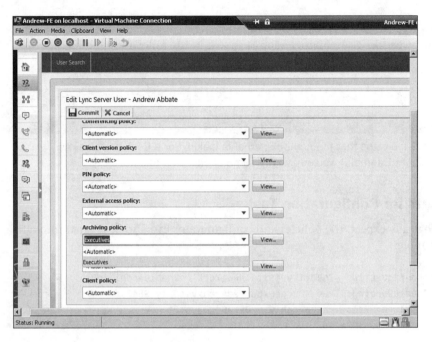

FIGURE 8.9   Choosing Archiving Policy

Using PowerShell for Configuration Tasks

For administrators who prefer to do all their configuration tasks through PowerShell, Lync Server 2010 supports the capability to read and modify the archive policy and archive configuration through cmdlets:

```
Get-CsArchivingConfiguration
Identity                  :Global
EnableArchiving           :ImAndWebConf
EnablePurging        :True
PurgeExportedArchivesOnly:False
BlockOnArchiveFailure     :True
KeepArchivingDataForDays  :14
```

These cmdlets can be modified through Set-CsArchivingConfiguration. For example, the following cmdlet updates the archive retention period to 15 days.

```
Set-CsArchivingConfiguration –Identity Global –KeepArchivingDataForDays 15
```

For the policy, use Get-CsArchivingPolicy:

```
Identity                  :Global
Description          :
ArchiveInternal           :True
ArchiveExternal           :True
```

This cmdlet returns the same set of information for each policy that has been defined.

To modify a policy, use Set-CsArchivingPolicy as shown in the following example:

```
Set-CsArchivingPolicy –Identity Global –ArchiveExternal:$False
```

> **NOTE**
>
> The use of the $ indicates that the ArchiveExternal is looking for a Boolean value. As such, using –ArchiveExternal:0 would have the same effect.

Using Cmdlets for Configuration Tasks

As one might logically expect, the policies and configurations can also be created through cmdlets, for example:

```
New-CsArchivingConfiguration –Identity "site:New York" –EnableArchiving
ImAndWebConf –EnablePurging:$True –PurgeExportedArchivesOnly:$False
–BlockOnArchiveFailure:$False –KeepArchivingDataForDays:21
–ArchiveDuplicateMessages:$False
```

Notice the last argument set in this command—ArchiveDuplicateMessages. This is a good example of where there are options available through the cmdlets that aren't exposed to the GUI tools.

The power of using cmdlets to manage an application, such as Lync Server 2010, becomes readily evident when you are dealing with a large implementation. By scripting the configuration of the entire environment, you are able to eliminate the human error introduced by having a distributed group of people perform repetitive tasks. Similarly, the script written to perform the configuration immediately becomes the documentation of the configuration. If later changes need to occur, you can perform queries to find the objects and modify them at the same time. If you plan to manage the environment in this manner, it becomes helpful to put some thought into a logical naming convention for policies and configurations. This enables you to search on some common value in the policies and configurations to select them for modification.

In a similar manner, PowerShell-based cmdlets make it easy to pull configuration reports from a large implementation. For example, imagine that your company announced a policy that all IMs will be retained for at least 30 days. More than likely, someone will ask you to make sure all your configurations retain messages for at least 30 days. Rather than scrolling through the GUI to find configurations with values under 30, you could simply run a cmdlet such as the following to produce a report of all configuration where the CachePurgingInterval is less than 30 days:

```
Get-CsArchivingConfiguration ¦ Where {$_.CachePurgingInterval –lt "30"} ¦ select
Identity
```

However, if you were going to do that, why not fix it all on one shot?

```
$Array=Get-CsArchivingConfiguration ¦ Where {$_.CachePurgingInterval -lt "30"}
Foreach ($Name in $Array)
{
$Var = $Name.Identity
Set-CsArchivingConfiguration -Identity $var -CachePurgingInterval:30
}
```

This report searches all configurations in the topology and sets any that have a CachePurgingInterval of less than 30 to 30 without touching any that were already higher than 30.

Administration

This section reviews common administration tasks for the Lync Server 2010 Archiving role including Data Export and Purge Mode.

In general, there isn't much day-to-day administration of the Lync Server 2010 Archiving Server role. Instead, this section focuses on the management of data stored in the Archiving database.

One of the most common tasks you perform against the Archiving Server is exporting content from the Archive database. This is performed through the Lync Server Management Shell using the Export-CsArchivingData commandlet as follows:

```
Export-CsArchivingData -DBInstance SQLSRV -StartDate 02/02/2010
-OutputFolder "C:\Archiving" -UserUri Andrew@Companyabc.com
```

This command exports all sessions pertaining to the UserURI defined in the cmdlet. The output is a series of .eml files that are created in the OutputFolder path.

Troubleshooting

The Archiving Server role is fairly straightforward; however, there are a few things that commonly go wrong during deployment. This section covers the common issues and areas to check if you find your Archiving Server deployment not going smoothly.

Because there are a lot of server-to-server connections involved in a Archiving Server deployment, the most obvious source of problems is ensuring proper permissions. Also, ensure that usernames and passwords are typed correctly. When in doubt, re-enter the usernames and passwords used for database access for the Archiving Server. Also, ensure the accounts aren't subject to password expiration in Active Directory.

When connecting to the web-based Control Panel, make sure you tell IIS on that system to use the correct SSL certificate. Assigning a certificate through the Lync Server 2010 setup process won't alter the cert used by IIS, only the one used by Lync Server 2010.

Ensure that the correct pool is assigned to send data to the Archiving Server. An Archiving Server can be deployed with no pool assignment, which results in no data collected for reporting.

The Lync Server event log is also a good place to check for errors. From the Start menu, select **Administrative Tools,** and select **Event Viewer.** Expand the **Applications and Services Logs** item and select **Lync Server.** All events related to Lync Server 2010 functions reside here. Often the error description is enough to identify the problem and determine the resolution.

If you suspect that your Archiving Server isn't working properly, set the configuration for a test site to Critical Mode, which is to say set **Block on Archive Failure** to **true.** Then send IMs between two accounts in the site with this configuration. If the IMs go through, Archiving is working correctly. If the messages state that the recipient is unable to be reached, even though the recipient shows at available in the presence, Archiving isn't working properly.

One common cause for Archiving to fail is that the Front End Server isn't able to install the Archiving agent properly due to a problem with the Message Queuing service. You might see event ID 30517 in the Lync Server logs or you might see event ID 30509. Although the FE role requires Message Queuing Service, it doesn't require Message Queuing Directory Integration. However, the Archiving agent does require this. The fix is to simply install the additional feature on the Front End servers that are targets for Archiving. Another common configuration mistake is to enable Windows Firewall on one or more components of Lync Server 2010 after the installation has occurred. As such, necessary firewall ports might not be open.

For a good list of necessary firewall ports for Windows Server 2008 Firewall needed to support Lync Server 2010, see Chapter 12, "Firewall and Security Requirements."

Best Practices

The following are the best practices from this chapter:

- ▶ Leverage the Archiving Server to record messages for key employees.

- ▶ Be sure to understand compliance regulations around archiving that you might need to follow in Lync Server 2010.

- ▶ Although the Lync Server 2010 Control Panel might seem easier to use at first, there are many functions that can only be accomplished in the management shell.

- ▶ A single Archiving Server can archive for multiple Front End pools. However, in larger deployments, a dedicated Archiving Server per pool might be required.

- ▶ For larger deployments, use a dedicated SQL Archiving Server.

- ▶ When possible, perform your configurations through the management shell to simplify bulk tasks and keep a record of what changes were made.

▶ Always publish a new topology before making changes or installing a new server role.

▶ Make sure you have enough storage to maintain the archive for the expected period.

▶ Be aware of any existing retention policies that might conflict with your plans for archiving in Lync Server 2010.

Summary

In this chapter we've seen how archiving works in Microsoft Lync Server 2010 and how it can be used to comply with regulatory compliances or to simply maintain a history of conversations used within an environment. By properly planning for the Archive Server role and by implementing it based on best practices, companies can enjoy the benefits of the Archive Server and can depend on it to be available should they configure it to be used in critical mode.

While the configuration and administration of the Archive Server role is relatively straightforward, it is still recommended that administrators familiarize themselves with this entire chapter before deploying the Archive Server role to reduce the chances of anything going wrong.

Director

The Microsoft Lync Server Director role has been included in the Lync Server product ever since Live Communications Server 2005, Service Pack 1, but it typically has been the least deployed server roles. Whether it is a matter of not understanding the benefits or not knowing the role is unknown, but the bottom line is that a Director provides several improvements to any Lync Server topology.

This chapter focuses on the Director role and how it interacts with other components of Lync Server. The benefits of a Director are explained from an internal perspective and an external viewpoint where it adds a degree of security and stability to the environment.

This chapter also discusses the steps required to prepare a server for the Director role and how to install a Director in the environment. The components of a Director role are examined and guidelines for troubleshooting common issues with a Director are provided for reference.

Director Overview

The Director role in Lync Server is a specialized subset of the Front End Server, which provides authentication and redirection services. Unlike a Front End Server, it is not possible to home user accounts on a Director pool, and it provides no user services to endpoints. The primary function is to authenticate endpoints and "direct" users to the pool where their user account is homed.

When a client signs in to a Director, he is first authenticated and then informed which pool to register. Directors are beneficial for deployments where multiple pools exist because they provide a single point of authentication for the endpoints. When external access is used, a Director serves as the next hop server between Edge Servers and the Front End pools.

Dedicated Role

The Director role in Lync Server has changed slightly and is much more specialized than in the previous releases of Communications Server. In prior versions, users installed the Director role the same way as a Front End Server followed by a series of manual steps to deactivate most of the Front End Services. These steps were well documented, but it was up to the administrator to follow them correctly. It was impossible to prevent administrators or help desk users from homing new user accounts on a Director pool because they appeared just like any other front-end pool choice when enabling user accounts.

Now, in Lync Server, the Director is a dedicated role separate from a Front End Server. It can be installed like any other role and does not require manual deactivation steps. This separation not only improves the ease of deploying a Director, but increases the security and stability of the role by not installing unnecessary components and leaving deactivation to the administrator.

Benefits of a Director

When multiple front-end pools are deployed, an administrator must decide which pool, or pools, the SRV records required for automatic client sign-in will point to. Without a Director, the pool selected with the lowest SRV record priority becomes the central point of authentication for all users. Users not homed to this pool are authenticated and provided with the name of the pool where their account is hosted. Then the endpoints register to their home pool instead of the pool used for automatic client sign-in. This is usually how a Director performs. Without a dedicated Director, a pool is tasked with handling authentication and Director duties for all other pools in the deployment.

The benefit of a dedicated Director from an internal perspective is that initial authentication requests are offloaded from Front End Servers. In many environments, offloading authentication requests can be negligible. In deployments near capacity of the hardware, this enables the Front End Servers to focus on other core services such as messaging, conferencing, and voice.

> **NOTE**
>
> Internal traffic to a Director varies based on time of day. In the morning as users sign in to endpoints for the start of the work day, a Director is busier than during the late afternoon when users are already signed in to their pools.

Internal Endpoint Sign-In Process

There is no logic in an endpoint to indicate it is initially connecting to a Director and not a Front End Server. This means that the same DNS records, authentication methods, and signaling are used from the endpoint's perspective. The Director first authenticates the user and then provides the name of the pool that the endpoint should register to instead of which point the client will attempt another sign-in to the pool the Director provided. The sign-in process looks like the following:

1. The endpoint resolves DNS SRV records for automatic configuration and attempts to connect to the Director.
2. The Director verifies the user's credentials.

> **NOTE**
>
> If the credentials are not valid, the endpoint does not authenticate and the connection terminates.

3. If the credentials are verified successfully, the Director checks what pool the user's account is homed to and provides the name of the pool to the endpoint.
4. The Director closes the session with the endpoint.
5. The endpoint attempts to authenticate again to the front end pool that the Director indicated.

After a Director authenticates an endpoint and provides the name of the correct front end pool, it removes itself from the communication path. An endpoint communicates with its own front end pool after receiving the information. Figure 9.1 demonstrates how a Director authenticates internal users and then removes itself from the communication path.

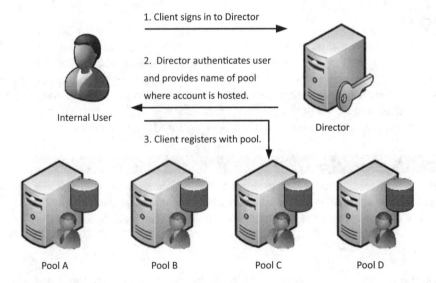

Internal Pools

FIGURE 9.1   Director Sign-In Process

External Access

Another strong benefit of using a Director is its capability to serve as a barrier between internal pools and external traffic. To understand the benefit, note that Edge Servers do not authenticate external user requests across the Internet and merely pass traffic to an internal server to handle authentication. Without a Director, external traffic authenticates by a Front End pool, or, in other words, anonymous Internet traffic is allowed to communicate with an internal domain member server.

Instead of allowing authentication requests from an Edge Server to pass directly to a Front End pool, a Director can be placed between a communication path to authenticate users before external traffic reaches a Front End Server. In situations where multiple internal pools exist and all leverage a single Edge Server pool, a Director also points user requests to the correct pool or next hop. Unlike the internal scenario, a Director used as a next hop stays in the communication path at all times, which ensures the protection of internal pools. Figure 9.2 shows how a Director sits in the communication path from remote users to a Front-End pool.

Front End   Director   Access Edge   Internet   External User
Server   Server

FIGURE 9.2   Director Placement for Edge Servers

Denial of Service

A compelling reason to deploy a Director is that it provides some isolation for Front End pools from the Edge Servers and Internet. If there was a denial of service attack against the Edge Servers, only the Edge Servers and Director would be affected. This separation enables the front-end pools to continue operating as normal without being affected by the attack. If a Director was not deployed as the next hop from an Edge Server, an attack could potentially impact a front-end pool and cause a much larger disruption to user services.

> **NOTE**
>
> When defining External Access through a single Edge Server, or pool or Edge Servers, the Topology Builder checks whether a Director exists within the same site definition. If so, it automatically is suggested as the next hop from the Edge Server pool.

Placement

A Director pool should be located where the majority of the user base exists because it is the initial point of sign-in for all users. It makes sense to place a Director in a datacenter with a Front End pool, but it's unnecessary to use a Director in branch offices with small user counts.

Another recommendation when planning for placement is to use a Director in any location where an Access Edge Server role exists. As unauthenticated traffic from the Internet passes to the internal network, the Director is a short hop away from the Edge Server and can authenticate the traffic quickly. If the Director is in another location, traffic from an Edge Server has to traverse a WAN connection before being authenticated.

> **NOTE**
>
> In remote locations where it makes sense to deploy a Web Conferencing and A/V Edge Server to support local media paths, it isn't necessary to deploy a Director. This is because the signaling traffic a Director sees is only used between the Access Edge Server role and front end pools, unlike media paths that flow directly between endpoints. Figure 9.3 shows how a Director in one site still serves a remote user in another site for signaling traffic.

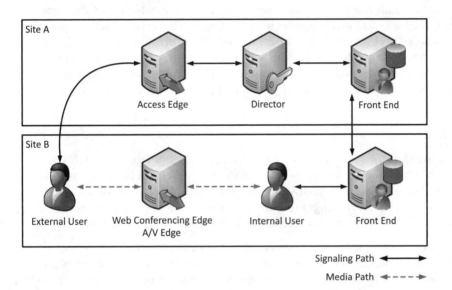

FIGURE 9.3   Signaling and Media Paths with a Director and Conferencing Edge Server in Additional Site

Standard Edition Versus Enterprise Edition

In previous versions of Office Communications Server, an administrator had the option to deploy both Standard Edition and Enterprise Edition Directors, which caused some confusion around deployment methods and licensing. In Office Communications Server 2007, multiple Directors could be deployed either as an array of multiple Standard Edition Front Ends, or as a pool of multiple Enterprise Edition servers with a dedicated back-end SQL server database. Office Communications Server 2007 R2 simplified these options, and the only option for Director high availability was a pool of Enterprise Edition servers. This model was problematic because a pool of Directors created its own databases, which matched the name as the front end pool. To alleviate this issue, a separate SQL instance was required to separate the two.

In Lync Server, this is simplified so that Directors no longer have a Standard Edition or Enterprise Edition designation. The deployment model closely resembles the array of Standard Edition Servers option, which was removed from Office Communications Server 2007 R2, where each server has a local database instance. This solves the duplicate database name issue and makes the deployment significantly easier because SQL server sets are not required. The Director role also does not require a Standard or Enterprise Edition license in Lync Server 2010.

Back End Database

In Lync Server, each Director stores its information in a local SQL Server 2008 Express database instance. This change alleviates an issue found in previous releases where a Director used the same back-end database name as the Front End Servers. When the Front Ends and Directors used the same database name, it became impossible to use the same SQL Server instance for both functions, which meant a new SQL Server or SQL instance had to be provisioned exclusively for the Director pool. The other downside was that a Director has a relatively low usage of the SQL Server, so providing an exclusive server or instance was generally considered a waste of resources. The change to a local database instance in Lync Server enables more businesses to include the Director role in their deployments.

Web Services

In Lync Server, the Director role is capable of providing a subset of Front End web services to the endpoints. A primary use for this scenario is the Client Version filter used to check the version of software endpoints sign-in with and potentially block older or unwanted versions from successfully connecting. In some cases, the filter is used to provide the client with a link to a web page or automatically provide an update for the software.

The device update service is another web service that can be deployed on a Director. When the DNS records for client updates points to a Director, the phone endpoints can download firmware updates from there instead of a Front End Server. Depending on the workload of Front End Servers in the environment, it might be beneficial to use a Director for these functions.

> **WARNING**
>
> The Director role cannot be collocated with any other server role in Lync Server. It must be installed on a server with no other roles to be fully supported by Microsoft.

Director Installation

Installing the Director role is similar to deploying any other role in Lync Server. Most of the installation process consists of completing the prerequisite work and installing the server, which can be a quick process. A Director can be introduced into the environment at any time and does not necessarily need to be deployed from the start. If Edge services are deployed, it usually makes sense to deploy a Director at the same time.

Prerequisites

A Director requires the same prerequisite software as a Front End Server because it is still a subset of the Front End role. The different hardware, operating system, and software prerequisites are discussed in this section.

Hardware Requirements

This section discusses the recommended minimum hardware requirements for Lync Server servers.

The Lync Server Director processor requirements are as follows:

- ▶ Dual processor, quad-core 2.0 GHz or faster
- ▶ Four-way processor, dual-core 2.0 GHz or faster

> **NOTE**
>
> Lync Server is only a 64-bit application and requires a 64-bit-capable processor. This is generally not an issue with modern hardware, but be sure to verify that legacy hardware supports a 64-bit operating system before attempting to use it for a Director.

The Lync Server Director memory requirements are as follows:

- ▶ 12 GB RAM

    The Lync Server Director disk requirements are as follows:

- ▶ 10K RPM HDD
- ▶ Local storage with at least 72 GB free space

The Lync Server Director network requirements are as follows:

- ▶ Dual 1 gigabit per second (Gbps) network adapters (recommended)
- ▶ Single 1 gigabit per second (Gbps) network adapter (supported)

> **NOTE**
>
> When using multiple network adapters, it is recommended to use them only for fault tolerance. This means network adapters should be used for failover only and not be teamed for greater throughput.

Operating System Requirements

The Lync Server Director supports the following operating systems:

- ▶ Windows Server 2008, x64 Standard Edition with Service Pack 2
- ▶ Windows Server 2008, x64 Enterprise Edition with Service Pack 2
- ▶ Windows Server 2008, x64 Datacenter Edition with Service Pack 2
- ▶ Windows Server 2008 R2, Standard Edition
- ▶ Windows Server 2008 R2, Enterprise Edition
- ▶ Windows Server 2008 R2, Datacenter Edition

> **NOTE**
>
> The Datacenter editions of both Windows Server 2008, x64 with Service Pack 2 and Windows Server 2008 R2 are supported by Microsoft, but they have not been fully tested for use with Lync Server.

The Windows Server Core, Web, and High Performance Computing editions for any operating system version are not supported for deployment.

Software Requirements

The Lync Server Director requires the following components to be installed:

- ▶ .NET Framework 3.5
- ▶ Visual C++ 2008 Redistributable
- ▶ PowerShell 2.0
- ▶ Windows Installer 4.0
- ▶ WinRM 2.0
- ▶ BITS 4.0

Server Roles and Features

In addition to the operating system and software requirements listed previously, a Director requires several Windows server roles, role services, and features to be installed. The following IIS role services are required for a Director installation:

- ▶ Static content
- ▶ Default document
- ▶ Directory browsing
- ▶ HTTP errors

- ▶ HTTP redirection

- ▶ ASP.net

- ▶ .NET extensibility

- ▶ ISAPI extensions

- ▶ ISAPI filters

- ▶ HTTP logging

- ▶ Logging tools

- ▶ Request monitor

- ▶ Tracing

- ▶ Basic authentication

- ▶ Windows authentication

- ▶ Request filtering

- ▶ Static content compression

- ▶ IIS management console

- ▶ IIS management scripts and tools

Installing Server Roles

Windows PowerShell can be used to automate installation of the prerequisite roles and features instead of using the Windows Server Manager graphical. The following steps show how to use PowerShell for this purpose:

1. Log on to the server with an account that has administrative credentials.
2. Click **Start** and navigate to **All Programs, Accessories, and Windows PowerShell**.
3. Right-click the Windows PowerShell shortcut and select **Run as administrator**.
4. Select **Yes** when prompted by User Account Control.
5. Run the following command to make the server manager:

   ```
   Import-Module ServerManager
   ```

6. Run the following command to install the Windows features and IIS role services required:

   ```
   Add-WindowsFeature,RSAT-ADDS-Tools,RSAT-Web-Server,Web-Server,Web-Http-
   Redirect,Web-Asp-Net,Web-Net-Ext,Web-ISAPI-Ext,Web-ISAPI-Filter,Web-
   Log-Libraries,Web-Http-Tracing,Web-Basic-Auth,Web-Windows-Auth,Web-
   Scripting-Tools –Restart
   ```

7. The server restarts when installation is complete.

6

Create Director Pool

After the server is prepared for installation, the topology must be edited and published to reflect the new Director pool. This involves editing the existing topology if it exists and then republishing the topology so that all other servers in the environment are aware of the new Director pool.

Edit Topology

The next step in deploying a Director is to edit the existing Lync Server topology. To edit the topology, use the following steps:

> **NOTE**
>
> If the Topology Builder is not already installed on the local computer or another computer in the environment, it can be installed from the Lync Server media.

1. Open the Lync Server Topology Builder.
2. When prompted to import an existing topology from Active Directory, select **OK**.
3. Expand the Site node where the Director will be deployed.
4. Right-click the **Director Pools** node and select **New Director Pool**.
5. Enter the fully qualified name of the Director pool in the **Pool FQDN** field.
6. Select whether the new Director pool will be a **Multiple computer pool** or **Single computer pool**, and click **Next**.
7. If **Multiple computer pool** was selected, click the **Add** button, enter the fully qualified name of the Director in **the Computer FQDN** field, and click **OK**.
8. Click the **Add** button and repeat for additional Directors, which will part of the same pool.
9. Click the **Next** button to continue.
10. Define the share to use for the new Director pool or create a new one. Then click **Next**.
11. Review the Web Services URL for the Director pool.

> **NOTE**
>
> The internal web services FQDN must be changed to a name different from the pool FQDN if DNS load balancing is used. If a hardware load balancer will be used to balance all SIP and HTTPS traffic, or if the pool will only consist of a single member, the web services FQDN does not need to be changed.

12. Click **Finish** when ready. Figure 9.4 shows what a sample topology with a Director pool might look like.

Publish Topology

After the topology has been modified to include the Director pool, the configuration can be published. This step publishes the changes to the Central Management Store and all existing Lync Servers update their local configuration stores to match.

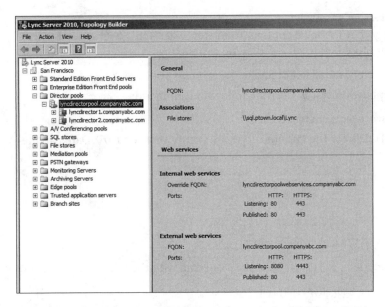

FIGURE 9.4   Defining a Director Pool in Lync Server Topology Builder

1. Ensure that the Lync Server Topology Builder is still open and contains the Director pool recently added.
2. Click the top node of the management console, Lync Server.
3. Click the **Action** menu and select **Publish**, or select **Publish** from the Actions pane on the right side of the console.
4. Click **Next** to begin publishing the topology.
5. When the log indicates a successful update, click **Finish** to complete the wizard.

Install Server

At this point, the target server should be fully prepared and meet all prerequisites. Refer to the "Prerequisites" section earlier in this chapter for a full list of the Director requirements.

Install Local Configuration Store

To install server roles in Lync Server, the target server must have a local configuration store installed and populated with the topology information.

1. Insert the Lync Server media on the server to be used as an Edge Server and launch Setup.exe found in the Setup\amd64 folder.
2. Enter a location for the installation files to be cached, and click **Install**.
4. Click **Install or Update Lync Server system.**
5. Under **Step 1: Install Local Configuration Store**, click **Run**.
6. Select **Retrieve configuration automatically from the Central Management Store** and click **Next**.
7. Click **Finish** after the local store is successfully created.

Update and Verify Configuration Store

The following steps verify that the local configuration store has been synchronized with the Central Management Store before server roles are installed.

1. Launch the Lync Server Management Shell.

2. Check the CMS replication status with the following command:

   ```
   Get-CSManagementStoreReplicationStatus
   ```

3. Check the ReplicaFQDN for the current server and verify that the UpToDate parameter reads True.

   ```
   UpToDate            : True
   ReplicaFQDN         : lyncdirector1.companyabc.com
   IsDeleted           : False
   LastStatusReport    : 7/3/2010 10:02:17 PM
   LastUpdateCreation  : 7/3/2010 10:02:10 PM
   ```

4. If the UpToDate parameter is False, update the store data with the following command:

   ```
   Invoke-CSManagementStoreReplication
   ```

5. Check the replication status again and verify that it is now updated and in sync with the Central Management Store.

> **WARNING**
>
> If the local store is not in sync with the central store, the installation of Lync Server components will not proceed.

Install Lync Server Components

The following steps enable the server to read the topology information from the local configuration store and then install the server roles matching its own FQDN.

1. Under **Step 2: Setup or Remove Lync Server Components**, click the **Run** button.

2. Select **Next** to begin the Director installation published in the topology.

3. Click **Finish** when the installation completes.

Create Certificates

Like all other roles in Lync Server, the Director communicates to other servers in the organization using Mutual Transport Layer Security (MTLS). To leverage MTLS, the Director needs one certificate installed meeting a few requirements. A separate certificate can be used for each function, or a single certificate meeting the following requirements can be used:

▶ The Director pool fully qualified domain name should be the subject name.

▶ The individual pool member fully qualified names should be included as a subject alternative name.

▶ If the internal or external web services FQDN differs from the pool name, it should be included as a subject alternative name.

▶ All supported SIP domains must be entered as a subject alternative name in the format sip.<SIP domain>.

NOTE

The certificate wizard in Lync Server automatically populates the subject name and required subject alternative names based on the published topology, which greatly simplifies certificate confusion created by prior versions. If only one certificate is used for the default, internal web services, and external web services, the subject alternative names must be manually added when running the wizard.

Use the following steps to request and assign the necessary certificates:

1. Under **Step 3: Request, Install, or Assign Certificate**, click the **Run** button.

2. Highlight **Default** certificate and click **Request**.

3. Click **Next** to begin the wizard.

4. Select either **Send the request immediately to an online certification authority** or **Prepare the request now, but send it** later if an offline request will be generated. Click Next.

5. If creating an online request then select a certification authority detected in the environment and click **Next**.

6. **Specify alternate credentials for the certification authority** if required or click **Next** to use the currently logged on credentials.

7. Select **Use an alternate certificate template for the selected certification authority** if necessary. The default is to not select this option which will use the WebServer template. Click **Next**.

8. Enter a **Friendly Name** for the certificate such as Director.

9. Select a key **Bit Length** of 1024, 2048, or 4096.

10. If the certificate is exportable, select the **Mark the certificate's private key as exportable** check box.

11. Enter an **Organization** name, typically the name of the business.

12. Enter an **Organizational Unit** name, typically the name of a division or department, and click **Next**.

13. Select a **Country**, enter a **State or Province**, enter a **City or Locality**, and click **Next**.

14. Review the automatically populated subject and subject alternative names. Click **Next**.

15. Place a check mark next to any SIP domains that will use the Director pool for automatic sign-in and click **Next**.

16. Include additional subject alternative names if necessary. Click **Next**.

17. Click **Next** to complete the request, and then click **Finish** to complete the wizard.

> **TIP**
>
> After completing the wizard, it might be necessary to run through it at least two more times—once to generate an internal web services certificate and once to generate an external web services certificate. It's also possible to use the same certificate for all three functions if the internal and external web service URLs match the pool FQDN.

If the certificates are issued from an online certificate authority, they should be installed automatically. If an offline request is issued, the wizard must be re-run with the option to complete an offline request.

Assign Certificates

After creating the necessary certificates, the Director services must have certificates assigned to them. This process binds each certificate either to the Front End Service or IIS websites, depending on the selection. The following steps show how to assign a certificate:

1. Under **Step 3: Request, Install, or Assign Certificate**, click the Run button.

2. Highlight **Default** certificate and click **Assign an existing certificate**.

3. Click **Next** to begin the wizard.

4. Highlight the certificate to be assigned and click **Next**.

5. Click **Next** to confirm the selection.

6. Click **Finish** when the wizard completes.

Start Services

After the necessary certificates are requested and assigned, the Lync Server Director services can be started.

1. Below **Step 4: Start Services**, click the **Run** button.

2. Click **Next** to start the Lync Server services.

3. Click **Finish** to complete the wizard.

At this point, the Director installation is complete and functional. The Director pool is not used automatically by internal clients, so the DNS SRV records for automatic client sign-in must be updated to point users to the new Director pool.

▶ See Chapter 5, "Microsoft Lync Server 2010 Front End," for the SRV record requirements.

Director Configuration

After a Director pool is installed, there generally is not much configuration left to do. This section discusses some of the configuration options available to a Director and addresses items administrators should be aware of when configuring a Director.

Certificate Requirements

The Director role in Lync Server is much like any other role in that it uses certificates for communication to other servers and for client services. There are three different types of certificates a Lync Server Director requires, each with slightly different naming requirements. Typically, the same certificate will be assigned to each three functions.

- ▶ **Default**—The default certificate is used for MTLS communications between servers and for securing SIP signaling in client communications. The certificate contains the server name in the subject field, the pool name as a subject alternative name, and internally supported SIP domains as a subject alternative name in the sip.<SIP Domain> format.

- ▶ **WebServicesInternal**—The WebServicesInternal certificate is used to secure communication for internal clients to the web services. This certificate contains the internal web services that FQDN defined in the topology for the pool. This certificate is bound to the internal web services' website in IIS.

- ▶ **WebServicesExternal**—The WebServicesExternal certificate is used to secure communication for external clients to the web services. This certificate contains the external web services FQDN defined in the topology for the pool. This certificate is bound to the external web services' website in IIS.

SRV Records

An issue with the architecture of Office Communications Server 2007 and 2007 R2 was that clients used only a single DNS SRV record. If a Director was in use, the SRV record typically pointed to it to ensure users signed in to a Director first and not directly to a front end pool. On one hand, this provided the administrator with control over where users initially authenticated to, but on the flip side this represented a single point of failure. If there was an issue with the Director or pool of Directors, clients would not be able to sign in. This dilemma can be mitigated in a few ways with Lync Server; either by adding more nodes to a pool or by using multiple SRV records with different priorities.

Now, endpoints recognize multiple SRV records for automatic sign-in with different priorities. If one pool or host is unavailable, they will try the next host. This means that organizations can deploy a Director with the lowest priority SRV record, but also have the automatic sign-in backup be a front-end pool with a higher priority in case the Director pool is unavailable. There is also the potential to use two Director pools with different priorities, but this is necessary only for the most stringent of availability requirements.

> **NOTE**
>
> When resolving SRV records in DNS, clients prefer the record with the lowest priority value. The terminology is a bit deceiving, so be sure to place a Director pool as the lowest priority to ensure it is used before any other pool with a higher priority.

Web Services FQDN Overrides

When creating a Director pool in the Topology Builder, the web services FQDNs are automatically provisioned with an option to override the internal and external FQDNs. When a single Director is deployed, overriding the FQDN is generally unnecessary, but when multiple Directors are deployed, it might be necessary to change the URLs depending on load-balancing methods.

If a traditional load balancer is used for the SIP, HTTP, and HTTPS traffic, it is acceptable to use the pool FQDN suggested by the Topology Builder. This works great because all of the traffic is destined for the same virtual IP hosted by the load balancer. This kind of configuration is shown in Figure 9.5.

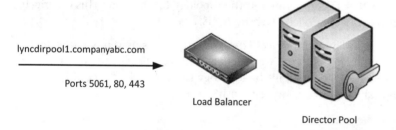

FIGURE 9.5   Using a Hardware Load Balancer for Director Traffic

Within Lync Server, a DNS load balancing for SIP traffic option exists, but a hardware load balancer is still necessary for balancing HTTP and HTTPS traffic. This configuration means that there is a split in the services and one FQDN must resolve to the pool for SIP traffic and another FQDN is necessary for the web services traffic. These two FQDNs resolve to different locations; the pool name always resolves to Director pool member servers and the web services FQDN resolves to a load-balancer virtual IP. This kind of scenario is shown in Figure 9.6.

The web services can also be configured differently for internal and external traffic depending on existing infrastructure. For example, an organization might use a combination of DNS load balancing and a hardware load balancer for all internal pool load balancing, so overriding the internal FQDN is required internally.

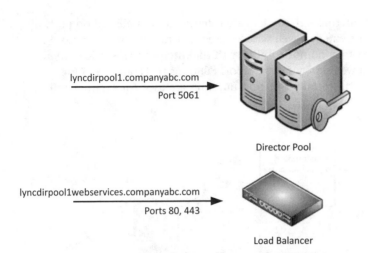

lyncdirpool1.companyabc.com

Port 5061

Director Pool

lyncdirpool1webservices.companyabc.com

Ports 80, 443

Load Balancer

FIGURE 9.6   Using a Combination of DNS and Hardware Load Balancing for Director Traffic

In this example, consider a reverse proxy scenario where the reverse proxy has its own form of built-in load balancing such as with Microsoft Forefront Threat Management Gateway. It can resolve the web services directly to the pool FQDN because SIP traffic is not carried through the reverse proxy. A reverse proxy sending external traffic to the Director pool that uses a load balancer internally is shown in Figure 9.7.

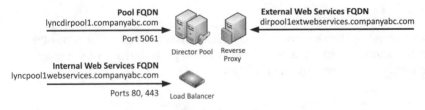

Pool FQDN
lyncdirpool1.companyabc.com

Port 5061

Director Pool   Reverse
                Proxy

External Web Services FQDN
dirpool1extwebservices.companyabc.com

Internal Web Services FQDN
lyncpool1webservices.companyabc.com

Ports 80, 443   Load Balancer

FIGURE 9.7   External and Internal Web Services Names

Web Services Ports

When configuring the internal and external web services for a Director, options exist to define the listening ports and the published ports. The differences between the two are outlined here:

▶ **Listening ports**—Ports that the IIS services bind to on the Lync Server.

▶ **Published ports**—Ports used by clients to access the services. These ports might be redirected by a load balancer, reverse proxy, or firewall to the listening port on a server.

In a default installation, the internal web services are listening and published on ports 80 and 443. However, because the external web services use a separate IIS site, they need to run on alternate ports so that they do not conflict with the internal web services. In a default scenario, the external web services run on port 8080 for HTTP and 4443 for HTTPS. Figure 9.8 shows how the different IIS port bindings are used for external and internal traffic.

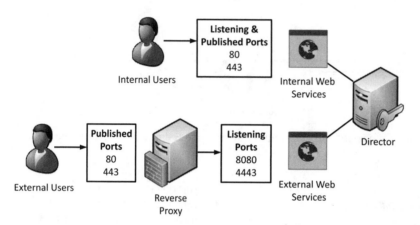

FIGURE 9.8   Listening and Published Ports for Web Services

Reverse Proxy

To support external access to the Director web services, use a reverse proxy. It is possible to allow Internet traffic directly to the external web services ports, but a reverse proxy helps to increase security by inspecting the HTTP and HTTPS traffic and filtering any malicious requests.

▶ Refer to Chapter 6, "Microsoft Lync Server 2010 Edge," for configuration of a reverse proxy such as Microsoft Forefront Threat Management Gateway.

High Availability

Redundancy for the Director role is provided in the same way as with Front End Servers and requires adding more Directors to a pool. Also like a front-end pool, up to 10 servers can be defined in a Director pool. Load balancing is achieved through the same methods as Front End Servers by providing multiple IP addresses, which resolve to the pool name of the Directors. If one IP address is unavailable, the endpoint attempts to log in to another IP address provided for the pool in DNS.

Adding Directors to a Pool

Adding an additional Director to a pool is much like creating the initial pool. The topology must first be updated and published to reflect the change. Follow the steps described previously to import the existing topology in Topology Builder, and then use the following steps to include an additional pool member:

1. Expand the **Director Pools** node.
2. Right-click the Director pool name and select **New Server**.
3. Enter the **fully qualified domain name** of the new Director.
4. Either select **Use all configured IP addresses** or **Limit service usage to selected IP addresses**, and enter the IP addresses to be used by the Lync Server services.
5. Click **OK** when complete.

Now, publish the topology again and proceed with the Director installation using the same steps defined in the "Install Server" section earlier in this chapter.

Director Administration

Administration of the Director role in Lync Server can be performed through a combination of the Lync Server Control Panel and the Lync Server Management Shell. This section discusses management of Director services and possible uses for the web services included in a Director installation.

Topology Status

A relatively easy method of checking the health status of a Director server or pool exists through the Lync Server Control Panel. To check the status of a Director pool, perform the following steps:

1. Open **the Lync Server Control Panel**.

2. Click **Topology**.

3. Highlight the server in question, and click the **Get service status** button.

4. Double-click the server to drill down further and check the status of individual services such as the Registrar or web services. Figure 9.9 shows what the Lync Server Control Panel looks like.

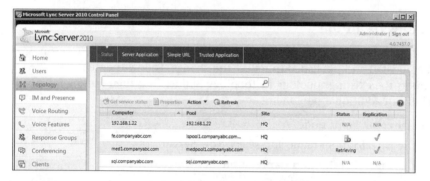

FIGURE 9.9   Lync Server Control Panel Topology Status Example

Services Management

Managing the Lync Server services is the extent of administration involved with a Director after it is installed and configured. Administrators can start, stop, or drain the Director servers either from the Lync Server Control Panel or the Lync Server Management Shell. Stopping the services ends all user sessions, but draining the services enables existing connections to continue, but stop accepting new connections. This enables an administrator to prepare a server for maintenance without immediately impacting users.

To manage the Lync Server services, perform the following steps:

1. Open **the Lync Server Control Panel**.

2. Highlight the server to be modified.

3. Click **Action** and either select **Start all services**, **Stop all services**, or **Prevent new connections for all services**.

4. Alternatively, double-click the server to drill down further and manage the individual services.

Load-Balancer Drain

Draining a hardware load-balancer's connections to a pool server is a task that should be done in conjunction with the Prevent new connections for all services option in the Lync Server Control Panel. The Lync Server services have no method of managing a hardware load balancer, so if one is used for the web services traffic, it must be started, stopped, and drained independently.

Client Version Filter

One potential use for a Director is to control the client versions connecting to the Lync Server infrastructure. Because the Director is an initial sign-in point for any client, perform a filter check at the sign-in point. To manage which types of clients can connect to a Director, perform the following steps:

1. Open the **Lync Server Control Panel**.
2. **Click Clients**.
3. Ensure **Client Version Policy** is highlighted, click **New**, and select **Pool policy**.

> **NOTE**
>
> If a policy is edited at the Pool level, such as in the previous example, it only applies to the selected service and pool. The example only enforces the client version filter at the Director, meaning that an endpoint could sign in to a front end pool directly without a client check. Edit the global policy if the client filtering is performed on all pools.

4. Highlight the Director pool name, and click **OK**.
5. Highlight a client application, such as **Office Communicator**, and click **Modify**.
6. Note the **Action** at the end of the screen. This can be modified to block or allow with the option to present a URL to the user, or even upgrade the application at sign-in. Click **OK** to save any changes.
7. Add, modify, or remove any specific client applications and versions that the Director pool should check and click **Commit**.
8. Click the **Client Version Configuration** menu option.
9. Highlight the **Global Policy**, click **Edit** and then **Modify**.
10. The default action applies to any client application not listed within the Client Version Policy. By default, any client application not listed in the Client Version Policy will be allowed to sign in. Figure 9.10 shows a sample configuration where all Office Communicator versions will be allowed, but told an upgrade is available.

Authentication Methods

A Director has the capability to use Kerberos, NTLM, or a combination of both to authenticate user traffic. Kerberos or NTLM can be used for authenticating users internally, but only the NTLM authentication protocol can be used to authenticate remote or external users. In the event of an Active Directory failure, clients can use a certificate issued by Lync Server to authenticate to servers.

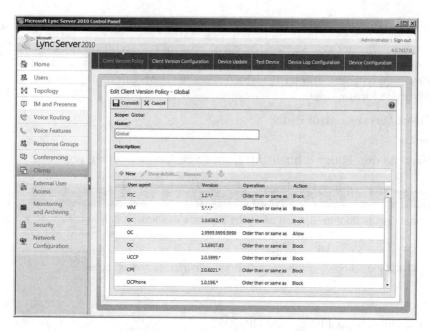

FIGURE 9.10   The Client Version Filter in Lync Server

NOTE

A certificate is neither issued by nor used by a public key infrastructure. The only purpose for the certificate is in relation to authenticating Lync Server endpoints.

To configure the setting, open the Lync Server Control Panel and perform the following steps:

1. Open the **Lync Server Control Panel**.
2. Click **Security**.
3. Click **Registrar**.
4. Click **New** and select the Director Registrar service.
5. Select the appropriate checkboxes to enable Kerberos, NTLM, or certificate authentication, and click **Commit**. An example of editing the Global policy that applies to all servers is shown in Figure 9.11.

FIGURE 9.11   Authentication Options in Lync Server

Director Best Practices

The following are best practices from this chapter:

▶ Implement a Director pool when multiple pools exist internally. A Director provides a single point of initial sign-in for all pools and offloads authentication duties from Front End Servers.

▶ Use a Director as the next hop in any location with an Access Edge Server. This provides a degree of separation from the front end pools and protects the internal infrastructure from attack. Users are also authenticated at the Director when logging in remotely, so a Front End Server does not have to handle authentication requests.

▶ Order SRV records so that a Director pool has the lowest priority. Front-end pools should have a higher priority value so that clients first try to sign in to the Director pool.

▶ Plan for high availability in the environment from the start even if not implementing multiple pool member initially. Completing the planning work up front makes adding high availability at a later time much easier.

▶ Use multiple Directors within a pool to provide high availability.

▶ Carefully plan certificate names to match pool and web service URL requirements.

Summary

The Director role in Lync Server has some clear advantages over prior versions, namely the simplicity involved in deploying a Director and the introduction of a dedicated role with only the required components. A Director can add value to almost any Lync Server deployment and because it requires no additional licensing, it becomes an even more attractive option for organizations.

Organizations are most likely to deploy a Director in their Lync Server environment when they fully understand the benefits of the role and the value it adds. For organizations where multiple internal pools exist, a Director can improve the environment by acting as a single point of initial authentication and offload that responsibility from the front end pools. Other businesses might deploy a Director because of the security benefits from an external perspective where it acts as a barrier between the front end pools and Access Edge Servers.

Either way, usage of the Director role likely increases in Lync Server deployments because it becomes critical to stabilize and protect the services that the Lync Server infrastructure provides to users.

PART III

External Dependencies

IN THIS PART

Dependent Services

Lync Server, like most Microsoft applications, depends on a number of other infrastructure services. To operate properly, Lync Server integrates with Active Directory to store configuration information on user objects. It depends on DNS for finding hosts and services, it depends on Public Key Infrastructure (PKI) to provide certificates, and it depends on the network to connect clients to servers. This chapter covers some of those dependencies and helps Lync Server administrators understand and configure these items.

Active Directory

Almost any application build by Microsoft has a high level of integration and dependency with Active Directory; Lync Server is no exception. Lync Server cannot be installed without Active Directory and it needs certain attributes available in Active Directory. Lync Server provides wizards that help administrators properly prepare and configure Active Directory to properly support Lync Server. Following these configurations, in order, makes it easy for an administrator to deploy Lync Server successfully.

Active Directory requirements include

▶ All Domain Controllers (DC) in the forest must be 2003 SP2 or higher.

▶ The domain functional level for domains containing Lync Server must be 2003 Native or higher (not 2003 Interim).

▶ The forest functional level for the forest must be 2003 Native or higher (not 2003 Interim).

Schema Extensions

To provide the necessary attributes used by Lync Server, it is necessary to extend the schema with the provided extensions. This process is easiest to run on a system destined to be a Lync Server, and by someone who is currently a member of the Schema Administrators group must perform it. If you add your account to Schema Administrators for installing Lync Server, be sure to log off and on to ensure you have a Kerberos ticket that reflects the recent group membership change. Prior to extending the schema, first install the following components:

▶ .NET 3.5 SP1

▶ Active Directory Domain Services (does not need to be promoted)

From the Lync Server installation media, follow these steps:

1. Launch Setup.exe.

2. When the wizard displays, browse to your intended installation location. Choose whether to check for updates, and then click **OK**.

3. When prompted, carefully read the software license terms, and then click the **I accept the terms in the license agreement** option if you agree to the terms. Then click **OK**.

4. When the Deployment Wizard launches, it determines the current state of the environment and prompts you for installations as needed. In the case of a fresh installation, you are offered the opportunity to prepare Active Directory. Click **Prepare Active Directory**, as shown in Figure 10.1.

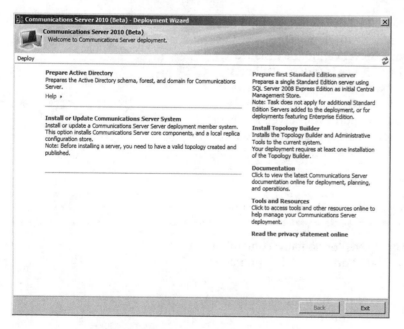

FIGURE 10.1   Running the Deployment Wizard

> **NOTE**
>
> Be sure the Schema Master role is available and that you have Schema Admin credentials.

5. Assuming the prerequisites are met, click **Run** on Step 1: Prep Schema, which will launch the wizard shown in Figure 10.2.

6. Click **Next**.

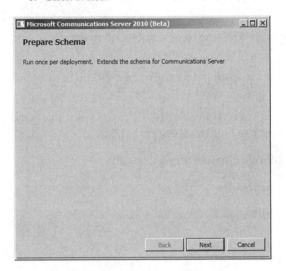

FIGURE 10.2   Preparing the Schema

7. When the commands are executed, click Finish.

8. Using tools such as Repadmin or ADSIEDIT, spot check DCs to ensure that the updated schema partition has replicated.

New Active Directory classes created include

▶ **msRTCSIP-GlobalTopologySettings**—This class is a container that holds global topology setting objects.

▶ **msRTCSIP-GlobalTopologySetting**—The local global topology setting object.

▶ **msRTCSIP-ConnectionPoint-Generic**—SCP to specify computer as a Live Lync Server.

New Active Directory attributes include

▶ **msRTCSIP-TenantId**—This attribute is a unique identifier of the tenant. This identifier should be unique across all tenants.

▶ **msRTCSIP-UserPolicies**—This attribute is used to store name-value pairs.

10

▶ **msRTCSIP-OwnerUrn**—This attribute is the Uniform Resource Name (URN) of the owner for the application contact.

▶ **msRTCSIP-TargetUserPolicies**—This attribute is used to store name-value pairs for target policies on a Lync Server user.

▶ **msRTCSIP-DeploymentLocator**—This attribute is used in a split-domain topology and contains a fully qualified domain name (FQDN).

▶ **msRTCSIP-PrivateLine**—This attribute contains the device ID of a private line device.

▶ **msRTCSIP-AcpInfo**—This attribute is used to store user audio conferencing provider information.

▶ **msRTCSIP-GroupingID**—This attribute is a unique identifier of a group, used to group address book entries.

▶ **ms-Exch-UC-Voice-Mail-Settings**—This multivalued attribute holds voice mail settings. This attribute is shared with Exchange Unified Messaging (UM).

The following Active Directory classes are modified to add a mayContain:

▶ **Organizational-Unit**

    ▶ add mayContain msRTCSIP-TenantId

▶ **User**

    ▶ add mayContain msRTCSIP-AcpInfo

    ▶ add mayContain msRTCSIP-GroupingID

    ▶ add mayContain msRTCSIP-ApplicationOptions

    ▶ add mayContain msRTCSIP-OwnerUrn

    ▶ add mayContain msRTCSIP-UserPolicies

    ▶ add mayContain msRTCSIP-TargetUserPolicies

    ▶ add mayContain msRTCSIP-TenantId

▶ **Contact**

    ▶ add mayContain msRTCSIP-AcpInfo

    ▶ add mayContain msRTCSIP-OwnerUrn

    ▶ add mayContain msRTCSIP-GroupingID

    ▶ add mayContain msRTCSIP-UserPolicies

    ▶ add: mayContain msRTCSIP-TargetUserPolicies

    ▶ add mayContain msRTCSIP-TenantId

▶ **Group**

    ▶ add mayContain msRTCSIP-GroupingID

    ▶ add mayContain msRTCSIP-TenantId

▶ **msRTCSIP-GlobalTopologySetting**

    ▶ add mayContain msRTCSIP-BackEndServer

    ▶ add mayContain msRTCSIP-ServerVersion

    ▶ add mayContai-msRTCSIP-ExtensionData

▶ **Mail-Recipient**

    ▶ add mayContain ms-Exch-UC-Voice-Mail-Settings

Forest Prep

After the schema has been updated, the setup enables you to continue the remaining steps. The next logical step is to prepare the forest for the Lync Server installation. Continuing with the existing Deployment Wizard, follow these steps:

1. Click **Run** on Step 3: Prepare Current Forest. The Prepare Forest task will launch as shown in Figure 10.3.

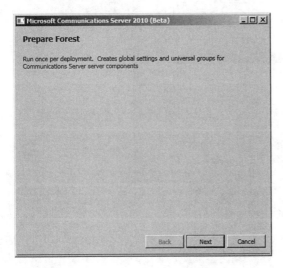

FIGURE 10.3   Preparing the Forest

2. Click **Next**.
3. When the commands are executed, click **Finish**.
4. Verify that the changes Forest Prep performed have replicated.

> **TIP**
>
> An easy way to do this is to use ADSIEdit or Ldp to check multiple DCs to see whether the new CS and RTC groups are present.

Domain Prep

As with most Microsoft applications, after the forest is prepared, the domain must be prepared. Important to note is that the steps domain prep performs are different from those in forest prep. So even if a forest is comprised of a single domain, it is necessary to perform both tasks. Domain prep should be performed on all domains that host Lync Server users or servers.

1. Click **Run** on Step 5: Prepare Current Domain.
2. When the commands are executed, click **Finish**.
3. Verify replication of the Access Control Entries set by Domain Prep, and then click Exit. This will return you to the Deployment Wizard, as shown in Figure 10.4.

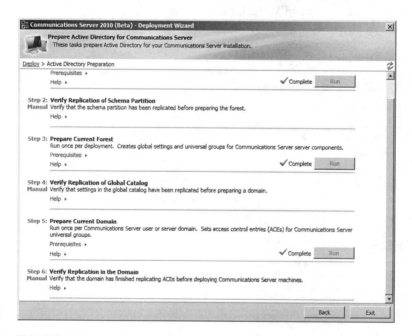

FIGURE 10.4   Verifying Replication

2010 Security Groups

Domain Prep performs several tasks, including setting permissions on various objects and containers and creating several groups for use with Lync Server. The groups created are detailed lists.

The service groups are

▶ **RTCHSUniversalServices**—Includes service accounts used to run Front End Server and enables servers read/write access to Lync Server global settings and Active Directory user objects

▶ **RTCComponentUniversalServices**—Includes service accounts used to run conferencing servers, web services, Mediation Server, Archiving Server, and Monitoring Server

▶ **RTCProxyUniversalServices**—Includes service accounts used to run Lync Server Edge Servers

The administration groups are

▶ **RTCUniversalServerAdmins**—Allows members to manage server and pool settings

▶ **RTCUniversalUserAdmins**—Allows members to manage user settings and move users from one server or pool to another

▶ **RTCUniversalReadOnlyAdmins**—Allows members to read server, pool, and user settings

The infrastructure groups are

▶ **RTCUniversalGlobalWriteGroup**—Grants write access to global setting objects for Lync Server.

▶ **RTCUniversalGlobalReadOnlyGroup**—Grants read-only access to global setting objects for Lync Server.

▶ **RTCUniversalUserReadOnlyGroup**—Grants read-only access to Lync Server user settings.

▶ **RTCUniversalServerReadOnlyGroup**—Grants read-only access to Lync Server settings. This group does not have access to pool-level settings; it accesses only settings specific to an individual server.

Forest preparation then adds service and administration groups to the appropriate infrastructure groups, as follows:

RTCUniversalServerAdmins is added to RTCUniversalGlobalReadOnlyGroup, RTCUniversalGlobalWriteGroup, RTCUniversalServerReadOnlyGroup, and RTCUniversalUserReadOnlyGroup.

RTCUniversalUserAdmins is added as a member of RTCUniversalGlobalReadOnlyGroup, RTCUniversalServerReadOnlyGroup, and RTCUniversalUserReadOnlyGroup.

RTCHSUniversalServices, RTCComponentUniversalServices, and RTCUniversalReadOnlyAdmins are added as members of RTCUniversalGlobalReadOnlyGroup, RTCUniversalServerReadOnlyGroup, and RTCUniversalUserReadOnlyGroup.

Forest preparation also creates the following role-based access control (RBAC) groups:

- ▶ CSAdministrator
- ▶ CSArchivingAdministrator
- ▶ CSBranchOfficeTechnician
- ▶ CSHelpDesk
- ▶ CSLocationAdministrator
- ▶ CSResponseGroupAdministrator
- ▶ CSRoleAdministrator
- ▶ CSServerAdministrator
- ▶ CSUserAdministrator
- ▶ CSViewOnlyAdministrator
- ▶ CSVoiceAdministrator

Domain Name System

Lync Server utilizes DNS as the method for resolving names to IP addresses and for identifying servers that provide specific services.

Although there are various ways to install and configure DNS, the most straightforward and complete process involves invoking the Add Roles Wizard and the subsequent Configure a DNS Server Wizard. The process detailed in this section illustrates the installation of a standard zone. Multiple variations of the installation are possible, but this particular scenario is illustrated to show the basics of DNS installation.

Install and Configure DNS on Windows Server 2008 R2

Installation of DNS on Windows Server 2008 R2 is straightforward, and no reboot is necessary. To install and configure the DNS service on a Windows Server 2008 R2 computer, follow these steps:

1. Launch Server Manager.
2. Select the Roles node and click the **Add Roles** link.
3. Click **Next** on the Before You Begin page.
4. Select the **DNS Server role** check box and click **Next**.
5. Click **Next** on the Introduction to DNS Server page.
6. Click **Install** on the Confirmation page to install the DNS role.
7. Click **Close** to exit the Add Roles Wizard.

The DNS role is installed on the Windows Server 2008 R2 server, but it has not been configured. To configure the role, execute the following steps:

1. Launch Server Manager.

2. Expand the roles, DNS server, DNS nodes, and then select the DNS server name.

3. Select **Action, Configure a DNS Server**.

4. On the Welcome page for the Configure a DNS Server Wizard, click **Next** to continue.

5. Select **Create Forward and Reverse Lookup Zones (Recommended for Large Networks)**, and then click **Next**.

6. Select **Yes, Create a Forward Lookup Zone Now (Recommended)**, and then click **Next**.

7. Select the type of zone to be created—in this case, choose Primary Zone—and then click **Next**. If the server is a writable domain controller, the Store the Zone in Active Directory check box is available.

8. If you are storing the zone in Active Directory, select the replication scope, and then click **Next**.

9. Type the FQDN of the zone in the Zone Name box, and then click Next.

10. At this point, if creating a non–AD–integrated zone, you can create a new zone text file or import one from an existing zone file. In this case, choose **Create a New File with This File Name** and accept the default. Click **Next** to continue.

11. The subsequent page allows a zone to either accept or decline dynamic updates. For this example, enable dynamic updates by selecting the **Allow Both Nonsecure and Secure Updates** option button, and then clicking **Next**.

12. The next page allows for the creation of a reverse lookup zone. Here, select **Yes, Create a Reverse Lookup Zone Now**, and then click **Next**.

13. Select **Primary Zone** for the reverse lookup zone type, and then click **Next**.

14. If storing the zone in Active Directory, select the replication scope, and then click **Next**.

15. Accept the default IPv4 Reverse Lookup Zone, and then click **Next**.

16. Type the network ID of the Reverse Lookup Zone, and then click **Next**.

NOTE

The network ID is typically the first set of octets from an IP address in the zone. If a Class C IP range of 192.168.3.0/24 is in use on a network, you enter the values 192.168.3.

10

17. Again, if creating a non–AD–integrated zone, you are offered the option to create a new zone file or to utilize an existing file. For this example, choose **Create a New File with This File Name**, and then click **Next** to continue.

18. Again, you are presented the option for dynamic updates. For this example, select **Allow Both Nonsecure and Secure Updates**, and then click **Next** to continue.

19. The next page deals with the setup of forwarders, which are normally used when only part of DNS is delegated to Active Directory. In this example, choose **No, It Should Not Forward Queries**, and then click **Next** to continue.

20. The final window displays a summary of the changes that are made and the zones that are added to the DNS database. Click **Finish** to finalize the changes and create the zones.

DNS Records Lync Server Uses

Lync Server utilizes DNS for several purposes. Not only do traditional hostname-to-IP address lookups occur, Lync Server utilizes specialized DNS records to identify particular services much like Active Directory does. Lync Server is even able to use DNS round robin to provide load balancing between sites. Some record examples include

▶ A or address records

▶ PTR or pointer records

▶ SRV or service location records

Lync Server requires registration of hostnames of servers as A records. Administrators implementing the DNS load-balancing features of Lync Server are required to specify the server FQDN and the cluster FQDN using the same IP address for each server in the cluster and A records for all clusters that contain an Enhanced registrar. For example:

ClusterNode1.companyabc.com	A	10.1.1.2
RegistrarCluster.companyabc.com	A	10.1.1.2
ClusterNode2.companyabc.com	A	10.1.1.3
RegistrarCluster.companyabc.com	A	10.1.1.3

The more unusual DNS records used by Lync Server are SRV records. These are used to identify resources of a particular type that are either providing a specific service or that are in a particular location. This is where the subdomains come into play. For example:

_sipinternal._tcp.companyabc.com

SRV records hold additional information, such as

Domain: Companyabc.com

Service: _sipfederationtls

Protocol: _tcp

Priority: 10

Weight: 100

Port number: 5061

Host offering this service: FQDN of host

This enables a client to ask DNS where to find a host providing a specific service, and DNS can return one or more answers. By using Priority and Weight, one can enforce a behavior of how loads are shared or directed.

Public Key Infrastructure

Lync Server utilizes SSL certificates to protect connections by authenticating the endpoint and then encrypting transmissions. Lync Server can utilize either public or private certificates. This is to say that a Lync Server administrator has the option to purchase certificates from a publicly trusted third party such as Verisign or Digicert or he can choose to issue his own certificates from an internally developed PKI.

A PKI consists of hardware and software in addition to policies and procedures to create and manage digital certificates. Although a full explanation of how to plan and manage a PKI goes beyond the scope of this chapter, the decisions for how a PKI is built determine how far it can be trusted to secure identities and information.

Understanding PKI Roles

Most PKIs consist of many roles. Some roles are optional and based on the level of assurance desired, but it is useful to understand PKI terminology. Following are some terms you should know:

▶ **Certificate Authority (CA)**—An entity that issues digital certificates that certify ownership of a public key by the named subject of the certificate.

▶ **Root CA**—The first CA in a PKI, this role anchors the CA hierarchy. The entire PKI is only as trustworthy as the Root CA. Any user, computer, or service that trusts the Root CA implicitly trusts any certificate issued by other CAs in the hierarchy.

▶ **Policy CA**—Typically located at the second tier of a CA hierarchy, the Policy CA's job is to issue certificates to other CAs, not to end consumers. The Policy CA defines the rules by which the lower tier CAs operate. Policy CAs are typically used only in wide-reaching PKIs.

▶ **Issuing CA**—The Issuing CA is the CA that provides certificates to the end consumer. The Issuing CA can issue certificates only for which it has templates defined.

Understanding Certificates

Digital certificates are a form of electronic credentials that validate the identity of entities on a network. Certificates allow a public key to be signed by a trusted authority to vouch for another entity's identity. Certificates can be used for different purposes depending on the Object Identifier (OID) assigned to the certificate by a template. This allows a certificate to be used for authentication, encryption, or data integrity.

The best way to understand how this process works is to compare it to a process with which people are already familiar. The process parallels nicely to the idea of a driver's license.

A driver's license is a well-accepted form of identification for people. To request a driver's license, you need to go to the DMV. The DMV acts like a registration authority because it validates the identity of the requestor. The DMV is allowed to issue only one type of item: a driver's license. The license has a standardized appearance and standard information. This is similar to the concept of a certificate template on a CA. It defines what information must be gathered and what information can go into the certificate. The local DMV acts like an Issuing CA, and the state-level DMV acts like a Root CA and a Policy CA in that it sets forth the standards for what the local DMV is allowed to issue.

After a user is issued a driver's license, he can present it to other entities as a form of identity validation. This is functionally equivalent to authentication. Although the entity that looks at the license can't personally authenticate the card holder, he is able to compare the identity on the license to the information available about the license holder. Because the entity trusts the DMV, it can assume that the DMV did a sufficient job of validating the identity of the card holder and trust that the DMV vouches for the identity of the card holder. This is the same way in which a computer trusts the identity of another computer based on the certificate it holds. If the queried information on the computer matches what is in the certificate and if the Root CA at the top of the CA hierarchy is trusted, the connection is trusted.

> **NOTE**
>
> This process allows a client to be sure that the server to which he is connecting is the server he thinks it is. Without this type of authentication, a client can be redirected to a malicious host and can potentially send sensitive information to an untrustworthy host. This is typically called a man in the middle attack; the use of certificates is an excellent way to prevent this situation.

Installing Certificate Services

Although certificate services are offered by a number of vendors, this chapter covers only the installation of Microsoft Certificate Services because it is the most commonly used CA for Microsoft products. In smaller scenarios, an Enterprise Root CA can be provisioned, although in many cases, those smaller organizations might still want to consider a standalone Root and a subordinate Enterprise CA. For the single Enterprise Root CA scenario, however, the following steps can be taken to provision the CA server:

1. Open Server Manager (click **Start, All Programs, Administrative Tools, Server Manager**).

2. In the Nodes pane, select **Roles**, and then click the **Add Roles** link in the tasks pane.

3. On the welcome page, click **Next**.

4. On the Select Server Roles page, check the box for **Active Directory Certificate Services**, and then click **Next**.

5. Review the information about AD CS on the Introduction page, and then click **Next** to continue.

6. On the Select Role Services page shown in Figure 10.5, choose which role services are required. A base install needs only the Certificate Authority role. Click **Next** to continue.

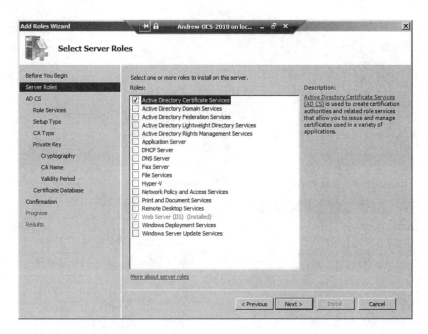

FIGURE 10.5   Installing AD CS

7. Select whether to install an Enterprise (integrated with AD DS) CA or a Standalone CA on the subsequent page. In this example, you install a domain-based Enterprise Root CA. Click **Next** to continue.

8. On the Specify CA Type page, specify the CA type, as shown in Figure 10.6. In this case, you install a Root CA on the server. Click **Next** to continue.

9. On the following Set Up Private Key page, you can choose whether to create a new private key from scratch or reuse an existing private key from a previous CA implementation. In this example, we create a new key. Click **Next** to continue.

10. On the Configure Cryptography for CA page, enter the private key encryption settings, as shown in Figure 10.7. Normally, the defaults are fine, but there might be specific needs to change the Crypto Service Provider (CSP), key length, or other settings. Click **Next** to continue.

10

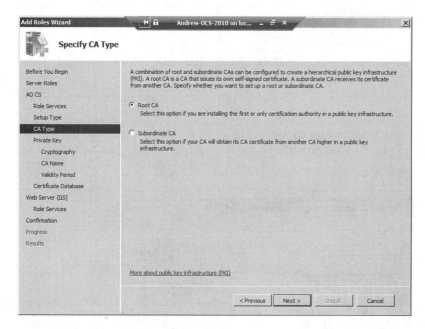

FIGURE 10.6   Specifying a CA Type

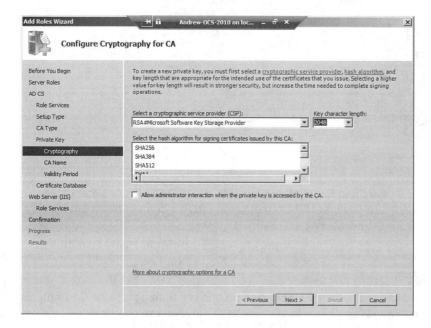

FIGURE 10.7   Choosing Cryptography Settings

11. Choose a common name to identify the CA. Keep in mind that this name displays on all certificates the CA issues. For this example, enter the common name **CompanyABC-CorpCA**. Click **Next** to continue.

12. Set the validity period for the certificate to be installed on this CA server. If this is a Root CA, the server has to reissue the certificate chain after the expiration period has expired. In this example, a 5-year validity period is used, although many production scenarios have a 20-year CA created for the root. Click **Next** to continue.

13. Specify a location for the certificate database and log locations, and then click **Next** to continue.

14. Review the installation selections on the confirmation page, as shown in Figure 10.8, and then click **Install**.

FIGURE 10.8   Reviewing AD CS Installation Options

15. Click **Close** when the wizard is complete.

16. After you install AD CS, additional CAs can be installed as subordinate CAs, and the administration of the PKI can be performed from the CA console (choose **Start**, **All Programs**, **Administrative Tools**, **Certification Authority**).

Certificate Types for Lync Server

Certificates have traditionally been a difficult subject for earlier versions of Communication Server. For many administrators, OCS 2007 was likely their first exposure to Subject Alternate Name (SAN) certificates. A SAN certificate differs from traditional certificates in one way: SAN certificates contain multiple names where traditional certificates contain only one name. By containing multiple names, a SAN certificate can correctly answer to a hostname, a service name, or a load-balanced name. This greatly simplifies load balancing and geographic redundancy by allowing a system to respond to multiple names using a single certificate when a secure connection is desired.

10

Lync Server provides a wizard for requesting, installing, and assigning certificates. This wizard is reachable when installing CS system components. For example:

1. Launch Setup from the Lync Server install media.

2. Click **Install or Update Lync Server System**.

3. Assuming the Local Configuration Store is installed and at least one component has been installed, click **Run** on Step 3 to request a new certificate.

4. Click **Request** to request a certificate.

5. The Request Wizard launches. Click **Next**.

6. If you are going to use a third-party certificate, choose **Prepare the request now, but send it later (offline certificate request)**. If you utilize your own CA, you can select **Send the request immediately to an online Certificate Authority**.

7. In this example, you use an offline CA. When prompted, browse to a location where you can store the certificate request file. After it is selected, click **Next**.

8. By default, the wizard creates a request for a WebServer (SSL) certificate. Click **Next**.

9. Enter a friendly name for the certificate. This makes it easier to identify later. Choose a bit length for the certificate. If you need to export the private key later, select the check box. This is typically used when a single SAN cert is imported onto multiple computers. Click **Next**.

10. Enter information for organization and organizational unit. With most external CAs, these values have been defined as naming constraints and must match values you've already defined with your certificate provider. Click **Next**.

11. Pick your country from the drop-down menu, and then enter information for the State/Province and City/Locality options. Click **Next**.

12. Review the names that are populated into the certificate as shown in Figure 10.9, and then click **Next**.

13. If you use auto-logon without DNS SRV entries, if you perform strict domain matching, or if you plan to deploy OC Phone edition devices, you need to check the box to add additional SANs per SIP domain as shown in Figure 10.10. Click **Next**.

14. Any additional Subject Alternate Names outside those determined by the wizard can be added. After they are added, click **Next**.

15. Review the Certificate Request Summary, and then click **Next**.

16. After the commands are executed, click **Next**.

17. This generates the certificate request file. Depending on your certificate provider, you might upload this file or copy and paste the text contained in the file when requesting your certificate. The text version of the request is shown in Figure 10.11. Click **Finish**.

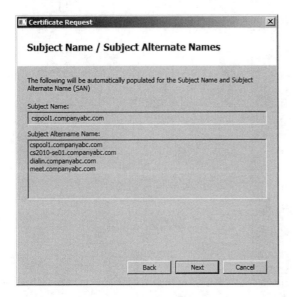

FIGURE 10.9   Reviewing Subject Alternate Names

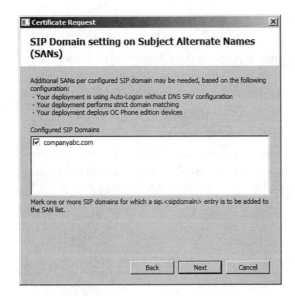

FIGURE 10.10   Configuring SIP Domains on SANs

FIGURE 10.11   Text Version of a Request File

After the certificate has been returned signed by the vendor, it is necessary to import the certificate and assign it:

1. From the Start menu, click **All Programs**, **Microsoft Lync Server**, **Lync Server Deployment Wizard**.
2. Click **Install or Update Lync Server System**.
3. Click **Run** on Step 3: Request, Install or Assign Certificates.
4. Click **Import Certificate** in the lower portion of the wizard.
5. Click **Browse** and navigate to the certificate that the vendor sent. If there is a private key contained in the file (for example, if it was exported by a different Lync Server) select the appropriate check box, and if a password was set on the export, enter it in the field provided. Click **Next**.
6. Review the summary and click **Next**.
7. When the command has executed, click **Finish**.
8. In the Certificate Wizard, click **Assign**.
9. Click **Next**.
10. Choose the certificate you want to assign as shown in Figure 10.12, and then click **Next**.

TIP

This is where the friendly name comes in handy. If you aren't sure which certificate to use, you can view certificate details and look for the correct Subject Alternate Names.

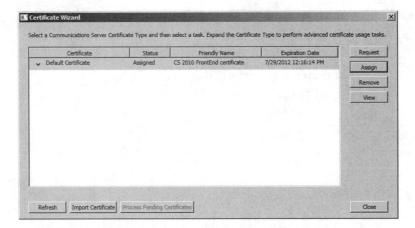

FIGURE 10.12   Assigning Certificates

11. Review the certificate summary, and then click **Next**.

12. After the command has executed, click **Finish**.

    Lync Server now has an assigned default certificate, as shown in Figure 10.13.

13. Click **Close** to end the Certificate Wizard.

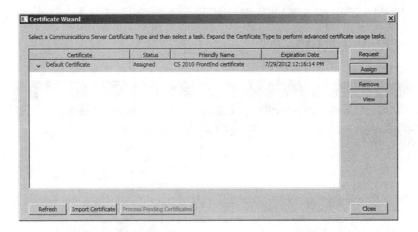

FIGURE 10.13   Viewing the Assigned Certificate

Understanding the Lync Server Certificate

Viewing the certificate issued for Lync Server will help one understand what certificates are and how they get used. The easiest way to look at locally installed certificates is with the Certificates MMC.

1. From the Run line, type **MMC**. Press **Enter**.
2. From the File menu, choose **Add/Remove Snap-In**.
3. From the available snap-ins, add **Certificates**.
4. When prompted, select **Computer Account**, and then click **Finish**.
5. Choose **Local Computer**. Click **Finish**.
6. Click **OK**.
7. Expand **Certificates (Local Computer)**.
8. Expand **Personal**.
9. Click **Certificates**.
10. Double-click the certificate to be viewed.

This view shows some basic information about the certificate. At the top, the certificate explains its intended purposes. Certificates are often used to ensure the identity of a remote system and the Lync Server certificate is no different. The certificate shows who it was issued to and who it was issued by. This is how other systems can trust a system using this certificate. They can check to see whether the name they asked for is listed in the certificate and whether the certificate was issued by a hierarchy that they trust.

The certificate also lists its validity period. This is important to realize as the certificate eventually expires. When it does, no other systems trust the certificate. Figure 10.14 shows that the system holds the private key that corresponds to this certificate. This gives one the potential to export the certificate and the associated public and private keys so that the same certificate can be used on other systems. This is common in situations where the certificate is used on load-balanced systems.

> **NOTE**
>
> By listing the load-balanced name in the certificate, clients connecting to any member of the load-balanced group trust the certificate, connect properly, and establish an encrypted session.

The Details tab on the certificate offers much more information, as follows:

▶ **Version**—This is the type of template used to generate the certificate. Higher version numbers offer more customization of the template.

▶ **Serial number**—This is a unique value used to identify a certificate.

▶ **Signature algorithm**—This is the algorithm used to sign the certificate.

▶ **Signature hash algorithm**—This is the algorithm used to create the signature hash.

▶ **Issuer**—This is the canonical name of the CA that issued the certificate.

▶ **Valid from, Valid to**—These values establish the lifespan of the certificate.

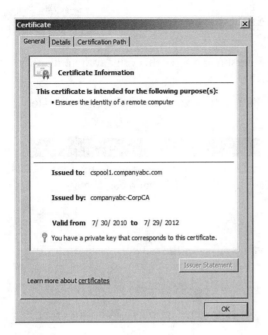

FIGURE 10.14   Viewing a Certificate

▶ **Subject**—This is a canonical representation of the name of the certificate, including location information. It is important that the full name be unique if you are replacing another certificate that is still valid.

CAUTION

Most providers revoke an existing certificate if a new one is generated with the same subject name. This can cause an outage if you do not plan for it. Typically, a certificate provider allows you to register multiple OU values for naming constraints to avoid a perfect match to the subject name.

▶ **Public Key**—This is the value remote systems use to encrypt data destined for the holder of the private key.

▶ **Certificate Template Name**—This is the name of the template the CA uses to issue the certificate.

▶ **Enhanced Key Usage**—This maps to a standard set of OIDs that define what a key can be used for. In the case of the Lync Server certificate, the value is 1.3.6.1.5.5.7.3.1, which means server authentication.

▶ **Subject Key Identifier**—Path validation software uses this value by helping to identify certificates that contain a particular public key.

10

▶ **Subject Alternative Name**—This is the field that lists the names to which the certificate can correctly match.

▶ **Authority Key Identifier**—Path validation software uses this value to help identify the next certificate up in a certificate chain.

▶ **CRL Distribution Points**—This field tells a system where to check for Certificate Revocation Lists (CRLs).

CAUTION

At least one of these paths needs to be reachable by a system that needs to trust the certificate. If a CRL can't be found, the client is not able to verify that a certificate hasn't been revoked and won't trust it.

▶ **Authority Information Access**—This value provides the network location for the issuing CA's certificate.

▶ **Key Usage**—This field defines what the keys can be used for.

▶ **Thumbprint algorithm**—The algorithm used to generate the thumbprint of the certificate.

▶ **Thumbprint**—A unique value identifying the certificate. Most applications that use certificates identify them by the thumbprint.

▶ **Friendly name**—This is a name given to the certificate by the requestor to more easily identify a certificate. Administrators quickly realize that it's much easier to spot a certificate by its friendly name than it is to use its thumbprint.

The last tab on the certificate is the Certification Path as shown in Figure 10.15. This is the quick-and-easy way to ensure a certificate is valid. Not only is there a simple statement of the certificate's status, but if that status is invalid, you can quickly look at the chain to see where the problem is. You can even look at upstream certificates from the chain and view the same level of details on those. This makes it easier to troubleshoot issues such as expired intermediate CAs or inaccessible CRLs.

Network Dependencies

Lync Server, a product that provides voice, video, and text services over a network, has many dependencies on the network to provide functionality. Although concepts such as connectivity and sufficient bandwidth are obvious, other dependencies exist, including services such as DHCP, network site definitions, and configuration of specific features on the network switches.

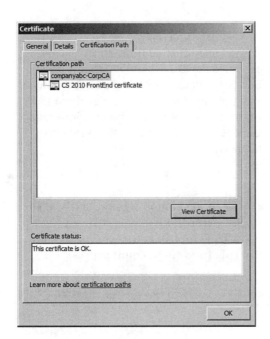

FIGURE 10.15   Viewing the Trust Chain

Supporting Lync Server with DHCP

Although soft clients inherit their connectivity from the host they are connected to, specialized devices such as VoIP desk phones are likely managed centrally by the Lync Server administrator. Traditionally, these devices are configured via DHCP to allow them to connect properly and to let the device know where to look for firmware of software updates. Microsoft recommends several DHCP options for use with Communicator Phone Edition devices. These are

- ▶ **Option 43**—CS Pool Certificate Provisioning Service URL—Specifies the internal (Uniform Resource Locator) URL in the form https://CSWebPoolDFQDN:443/CertProv/CertProvisioningService.svc.

- ▶ **Option 120**—FQDN for the CA Pool Registrar—Specifies the pool fully qualified domain name for the pool that acts as the first logon server for the device, usually a Director pool.

- ▶ **Option 43**—VLAN ID—Allows the configuration of a Virtual Local Area Network (VLAN) ID. Do not use this if you use Link Layer Discovery Protocol (LLDP)-enabled switches for providing VLAN IDs.

- ▶ **Option4**—TimeServer—Points the device to a time server to keep it in sync with other systems.

Segregation of Traffic

To ensure the best audio quality, it is highly recommended that administrators separate VoIP traffic from other network traffic by placing voice devices on a VLAN that is dedicated to voice functions. Similarly, users with USB-based devices should connect to a wired network rather than a wireless network. By keeping phone devices on a segregated VLAN, it is easier to layer services such as Quality of Service (QoS) onto the network segment to ensure the best possible voice quality for end users. It also makes it simpler to monitor devices because they are logically grouped at the network level.

Switch Configurationss

Because IP phones running the Communicator 2010 Phone Edition support LLDP-MED (Link Layer Discovery Protocol-Media Endpoint Discovery) and PoE (Power over Ethernet), you have to utilize switches that support IEEE802.1AB and ANSI/TIA-1057 to take advantage of LLDP-MED. Similarly, to utilize PoE, the switches must support PoE802.3AF or 802.3at.

If using LLDP-MED, be sure to set LLDP-MED network policy to the correct voice VLAN ID.

Defining Network Sites

Not unlike Active Directory or Exchange, Lync Server needs to define network sites and associated subnets to make decisions about where to access a resource or how to route a call. All subnets in a network should be defined and associated with a correct network site in Lync Server. This is easily handled by a simple comma-separated value file and the Lync Server cmdlets in PowerShell. For example, the CSV file might be called subnet.csv and contain

```
IPAddress, mask, description, NetworkSiteID
10.1.1.0, 24, "NA:Subnet in Dublin", Dublin
10.1.2.0, 24, "NA:Subnet in Lompoc", Lompoc
10.1.3.0, 24, "NA:Subnet in Ocean Springs", Ocean_Springs
10.1.4.0, 26, "EU:Subnet in London", London
```

These values can be easily imported into the Lync Server network's definitions via this command:

```
import-csv subnet.csv ¦ foreach {New-CSNCSSubnet $_.IPAddress -MaskBits $_.mask
-Description $_.description -NetworkSiteID $_.NetworkSiteID}
```

This script can be scheduled to run regularly, and when new sites or subnets are added to the network, the csv file is updated and the script keeps the network definitions current.

CHAPTER 11

SQL

Lync Server, like many Microsoft applications, depends on SQL as a back-end storage mechanism for topology, configuration, and application information. Most administrators will likely choose SQL 2008R2 as their SQL of choice based on the fact that it contains the latest tools, technologies, and security features from Microsoft. This chapter covers installation of SQL 2008 R2 as it pertains to a Lync Server implementation and introduces Lync Server administrators to some management tasks of SQL 2008 R2.

Installing SQL 2008 R2

To install SQL 2008 R2, perform the following steps:

1. Double-click **Setup** on the SQL 2008 R2 DVD.

2. If the .NET framework is not already present, the wizard requests it. Click **OK** to enable the wizard to install the .NET framework.

3. When the SQL Server Installation Center displays, as shown in Figure 11.1, click **Installation** in the left pane, and then click **New installation or add features to an existing installation**.

4. After the Setup Support Rules Wizard runs, and if all checks pass, click **OK**.

5. When the wizard prompts, enter your product key and click **Next**.

6. Read the licensing terms. If you agree, check the box next to **I accept the license terms** and then click **Next**.

7. Click **Install** to set up the support files.

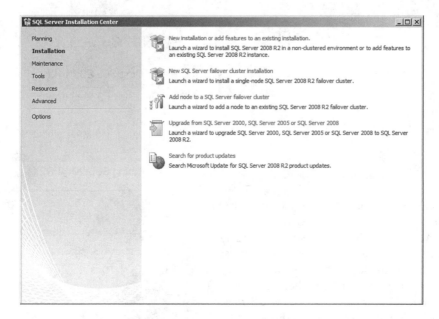

FIGURE 11.1   The SQL Server Installation Center

8. When the support rules are completed, review the status. If all operations pass, click **Next**. Otherwise, click the status for additional information and perform the recommended remediation.

9. When the Setup Role wizard launches, as shown in Figure 11.2, **choose SQL Server Feature Installation** and click **Next**.

10. Select the features you want to install and select the paths to which they should be installed. The features chosen depend on the roles you plan to use in Lync Server. Click **Next**.

11. If all operations pass, click **Next**. Otherwise, click the status for additional information and perform the recommended remediation.

12. Choose **Default Instance** and click **Next**.

13. Review the disk space usage summary and click **Next**.

14. Choose the accounts to use for running the SQL services as shown in Figure 11.3 and enter passwords if they are to be named accounts. Leave the startup types as default. Click **Next**.

15. Choose the authentication mode to be used, as shown in Figure 11.4.

TIP

Choose mixed mode if your environment doesn't have a policy against local SQL SA accounts. This enables a local way to authenticate SQL should the system be unable to contact the domain. Set a complex password if a local SA will be used.

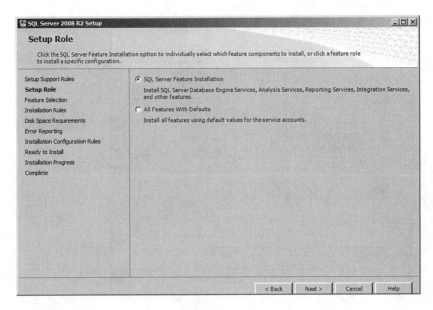

FIGURE 11.2   The Setup Role Wizard

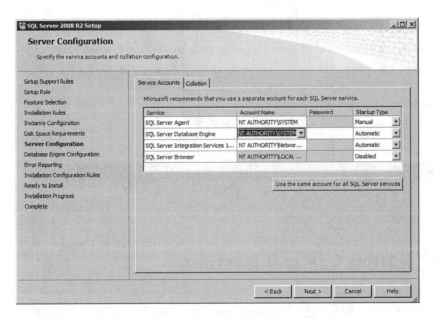

FIGURE 11.3   Configuring SQL Service Accounts

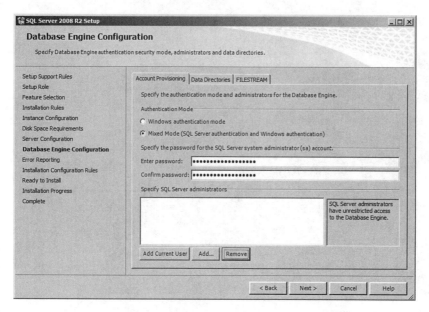

FIGURE 11.4   Choosing an Authentication Mode

16. Add SQL Server administrators, and then click **Next**.

17. Choose whether to participate in error reporting back to Microsoft. Click **Next**.

18. If all configuration operations pass, click **Next**. Otherwise, click the status for additional information and perform the recommended remediation.

19. Review the feature summary and click **Install**.

20. When the installation is completed, click **Close**.

TIP

Don't forget to run Windows Update to look for SQL-related patches.

SQL 2008 R2 Backup and Restore

To allow for recoverability of Lync Server and to ensure that information such as CDR records and IM archives are available for long periods of time, regularly back up the SQL databases associated with those functions.

There are many ways to back up SQL, including native Windows Server 2008 backup, SQL-based jobs that output the DB into a flat file, and third-party backup solutions that support SQL 2008 R2.

> **NOTE**
>
> For the purposes of this chapter, we cover Windows Server 2008's native backup and SQL 2008 R2's native backup.

Backing Up SQL through Windows Server 2008

Windows Server 2008 and Windows Server 2008 R2 contain a native backup application called Windows Server Backup. Because Windows Server Backup is not installed by default, it is necessary to add this feature by performing the following steps:

1. Click the **Server Manager** icon.
2. In the left pane, click **Features**.
3. In the right pane, click **Add Features**.
4. Scroll down to Windows Server Backup Features, and select the check box to its left as shown in Figure 11.5. Click **Next**.

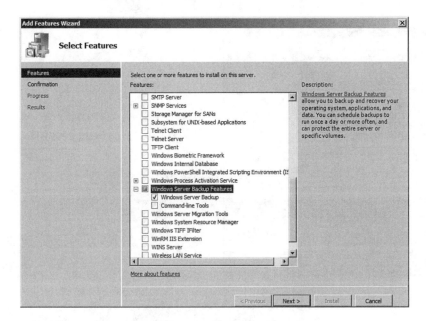

FIGURE 11.5   Adding the Windows Server Backup Feature

5. Click **Install**.
6. When the installation is completed successfully, click **Close**.
7. Close Server Manager.

Now that the Windows Server Backup feature is installed, it can be used to back up SQL:

1. Click **Start**, **Administrative Tools**, and **Windows Server Backup**.
2. In the Action pane at the far right, click **Backup Once**.
3. In the Backup Options Wizard, choose either **Scheduled backup options** to repeat previous settings or choose **Different options** to make a backup with different options. Click **Next**.

> **NOTE**
>
> If this is the first time Windows Server Backup is used, the Scheduled backup options choice is not available.

4. When prompted, choose either a Full Server or Custom backup. If you choose Custom, be sure to include the drive containing SQL. Click **Next**.
5. Choose the destination type, either local drives or a remote share. Click **Next**.
6. Specify the remote location and click **Backup**, which will start a backup as shown in Figure 11.6.

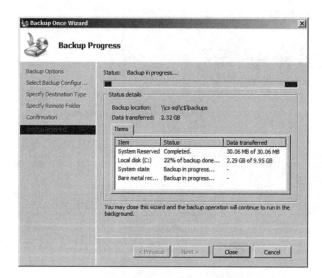

FIGURE 11.6   Running a Backup

> **NOTE**
>
> If you do not have rights to the target location, click **Next** and then you will be prompted for credentials. Enter them and click **OK**. Then click **Backup**.

7. When the backup is completed, click **Close**.

Backing Up SQL through SQL Server Management Studio

Another way to back up SQL is by using the native functions of SQL 2008 R2 to create a flat file backup that can be picked up by another backup application. This is especially useful if an environment already has a centralized backup infrastructure that doesn't support SQL natively.

To back up SQL through the SQL Server Management Studio, perform the following steps:

1. Click **Start**, All Programs, Microsoft SQL Server 2008 R2, SQL Server Management Studio.

2. Connect to the appropriate instance of the Microsoft SQL Server Database Engine and provide the necessary credentials, as shown in Figure 11.7.

FIGURE 11.7   Connecting to SQL

3. Expand **Databases** in the left pane.

4. Right-click the database you want to back up, choose **Tasks**, and click **Back Up** as shown in Figure 11.8.

5. Verify the name of the database you selected and choose a backup type.

TIP

In step 5, define a backup destination and optionally set an expiration for the backup set. You can alter the name of the backup set if desired. Also enter a meaningful description of the backup.

---

6. Click **Options** in the left pane to view additional options. Set these as desired as shown in Figure 11.9 and click **OK**.

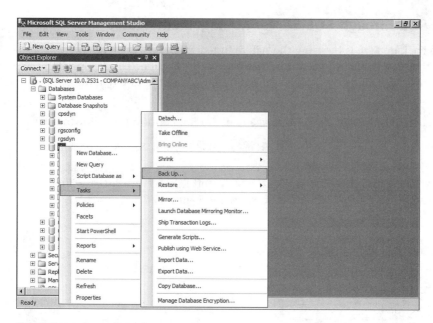

FIGURE 11.8   Backing Up a Database in SQL

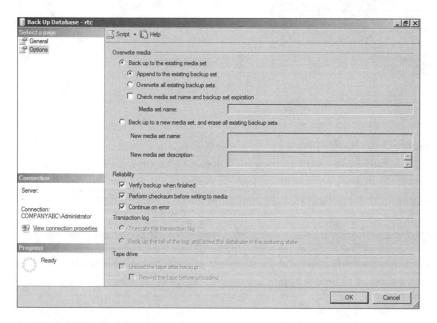

FIGURE 11.9   Configuring Backup Options

> **NOTE**
>
> SQL administrators have the option to click Script on the Backup Wizard after the job is configured to have the system create a backup script that can be called again in the future. This script can be executed through SQL Server Management Studio, as shown in Figure 11.10.

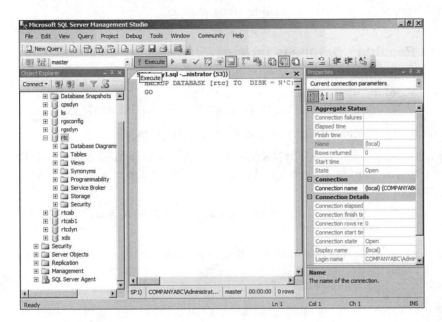

FIGURE 11.10   Scripting a Backup in SQL

7. When the backup completes, click **OK**.

The following is a sample backup script created with the Management Studio:

```
BACKUP DATABASE [rtc] TO DISK = N'C:\Program Files\Microsoft SQL
Server\MSSQL10.MSSQLSERVER\MSSQL\Backup\rtc.bak' WITH DIFFERENTIAL ,
NOFORMAT, NOINIT, NAME = N'rtc-Differential Database Backup', SKIP,
NOREWIND, NOUNLOAD, STATS = 10
GO
```

Managing and Maintaining SQL 2008 R2

To keep Lync Server operating smoothly and with optimal performance, Lync Server administrators should conduct regular maintenance on each SQL Server database. Such maintenance tasks include rebuilding indexes, checking database integrity, updating index statistics, and performing internal consistency checks and backups. Administrators can perform database maintenance tasks either by executing Transact-SQL commands or by running the Database Maintenance Wizard.

This section provides information and recommendations for maintaining the databases that host Lync Server data and configurations. Later in this section, administrators learn how to automate and schedule the major maintenance tasks by creating database mainte-nance plans through SQL Server Database Maintenance Wizard.

Checking and Repairing Database Integrity

DBCC CHECKDB is the most frequently used validation command for checking the logical and physical integrity of the whole database. Essentially, DBCC CHECKDB is a superset command that actually runs CHECKALLOC, CHECKTABLE, and CHECKCATALOG.

The following are some recommendations for using DBCC CHECKDB:

▶ Administrators should run DBCC CHECKDB rather than the individual operations because it identifies most of the errors and is generally safe to run in a production environment.

▶ After running DBCC CHECKDB, administrators should run it again with the REPAIR argument to repair reported errors.

▶ DBCC CHECKDB can be time-consuming and it performs schema locks that prevent metadata changes; therefore, it is highly recommended that administrators run it during nonproduction hours.

▶ The command should run on a table-by-table basis if it is used to perform consis-tency checks on large databases.

Monitoring and Reducing Fragmentation

Although indexes can speed up the execution of queries, some overhead is associated with them. Indexes consume extra disk space and involve additional time to update themselves any time data is updated, deleted, or inserted in a table.

When indexes are first built, little or no fragmentation should be present. Over time, as data is inserted, updated, and deleted, fragmentation levels on the underlying indexes may begin increase.

When a data page of data is completely full and further data must be added to it, a page split occurs. To make room for the new data, SQL Server creates another data page some-where else in the database (not necessarily in a contiguous location) and moves some of the data from the full page to the newly created one.

The effect of this is that the blocks of data are logically linear but physically nonlinear. Therefore, when searching for data, SQL Server has to jump from one page to somewhere else in the database looking for the next page it needs instead of going straight from one page to the next. This results in performance degradation and inefficient space utilization.

Monitoring Fragmentation

The fragmentation level of an index is the percentage of blocks that are logically linear and physically nonlinear. In SQL Server 2008 R2, SQL Server 2008, or SQL Server 2005, administrators can use the sys.dm_db_index_physical_stats dynamic management function and keep an eye on the avg_fragmentation_in_percent column to monitor and measure the fragmentation level. The value for avg_fragmentation_in_percent should be as close to zero as possible for maximum performance. However, values from 0% to 10% may be acceptable.

Reducing Fragmentation

In the previous version of Communications Server, it was recommended to track and reduce the fragmentation level by running the database statistics timer job, which updates the query optimization statistics and rebuilds all indexes in the content databases every time it runs. Another option was reorganizing or rebuilding the indexes on a regular basis using the SQL Server 2008 or SQL Server 2005 Maintenance Wizard.

In Lync Server, administrators no longer need to worry about fragmentation because Lync Server can do that on their behalf through the health analyzer. The health analyzer performs health checks based on timer jobs and self-heals the database index fragmentation automatically.

Shrinking Data Files

In SQL Server 2005 and SQL Server 2008/R2, administrators can reclaim free space from the end of data files to remove unused pages and recover disk space.

CAUTION

However, shrinking data files is not recommended unless the content database has lost at least half of its content. This typically happens after activities that create whitespace in the content database, such as moving a site collection from a content database to another one or deleting a massive amount of data. Shrinking Lync Server databases other than content databases is not recommended because they do not generally experience as many necessary deletions to contain considerable free space.

Shrinking a Database by Using SQL Server 2008 R2 Management Studio

The following steps show how to shrink a database by using SQL Server 2008 R2 Management Studio:

1. Click **Start, All Programs, Microsoft SQL Server 2008 R2**, and **SQL Server Management Studio**.

2. Connect to the desired SQL Server database engine instance and expand that instance.

3. Expand **Databases**, right-click the database to be shrunk, click **Tasks**, click **Shrink**, and click **Files**.

4. Select the file type and filename from the dialog box shown in Figure 11.11.

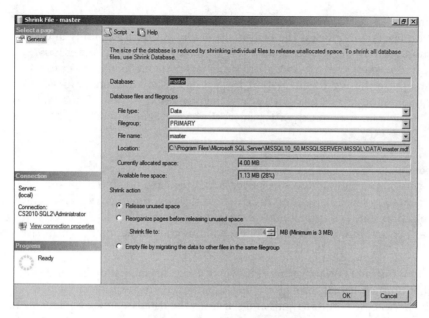

FIGURE 11.11   Selecting the File Type and Filename

a. Optionally, select **Release unused space**. Selecting this option causes unused space in the file to be released to the operating system and shrinks the file to the last allocated extent. This reduces the file size without moving data.

b. Optionally, select **Reorganize files before releasing unused space**. If this option is selected, the **Shrink file** option must be set to **value**. Selecting this option causes unused space in the file to be released to the operating system and relocates rows to unallocated pages.

c. Optionally, select **Empty file by migrating the data to other files in the same filegroup**. Selecting this option moves all data from the specified file to other files in the file group. The empty file can then be deleted. This option is the same as executing DBCC SHRINKFILE with the EMPTYFILE option.

5. Click **OK**.

Creating SQL Server Maintenance Plans

Maintaining Lync Server back end databases can significantly improve the health and performance of Lync Server servers. Unfortunately, administrators often do not perform regular database maintenance because maintaining Lync Server environments involves several maintenance tasks.

Fortunately, Microsoft has provided maintenance plans as a way to automate these tasks. A maintenance plan performs a comprehensive set of SQL Server jobs that run at scheduled intervals. Specifically, the maintenance plan conducts scheduled SQL Server maintenance tasks to ensure that databases are performing optimally, regularly backed up, and checked for anomalies.

> **TIP**
>
> Administrators can use the Maintenance Plan Wizard (included with SQL Server) to create and schedule these daily tasks. In addition, the wizard can configure database and transaction log backups.

Administrators should set maintenance operations or maintenance plans to run during off-hours to minimize the performance impact on users.

Configuring a SQL Server 2008 R2 Database Maintenance Plan

The following steps show how to configure a SQL Server 2008 R2 database maintenance plan:

1. Click **Start, All Programs, Microsoft SQL Server 2008 R2**, and **SQL Server Management Studio**.

2. Connect to the desired SQL Server database engine instance.

3. Expand **Management**, right-click **Maintenance Plans**, and then click **Maintenance Plan Wizard**.

4. On the Welcome to the Database Maintenance Plan Wizard screen, click **Next** to continue.

5. On the Select a Target Server Plan Properties screen shown in Figure 11.12, enter a name and description for the maintenance plan.

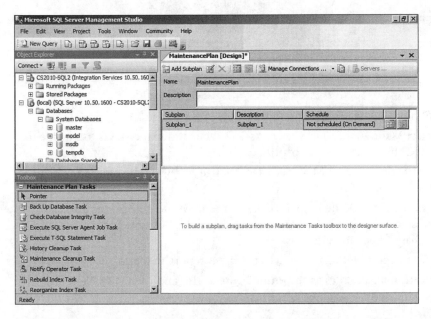

FIGURE 11.12   Enter a Name and Description for the Maintenance Plan

6. Decide whether to configure one or more maintenance plans.

   To configure a single maintenance plan, select **Single schedule for the entire plan or no schedule**. This option is selected in this example.

   To configure multiple maintenance plans with specific tasks, select **Separate schedules for each task**. This option is selected in this example.

7. Click **Change** to set a schedule for one or more of the plans. The Job Schedule Properties dialog box displays, as shown in Figure 11.13.

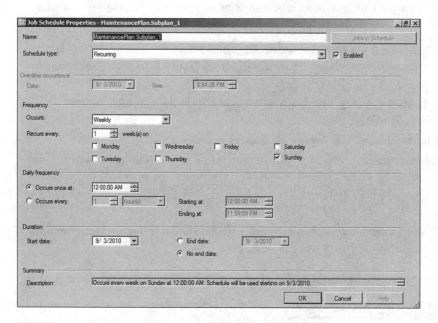

FIGURE 11.13   Set a Schedule for One or More of the Plans

8. Complete the schedule, click **OK**, and then click **Next** to continue.

9. On the Select Maintenance Tasks screen, select the maintenance tasks to include in the plan, and then click **Next** to continue.

10. In the Select Maintenance Task Order page, change or review the order in which the tasks will be executed. Select a task, and then click **Move up** or **Move down**.

11. When tasks are in the desired order, click **Next**. The wizard guides you through setting the details for each task. For example, Figure 11.14 shows the configuration of the Database Check Integrity Task.

12. On the Select Report Options page, select **Write a report to a text file**.

13. Select a location for the files as shown in Figure 11.15, and then click **Next** until the wizard is completed.

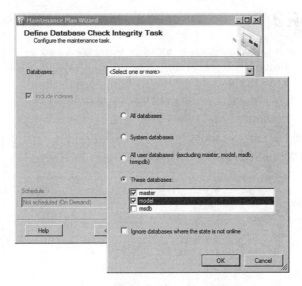

FIGURE 11.14   Configuration of the Database Check Integrity Task

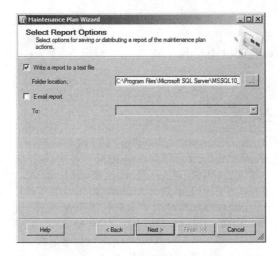

FIGURE 11.15   Select a Location for the Files

NOTE

Administrators should include the Database Check Integrity maintenance task for all Lync Server databases and the Maintenance Cleanup Task maintenance task in their plans. It is also recommended not to select the option to shrink the database, primarily because automatically shrinking databases on a periodic basis leads to excessive fragmentation and produces I/O activity, which can negatively influence the performance of Lync Server.

Monitoring SQL 2008 R2

Lync Server administrators need to know how to proficiently monitor SQL Server performance and storage in Lync Server environments. Understanding monitoring strategies and tools enables administrators to shift from reactively dealing with issues to proactively troubleshooting and fixing problems before the server gets to the point where end users are affected.

This section walks administrators through a range of monitoring tools to efficiently and powerfully monitor, maintain, and troubleshoot SQL Server in Lync Server environments. Topics in this section include

- ▶ WMI

- ▶ Event logs

- ▶ Dynamic management views

- ▶ Reliability and performance monitor

- ▶ Activity monitor

- ▶ Management data warehouse

With a vast range of monitoring tools available, choosing the right tool for the job is an important skill.

Windows Management Instrumentation

Windows Management Instrumentation (WMI) is a Microsoft implementation of Web-Based Enterprise Management (WBEM), an industry initiative that establishes management infrastructure standards. WMI supplies administrators with the tools to explore, understand, and use various system devices, resources, and applications of Microsoft operating systems and servers. WMI includes a rich infrastructure that enables efficient and scalable monitoring, data collection, and problem recognition. Think of WMI as a set of functionalities embedded into Microsoft operating systems and servers—including SQL Server—that allows for local and remote monitoring and management.

WMI is a huge initiative and certainly deserves an entire book of its own. However, what administrators need to know is that the architecture of WMI enables extensibility through the use of providers, which are Dynamic Link Library files that interface between WMI and software or hardware components.

Each provider contains a set of WMI classes. Each WMI class represents a manageable entity, exposes information through properties, and enables the execution of some actions through methods. Because a provider is designed to access some specific management information, the WMI repository is logically divided into several areas called *namespaces*. Each namespace contains a set of providers with their related classes specific to a management area.

Administrators should also know that SQL Server, as part of its installation process, adds two providers to the WMI repository (WMI Provider for Configuration Management and WMI Provider for Server Events):

▶ The WMI Provider for Configuration Management enables administrators to use WMI to manage SQL Server services, SQL Server client and server network settings, and server aliases. For example, after a connection is established with the WMI provider on a remote computer, not only is it possible to retrieve information about SQL Server instances, but it's also possible to perform actions on them such as starting and stopping the instances.

▶ The WMI Provider for Server Events enables administrators to use WMI to monitor events in SQL Server. Included are Data Definition Language (DDL) events that occur when databases are created, altered, or dropped and when tables are created, altered, or dropped, for example. Additionally, software developers can write code that responds to these events, and they can even author their own set of monitoring tools. Administrators can also create a SQL Server Agent alert that is raised when a specific SQL Server event occurs that is monitored by the WMI Provider for Server Events.

TIP

WMI enables scripting languages such as VBScript or Windows PowerShell or even the WMI command-line utility (Wmic.exe) to manage local and remote servers. This enables administrators to query management information through a SQL-like language called the WMI Query Language (WQL).

To explore the available namespaces, classes, and events, administrators can use a tool such as WMI Explorer.

Event Logs

An additional aspect of monitoring that is often disregarded by some administrators is monitoring the various log files available. SQL Server logs certain system events and user-defined events to the SQL Server error log and the Microsoft Windows application log.

Administrators can use information in the SQL Server error log to troubleshoot problems related to SQL Server. In fact, browsing the SQL Server logs for irregular entries is an essential administration task; preferably, it should be carried out on a daily basis to help administrators spot current or potential problem areas. An application-aware solution, such as Microsoft's System Center Operations Manager (SCOM), helps to automate the process of monitoring SQL (and Lync Server) logs.

SQL Server error log files are simple text files stored on disk, but it is good practice to examine them by using SQL Server Management Studio or by executing the xp_readerrorlog extended stored procedure to prevent SQL operations from being blocked by opening one of the files in a text editor.

A new error log file is created each time an instance of SQL Server is started; however, the sp_cycle_errorlog system stored procedure can be used to cycle the error log files without having to restart the instance of SQL Server.

The Windows application log describes events that occur on the Windows operating system, as well as other events related to SQL Server and SQL Server Agent. Administrators can use the Windows Event Viewer to view the Windows application log and to filter the information. These event logs are another place that administrators look for information about issues that take place with SQL Server.

In the past, administrators had to view the SQL Server and Windows event logs independently. However, the SQL Server Management Studio Log File viewer makes it possible for administrators to combine both sets of logs into a united view.

Using the SQL Server Log File Viewer

The following steps show how to view the log files using SQL Server Management Studio:

1. Click **Start, All Programs, Microsoft SQL Server 2008 R2,** and **SQL Server Management Studio**.

2. Connect to the desired SQL Server database engine instance and expand that instance.

3. In Object Explorer, expand **Management**.

4. Right-click **SQL Server Logs**, click **View**, and then select either **SQL Server Log** or **SQL Server and Windows Log**.

5. Double-click a log file, such as the one shown in Figure 11.16.

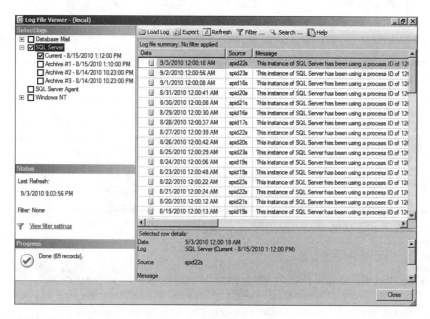

FIGURE 11.16   Select a Log File

In production environments, log files can get quite large and take a long time to open. To avoid huge log files, cycle them on a regular basis. Restarting the SQL Server service is not good practice. Alternatively, the log file can be automatically cycled using the sp_cycle_errorlog system stored procedure. The more writes to the error log, the more often it should be cycled.

To automate the log-cycling process, administrators can use the SQL Server Agent to create a new agent job with a single T-SQL task to execute the stored procedure, or they can include it in a regular daily or weekly maintenance plan. Maintenance plans are covered in-depth earlier in this chapter in "Managing and Maintaining SQL 2008 R2."

Number of Log Files to Maintain

To keep as much historical information as possible, administrators should configure the number of log files to be retained; this number depends on the amount of disk space available and the amount of activity on the server.

The following steps show how to configure the number of log files to be retained:

1. Click **Start, All Programs, Microsoft SQL Server 2008 R2**, and **SQL Server Management Studio**.

2. Connect to the desired SQL Server database engine instance and expand that instance.

3. In Object Explorer, expand **Management**.

4. Right-click **SQL Server Logs** and click **Configure**.

5. As shown in Figure 11.17, select the check box to limit the number of error logs created before they are recycled. SQL Server retains backups of the previous six logs unless you check this option and specify a different maximum number of error log files.

6. Specify a different maximum number of error log files, and click **OK**.

Dynamic Management Views

Another area to retrieve monitoring information is the Master database, which is where SQL Server stores most of its configuration information. It is not a good idea to directly query the master database because Microsoft could change the structure of the master database from version to version or even in service pack releases. Rather than developers building solutions that rely on the Master database schema and risking changes in a service pack ruining the solution, Microsoft has created a set of dynamic management views and functions.

Dynamic management views and functions return valuable information that can be used to monitor the health of a server instance, diagnose problems, and tune performance. They give administrators an easy way to monitor what SQL Server is doing and how it is performing by providing a snapshot of the exact state of SQL Server at the point they are queried. They replace the need to query the system tables or to use other inconvenient methods of retrieving system information in use prior to SQL Server 2005. SQL Server 2005 introduced DMVs, and the latest release, SQL Server 2008 (and SQL Server 2008 R2), includes additional DMVs.

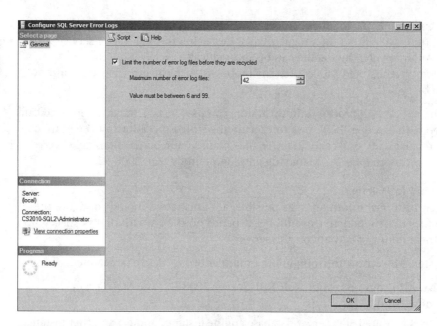

FIGURE 11.17   Limit the Number of Error Logs Created before They Are Recycled

> **NOTE**
>
> Whenever an instance starts, SQL Server saves state and diagnostic data into DMVs.
> When an instance restarts, the information flushes from the views and new data loads.

DMVs and functions are part of the sys schema in the Master database. Administrators can find a list of dynamic views in SQL Server Management Studio under **Master**, **Views**, **System Views**, and the dynamic functions are located under **Master**, **Programmability**, **Functions**, **System Functions**, **Table-valued Functions**. Each dynamic object's name has a dm_ prefix.

For example, earlier in this chapter, in "Managing and Maintaining SQL 2008 R2," the sys.dm_db_index_physical_stats dynamic management function was used to determine the fragmentation percentage of the indexes for efficient database maintenance.

> **NOTE**
>
> For more details about DMVs and functions, refer to *SQL 2008 R2 Unleashed*.

Reliability and Performance Monitor

One of the Windows tools that administrators should be skilled at using is the Reliability and Performance Monitor. Administrators who used Perfmon in Windows Server 2003 might find the Reliability and Performance Monitor in Windows Server 2008 (the tool is called just Performance Monitor in Windows Server 2008 R2) a bit confusing when they first explore it. However, in addition to all the features included in previous versions, it now presents new functionality that can make performance troubleshooting easier and powerful because it provides a more detailed view of Windows server performance and per-instance SQL Server–specific counters.

The Reliability and Performance Monitor can monitor resource usage for the server and provide information specific to SQL Server either locally or for a remote server. It provides a massive set of counters that can be used to capture a baseline of server resource usage, and it can monitor over longer periods to help discover trends. It can also detect abnormal values at a glance for key performance counters on critical SQL Server instances. Additionally, administrators can configure it to produce alerts when preset thresholds are surpassed.

After opening the Reliability and Performance Monitor, shown in Figure 11.18, the % Processor Time counter from the Processor object is automatically monitored in real time with a one-second refresh interval. Additional counters can be appended to the graph by clicking the green plus icon on the toolbar and navigating through objects, which classify the counters into groups.

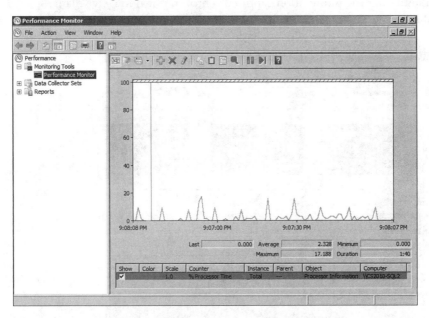

FIGURE 11.18   The Reliability and Performance Monitor

NOTE

When a SQL Server instance is installed on a server, it adds more than 1,000 new performance counters to the Performance Monitor section of the Reliability and Performance Monitor. Of the many performance counters that can be selected when troubleshooting a SQL Server instance, choosing the appropriate key indicators can significantly help administrators quickly isolate bottlenecks and direct their investigation to the appropriate resources for corrective actions.

Additionally, administrators can capture performance counters to log files for long-term analysis by creating Data Collector Sets.

> **NOTE**
>
> Creating Data Collector Sets is beyond the scope of this chapter; for more information about this topic, refer to *SQL 2008 R2 Unleashed*.

Activity Monitor

Undoubtedly, the Reliability and Performance Monitor is a great tool for administrators to monitor resource usage; however, an administrator should first leverage the SQL Server Activity Monitor, shown in Figure 11.19, when needing to gain insight into a SQL Server system's performance. In SQL Server 2008, the Activity Monitor introduced a new performance dashboard with intuitive graphs and performance gauges with drill-down and filtering capabilities. The new tool's look and feel is similar to the Reliability and Performance Monitor, but the information captured is broken down into five main sections dedicated to SQL Server performance monitoring.

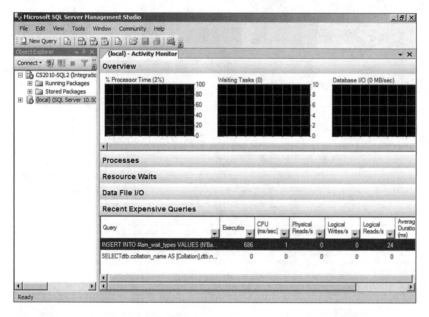

FIGURE 11.19   The Activity Monitor

The sections are Overview, Processes, Resource Waits, Data File I/O, and Recent Expensive Queries. In SQL Server 2008 R2, right-click a SQL Server instance within Object Explorer and specify the Activity Monitor to launch the tool, as shown in Figure 11.19.

▶ **Overview**—This section shows the graphical display of Processor Time (%), Number of Waiting Tasks, Database I/O (MB/Sec), and the Number of Batch Requests/second.

11

▶ **Processes**—This section lists all the active users who are connected to the SQL Server database engine. This is beneficial for administrators because they can click the session IDs, run a SQL Server Profiler trace to capture all its activities, or even kill a specific process.

▶ **Resource Waits**—This section displays resource waits vertically, based on wait categories: CPU, SQLCLR, Network I/O Latch, Lock, Logging, Memory, Buffer I/O, Buffer Latch, and Compilation. From a horizontal perspective, the Wait Time, Recent Wait Time, Average Waiter Counter, and Cumulative Wait Time metrics are published for each Wait Category. Analogous to the Processes section, data can be filtered based on items within a column.

▶ **Data File I/O**—This displays disk-level I/O information related to all the data and log files of user and system databases. Administrators can use this to rapidly recognize databases that are performing badly because of disk bottlenecks.

▶ **Recent Expensive Queries**—This last section gives administrators the opportunity to capture the queries that are performing the worst and negatively influencing a SQL Server instance. Approximately 10 to 15 of the worst and most expensive queries are displayed in the performance dashboard. The actual query is displayed with augmenting metrics such as Execution in Minutes, CPU ms/sec, Physical Reads/sec, Logical Write/sec, Logical Reads/sec, Average Duration in ms, and Plan Count. It is also possible to right-click the most expensive query and show the execution plan.

Data Collectors

The Management Data Warehouse provides administrators with a simple mechanism to track statistics over time. By implementing the Management Data Warehouse, administrators can monitor performance and do trend analysis for the SQL Server 2008 R2 instances they manage.

The Management Data Warehouse is a relational database inside the SQL Server 2008 R2 instance that holds a variety of performance-related statistics. The performance statistics in the Management Data Warehouse are gathered via special data-gathering routines, known as *data collections*. The Management Data Warehouse can include data collection information from a sole instance or can alternatively hold data collected from multiple instances. The data collection process depends on prebuilt SSIS routines and SQL Server Agent jobs, which diminishes the number of tasks administrators need to do to build and maintain a database that contains performance statistics.

SQL Server 2008 R2 provides the following system data collection definitions:

▶ Disk usage

▶ Query activity

Server Activity

Each of these data collection definitions identifies the data to be collected, how often it should be collected, and how long it should be kept in the Management Data Warehouse.

Data collections can be run manually, on a schedule, or continually. Manual and scheduled data collections collect and upload data into the Management Data Warehouse on the same schedule. These types of data collections are known as *noncached collections*. When a data collection runs continually, data is cached in a directory and then uploaded to the Management Data Warehouse from time to time. These are known as *cached collections*.

> **NOTE**
>
> Microsoft has also provided standard reports to enable administrators to drill down into data gathered for each of these collections using SQL Server Management Studio.

Summary

As shown in this chapter, SQL is an integral part of Lync Server 2010 and by properly monitoring and maintaining the SQL Server, one ensures that Lync Server 2010 will continue to run smoothly and perform well for the end users. By creating maintenance plans and performing regular backups, SQL can be fairly trouble free for administrators. Proper monitoring of SQL reduces the chances of unhappy surprises in the Lync Server 2010 deployment. For additional information on SQL, the book *SQL 2008 R2 Unleashed* is highly recommended.

CHAPTER 12

Firewall and Security Requirements

Most companies deploy Lync Server so that they can support IM and conferencing services with users that connect outside the corporate network. To properly protect the Lync Server systems from attack, apply a layered approach to security. In the case of Lync Server, this means a combination of local firewalls, network firewalls, reverse proxies, and a responsible methodology for provisioning access to shares and services.

This chapter lays out approaches for applying layers of security onto the Lync Server systems. Although securing a system and configuring accounts for least privilege can be a fair amount of effort, the benefits reaped in terms of security greatly outweigh the efforts.

Using Network Layer Firewalls with Lync Server

Wikipedia defines a *firewall* as a part of a computer system or network that is designed to block unauthorized access while permitting authorized communications. It is a device or set of devices configured to permit or deny computer applications based on a set of rules and other criteria.

There are several types of firewall techniques including

▶ **Packet filtering**—Packet filtering inspects packets as they are passed through the network and rejects or accepts these packets based on defined rules. Typically, these rules are in the form of source address to destination address on port XYZ, allow. Packet-filtering firewalls are generally fast but can be difficult to configure for applications that dynamically choose ports for communications after an initial handshake.

▶ **Application gateway**—Application gateways apply security enforcement to specific applications. In other words, the gateway understands the applications and can recognize its packets. It makes its decisions based on which applications are allowed to pass through the firewall. Application gateways can be relatively easy to configure but are generally processor intensive and thus cannot handle as much throughput as a packet-filtering firewall.

▶ **Proxy/reverse proxy server**—A proxy server intercepts all messages entering and leaving the network. It inspects the packets and then continues the conversation on behalf of the protected system. In this way, packets never go directly from the source to the protected destination or from the protected source directly to the uncontrolled destination. Not unlike applications gateways, proxy servers are processor intensive.

Network-Based Firewalls

Most implementations of Lync Server involve some form of a network-based firewall, usually in the DMZ (Demilitarized Zone). The purpose of this device is to ensure that only the necessary services on the Lync Server systems are made available externally. Although an administrator might want external users to reach an Edge Server on port 443 for a web-based client, it is probably not desirable for users on the Internet to be able to map a drive to the Edge Server on port 445.

To maximize security, it is fairly common to configure the external services of Lync Server so that not only is there a firewall between the Internet and the Lync Server servers, but that there is also a firewall between the internal network and the Lync Server servers. This can be accomplished either with dual firewalls, or by placing the Lync Server servers into a DMZ on a three or more legged firewall. Dual firewalls are technically more secure because if an attacker compromised the firewall that was exposed externally, he or she must still compromise a second firewall before having access to the internal hosts.

The first step in implementing this type of firewall for Lync Server is to understand what services you plan to make available from outside the network and then to determine exactly which ports and protocols need to be opened on the firewall.

Considerations with Network Address Translation and Lync Server

If a single Edge Server is placed behind a firewall, it is acceptable to enable NAT. NAT effectively takes packets bound for the firewall and forwards them to hosts inside the firewall based on port rules. This enables a company with limited numbers of routable IP addresses to support multiple services with fewer IP addresses. It also provides a layer of security by requiring the firewall to process the packet first before it reaches the eventual destination. In addition, it enables protected systems to hide their IP information because they never appear to be a source of a packet to a system on the Internet; the firewall always appears to be the source.

> **TIP**
>
> If you enable NAT for the external firewall, configure firewall filters that are used for traffic from the Internet to the Edge Server with destination network address translation (DNAT). Similarly, configure and filter for traffic going from the Edge Server to the Internet with source network address translation (SNAT). Important to note is that the inbound and outbound filters for this purpose must use the same internal and external addresses. If externally, the Edge is 11.22.33.44 and is mapped to an Edge Server at 10.1.1.44. The mapping for the Edge to talk to the Internet needs traffic from 10.1.1.44 to come from 11.22.33.44. Although this might seem obvious, there are many situations where all internal hosts appear to come from the same IP address. This is called *PAT* or *Port Address Translation* or is sometimes called *NAT overload*.

> **CAUTION**
>
> If multiple Edge Servers are deployed in a load-balanced fashion, the external firewall cannot be configured for NAT. Regardless of the use of load balancers or not, an internal firewall used to protect Edge Servers cannot be NAT enabled for the internal IP address of an Edge Server.

Ports to Open

The specific ports needed to open on a firewall vary somewhat depending on what services are placed into the DMZ and which services need to be accessible from the Internet. This section summarizes commonly deployed DMZ roles and the ports necessary to support them. The description calls out the port, traffic type, type of firewall it applies to (internal or external), and the purpose for the opening.

Audio/Video Edge Service Port Ranges

TCP 50,000 through 59,999—Incoming, these ports are needed for connections with Federated partners running Lync Server. Federated partners still running OCS 2007 also need UDP 50,000 through 59,999. This is to support RTP (Real-Time Transport Protocol). Federated A/V to a partner running an OCS 2007 R2 edge environment works over 3478/UDP or 443/TCP. This applies to the external firewall.

TCP 443 (STUN/TCP)—Outbound, for media transfer between internal users and external users. This applies to both the internal and external firewalls.

UDP 3478 (STUN/UDP)—Inbound and outbound for media exchange between internal users and external users. This applies to both the internal and external firewalls.

TCP 5062 (SIP/MTLS)—Outbound, for authentication of A/V users. This applies to the internal firewall.

Access Edge Service Port Ranges

TCP 5061 (TCP/MTLS)—Incoming and outgoing, usually to a director or the virtual IP of a load balancer. This applies to the internal firewall.

UDP 53 (DNS)—Outgoing, to enable the Access Edge to find other systems. The Access Edge should be configured to use an external DNS, to avoid unnecessary openings in the internal firewall. This might require using the host file to find systems also in the DMZ. This applies to the external firewall.

TCP 80 (HTTP)—Outgoing, to enable the system to download Certificate Revocation Lists. This applies to the external firewall.

TCP 443 (HTTPS)—Outgoing, to enable the system to download Certificate Revocation Lists that are published with SSL. This applies to the external firewall.

TCP 5061 (SIP/MTLS)—Incoming and outgoing. This applies to the external firewall.

Web Conferencing Edge Service

TCP 8057 (PSOM/MTLS)—Outbound, for communications between Web Conferencing Servers and the Web Conferencing Edge Service. This applies to the internal firewall.

TCP 443 (PSOM/TLS)—Inbound for access of remote, anonymous, and federated users into internal Web Conferences. This applies to the external firewall.

All Edge Servers

TCP 4443 (HTTPS)—Inbound, to enable for replication of configuration data to Edge Servers from the Central Management Server. This applies to the internal firewall.

Using Operating System Firewalls with Lync Server

In Windows Server 2003 SP1, Microsoft introduced an integrated firewall into the Windows operating system. As with most Microsoft products, it has improved with each iteration. Flash forward to Windows Server 2008 and you find that the integrated firewall is quite good. Lync Server does an excellent job of integrating into the Windows Server Firewall at the time of installation.

Layering an operating system layer firewall with a network layer firewall is an excellent way to improve overall security of a system with minimal expense. By layering these two together, if the network firewall becomes compromised, the attacker has to pierce the OS layer firewall to compromise the systems. Similarly, given that many attack vectors can come from within the company itself, the OS layer firewall offers protection from trusted systems that might become compromised.

Configuring the Windows Server 2008 Firewall for Lync Server

If the Windows Firewall is enabled and started at the time of installation of Lync Server components, the necessary exceptions will be created automatically.

> **CAUTION**
>
> Although many administrators are tempted to disable the Windows Firewall, it is certainly worth leaving it in place with the necessary rules configured. If you are convinced you don't want to use the Windows Firewall, and don't plan to use a third-party operating system layer firewall, leave the Windows Firewall service running, but configure the rules to allow all traffic to pass unhindered. This prevents possible problems interacting with the Windows Filtering Platform.

For administrators who installed Lync Server without the firewall on and want to enable it and backfill the rules, Table 12.1 details the rules created to support various Lync Server roles.

TABLE 12.1   Lync Server 2010 Firewall Rules

Name	Program	Protocol	Local Port	Remote Port
OCS SQL RTC Access	C:\Program Files\Microsoft SQL Server\MSSQL10.RTC\MSSQL\Binn\ sqlservr.exe	TCP	Any	Any
OCS SQL RTC Access	C:\Program Files\Microsoft SQL Server\MSSQL10.RTC\MSSQL\Binn\ sqlservr.exe	UDP	Any	Any
OCS SQL RTC Access	C:\Program Files\Microsoft SQL Server\MSSQL10.RTC\MSSQL\Binn\ sqlservr.exe	TCP	Any	Any
OCS SQL RTC Access	C:\Program Files\Microsoft SQL Server\MSSQL10.RTC\MSSQL\Binn\ sqlservr.exe	UDP	Any	Any
SQL Browser	Any	UDP	1434	Any
CS FTA	C:\Program Files\Microsoft Lync Server 2010\File Transfer Agent\ FileTransferAgent.exe	Any	Any	Any
CS master	C:\Program Files\Microsoft Lync Server 2010\Master Replicator Agent\ MasterReplicatorAgent.exe	Any	Any	Any
CS OcsAppServer Host.exe	C:\Program Files\Microsoft Lync Server 2010\Application Host\ OcsAppServerHost.exe	Any	Any	Any
CS Replica	C:\Program Files\Microsoft Lync Server 2010\Server\Replica Replicator Agent\ReplicaReplicatorAgent.exe	Any	Any	Any

TABLE 12.1   Lync Server 2010 Firewall Rules

Name	Program	Protocol	Local Port	Remote Port
CS rtcappsrv	C:\Program Files\Microsoft Lync Server 2010\Application Host\ OcsAppServerMaster.exe	Any	Any	Any
CS rtcasmcu	C:\Program Files\Microsoft Lync Server 2010\OCSMCU\Application Sharing\ASMCUSvc.exe	Any	Any	Any
CS rtcavmcu	C:\Program Files\Microsoft Lync Server 2010\OCSMCU\AV Conferencing\ AVMCUSvc.exe	Any	Any	Any
CS rtcdatamcu	C:\Program Files\Microsoft Lync Server 2010\Web Conferencing\ DataMCUSvc.exe	Any	Any	Any
CS rtcimmcu	C:\Program Files\Microsoft Lync Server 2010\OCSMCU\IM Conferencing\ IMMCUSvc.exe	Any	Any	Any
CS rtcmedsrv	C:\Program Files\Microsoft Lync Server 2010\Mediation Server\ MediationServerSvc.exe	Any	Any	Any
CS rtcmeetingmcu	C:\Program Files\Microsoft Lync Server 2010\OCSMCU\Web Meeting Conferencing\MeetingMCUSvc.exe	Any	Any	Any
CS rtcsrv	C:\Program Files\Microsoft Lync Server 2010\Server\Core\RTCSrv.exe	Any	Any	Any
CS TCP13457	Any	TCP	13457	Any
CS TCP135	Any	TCP	135	Any
CS TCP443	Any	TCP	443	Any
CS TCP444	Any	TCP	444	Any
CS TCP4443	Any	TCP	4443	Any
CS TCP445	Any	TCP	445	Any
CS TCP80	Any	TCP	80	Any
CS TCP8060	Any	TCP	8060	Any
CS TCP8061	Any	TCP	8061	Any
CS TCP8080	Any	TCP	8080	Any

TABLE 12.1   Lync Server 2010 Firewall Rules

Name	Program	Protocol	Local Port	Remote Port
Remote Administration (NP-In)	System	TCP	445	Any
Remote Administration (RPC)	%SystemRoot%\system32\svchost.exe	TCP	RPC Dynamic Ports	Any
Remote Administration (RPC-EPMAP)	%SystemRoot%\system32\svchost.exe	TCP	RPC Endpoint Mapper	Any
Remote Desktop (TCP-In)	System	TCP	3389	Any
Remote Service Management (NP-In)	System	TCP	445	Any
Remote Service Management (RPC)	%SystemRoot%\system32\services.exe	TCP	RPC Dynamic Ports	Any
Remote Service Management (RPC-EPMAP)	%SystemRoot%\system32\svchost.exe	TCP	RPC Endpoint Mapper	Any
Secure Socket Tunneling Protocol (SSTP-In)	System	TCP	443	Any
World Wide Web Services (HTTPS Traffic-In)	System	TCP	443	Any
Windows Firewall Remote Management (RPC)	%SystemRoot%\system32\svchost.exe	TCP	RPC Dynamic Ports	Any
Windows Firewall Remote Management (RPC-EPMAP)	%SystemRoot%\system32\svchost.exe	TCP	RPC Endpoint Mapper	Any
Windows Remote Management - Compatibility Mode (HTTP-In)	System	TCP	80	Any

12

TABLE 12.1 Lync Server 2010 Firewall Rules

Name	Program	Protocol	Local Port	Remote Port
Windows Remote Management (HTTP-In)	System	TCP	5985	Any
World Wide Web Services (HTTP Traffic-In)	System	TCP	80	Any

Using Reverse Proxies with Lync Server

Reverse proxies, such as ISA 2006 SP1 or Forefront Threat Management Gateway (TMG), are excellent ways to securely publish applications, such as Lync Server, to users on the Internet. By controlling specific ports to pass traffic and limiting destination URLs to only the desired paths, you can safely pass traffic from the Internet to Lync Server roles. The following sections discuss how to configure reverse proxies to work with Lync Server.

Configuring ISA 2006 SP1 to Support Lync Server

Although it has been around for a while, many environments already have ISA 2006 SP1 deployed for protecting applications, such as Exchange, SharePoint, or IIS. As such, it is typical for these environments to leverage their existing ISA implementation to publish Lync Server. The typical reasons for deploying a reverse proxy, such as ISA for Lync Server, include the following:

▶ Enabling external users to expand distribution groups

▶ Enabling external users to download meeting content

▶ Enabling external devices to connect to Device Update Service for updates

▶ Enabling remote users to download files from the Address Book Service

Assuming ISA 2006 SP1 is already installed and network cards are already configured, the following steps outline how to publish a Lync Server Edge Server deployment through ISA 2006 SP1:

▶ Configure a web farm FQDN

▶ Request and configure SSL certificates

▶ Create a web server publishing rule

▶ Configure authentication and certification on IIS virtual directories

▶ Create an external DNS entry

▶ Verify access

Configure Web Farm FQDN

During the setup of Enterprise pools and Standard Editions servers, there is an option to configure an external web farm Fully Qualified Domain Name (FQDN) on the web farm FQDN's page during the Create Pool Wizard (or the Deploy Server Wizard). If an URL was not chosen during this process, it is necessary to configure the settings using the following procedure:

1. Click **Start, App Programs, Microsoft Communications Server 2010,** and **Communications Server Topology Builder.**

2. Choose **Download Topology from existing deployment** and click **OK.**

3. In Topology Builder, in the console tree, navigate to your Enterprise or Standard pool, and right-click the name of the pool.

4. Click **Edit Properties.**

5. In the middle of the Edit Properties screen, there is a field under external web services titled FQDN. Enter the FQDN to be used for Web Services and click **OK.**

6. In the left pane, right-click **Lync Server,** and click **Publish topology.**

7. Click **Next.**

8. Select the database where the topology will live, and click **Next.**

9. Click **Finish.**

Request and Configure SSL Certificates

Depending on where your SSL certificates are coming from, it might be necessary to install the Root Certificate Authority's certificate into the Root Trust Container on the ISA 2006 SP1 server.

In the case of an SSL certificate that comes from a well-known vendor, odds are the Root CA is already in the Windows trust list. If the SSL certificate comes from a lesser known third-party CA, you can typically download the Root CA's certificate from the vendor in question. In the case of an internal PKI, export the Root CA's certificate with these steps:

1. Log on to the Root CA.

2. From the Start menu, go to the run line, type **MMC,** and press **Enter.**

3. From the File menu, click **Add/Remove Snap-in.**

4. Click **Add.**

5. Select **Certificates,** and then click **Add.**

6. Choose **Computer** account and click **Finish.**

7. Click **Close** and then click **OK.**

8. Expand **Certificates (Local Computer), Personal,** and **Certificates.**

9. In the right pane, look for the Root CA certificate. It will be issued to itself and issued by itself. Right-click the **Root CA** certificate.

10. Click **All Tasks,** and choose **Export.**

11. When the Certificate Export Wizard launches, click **Next**.

12. When asked about exporting the private key, click **NO, do not export the private key**. Click **Next**.

WARNING

In step 12, it is important not to export the private key or else it could potentially be used to impersonate the Root CA.

---

13. Select the format for the export, typically **DER Encoded Binary X.509 (CER)**, and click **Next**.

14. Browse to a location where you will save the certificate, and give it a name to save under. Click **Next**.

15. Click **Finish**, and click **OK**.

The .cer file that was exported is the public key certificate of the Root CA. This is used to identify the Root CA. This certificate will be imported into any system that needs to trust certificates whose chains are initially anchored by this CA.

In the case of an Active Directory–integrated Root CA, often called an *Enterprise Root CA*, the root certificate is already trusted by all domain members. Because PKI best practices call for the Root CA to be offline when not in use, it is often necessary to perform the import manually or else to push out the root certificate through Group Policy. Because ISA 2006 SP1 is typically deployed in a workgroup rather than a domain, it can't benefit from the Group Policy method, so it is necessary to manually install the Root CA certificate with the following steps:

1. Log on to the ISA 2006 SP1 server.

2. From the Start menu, go to the run line, type **MMC**, and press **Enter**.

3. From the File menu, click **Add/Remove Snap-in**.

4. Click **Add**.

5. Select **Certificates**, and click **Add**.

6. Choose **Computer** account, and click **Finish**.

7. Click **Close**, and click **OK**.

8. Expand **Certificates (Local Computer)**, **Trusted Root Certification Authorities**, and **Certificates**, as shown in Figure 12.1.

9. In the right pane, right-click on an empty space, click **All Tasks**, and select **Import**.

10. When the Certificate Import Wizard appears, click **Next**.

11. Browse to the location where the Root CA certificate is located, as shown in Figure 12.2. Typically, this is removable media because the ISA 2006 SP1 server likely doesn't have connectivity to a location where such a certificate would usually be stored. Click **Next**.

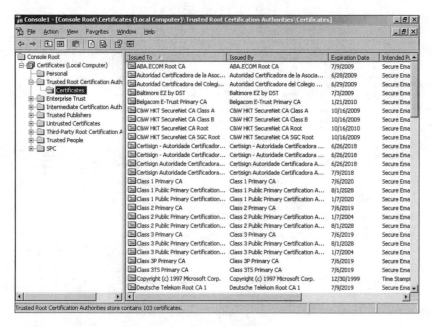

FIGURE 12.1   Trusted Root Certificate Authorities

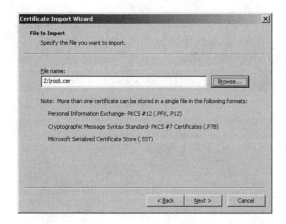

FIGURE 12.2   Importing the Certificate File

12. Select **Place all certificates in the following store and leave the value set to Trusted Root Certification Authorities**, and click **Next**.

13. Click **Finish**, and **OK** and the Root CA will appear in the trusted container, as shown in Figure 12.3.

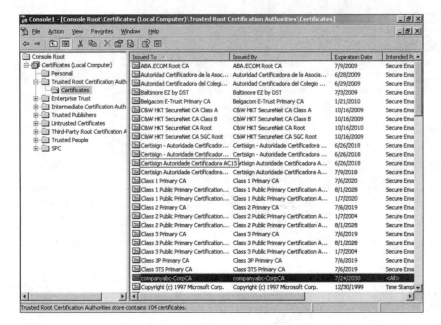

FIGURE 12.3   Viewing the Newly Trusted Root CA

The next step is to export the Edge Server's SSL certificates in the same manner as the Root CA's certificate was exported in the previous example. It is then copied to the ISA 2006 SP1 server and imported into its Personal store for the computer account, using essentially the same steps as the Root CA certificate import in the previous example. This makes the certificate available for later configuration of ISA 2006 SP1.

Configure Web Publishing Rules

Web publishing rules are used by ISA Server to securely publish internal resources over the Internet. In addition to providing web service URLs for the various Lync Server virtual IIS directories, it is necessary to create publishing rules for simple URLs. For each simple URL, it is necessary to create an individual rule on the reverse proxy that references that URL. The following procedures can be used to create web publishing rules:

1. Log on to the ISA 2006 SP1 server.
2. Click **Start, All Programs, Microsoft ISA Server**, and **ISA Server Management**.
3. In the left pane, expand the name of the ISA Server.
4. Right-click **Firewall Policy**, click **New**, and click **Web Site Publishing Rule**.
5. On the Welcome to the New Web Publishing Rule page, enter a name for the publishing rule that will be easy to reference in the future. Click **Next**.

6. On the Select Rule Action page, choose **Allow**. Click **Next**.

7. On the Publishing Type page, choose **Publish a single Web site or load balancer**. Click **Next**.

8. On the Server Connection Security page, choose **Use SSL to connect to the published Web server or server farm**. Click **Next**.

9. On the internal Publishing Details page, enter the FQDN of the internal web farm where meeting content and the Address Book are hosted in the internal Site name box.

> **NOTE**
>
> The ISA Server must be able to resolve the FQDN entered in step 9. If the ISA Server will not be able to reach a DNS server that can resolve the FQDN, you will need to select **Use a computer name or IP address to connect to the published server** and then enter the IP address in the Computer name or IP address box.

10. On the internal Publishing Details page, enter /* as the path of the published folder, as shown in Figure 12.4. Click **Next**.

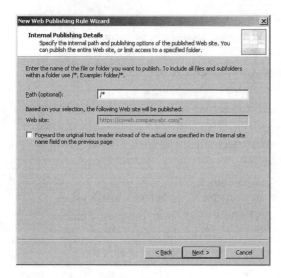

FIGURE 12.4   Updating the Path

11. On the Public Name Details page, verify that **This domain name** is selected under **Accept Requests for**. Type the FQDN of the external web farm into the Public Name box, as shown in Figure 12.5. Click **Next**.

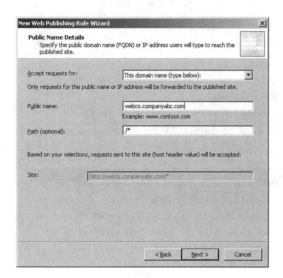

FIGURE 12.5   Completing the New Web Publishing Rule Wizard

12. On the Select Web Listener page, click **New**.

13. On the Welcome to the New Web Listener Wizard page, enter a name for the new web listener in the Web listener name box. Click **Next**.

14. On the Client Connection Security page, choose **Require SSL secured connections with clients**. Click **Next**.

15. On the Web Listener IP address page, select **external**, and click **Select IP Addresses**.

16. On the external Listener IP selection page, select **Specified IP address on the ISA Server computer in the selected network**, select the IP address, and click **Add**. Click **Next**.

17. On the Listener SSL Certificates page, click **Assign a certificate for each IP address**, and select the IP address that was added in step 16. Click **Select Certificate**.

18. On the Select Certificate page, select the certificate matching the public name selected in step 11, as shown in Figure 12.6 and click **Select**. Click **Next**.

19. On the Authentication Setting page, select **No Authentication**. Click **Next**.

20. On the Single Sign On Setting page, click **Next**.

21. On the Completing the Web Listener Wizard page, verify the information and click **Finish**.

22. On the Authentication Delegation page, select **No Delegation, but client may authenticate directly**. Click **Next**.

23. On the User Set page, click **Next**.

24. On the Completing the New Web Publishing Rule Wizard page, verify the rule settings and click **Finish**.

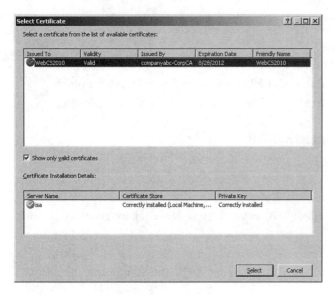

FIGURE 12.6   Selecting the Certificate

25. Click **Apply,** as shown in Figure 12.7 to save the changes and update the configuration.

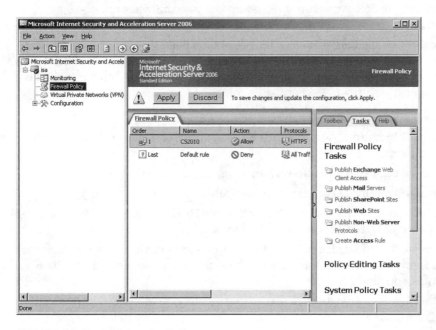

FIGURE 12.7   Applying the Policy

To modify the properties of the web publishing rule, perform the following steps:

1. Log on to the ISA 2006 SP1 server.

2. Click **Start, All Programs, Microsoft ISA Server**, and **ISA Server Management**.

3. In the left pane, expand the name of the ISA Server and click **Firewall Policy**.

4. In the details page, right-click the secure web server publishing rule, and click **Properties**.

5. On the Properties page, click the **From** tab.

6. In the This rule applies to traffic from these sources list, click **Anywhere**, and click **Remove**.

7. Click **Add**.

8. In the Add Network Entities dialog box, expand Networks, click **external**, click **Add**, and click **Close**.

9. Click the **To** tab.

10. Select the **Forward the original host header instead of the actual one** check box.

11. Click the **Bridging** tab.

12. Select the **Redirect request to SSL port** check box and specify port **443**.

13. Click the **Public Name** tab.

14. Add the **Subject Alternate Names** to this field.

15. Click **Apply**, and click **OK**.

16. Click **Apply** in the details pane to save and update the configuration.

Configure Authentication and Certification on IIS Virtual Directories

To correctly pass SSL encrypted packets through the reverse proxy into the IIS directories on the Lync Server servers, make sure that certification is properly configured on IIS. This task can be performed with the following steps:

1. Log in to a published Lync Server server.

2. Click **Start, All Programs, Administrative Tools** and select **Internet Information Services (IIS) Manager**.

3. In the IIS manager, expand the **ServerName**, and expand **Sites**.

4. Click **Communications Server external Web Site**.

5. In the Actions pane, click **Bindings**. Verify that the HTTPS is associated with port 4443, as shown in Figure 12.8 and click **HTTPS**.

6. In the Edit Site Binding dialog box, verify that the correct certificate is associated, as shown in Figure 12.9. This should be the certificate used in the previous ISA 2006 SP1 Listener configuration.

7. On the Directory Security tab, click **Server Certificate** located under Secure Communications.

8. On the Welcome to the Web Server Certificate Wizard page, click **Next**.

9. On the Server Certificate page, click **Assign an existing certificate**, and click **Next**.

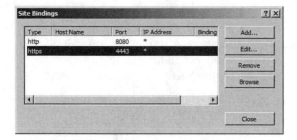

FIGURE 12.8   Verifying the HTTPS Port

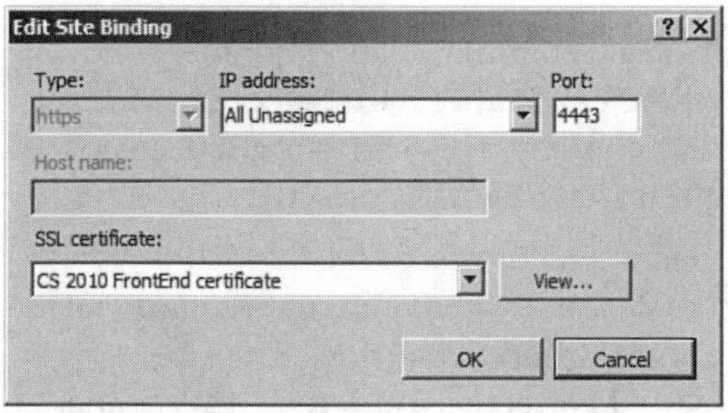

FIGURE 12.9   Verifying the SSL Certificate

10. On the SSL Port page, verify that the value is set to **4443** in the **SSL port this Web site should use** box and click **Next**.

11. On the Certificate Summary page, verify the settings, and click **Next**.

12. Click **Finish**.

13. Click **OK** to close the Default Web Site Properties dialog box.

Create a DNS Record in the External DNS

For clients on the Internet to find Lync Server services, add an Address (A) record to an external DNS that is authoritative for the DNS domain that services Lync Server externally. This includes (A) or (SRV) records, as described in Chapter 10, "Dependent Services."

NOTE

The procedure for creating records depends on the DNS server used. In the case of an externally hosted DNS, it might be as simple as calling your service provider and requesting the records.

Keep in mind that it might take several minutes to as much as a few hours for the new records to propagate to an external DNS server and become available to clients.

12

Verify Access

Before making Lync Server available externally, the administrator should verify that the environment is working correctly through the reverse proxy. Assuming the firewall rules are in place and that the necessary DNS records are available externally, the following procedure helps administrators determine whether their environment is configured correctly:

1. From an externally connected computer, open a web browser and type https:// externalwebfarmFQDN/abs/ where externalwebfarmFQDN is the external FQDN of the web farm that hosts the Address Book Service. If the URL returns an HTTP challenge, the site is configured correctly. You receive this challenge because the Address Book Server folder is configured to use Microsoft Windows Integrated Authentication.

2. From an externally connected computer, open a web browser and type https:// externalwebfarmFQDN/conf/Tshoot.html where externalwebfarmFQDN is the external FQDN of the web farm that hosts meeting content. This URL should display the troubleshooting page for web conferencing if it is configured correctly.

3. From an externally connected computer, open a web browser and type https:// externalwebfarmFQDN/GroupExpansion/service.asmx where externalwebfarmFQDN is the external FQDN of the web farm that hosts Group Expansion. If the URL returns an HTTP challenge, the site is configured correctly. You receive this challenge because the Address Book Server folder is configured to use Microsoft Windows Integrated Authentication.

Configuring TMG to Support Lync Server

Forefront TMG is the logical successor of ISA 2006 SP1 and is the other primary choice for use as a reverse proxy with Lync Server. The high-level steps for publishing Lync Server with Forefront TMG are the same as those for ISA 2006 SP1. The specific steps that vary due to the slightly different interface are detailed in the following sections.

TIP

Because Forefront TMG is a native 64-bit application, whereas ISA 2006 SP1 is a 32-bit application, it has the potential to service a much larger number of connections and could be a key decision point for large deployments.

Configure Web Publishing Rules

Web publishing rules are used by Forefront TMG Server to securely publish internal resources over the Internet. In addition to providing web service URLs for the various Lync Server virtual IIS directories, it is also necessary to create publishing rules for simple URLs. For each simple URL, it is necessary to create an individual rule on the reverse proxy that references that URL. The following procedures can be used to create web publishing rules:

1. Log on to the Forefront TMG Server.

2. Click **Start**, **All Programs**, **Microsoft Forefront TMG**, and **Forefront TMG Management**.

3. In the left pane, expand the name of the **TMG Server**.

4. Right-click **Firewall Policy**, click **New**, and click **Web Site Publishing Rule**, as shown in Figure 12.10.

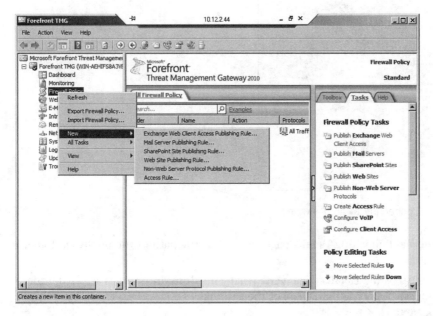

FIGURE 12.10   Creating a New Website Publishing Rule

5. On the Welcome to the New Web Publishing Rule page, enter a name for the publishing rule that will be easy to reference in the future. Click **Next**.

6. On the Select Rule Action page, choose **Allow**. Click **Next**.

7. On the Publishing Type page, select **Publish a single Web site or load balancer** and click **Next**.

8. On the Server Connection Security page, choose **Use SSL to connect to the published Web server or server farm**. Click **Next**.

9. On the internal Publishing Details page, enter the FQDN of the internal web farm where meeting content and the Address Book are hosted in the internal Site name box.

NOTE

The ISA Server must be able to resolve the FQDN entered in step 9. If the ISA Server will not be able to reach a DNS server that can resolve the FQDN, select **Use a computer name or IP address to connect to the published server** and then enter the IP address in the **Computer name or IP address** box, as shown in Figure 12.11.

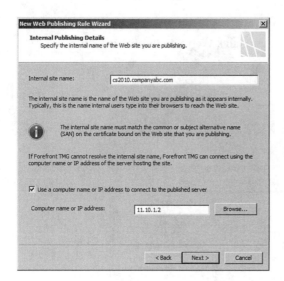

FIGURE 12.11   Connecting to an IP Address

10. On the internal Publishing Details page, enter /* as the path of the published folder. Click **Next**.

11. On the Publish Name Details page, verify that **This domain name** is selected under Accept Requests for. Type the FQDN of the external web farm into the Public Name box. Click **Next**.

12. On the Select Web Listener page, click **New**.

13. On the Welcome to the New Web Listener Wizard page, enter a name for the new web listener in the **Web listener name** box. Click **Next**.

14. On the Client Connection Security page, choose **Require SSL secured connections with clients**. Click **Next**.

15. On the Web Listener IP address page, select **external**, and click **Select IP Addresses**.

16. On the external Listener IP selection page, select **Specified IP address on the TMG Server computer in the selected network**, select an IP address, and click **Add**. Click **Next**.

17. On the Listener SSL Certificates page, click **Assign a certificate for each IP address**, and select the IP address that was added in step 16. Click **Select Certificate**.

18. On the Select Certificate page, select the certificate matching the public name selected in step 11, as shown in Figure 12.12 and click **Select**. Click **Next**.

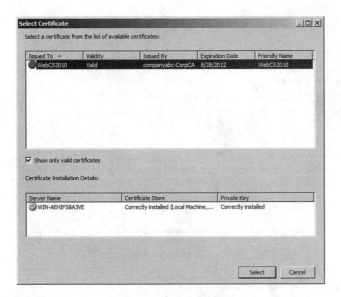

FIGURE 12.12   Selecting the Certificate

19. On the Authentication Settings page, select **No Authentication**. Click **Next**.

20. On the Single Sign On Settings page, click **Next**.

21. On the Complete the New Web Listener Wizard page, click **Finish**.

22. Returning to the Select Web Listener page, select the listener that was just created and click **Next**.

23. On the Authentication Delegation page, select **No delegation but the client may authenticate directly**. Click **Next**.

24. On the User Sets page, click **Next**.

25. On the Completing the New Web Publishing Rule Wizard page, verify the rule settings and click **Finish**.

26. Click **Apply** to save the changes, as shown in Figure 12.13 and update the configuration.

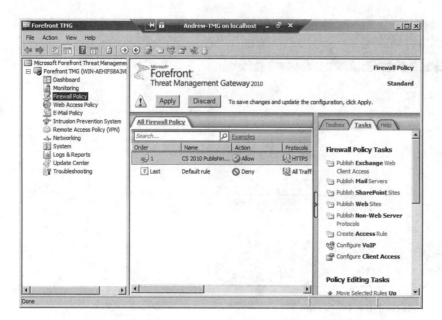

FIGURE 12.13   Applying the Firewall Policy

Securing Service Accounts

Most Microsoft applications use service accounts, and Lync Server is no exception. Although some applications use service accounts running as System or Network Service, many IT groups prefer to use named accounts for services. This often results in simplified management of permissions because accounts can use descriptive names and it makes it easier to apply local policies to these service accounts. It also enables you to create a single domain-based service account to use across multiple servers. This also makes it easier to ensure that rights are consistent across multiple servers in the same deployment. Regardless of the methodology used, it is worthwhile to put some effort toward securing the service accounts.

CAUTION

In too many environments, service accounts are given high-level rights to avoid taking the time to determine granular rights. Often in these situations, multiple members of IT are familiar with the logon name and password of these service accounts because they might be used for configuring certain applications. This results in multiple people having access to a high privilege account with no accountability because there is no way to know which person used the account. This is generally considered a bad idea for security.

Configuring Service Accounts with Least Privilege

As a general rule, when creating service accounts to work with applications, special care should be taken to ensure that the services have only the rights they need to do their jobs. Rather than simply making a service account a local administrator on a given server, take the time to determine what rights it actually needs and grant them through the Local Security Policy editor.

1. Click **Start**, **Administrative Tools**, and **Local Security Policy**.
2. Expand **Local Policies**.
3. Click **User Rights Assignment**, as shown in Figure 12.14.

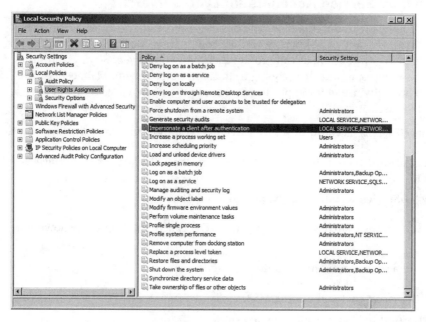

FIGURE 12.14   Viewing User Rights Assignment

4. Choose a right that needs to be granted from the right pane and double-click it.
5. On the Local Security Setting tab, click **Add User or Group**.
6. Add the service account into the available window, and click **Check Names**. Click OK.
7. Click **OK** again to grant the right.

Some local rights that are typically granted for applications include

▶ Access this computer from the network

▶ Allow log on locally

▶ Back up files and directories

▶ Generate security audits

▶ Load and unload device drivers

▶ Log on as a service

These types of granular rights can easily replace the need to make a service account a local administrator on a server. Coupling limited rights with a Managed Service Account can greatly reduce the possibility of a high privilege account from becoming comprimised and used to take control of a system.

Utilizing Managed Service Accounts for Lync Server

Active Directory 2008 R2 introduced a new type of service account known as a managed service account. Managed service accounts work like computer accounts in Active Directory. That is to say, they automatically rotate their passwords every 30 days, and they cannot be used by a person to interactively log in to a computer system. Managed service accounts are exceptionally useful for applications that require named accounts and have a need for heightened security.

To create a managed service account in Active Directory, you must use PowerShell:

1. Click **Start**, **Administrative Tools**, and **Active Directory Module for Windows PowerShell**.
2. Type **New-ADServiceAccount MSAName–enabled $true**.

This creates an MSA in the Managed Service Accounts OU called MSAName, as shown in Figure 12.15.

To use this MSA on a server, perform the following steps:

1. Log on to the server that will use the MSA.
2. Click **Start**, **Administrative Tools**, and **Services**.
3. When prompted for permissions, click **Continue**.
4. Right-click the service that will use the MSA and click **Properties**.
5. Click **Log On** tab, click This Account, and type the name of the MSA in the format of *domain\MSAname*. Click **OK**.
6. Select the service and click **Start the Service**. Verify that the MSA name appears in the Log On As column.

From this point forward, the service account updates its own password every 30 days, as a computer account does in Active Directory. This results in a secure password that isn't known by any administrator on the network.

Note that only one computer can use a particular Managed Service Account, so if you have a need for multiple computers to use a Managed Service Account, configure one MSA per system that needs to use one.

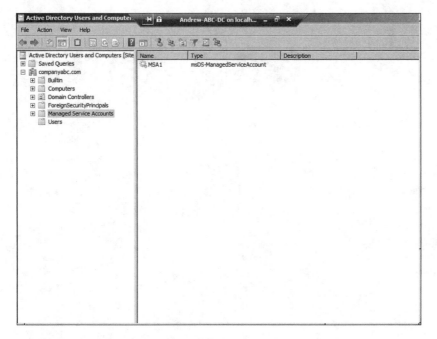

FIGURE 12.15   Creating a Managed Service Account

Summary

As shown seen in this chapter, properly securing a Lync Server 2010 implementation is a valuable process because it protects the servers from potential exploitation. By utilizing existing technologies such as firewalls and proxies, one can greatly reduce the attack surface of Lync Server 2010. Through the use of limited rights and managed service accounts, one can greatly reduce the possibility of unauthorized users gaining access to the new system.

Configuring protective features in the operating system is a relatively painless process that can go a long way toward securing the overall implementation. Tasks as simple as limiting rights to shares and controlling services will also serve to reduce the attack surface of a Lync Server 2010 deployment. As mentioned in this chapter, this process of locking down systems is especially important if hosts will be accessed from outside the organization or if sensitive information will be communicated within Lync Server 2010.

PART IV
Administration and Management

IN THIS PART

Monitoring Microsoft Lync Server 2010

Overview

System Center Operations Manager (OpsMgr) 2007 R2 provides the best-of-breed approach to monitoring and managing Lync Server 2010 within the environment. OpsMgr helps to identify specific environmental conditions before they evolve into problems through the use of monitoring and alerting components.

OpsMgr provides a timely view of important Lync Server 2010 conditions and intelligently links problems to knowledge provided within the monitoring rules. Critical events and known issues are identified and matched to technical reference articles in the Microsoft Knowledge Base for troubleshooting and quick problem resolution. The management pack also provides for synthetic transactions to monitor services end-to-end.

The monitoring is accomplished using standard operating system components such as Windows Management Instrumentation (WMI), Windows event logs, and Windows performance counters, along with Lync Server 2010–specific API calls and PowerShell cmdlets. OpsMgr-specific components are also designed to perform synthetic transactions and track the health and availability of network services.

In addition, OpsMgr provides a reporting feature that enables administrators to track problems and trends occurring on the network. Reports can be generated automatically, providing network administrators, managers, and decision makers with a current and long-term historical view of environmental trends. These reports can be delivered through e-mail or stored on file shares to power web pages.

The following sections focus on defining OpsMgr as a monitoring system for Lync Server 2010. This chapter provides specific analysis of the way OpsMgr operates and presents OpsMgr design best practices, specific to deployment for Lync Server 2010 monitoring.

OpsMgr Lync Server 2010 Monitoring

Operations Manager 2007 R2 includes one of the best management packs for monitoring and maintaining Lync Server 2010. This management pack was developed by the product group and includes information about the product.

The Lync Server 2010 management pack monitors all the Lync Server 2010 server roles and has separate views for each of the roles to enable targeted monitoring in the console. The Lync Server 2010 management includes the following features:

- **Automatic Lync topology discovery through the Central Discovery script**—The Central Discovery script is a PowerShell script that runs on an automatically selected Central Discovery Watcher Node. This is the Front End pool where the Central Management Store is installed. The script automatically discovers and initiates monitoring of all Lync roles, components, and services.

- **Automatic monitoring of pools**—Front End and Edge pools are discovered automatically and monitored for a variety of availability, configuration, performance, and security conditions.

- **Automatic alerting**—The Lync Server management alerts on thousands of different conditions, enabling the administrator to immediately be aware of any potential problems in the infrastructure.

- **Synthetic transactions to simulate user traffic**—The management pack leverages the built-in Lync Server synthetic transaction PowerShell cmdlets.

The Microsoft Lync Server Management Pack monitors all aspects of the Microsoft Lync Server infrastructure. The management pack structures the monitoring into the services paradigm used by Lync Server. These services include

- Application Service
- Archiving Service
- Central Management Service
- Conferencing Service
- Core Service
- Edge Service
- Mediation Service
- Provisioning Service
- Registration Service
- User Service
- Web Service

On all these services, administrators can generate availability reports to ensure that the servers and systems are meeting the Service Level Agreements (SLAs) set by the organization.

For each of the services, the management pack has views for

- Service alerts

- Service performance

- Service state

In addition, the OpsMgr platform monitors the Lync Server 2010 dependencies to ensure that the Lync Server 2010 infrastructure doesn't fail due to a failure of the dependent systems such as the operating system, Active Directory, DNS, and IIS. The features of the management packs for the following major systems include

- **Windows Operating System Management Pack**—Monitors and alerts all the major elements of the Windows server that Lync Server 2010 runs on, including processor, memory, network, disk, and event logs. It gathers performance metrics and alerts on thresholds, and critical events.

- **Active Directory Management Pack**—Monitors and alerts on Active Directory key metrics such as replication latency, domain controller response times, and critical events. The management pack generates synthetic transactions to test the response time of the PDC emulator, LDAP, and other domain services.

- **DNS Management Pack**—Monitors and alerts on DNS servers for resolution failures and latency, and critical events.

- **IIS Management Pack**—Monitors and alerts on IIS services, application pools, performance, and critical events.

What Is New in OpsMgr R2?

System Center Operations Manager 2007 R2 released in spring 2009 and includes many new improvements on the previous version, Operations Manager 2007 Service Pack 1. Some of these improvements include

- **Cross platform support**—This supports non-Microsoft platforms such as UNIX and Linux. This enables administrators to have a single-pane view of their entire IT environment in OpsMgr.

- **Integration with System Center Virtual Machine Manager 2008**—This integrates with the VMM 2008 and enables synergies such as Performance Resource and Optimization (PRO) Tips, which provide virtual machine recommendations based on observed performance and the capability to implement the recommendation at the click of a button.

▶ **Notifications**—The notification system has been revamped and now includes an Outlook rule–style interface. Notifications can be generated for specific alerts, and notifications can be sent out as high-priority emails.

▶ **Overrides view**—Rather than hunt for overrides within all the management packs, OpsMgr R2 has an authoring view that shows all the overrides defined in the system.

▶ **Improved management pack maintenance**—OpsMgr 2007 R2 enables Microsoft management packs to be browsed, downloaded, and imported directly from the console. It even includes versioning, dependency checks, and the capability to search from management pack updates.

▶ **Service level monitoring**—Applications can be defined from various monitored objects and the service level of the application, and be monitored and reported on against defined target SLAs.

▶ **Better scaling of URL monitoring**—The URL monitor now scales to thousands of websites without undue performance impact.

▶ **Improved database performance**—The overall performance of the database and console has been dramatically improved.

These improvements bring the platform to a new level of performance and interoperability while retaining the look and feel of the original Operations Manager 2007 tool.

How OpsMgr Works

OpsMgr is a sophisticated monitoring system that effectively allows for large-scale management of mission-critical servers. Organizations with a medium-to-large investment in Microsoft technologies will find that OpsMgr allows for an unprecedented capability to keep on top of the event log messages that occur on a daily basis. In its simplest form, OpsMgr performs two functions: processing monitored data and issuing alerts and automatic responses based on that data.

The model-based architecture of OpsMgr presents a fundamental shift in the way a network is monitored. The entire environment can be monitored as groups of hierarchical services with interdependent components. Microsoft, in addition to third-party vendors and a large development community, can leverage the functionality of OpsMgr components through customizable monitoring rules.

OpsMgr Functionality

OpsMgr provides for several major pieces of functionality as follows:

▶ **Management packs**—Application-specific monitoring rules are provided within individual files called *management packs*. For example, Microsoft provides management packs for Windows server systems, Exchange Server, SQL Server, SharePoint,

DNS, and DHCP, along with many other Microsoft technologies including Lync Server 2010. Management packs are loaded with the intelligence and information necessary to properly troubleshoot and identify problems. The rules are dynamically applied to agents based on a custom discovery process provided within the management pack. Only applicable rules are applied to each managed server.

▶ **Event monitoring rules**—Management pack rules can monitor for specific event log data. This is one of the key methods of responding to conditions within the environment.

▶ **Performance monitoring rules**—Management pack rules can monitor for specific performance counters. This data is used for alerting based on thresholds or archived for trending and capacity planning. The performance graph in Figure 13.1 shows IM Performance Latency data for the LS1 Server. There was a brief spike in latency at approximately 6:15 a.m., but the latency is normally under less than 0.05ms.

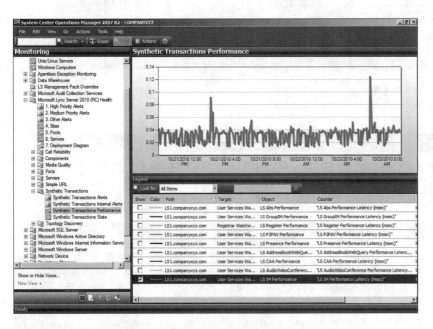

FIGURE 13.1   Operations Manager 2007 R2 Performance Charts

▶ **State-based monitors**—Management packs contain monitors, which allow for advanced state-based monitoring and aggregated health rollup of services. Monitors also provide self-tuning performance threshold monitoring based on a two- or three-state configuration. Figure 13.2 shows the health explorer for the LS1 Server. The Lync Server Application Sharing service is stopped.

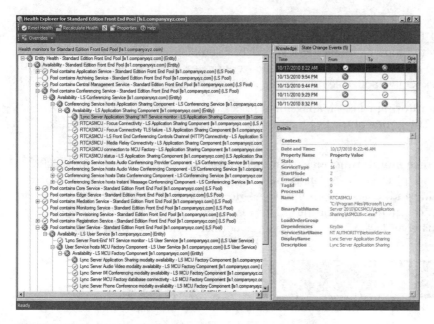

FIGURE 13.2   Health Explorer

TIP

The health explorer drills down to the states that are unhealthy, leaving all the other states collapsed for ease of troubleshooting.

NOTE

The health explorer in Figure 13.2 also shows the state change events over time. This enables reoccurring or intermittent problems to be tracked. In Figure 13.2, the service was stopped on 10/11/2010 and 10/13/2010 as well as 10/17/2010.

▶ **Alerting**—OpsMgr provides advanced alerting functionality by enabling email alerts, paging, short message service (SMS), instant messaging (IM), and functional alerting roles to be defined. Alerts are highly customizable, with the capability to define alert rules for all monitored components.

▶ **Reporting**—Monitoring rules can be configured to send monitored data to both the operations database for alerting and the reporting database for archiving.

▶ **End-to-end service monitoring**—OpsMgr provides service-oriented monitoring based on System Definition Model (SDM) technologies. This includes advanced object discovery and hierarchical monitoring of systems.

Processing Operational Data

OpsMgr manages Lync Server 2010 infrastructures through monitoring rules used for object discovery, Windows event log monitoring, performance data gathering, and application-specific synthetic transactions. Monitoring rules define how OpsMgr collects, handles, and responds to the information gathered. OpsMgr monitoring rules handle incoming event data and enable OpsMgr to react automatically, either to respond to a predetermined problem scenario, such as a failed hard drive, with predefined corrective and diagnostics actions (for example, trigger an alert, execute a command or script, and so on) to provide the operator with additional details based on what was happening at the time the condition occurred.

Generating Alerts and Responses

OpsMgr monitoring rules can generate alerts based on critical events, synthetic transactions, or performance thresholds and variances found through self-tuning performance trending. An alert can be generated by a single event or by a combination of events or performance thresholds. Alerts can also be configured to trigger responses such as e-mail, pages, Simple Network Management Protocol (SNMP) traps, and scripts to notify you of potential problems. In brief, OpsMgr is completely customizable in this respect and can be modified to fit most alert requirements.

A sample alert is shown in Figure 13.3. The alert indicates that the Lync Server Application Sharing service is not running.

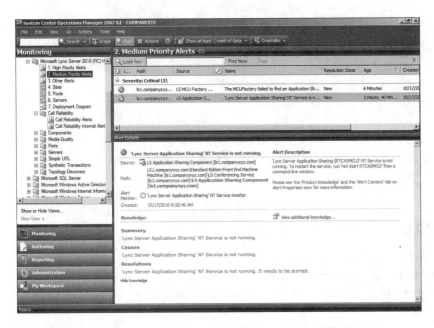

FIGURE 13.3   Operations Manager 2007 R2 Lync Server 2010 Alert

---

TIP

The alert details show the cause of the alert and recommended resolutions. This helps guide new administrators to quickly solve the problem, even if they are not familiar with the application in question. This alert corresponds to the unhealthy state shown in Figure 13.2.

The alerts are dynamic and automatically resolve themselves if the condition that generated the alert is resolved. After starting the Lync Server Application Sharing Service on LS1, the alert was closed automatically and the state transitioned to healthy. Figure 13.4 shows the health explorer state, including the time the service was started at 11:05 a.m. on 10/17/2010.

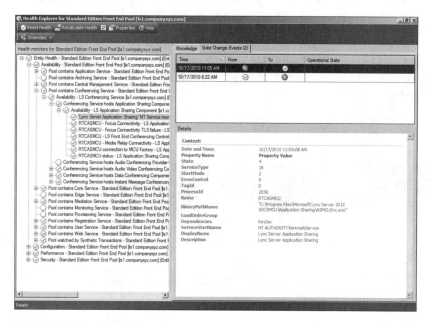

FIGURE 13.4   Health Explorer Health State

OpsMgr Architecture

OpsMgr is primarily composed of five basic components: the operations database, reporting database, Root Management Server, management agents, and Operations Console. These components make up a basic deployment scenario. There are also several optional components that provide functionality for advanced deployment scenarios.

OpsMgr was specifically designed to be scalable and can subsequently be configured to meet the needs of any size company. This flexibility stems from the fact that all OpsMgr components can either reside on one server or can be distributed across multiple servers.

Each of these various components provides specific OpsMgr functionality. OpsMgr design scenarios often involve the separation of parts of these components onto multiple servers. For example, the database components can be delegated to a dedicated server, and the management server can reside on a second server.

The following list describes the different OpsMgr components:

▶ **Operations database**—The operations database stores the monitoring rules and the active data collected from monitored systems. This database has a seven-day default retention period.

▶ **Reporting database**—The reporting database stores archived data for reporting purposes. This database has a 400-day default retention period.

▶ **Root Management Server**—This is the first management server in the management group. This server runs the software development kit (SDK) and Configuration service, and is responsible for handling console communication, calculating the health of the environment, and determining what rules should be applied to each agent.

▶ **Management Server**—Optionally, an additional management server can be added for redundancy and scalability. Agents communicate with the management server to deliver operational data and pull down new monitoring rules.

▶ **Management agents**—Agents are installed on each managed system to provide efficient monitoring of local components. Almost all communication is initiated from the agent with the exception of the actual agent installation and specific tasks that run from the Operations Console. Agentless monitoring is also available with a reduction of functionality and environmental scalability.

▶ **Operations Console**—The Operations Console is used to monitor systems, run tasks, configure environmental settings, set author rules, subscribe to alerts, and generate and subscribe to reports.

▶ **Web Console**—The Web Console is an optional component used to monitor systems, run tasks, and manage maintenance mode from a web browser.

▶ **Audit Collection Services**—This is an optional component used to collect security events from managed systems; this component is composed of a forwarder on the agent that sends all security events, a collector on the management server that receives events from managed systems, and a special database used to store the collected security data for auditing, reporting, and forensic analysis.

▶ **Gateway Server**—This optional component provides mutual authentication through certificates for nontrusted systems in remote domains or workgroups.

▶ **Command shell**—This optional component is built on PowerShell and provides full command-line management of the OpsMgr environment.

▶ **Agentless Exception Monitoring**—This component can be used to monitor Windows and application crash data throughout the environment and provides insight into the health of the productivity applications across workstations and servers.

13

► **Connector Framework**—This optional component provides a bidirectional web service for communicating, extending, and integrating the environment with third-party or custom systems.

The Operations Manager 2007 architecture, with all the major components and their data paths, is shown in Figure 13.5.

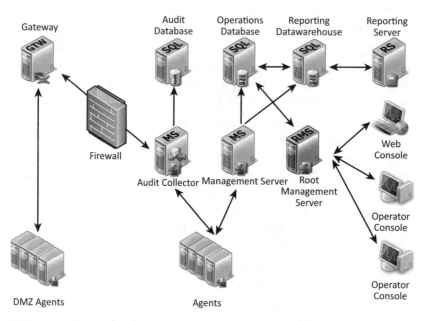

FIGURE 13.5   Operations Manager 2007 R2 Architecture

Understanding How OpsMgr Stores Captured Data

OpsMgr uses two Microsoft SQL Server databases for all collected data. Both databases are automatically maintained through OpsMgr-specific scheduled maintenance tasks.

The operations database stores all the monitoring rules and is imported by management packs and operational data collected from each monitored system. Data in this database is retained for seven days by default. Data retention for the operations database is lower than the reporting database to improve efficiency of the environment.

> **TIP**
>
> The operations database must be installed as a separate component from OpsMgr. However, it can physically reside on the same server, if needed.

The reporting database stores data for long-term trend analysis and is designed to grow much larger than the operations database. Data in the reporting database is stored in three states: raw data, hourly summary, and daily summary. The raw data is stored only for 14 days, whereas both daily and hourly data are stored for 400 days. This automatic summarization of data allows for reports that span days or months to be generated quickly.

Determining the Role of Agents in System Monitoring

The agents are the monitoring components installed on each managed computer. They monitor the system based on the rules and business logic defined in each of the management packs. Management packs are dynamically applied to agents based on the different discovery rules included with each management pack.

Defining Management Groups

OpsMgr uses the concept of management groups to logically separate geographical and organizational boundaries. Management groups enable you to scale the size of OpsMgr architecture or politically organize the administration of OpsMgr.

At a minimum, each management group consists of the following components:

- ▶ An operations database
- ▶ An optional reporting database
- ▶ A Root Management Server
- ▶ Management agents
- ▶ Management consoles

OpsMgr can be scaled to meet the needs of different-sized organizations. For small organizations, the OpsMgr components can be installed on one server with a single management group. In large organizations, on the other hand, the distribution of OpsMgr components to separate servers enables the organizations to customize and scale their OpsMgr architecture. Multiple management groups provide load balancing and fault tolerance within the OpsMgr infrastructure. Organizations can set up multiple management servers at strategic locations to distribute the workload among them.

> **NOTE**
>
> The general rule of thumb with management groups is to start with a single management group and add more management groups only if they are absolutely necessary. Administrative overhead is reduced, and there is less need to re-create rules and perform other redundant tasks with fewer management groups.

How to Use OpsMgr

Using OpsMgr is relatively straightforward. The OpsMgr monitoring environment can be accessed through three sets of consoles: an Operations Console, a Web Console, and a command shell. The Operations Console provides full monitoring of agent systems and administration of the OpsMgr environment, whereas the Web Console provides access only to the monitoring functionality. The command shell provides command-line access to administer the OpsMgr environment.

Managing and Monitoring with OpsMgr

As mentioned in the preceding section, two methods are provided to configure and view OpsMgr settings. The first approach is through the Operations Console and the second is through the command shell.

Within the Administration section of the Operations Console, you can easily configure the security roles, notifications, and configuration settings. Within the Monitoring section of the Operations Console, you can easily monitor a quick up/down status, view active and closed alerts, and confirm overall environment health.

In addition, a web-based monitoring console can be run on any system that supports Microsoft Internet Explorer 6.0 or higher. This console can be used to view the health of systems, view and respond to alerts, view events, view performance graphs, run tasks, and manage maintenance mode of monitored objects. New to OpsMgr 2007 R2 is the capability to display the health explorer in the Web Console.

Reporting from OpsMgr

OpsMgr management packs commonly include a variety of preconfigured reports to show information about the operating system or the specific application to which they were designed to work. These reports are run in SQL Reporting Services. The reports provide an effective view of systems and services on the network over a custom period, such as weekly, monthly, or quarterly. They can also help you monitor your networks based on performance data, which can include critical pattern analysis, trend analysis, capacity planning, and security auditing. Reports also provide availability statistics for distributed applications, servers, and specific components within a server.

Reports are particularly useful for executives, managers, and application owners. These reports show the availability of any object within OpsMgr, including a server (see Figure 13.6), a database, or even a service such as Lync Server 2010 that includes a multitude of servers and components. The availability report in Figure 13.6 shows that the LS1 Server was available until after 8:00 a.m. and then was down through 11:00 a.m.

The reports can be run on demand or at scheduled times and delivered through e-mail. OpsMgr can also generate HTML-based reports that can be published to a web server and viewed from any web browser. Vendors can also create additional reports as part of their management packs.

Using Performance Monitoring

Another key feature of OpsMgr is the capability to monitor and track server performance. OpsMgr can be configured to monitor key performance thresholds through rules that are set to collect predefined performance data, such as memory and CPU usage over time. Rules can be configured to trigger alerts and actions when specified performance

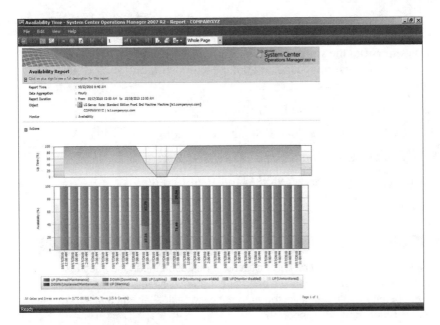

FIGURE 13.6   Availability Report

thresholds have been met or exceeded, enabling network administrators to act on potential performance issues. Performance data can be viewed from the OpsMgr Operations Console.

In addition, performance monitors can establish baselines for the environment and then alert the administrator when the counter subsequently falls outside the defined baseline envelope.

Using Active Directory Integration

Active Directory integration provides a way to install management agents on systems without environmental-specific settings. When the agent starts, the correct environmental settings, such as the primary and failover management servers, are stored in Active Directory. The configuration of Active Directory integration provides advanced search and filter capabilities to fine-tune the dynamic assignment of systems.

Integrating OpsMgr Non-Windows Devices

Network management is not a new concept. Simple management of various network nodes has been handled for quite some time through the SNMP. Quite often, simple or even complex systems that use SNMP to provide for system monitoring are in place in an organization to provide for varying degrees of system management on a network.

OpsMgr can be configured to integrate with non-Windows systems through monitoring of syslog information, log file data, and SNMP traps. OpsMgr can also monitor TCP port communication and website transaction sequencing for information-specific data management.

New to OpsMgr 2007 R2 is the capability to monitor non-Microsoft operating systems such as Linux and UNIX, and the applications that run on them, such as Apache and MySQL. OpsMgr monitors the file systems, network interfaces, daemons, configurations, and performance metrics. Operations Manager 2007 R2 supports monitoring of the following operating systems:

▶ HP-UX 11i v2 and v3 (PA-RISC and IA64)

▶ Sun Solaris 8 and 9 (SPARC) and Solaris 10 (SPARC and x86)

▶ Red Hat Enterprise Linux 4 (x86/x64) and 5 (x86/x64) Server

▶ Novell SUSE Linux Enterprise Server 9 (x86) and 10 SP1 (x86/x64)

▶ IBM AIX v5.3 and v6.1

NOTE

The previous operating systems are *first-class citizens* in Microsoft's parlance because they are treated as equals with the Windows operating systems. Agents can be pushed from the console, operations data is collected automatically, tasks can run against the agents, and all major functions are supported.

Special connectors can be created to provide bidirectional information flows to other management products. OpsMgr can monitor SNMP traps from SNMP-supported devices as well as generate SNMP traps to be delivered to third-party network management infrastructures.

Exploring Third-Party Management Packs

Software and hardware developers can subsequently create their own management packs to extend OpsMgr's management capabilities. These management packs extend OpsMgr's management capabilities beyond Microsoft-specific applications. Each management pack is designed to contain a set of rules and product knowledge required to support its respective products. Currently, management packs have been developed for APC, Cisco, Citrix, Dell, F5, HP, IBM, Linux, Oracle, Solaris, UNIX, and VMware to name a few.

▶ A complete list of management packs can be found at the following Microsoft site: http://pinpoint.microsoft.com/en-US/systemcenter/managementpackcatalog.

OpsMgr Component Requirements

Each OpsMgr component has specific design requirements, and a firm knowledge of these factors is required before beginning the design of OpsMgr. Hardware and software requirements must be taken into account, as well as factors involving specific OpsMgr components, such as the Root Management Server, gateway servers, service accounts, mutual authentication, and backup requirements.

Exploring Hardware Requirements

Having the proper hardware for OpsMgr to operate is a critical component of OpsMgr functionality, reliability, and overall performance. Nothing is worse than overloading a brand-new server only a few short months after its implementation.

The industry standard generally holds that any production servers deployed should remain relevant for three to four years following deployment. Stretching beyond this time-frame might be possible, but the ugly truth is that hardware investments are typically short term and need to be replaced often to ensure relevance. Buying a less-expensive server might save money in the short term, but could potentially increase costs associated with downtime, troubleshooting, and administration.

That said, the following are the Microsoft-recommended minimums for any server running an OpsMgr 2007 server component:

▶ 2.8 GHz processor or faster

▶ 20 GB of free disk space

▶ 2 GB of random access memory (RAM)

These recommendations apply only to the smallest OpsMgr deployments and should be seen as minimum levels for OpsMgr hardware. More realistic deployments have the following minimum levels:

▶ 2–4 2.8 GHz Cores

▶ 64-bit Windows operating system

▶ 64-bit SQL Server

▶ 60 GB free disk space on RAID 1+0 for performance

▶ 4–8 GB RAM

CAUTION

Operations Manager 2007 R2 is one of Microsoft's most resource-intensive applications, so generous processor, disk, and memory are important for optimal performance. Future expansion and relevance of hardware should be taken into account when sizing servers for OpsMgr deployment to ensure that the system has room to grow as agents are added and the databases grow.

Determining Software Requirements

OpsMgr components can be installed on either 32-bit or 64-bit versions of Windows Server 2008. The database for OpsMgr must be run on a Microsoft SQL Server 2005 or Microsoft SQL Server 2008 server. The database can be installed on the same server as OpsMgr or on a separate server, which is discussed in more detail in following sections.

> **TIP**
>
> OpsMgr itself must be installed on a member server in a Windows Active Directory domain. It is commonly recommended to keep the installation of OpsMgr on a separate server or set of dedicated member servers that do not run any other applications that can interfere in the monitoring and alerting process.

A few other factors critical to the success of an OpsMgr implementation are as follows:

- Microsoft .NET Framework 2.0 and 3.0 must be installed on the management server and the reporting server.

- Windows PowerShell.

- Microsoft Core XML Services (MSXML) 6.0.

- WS-MAN v1.1 (for UNIX/Linux clients).

- Client certificates must be installed in environments to facilitate mutual authentication between non-domain members and management servers.

- SQL Reporting Services must be installed for an organization to be able to view and produce custom reports using OpsMgr's reporting feature.

OpsMgr Backup Considerations

The most critical piece of OpsMgr, the SQL databases, should be regularly backed up using standard backup software that can effectively perform online backups of SQL databases. If integrating these specialized backup utilities into an OpsMgr deployment is not possible, it is necessary to leverage built-in backup functionality found in SQL Server.

Advanced OpsMgr Concepts

OpsMgr's simple installation and relative ease of use often disguises the potential complexity of its underlying components. This complexity can be managed with the right amount of knowledge of some of the advanced concepts of OpsMgr design and implementation.

Understanding OpsMgr Deployment Scenarios

As previously mentioned, OpsMgr components can be divided across multiple servers to distribute load and ensure balanced functionality. This separation enables OpsMgr servers to come in four potential flavors, depending on the OpsMgr components held by these servers. The four OpsMgr server types are as follows:

- **Operations Database Server**—An Operations Database Server is simply a member server with SQL Server 2005 installed for the OpsMgr operations database. No other OpsMgr components are installed on this server. The SQL Server 2005 component can be installed with default options and with the system account used for authentication. Data in this database is kept for four days by default.

▶ **Reporting Database Server**—A Reporting Database Server is simply a member server with SQL Server 2005 and SQL Server Reporting Services installed. This database stores data collected through the monitoring rules for a much longer period than the operations database and is used for reporting and trend analysis. This database requires significantly more drive space than the operations database server. Data in this database is kept for 13 months by default.

▶ **Management Server**—A Management Server is the communication point for both management consoles and agents. Effectively, a management server does not have a database and is often used in large OpsMgr implementations that have a dedicated database server. Often, in these configurations, multiple management servers are used in a single management group to provide for scalability and to address multiple managed nodes.

▶ **All-in-one server**—An all-in-one server is effectively an OpsMgr server that holds all OpsMgr roles, including the databases. Subsequently, single-server OpsMgr configurations use one server for all OpsMgr operations.

Multiple Configuration Groups

As previously defined, an OpsMgr management group is a logical grouping of monitored servers that are managed by a single OpsMgr SQL database, one or more management servers, and a unique management group name. Each management group established operates separately from other management groups, although they can be configured in a hierarchical structure with a top-level management group able to see connected lower-level management groups.

The concept of connected management groups enables OpsMgr to scale beyond artificial boundaries and gives a great deal of flexibility when combining OpsMgr environments. However, certain caveats must be taken into account. Because each management group is an island, each must subsequently be manually configured with individual settings. In environments with a large number of customized rules, for example, a manual configuration creates a great deal of redundant work in the creation, administration, and troubleshooting of multiple management groups.

Deploying Geographic-Based Configuration Groups

Based on the factors outlined in the preceding section, it is preferable to deploy OpsMgr in a single management group. However, in some situations an organization needs to divide its OpsMgr environment into multiple management groups. The most common reason for division of OpsMgr management groups is division along geographic lines. In situations in which wide area network (WAN) links are saturated or unreliable, it might be wise to separate large islands of WAN connectivity into separate management groups.

Simply being separated across slow WAN links is not a good reason to warrant a separate management group, however. For example, small sites with few servers do not warrant the creation of a separate OpsMgr management group, with the associated hardware, software, and administrative costs. However, if many servers exist in a distributed, generally well-connected geographical area, that might be a case for the creation of a management group. For example, an organization can be divided into several sites across the United States, but decide to divide the OpsMgr environment into separate management groups for East Coast and West Coast to roughly approximate their WAN infrastructure.

Smaller sites that are not well connected but are not large enough to warrant their own management group should have their event monitoring throttled to avoid being sent across the WAN during peak usage times. The downside to this approach, however, is that the reaction time to critical event response is increased.

Deploying Political or Security-Based Configuration Groups

The less common method of dividing OpsMgr management groups is by political or security lines. For example, it might become necessary to separate financial servers into a separate management group to maintain the security of the finance environment and allow for a separate set of administrators.

Politically, if administration is not centralized within an organization, management groups can be established to separate OpsMgr management into separate spheres of control. This keeps each OpsMgr management zone under separate security models.

As previously mentioned, a single management group is the most efficient OpsMgr environment and provides for the least amount of redundant setup, administration, and troubleshooting work. Consequently, avoid artificial OpsMgr division along political or security lines, if possible.

Sizing the OpsMgr Database

Depending on several factors, such as the type of data collected, the length of time that collected data will be kept, or the amount of database grooming that is scheduled, the size of the OpsMgr database grows or shrinks accordingly.

> **TIP**
>
> It is important to monitor the size of the database to ensure that it does not increase beyond the bounds of acceptable size. OpsMgr can be configured to monitor itself, supplying advance notice of database problems and capacity thresholds. This type of strategy is highly recommended because OpsMgr can easily collect event information faster than it can get rid of it.

The size of the operations database can be estimated through the following formula:

```
(Number of agents x 5 MB x retention days) + 1,024 overhead = estimated database size
```

For example, an OpsMgr environment monitoring 1,000 servers with the default seven-day retention period has an estimated 35 GB operations database:

```
(1,000 * 5 * 7) + 1,024 = 36,024 MB
```

The size of the reporting database can be estimated through the following formula:

```
(Number of agents x 3 MB x retention days) + 1,024 overhead = estimated database size
```

The same environment monitoring 1,000 servers with the default 400-day retention period has an estimated 1.1 TB reporting database:

```
(1,000 * 3 * 400) + 1,024 = 1,201,024 MB
```

> **CAUTION**
>
> It is important to understand that these estimates are rough guidelines only and can vary widely depending on the types of servers monitored, the monitoring configuration, the degree of customization, and other factors.

Defining Capacity Limits

As with any system, OpsMgr includes limits that should be taken into account before deployment begins. Surpassing these limits might be cause for the creation of new management groups and should subsequently be included in a design plan. These limits are as follows:

- ▶ **Operations Database**—OpsMgr operates through a principle of centralized, rather than distributed, collection of data. All event logs, performance counters, and alerts are sent to a single centralized database, and there can subsequently be only a single operations database per management group. Considering the use of a backup and high-availability strategy for the OpsMgr database is, therefore, highly recommended to protect it from outage. It is recommended to keep this database with a 50 GB limit to improve efficiency and reduce alert latency.

- ▶ **Management servers**—OpsMgr does not have a hard-coded limit of management servers per management group. However, it is recommended to keep the environment between three to five management servers. Each management server can support approximately 2,000 managed agents.

- ▶ **Gateway servers**—OpsMgr does not have a hard-coded limit of gateway servers per management group. However, it is recommended to deploy a gateway server for every 200 nontrusted domain members.

- ▶ **Agents**—Each management server can theoretically support up to 2,000 monitored agents. In most configurations, however, it is wise to limit the number of agents per management server, although the levels can be scaled upward with more robust hardware, if necessary.

- ▶ **Administrative Consoles**—OpsMgr does not limit the number of instances of the Web and Operations Console; however, going beyond the suggested limit might introduce performance and scalability problems.

Defining System Redundancy

In addition to the scalability built in to OpsMgr, redundancy is built in to the components of the environment. Proper knowledge of how to deploy OpsMgr redundancy and place OpsMgr components correctly is important to the understanding of OpsMgr redundancy.

The main components of OpsMgr can be made redundant through the following methods:

▶ **Management Servers**—Management servers are automatically redundant and agents failover and failback automatically between them. Simply install additional management servers for redundancy. In addition, the Root Management Server (RMS) acts as a management server and participates in the fault tolerance.

▶ **SQL databases**—The SQL database servers hosting the databases can be made redundant using SQL clustering, which is based on Windows clustering. This supports failover and failback.

▶ **Root Management Server**—The RMS can be made redundant using Windows clustering. This supports failover and failback.

Having multiple management servers deployed across a management group enables an environment to achieve a certain level of redundancy. If a single management server experiences downtime, another management server within the management group takes over the responsibilities for the monitored servers in the environment. For this reason, it might be wise to include multiple management servers in an environment to achieve a certain level of redundancy if high uptime is a priority.

The first management server in the management group is called the *Root Management Server*. Only one RMS can exist in a management group, and it hosts the SDK and Configuration service. All OpsMgr consoles communicate with the management server, so its availability is critical. In large-scale environments, the RMS should leverage Microsoft Cluster technology to provide high availability for this component.

> **CAUTION**
>
> Because there can be only a single OpsMgr database per management group, the database is subsequently a single point of failure and should be protected from downtime. Using Windows Server 2008 clustering or third-party fault-tolerance solutions for SQL databases helps to mitigate the risk involved with the OpsMgr database.

Monitoring Nondomain Member Considerations

DMZ, workgroup, and nontrusted domain agents require special configuration, such as certificates to establish mutual authentication. Operations Manager 2007 requires mutual authentication; that is, the server authenticates to the client and the client authenticates to the server to ensure that the monitoring communications are not hacked. Without mutual authentication, a hacker can execute a man-in-the-middle attack and impersonate either the client or the server. Thus, mutual authentication is a security measure designed to protect clients, servers, and sensitive Active Directory domain information, which is exposed to potential hacking attempts by the all-powerful management infrastructure. However, OpsMgr relies on Active Directory Kerberos for mutual authentication, which is not available to nondomain members.

> **NOTE**
>
> Lync Edge servers are commonly placed in the DMZ and are not domain members, so every Lync Server 2010 environment needs to deploy certificate-based authentication for proper monitoring.

In the absence of Active Directory, trusts, and Kerberos, OpsMgr 2007 R2 can use X.509 certificates to establish the mutual authentication. These can be issued by any PKI, such as Microsoft Windows Server 2008 Enterprise CA.

Installing agents on Edge Component servers is discussed later in the chapter in the "Installing Edge Component Monitoring Certificates" section.

Securing OpsMgr

Security has evolved into a primary concern that can no longer be taken for granted. The inherent security in Windows 2008 is only as good as the services that have access to it; therefore, you should perform a security audit of all systems that access information from servers. This concept holds true for management systems as well because they collect sensitive information from every server in an enterprise. This includes potentially sensitive event logs that could be used to compromise a system. Consequently, securing the OpsMgr infrastructure should not be taken lightly.

Securing OpsMgr Agents

Each server that contains an OpsMgr agent and forwards events to management servers has specific security requirements. Server-level security should be established and should include provisions for OpsMgr data collection. All traffic between OpsMgr components, such as the agents, management servers, and database, is encrypted automatically for security, so the traffic is inherently secured.

In addition, environments with high security requirements should investigate the use of encryption technologies such as IPSec to scramble the event IDs sent between agents and OpsMgr servers, to protect against eavesdropping of OpsMgr packets.

OpsMgr uses mutual authentication between agents and management servers. This means that the agent must reside in the same forest as the management server. If the agent is located in a different forest or workgroup, client certificates can be used to establish mutual authentication. If an entire nontrusted domain must be monitored, the gateway server can be installed in the nontrusted domain, agents can establish mutual authentication to the gateway server, and certificates on the gateway and management server can be used to establish mutual authentication. In this scenario, you can avoid placing a certificate on each nontrusted domain member.

Understanding Firewall Requirements

OpsMgr servers deployed across a firewall have special considerations that must be taken into account. Port 5723, the default port for OpsMgr communications, must specifically be opened on a firewall to enable OpsMgr to communicate across it.

Table 13.1 describes communication for this and other OpsMgr components.

TABLE 13.1   OpsMgr Communication Ports

From	To	Port
Agent	Root Management Server	5723
Agent	Management server	5723
Agent	Gateway server	5723
Agent (ACS forwarder)	Management server ACS collector	51909
Gateway server	Root Management Server	5723
Gateway server	Management server	5723
Management or Gateway server	UNIX or Linux computer	1270
Management or Gateway server	UNIX or Linux computer	22
Management server	Operations Manager database	1433
Management server	Root Management Server	5723, 5724
Management server	Reporting data warehouse	1433
Management server ACS collector	ACS database	1433
Operations Console	Root Management Server	5724
Operations Console (reports)	SQL Server Reporting Services	80
Reporting server	Root Management Server	5723, 5724
Reporting server	Reporting data warehouse	1433
Root Management Server	Operations Manager database	1433
Root Management Server	Reporting data warehouse	1433
Web Console browser	Web Console server	51908
Web Console server	Root Management Server	5724

The agent is the component that ports need to be opened most often, which is only port 5723 from the agent to the management servers for monitoring. Other ports, such as 51909 for ACS, are more rarely needed. Figure 13.7 shows the major communications paths and ports between OpsMgr components.

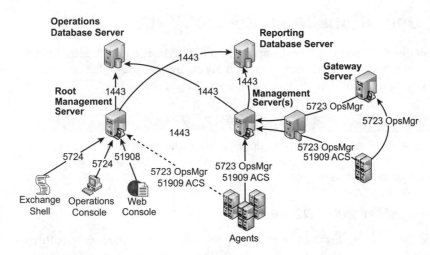

FIGURE 13.7   Communications Ports

Outlining Service Account Security

In addition to the aforementioned security measures, security of an OpsMgr environment can be strengthened by the addition of multiple service accounts to handle the different OpsMgr components. For example, the Management Server Action account and the SDK/Configuration service account should be configured to use separate credentials to provide for an extra layer of protection in the event that one account is compromised.

▶ **Management Server Action account**—The account responsible for collecting data and running responses from management servers.

▶ **SDK and Configuration service account**—The account that writes data to the operations database; this service is also used for all console communication.

▶ **Local Administrator account**—The account used during the agent push installation process. To install the agent, local administrative rights are required.

▶ **Agent Action account**—The credentials that the agent runs as. This account can run under a built-in system account, such as Local System, or a limited domain user account for high-security environments.

▶ **Data Warehouse Write Action account**—The account used by the management server to write data to the reporting data warehouse.

▶ **Data Warehouse Reader account**—The account used to read data from the data warehouse when reports are executed.

▶ **Run As accounts**—The specific accounts used by management packs to facilitate monitoring. These accounts must be manually created and delegated specific rights as defined in the management pack documentation. These accounts are then assigned as run-as accounts used by the management pack to achieve a high-degree of security and flexibility when monitoring the environment.

Installing Operations Manager 2007 R2

As discussed in the previous section, Operations Manager 2007 R2 is a multitier and multi-component application that can be deployed in a variety of architectures. This enables OpsMgr to support scaling from a small organization to a large enterprise.

> **NOTE**
>
> For the purposes of this chapter, an all-in-one single-server install is used. This allows for monitoring of small- to medium-sized Lync Server 2010 organizations spanning a handful of servers up to 50 servers.

Single Server OpsMgr 2007 R2 Install

This section steps through the install of OpsMgr and Reporting on a single-server configuration. The specification for a single-server configuration to support 50 Lync Server 2010 servers is

- ► 2 x 2.8GHz Cores
- ► 8 GB RAM
- ► 4 Drive RAID 0+1 Disk (200+ GB Space)

These hardware requirements ensure that the system can perform to specification. Note that the Lync Server 2010 servers generate a heavier load than other server types such as domain controllers or web servers. This configuration can support 50 Lync Server 2010 servers or 250 servers of other types.

> **NOTE**
>
> If the configuration is to be virtualized on a Windows Server 2008 Hyper-V host or a VMware ESX host, a single server configuration is not recommended. Instead, use a two-server configuration, and install SQL Server 2008 on the second server to balance the load.

The steps in this section assume that the single server has been prepared with the following:

- ► Windows Server 2008 operating system installed
- ► Web role with the appropriate features installed

> **NOTE**
>
> To install SQL Reporting Services and the web components of OpsMgr 2007 R2, the following Windows Server 2008 Web role features need to be installed: Static Content, Default Document, HTTP Redirection, Directory Browsing, ASP, ASPNet, ISAPI Extension, ISAPI Filters, Windows Authentication, IIS Metabase, and IIS 6 WMI.

- Windows PowerShell feature installed

- SQL Server 2008 with Reporting Services installed

- An OpsMgr service account with local administrator rights to the server and system administrator rights to the SQL Server 2008 created

The preceding steps prepare the system for the install of OpsMgr R2. The next section discusses the prerequisite checker and includes information about additional requirements and how to check them.

> **NOTE**
>
> Before installing, it is important to run the built-in prerequisite checker. This utility is available on the OpsMgr installation media and confirms a host of software prerequisites before attempting the actual installation. This gives the administrator time to download and install the necessary software, rather than the installation failing in the middle of configuration.

Prerequisite Checker

This section assumes a Windows Server 2008 and SQL Server 2008 server will be used for the single-server installation, but the prerequisite checker looks at more general requirements based on the OpsMgr-supported platforms. The prerequisite checker looks for the following software on a single-server configuration:

- Windows Server 2003 Service Pack 1 or Windows Server 2008

- Microsoft SQL Server 2005 Service Pack 1 or SQL Server 2008

- Microsoft SQL Server 2005 Reporting Services Service Pack 1 or SQL Server 2008 Reporting Services

- World Wide Web service running and set for automatic startup

- WS-MAN v1.1

- NET Framework 2.0 and .NET Framework 3.0 components

- Windows PowerShell

- Key hotfixes

To use the Prerequisite Viewer for a single-server configuration, perform the following steps:

1. Log on with an account that has administrator rights.
2. Insert the Operations Manager 2007 R2 installation media.
3. The setup starts automatically or launches SetupOM.exe.
4. Click **Check Prerequisites** to start the Prerequisite Viewer.
5. Select **Operational Database**, **Server**, **Console**, **Power Shell**, **Web Console**, **Reporting**, and **Data Warehouse**. Click **Check**.

NOTE

The prerequisite checker findings display and have active links that can be clicked to get specific guidance, and links to download software and hotfixes.

6. When you finish with the Prerequisite Viewer, click **Close**.

Remediate all the guidance in the prerequisite checker before proceeding to the installation. The guidance includes warnings, particularly with some of the hotfixes. Leaving out hotfixes might enable the installation to proceed but might make the OpsMgr application less stable. All recommendations should be applied to ensure the most stable platform possible. If any of the installations require a reboot, run the prerequisite checker again.

When the server meets all the prerequisites and is ready for installation, the steps to run the install are as follows:

1. Log on with the OpsMgr service account.
2. Launch **SetupOM.exe** from the OpsMgr installation media.
3. Click **Install Operations Manager 2007 R2**.
4. Click **Next**.
5. Accept the license agreement and click **Next**.
6. Enter the CD key if required and then click **Next**.
7. When the Custom Setup page displays, leave the components set to their defaults, and then click **Next**.
8. Type the management group name in the Management Group box and click **Next**.
9. Select the instance of SQL Server on which to install the Operations Manager 2007 R2 database (choose the local system because this is a single-server install) and then click **Next**.
10. Leave the default database size of 1,000 MB and then click **Next**.
11. Select **Domain or Local Computer Account**, type the user account and password, select the domain or local computer from the list, and then click **Next**.
12. On the SDK and Config Service Account page, select **Domain or Local Account**, type the user account and password, select the domain or local computer from the list, and then click **Next**.
13. On the Web Console Authentication Configuration page, select **Use Windows Authentication** and click **Next**.
14. On the Operations Manager Error Reports page, leave **Do You Want To Send Error Reports to Microsoft** cleared and click **Next** to not send Operations Manager 2007 R2 error reports to Microsoft.
15. On the Customer Experience Improvement Program page, leave the default option of **I Don't Want to Join the Program** selected and then click **Next**.
16. On the Ready to Install page, click **Install**.

17. When the Completing the System Center Operations Manager 2007 R2 Setup Wizard page appears, leave the **Backup Encryption Key** box selected to back up the encryption key.

> **NOTE**
>
> A copy of the encryption key is needed to promote a management server to the role of the root management server if a failure of the RMS occurs.

18. Leave **Start the Console** selected to open the Operations console.
19. Click **Finish**.

Operations Manager 2007 R2 is now installed in a single-server configuration. This configuration can manage up to 250 servers.

Importing Management Packs

After the initial installation, OpsMgr includes only a few management packs. The management packs contain all the discoveries, monitors, rules, knowledge, reports, and views that OpsMgr needs to effectively monitor servers and applications. One of the first tasks after installing OpsMgr 2007 is to import management packs into the system.

There are several management packs in the Internet catalog on the Microsoft website. These include updated management packs, management packs for new products, and third-party management packs. Only load the management packs that are going to be used because each additional management pack increases the database size, adds discoveries that affect the performance of agents, and in general clutters up the interface.

The key management packs for a Lync Server 2010 environment follow:

- ▶ Windows Server Core OS
- ▶ Windows Server Active Directory
- ▶ Windows Server Domain Naming Service
- ▶ Windows Server IIS
- ▶ SQL Server
- ▶ Lync Server 2010

For each of these management packs, it is important to load the relevant versions only. For example, if the environment includes Windows Server 2008, load only the Windows Server Core OS 2008 management pack. If the environment includes both Windows Server 2003 and Windows Server 2008, load both the Windows Server Core OS 2003 and the Windows Server Core OS 2008.

In versions of OpsMgr prior to R2, the management packs had to be downloaded from the Microsoft website one by one, the MSI installed one by one, and the management packs imported one by one. Dependencies were not checked unless additional steps were taken to consolidate the management pack files prior to importing. This was a labor-intensive process. Also, there was no easy way to check for updates to already installed management packs.

In OpsMgr 2007 R2, a new Management Pack Import Wizard was introduced. This wizard connects directly to the Microsoft management pack catalog and downloads, checks, and imports management packs. It even performs checks to ensure that the management packs are the latest versions. This is a huge improvement over the old method to import management packs.

To import the key management packs, perform the following steps:

1. Launch the **Operations Console**.
2. Select the **Administration** section.
3. Select the **Management Packs** folder.
4. Right-click the **Management Packs** folder and select **Import Management Packs**.
5. Click the **Add** button and select **Add from Catalog**.
6. Click the **Search** button to search the entire catalog.

NOTE

The View pull-down in the Management Pack Import Wizard includes four options, which are All Management Packs in the Catalog, Updates Available for Installed Management Packs, All Management Packs Released in the Last 3 Months, and All Management Packs Released in the Last 6 Months. The Updates option checks against the already-installed management packs and enables the download of updated versions of these.

---

7. Select the key management packs from the preceding list and click **Add** for each of them. Each of the major management packs might include a number of submanagement packs for discovery, monitoring, and other breakdowns of functionality.
8. After adding management packs, click **OK**.
9. The wizard now validates the added management packs, checking for versions, dependencies, and security risks. It enables problem management packs to be removed and dependencies to be added to the list.
10. Click **Install** to begin the download and import process. Progress shows for each of the management packs imported.
11. After all the management packs complete, click **Close** to exit the wizard.

After the import completes, the management packs take effect immediately. Agents discover based on the schedule specified in the management packs, and monitors and rules deploy.

Deploying OpsMgr Agents

OpsMgr agents are deployed to all managed servers through the OpsMgr Discovery Wizard, or by using software distribution mechanisms such as Active Directory GPOs or System Center Configuration Manager 2007. Installation through the Operations Console uses the fully qualified domain name (FQDN) of the computer.

When searching for systems through the Operations Console, you can use wildcards to locate a broad range of computers for agent installation. Certain situations, such as monitoring across firewalls, can require the manual installation of these components.

The Discovery Wizard can discover and configure monitoring for Windows computers, UNIX/Linux computers, and network devices. It pushes agents to Windows and UNIX/Linux computers, if the proper rights are provided, such as an account with local administrator rights or a root account.

To install domain member agents using the Discovery Wizard, perform the following steps:

1. Launch the **Operations Console** and select the **Administration** section.

2. Right-click the top-level **Administration** folder and select **Discovery Wizard**.

3. Select the Windows computers and click **Next**.

4. Select **Automatic computer discovery** and click **Next**. This scans the entire Active Directory domain for computers.

5. Leave the **Use selected Management Server Action Account** and click **Discover**. This starts the discovery process.

6. After the discovery runs (this might take a few minutes), the list of discovered computers displays. Select the devices that should have agents deployed to them.

NOTE

The list includes only systems that do not already have agents installed. If a computer has an agent installed, the wizard excludes it from the list of devices.

7. Click **Next**.

8. Leave the **Agent installation** directory and the **Agent Action Account** at the defaults, and click **Finish**.

9. The Agent Management Task Status window appears, listing all the computers selected and the progress of each installation. As shown in Figure 13.8, the LS1.companyxyz.com agent installation task starts.

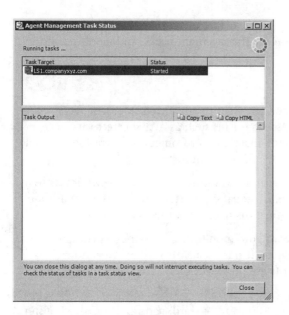

FIGURE 13.8   Agent Installation Progress

10. Click **Close** when the installation completes.

Even if the window is closed before the installs complete, the results of the installs can be viewed in Task Status view in the Monitoring section of the Operations Console.

The agent deployment is efficient, and a large number of computers can be selected for deployment without any issues. The agents start automatically and monitor as they are discovered.

After installation, it might be necessary to wait a few minutes before the information from the agents is sent to the management server.

During the next few minutes after installation, the agent contacts the management server and establishes a mutually authenticated, encrypted communication channel with the assigned management server. If the agent was pushed through a software delivery system such as System Center Configuration Manager 2007, the agent determines the management server through Active Directory–integrated discovery.

The agent downloads rules to discover the various applications and components it's hosting, enabling the correct application-specific management packs to be applied. This discovery process runs periodically to ensure that the correct rules are always applied to the server.

SCOM Dip Stick Health Checks

When driving, the conscientious driver goes through a set of basic automobile checks, including the following:

▶ Check the oil level with the dip stick.

▶ Check the tire pressure.

▶ Check the gasoline level.

These are sometimes referred to as the *dip stick health checks* because the automobile oil level is checked with a dip stick.

Like any other complicated technology, Operations Manager 2007 can have problems in a variety of ways ranging from running out of disk space, to failing to send email notifications, to having agents stopped, and so forth. To make sure that Operations Manager is functioning properly, a set of dip stick health checks can be performed to make sure everything is running smoothly.

These are the tasks that the OpsMgr administrator should do every day to verify the health and proper operation of the OpsMgr infrastructure:

1. Verify that you have received notifications by e-mail. Confirm that you are getting notifications within the normal range. Too many notifications is a bad sign and too few (or none) is also a bad sign.

2. Review OpsMgr daily reports sent by e-mail or in the console. If using the console, the reports are stored in the Favorites folder in the Reporting space.

   ▶ Refer back to Chapter 9, "Director," for more information about how to set up these reports.

3. In the Operations Manager console, review the **Active Alerts** view. This shows you new alerts.

4. In the Operations Manager console, review the **All Alerts** view. This shows you both new and closed alerts.

5. In the Operations Manager console, review the **Agent Health State** view in the \Operations Manager\Agent node. Investigate Critical, Warning, or Not Monitored states.

6. In the Operations Manager console, review the **Active Alerts** view in the \Operations Manager\Agent node. Investigate Critical or Warning alerts.

7. In the Operations Manager console, review the **Management Server Health State** view in the \Operations Manager\Management Server node. Investigate Critical, Warning, or Not Monitored states.

8. In the Operations Manager console, review the **Active Alerts** view in the \Operations Manager\Management Server node. Investigate Critical or Warning alerts.

After reviewing these health check points, an administrator can be confident that the Operations Manager 2007 R2 infrastructure is functioning properly.

The second check recommends reviewing the daily reports. The recommended Operations Manager health reports to review on a daily basis are as follows:

▶ **Alert Logging Latency report**—This report tells you the length of time between a raised event to a generated alert. This should be under 30 seconds.

▶ **Send Queue % Used Top 10 report**—This report tells you whether agents are having trouble uploading their data to the management servers. These queues should be less than 1 percent.

▶ **Top 10 Most Common Alerts report**—This report analyzes the common alerts that are generated and are good for identifying alert-tuning opportunities.

▶ **Daily Alert report**—This report gives you a complete list of alerts that were generated. This is detailed, but is good for chasing down problems uncovered in other checks.

These checks should give a good sense of the operational health of the SCOM infrastructure.

Installing Edge Component Monitoring Certificates

Monitoring the Edge Server role requires an install of certificate-based mutual authentication. This process has several steps, but is straightforward. To install and configure certificates to enable the Edge Transport servers to use mutual authentication, complete the following five major tasks:

1. Create a Certificate Template to issue the correct format of X.509 certificates for Operations Manager to use for mutual authentication.

2. Request the Root CA certificate to trust the CA and the certificates it issues. This is done for each Edge Transport server and possibly for the management servers if not using an enterprise CA.

3. Request a certificate from the Root CA to use for mutual authentication. This is done for each Edge Transport server and for each management server.

4. Install the Operations Manager agent manually. This is done for each Edge Transport server.

5. Configure the agent to use the certificate. This is done for each Edge Transport server and for each management server.

These various X.509 certificates are issued from a certificate authority.

Create Certificate Template

This task creates a certificate template named Operations Manager that can be issued from the Windows Server 2008 certification authority web enrollment page. The certificate template supports Server Authentication (OID 1.3.6.1.5.5.7.3.1) and Client Authentication (OID 1.3.6.1.5.5.7.3.2), and enables the name to be manually entered rather than auto-generated from Active Directory because the Edge Transport will not be an Active Directory domain member.

The steps to create the security template follow:

1. Log on to CA, which is DC1.companyxyz.com in this example.
2. Launch **Server Manager**.
3. Expand **Roles**, **Active Directory Certificate Services**, and select **Certificate Templates** (fqdn).
4. Right-click the **Computer** template and select **Duplicate Template**.
5. Leave the version at **Windows 2003 Server, Enterprise Edition** and click **OK**.
6. In the **General** tab in the **Template** display name, enter **Operation Manager**.
7. Select the **Request Handling** tab and mark the **Allow Private Key to Be Exported** option.
8. Select the **Subject Name** tab and select **Supply** in the request. Click **OK** at the warning.
9. Select the **Security** tab, select **Authenticated Users**, and select the **Enroll** check box.
10. Click **OK** to save the template.
11. Select the Enterprise PKI to expose the CA.
12. Right-click the CA and select **Manage CA**.
13. In the certsrv console, expand the CA, right-click the **Certificates Templates**, and select **New, Certificate Template to Issue**.
14. Select the **Operations Manager** certificate template and click **OK**.

The new Operations Manager template is now available in the Windows Server 2008 web enrollment page.

Request the Root CA Server Certificate

This enables the Edge Transport Server to trust the Windows Server 2008 CA. This does not need to be done on the OpsMgr management servers because the Windows Server 2008 CA is an Enterprise CA, and all domain members automatically trust it. If the CA is not an enterprise CA, complete the steps for the management servers as well.

To request and install the Root CA certificate on the Lync Server 2010 Edge Role server, execute the following steps:

1. Log on to the Edge Transport Server (LS2.companyxyz.com, in this example) with local administrator rights.
2. Open a web browser and point it to the certificate server, in this case https://dc1.companyxyz.com/certsrv. Enter credentials if prompted.
3. Click the **Download a CA certificate, certificate chain, or CRL** link (see Figure 13.9).

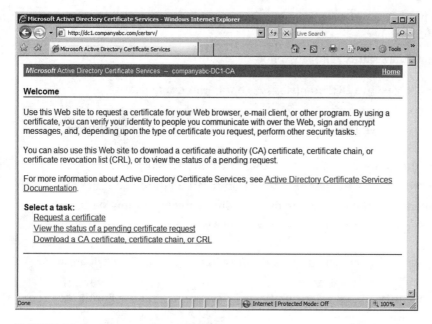

FIGURE 13.9   Download Root CA Certificate

4. Click the **Download CA certificate** link.

NOTE

If the certificate does not download, add the site to the Local Intranet list of sites in IE.

---

5. Click **Open** to open the CA certificate.
6. Click **Install Certificate** to install the CA certificate.
7. In the Certificate Import Wizard screen, click **Next**.
8. Select the **Place all certificates in the following store** radio button.
9. Click **Browse**.
10. Click the **Show physical stores** check box.
11. Expand the **Trusted Root Certification Authorities** folder and select the **Local Computer store**.
12. Click **OK**.
13. Click **Next**, **Finish**, and **OK** to install the CA certificate.
14. Close any open windows.

Repeat for all Edge Transport servers. Now the Edge Transport servers trust certificates issued by the certification authority. The next step is to request the certificates to use for the mutual authentication for all servers.

Request a Certificate from the Root CA Server

Each of the management servers and the servers in the DMZ (that is, the Edge Transport servers) need to be issued certificates to use for communication.

Perform the following steps to request a certificate:

1. Log in as an administrator, open a web browser, and point it to the certificate server (in this case, https://dc1.companyxyz.com/certsrv).
2. Click the **Request a Certificate** link.
3. Click the **advanced certificate request** link.
4. Click the **Create and Submit a request to this CA** link.
5. In the Type of Certificate Template field, select **Operations Manager**.
6. In the Name field, enter the **FQDN** (Fully Qualified Domain Name) of the target server.

> **NOTE**
>
> Go to the actual server to get the name. On the server, go to Computer Properties > Computer Name. Copy the full computer name and paste it into the Name field of the form.

7. Click **Submit**.
8. Click **Yes** when you get the warning pop-up box.
9. Click **Install this certificate**.
10. Click **Yes** when you see the warning pop-up box. The certificate is now installed in the user certificate store.

> **NOTE**
>
> The certificate was installed in the users' certificate store but needs to be in the local computer store for Operations Manager. The capability to use the web enrollment to directly place the certificate into the local computer store was removed from the Windows Server 2008 web enrollment, so the certificate must be moved manually.

11. Select **Start**, **Run**, and enter **mmc** to launch an MMC console.
12. Select **File** and **Add/Remove Snap-In**.
13. Select **Certificates** and click **Add**.
14. Select **My User Account** and click **Finish**.
15. Select **Certificates** again and click **Add**.
16. Select **Computer** account and click **Next**.
17. Select the **Local** computer, click **Finish**, and **OK**.

18. Expand the **Certificates—Current User, Personal**, and select the **Certificates** folder.

19. In the right pane, right-click the certificate issued earlier (in this example, EX3.companyxyz.com) and select **All Tasks, Export**. The certificate can be recognized by the certificate template name Operations Manager.

20. At the Certificate Export Wizard, select **Next**.

21. Select **Yes, export the private key**. Click **Next**.

22. Click **Next**.

23. Enter a password and click **Next**.

24. Enter a directory and filename (such as c:\EX1cert.pfx) and click **Next**.

25. Click **Finish** to export the certificate. Click **OK** in the pop-up box.

26. Expand the **Certificates (Local Computer), Personal**, and select the **Certificates** folder.

NOTE

If this is the first certificate in the local computer store, the Certificates folder will not exist. Simply select the Personal folder instead, and the Certificates folder will be created automatically.

---

27. Right-click in the right pane and select **All Tasks, Import**.

28. In the Certificate Import Wizard, select **Next**.

29. Click **Browse** to locate the certificate file saved earlier. Change the file type to **Personal Information Exchange (pfx)** to view the file. Click **Next**.

30. Enter the password used earlier, select **Mark This Key as Exportable**, and click **Next**.

31. Click **Next**.

32. Click **Finish** and **OK** in the pop-up box to complete the import.

The previous steps need to be completed for each Edge Component server and for each management server.

Install the Agent on the Lync Edge Server

The agent needs to be installed manually on each Lync Edge server. Normally agents are pushed by the Operations Manager console, but Edge servers typically reside in the DMZ and are not members of the domain.

Perform the following steps to manually install the agent:

1. Log on as an administrator and insert the OpsMgr 2007 R2 installation media.

2. At the AutoPlay menu, select **Run SetupOM.exe**.

3. Select **Install Operations Manager 2007 R2 Agent** from the menu.

4. Click **Next**.

5. Click **Next** to accept the default directory.

6. Click **Next** to Specify Management Group Information.

7. Type in the Management Group Name and FQDN of the Management Server. Keep the default Management Server port as **5723**. The example shown in Figure 13.10 has COMPANYXYZ as the management group name and scom1.companyxyz.com as the management server.

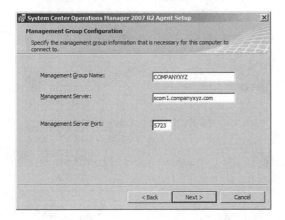

FIGURE 13.10   Manually Entered Management Group Information

8. Click **Next**.

9. Click **Next** at the Agent Action Account page to leave the Local System as the action account.

10. Click **Install** to complete the installation.

11. When the installer finishes, click **Finish**.

Complete the previous steps for each Lync Server 2010 Edge server.

The agent is installed but will not communicate correctly with the management server. This is because the agent has not been configured to use the certificate for mutual authentication. This task is discussed in the next section.

Configure the Agent to Use the Certificate

After the agent is installed, it still needs to be configured to use the correct certificate. The OpsMgr installation includes a utility called MOMCertImport.exe that configures the agent to use certificates for authentication and which certificate in the local computer store to use. The tool does not do any validation checking of the certificate itself, so care needs to be taken that the correct certificate is selected.

Perform the following steps to configure the agent to use a certificate:

1. Log on as an administrator on the Edge Transport server and insert the OpsMgr 2007 R2 installation media.

2. At the AutoPlay menu, select **Run SetupOM.exe**.

3. Select **Browse This CD** from the menu.

4. Select the **SupportTools** directory and the **AMD64** directory.

> **NOTE**
>
> Lync Server 2010 is a 64-bit application, so AMD64 is the correct folder for the 64-bit binaries. If the procedure is run for other servers, select the appropriate directory for the binaries, such as i386.

5. In the directory, double-click **MOMCertImport.exe**.

6. In the pop-up window, select the certificate issued previously and click **OK**. Use the **View Certificate** button to view the certificate details if the correct certificate is not obvious.

The Operation Manager service restarts automatically to have the selected certificate take effect. The preceding steps need to be repeated for each Edge Transport server and for each management server.

The Operations Manager event log can be viewed with the Windows Event Viewer. It is named Operations Manager and is located in the Applications and Services Logs folder in the tool. Any problems with the certificate are shown in the log immediately following the start of the System Center Management service.

Installing the Lync Server 2010 Management Pack

The installation of the Lync Server 2010 management pack is done through the management pack import process, which was used earlier in the chapter to import key management packs.

However, before installing the Lync Server management pack, certain requirements should be met to ensure that the management pack imports and deploys smoothly.

Before Installing the Management Pack

There are some requirements that should be made prior to installing the management pack. The Lync Server 2010 management pack requires the following:

▶ Lync Server 2010 is deployed.

▶ OpsMgr 2007 R2 agents is deployed to all Front End and Edge servers.

▶ Agent proxy is enabled on the Front End servers.

▶ Agent proxy is enabled on the synthetic transaction watcher node.

In most environments, agent proxy is not already enabled. Operations Manager 2007 R2 has a variety of security measures built in to the product to prevent security breaches. One measure in particular is the prevention of impersonation of one agent by another. That is, an agent SERVER1 cannot insert operations data into the database about SERVER2. This could constitute a security violation, where SERVER1 can maliciously generate fraudulent emergencies by making it appear that SERVER2 has operational issues.

Although this is normally a good feature, this can be a problem if, in fact, SERVER1 is monitoring SERVER2 from a client perspective. This is the case with the Lync Server management pack and so agent proxy must be turned on for the management pack to function properly.

To enable agent proxy for a computer, complete the following steps:

1. Open the **Operations Manager 2007 R2** console.
2. Select the **Administration** section.
3. Select the **Agent Managed** node.
4. Right-click the agent in the right pane and select **Properties**.
5. Click the **Security** tab.
6. Check the **Allow This Agent to Act as a Proxy and Discover Managed Objects on Other Computers** check box.
7. Click **OK** to save.

Repeat the steps for all agents that need to act as proxy agents (for example, all Lync Server 2010 front end, edge, and synthetic transaction watcher nodes).

Import the Management Pack

Several management packs are in the Internet catalog on the Microsoft website. The Lync management pack can be downloaded and imported from a file or installed using the Management Pack Wizard.

To import the Lync Server 2010 management pack from the file, perform the following steps:

1. Launch the **Operations Console**.
2. Select the **Administration** section.
3. Select the **Management Packs** folder.
4. Right-click the **Management Packs** folder and select **Import Management Packs**.
5. Click **Add** and select **Add from Disk**.
6. At the prompt to search the online catalog for any management pack dependencies, click **Yes**.
7. Browse to the Lync Server 2010 management pack, which has the filename **Microsoft.LS.2010.Monitoring.mp**.
8. Click **Open**.

9. The wizard now validates the Lync Server 2010 management pack, checking for version conflicts, dependencies, and security risks.

10. Click **Install** to begin the import process.

11. After all the management pack is imported, click **Close** to exit the wizard.

After the import completes, the management pack takes effect immediately. Agents begin discovering based on the schedule specified in the management packs and monitors and rules begin deploying.

Verify Central Discovery Script

The central discovery script runs automatically on the Lync Front End Server with the Central Management Store. This enables the management pack to discover all the roles, components, and services to be monitored.

The process of selecting the server is

1. Detect the Lync Server 2010 server Front End pool with the Central Management Store installed.

2. Discover all Front End servers.

3. Select the active master of the pool.

4. Use the active master to discover all the roles and components in the Lync Server 2010 topology.

This process occurs automatically. To confirm that the process completed without any problems, execute the following steps after importing the Lync Server management pack:

1. Launch the **Operations Manager** console.

2. Select the **Monitoring** space.

3. Expand the **Microsoft Lync Server 2010** folder.

4. Expand the **Topology Discovery** folder.

5. Select the **Discovery State** view.

6. Confirm that the LS Discovery Script state is Healthy, as shown in Figure 13.11.

Enable Edge Server Role Discovery

The Lync Server Edge role discovery is not enabled by default. Even with an agent installed on the edge server and the Lync Server 2010 management pack deployed, the Edge Server role will not be discovered.

The Edge Server role discovery is enabled using an override on the Central Topology Discovery rule.

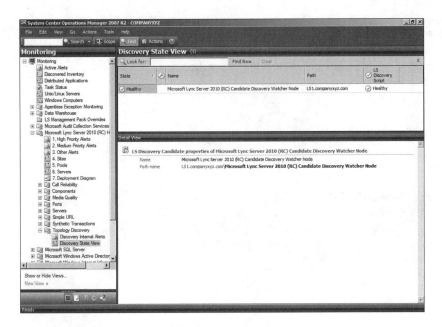

FIGURE 13.11   Lync Server Discovery Script State

To enable Edge role discovery, execute the following steps:

1. Launch the **Operations Manager Console**.

2. Select the **Authoring** space.

3. Expand the **Management Pack Objects** tree.

4. Select the **Object Discoveries** node.

5. In the Look For field, type **LS Central Topology Discovery** and click **Find Now**.

6. Right-click the first LS Central Topology Discovery rule and select **Overrides**, **Override the Object Discovery**, and **For All Objects of Class: LS Discovery Script**.

NOTE

There are multiple instances of the LS Central Topology Discovery rule returned. It doesn't matter which one is selected.

7. Select the destination management pack.

> **NOTE**
>
> Do not use the Default Management Pack because doing so creates problems for removing or updating the management pack in the future. Use or create a management pack dedicated for the Lync Server overrides.

8. Check the **DiscoverEdgeServerRole** box and change the **Override Value** to **True**, as shown in Figure 13.12.

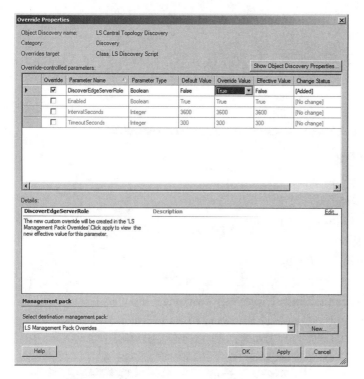

FIGURE 13.12   Edge Discovery Override

9. Click **OK** to save the override.

This now enables the Lync Server 2010 Edge Server role to be discovered and monitored. It can take some time for the Edge role to be discovered after the override is configured.

Configuring and Verifying Synthetic Transactions

Synthetic transactions are not enabled by default. The synthetic transactions are PowerShell cmdlets that allow for monitoring by simulating connections between two users. This enables the availability and performance of a pool to be tested.

Configuring synthetic transactions require several manual steps, including setting up the test users, configuring the synthetic transactions, configuring the watcher node to be discovered by the Operations Manager management pack, and optionally overwriting default performance threshold values for the watcher node.

To configure the Lync Server synthetic transactions:

1. Create two test user accounts and enable them for Lync services (for example, LSTest1 and LSTest2).

> **NOTE**
>
> The load on the watcher node can be significant.

13

2. On the intended synthetic transaction watcher node, launch the **Lync Server Management Shell**.

3. Enter the **New-CsHealthMonitoringConfiguration -TargetFQDN <PoolFQDN> -FirstTestUserSipUri <FirstUserSipUri> -SecondTestUserSipUri <SecondUserSipUri> -Verbose** command. For example, for the ls1.companyxyz.com pool and users LSTest1 and LSTest2, the command is shown in Figure 13.13.

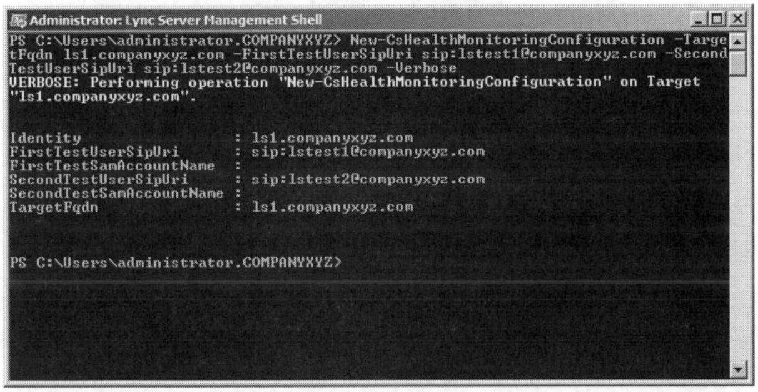

FIGURE 13.13   Synthetic Transaction Enable

> **NOTE**
>
> The test account SIP URI must be prefixed with the SIP:, as in sip:lstest1@companyxyz.com.

4. Confirm that the synthetic transaction is working by entering the **Test-CsRegistration <PoolFQDN> -verbose** command. For example, for the ls1. companyxyz.com pool, the command is shown in Figure 13.14.

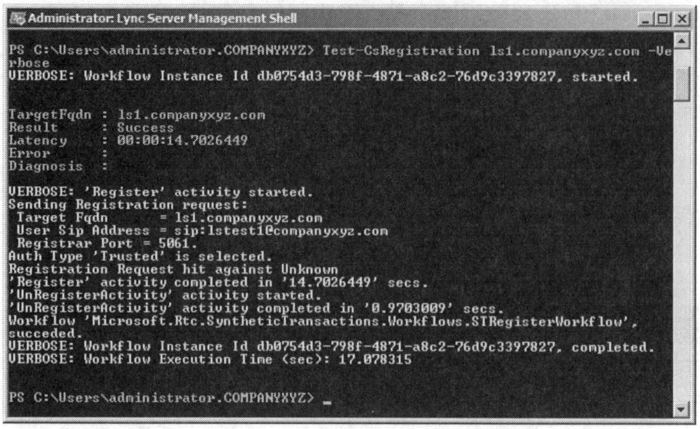

FIGURE 13.14   Synthetic Transaction Testing

5. The Result field shows Success, indicating that the synthetic transaction is configured properly.

6. Operations Manager 2007 R2 does not discover the watcher node automatically. A set of registry keys must be created to force the discovery. Set the registry keys for watcher node discovery by executing the following cmdlets from Communications Server Management Shell:

```
New-Item -Path "HKLM:\Software\Microsoft\Real-Time Communications\Health" and
"New-ItemProperty -Path "HKLM:\Software\Microsoft\Real-Time
Communications\Health" -Name"IsSTWatcherNode" -Value true ¦ Out-Null"
```

7. To enable the optional logging on the watcher node, run the PowerShell command:

```
New-ItemProperty -Path "HKLM:\Software\Microsoft\Real-Time
Communications\Health" -
    Name "LogOpsMgr" -PropertyType DWord -value 2 .
```

The watcher node is discovered by Operations Manager. The synthetic transaction shows state, generates alerts, and gathers latency performance data for IM, presence, address book, conferencing, and other client-facing services. Figure 13.15 shows a sample of the wealth of synthetic transaction information that is generated.

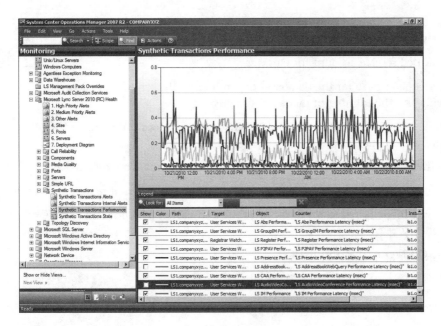

FIGURE 13.15   Synthetic Transaction Performance Information

Best Practices

The following are best practices from this chapter:

▶ Deploy System Center Operations Manager 2007 R2 for monitoring Lync Server 2010.

▶ Install the Windows Operating System, Active Directory, DNS, IIS, and Exchange management packs into OpsMgr to monitor network systems and applications that Lync Server 2010 depends on.

▶ Deploy Operations Manager Components on Windows 64-bit and SQL 64-bit for optimal performance.

▶ Create override management packs for each application management pack, such as the Lync Server 2010 management pack. Don't use the default management pack.

▶ Take future expansion and relevance of hardware into account when sizing servers for OpsMgr deployment.

▶ Keep the installation of OpsMgr on a separate server or a set of separate dedicated member servers that do not run any other separate applications.

▶ Use SQL Server Reporting Services to produce custom reports using OpsMgr's reporting feature.

▶ Start with a single management group and add on additional management groups only if they are absolutely necessary.

▶ Use a dedicated service account for OpsMgr.

▶ Allocate adequate space for the databases depending on the length of time needed to store events and the number of managed systems.

▶ Monitor the size of the OpsMgr database to ensure that it does not increase beyond the bounds of acceptable size.

▶ Leverage the reporting database to store and report on data over a long period.

▶ Modify the grooming interval to aggressively address environmental requirements.

▶ Configure synthetic transactions to monitor the end-user experience and latency of service delivery.

▶ Configure OpsMgr to monitor itself.

Summary

System Center Operations Manager 2007 R2 is key to managing Lync Server 2010. It can also be used in Windows Server 2003, Windows Server 2008, or mixed environments to provide for automated monitoring of all vital operating system, application, and network functionality. This type of functionality is instrumental in reducing downtime and getting the most out of a Lync Server 2010 investment. In a nutshell, OpsMgr is an effective way to gain proactive, rather than reactive, control over the entire environment.

CHAPTER 14

Backup and Restore of Microsoft Lync Server 2010

Real-time communication has evolved into a business-critical function. This becomes even more important as enterprises look to Lync Server to replace its legacy PBX system and function as an enterprise voice platform. As with any business-critical service, it must be backed up. Even more important, it must be backed up in a way that restoration of service is both straightforward and quick. After all, telephone service has the same expectations as electricity: always on. A good backup strategy is a solid way to meet those expectations.

> ▶ If you are looking for information specific to virtualization and snapshotting as a backup process, a full review of the topic is included in Chapter 25, "Virtualization."

This chapter highlights not only the best practices in creating a backup strategy for Lync Server, but also how to implement that strategy in your environment. It starts with a discussion of Lync Server backup strategy, followed by backup and restore processes. Finally, this chapter concludes with troubleshooting and best practices.

Backup and Restore Strategy

Simply backing up a server is not a viable strategy in and of itself nor is redundancy a suitable substitution for a good backup strategy. A good backup strategy considers uptime and restoration Service Level Agreements (SLA) and the impact of an extended outage.

As in previous versions, there are multiple facets to backing up Lync Server. Obviously, the SQL databases must be backed up. Fortunately, this process is fairly straightforward. There is nothing unique about backing up a Lync Server database compared to another SQL database. However, the Central Management Server (CMS) database must be backed up, too. In contrast, the local SQL express instances on each server role do not need to be backed up because they contain no unique information.

The next consideration is backing up the Lync Server configuration. The familiar LCSCmd process is gone, but it is replaced with the more powerful Lync Server cmdlets. Finally, one must consider a traditional full backup of each of the individual servers. However, in some environments, traditional backups may not be a requirement.

For most, environments in Table 14.1 outlines the best practices related to backup strategy.

TABLE 14.1   Best Practices for Backup Strategies

Type	Frequency
SQL database	Nightly
CMS	Every time a change is made, or at least monthly
Server backup	Weekly

> **NOTE**
>
> In environments that have no downtime, additional steps might be required. However, these types of scenarios are not the norm and are out of the scope of this chapter.

Backup Processes

This section includes the steps necessary to back up your Lync Server environment. As mentioned previously, backing up the environment is a multistep process. This section covers each step in detail. Of course, these steps are adequate for most eveninronments. Environments with special requirements might require a more exotic solution to back up and restore.

Backing Up Lync Server Databases

The good news is there is nothing unique about the Lync Server databases stored in SQL Server. They can be backed up and restored like any other database. Although this section does not cover the SQL database process in depth, it summarizes the process for CS administrators who might not be familiar with the process.

> **NOTE**
>
> Keep in mind that each pool has a unique database and must be backed up separately.

As in previous versions, data is stored in the RTC database. Backups can be done in the SQL Management Studio GUI, scripted using TSQL, or by using a SQL-specific backup agent such as Microsoft Data Protection Manager 2010. Because there are many different enterprise backup products, this section reviews the first two options. Users with an enterprise backup platform should follow the instrutions for SQL backup from their platform vendors.

Backing Up the RTC Database

For a given front end pool, the only database that needs to be backed up is the RTC database. If you choose to deploy Monitoring or Archiving services, those databases need to be backed up in the same manner. To back up the RTC database using the SQL Management Studio GUI, first log in to your SQL server and follow the steps that follow:

1. Open the SQL Management Studio tool and connect to the appropriate SQL instance where the RTC database is stored.

2. Expand **Databases** and find the **RTC** database.

3. Right-click the **RTC** database and select **Tasks, and** then select **Back Up.**

4. In the window that displays, ensure the RTC database is selected and the backup type is Full. Ensure the appropriate destination is selected, too. A proper configuration of this screen is shown in Figure 14.1.

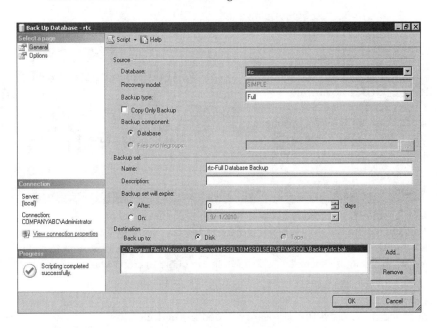

FIGURE 14.1   SQL Database Backup General Options

5. In the left column, select the **Options** item. Most of the items can be left at their default settings; however, it is recommended you enable the **Verify backup when finished** box, as shown in Figure 14.2. Because the RTC database is not very large, this process does not require much additional time.

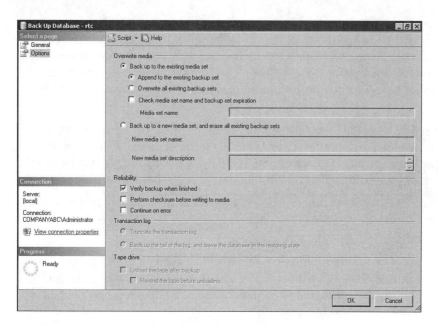

FIGURE 14.2 SQL Database Backup Other Options

6. Click **OK** to begin the backup.

7. A pop-up should display with the message, "The backup of database "rtc' completed successfully." Click **OK** to continue.

Create TSQL Script to Back Up the RTC Database

There are two ways to create the TSQL script for backing up the RTC database. If you are familiar with TSQL, it's simple to write the script and set it as a job.

TIP

If you are not familiar with TSQL, there is a way to have the SQL Management studio write the script for you. Follow steps 1–5 in the preceding section. However, instead of clicking **OK**, click the **Script** button at the top of the window and choose **Script Action to New Query Window** as shown in Figure 14.3. Simply run the query to create the backup.

For the process outlined previously, the script is included in the following:

```
BACKUP DATABASE [rtc] TO DISK = N'C:\Program Files\Microsoft SQL
Server\MSSQL10.MSSQLSERVER\MSSQL\Backup\rtc.bak' WITH NOFORMAT, NOINIT, NAME
= N'rtc-Full Database Backup', SKIP, NOREWIND, NOUNLOAD, STATS = 10
GO
declare @backupSetId as int
select @backupSetId = position from msdb..backupset where
```

```
database_name=N'rtc' and backup_set_id=(select max(backup_set_id) from
msdb..backupset where database_name=N'rtc' )
if @backupSetId is null begin raiserror(N'Verify failed. Backup information
for database ''rtc'' not found.', 16, 1) end
RESTORE VERIFYONLY FROM DISK = N'C:\Program Files\Microsoft SQL
Server\MSSQL10.MSSQLSERVER\MSSQL\Backup\rtc.bak' WITH FILE = @backupSetId,
NOUNLOAD, NOREWIND
GO
```

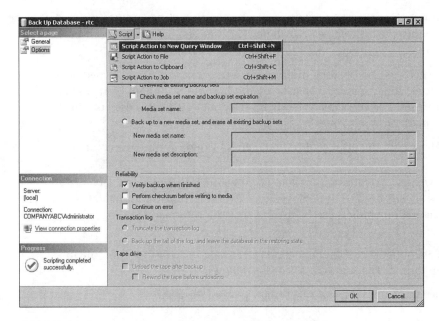

FIGURE 14.3   Creating a TSQL Script for Database Backup

Backing Up the Central Management Store

As mentioned previously, the long-lived LCSCmd.exe commands are gone and replaced with Lync Server Management Shell cmdlets. Specifically, the cmdlets for backing up the Central Management Store (CMS) are Export-CsConfiguration and Export-CsLisConfiguration, which export the overall configuration and the E911configuration, respectively.

▶ The process for restoring service from the exported configuration is covered later in the "Restore Processes" section of this chapter.

The Export-CsConfiguration cmdlet exports the Lync Server global configuration. In previous versions, much of this information was stored in Active Directory; however, for Lync Server, it's stored in the CMS. The CMS should be backed up after every configuration change or at a regular interval to ensure it can be easily restored in case of failure. There are two syntaxes for the command and both are displayed in the following:

```
Export-CsConfiguration - Filename <string> [-Force <SwitchParameter>] [-
LocalStore <SwitchParameter>]
Export-CsConfiguration –AsBytes <SwitchParameter> [-Force <SwitchParameter>]
 [-LocalStore <SwitchParameter>]
```

The parameters are defined as follows:

> ▶ **Filename**—Path to the .zip file to be created. For example, "C:\CsConfig.zip". You must use either the –FileName or –AsBytes flag, but you cannot use both in the same command.

> ▶ **AsBytes**—Returns CS Topology information as a byte array. The returned data must then be stored in a variable to be used by the Import-CsConfiguration cmdlets. You must use either the –FileName or –AsBytes flag, but you cannot use both in the same command.

> ▶ **Force**—Suppresses the display of nonfatal errors when running the command.

Normally, you wait for a replication cycle to occur before building a new server role. However, if new servers need to be deployed quickly, the Export-CSConfiguration and Import-CsConfiguration cmdlets can be used in succession to manually copy the topology to the new system.

The Export-CsLisConfiguration cmdlet exports E911 data to a configuration file in compressed .zip format. The syntax is defined as follows:

```
Export-CsLisConfiguration –Filename <string> [<CommonParameter>]
```

The parameters are defined as follows:

> ▶ Filename—Path to the .zip file to be created.

> ▶ CommonParameter—Any of the Cs common parameters including Verbose, Debug, ErrorAction, ErrorVariable, Warningaction, WarningVariable, OutBuffer, and OutVariable.

With these two files, a disaster recovery scenario becomes realistic. Without them, you are assured of starting over from scratch.

Backing Up Lync Server Servers

Although there are numerous enterprise backup solutions, this section focuses on the one included with Windows Server 2008 R2—namely Windows Server Backup. This tool is similar to NTBackup.exe, which has been used for years as a Windows backup solution.

Windows Server Backup must be added as a feature before it can be used. From the Server Manager tool, right-click **Features**, and then select **Add Features**. In the window that displays, put a check mark sext to Windows Server Backup Features. Click **Next**, and then click **Install to finish the installation**. A reboot is not required before using the feature.

When you launch Windows Server Backup from the Start menu, you see a screen similar to Figure 14.4. The following steps review the process to create a one-time server backup. The tool can also be used to create scheduled recurring backups.

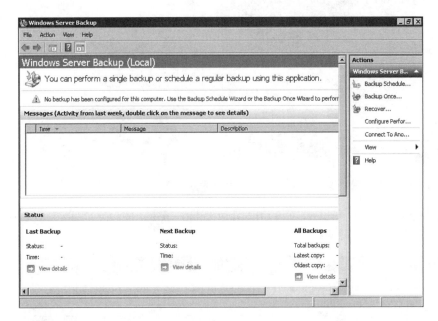

FIGURE 14.4   Windows Server Backup

To create a one-time server backup using the built-in Windows Server Backup tool, follow the steps that follow:

1. In the Windows Server Backup MMC, click **Backup Once** in the right action pane.

2. At the first screen, click **Next**.

3. For most installations, select **Full Server**, and then click **Next**.

TIP

It is generally recommended you store your backups in a location other than the local disk of the server. In the case of a server failure, all backups would be lost. This can be a SAN disk or something as simple as a share on another system. Select **Remote Shared Folder, and** then click **Next**.

---

4. For the purpose of this example, we save the backup to a share on another server, as shown in Figure 14.5. Select the **Do Not Inherit** option to limit access to a specific account.

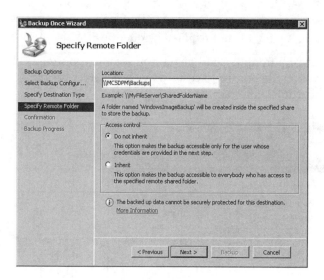

FIGURE 14.5   Save the Backup to a Location Other Than the Local Server

5. In the login prompt that displays, enter the appropriate credentials for an account that should have access to backup files.

NOTE

Often this is a service account. Note that this account must have write access to the location where the backup is stored.

---

6. Ensure everything is correct on the Confirmation screen, as shown in Figure 14.6. Then click **Backup** to start the backup process.

7. The Backup Progress screen displays and shows the backup progress, as shown in Figure 14.7.

8. When the backup process completes, click **Close** to close the window and finish the job.

The Windows Server Backup console shows the success backup and its timestamp in the Messages window. The Last Backup section also includes a "Successful" message and the timestamp.

This process can be done on all the Lync Server roles. However, as noted previously, SQL database backup is a different and unique process.

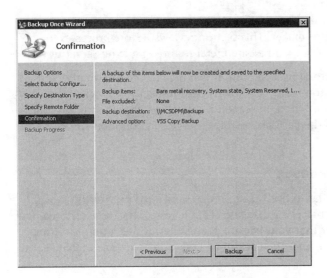

FIGURE 14.6   Windows Server Backup Confirmation

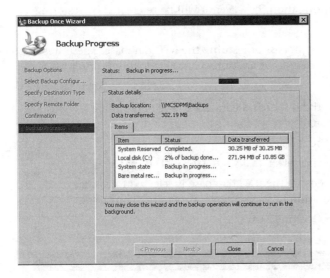

FIGURE 14.7   Windows Server Backup Progress

Restore Processes

Now that you have learned how to back up your data and systems, this section goes over the processes to restore that data. One can easily argue that restore is the most important part. If for no other reason, a successful restore implies a successful backup is available.

In many cases, a restore is the logical reversal of the backup process. However, there are still some decisions the administrator makes. This section reviews restore processes for databases, restoring or moving the CMS, and a bare metal restore of a Lync Server server.

Although it is simple to devise a strong backup plan, it is more challenging to plan for restoring service. There are simply too many unknowns with respect to the reason for the restore to plan for immediate restoration in all scenarios. There are literally infinite solutions available. This section covers the basics of restoring service in common situations.

Restoring Lync Server Databases

The database restore process is similar to the backup process outlined previously. Again, there is nothing unique about a Lync Server database. That is to say, it can be restored like any other SQL database. Remember that your backup process performed a point-in-time backup, meaning any changes made after the backup was performed are not included and will not be restored.

For the front end pool, only the RTC database needs to be restored. The RTCDyn database contains transient information and is re-created by the Front End Server. The RTCConfig database contains configuration information; however, it will be re-created by restoring the CMS in the next step.

The following steps walk through the process of restoing the RTC database. These steps assume the server is up and stable. These steps are not a complete instruction set for server replacement.

1. Open the SQL Management Studio tool and connect to the appropriate SQL instance where the RTC database is stored.
2. Expand **Databases** and find the **RTC** database.
3. Right-click the **RTC** database and select **Tasks – Restore – Database**.
4. In the window that displays, ensure the RTC database is selected for source and destination. A proper configuration of this screen is shown in Figure 14.8.
5. In the left column, select the **Options** item.

TIP

Most of the items can be left at their default settings. However, it is recommended to select the **Overwite the Existing Database** check box. This ensures there is no lingering garbage from a previous corrupted database.

---

6. Click **OK** to restore the database.

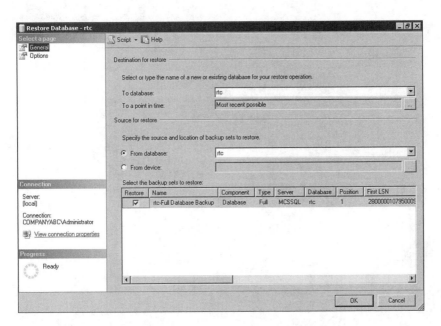

FIGURE 14.8   SQL Database Restore General Options

Create TSQL Script to Restore the RTC Database

There are two ways to create the TSQL script for restoring the RTC database. If you are familiar with TSQL, it's fairly simple to write the script and set it as a job.

TIP

If you are not familiar with TSQL, there is a way to have the SQL Management studio write the script for you. Follow steps 1–5 as shown previously. However, instead of clicking **OK**, click the **Script** button at the top of the window and choose **Script Action to New Query Window,** as shown in Figure 14.9. Simply run the query to create the backup.

For the process outlined previously, the script is included here.

```
RESTORE DATABASE [rtc] FROM DISK = N'C:\Program Files\Microsoft SQL
Server\MSSQL10.MSSQLSERVER\MSSQL\Backup\rtc.bak' WITH FILE = 1, NOUNLOAD,
REPLACE, STATS = 10
GO
```

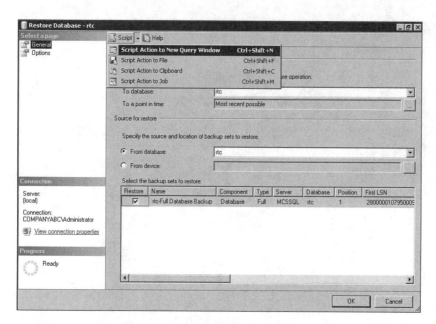

FIGURE 14.9   Creating a TSQL Script for Database Restore

Restoring the Central Management Store

Just like backing up the CMS, the restore process is performed with Lync Server Command Shell cmdlets. If you are looking to simply restore a known good configuration, use the Import-CsConfiguration and Import-CsLisConfiguration cmdlets. However, if the CMS is offline permanently or you simply want to move the CMS to a different pool, use the Move-CsManagementServer cmdlet.

The Import-CsConfiguration cmdlet imports the Lync Server global configuration from a exported file. There are two syntaxes for the command and both are displayed in the following:

```
Import-CsConfiguration - Filename <string> [-Force <switchParameters>
Export-CsConfiguration -ByteInput <Byte[]>
```

The parameters are defined as follows:

▶ **Filename**—Path to the .zip file to be imported. You must use either the –FileName or –AsBytes flag, but you cannot use both in the same command.

▶ **ByteInput**—Imports the topology based on a byte array stored in a variable from the export-CsConfiguration cmdlet. You must use either the –FileName or –AsBytes flag, but you cannot use both in the same command.

▶ **Force**—Suppresses the display of nonfatal errors when running the command.

If you want to move the CMS or you need to in a disaster recovery scenario, you'll use the Move-CsManagementServer cmdlet.

> **CAUTION**
>
> It is important to note that the Move-CsManagementServer cmdlet must be run from the server that becomes the new CMS owner. It cannot be run from a different system or the system where the CMS currently resides.

The syntax for the command is as follows:

```
Move-CsManagementServer –Confirm [<SwitchParameter>] [-CsConfiguration
<String>] [-CsLisConfiguration <String>] [-Force <switchParameter>] [-Report
<String>]
```

The parameters are defined as follows:

▶ **Confirm**—Prompts the user for confirmation before executing the command.

▶ **CsConfiguration**—Full path to the Lync Server .zip file created by the Export-CsConfiguration command.

▶ **CsLisConfiguration**—Full path to the Lync Server .zip file created by the Export-CsLisConfiguration command.

▶ **Force**—Forces the management server to move even if the existing database is offline. This parameter is required in a disaster recovery situation. Note that some data may be lost when using the force switch, so it should be used only as a last resort.

▶ **Report**—Creates an HTML log file at the specified location.

In a nondisaster recovery scenario where you are just moving the CMS to another server, the command is simple:

```
Move-CsManagementServer
```

However, in a disaster recovery scenario it would look more like this:

```
Move-CsManagementServer -CsConfiguration "C:\backup\CSConfiguration.zip" -
CsLisConfiguration "C:\backup\CSLisConfiguration.zip -Force -Report
"C:\logs\MoveCMS.html"
```

Of all the various restore processes, these tools are the most powerful. Armed with them, an administrator can recover from nearly any scenario.

14

Restoring Lync Server Servers

Earlier in this chapter, the server backup process process was outlined. This section covers the server restore process using the same tool, Windows Server Backup. Even if you are only restoring and not performing any actual backup tasks, Windows Server Backup must be added as a feature before it can be used. From the Server Manager tool, right-click **Features** and select **Add Features**. In the window that displays, select the **Windows Server Backup Features** check box. Click **Next, and** then click **Install** to finish the installation. A reboot is not required before using the feature.

Launch Windows Server Backup from the Start menu. Follow these steps to restore the server:

1. In the right action pane, click **Recover**.
2. Choose whether the backup file is located locally or on another server. Following the backup process previously outlined, it is stored on another server. Choose this option, and then click **Next**.
3. Choose **Remote Shared Folder**, and then click **Next**.
4. Enter the UNC path to the share. For the example shown, it is **\\MCSDPM\Backups**.
5. Choose the appropriate date of the backup you want to restore. The text at the top of the page shows the dates of the oldest and newest backups. Click **Next**.
6. Select **System State** and click **Next**.
7. Select **Original location** and click **Next**.
8. Click **Recover**.

After the system reboots, follow the same process, but choose to recover the volume.

Alternatively, an administrator can load the Windows 2008 R2 OS disc and start the Windows Recovery Environment. This allows a bare metal recovery. Assuming the same or identical hardware, this is the best way to ensure a successful recovery.

Troubleshooting

The backup process is straightforward; it's usually the restore process that is challenging. This section reviews common issues and areas to check should the process not go smoothly.

When running the Lync Server cmdlets, ensure you started the command shell in Administrator mode. Many cmdlets won't work unless executed in an elevated privilege environment. The errors can often be cryptic and not explicitly say they failed because of a shell permissions issue.

Often, even after a clean restore, a server may not respond as expected. In this scenario, it is recommended to uninstall the Lync Server binaries from the system using the **Programs and Features** item in the Control Panel. After a reboot, reinstall Lync Server. The server pulls clean data from the CMS and should begin to function correctly.

A disaster recovery situation is not the best time to find out that your backups were not successful. Monitor the backup logs and be diligent in ensuring a good backup is always available. Despite the extra time required, always verify a backup to ensure its validity.

Best Practices

The following are the best practices from this chapter:

▶ Have a good backup plan and a tested disaster recovery plan before you need it. Run through the plan and processes regularly.

▶ When running the Move-CsManagementServer cmdlet, only use the –force switch in a disaster recovery scenario.

▶ Always run the Move-CsManagementServer cmdlet from the server you want to move the CMS to, not the server you are moving from.

▶ If you are restoring to the same or identical hardware, perform a bare metal restore using the Windows Recovery Environment.

▶ Always store your backup files on a separate server. This ensures that a server failure does not take all backup files with it.

▶ Run the Export-CsConfiguration cmdlet after each configuration change to ensure a good backup is always available.

▶ It is a best practice to test the restore process in an isolated lab environment from time to time so that administrators are familiar with the process and that the backups are reliable.

14

Administration of Microsoft Lync Server 2010

Administration of Lync Server 2010 is a welcome relief for those who spend time managing a Live Communications Server or Office Communications Server deployment. The older products were based on a Microsoft Management Console snap-in that was not intuitive and often required many clicks to perform simple tasks. This chapter covers some of the improvements found in Lync Server 2010, such as the Lync Server Control Panel and the Lync Server Management Shell.

The addition of the Lync Server Management Shell follows the precedent set by the Microsoft Exchange Server team, and the Lync team has taken another cue by including role-based access control (RBAC) in this release. The Lync RBAC differs slightly from Exchange RBAC and is compared in this chapter.

Also discussed is the new topology model where all server planning and configuration are performed centrally. Building a topology using the Topology Builder and storing the configuration in the new Central Management Store (CMS) is explained in this chapter. The new scope-based policies are covered as well.

Common management tasks, such as draining servers or configuring quality of service settings, are detailed in this chapter. Finally, common troubleshooting steps are described with examples and how to use the Lync Server Logging Tool is covered.

Administration Overview

The life of a Lync Server administrator varies depending on the role within the organization, and this is where Lync Server 2010 shines over previous versions. Instead of resorting to a complex and difficult management console or Visual Basic script files, there is now an improved user interface backed by a management shell based on Windows PowerShell just as in Exchange Server since 2007. Combined with the new role-based access control, administrators can tackle delegated specific tasks either in the Lync Server Control Panel or leverage the Lync Server Management Shell command-line interface.

Lync Server Control Panel

A fairly drastic shift with Lync Server 2010 has been the initiative to completely remove the emphasis on managing servers using the Microsoft Management Console (MMC). With Lync Server 2010, the MMC console is replaced with the Lync Server Control Panel (LSCP), which is a web-based management interface that uses the Microsoft Silverlight runtime for management tasks. Figure 15.1 shows the layout of the new interface.

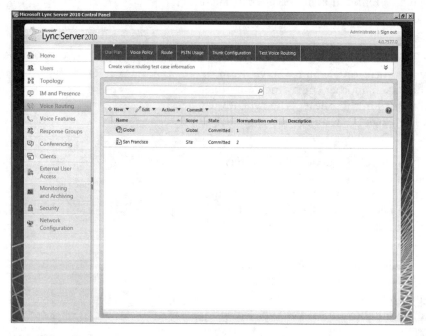

FIGURE 15.1   Lync Server Control Panel Interface

This change has several benefits that are immediately visible to administrators familiar with installing the old management tools on a separate workstation. Installation of the administrative tools took manually going through four to five different installation package prerequisites before the OCS administrative tools could be installed. Instead, the requirement now is that the end user have the latest Silverlight plug-in for the web browser.

From within the Lync Server Control Panel, administrators have a centralized dashboard for all management activities. This includes managing user accounts and policies that control what features are available to users.

> **NOTE**
>
> Opening the Lync Server Control Panel is similar to opening a web browser to the administrative web page. By default Internet Explorer does not pass credentials to a site unless specifically allowed, so administrators are prompted for credentials each time. To prevent the prompt for credentials, add the Lync administrative URL to the Local Intranet Zone in Internet Explorer. By default, this is https://<Pool FQDN or admin simple URL>.

The Lync Server Control Panel is divided into several sections, and each section has subsections for specific actions or policies. An overview of the options available within each section is described in the following:

- **Users**—Enable or disable users for Lync services, assign policies to users, and move users between pools.

- **Topology**—Provides a health overview of the deployment and reports on the status of all services. The different server applications and trusted applications are displayed in this section.

- **IM and presence**—Provides the file transfer, and intelligent IM filter settings.

- **Voice routing**—Contains settings for dial plans, voice policies, routes, trunk configuration, and PSTN usages. This section also contains test cases for assessing whether dial plans and routing are working as expected.

- **Voice features**—Contains settings for the new voice applications such as call park and unassigned number routing.

- **Response groups**—Links to the management interface for Response Group configuration. Queues and groups can be added or modified in this section as well.

- **Conferencing**—Configure conferencing policies, meeting configuration, dial-in access numbers, and PIN policies.

- **Clients**—Control Lync client versioning and updates. Firmware updates for Lync Phone Edition phones are also managed in this section.

- **External user access**—Contains external access policies controlling federation and public IM connectivity. Federated domains and allowed public IM networks are configured within this section.

▶ **Monitoring and archiving**—Configures settings for Call Detail Records, Quality of Experience monitoring, and instant message archiving.

▶ **Security**—Control authentication methods for clients and PIN policies for Lync Phone Edition devices.

▶ **Network configuration**—Configures the topology used for Call Admission Control, Media Bypass, and E-911.

CAUTION

Although the Lync Server Control Panel has its advantages over MMC management tasks, there are also some downsides, such as the fact that there is no right-click functionality available. This might be an adjustment that helps drive more administrators to learn the Lync Server Management Shell instead.

Lync Server Management Shell

A big change to Lync Server 2010 is the addition of the Lync Server Management Shell (LSMS). The LSMS is built on Microsoft's PowerShell command and scripting environment and is really the core of what drives Lync Server 2010 management. Many administrators will use the Lync Server Control Panel (LSCP) by default because they are more familiar with a graphical user interface, but as time goes on it should become apparent that much of Lync server management can be done in a more efficient manner through the LSMS.

Many organizations that use Microsoft Exchange Server are already familiar with how the Management Shell operates. When Microsoft first introduced the Exchange Management Shell as part of Exchange Server 2007, many administrators were frustrated and even intimidated by having some functionality only available in a command-line interface. The same is now true with the LSMS for previous administrators of LCS and OCS. Oftentimes, the same team within an organization who manages Exchange is responsible for managing Lync. If administrators have experience with the Exchange Management Shell, the change might not seem quite as drastic. For those entirely new to a command-line interface, it might take some time to feel comfortable.

Benefits of the Management Shell

For administrators primarily familiar with using graphical user interface (GUI) tools to manage systems, the LSMS might seem a bit intimidating at first, but Lync Server administrators new to PowerShell should spend some time getting acquainted with the new command-line based toolset for several reasons. First, some tasks and actions simply do not exist within the LSCP, so for these types of features, administrators must resort to using the LSMS. For example, in Live Communications Server and Office Communications Server, changing the port that a Front End Server used for SIP communication involved just a few check boxes within the management console. With Lync Server 2010, the only way to modify the port or add an additional port is to use the LSMS.

> **NOTE**
>
> A good example is when administrators want to allow a Lync Server Front End to also listen on port 5060 for unencrypted SIP communication in addition to the standard 5061 for SIP over TLS. This isn't possible in the Lync Server Control Panel, but to enable this feature using the Lync Server Management Shell, use the following cmdlet:
>
> Set-CsRegistrar registrar:<Pool FQDN> -SipServerTcpPort 5060

Another major benefit of the LSMS is that bulk tasks are much easier to accomplish. With the older products, a task such as moving users between pools or modifying assigned policies was typically done through the management consoles and involved running through multiple pages of a wizard. Selecting the correct users to modify was also somewhat difficult because there was no breakdown of groups or divisions within the GUI. In the end, it was apparent that performing bulk tasks needed some attention from the product group. With the LSMS, administrators have an incredible amount of flexibility in how to perform certain tasks. It is easy for administrators to select a group of users based on an attribute and modify all policies or move users quickly.

> **NOTE**
>
> Although bulk changes are easy to make with the LSMS, that also means it can be easy to make a mistake and have it affect many user accounts. Be sure to always test bulk changes on a smaller subset of users. If possible, have a test or development environment where bulk changes can be verified before they run against the production systems.

> **TIP**
>
> Some organizations familiar with PowerShell use custom scripts to provision new user accounts. Scripting these kinds of operations greatly reduces the chance for a human error to affect the account creation.

Just imagine how many times the wrong dial plan, voice policy, or conferencing policy can be applied to a new account when left as a manual process. For small organizations this isn't typically an issue, but for larger companies having a standardized, automated method is a necessity.

This kind of PowerShell-based provisioning has been fairly typical for Exchange mailboxes since Exchange 2007. Because OCS did not have any native PowerShell support, organizations were forced to continue using VBScript or some other method to automatically enable new accounts for OCS. With the LSMS, an entire workflow script can be used to create new accounts. When a new user joins the company, a PowerShell script is used to automatically create the new user account, place it in the correct organizational unit, provision a home folder, create an Exchange mailbox on the correct database, enable the user for Lync, and assign the correct voice and conferencing policies. Not only is the chance for error reduced, but consider how much time is saved by not requiring extra work.

Management Shell Basics

Tasks are performed in PowerShell through commands called *cmdlets*. Cmdlets each have a specific function and begin with a verb, such as Get or Set, indicating what action will be taken. The remainder of the cmdlet determines what specific object will be viewed or acted upon. The Lync Server Management Shell is built on top of the Windows PowerShell engine, meaning that everything you can do within Windows PowerShell can also be done within the Lync Server Management Shell. The opposite, however, is not true.

> **NOTE**
>
> When loading the Lync Server Management Shell, an extensive list of more than 500 custom cmdlets is loaded on top of the base PowerShell cmdlets available. These new cmdlets are specific to Lync Server and enable administrators to manage Lync components through the Management Shell.

Most of the cmdlets within the Lync Server Management Shell (LSMS) are consistent in their naming approach because they follow a format consisting of a verb, a hyphen, the letters "Cs," and lastly, an item. This might seem long, but it makes sense when you view the actual cmdlets. Commands to view the configuration or properties of an item all begin with Get and when changing or assigning new properties, the cmdlet begins with Set. For example, to view the properties of a particular Lync user account, the cmdlet Get-CsUser can be used. To set one of the properties for a user account, such as a phone number, the Set-CsUser cmdlet can be used.

> **NOTE**
>
> All the cmdlets in Lync Server 2010 include the Cs designator, which stands for Communications Server. The actual name change from Communications Server 14 to Lync Server happened fairly late in the product life cycle, and the cmdlet naming was never updated.

The first parameter in any cmdlet is referred to as the *identity*, which signifies what object will be acted upon. Not all Get cmdlets require an identity to be provided and, when omitted, it will return a list of all the matching objects. For example, running Get-CsUser –Identity sip:tom@companyabc.com returns the properties of only a single user, but simply running Get-CsUser with no identity specified returns a list of all users and their properties.

When using a Set command though, an identity must be specified so that the Management Shell knows which object should be modified. Additionally, the attribute of the object being modified must be specified. Only the attribute being changed must be included, so if other attributes are staying the same there is no need to include them. For example, if a user needs to be enabled for Enterprise Voice and assigned a Line URI, the command looks like the following string:

```
Set-CsUser -Identity sip:tom@companyabc.com - EnterpriseVoiceEnabled $true
-LineUri tel:+12223334444
```

Commands can also be strung together, or "piped" to one another. When piped to another cmdlet, the object passed from the first cmdlet is assumed to be the identity in the second cmdlet. Continuing the previous example, an equivalent command to the Set-CsUser example is the following string:

```
Get-CsUser -Identity sip:tom@companyabc.com ¦ Set-CsUser
-EnterpriseVoiceEnabled $true -LineUri tel:+12223334444
```

This might not seem beneficial when a single user is involved, but when piping multiple objects to another cmdlet they will each run through the destination cmdlet. Consider a scenario where an organization wants to enable all users who have a display name starting with the letter T for Enterprise Voice. First, the Get-CsUser cmdlet is used, but to return only the users whose display name begins with T, a Filter parameter is used. For those familiar with filtering using the Where-Object cmdlet, the Filter parameter uses the same syntax and operators. The Where-Object cmdlet can also be used here, but the built-in Filter parameter is more straightforward.

```
Get-CsUser -Filter {DisplayName -like "T*"}
```

This can be built on even further by piping the results to a Set-CsUser cmdlet where the users can be enabled for Enterprise Voice:

```
Get-CsUser -Filter {DisplayName -like "T*"} ¦ Set-CsUser -EnterpriseVoiceEnabled
$true
```

This short string of cmdlets can enable thousands of users for Enterprise Voice in a much faster method than using the Lync Server Control Panel.

Tips and Tricks

There are quite a few shortcuts and tricks that can be used within the Lync Server Management Shell to save time. This section discusses a few tips that might make using the Management Shell a bit easier and more efficient.

Use the Tab Key

Instead of typing a full cmdlet name, begin typing the first few letters after the action verb and press the Tab key. The Management Shell automatically cycles through the cmdlets that match the string already entered. For example, typing Get-CsP and then pressing Tab automatically changes to Get-CsPinPolicy. Pressing Tab again changes to Get-CsPool. Use Tab to go forward through the list and press Shift+Tab to cycle backward. The Tab key can also auto-complete parameters inside the cmdlet, so it is handy when recalling the exact parameter name.

Skip the Identity

Although the identity can make retrieving an object specific and is a required parameter when changing an object, it's not required to type the entire identity parameter. If the identity is not explicitly referenced, the first string after the cmdlet is assumed to the identity. For example, the following two commands are equivalent in functionality, but one requires fewer characters:

```
Get-CsVoicePolicy –Identity Executives
Get-CsVoicePolicy Executives
```

Surround Spaces with Quotation Marks

When referencing objects or names that have spaces or special characters, make sure the entire text string is enclosed in quotation marks or single quotation marks. When PowerShell detects a space, it assumes the next character will be the beginning of a new parameter. Without surrounding the text string in quotation marks, it might lead to commands that fail. Both single and double quotation marks are acceptable. For example, when trying to retrieve the user Tom Pacyk, this command generates an error:

```
Get-CsUser Tom Pacyk
```

To successfully return the correct user, use the following command:

```
Get-CsUser "Tom Pacyk"
```

Leverage Get-Help

Included within all the Lync Server Management Shell cmdlets is a built-in help reference. To retrieve assistance with any cmdlet, simply type Get-Help followed by the name of the cmdlet. For example, to get assistance with the Set-CsDialPlan cmdlet, type

```
Get-Help Set-CsDialPlan
```

This help request returns a description of the cmdlet's purpose, the full syntax and parameters available in the cmdlet, and a summary of what the cmdlet does. More information can also be requested using the –Examples, -Detailed, and –Full flags at the end of the command. –Examples returns sample commands with the correct syntax, -Detailed returns a description of each parameter, and –Full returns the complete documentation available.

Having this help reference available without manually searching through documentation is incredibly useful. It can also come in handy when you're having trouble remembering a specific cmdlet name. In these cases, wildcards can be used to search through the documentation for a match. For example, the following command returns a list that displays Set-CsBandwidthPolicyServiceConfiguration and Set-CsBlockedDomain:

```
Get-Help Set-CsB*
```

Role-Based Access Control

Just as in Exchange Server 2010, Lync Server 2010 has introduced the concept of role-based access control (RBAC). RBAC allows for a degree of flexibility in management of the infrastructure simply not possible with a traditional approach to administration control. In prior versions of the product, an administrator typically had full control of the environment and was able to modify any part of a deployment. With RBAC, permissions can be defined in a more granular method so that different levels of administrators can be delegated specific settings to manage.

Lync Versus Exchange RBAC

The basis for role-based access control is to provide a specific set of permissions and actions allowed to a group. For those familiar with Exchange 2010 RBAC, it should be apparent that the Lync version is not nearly as flexible. Exchange 2010 administrators can define the exact cmdlets and attributes allowed for each management role. With Lync Server 2010, administrators can only base new roles on an existing template. Individual cmdlets cannot be added or removed. Assignment of a management role can only be done by placing user accounts within a security group.

Default Roles

Lync Server 2010 ships with several predefined RBAC roles. These roles exist in any deployment after the preparation steps have been completed and have a global scope. The default RBAC roles in Lync Server 2010 include the following:

▶ **CsAdministrator**—This is the equivalent of RTCUniversalServerAdmins from OCS 2007. Users assigned this role have complete control over any part of the system. They can modify the topology, manage user accounts, and create additional RBAC roles. The CS Administrators group in Active Directory is assigned this role.

▶ **CsUserAdministrator**—This role relates to the RTCUniversalUserAdmins group from OCS 2007. This role is geared toward help desk administrators and allows for enabling or disabling users for Lync. This role can also move users between pools and assign policies to accounts. The CS User Administrators group in Active Directory is assigned this role.

▶ **CsVoiceAdministrator**—Users assigned to this role can manage any of the voice features found in Lync Server 2010. This includes creation and modification of dial plans, routes, voice policies, and PSTN usages. Typically this is assigned to telephony or voice team users. The CS Voice Administrators group in Active Directory is assigned to this role.

▶ **CsServerAdministrator**—This role can manage individual Lync servers. It is geared towards users who manage, monitor, and troubleshoot Lync servers. It is slightly a step below the CsAdministrator role because no changes that globally affect the deployment, such as topology modifications, are permitted. This role typically is assigned to users who are responsible for day-to-day operations and management of Lync servers. The CS Server Administrators group in Active Directory is assigned to this role.

▶ **CsViewOnlyAdministrator**—Permits read-only access to the Lync Server deployment. This includes topology, pool, server, and user configuration, but no changes can be made. The CS View-Only Administrators group in Active Directory is assigned to this role.

▶ **CsHelpDesk**—This role is slightly more advanced than CsViewOnlyAdministrator and includes the capability to perform basic troubleshooting. This role cannot modify any user properties or assign policies as CsUserAdministrator can. The CS Help Desk group in Active Directory is assigned to this role.

▶ **CsArchivingAdministrator**—Allows for modifying the archiving policies and configuration within the organization. This role is intended for compliance or legal department users who are responsible for archiving policies. The CS Archiving Administrators group in Active Directory is assigned to this role.

▶ **CsResponseGroupAdministrator**—This role permits modification of Response Group queues, agent groups, and workflows. It is intended for users who are responsible for a small call center or the interactive voice response (IVR) systems in the organization. The CS Response Group Administrators in Active Directory is assigned to this role.

▶ **CsLocationAdministrator**—This role has the capability to modify and associate the locations and network subnets involved in E-911. The CS Location Administrators group in Active Directory is assigned to this role.

> **NOTE**
>
> Do not modify the default RBAC roles. Instead, create new roles to suit the needs of each organization.

Creating New Roles

Organizations can build on the default RBAC roles by creating their own custom roles. To create a new role, use the following steps:

1. Create a security group with the same name as what the role will be named.

2. Identify a pre-existing RBAC role that contains most of the cmdlets required for the new role. It will serve as a template for the new role.

3. Decide on a Lync server scope for the new role. This can be a global site, a single site, or multiple sites.

4. (Optional) Decide on an organization scope for the new role. A role can be limited to affect only user accounts within a specific OU in Active Directory.

To create a new RBAC role, use the following syntax within the Lync Management Shell:

```
New-CsAdminRole –Identity <AD Security Group Name> -Template <Pre-Existing
Role Name> -ConfigScopes <Lync Configuration Scope> -UserScopes
<Organizational Units>
```

For example, to create a new role called SanFranciscoUserAdmins scoped to the SF site and the SF OU, use the following syntax:

```
New-CsAdminRole –Identity SanFranciscoUserAdmins –Template
CsUserAdministrators –ConfigScopes "site:SF" –UserScopes "OU=SF
Users,OU=Company ABC,DC=companyabc,DC=com"
```

Topology Model

Lync Server 2010 has made some significant changes to how the deployment is managed. Instead of individually installing and configuring servers, the deployment is managed centrally through the Topology Builder. This shift in management helps make administration easier for organizations and limits the potential for mistakes.

In prior versions of the product, administrators had to log on to each server in the topology and manually configure options such as next hops, monitoring associations, and service ports. With Lync Server 2010, the configuration is completed in advance and then published to the Central Management Store (CMS).

When a server is deployed, it installs SQL Server Express. A local copy of the CMS is then replicated to this SQL instance so that the server can reference the entire topology. When the administrator begins installation, the server reads the topology and installs any roles within the topology that match the fully qualified domain name of itself.

NOTE

The only configuration required to link or associate servers with each other is performed automatically during the installation process. This helps reduce the chance for incorrect settings that cause unpredictable or problematic behavior for the servers.

To review, the deployment model with Lync Server follows the following high-level steps:

1. Administrator creates topology by defining all sites, servers, and gateways in the deployment.

2. The topology is then published to the Central Management Store.

3. A Lync server installs the SQL Express engine and creates a local replica of the CMS.

4. The Lync server reads the local CMS replica and installs the roles matching its FQDN.

Central Management Store

The previous section referenced the Central Management Store. To understand the responsibility of the CMS, it is important to understand how prior versions of the product operated where server and service configuration was stored within Active Directory. Live Communications Server and Office Communications Server both stored configuration information within the System partition of the forest root domain. In many cases, this was acceptable, but it caused performance problems in scenarios where a remote office had poor connectivity to a domain controller in the forest root domain. This was because the System container is not replicated to all domain controllers in the forest, so servers could be required to leverage WAN links to read settings even if a domain controller existed locally.

To mitigate these problems, Office Communications Server 2007 R2 recommended migrating the settings to the Configuration container instead, which is replicated to all domain controllers in the forest. This solved the problem, but organizations had a confusing manual migration path to move settings to the new container and often skipped this step. Furthermore, organizations could not move the settings after installing OCS 2007 R2, so they were stuck in this state with performance problems.

With Lync Server 2010, the settings for the deployment have moved from Active Directory to the CMS, which is just an additional SQL database. The CMS must be populated before the first pool is created and is done automatically if the first pool is a Standard Edition server. The CMS can be stored on the same SQL server and instance acting as a Back End server for a pool, and after installation the CMS can be moved to another server at any time.

As indicated earlier, when a server is prepared for a Lync Server installation, the first action it takes is to install a local replica of the CMS. As changes occur in the CMS, these changes are synchronized out to all members of the topology, which removes the need for servers to maintain a constant connection to a centralized configuration store. Servers synchronize the changes regularly and use the information stored locally instead of contacting a central point for settings, which improves performance and stability.

Topology Builder

New to Lync Server 2010 is the Topology Builder application. The Topology Builder is a centralized configuration point for adding servers to the deployment or changing configuration. All naming, IP addressing, and association of servers are performed through the Topology Builder so that administrators do not need to individually configure servers.

This helps reduce the number of errors made during configuration of pools with multiple members.

Each server site is defined within the Topology Builder, and then each specific server role is defined and associated with a site. When completed, administrators can publish the topology to the CMS where it can be read by servers.

TIP

The Lync Server 2010 Planning Tool can export the planning topology to an XML file, which can then be imported into the Topology Builder. This enables an administrator to quickly plan, build, and publish a configuration in a streamlined workflow. Figure 15.2 shows the layout of the Topology Builder.

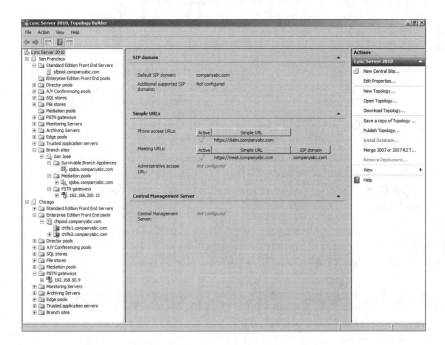

FIGURE 15.2   Topology Builder

Scopes

A new concept in Lync Server 2010 is the idea of scopes, which help define the boundary of a policy. Scopes are applied based on the topology built within the Topology Builder. The highest level that exists is the Global level. Within the Global level are sites, which represent physical locations where pools exist. Sites typically are datacenters where the Front End pool servers reside. Each site then contains the pools that make up the deployment. A site can have one pool or multiple pools. This arrangement is depicted in Figure 15.3.

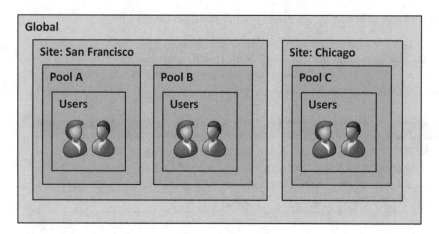

FIGURE 15.3   Lync Scopes

After the topology is defined, default policies for many different aspects of Lync Server 2010 are created. For example, global policies are created for Voice Policies, Conferencing Policies, and External Access Policies.

Global policies apply to all sites, pools, and users by default. Additional policies can be created at any of the other scopes as well, giving flexibility on overriding the defaults. The benefit of applying policies to a site or pool scope is that the additional task of assigning a policy directly to the users is no longer required. Instead, policies defined at a higher level are automatically applied to all scopes below as long as the lower scope does not have a policy already defined.

Administrators can still create new policies and assign them directly to a user account to override any global or site policies. This might be necessary to grant executives or VIP users a higher level of access than the default for everyone else in the site.

> **NOTE**
>
> In terms of priority, the policy assigned closest to the user account takes precedence. User policies override pool policies, pool policies override site policies, and site policies override the global policy. Policies automatically trickle down from the global level unless a policy exists closer to the user.

Management Tasks

There are some tasks that any administrator of Lync Server 2010 will manage at some point. This section covers some of these items that don't occur on a daily basis, but might be required at some point.

Server Draining

A new and useful feature to Lync Server 2010 is the concept of draining a server when preparing it for maintenance. This enables an administrator to prepare a server for maintenance without immediately affecting users. Existing sessions on the server are ended immediately and users will be transferred to a different server within the pool.

To prepare a server for maintenance, use the following steps:

1. Open the **Lync Server Control Panel**.
2. Click **Topology**.
3. Highlight the server to be modified.
4. Click **Action** and select **Prevent new connections for all services**.
5. Alternatively, double-click the server to drill down further and manage the individual services.

> **NOTE**
>
> Preventing new connections is a feature that only works with DNS load balancing and has no effect on whether a hardware load balancer continues to send traffic to a server. If using a hardware load balancer, perform the draining steps there instead.

This feature also does not cover load balancing of the web component services. The hardware load balancer used to distribute traffic to these services must also be drained to prevent new connections to the server prepared for maintenance.

Database Import/Export

A tool familiar to many LCS and OCS administrators is the database import/export tool called dmbimpexp.exe. This tool enables administrators to import or export user contact lists using XML files. Typically a SQL server backup captures the rtc database that contains the user contact lists, but having the XML version available can be useful when restoring from a backup that is slow or unavailable.

> **NOTE**
>
> It's a good idea to schedule a task to export the contact list from a pool from time to time. In a disaster scenario where users must be forcibly moved to another pool, the contact list information is lost. If organizations keep a current copy of the user contact lists from this tool, it can be used to restore the lists almost immediately. This enables users to be up and running on a new pool with their original contact list while the old pool is restored.

15

The dbimpexp tool is installed on servers in the <Lync Installation Drive>\Program Files\Common Files\Microsoft Lync Server 2010\Support folder. In cases where moving user contact lists between different Lync servers this works great, but for scenarios where users might be moved from OCS to Lync, the tool must be copied to the OCS server. The program can also be found on the Lync installation media within the Support folder.

> **NOTE**
>
> When moving user contact lists with dbimpexp, always use the version provided with the recent product release. For instance, when moving between OCS and Lync, use the dbimpexp version provided on the Lync media. When moving between LCS and OCS, use the OCS version.

There are many options when running dbimpexp, but the basic functionality is fairly straightforward. For a full list of the options available, see the dbimpexp-readme.html file included in the same folder as the executable.

To export all user contact lists to an XML file on a Standard Edition pool, use the following syntax:

```
dbimpexp.exe /hrxmlfile:"<Path and Filename>.xml"
```

To export all user contact lists to an XML file on an Enterprise Edition pool, one additional parameter is required. Use the following syntax:

```
dbimpexp.exe /hrxmlfile:"<Path and Filename>.xml" /sqlserver:"<SQL Server
FQDN and Instance Name if Named>"
```

After the contact lists are exported to XML and safe, they can be applied back to the users at any time. A scheduled task can easily perform this action on a nightly or weekly basis. Importing the contact lists is just as simple as the export procedure. By default, the contents of the XML file are merged with a user's existing contacts, but the /delete option can be used to empty the contact list before performing an import.

To import all user contact lists from an XML file on a Standard Edition pool, use the following syntax:

```
dbimpexp.exe /import /hrxmlfile:"<Path and Filename>.xml" /restype:all
```

To import all user contact lists from an XML file on an Enterprise Edition pool, one additional parameter is required. Use the following syntax:

```
dbimpexp.exe /import /hrxmlfile:"<Path and Filename>.xml" /sqlserver:"<SQL
Server FQDN and Instance Name if Named>" /restype:all
```

This is a powerful tool and can have a visible impact on user accounts if used incorrectly, so run some test scenarios before doing these changes in bulk. The export and import procedures can be targeted to only a single user by using the /user:<SIP Address> parameter.

Configuring Quality of Service

Quality of Service (QoS) can be used in networks where the media traffic used by Lync Server 2010 servers and clients should have a higher priority than other traffic using the same infrastructure. This is done by having the Lync servers and endpoints tag their media traffic packets with a specific Differentiated Services Code Point (DSCP) value. Routers within the network are then configured to prioritize traffic based on the DSCP values included with packets.

DSCP marking in Lync Server 2010 is done by using the policy-based QoS first introduced with Windows Server 2008 and Windows Vista. These policies are controlled through Windows Group Policy and can mark traffic with DSCP codes based on application names and port ranges. Because these policies can be centrally managed and controlled by the organization, it should be acceptable to trust the markings sent from client endpoints. Using a separate port range for each type of traffic enables the policy-based QoS to tag the traffic appropriately. For example, audio traffic using one port range can be assigned a DSCP code with higher priority than the port range used for video or application sharing.

15

> **NOTE**
>
> Network equipment is typically configured to ignore or not trust DSCP markings from computers on the regular data network. Because Lync is a softphone and operates using the same VLAN as PCs, the markings from machines on the data VLAN must be trusted to use QoS with Lync.

Server Configuration

Lync servers operate similarly to clients and tag media traffic through the use of policy-based QoS in Group Policy. Each media type has one of the following default port range assigned:

▶ Audio (49,152–57,500)

▶ Video (57,501–65,535)

▶ Application sharing (49,152–65,535)

These port ranges can then be matched through policy-based QoS and assigned a DSCP marking. The default port range for application sharing overlaps with both audio and video. If application sharing is tagged differently than either traffic, a separate port range must be configured. Port ranges for each media type can be configured using the Set-CsConferenceServer and Set-CsMediationServer cmdlets.

For example, to separate application sharing into its own port range, run the following command:

```
Set-CsConferenceServer -AppSharingPortStart 32768
```

This changes application sharing to use ports 32,768–49,151 while keeping the same amount of ports available.

Client Configuration

QoS tagging of the media is performed by the Lync client itself, so it must be provisioned in a way that it understands what ports to use for each type of traffic. By default, no tagging is done and all traffic uses the port range 1,024–65,535. The Lync client supports using different port ranges for the following types of traffic and recommends a minimum number of ports for each modality. Using port ranges that are below the recommended minimums increases the chance for a media request to fail.

▶ Audio (20 ports required)

▶ Video (40 ports required)

▶ Application sharing (4 ports required)

▶ File transfer (4 ports required)

First, to enable separate port ranges for each media type, run the following command:

```
Set-CsConferencingConfiguration -ClientMediaPortRangeEnabled $true
```

Next, define a unique port range for each type of traffic. As an example, the ports used on the client side can be the same as on the server. The sample numbers used here are well beyond the minimum number of ports required and are used only to show how the default port ranges can be moved. The port ranges used should be limited to the recommended sizes for ease of management and troubleshooting.

```
Set-CsConferencingConfiguration -ClientAudioPort 49152 -ClientAudioPortRange
8348 -ClientVideoPort 57501 -ClientVideoPortRange 8034 -ClientAppSharingPort
32768 -ClientAppSharingPortRange 16383 -ClientFileTransferPort 24733
-ClientFileTransferPortRange 8034
```

Creating a QoS Policy

After modifying the Lync clients and servers to use specific port ranges, QoS policies must be created to add the appropriate DSCP value to traffic originating from each port range. The steps required to use policy-based QoS through Group Policy are similar, but the port ranges used for servers and clients will likely differ. Create at least two separate policies: one for servers and one for clients. To create a new policy, perform the following steps:

1. Open a new Group Policy object.

2. Expand **Computer Configuration, Windows Settings**, and then click **Policy-Based QoS**.

3. Right-click **Policy-Based QoS** and select **Create new policy**.

4. Enter a name for the policy, such as **Lync Audio**.

5. Enter a DSCP value, such as **46** and click **Next**.

6. To limit the tagging only to Lync clients, select **Only applications with this executable name** and enter **communicator.exe**. Click **Next**.

7. Allow the policy to apply to **any source IP address** and **any destination IP address**.

8. In the **Select the protocol this QoS policy applies to**, select **TCP and UDP**.

9. In the **Specify the source port number** section, select **From this source port number or range** and enter the range used for audio traffic, such as 49152:57500.

10. Click **Finish** to complete the policy.

Repeat these steps for each type of media using a unique port range, which should be tagged differently. Figure 15.4 demonstrates what a policy with separate audio and video settings looks like.

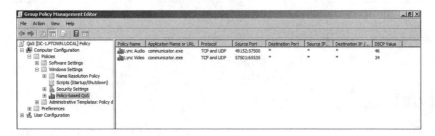

FIGURE 15.4   Policy-Based QoS

NOTE

The A/V Edge service behaves a bit differently. First, because it typically is not part of the domain, it might be necessary to create the policies locally on each server. Second, the port range used to define each service should be specified as a *destination* port instead of source port. This ensures traffic, which the Edge server uses to communicate to a Front End pool, is marked correctly.

Windows XP QoS

Because QoS policies can be created only on Windows Vista or later operating systems, the process for enabling QoS on Windows XP is slightly different. Windows XP QoS marking is also not as flexible as policy-based QoS and can only mark audio traffic as SERVICE-TYPE_GUARANTEED and video as SERVICETYPE_CONTROLLEDLOAD.

15

First, verify the QoS packet scheduler is installed on the client. Secondly, run the following command on a Lync server:

```
Set-CsMediaConfiguration -EnableQoS $true
```

Before the Lync client attempts to tag packets, the DSCP values should be modified using Group Policy.

1. Open a new Group Policy object.

2. Expand **Computer Configuration, Administrative Templates, Network, QoS Packet Scheduler**, and click **DSCP value of conforming packets**.

3. Double-click **Guaranteed service type**.

4. Select **Enabled** and enter a DSCP value such as **46**.

Repeat these steps for the Controlled load service type to tag video media.

Lync Phone Edition QoS

The final client type that can use QoS settings is the Lync Phone Edition client, which can run on third-party partner hardware. Lync Phone Edition settings are determined through in-band signaling to the devices. In addition to a DSCP value for audio traffic, the Lync Phone Edition clients also support 802.1p. To set the Lync Phone Edition QoS settings, use the following command on a Lync server:

```
Set-CsUcPhoneConfiguration -VoiceDiffServTag 46 -Voice8021p 5
```

Troubleshooting

Troubleshooting a Lync Server installation might become necessary in the event that users are unable to sign in or features seem to not work correctly. This section discusses the key components to check when issues arise. Common troubleshooting tools and tips are also provided, which should resolve many issues.

Certificates

Incorrectly issued certificates were a common issue in Office Communications Server deployments, but these issues should mostly be mitigated with the new Lync Server wizards. The option to manually request and modify the certificate still exists, which might lead to some problems.

Follow the following guidelines to rule out any certificate issues:

▶ **Subject and subject alternative names**—Ensure that the required subject name and subject alternative names have been entered for each role. The guidance for each role varies, so verify the names required when deploying a new server. Always use the certificate wizard suggested names if possible. Wildcard certificates are still technically unsupported for most scenarios.

- ▶ **Key bit length**—The certificate bit length must be 1024, 2048, or 4096 to be supported by Lync Server 2010.

- ▶ **Template**—The template used to issue the certificate should be based on the web server template. If the Lync Server 2010 certificate wizard is used, the correct template will automatically be applied.

- ▶ **Private key**—The server certificate must have the private key associated to be used by Lync Server 2010. In situations where certificates are exported or copied between servers, export the private key with the certificate.

- ▶ **Certificate chain**—The server must be able to verify each certificate up to a Trusted Root Certification Authority. Additionally, because the server is presenting the certificate to clients, it must contain each intermediate certificate in the certificate chain.

- ▶ **Certificate store**—All certificates used by a server must be located in the Personal section of the local computer certificate store. A common mistake is to place certificates in the Personal section of the user account certificate store.

- ▶ **Certificate trust**—Be sure the clients and servers communicating with the server all contain a copy of the top-level certificate authority of the chain in their Trusted Root Certification Authority local computer store. When the certification authority is integrated with Active Directory this is generally not an issue, but when using an offline or nonintegrated certificate authority it might be necessary to install root certificates on clients and servers.

DNS Records

Successful operation of Lync servers is heavily dependent on correctly configuring DNS. All necessary DNS records should exist and resolve to the correct locations. Verify that all servers have a host record configured in DNS. Separate web components URLs and simple URLs are not automatically entered and must be manually created by an administrator.

Use the following sample nslookup sequence within a command prompt to check the host record of the pool:

```
nslookup
set type=a
lyncdirpool1.companyabc.com
```

A successful query returns a name and IP address. Verify that the IP returned matches the IP addresses assigned to the servers or load balancer and that no extra, or surprise, IP addresses are returned.

To verify the SRV record required for automatic client sign-in internally, the syntax is slightly different. The following is another sample nslookup sequence:

```
nslookup
set type=srv
_sipinternaltls._tcp.companyabc.com
```

15

A successful query returns a priority, weight, port, and server hostname. Verify that the server name matches the pool name and the correct port is returned.

Logs

A good source of information in troubleshooting any server issue are the event logs. Lync Server 2010 creates a dedicated event log for informational activities, warnings, and errors within the standard Windows Server Event Viewer console. To view this event log, use the following steps:

1. Click **Start**.
2. Type **eventvwr.msc** and click **OK** to open the Event Viewer Microsoft Management Console.
3. Expand the **Applications and Services Logs** folder.
4. Click the **Lync Server** log.
5. Examine the log for warning or error events, which might provide additional insight into any issues.

Lync Server Management Shell

The Lync Server 2010 Management Shell provides several cmdlets, which are used to test various functions of a server. A useful cmdlet for verifying the overall health of a server is Test-CSComputer Server, which verifies that all services are running, the local computer group membership is correctly populated with the necessary Lync Server Active Directory groups, and the required Windows Firewall ports have been opened. The Test-CSComputer cmdlet must run from the local computer and uses the following syntax:

```
Test-CSComputer –Report "C:\Test-CSComputer Results.xml"
```

After running the cmdlet, open the generated XML file to view a detailed analysis of each check.

Synthetic Transactions

A new feature in Lync Server 2010 is the introduction of synthetic transactions, which are a set of PowerShell cmdlets used to simulate actions taken by servers or users in the environment. These synthetic transactions enable an administrator to conduct realistic tests against a service. In the case of a Director, the most useful synthetic transaction is the Test-CSRegistration cmdlet, which simulates a user signing in to the specified server.

The Test-CSRegistration cmdlet requires providing a target server, user credential, and SIP address. A registrar port can optionally be included. The user credential parameter's username and password must be collected by an authentication dialog and saved to a variable as in the following command:

```
$Credential = Get-Credential "COMPANYABC\tom"
```

After the credentials are collected, the cmdlet can be run with the user credential variable previously saved.

```
Test-CSRegistration -TargetFQDN lyncpool1.companyabc.com -UserCredential
 $Credential -UserSipAddress "sip:tom@companyabc.com" -RegistrarPort 5061
-Verbose
```

LISTING 15.1   Test-CSRegistration Example

```
TargetFQDN    : lyncpool1.companyabc.com
Result        : Success
Latency       : 00:00:10.9506726
Error         :
Diagnosis     :
```

As seen in the output, the registration test was successful.

Telnet

Telnet is a simple method of checking whether a specific TCP port is available from a client machine. From a machine that is having trouble contacting a server, use the following steps to verify connectivity to the Registrar service:

1. Open a command prompt.
2. Type the following command:

   ```
   telnet <Director pool FQDN> 5061
   ```

If the window goes blank and only a flashing cursor is seen, it means the connection was successful and the port can be contacted without issue. If the connection fails, an error is returned. Check that the services are running on the Director and that no firewalls are blocking the traffic.

> **TIP**
>
> The Telnet client is not installed by default in Windows Vista, Windows 7, Windows Server 2008, or Windows Server 2008 R2. On a desktop operating system, it must be installed using the Turn Windows Features on or off option found in Programs and Features. On a server operating system, it can be installed through the Features section of Server Manager.

Time

A key component of any service running successfully in Lync Server 2010 is the computer time. Verify that the clocks on the Lync Server 2010 servers are correctly set and have the appropriate time zones configured. If the clocks between a server and client are off by more than five minutes, authentication will begin to fail, which might prevent users from logging on successfully.

Services

Basic troubleshooting always begins with making sure the Lync Server services are all running. When services are in a stopped state, users will see many issues such as being unable to sign in or connect to the server. Verify that the following services are configured to start automatically and are running. Verification of the services can be done either through the traditional Services MMC or through the Lync Server Management Shell.

To verify the services are running, open the Lync Server Management Shell and run the Get-CsWindowsService cmdlet. This cmdlet returns both the service status and how many active connections exist, which can be valuable information when draining a server for maintenance.

```
PS C:\> Get-CsWindowsService
Status Name              Activity Level
Running MASTER
Running REPLICA
Running RTCSRV            Incoming requests per second=0
Running RTCCAA            Concurrent Calls=0
Running RTCCAS            Concurrent Conferences=0
Running RTCRGS            Current Active Calls=0
Running RTCPDAUTH
Running RTCPDPCORE        Active Client Connections=0
Running RTCCPS            Total Parked Calls=0
Running RTCATS            Current Active Calls=0
Running RTCIMMCU          Active Conferences=0
Running RTCDATAMCU        Active Conferences=0
Running RTCAVMCU          Number of Conferences=0
Running RTCASMCU          Active Conferences=0
Running RTCMEDSRV         Current Outbound Calls=0
Running RTCMEETINGMCU     Active Conferences=0
Running FTA
```

The following command quickly identifies nonrunning services by skipping the activity check:

```
Get-CsWindowsService –ExcludeActivityLevel ¦ Where-Object {$_.Status –ne "Running"}
```

Lync Server Logging Tool

When all else fails and the problem cannot be diagnosed, perform a diagnostic trace of the server traffic. Included with the installation of any Lync Server role is the Lync Server Logging Tool. This application can be found within the Start menu under the Microsoft

Lync Server 2010 program group. This tool is valuable when troubleshooting Lync Server problems because it provides insight into what is happening at the protocol level.

The most common type of tracing done with this tool is to capture the SIP traffic between servers or clients to determine a potential problem. Other traditional types of tracing tools, such as Wireshark, are unable to analyze the Lync Server SIP traffic because it is encrypted using TLS security. When running the logging tool locally on a server, it is able to decrypt the TLS security so that all the SIP messaging becomes readable. Running the Lync Server Logging Tool does not disrupt the server traffic and can be done while users are actively using the system.

To get started, open the Lync Server Logging Tool (see Figure 15.5).

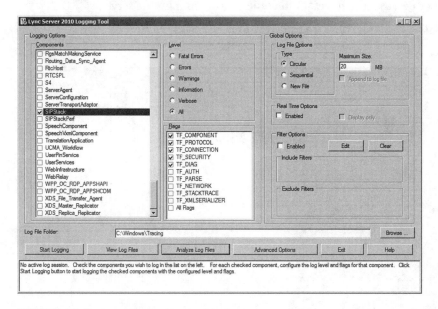

FIGURE 15.5   Lync Server Logging Tool

To capture the SIP traffic, perform the following steps:

1. Check the box labeled **SIP Stack**.

2. Click **Start Logging**.

3. Reproduce the issue that is driving the troubleshooting.

4. Click **Stop Logging** when the issue has been experienced again.

At this point, an administrator has two options. The first is to click View Log Files to display the logs in text format. This can be difficult to read and troubleshoot because SIP conversations include many lines. For a better experience, first install the Lync Server 2010 Resource Kit Tools. The Snooper tool provides a much cleaner view of a SIP conversation.

1. After the Resource Kit Tools are installed, click the **Analyze Log Files** button.

2. Verify that the SIP Stack is still selected and click **Analyze**.

3. Snooper should open automatically and display the conversation. Click the **Messages** tab to view the SIP conversation.

A message-by-message view of the conversation is located on the left side. Clicking any of the lines change the view in the right-side pane to display the entire SIP message selected. Error messages are highlighted in red for easy identification. A search bar, where keywords such as a username or phone number are entered, is located at the top of the window. After entering a search string and pressing Enter, the view is filtered to only display messages with that string. This kind of filtering can be useful when searching for problems with a single user because it removes all the other traffic through the server.

Figure 15.6 displays a sample SIP trace using the Snooper tool.

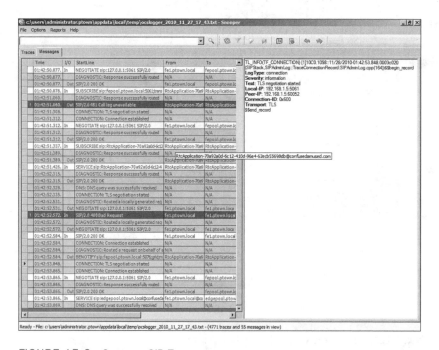

FIGURE 15.6   Snooper SIP Trace

NOTE

The example traces a SIP conversation, but the Lync Server Logging Tool is capable of tracing every component of the product. When opening the tool, all the different components are displayed and can be selected. Many of the names are tough to decipher, and most only need to be traced when requested by a Microsoft support professional. In many cases, tracing the SIP Stack determines the main issue.

Best Practices

The following are best practices from this chapter:

▶ Use the new Lync Server Management Shell for bulk administration tasks or to perform tasks more quickly than possible within the Lync Server Control Panel.

▶ Create RBAC roles, which are scoped appropriately for administrators within the organization. Different sets of users can be managed by different administrators easily with this new flexibility.

▶ Use the Lync Server Planning Tool to create a topology that can be imported to the Lync Server Topology Builder and saved in the Central Management Store. This helps reduce the time involved in planning and creating a topology while improving the likelihood for success.

▶ Use Quality of Service on Lync servers and clients to help improve media quality on unreliable or oversaturated networks.

▶ Use synthetic transactions to test Lync Server services easily. These PowerShell cmdlets do not require a test workstation, but can simulate user activities against the server.

▶ Become familiar with the Lync Server Logging Tool and how to diagnose issues with SIP tracing. This greatly improves the speed and accuracy in resolving problems.

Summary

It should be apparent that the new changes to the administration model are going to make lives easier within many organizations. Although the Lync Server Control Panel certainly has its nuances, such as no right-click functionality, the layout and organization are welcome changes. For the tasks that are tedious to perform in a user interface, administrators now have the full power of the Lync Server Management Shell at their disposal. This automates batch tasks or enables organizations to develop standard new user creation scripts based on PowerShell.

The topology model also helps to reduce the number of errors or anomalies created by requiring administrators to configure servers individually in prior versions. This centralized approach to setup ensures all pool members are identical and that the topology should work before ever being placed into production. Scope-based policies enable organizations to standardize on global or site policies easily, ensuring users are not assigned different policies.

A good portion of any Lync Server administrator's life includes some troubleshooting, so becoming familiar with the most common issues and tools is highly recommended. The new synthetic transactions can help administrators stay on top of problems before they become major issues and the Lync Server Logging Tool is a valuable resource for diagnosing errors.

PART V

Migrating from Older Versions

IN THIS PART

Migrating from LCS and OCS

Overview

Much like Microsoft Exchange, there's only one way to do an upgrade or migration to Lync Server 2010. The upgrade process is a migration in that Lync must be built on separate servers in parallel to the existing deployment. Also similar to Microsoft Exchange, the upgrade should be done from the outside in. The process is straightforward, with only a few challenging areas. The lack of options can be a blessing in that there is less to go wrong when there is only one right way to do something.

If your organization is still using Live Communications Server (LCS) 2003 or 2005, you need to crawl out from under that rock and upgrade to Office Communications Server (OCS) 2007 R2 as an interim step before moving on to Lync Server 2010. A high-level discussion of the LCS-to-OCS process is included in the "Office Communications Server 2007 R2" section that follows.

Assuming OCS 2007 R2 is already in place, the Lync Architect will plan the architecture outside in, starting with the Edge Server. The Lync 2010 Edge Server can proxy connections for users in both Lync Server 2010 pools and OCS 2007 R2 pools. This means there is no need to maintain separate Edge Servers during the coexistence period.

> ▶ Edge Servers are covered in more detail in the "Edge Server Migration to Lync Server 2010" section of this chapter.

This chapter highlights the full lifecycle of the migration process starting with importing the configuration, moving to the Edge Server, and then the internal servers. Finally, the chapter concludes with troubleshooting and best practices.

NOTE

Where the migration is a simple rip-and-replace, such as the Archiving Server role, the topic is not covered in great detail in this chapter.

Office Communications Server 2007 R2

As mentioned, there is no direct migration path from LCS 2003 or 2005 to Lync Server 2010. An intermediate step of migrating to OCS 2007 R2 is required. Although the focus in this book is on Lync, it would be remiss to disregard this step completely, so this section reviews the OCS 2007 R2 process at a high level. A key issue is that the administrator must install the OCS 2007 R2 schema and server(s) before installing the Lync Server schema.

Although there are a few client-side issues for coexistence, assume this is a short-term intermediate step on the way to Lync and that the Lync client is rolled out before going live. On the server-side, administrators want to make sure they are on at least LCS 2005 Service Pack 1. Also, if any coexistence is required, an MTLS certificate is required on the LCS server to communicate with OCS, and users should not be enabled for enhanced presence until the Communicator 2007 client or later is deployed.

These preparation steps use LCSCmd, which can be found on the OCS 2007 R2 installation media at the following path: Setup\amd64. The first step is to extend the schema. Next, ensure the user is a member of the Schema Admins group and the commands are either run on the Schema Master or that Remote RPC is enabled on the Schema Master server. Then, run the following command:

```
LCSCmd /Forest /Action:SchemaPrep
```

After that command finishes, wait until the changes replicate throughout the Active Directory forest. A different permutation of the LCSCmd can be used to determine the overall state of the schema preparation. To see the schema prep state, run the following command:

```
LCSCmd /Forest /Action:CheckSchemaPrepState
```

The next step is to prepare the Active Directory forest. This command requires being a member of the Enterprise Admins group. To prepare the forest, run the following command:

```
LCSCmd /Forest /Action:ForestPrep
```

Be sure to wait until the effect has replicated to all domain controllers in the forest. To check the state, run the following command:

```
LCSCmd /Forest /Action:CheckForestPrepState
```

The final preparation step is to prepare the domain. You need to run this step for each domain where you currently have LCS or plan to deploy OCS or Lync. To prepare the domain, run the following command:

```
LCSCmd /Domain[:<domain FQDN>] /Action:DomainPrep
```

Wait until the changes have propagated to all domain controllers in the domain before continuing. The state can be checked by running the following command:

```
LCSCmd /Domain[:<domain FQDN>] /Action:CheckDomainPrepState
```

The final step is to delegate installation permissions using the least necessary permissions model. This is important because many unified communications administrators are not also domain administrators. This process delegates the necessary permissions to install OCS 2007 R2.

To continue the installation process, perform the following steps:

1. From the Deployment Wizard, click **Delegate Setup and Administration** under Step 7.
2. Click the **Run** button under Delegate Setup Tasks.
3. At the Setup Delegation Wizard welcome dialog box, click **Next** to continue.
4. At the Authorize Group dialog box, choose the Trustee domain and enter a name of an existing Universal Security group. Members of that group receive permissions to activate the server. Click **Next** to continue.

NOTE

The group chosen must be a Universal Security group or installation fails.

5. At the OU Location dialog box, enter the full distinguished name (DN) of the organizational unit (OU) where the OCS Server computer accounts are located. For example, OU=OCS, OU=Servers, CN=Computers, DC=companyabc, DC=com.
6. After entering the DN of the server's OU, click **Next** to continue.
7. Enter the name of service accounts used for the session initiation protocol (SIP) and components services. These accounts should be created in advance in Active Directory.
8. Review the information in the subsequent dialog box, and then click **Next** to begin setup.
9. Click **Finish**.

Install Office Communications Server 2007 R2

After the preparation steps are complete, it's time to move on to installing OCS 2007 R2.

NOTE

Because the context is to provide only a short-term interim step to Lync Server 2010, only the front-end process is covered in this chapter. That is all that is necessary for most deployments.

First, the administrator must install the prerequisites. This can be easily scripted for Windows Server 2008 x64 or Windows Server 2008 R2 using the following commands:

```
Servermanagercmd -i web-server
Servermanagercmd -i web-webserver
Servermanagercmd -i web-common-http
Servermanagercmd -i web-static-content
Servermanagercmd -i web-dir-browsing
Servermanagercmd -i web-http-errors
Servermanagercmd -i web-http-redirect
Servermanagercmd -i web-health
Servermanagercmd -i web-http-logging
Servermanagercmd -i web-request-monitor
Servermanagercmd -i web-security
Servermanagercmd -i web-basic-auth
Servermanagercmd -i web-windows-auth
Servermanagercmd -i web-digest-auth
Servermanagercmd -i web-filtering
Servermanagercmd -i web-performance
Servermanagercmd -i web-stat-compression
Servermanagercmd -i web-mgmt-tools
Servermanagercmd -i web-mgmt-console
Servermanagercmd -i web-mgmt-compat
Servermanagercmd -i web-metabase
Servermanagercmd -i web-wmi
Servermanagercmd -i web-lgcy-scripting
Servermanagercmd -i web-lgcy-mgmt-console
Servermanagercmd -i rsat
Servermanagercmd -i rsat-addc
Servermanagercmd -i rsat-role-tools
Servermanagercmd -i rsat-web-server
Servermanagercmd -i was
Servermanagercmd -i was-process-model
```

After all the prerequisites have been satisfied and the Active Directory schema has been extended, the process for installing an OCS 2007 R2 server can begin. To begin this process, perform the following steps:

1. From the Deployment Wizard, click **Deploy Standard Edition Server**.

2. Under Step 2, click **Run**.

3. Click **Deploy Server** at the screen that appears and click **Next** on the first screen. Leave the installation folder at the default, and then click **Next** to continue.

4. Select the appropriate Application Configuration. The default is all services selected.

5. At the account information field, select **Use an Existing Account**, and enter the service account information entered in the previous steps for delegation.

6. At the Component Service Account dialog box, choose **Use an Existing Account**, and then enter the second service account created during the delegation steps and its password. Click **Next** to continue.

7. In the Web Farm FQDNs dialog box, enter the internal and external FQDNs of the farm. Click **Next** to continue.

8. Enter the database and log information into the fields in the Database File dialog box. Click **Next** to continue.

9. Click **Next** at the Ready to Deploy dialog box.

10. Click **Finish**.

Some basic configuration is required; however, it is minimal because OCS 2007 R2 is used only to bridge LCS and Lync. With OCS 2007 R2 now in place, the administrator can move all the users from the legacy LCS pool to the OCS pool. After the users are moved to the OCS pool, follow the instructions in the next section to migrate users and configure the Lync pool.

Edge Server Migration to Lync Server 2010

The Edge Server upgrade process is actually the easiest part of the overall migration process; it's a direct replacement. A Lync 2010 Edge Server can proxy connections for both Lync Server 2010 Front End pools and OCS 2007 R2 pools, meaning there is no need to run both versions of Edge in parallel during the coexistence period.

However, because the Lync Edge Server can use just one external IP address and the OCS 2007 R2 Edge Server requires three, there are some design considerations. In addition, the Edge Server build process is covered in detail in Chapter 6, "Microsoft Lync Server 2010 Edge." This section covers the changes that need to be made for migrating from the OCS 2007 R2 Edge Server to a Lync 2010 Edge Server.

> ▶ The design considerations mentioned in the previous paragraph and a full review of the Edge Server design process are covered in Chapter 27, "Planning for Deploying External Services."

Configure Internal Pools

After a successful Edge Server installation, the next step is to set the internal pools to use it. The easiest way is to reset the global Edge Server and Federation settings using the OCS 2007 R2 management console, as shown in Figures 16.1 and 16.2.

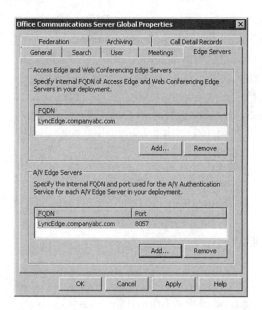

FIGURE 16.1   Adding the New Lync Edge Server

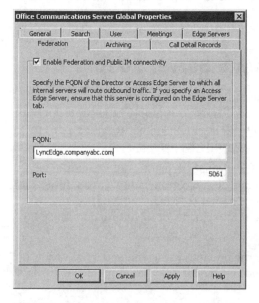

FIGURE 16.2   Resetting the Global Federation Route to Point to a Lync Edge Server

If the administrator chose to overwrite the global settings with pool-specific settings, those need to be changed, too.

Under Pool Settings, the administrator needs to point the AV Authentication service to the new Edge Server, as shown in Figure 16.3. This needs to be done for each pool.

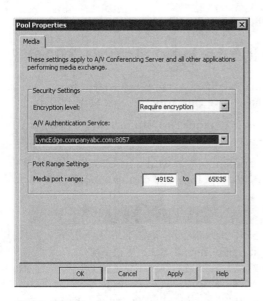

FIGURE 16.3   Configuring the OCS Pool A/V Authentication Service

Repoint DNS Records

Finally, the administrator must repoint the appropriate DNS records to the new Edge Server, such as sip.companyabc.com. In addition to the new DNS records listed in Chapter 6, the existing SRV records need to be modified. The SRV records required and what they should be changed to follows:

▶ To review a list of the existing SRV records, refer to Chapter 6.

▶ For remote user access

  ▶ _sip._tls.companyabc.com points to port 443 for the FQDN of the Remote Access Service on the Edge Server.

▶ For federation

▶ _sipfederationtls._tcp.companyabc.com points to port 5061 for the FQDN of the Remote Access Service on the Edge Server.

> **NOTE**
>
> If an organization has partners that do not use open federation, they will need to update their Edge Server federation settings with the name of the new Lync Edge Server.

It is a good idea to test the edge services at this time before upgrading the internal servers.

Front End and User Migration to Lync Server 2010

The Front End Server migration is a bit more involved and requires more steps to complete successfully. The first step is to prepare Active Directory for Lync Server 2010.

▶ Refer to Chapter 5, "Microsoft Lync Server 2010 Front End," to review the necessary steps to build a Lync Server 2010 Front End.

After the Central Management Store is created and populated with a base topology, the administrator must import the legacy OCS 2007 R2 topology and configuration.

> **NOTE**
>
> Before proceeding, ensure the OCS WMI Backward Compatability pack is installed. It is located on the Lync Server installation media at Setup\amd64\Setup\OCSWMIBC.msi.

On the Front End Server, open the Lync Management Shell and enter the following command. Note the whole process can also be accomplished in the Lync Topology Builder GUI by selecting the Lync Server 2010 menu item at the top-left and then selecting Merge 2007 or 2007 R2 Topology in the right Action pane.

```
Merge-CsLegacyTopology –TopologyXmlFileName C:\TopologyFiles\
➥MergedTopology.xml -Verbose
```

This command exports the existing OCS 2007 R2 topology and configuration to an XML file. This includes all Forest and Pool Server configuration data, including items such as location profiles, voice routes, and gateway devices. Now the information needs to be published to the new Lync topology. Run the following command to publish the legacy configuration information to the existing topology:

```
Publish-CsTopology –FileName C:\TopologyFiles\MergedTopology.xml -Verbose
```

Finally, the information must be imported to the topology. To do so, enter the following command:

```
Import-CsLegacyTopology -Verbose
```

If you have existing conferencing directories, you can import them using a similar command as shown in the following:

```
Import-CsLegacyConferenceDirectory -Verbose
```

Now when you view your Lync topology in Topology Builder, you can see a legacy site added on the left pane menu called BackCompatSite. This includes settings for the OCS 2007 R2 servers and configuration. As appropriate, the configuration items are also added to Lync containers and applied to existing and future Lync servers, as shown in Figure 16.4.

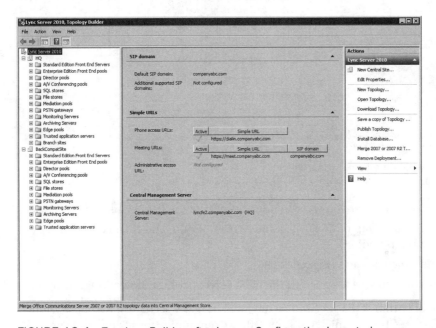

FIGURE 16.4   Topology Builder after Legacy Configuration Imported

Before moving on, the topology must be republished with the new OCS 2007 R2 data. Select your site, right-click, click **topology**, and then click **publish**. Follow the wizard to republish the topology, and then click **Finish** when the job is complete.

Migration Process

Now the administrator is ready to begin migrating users to Lync Server 2010. The steps that follow outline the user migration process using the Lync Server Control Panel:

1. From the Start menu, open the **Lync Server Control Panel.**
2. Click the **Users** tab on the left menu bar.
3. In the main pane, click **Add Filter.**
4. Set **Legacy User** equal to **True**, as shown in Figure 16.5.

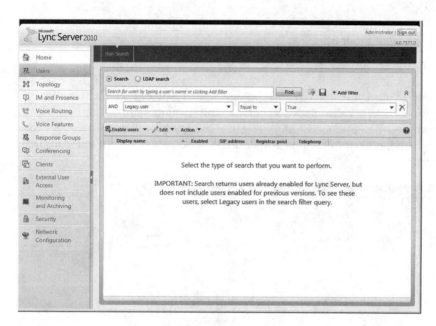

FIGURE 16.5   Setting the Legacy User Filter

5. Enter the name of a user you want to migrate or leave the field blank to find all users.

6. Select the user or group of users, click the **Action** button, and then choose **Move Selected Users to Pool**.

7. Choose the Lync pool and then click **OK**.

8. The user should now be assigned to the Lync Server pool, as shown in Figure 16.6.

Users aren't the only things that need to be migrated in many scenarios. Response Group configuration also needs to be migrated from Office Communications Server to Lync Server 2010. The Move-CsRgsConfiguration cmdlet is used to migrate the Response Group to Lync. An example is shown in the following:

```
Move-CsRgsConfiguration –Source "ocsr2.companyabc.com" –destination
"Lyncfe2.companyabc.com" -verbose
```

Ensure this command completes successfully by running the Get-CsRgsConfiguration cmdlet. The syntax is as follows:

```
Get-CsRgsConfiguration –Identity <RgsIdentity>
```

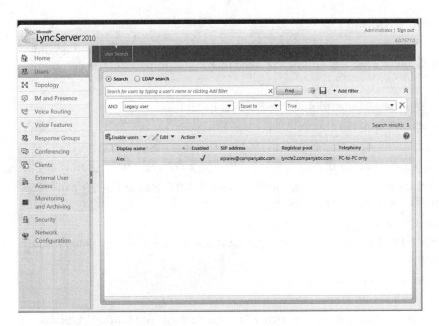

FIGURE 16.6   Successfully Migrated User

Automatic Client Upgrade

Administrators are encouraged to make the client upgrade process as simple as possible for end users. There are two recommended methods:

- Using System Center Configuration Manager (SCCM) to push the new client package

- Using the Client Version Policy to offer an upgrade when a user signs in with a legacy client

The Lync client can be packaged and pushed by SCCM similar to most other programs. There are no caveats other than this process also uninstalls any legacy clients, including OCS Communicator. The Client Version Policy has an option to either refer the user to a URL where the new client can be installed or to push the client directly from any web location accessible from the client. This option is configured in the Lync Server Control Panel under the Clients tab in the Client Version Policy section.

> **NOTE**
>
> Ensure that the location chosen by the administrator is available to users both internally and externally.

Decommission Process

The final step is to delete the BackCompatSite in the Lync Topology Builder and decommission the OCS 2007 R2 Servers. Follow the steps that follow to perform the decommission process:

1. Open the Topology Builder tool on the Lync Front End Server.
2. Select the **BackCompatSite**.
3. Click **Delete** in the right Action pane.
4. A warning pops up saying the site is not empty. Click **OK** to delete it anyway.
5. Republish the topology by clicking the **Lync Server 2010** item in the left pane. Then click **Publish Topology** in the right Action pane.
6. Click **Next** to begin the process.
7. Ensure that it finishes successfully and the BackCompatSite object is deleted from the topology.
8. Log in to the OCS 2007 R2 Server.
9. Open the OCS 2007 R2 MMC.
10. Expand the **forest** and then choose either **Enterprise Pools** or **Standard Edition Servers**, whichever is appropriate.
11. Expand the **pool** and select the first **Server**. Then expand the **Deactivate** menu on the right side of the MMC as shown in Figure 16.7.

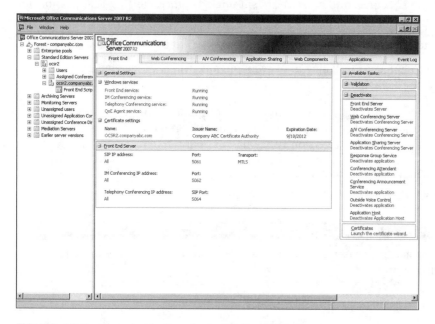

FIGURE 16.7   Preparing to Deactivate the First OCS Server

12. The administrator deactivates all services for each Front End Server. Start at the bottom of the list and select **Application Host** to deactivate the application host.

13. Click **Next** four times to complete the wizard and begin the process. Note that the administrator might need to check the **Force Deactivation of Application Host** box if applications still run on the OCS 2007 R2 Server. When the process is complete, click **Finish** to close the wizard.

14. Expand the **Deactivate** menu again and select **Application Sharing Server**.

15. Click **Next** three times to go through the wizard. Click **Finished** when it is completed.

16. Expand the **Deactivate** menu again and select **A/V Conferencing Server**.

17. Click **Next** three times to go through the wizard. Click **Finished** when it is completed.

18. Expand the **Deactivate** menu again and select **Web Conferencing Server**.

19. Click **Next** twice to go through the wizard. Click **Finished** when it is completed.

20. Expand the **Deactivate** menu again and select **Web Components Server**.

21. Click **Next** three times to go through the wizard. Click **Finished** when it is completed.

22. Expand the **Deactivate** menu again and select **Front End Server**. Ensure that the Conferencing Directory is deleted. It might need to be manually deleted from the **Assigned Conference Directories** menu item.

23. Click **Next** four times to go through the wizard. Click **Finished** when it is completed.

24. Perform steps 11–23 for all servers in a multiserver deployment.

25. This process deletes the server and pools for a Standard Edition deployment. For an Enterprise pool deployment, right-click the pool and select **Remove Pool**.

26. The final step is to uninstall the OCS 2007 R2 binaries from the server and power it off.

After these steps are complete, the OCS 2007 R2 infrastructure is fully decommissioned, and administrators can focus on tuning their Lync Server 2010 environment.

Troubleshooting

As with any migration, there's a lot that can go wrong regardless of how well planned in advance. The most important item to check is to ensure that Active Directory is healthy and functioning properly. A close second is ensuring all the required manual DNS changes have been made and DNS works flawlessly. The added convenience of the Deployment Wizard doesn't lessen the importance of certificates. They are still core to all server and server-client communications.

Be sure to check the various log files that are created. It's great news that nearly every action, whether done in the Lync Control Panel or the Lync Management Shell, creates a detailed XML log file in the Windows temp directory. Administrators should review these regularly to gain insight into their deployments and understand any errors that occur. The Lync Server event log is also a good place to check for errors. From the **Start** menu, select

16

Administrative Tools, and then select **Event Viewer**. Expand the **Applications and Services Logs** item and then select **Lync Server**. All events related to Lync Server functions reside here. Often the error description is enough to identify the problem and make clear the resolution.

Some tools need to be installed manually to perform some aspects of the migration process. For example, the OCSWMIBC package must be manually installed before migrating the Response Group configuration to Lync Server.

Best Practices

The following are the best practices from this chapter:

▶ Perform an Active Directory health check before beginning the upgrade and migration process. Resolve any issues before starting the process.

▶ Although the Communications Server 2010 Control Panel might seem more familiar at first, there are many functions that can be accomplished only in the Management Shell.

▶ Always install the SQL backward compatibility pack to ensure all cmdlets run correctly.

▶ Resolve any errors in the OCS 2007 R2 infrastructure before merging the topology to Lync Server 2010.

▶ Publish the topology often and after each significant configuration change.

▶ Ensure all users and other objects, such as Exchange Unified Messaging Autoattendant accounts, are all migrated to Lync Server before beginning the OCS 2007 R2 decommission process.

▶ Use the Client Version Policy to restrict legacy clients and allow self-service upgrades.

Summary

As you have seen, the upgrade and migration process is straightforward. The Edge Server is a simple replacement. The Lync Edge Server role can proxy communication for Lync Server and OCS 2007 pools and connect with Lync and OCS 2007 clients. The Front End pool process requires a side-by-side upgrade, and then a migration of users from the OCS pool to the Lync Server pool. Users will maintain their current contact lists during the migration. In fact, users generally won't know they have been migrated unless they are prompted to upgrade their client post-migration.

PART VI

Voice

IN THIS PART

PBX Integration

As versions of Communications Server have come and gone, there has also been discussion around whether the product was fit to be a complete replacement for any existing voice infrastructure. In Lync Server, that discussion will certainly appear again, but more and more organizations will see that it currently meets their entire voice platform needs. The first step in either a migration or testing scenario is to provide integration with the existing voice services, which is what this chapter covers.

This chapter provides an overview of the integration possibilities and some background on basic telephony. In addition to providing an overview of the possible integration methods from how an administrator views the systems, the different end-user scenarios are examined to show what is possible from a user standpoint.

Some of the key improvements in Lync Server that make it possible to use as the only voice infrastructure are also discussed in this chapter. These improvements are items that caused many organizations to pass on using prior versions Communications Server as the primary voice platform, but have now been implemented, making this product a compelling voice platform for businesses.

Telephony Overview

To understand the options existing to integrate Lync Server with an existing voice infrastructure, it is important to understand some fundamentals of telephony. This section discusses some basic concepts in telephony and how they apply to Lync Server.

Public Switched Telephone Network

The Public Switched Telephone Network (PSTN) is the common network of telephony systems across the world. Similar to the Internet, it can be considered a cloud through which phone systems (as opposed to computers) are connected. Protocol standards implemented across many different vendors is what allows for a common set of services such as making and receiving phone calls to work across the PSTN regardless of where the calls are placed. Connections to PSTN are analog phone lines, cellular connections, satellite based, or any other form, as shown in Figure 17.1. The PSTN serves as the backbone for voice services around the world.

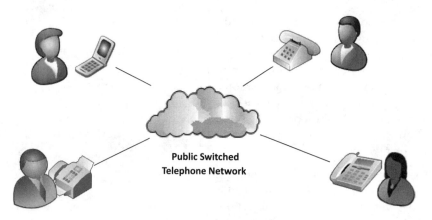

Public Switched Telephone Network

FIGURE 17.1   The Public Switched Telephone Network

Private Branch Exchange

A Private Branch Exchange (PBX) is a device that organizations typically have on-premise, which enables them to connect internal phones, fax machines, or devices together. The PBX on premise allows for users within the organization to call each other without traversing the PSTN and incurring charges. A PBX also usually has trunk lines that connect to the PSTN so that internal users can make and receive calls with PSTN users when required, as shown in Figure 17.2.

As telephony has evolved over the years, different types of PBXs have been used by companies. Usually they fall into one of three categories:

▶ **Traditional PBX**—A traditional PBX is one that does not have IP capabilities. These are generally very old or low-end systems with limited feature sets. These systems are usually entirely based on analog handsets for end users.

▶ **IP PBX**—An IP PBX is a system that is entirely based on Voice over IP (VoIP). It does not support analog devices natively and all endpoints are IP-based network devices.

▶ **Hybrid PBX**—Many PBXs have the capability to function as both a traditional PBX with analog endpoints and as an IP PBX through the purchase of expansion modules and software upgrades. These PBXs offer the most flexibility for an organization because they can connect many different types of devices, as shown in Figure 17.3 as the business transitions to IP telephony.

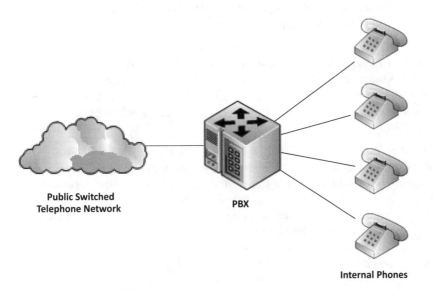

FIGURE 17.2   A Private Branch Exchange (PBX)

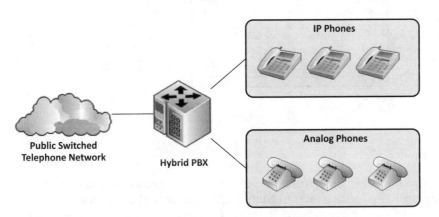

FIGURE 17.3   Hybrid PBX Connecting Analog and IP Phones

Signaling

To facilitate users who are able to call each other, there must be some information exchanged between the PBX and the end users, such as the phone number of the caller and the phone number of the callee. This is referred to as the *signaling information*, and usually contains more than just phone numbers. However, for the sake of this text, it can be considered what controls the calls. The signaling information is how a call is placed, transferred, or ended. The actual voice traffic, or the audio a user speaks and hears, is considered the media.

Signaling information can come in the form of in-band or out-of-band. *In-band* means the information shares the same channel or line as the media. The most common form of in-band signaling is dual-tone multi frequency signaling (DTMF), which is sent when pressing keys on a phone. Each key transmits a unique tone, indicating a different piece of information to the PBX.

Signaling can also be carried out-of-band, which is typical for PBX trunk lines to the PSTN or when connecting directly to another PBX. Out-of-band signaling uses a dedicated channel for the signaling information while the media or actual voice traffic is carried in different channels. Using a T1 connection as an example, there are 24 channels each with 64 kbps of bandwidth available. The first 23 channels carry the voice traffic, so 23 simultaneous calls are supported. The channel 24 carries the signaling information for all of the first 23 channels. This is considered out-of-band because the signaling and media are in separate channels on the connection, as shown in Figure 17.4.

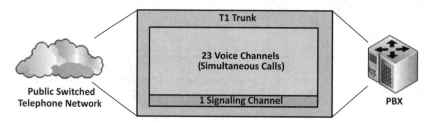

FIGURE 17.4   Out-of-Band Signaling

Voice over IP

As internal networks began to grow, Voice over IP (VoIP) based PBXs began to emerge. Instead of using traditional analog lines to connect internal users, the VoIP handsets connected to the PBX over the IP protocol, just like a computer or any other device on the network. This allowed voice and data traffic to share a common infrastructure, which cuts down on wiring and management overheard.

Just like with traditional PBXs, VoIP requires some form of signaling to control the calls. An early form of signaling used for VoIP was H.323, and the Media Gateway Control Protocol (MGCP) has also gained widespread adoption.

The Session Initiation Protocol, or SIP, has also emerged as a standard that many IP PBXs use for signaling. Lync Server uses SIP for all of its internal signaling and for integrations with other PBX vendors because it provides a common framework for controlling calls. Vendors can also implement extensions on top of SIP to provide additional signaling capabilities. These extensions make SIP extremely flexible, but can lead to interoperability problems between different IP PBXs because each vendor develops its own extensions.

Media

Although SIP meets the needs for signaling information, VoIP PBXs still require a method to transmit the media stream. The Real-Time Transport Protocol (RTP) is used in almost every VoIP implementation and was developed specifically for transmitting audio and video traffic across networks. Encryption of the media traffic was later added in the form of Secure Real-Time Transport Protocol (SRTP), which is what Lync Server uses by default to ensure that the media cannot be intercepted and played back.

SRTP only provides a standard for carrying the media traffic that can be of various media codecs. Media codecs are a way of translating audio and video data into bits that can be transmitted across a network. For two users to have an audio conversation, the codec used by both parties must match to correctly encode and decode the traffic. Although SRTP carries the real-time media, the parties must agree on a codec to have a conversation. Figure 17.5 displays this split of signaling and media traffic, which uses a specific codec such as RTAudio or G.711.

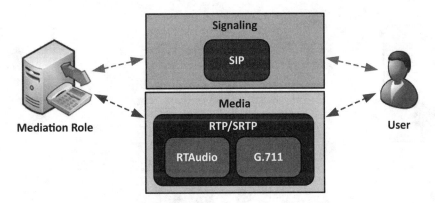

FIGURE 17.5   SIP Signaling and SRTP Media

Lync Server 2010 endpoints have the ability to use two different audio codecs. The default codec is Microsoft's proprietary RTAudio codec, which can dynamically adjust its bandwidth to ensure a certain level of call quality. Lync endpoints can now also take advantage of the G.711 codec in certain scenarios that many VoIP implementations have used for years.

When Lync endpoints cannot communicate directly with another endpoint, the Mediation Server role can be used to transcode between RTAudio and G.711 codecs in a media stream. This is typical for when Lync endpoints communicate to a Mediation Server via RTAudio, but the Mediation Server may communicate with a media gateway via G.711. The Mediation Server acts as a translator in these scenarios.

Integration Methods

There are a number of ways to integrate Lync Server with an existing PBX to support a period of coexistence either while evaluating Enterprise Voice or performing a complete migration to Enterprise Voice. A new Greenfield deployment is rare to come across, which is why many deployments require this coexistence situation for some time. This section discusses the options available to organizations looking to integrate Lync Server with their existing voice infrastructure.

Direct SIP

The easiest and generally most cost-effective way of integrating Lync Server with an existing PBX is if the PBX supports SIP trunks. Many IP PBXs support this functionality, and many other hybrid PBXs support SIP trunks with additional hardware and software upgrades.

In Direct SIP scenarios, the Mediation Server role (which can now be collocated with a Front End Server) serves as the conversion point between the two systems. The signaling on both sides of the server is SIP, but the Mediation role translates the media stream between G.711 on the PBX side and RTAudio on the Lync Server side. A logical overview of a Direct SIP connection is displayed in Figure 17.6.

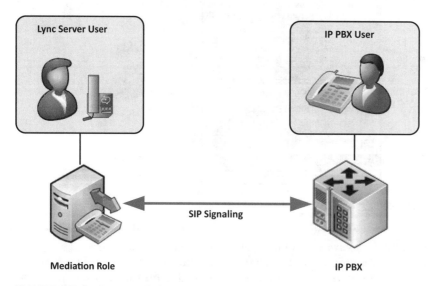

FIGURE 17.6   Direct SIP Integration

Direct SIP integration allows for a number of different end-user scenarios, which are discussed later in this chapter. What usually happens is specific extensions, or a range of extensions, will configure to be "owned" by Lync Server instead of the PBX. These extensions are configured on the old PBX to route across the SIP trunk to let Lync Server handle the call. It is the PBX's way of saying it is not responsible for these numbers, but it knows where they can be reached.

Media Gateways

If Direct SIP is not an option because the PBX does not support the feature or has no IP PBX capabilities, a third-party device called a *media gateway* can be used to complete the integration. Media gateways act as an intermediary between the PBX and Lync Server to help translate traditional PBX protocols to SIP traffic, which Lync Server understands. Media gateways are produced by many vendors today and provide a wide array of integration options for businesses looking to implement the voice features of Lync Server. They typically have traditional telephony connections for T1/E1 systems on the PBX side along with network adapters to communicate with Lync Server. This type of scenario is depicted in Figure 17.7.

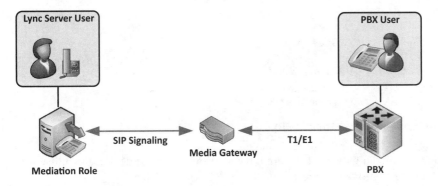

FIGURE 17.7   PBX Integration with Media Gateway

Also, as when configuring a Direct SIP trunk link, configuration of the old PBX is necessary so that it knows to route calls for specific extensions to the media gateway, which delivers the calls to Lync Server.

> **NOTE**
>
> An additional layer of complexity is involved because the media gateway must also be configured to route calls appropriately. On the other hand, the media gateway provides a degree of flexibility in call manipulation that sometimes is not possible natively with a PBX or Lync Server.

Depending on the media gateway and business requirements, it might be necessary to place the media gateway in front of the old PBX. This can potentially have a bigger impact on the organization, but can greatly simplify some of the routing configuration.

Some gateway vendors have software that can detect whether a user's extension is Enterprise Voice or a legacy phone by reading specific Active Directory attributes. This might not seem like a big advantage up front, but as users are migrated to Enterprise Voice it becomes advantageous not to have to constantly change routing rules on the PBX to indicate where an extension exists. This type of integration scenario is shown in Figure 17.8 where the media gateway becomes the link to the PSTN.

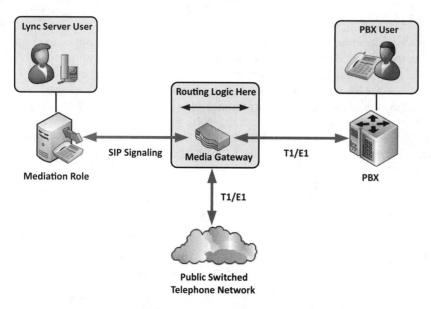

FIGURE 17.8   Media Gateway in Front of PBX

No matter where the media gateway is located, it can provide a great deal of flexibility for organizations looking to move to or test Lync Server Enterprise Voice.

Remote Call Control

Remote call control was the original form of PBX integration introduced with Live Communications Server 2005 and allows for users to control their legacy desk phone from Lync by clicking a contact in their contact list to dial. It also allows for their presence to be automatically updated to "In a call" when using the legacy phone.

> **NOTE**
>
> Support for new Remote Call Control implementations was originally going to be dropped in Lync Server, but the product team has adjusted its stance and will support new deployments. That said, it is a legacy technology and unlikely to be supported in future releases.

Remote call control does not give users the Enterprise Voice features for controlling calls, assigning delegates, or configuring call-forwarding settings. It also does not work remotely, so it can be used only inside the network, which limits its usefulness for remote workers.

Computer Supported Telecommunications Applications Gateway

A Computer Supported Telecommunications Applications (CSTA) Gateway was required to translate between older versions Communications Server and the PBX presence information. This gateway software usually involved an additional server component from the PBX vendor and additional user licensing. Lync Server instead uses the Get and Put verbs over SIP to control presence that can help to remove the dependency on the CSTA gateway, but a CSTA gateway might still be required depending on the PBX vendor. How the PBX and CSTA gateway integrate with Lync Server is shown in Figure 17.9.

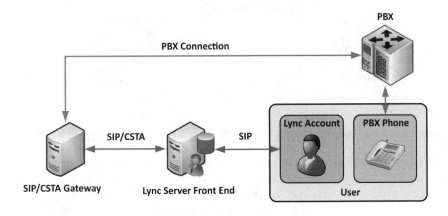

FIGURE 17.9   CSTA Gateway

Dual Forking

Dual forking is mentioned here only for clarity, but it is no longer a supported deployment option in Lync Server. The only IP PBX ever qualified for dual forking with Communications Server 2007 R2 was the Nortel CS 1000. Dual forking allowed a user to have the same extension in both the legacy PBX and Communications Server, and incoming calls always rang both systems. Figure 17.10 walks through the basic steps that occurred with dual forking. Again, this feature is not available in Lync Server 2010.

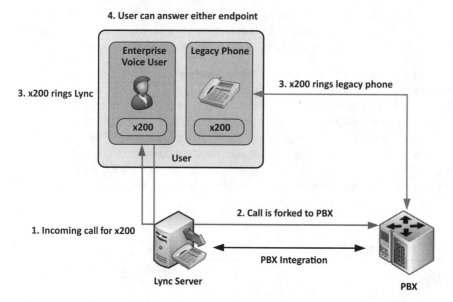

FIGURE 17.10   Dual Forking

NOTE

It is still technically possible with some PBX vendors to maintain the same extension in both systems, but this configuration is not supported by Microsoft. It requires complex translation patterns and dialing tricks in both systems, making it not a very scalable solution. It is generally much simpler to use two different extensions in migration or coexistence scenarios.

SIP Provider Trunking

The final integration method isn't so much integration with an existing PBX as it is a way to provide voice services between the end users without one of the other methods. SIP provider trunking involves using an ITSP (Internet Telephony Service Provider) to deliver voice services across the Internet to a Lync Server organization, similar to a service provider provisioning Internet access. If integration with an existing PBX is not possible with any of the other means, or if an organization wants to move away from the legacy PBX services and provider, an ITSP can replace those services. Figure 17.11 shows how a Lync user could call a PBX user using SIP trunking and the PSTN.

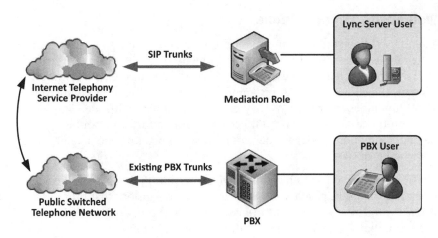

FIGURE 17.11   SIP Trunking

In this situation, Enterprise Voice users can communicate with users still hosted on the PBX, but only by traversing the PSTN.

> **CAUTION**
>
> This is not an optimal call path for users who are physically sitting next to each other on different systems, but does provide a connectivity option if no others exist. In a migration scenario, as fewer users remain on the legacy PBX, this becomes less of an issue.

End-User Scenarios

This section discusses the different types of PBX integrations from the perspective of an end-user. Organizations can deploy a mix of these scenarios to meet the needs of different users and don't have to pick just one path. For example, some users might be completely using Enterprise Voice, but others want to retain a legacy phone for use with audio conferencing.

Although users transition to Enterprise Voice, they might configure call-forwarding settings to simultaneously ring their legacy PBX phone. Certainly presenting more options to users makes managing the solution more difficult, but might be necessary. What scenarios are possible is dependent on the integration methods referenced previously.

Enterprise Voice

In this scenario, end users have full Enterprise Voice functionality and use only Lync Server endpoints as their phones. This state provides the most features and flexibility to the end-users. This is the state Enterprise Voice users are in for a new deployment with no existing PBX or when a migration is completed.

Enterprise Voice with Legacy Phone

In this scenario, end users have full Enterprise Voice functionality, but also retain a legacy PBX phone on their desks. This scenario is typical for migrations from a legacy PBX where a period of coexistence is required while users become accustomed to the new Lync Server endpoints. Users have the choice of which system to use when placing or receiving calls through the use of simultaneous ringing. As they grow more familiar with the Lync Server tools, they rely less on the legacy phone until it becomes unnecessary and can be removed. As the migration ends and legacy devices retired, the organization actually ends in the pure Enterprise Voice state.

Most implementations require a user to have two extensions during this period of coexistence. One extension is the user's primary, or publicly known extension, that other users dial and is associated with the user's account in Lync Server. The other is a secondary, or unpublished extension, that is only associated with the legacy phone.

When placing calls, users can choose whether to use Lync or the legacy phone. When calling from Lync, the callees see the call from the user's primary, published number in the organization, but calls coming from the legacy phone appear from the unpublished number. Figure 17.12 shows what could happen when users dial from either a Lync or PBX phone endpoint.

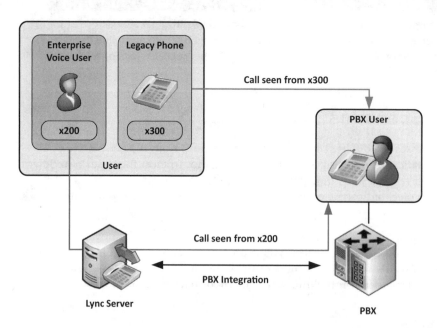

FIGURE 17.12   Enterprise Voice with Legacy Phone

Receiving calls on both devices in this scenario is accomplished through the users configuring simultaneous ringing within Lync. Inbound calls are routed first to the Lync Server account that determines what should happen to the call. Users generally set their Lync call-forwarding options to simultaneously ring the secondary extension associated with their legacy PBX phone. This enables them to answer incoming calls either with a Lync endpoint or on the legacy phone without the caller noticing where the call was picked up. As the migration period goes on, users can adjust their simultaneous ringing to stop ringing the legacy phone altogether. An example of how simultaneous ringing happens is shown in Figure 17.13.

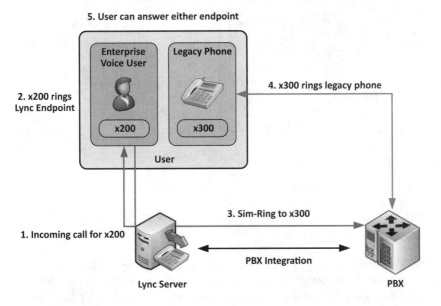

FIGURE 17.13   Simultaneous Ringing

17

> **TIP**
>
> Analyze peak capacity of the PBX and media gateways when planning for simultaneous ringing. As an example, a media gateway with two T1s configured to a legacy PBX might support an initial integration with Lync Server. Now when users have simultaneous ringing, it might be necessary to use up to twice the number of channels so four T1s might be required to support the coexistence.

Legacy Phone for Conferencing

Another option for organizations not looking to fully implement Enterprise Voice features or replace existing handsets is to leverage the conferencing features of Lync Server with their existing investments. This enables an organization to migrate away from a legacy or hosted conferencing system without changing the fundamental way users function. As shown in Figure 17.14, users are not enabled for Enterprise Voice, but instead retain their PBX desk phone.

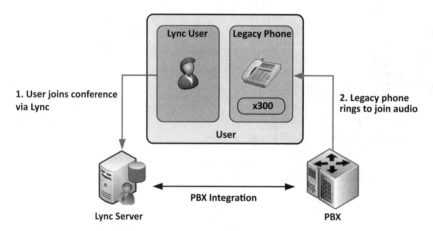

FIGURE 17.14   Legacy Phone for Conferencing

Users in this scenario have full access to the rich conference scheduling controls within Outlook and Lync, but instead of using a Lync endpoint to participate in audio conferences they can use their legacy desk phone. This is accomplished through the use of the Join audio conferences from setting within Lync. Users can elect to be called at a number published within Active Directory or enter a number manually. To join an audio conference through Lync, the user just answers the desk phone. A screenshot of configuring this dial-out ability is shown in Figure 17.15.

FIGURE 17.15   Join Settings

Legacy Phone Presence and Click-to-Call

A more limited set of features can be deployed to users that gives Click-to-Call functionality. This enables the end users to click a user within their Lync contact list and have it dial the user's number from their legacy PBX phone. Additionally, presence messages are integrated so that when a user places a call from the legacy phone, his or her presence in Lync automatically updates to In a Call. This is the scenario Remote Call Control provides to end-users.

> **CAUTION**
>
> This is one of the most basic integration options and does not provide a significant amount of flexibility or features to the end user. In this state, call-forwarding settings, delegation of calls, and advanced call control features are not available. The Click-to-Call features also do not work well for remote users because even if they initiate a call, it places the call from a desk phone inside the office, attached to the local PBX.

PBX Software Plugin

The final end-user scenario is where the PBX vendor uses the Lync Server APIs to develop add-on software for the desktop to integrate with Lync. Examples of this are Cisco's UC Integration for Lync (CUCI-Lync) and Avaya's Application Enablement Server (AES) products, which must be installed and managed separately from the Lync client.

> **CAUTION**
>
> These solutions might seem appealing to some organizations, but the plugins can introduce a layer of complexity in troubleshooting voice issues. The plugins do not give the end user Enterprise Voice functionality and are not much of an advantage over remote call control feature set.

17

Voice calls and traffic are still done entirely through the existing PBX and not through Lync Server. Instead of the native call controls provided by Lync, users will see a UI developed by the PBX vendor, which might confuse end users.

The main difference with these solutions over Remote Call Control is that the presence and phone control features are client-side as opposed to server-side. Instead of Lync Server integrating with a PBX for presence updates and phone control, the software plugin handles the call control and user presence updates, which means that no CSTA gateway is required.

Key Improvements

Lync Server has made some great strides to address some of the weaknesses for voice deployments in earlier versions. This section briefly discusses a few of the key improvements that will make replacing an existing PBX or integrating with an existing PBX significantly easier.

Media Bypass

The fact that the Mediation server role can now be collocated on a Front End Server significantly eases the infrastructure requirements for implementing Lync Server voice. The other big advancement is the capability for media bypass from Lync endpoints.

When possible, a Lync client will use the G.711 codec to communicate directly with an IP PBX or media gateway that eliminates the need for the Mediation server to be involved with converting between G.711 and RTAudio. This change should help reduce the number of hops, remove potential latency, and improve the overall voice quality. As shown in Figure 17.16, the SIP signaling information still flows through the Mediation server role, but the Lync endpoints can send their media directly to the IP PBX or media gateway.

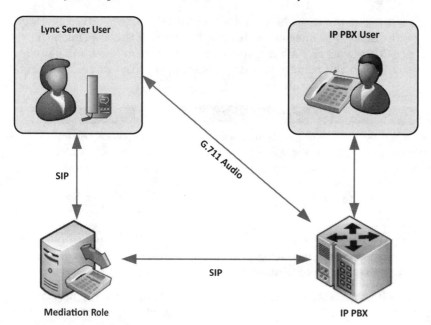

FIGURE 17.16   Media Bypass

Routing

In prior versions of Communications Server, each Mediation Server could only be associated with a single gateway, PBX, or SIP trunk. A new feature in Lync Server is the capability for a single Mediation Server to be associated with multiple gateways. This allows for a single Mediation Server to connect to multiple media gateways or IP PBXs, which can significantly reduce the amount of server hardware required to implement a redundant solution. An example of a Mediation Server connecting to two IP PBXs and a media gateway is shown in Figure 17.17.

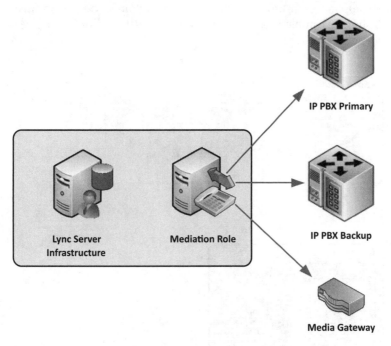

FIGURE 17.17   Multiple Routes from a Single Mediation Server

Caller ID Controls

Lync Server has the capability to manipulate the calling party phone number and display name. This was previously a feature that required using the PBX or a media gateway to manipulate the strings, but is now configurable by administrators.

This manipulation can also be configured to occur only for external calls so that calls between internal users display the actual user's extension, but a call to an external party can be masked as the main company line. If a user configures simultaneous ringing to a mobile number, the system allows for another internal user's caller ID to be presented to that mobile phone.

Survivable Branch Appliances

In Lync Server, third-party media gateway vendors will be producing devices called Survivable Branch Appliances (SBAs), which give a remote site's basic telephony features in the event of a WAN outage. Previously, when a remote site lost a WAN link, it caused users in that site to become disconnected from Communicator and unable to make phone calls. Now, the SBA can be connected to the PSTN and in the event of a WAN outage, users remain connected and are able to make and receive phone calls.

SBAs are first configured by administrators at the main site and then shipped to a branch office where they can be powered on and running with a few basic steps. The SBAs come in the form of stand-alone appliances or modules for switching equipment already located at a branch. Figure 17.18 shows a sample topology where an SBA exists in a branch office with its own PSTN connection.

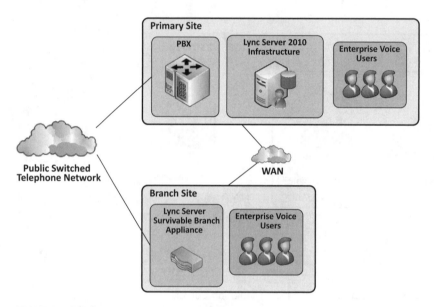

FIGURE 17.18   Survivable Branch Appliance

Analog Devices

Analog devices, such as fax machines or legacy phones, were not supported in prior versions of Communications Server, but this release supports these kinds of devices. Connectivity of the devices to the infrastructure is accomplished through the use of media gateways, which have these analog ports. Routing and policy enforcement of the devices is performed by Lync Server by connecting to the media gateway over IP.

Best Practices

The following are best practices from this chapter:

▶ First identify how an existing PBX can integrate with Lync server. A media gateway may be required.

▶ Evaluate the media gateway vendors and devices and vendors to find a feature set that meets the needs of the organization.

▶ Ensure that media gateways have enough channels to handle peak capacity, especially when using simultaneous ringing.

▶ Identify which features that end users are provisioned with prior to determining hardware requirements.

▶ Spend time training users on the integration and how to use the systems during a period of coexistence.

Summary

Lync Server provides a stronger and more flexible integration story that should make many organizations interested in pursuing an Enterprise Voice deployment. The additions, such as media bypass, routing to multiple gateways, and Caller ID controls, address many of the pain points from prior versions. The Survivable Branch Appliances also provide a strong story for branch office sites where they can now continue working without a WAN connection.

17

CHAPTER 18

Enterprise Voice

Lync Server 2010 makes a very strong case as a full-fledged phone system businesses can use to fulfill their voice needs. Microsoft has introduced significant improvements to the product that make Lync Server 2010 a compelling option as the solve Private Branch Exchange (PBX) in an organization.

This chapter discusses the Enterprise Voice enhancements found in Lync Server 2010. It also details the components required to configure a voice deployment such as dial plans, routing, and voice policies.

The new, advanced Enterprise Voice features such as Call Admission Control, Media Bypass, and Enhanced 911 are covered with instructions for how to configure each service to meet the needs of a business. Steps for preparing the topology to introduce branch sites with resilient voice services through an appliance or server are included. Response Group configuration is covered in this chapter with examples about how to configure both basic and interactive workflows.

▶ For a more detailed discussion about planning for each of these features, see Chapter 28, "Planning for Voice Deployment."

Mediation Server Overview

The Mediation Server role in Lync Server 2010 is responsible for providing voice features to end users that allow them to connect with the Public Switched Telephone Network (PSTN) or another PBX. The Mediation Server provides a number of benefits to a Lync Server 2010 deployment that are discussed in greater detail throughout this section.

Perhaps one of the biggest improvements in Lync is the fact that the Mediation Server can now be collocated with a Front End Server, reducing the number of servers required in a deployment. This chapter focuses on configuration of each voice component.

▶ For planning voice components, see Chapter 28.

Enterprise Voice

Enterprise Voice on a basic level is referred to as the feature that allows Lync endpoints to place and receive phone calls through the PSTN. Enterprise Voice differs from many other IP PBX vendors by providing a rich user interface that allows the end user to control advanced call functionality with only a few clicks. Comparable solutions from other vendors require logging in to separate systems or assistance from an administrator to accomplish the same task that an end-user can do in Lync Server 2010.

Users can forward calls to a mobile phone or alternative number with a click and even have the calls forwarded based on working hours defined in Outlook. Delegates can answer calls on behalf of a manager, and teams can route calls to each other easily. Presence is also integrated with Enterprise Voice so that users can have calls sent directly to voice mail if their presence is Do Not Disturb.

Media Bypass

Media Bypass allows Lync endpoints to communicate directly with an IP/PSTN gateway or SIP trunking provider. This feature is a big reason collocation of the Mediation Server with the Front End service is now supported. Instead of having the Mediation Server transcode every PSTN audio call from RTAudio to the G.711 codec, the Lync endpoints can send G.711 audio directly to an IP/PSTN gateway, bypassing Mediation Server entirely. This not only cuts down on the processing required for the Mediation Server, it also improves call quality by removing an additional hop and potential latency.

Call Admission Control

Call Admission Control functionality is another welcome feature in Lync Server 2010 that gives the administrator much more control over how voice and video are routed in the network. Lync Server 2010 provides Call Admission Control by defining network regions and bandwidth available between different sites. Administrators can limit both the total amount of bandwidth used for voice and video between sites and the bandwidth limit for each individual session. When a Lync client attempts to make a call, both endpoints check the bandwidth policy to verify the call can be placed. These limits enable organizations to protect a WAN link from becoming oversaturated and providing a poor end-user experience.

What happens when these limits are reached is also configurable by the organization. The first option attempted routes the call across the Internet using Edge Servers. PSTN rerouting can be used to automatically place the call through an IP/PSTN gateway instead of traversing the WAN link. Policies might also be assigned to users who allow them to override the bandwidth policy and still make a successful call.

Enhanced 911

Enhanced emergency services in Lync Server 2010 allow an emergency call to automatically provide location information to a dispatcher. Lync Server 2010 maintains a location information database consisting of subnet, switch, port, and wireless access points within an organization. These objects are then associated with a specific address and floor or suite number. When Lync endpoints are signed in, they can automatically detect the location based on this data. When users are outside of the organization and a location cannot be determined, users can enter a location and address manually. They can also be prohibited from making phone calls until a location is provided.

> **TIP**
>
> It is important to note that Lync cannot natively transmit the E-911 information to a dispatcher. The location data is actually sent first to a third-party emergency service routing provider web service that delivers the information to dispatchers.

Remote Survivability

Another big improvement in Lync Server 2010 is that remote sites can sustain the loss of a WAN connection. This is accomplished by provisioning a survivable branch appliance or survivable branch server in locations that do not have Front End services deployed. If a WAN link outage occurs and the branch can no longer access the Front End pool, the users remain signed in to the Lync endpoints and can still place and receive PSTN phone calls.

The survivable branch appliances that are produced by third-party Microsoft partners come in a variety of formats and capacities. The setup process for each varies slightly, but most of the configuration can be completed by an administrator in a central site.

> **TIP**
>
> When the appliance arrives at a branch, a technician with basic skills should be able to physically cable the appliance and run through a simple setup wizard to complete the installation.

Response Groups

Response Groups are a feature carried forward from OCS 2007 R2 with quite a few improvements. Response Groups enable organizations to create groups of call agents that belong to queues. Callers reach these queues by navigating a workflow that can be as simple as being routed to different agents based on the time of day. Workflows can also be more interactive and ask the callers a number of questions before routing calls to a queue.

With the Lync Server Management Shell, the depth of a workflow is unlimited and completely flexible. This should enable organizations to leverage Response Groups in a way

18

that meets their needs, as different as those might be from one business to the next. Custom audio prompts can be uploaded for the questions, or the native text-to-speech capabilities can be used so that administrators simply need to type a question into a text field.

Mediation Server Installation

In most cases, with Lync Server 2010, the Mediation Server role is actually collocated with a Front End Server, but it is still possible to deploy a standalone Mediation Server for performance benefits or when an isolated pool is required. This section discusses a standalone Mediation Server installation.

Prerequisites

A Mediation Server requires only the .NET Framework installation. No additional server components are needed.

Hardware Requirements

This section discusses the recommended minimum hardware requirements for Lync Server 2010 servers.

The Lync Server 2010 Mediation Server processor requirements are as follows:

▶ Dual processor, quad-core 2.0 GHz or faster

▶ Four-way processor, dual-core 2.0 GHz or faster

> **NOTE**
>
> Lync Server 2010 is only a 64-bit application and requires a 64-bit–capable processor. This is generally not an issue with any modern hardware, but be sure to verify legacy hardware that supports a 64-bit operating system before attempting to use it for a Mediation Server.

The Lync Server 2010 Mediation Server memory requirements are as follows:

▶ 16 GB RAM

The Lync Server 2010 Mediation Server disk requirements are as follows:

▶ 10K RPM HDD

The Lync Server 2010 Mediation Server network requirements are as follows:

▶ Dual, 1 gigabit per second (Gbps) network adapters (recommended)

▶ Single, 1 gigabit per second (Gbps) network adapter (supported)

> **TIP**
>
> When using multiple network adapters in a Mediation Server, each adapter should be placed on a separate subnet. If separate subnets cannot be provided, only a single adapter should be used.

Operating System Requirements

The Lync Server 2010 Mediation Server supports the following operating systems:

- ▶ Windows Server 2008, x64 Standard Edition with Service Pack 2

- ▶ Windows Server 2008, x64 Enterprise Edition with Service Pack 2

- ▶ Windows Server 2008, x64 Datacenter Edition with Service Pack 2

- ▶ Windows Server 2008 R2, Standard Edition

- ▶ Windows Server 2008 R2, Enterprise Edition

- ▶ Windows Server 2008 R2, Datacenter Edition

> **NOTE**
>
> The Datacenter editions of both Windows Server 2008 x64 with Service Pack 2 and Windows Server 2008 R2 are supported by Microsoft, but have not been fully tested for use with Lync Server 2010.

The Windows Server Core, Web, and High Performance Computing editions for any operating system version are not supported for deployment.

Software Requirements

The Lync Server 2010 Mediation Server requires the following components to be installed:

- ▶ .NET Framework 3.5

- ▶ Visual C++ 2008 Redistributable

- ▶ PowerShell 2.0

- ▶ Windows Installer 4.0

- ▶ WinRM 2.0

- ▶ BITS 4.0

Create Mediation Server Pool

After the server has been fully prepared for installation, the topology must be edited and published to reflect the new Mediation Server pool. This involves both editing the existing topology, if it exists, and then publishing that topology so that all other servers in the environment are aware of the new Mediation Server pool.

Edit Topology

The next step in deploying a Mediation Server is to edit the existing Lync Server topology. To edit the topology, use the following steps:

> **NOTE**
>
> If the Topology Builder is not already installed on the local computer or another computer in the environment, it can be installed from the Lync Server 2010 media.

18

1. Open the **Lync Server Topology Builder**.

2. When prompted to import an existing topology from Active Directory, click **OK**.

3. Expand the Site node where the Mediation Server is deployed.

4. Right-click the Mediation Server's node and select **New Mediation Server**.

5. Enter a **pool FQDN** and select either **Multiple computer pool** or **Single computer pool**.

6. Enter a **computer FQDN** for the server being used as a Mediation Server, click **Add**, and then click **Next**.

7. Select a **next hop pool** for the Mediation pool. This should be a Front End pool.

8. Select an **edge pool** for the Mediation pool to use with external voice traffic.

9. Click **New** to define a PSTN gateway to associate with the Mediation pool.

10. Enter a **gateway FQDN or IP address** and **Listening Port for IP/PSTN Gateway**. Select a **SIP Transport Protocol**, and then click **OK**.

11. Repeat for any additional gateways that are associated to this Mediation pool.

12. Click **Finish** when ready. Figure 18.1 shows a sample Mediation Server pool that has been added to the existing topology.

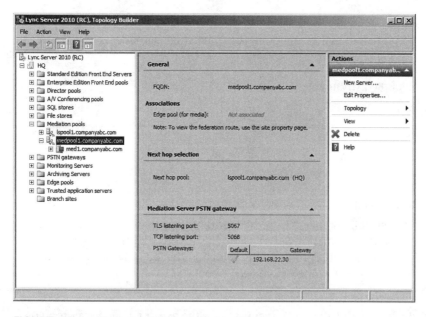

FIGURE 18.1   Mediation Server Added to Topology

Publish Topology

After the topology has been modified to include the Mediation Server pool and IP/PSTN gateways, the configuration can be published. The following steps publish the changes to the Central Management Store and all existing Lync Server 2010 servers update their local configuration stores to match:

1. Ensure the Lync Server Topology Builder is still open and contains the Mediation Server pool that was recently added.

2. Click the top node of the management console, **Lync Server 2010**.

3. Click the **Actions** menu, and then click **Publish**, or select Publish from the Actions pane on the right side of the console.

4. Click **Next** to begin publishing the topology.

5. When the log indicates a successful update, click **Finish** to complete the wizard.

Install Server

At this point, the target server should be fully prepared and meet all prerequisites.

▶ Refer to the "Prerequisites" section covered earlier in this chapter for a full list of the Mediation Server requirements.

Install Local Configuration Store

To install any server role in Lync Server 2010, the target server must first have a local configuration store installed and populated with the topology information.

1. Insert the Lync Server 2010 media on the server to be used as a Mediation Server and launch **Setup.exe** found in the Setup\amd64 folder.

2. Enter a location for the installation files to be cached, and then click **Continue installation without checking for updates**. Click **OK**.

3. Select **I accept the terms in the licensing agreement**, and then click **OK**.

4. Click **Install or Update Lync Server system**.

5. Under **Step 1: Install Local Configuration Store**, click **Run**.

6. Select **Retrieve directly from the Central Management Store** and then click **Next**.

7. Click **Finish** after the local store is successfully created.

Update and Verify Configuration Store

The following steps verify the local configuration store has been synchronized with the Central Management Store before any server roles are installed.

1. Launch the **Lync Server Management Shell**.

2. Check the CMS replication status with the following command:

```
Get-CSManagementStoreReplicationStatus
```

3. Check the ReplicaFQDN for the current server and verify the UpToDate parameter reads True.

18

```
UpToDate           : False
ReplicaFQDN        : med1.companyabc.com
IsDeleted          : False
LastStatusReport   : 7/3/2010 10:02:17 PM
LastUpdateCreation : 7/3/2010 10:02:10 PM
```

4. If the UpToDate parameter is False, initiate an update of the store data with the following command:

```
Invoke-CSManagementStoreReplication
```

5. Check the replication status again and verify it is now updated and in sync with the Central Management Store. If the local store is not in sync with the Central Store installation, the installation of the Lync Server components does not proceed.

Install Lync Server Components

The following steps enable the server to read the topology information from the local configuration store and then install the server roles matching its own FQDN.

1. Under **Step 2: Setup or Remove Lync Server Components**, click the **Run** button.

2. Click **Next** to begin the Mediation Server installation published in the topology.

3. Click **Finish** when the installation completes.

Create Certificates

Like all other roles in Lync Server, the Mediation Server communicates to other servers in the organization using Mutual Transport Layer Security (MTLS). To leverage MTLS, the Mediation Server needs one certificate installed that meets a few requirements:

▶ The subject name should contain the pool's FQDN.

▶ The pool name should be included as a subject alternative name.

▶ The fully qualified name of the server should be included as a subject alternative name.

> **NOTE**
>
> The Certificate Wizard in Lync Server 2010 automatically populates the subject name and any required subject alternative names based on the published topology, which greatly simplifies certificate confusion created by prior versions. If only one certificate is used for the default internal web services and external web services, the subject alternative names must be manually added when running the wizard.

Use the following steps to request and assign the necessary certificates:

1. Under **Step 3: Request, Install, or Assign Certificate**, click the **Run** button.

2. Highlight **Default** certificate and click **Request**.

3. Click **Next** to begin the wizard.

4. Select either **Send the request immediately to an online certification authority** or **Prepare the request now, but send it later** if an offline request will be generated. Click **Next**.

5. If creating an online request, select a certification authority detected in the environment and click **Next**.

6. **Specify alternate credentials for the certification authority** if required or click **Next** to use the currently logged on credentials.

7. Select **Use an alternate certificate template for the selected certification authority** if necessary. The default is to not select this option, which will use the WebServer template. Click **Next**.

8. Enter a **Friendly Name** for the certificate such as Mediation Server Pool.

9. Select a key **Bit Length** of 1024, 2048, or 4096.

10. If the certificate is exportable, select the **Mark the certificate's private key as exportable** check box.

11. Enter an **Organization** name, typically the name of the business.

12. Enter an **Organizational Unit** name, typically the name of a division or department, and click **Next**.

13. Select a **Country**, enter a **State or Province**, enter a **City or Locality**, and click **Next**.

14. Review the automatically populated subject and subject alternative names. Click **Next**.

15. Include additional subject alternative names if necessary. Click **Next**.

16. Click **Next** to complete the request, and then click **Finish** to complete the wizard.

If the certificates are issued from an online certificate authority, they should be installed automatically. If an offline request is issued, the wizard must be rerun with the option to complete an offline request.

Assign Certificates

After creating the necessary certificates, the Mediation Server services must have certificates assigned to them. The following steps show how to assign a certificate:

1. Under **Step 3: Request, Install, or Assign Certificate**, click the Run button.

2. Highlight **Default certificate** and click **Assign an existing certificate.**

3. Click **Next** to begin the wizard.

4. Highlight the certificate to be assigned and click **Next**.

5. Click **Next** to confirm the selection.

6. Click **Finish** once the wizard completes.

Start Services

After the necessary certificates are requested and assigned, the Lync Server Mediation Server services can be started.

1. Below **Step 4: Start Services**, click the **Run** button.
2. Click **Next** to start the Lync Server services.
3. Click **Finish** to complete the wizard.

At this point, the Mediation Server installation is complete and it should be functional. Be sure to configure any IP/PSTN gateways to interoperate with the Mediation Server pool.

Voice Routing

Voice routing in Lync Server 2010 is a complex melding of many different objects. These objects are linked in a way that determines exactly how a call is routed. Voice routing comprises the following objects:

▶ **Dial Plan**—Dial plans are the equivalent of location profiles from Office Communications Server. A dial plan contains a set of normalization rules to convert dial strings to a routable format and is assigned to users.

▶ **Normalization Rules**—Associated with a dial plan and converts the digits a user might dial into a common format that is then routable by the system.

▶ **Voice Policies**—Determines what voice features users are allowed to use, such as call forwarding, simultaneous ringing, and call transfer.

▶ **Routes**—Routes are used in Lync Server to direct calls through a specified gateway or a set of gateways.

▶ **PSTN Usages**—Usages are a class of call that is then associated with voice policies. If a user's voice policy does not contain a specific PSTN usage, the user is not allowed to place the call.

▶ **Gateways**—Gateway objects are a PSTN media gateway, an IP-PBX, or an Internet Telephony Service Provider. Any object that Lync Server sends calls to can be considered a gateway.

▶ **Trunk Configuration**—A logical connection representing the connection between a Lync Server and a PSTN gateway, IP-PBX, or Internet Telephony Service Provider.

▶ **Translation Rules**—Rules associated with a trunk configuration to manipulate dial strings before being sent across a trunk. These rules can manipulate the dial string sent across the trunk if the opposite end is not capable of handling E.164 numbers.

Dial Plan

A dial plan in Lync Server 2010 is associated with users and contains a set of normalization rules. Normalization rules are used to convert dial strings entered by users into a format routable by Lync. Dial plans can differ based on region or site depending on how users are used to dialing digits. Additional dial plans are usually created to accommodate different dialing habits based on sites or users. To create a new dial plan, use the following steps:

1. Open the **Lync Server 2010 Control Panel**.

2. Click **Voice Routing**.

3. Click **Dial Plan**.

4. A dial plan can be scoped to apply at the site level, to a specific pool, or even just to a specific set of users. Click **New**, and then select **Site dial plan**, **Pool dial plan**, or **User dial plan**.

5. Enter a simple name for the dial plan to uniquely identify it within the topology.

6. Enter a **Description** for the dial plan.

7. If the dial plan is associated with a Dial-in Conferencing Region, enter the name of that region.

8. If users need to use any kind of prefix to dial external numbers, enter those keys in the External access prefix field.

9. Click **OK** to save the dial plan.

Normalization rules can be added or modified at any time.

Normalization Rules

Normalization rules are associated with a dial plan and provide a way for administrators to translate dial strings users enter into full E.164 format. For instance, a country code and local area code might be automatically appended when a user tries to dial only seven digits. Many organizations used four- or five-digit internal extensions, and normalization rules can convert those dial patterns to a full E.164 number.

Administrators can either define the normalization rules using regular expressions or using the Normalization Rule tool. To create a new normalization rule, use the following steps:

1. On the **Edit Dial Plan** screen, click the **New** button in the **Associated Normalization Rules** section.

2. Provide a name for the rule and description for the rule.

> **NOTE**
>
> This example uses the Normalization Rule tool, but for more advanced pattern matching, click the Edit button at the bottom of the screen to manually enter the matching pattern and translation rule using regular expressions.

3. In the **Starting digits** field, enter the beginning digits of the string to be matched.

4. Specify a **Length** of the string to be matched. Options include matching at least a specific number of digits, exactly a certain number of digits, or any number of digits.

5. Specify a number of **Digits to remove** after a string matches the starting digits and length. These digits will be removed from the left side of the number.

6. Specify **Digits to add** after the selected number of digits have been removed.

18

7. If the pattern matches numbers that are internal to the organization, check the box **Internal extension**.

8. Click **OK** to save the translation rule and click **OK** again to save the trunk configuration.

Voice Policies

Voice policies in Lync Server 2010 are a way of controlling features and calling abilities of users. Voice policies are assigned to user accounts through a global, site, or direct method. The following options are available when creating a voice policy:

▶ **Enable call forwarding**—Enables users to forward calls to other users or devices.

▶ **Enable delegation**—Enables users to specify other users to answer and place calls on their behalf.

▶ **Enable call transfer**—Enables users to transfer calls to another user.

▶ **Enable call park**—Enables users to place a call on hold and pick it up from another phone or location by dialing a call park orbit number.

▶ **Enable simultaneous ringing of phones**—Enables users to simultaneously ring another user or phone number.

▶ **Enable team call**—Enables users to answer calls on behalf of another team member.

▶ **Enable PSTN reroute**—Enables users to place calls to be rerouted to the PSTN network when the Wide Area Network (WAN) network is congested or unavailable.

▶ **Enable bandwidth policy override**—Enables users to avoid limitations imposed by Call Admission Control policies.

▶ **Enable malicious call tracing**—Enables users to report malicious calls.

To create a new voice policy, complete the following steps:

1. Open the **Lync Server 2010 Control Panel**.

2. Click **Voice Routing**.

3. Click **Voice Policy**.

4. A voice policy can be scoped to apply at the site level or pool level. Click **New** and then select either **Site policy** or **User policy**.

5. If creating a Site policy, the name field is populated automatically and cannot be changed. Enter a description for the policy.

6. Select or do not select **Enable call forwarding**.

7. Select or do not select **Enable delegation**.

8. Select or do not select **Enable call transfer**.

9. Select or do not select **Enable call park**.

10. Select or do not select **Enable simultaneous ringing of phones**.

11. Select or do not select **Enable team call**.

12. Select or do not select **Enable PSTN reroute**.

13. Select or do not select **Enable bandwidth policy override**.

14. Select or do not select **Enable malicious call tracing**.

15. Click **OK** to save the voice policy. Associated PSTN usages can be added or modified at any time. Figure 18.2 displays a sample voice policy that allows all these features.

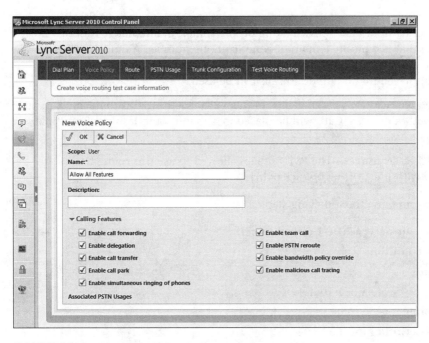

FIGURE 18.2   Creating a Voice Policy

Alternatively, the Lync Server Management Shell can be used to create a new voice policy:

```
New-CsVoicePolicy -Identity <Name> -AllowCallForwarding <$True | $False>
-AllowPSTNReRouting <$True | $False> -AllowSimulRing <$True | $False>
-EnableBWPolicyOverride <$True | $False> -EnableCallPark <$True | $False>
-EnableCallTransfer <$True | $False> -EnableDelegation <$True | $False>
-EnableMaliciousCallTracing <$True | $False> - EnableTeamCall <$True |
$False> -PSTNUsage <List of PSTN Usages associated with the policy>
```

Routes

Routes are used in Lync Server to direct calls through a specified gateway or a set of gateways. Routes are processed after numbers are normalized based on a dial plan and determine which gateway will place a call. Creating a new route has the following options:

▶ **Starting digits for numbers that you want to allow**—Routes are based on the beginning of the digit string, including the addition (+) symbol. Routes are matched based on a top-down matching algorithm, so the most specific routes should be highest in the route order.

▶ **Exceptions**—In some cases, using route priority might be difficult or some patterns should be excluded from traversing a specific gateway. The Exceptions option allows an administrator to exclude strings that would otherwise match the route.

▶ **Suppress caller ID**—This option enables an administrator to prevent the caller's actual caller ID from being passed along on the route. An alternative caller ID must be entered that is typically a main or generic phone number. A limitation here is this cannot be variable based on the calling party ID. Instead, only a single phone number displayed for all outbound calls can be used.

▶ **Associated gateways**—A list of gateways that calls matching this route and can be used for outbound calls. Calls will be placed in a round-robin fashion if multiple gateways are associated.

▶ **Associated PSTN usages**—The PSTN usages allowed to use this route. Usages are associated with users through voice policies.

To create a new route, use the following steps:

1. Open the **Lync Server 2010 Control Panel**.
2. Click **Voice Routing**.
3. Click **Route**.
4. Click **New** to create a new route.
5. Enter a **Name** for the route.
6. Enter a **Description** for the route.
7. In the **Starting digits for numbers that you want to allow** field, enter the beginning digits this route should match and then click **Add**.
8. Repeat this step for any additional patterns this route should handle.
9. If any numbers that might match this pattern should be excluded, click the **Exceptions** button and enter those numbers.
10. If the outbound caller ID should be altered for this route, check the box **Suppress caller ID** and enter an **Alternate caller ID**.
11. In the Associated gateways section, click the **Add** button, select the outbound gateways, and click **OK**.
12. In the Associated PSTN Usages field, click **Select**, choose any **PSTN Usages**, and click **OK**.
13. Click **OK** to save the route.

PSTN Usages

PSTN usage records are associated with routes and voice policies to provide a way to control which users are allowed to use specific routes. Voice policies are applied to users, which contain a list of PSTN usages. If a user dials a number that matches a route with one of those PSTN usages, the call will be placed. If not, the user will be unable to make the call.

To create a new PSTN usage record, use the following steps:

1. On the **Edit Voice Policy** screen, click the **New** button in the Associated PSTN Usages section.
2. Enter a **Name** for the PSTN usage.
3. Click the **Select** button in the Associated Routes section to associate the usage with an existing route. Alternatively, click **New** to create a new route for the usage.
4. Select a route and click **OK**.
5. Click **OK** to save the PSTN usage record.

Trunk Configuration

A *trunk* is a logical connection between the Mediation Server role and a PBX, PSTN gateway, or Internet Telephony Service Provider. The trunk settings apply to any gateway the site or pool is associated with, so if these settings vary across gateways, a new pool might be required for each unique set. Creating a new trunk configuration has the following options:

▶ **Scope**—A trunk can either be scoped so that it applies to entire Lync Server site or it can be restricted to only a specific Front End pool. A global trunk configuration also exists.

▶ **Maximum early dialogs supported**—This value is the number of forked responses the opposite end of the trunk can support in a single SIP INVITE that it sends to the Mediation Server.

▶ **Encryption support level**—Required means Secure Real-Time Transport Protocol (SRTP) must be used to encrypt the media traffic on the trunk, Optional means the Mediation Server attempts to use encryption if the gateway supports it, and Not Supported means the media traffic is not encrypted on the trunk.

▶ **Enable media bypass**—Use if endpoints are allowed to communicate directly with the opposite end of the trunk. This configuration is highly recommended to reduce processing on the Mediation Server.

▶ **Centralized media processing**—Use if the signaling and media traffic for this trunk terminate at the same IP address. If using Media Bypass is enabled, this option must also be selected.

▶ **Enable refer support**—Use if the trunk endpoint supports receiving SIP REFER requests from the Mediation Server.

To create a new trunk, complete the following steps:

1. Open the **Lync Server 2010 Control Panel**.
2. Click **Voice Routing**.
3. Click **Trunk Configuration**.
4. Click **New**, and then select either **Site** or **Pool** scope.
5. Enter a value for the **Maximum early dialogs supported** field.
6. Select an encryption support level.
7. Optionally, check the box for **Enable media bypass**
8. Optionally, check the box for **Centralized media processing**.
9. Optionally, check the box for **Enable referrer support**.
10. Click **OK** to save the trunk configuration. Translation rules can be applied at a later time after they are created.

Alternatively, the Lync Server Management Shell can be used to create a trunk configuration:

```
New-CSTrunkConfiguration -Identity <Name> -ConcentratedTopology
<$True¦$False> -EnableBypass <$True¦$False> -EnableReferSupport
<$True¦$False> -MaxEarlyDialogs <$True¦$False> -OutboundTranslationRulesList
<Collection of translation rules> -SRTPMode <Required¦Optional¦NotSupported>
```

There are also a number of parameters configurable for a trunk that are not exposed in the Lync Control Panel. These parameters can be set using only the New-CSTrunkConfiguration or Set-CSTrunkConfiguration cmdlets:

▶ **EnableMobileTrunkSupport**—True or false value to indicate whether the trunk is a mobile carrier.

▶ **EnableSessionTimer**—True or false value to indicate if each session is timed to determine whether it is currently active or not.

▶ **EnableSignalBoost**—True or false value to indicate whether the opposite end of the SIP trunk should boost the audio volume of packets sent to Lync. This feature works only if the opposite end of the SIP trunk supports the feature.

▶ **RemovePlusFromUri**—True or false value to indicate whether the Lync server should remove the plus prefix (+) from URIs before sending them across this SIP trunk.

▶ **RTCPActiveCalls**—True or false value to indicate whether the trunk sends RTP Control Protocol packets for active calls.

▶ **RTCPCallsOnHold**—True or false value to indicate whether the trunk sends RTP Control Protocol packets for calls placed on hold.

Translation Rules

Translation rules are a powerful new feature in Lync Server 2010 that enables digit manipulation to a PBX or media gateway. Lync Server recommends all numbers be the E.164 format, but a PBX or gateway might be configured for local dialing or require special access codes before accepting dial strings.

With translation rules on a trunk, an administrator can configure Lync Server to modify the dial string before sending it to the trunk. This ability is not available in Office Communications Server. For example, the translation rules can now remove a prefix such as +44 and replace it with 901144 before sending the string to the PBX. Administrators can either define the translation rules using regular expressions or using the Translation Rule tool.

To create a new translation rule, complete the following steps:

1. On the Edit Trunk Configuration screen, click the **New** button in the Associated Translation Rules section.
2. Provide a **Name** and a **Description** for the rule.

> **NOTE**
>
> This example uses the Translation Rule tool, but for more advanced pattern matching, click the Edit button at the bottom of the screen to manually enter the matching pattern and translation rule using regular expressions.

3. In the **Starting digits** field, enter the beginning digits of the string to be matched.
4. Specify a **Length** of the string to be matched. Options include matching at least a specific number of digits, exactly a certain number of digits or any number of digits.
5. Specify a number of **Digits to remove** after a string matches the starting digits and length.
6. Specify **Digits to add** after the selected number of digits have been removed.
7. Click **OK** to save the translation rule and click **OK** again to save the trunk configuration.

Export and Import Voice Configuration

Lync Server 2010 enables administrators to easily export and import the entire voice-routing configuration from a system. To export a configuration, use the following steps:

1. Open the **Lync Server 2010 Control Panel**.
2. Click **Voice Routing**.
3. From any of the submenu selections, click **Actions**, and then click **Export configuration**.
4. Select a location to save the configuration file, and then click **Save**. The file format has a VCFG extension.

To import a previously saved configuration file, use the following steps:

1. Open the **Lync Server 2010 Control Panel**.
2. Click **Voice Routing**.
3. From any of the submenu selections, click **Actions** and then click **Import configuration**.
4. Locate the configuration file and click **Open**.

NOTE

Like all other voice configuration changes, an imported configuration won't be active until published.

Test Cases

Test cases enable administrators to verify the voice configuration works as expected. To create a new voice routing test case, use the following steps:

1. Open the **Lync Server 2010 Control Panel**.
2. Click **Voice Routing**.
3. Click **Test Voice Routing**.
4. Click the **New** button to create a new test case.
5. Enter a **Name** for the case.
6. Enter a **Dialed number** to test. This is the number a user enters into the Lync client and is normalized based on the selection dial plan selected next.
7. Select a **Dial Plan**.
8. Select a **Voice policy**.
9. Enter an **Expected translation**. This is the string the dialed number to test string is expected to be translated to. If a normalization rule in the dial plan does not convert the dialed number to this string, the test is recorded as a failure.
10. Select an **Expected PSTN usage** for the test case. This field is optional. If the test case matches a PSTN usage other than the one selected here, the test is recorded as a failure.
11. Select an **Expected route** for the test case. This field is optional. If the voice test matches a route other than the one selected here, the test is recorded as a failure.
12. Click the **Run** button to begin the test.
13. To save the test case, click the **OK** button. Figure 18.3 shows a sample test case that has failed all tests. This indicates an administrator should modify the voice configuration before publishing the changes.

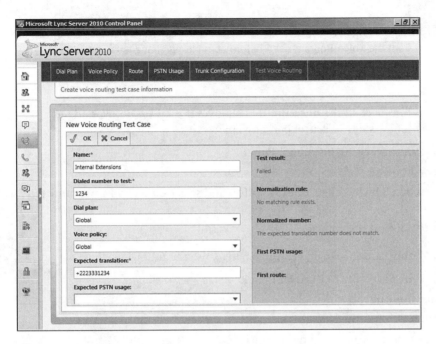

FIGURE 18.3   Failed Test Case

Publishing Changes

When making changes to voice configuration in Lync Server 2010, the changes are not actually active to clients until published. In other words, creating new routes or policies has no effect on the environment unless published by an administrator.

Before publishing occurs, the pending changes can be reviewed by using the following steps:

1. Open the **Lync Server 2010 Control Panel**.
2. Click **Voice Routing**.
3. From any submenu, click the **Commit** button, and then select **Review uncommitted changes**.
4. Click **Close** after reviewing the pending changes.

To publish the uncommitted changes, use the following steps:

1. Open the **Lync Server 2010 Control Panel**.
2. Click **Voice Routing**.
3. From any submenu, click the **Commit** button, and then select **Commit all**.
4. The uncommitted changes are displayed again on this screen. Click **Commit** to save the changes.

> **NOTE**
>
> Navigating away from the Voice Routing page before committing changes is cause for pending changes to be lost.

Another option is to cancel all the uncommitted changes if they are not working as expected. Use the follow steps to cancel pending changes:

1. Open the **Lync Server 2010 Control Panel**.
2. Click **Voice Routing**.
3. From any submenu, click the **Commit** button and select **Cancel all uncommitted changes**.
4. Click **OK** to confirm the choice.

If the intent is to only cancel a single pending change, use the following steps:

1. Open the **Lync Server 2010 Control Panel**.
2. Click **Voice Routing**.
3. Click the tab that has the changes you need to cancel.
4. Highlight the object you are going to cancel.
5. Click the **Commit** button and select **Cancel selected changes**.

Managing Enterprise Voice Users

Before a user has the ability to make and receive PSTN calls, he must be enabled for Enterprise Voice. After a user account has been enabled for Lync, the account can be optionally enabled for Enterprise Voice.

To enable an existing user for Enterprise Voice, use the following steps:

1. Open the **Lync Server 2010 Control Panel**.
2. Click **Users**.
3. Enter a search for a user who has been previously enabled for Lync and click **Find**.
4. Highlight the user to be enabled, click the **Edit** button, and then select **Show Details**.
5. Click **Telephony** and select **Enterprise Voice**.
6. Enter a **Line URI** for the user. The format for the Line URI should begin with tel:. For example, tel:+12345678901.
7. Select a **Dial plan policy** for the user.
8. Select a **Voice policy** for the user.
9. Click **Commit**. Figure 18.4 shows a sample user being enabled for Enterprise Voice abilities.

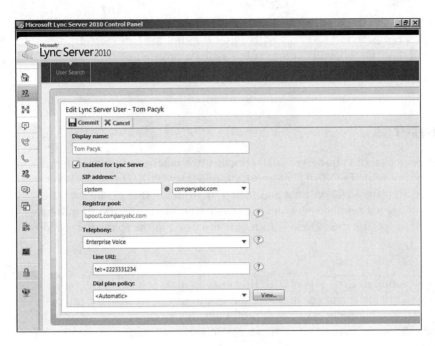

FIGURE 18.4   Enabling Users for Enterprise Voice

A user can also be enabled for Enterprise Voice using the Lync Server Management Shell:

```
Set-User –Identity <User Name> -EnterpriseVoiceEnabled $true –LineURI "tel:<E.164
➥number>"
```

Voice Policies

After creating voice policies with a user scope, they can be assigned to users through the Lync Control Panel or Lync Server Management Shell. Use the following command to assign a dial plan directly to a user:

```
Grant-CsVoicePolicy –Identity <User Name> -PolicyName <Voice Policy Name>
```

Dial Plans

After creating dial plans with a user scope, they can be assigned to users through the Lync Control Panel or Lync Server Management Shell. Use the following command to assign a dial plan directly to a user:

```
Grant-CsDialPlan –Identity <User Name> -PolicyName <Dial Plan Name>
```

Private Lines

Private phone lines in Lync Server 2010 are a new feature that enables an Enterprise Voice user to have a secondary phone extension associated with his account. This number is not published in address books, but the user can be reached through this number. Incoming calls indicate the call is to the private line and can have an alternative ringing sound associated. Private lines can be associated only with a user through the Lync Server Management Shell. Use the following command to assign a private line:

```
Set-CsUser -Identity <User Name> -PrivateLine tel:<Phone number>
```

Voice Features

The voice features section of Lync Server 2010 contains two new additions to Enterprise Voice that were not possible in Office Communications Server 2007. The first feature, call park, enables users to place a call on hold and pick it up from another extension. The second feature, unassigned numbers, enables the organization to route calls to numbers not associated with a specific user. These features are discussed in the following sections.

Call Park

Call park is a new feature in Lync Server 2010 that enables users to place a call on hold and then pick up that same call at another location or extension. To enable a call park, administrators must first configure a call park orbit table or a group of extensions to be used for parking calls. As users park calls, an extension is selected from these orbit tables and assigned to the call.

To create a new range for parking calls, use the following steps:

1. Open the **Lync Server 2010 Control Panel**.
2. Click **Voice Features**.
3. Click **Call Park**.
4. Click **New** to create a new number range.
5. Enter a **Name** for the range.
6. Enter a beginning and ending number for the **Number range**. The range can use up to nine total digits and can begin with a # or * so as not to overlap with existing extensions.
7. Select a **FQDN of destination server** from the selection box. Calls parked to the specified extension range are routed to this server or pool. Figure 18.5 shows a sample call park orbit range being configured.

Alternatively, the Lync Server Management Shell can be used to configure a new call park orbit:

```
New-CsCallParkOrbit -Identity <Range Name> -NumberRangeStart <First number
in the range> -NumberRangeEnd <Last number in the range> -CallParkService
<FQDN of the server hosting the Call Park service>
```

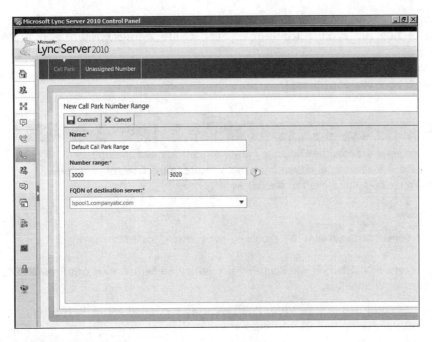

FIGURE 18.5   Call Park Orbit

Configuring additional call park settings can be performed only in the Lync Server Management Shell. Call park settings can be configured at a global level or applied to a specific site.

The following settings can be modified:

▶ **CallPickupTimeoutThreshold**—The amount of time a call that has been parked waits without answer before it rings back to the phone where the call was originally answered. This is to ensure a call is not parked and then forgotten.

▶ **EnableMusicOnHold**—True or false value that determines whether on-hold music is played to the caller while parked.

▶ **MaxCallPickupAttempts**—The number of times a call rings back to the phone where originally answered before it times out and is forwarded to a specified SIP URI.

▶ **OnTimeoutURI**—A SIP URI where calls that are not picked up are forwarded. This can be a user account for an operator or a Response Group address.

▶ To create a new site-specific setting, use the following cmdlet:

```
New-CsCpsConfiguration –Identity site:<Site Name> -
CallPickupTimeoutThreshold <hh:mm:ss> -EnableMusicOnHold <True ¦ False> -
MaxCallPickupAttempts <number of rings> -OnTimeoutURI sip:<SIP URI to route
unanswered calls>
```

18

Whether on-hold music is played is determined by the EnableMusicOnHold parameter, but the actual music on hold file is configured using the Set-CsCallParkMusicOnHoldFile cmdlet:

```
Set-CsCallParkMusicOnHoldFile –Service ApplicationServer:<FQDN of Front-End
Pool with music file> -Content <Byte[]>
```

> **NOTE**
>
> The Content parameter expects the audio file in byte format. To make the transfer easy, store the file in a variable, and then pass that variable to the Content parameter. Storing the audio file correctly looks like the following:

```
$AudioFile = Get-Content –ReadCount 0 –Encoding byte <Path and File Name>
```

Call Park is not a feature enabled on the default voice policy, so before users can leverage this feature, it must be enabled.

▶ Follow the steps outlined in the "Voice Policies" section covered earlier in this chapter to configure a voice policy to support call park.

> **NOTE**
>
> For call park number ranges to function properly, they must *not* normalize through a normalization rule associated in dial plans. It might be necessary to configure an additional normalization rule that matches the number range but returns the translation without modification. This kind of rule matches prior to any other rules that can potentially modify the entered number. This is where using a * or # prefix in the call park ranges can be helpful.

Unassigned Numbers

One feature that many organizations are interested in, but that Office Communications Server is unable to provide natively, is the ability to direct calls to unassigned numbers to an attendant or operator. If numbers are not assigned, those calls simply fail. In Lync Server 2010, administrators can define ranges of unassigned numbers and an action that occurs when someone dials one of those numbers.

> **NOTE**
>
> The ranges defined for unassigned numbers can actually contain numbers that are assigned to users. This does not interfere with call routing and can actually be helpful for when users leave or extensions are removed. This way, callers can still be routed appropriately if the extension no longer exists.

Calls that match an unassigned number range can be routed in only two different ways: Either an announcement can be played to the caller or the caller can be transferred to an Exchange Unified Messaging Auto Attendant extension.

To create a new unassigned number range, use the following steps:

1. Open the **Lync Server 2010 Control Panel**.
2. Click **Voice Features**.
3. Click **Unassigned Number**.
4. Click **New**.
5. Enter a **Name** identifying this range of numbers.
6. In the first **Number range** field, enter the first number in the range.
7. In the second **Number range** field, enter the last number in the range.
8. In the Announcement service field, select either **Announcement** or **Exchange UM**.

If configuring an announcement, follow these steps:

1. Click **Announcement service**.
2. Click **Select**.
3. Choose an application server in the organization with an audio announcement configured and then click **OK**.
4. Select an Announcement to be played and then click **OK**.
5. Click **OK** again to save the range definition.

If configuring an Exchange Unified Messaging transfer, follow these steps:

1. Click **Auto Attendant phone number**.
2. Click **Select**.
3. Choose a phone number to transfer callers to and then click **OK**.
4. Click **OK** again to save the range definition.

TIP

On the Unassigned number page, be sure to order the unassigned number ranges in the desired order. The ranges are matched starting from top to bottom, so if a range overlaps with another, the first range in the list is used.

Announcement Files

Before you can use a prerecorded audio file as an announcement, it must be imported using the Lync Server Management Shell. To import a file, first store the content in a temporary variable:

```
$MyAudioFile = Get-Content <File path and name> -ReadCount 0 -Encoding Byte
```

18

Then import the announcement file to the file share using the variable:

```
Import-CsAnnouncementFile –Parent service:ApplicationServer:<Front-End FQDN>
-Content $MyAudioFile
```

Network Configuration

The first step in configuring the three advanced Enterprise Voice features of Call Admission Control, Media Bypass, and Enhanced 911 is to define the network configuration. Each of these features relies on the network configuration to work correctly. The following section explains how to create the necessary network objects before configuring any of the advanced features.

Network Regions

A network region in Lync Server 2010 is generally a large area that encompasses a number of network sites. These are the hubs or backbones of the network. Each region is associated with a central site where a Lync Server 2010 Front End pool exists.

Use the following steps to create a new network region.

1. Open the **Lync Server 2010 Control Panel**.
2. Click **Network Configuration**.
3. Click **Region**.
4. Click the **New** button.
5. Enter a **Name** for the region.
6. Select a **Central Site** for the region. This is a site in the topology containing Lync Servers.
7. Select **Enable audio alternate path** if this region allows audio traffic to use alternative routes.
8. Select **Enable video alternate path** if this region allows video traffic to use alternative routes.
9. Click **Commit**. Network sites can be associated at a later time. A sample Network Region definition is displayed in Figure 18.6.

Alternatively, a new network region can be created with the Lync Server Management Shell:

```
New-CSNetworkRegion –Identity <Network Region Name> -CentralSite <Lync Site
Name> -Description <Region Description> -AudioAlternatePath <$True¦$False>
–VideoAlternatePath <$True¦$False>
```

Network Sites

A network site represents a particular office location that can be a main headquarters, a branch office, or a collection of buildings in a campus. Network sites typically have similar bandwidth and each site is then associated with a network region. The central site defined for the region is typically included as a site in the region because it is not done automatically.

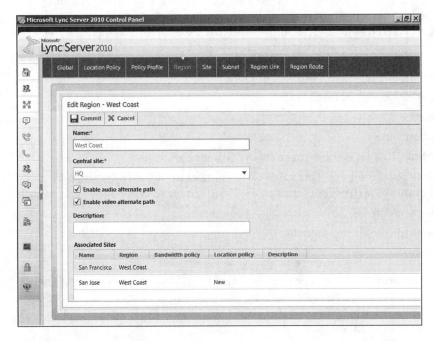

FIGURE 18.6   Network Region

Use the following steps to create a new network site:

1. Open the **Lync Server 2010 Control Panel**.
2. Click **Network Configuration**.
3. Click **Site**.
4. Click the **New** button.
5. Enter a **Name** for the site.
6. Enter a **Description** for the site.
7. Select a **Region** to associate the site with from the drop-down menu.
8. Bandwidth policy, location policy, and associated subnets can be added at a later time after those objects exist.
9. Press the **Commit** button.

Alternatively, a new network site can be created with the Lync Server Management Shell:

```
New-CSNetworkSite –NetworkSiteID <Site Name> -Description <Description of
site> -NetworkRegionID <Name of region to associate site with>
```

Network Subnets

Network subnets in Lync Server 2010 are the glue that binds a client connection to a specific network site, and region. When a Lync client performs an action that requires network awareness, the client IP address is examined and then used to determine the appropriate action based on the associated policies with the endpoint subnet.

Use the following steps to create a new network site:

1. Open the **Lync Server 2010 Control Panel**.
2. Click **Network Configuration**.
3. Click **Subnet**.
4. Click the **New** button.
5. Enter a **Subnet ID** that is the actual network IP address.
6. Enter a **Mask** for the subnet. This value is the number of bits used for the subnet mask. For example, if the subnet uses a 255.255.255.0 mask, enter 24 for this value.
7. Select a **Network site ID** to associate with the subnet.
8. Enter a **Description** for the subnet.
9. Click **Commit**.

Alternatively, a new network site can be created with the Lync Server Management Shell:

```
New-CSNetworkSubnet –SubnetID <Network Address> -MaskBits <Number of bits in
subnet mask> -NetworkSiteID <Associated network site>
```

After network regions, sites, and subnets have been created in the deployment, Call Admission Control, Enhanced 911, and Media Bypass can be configured.

Call Admission Control

After network regions, sites, and subnets have been created, Call Admission Control can be configured and enabled. Be sure to create all the necessary objects prior to proceeding with the Call Admission Control configuration. Call Admission Control enables clients to determine whether an audio or video call can actually be established based on available network bandwidth.

Bandwidth Policy Profiles

After creating the required network objects, the next step in configuring Call Admission Control is to create bandwidth policy profiles. Each bandwidth policy profile defines the total bandwidth limit for a site or region and the bandwidth limit per session for both audio and video.

Use the following steps to create a new bandwidth policy profile:

1. Open the **Lync Server 2010 Control Panel**.
2. Click **Network Configuration**.

3. Click **Policy Profile**.

4. Click the **New** button.

5. Enter a **Name** for the profile. Usually this is indicative of the link speed of the network to which it is applied.

6. Enter an **Audio limit** in kbps. This is the cumulative limit of all audio sessions.

7. Enter an **Audio session limit** in kbps. This is the limit applied to each audio session.

8. Enter a **Video limit** in kbps. This is the cumulative limit of all video sessions.

9. Enter a **Video session limit** in kbps. This is the limit applied to each video session.

10. Enter a **Description** for the bandwidth policy profile.

11. Click **Commit**.

Alternatively, a new bandwidth policy profile can be created using the Lync Server Management Shell:

```
New-CSBandwidthPolicyProfile -Identity <Name of profile> -Description
<Profile description> -AudioBWLimit <Total audio limit in kbps>
-AudioBWSessionLimit <Audio limit per session in kbps> -VideoBWLimit <Total
video limit in kbps> -VideoBWSessionLimit <Video limit per session in kbps>
```

Associate Bandwidth Policy Profile

After creating the required bandwidth policy profiles, they must be associated with network sites. To use the Lync Server Control Panel to perform this task, use the following steps:

1. Open the **Lync Server 2010 Control Panel**.

2. Click **Network Configuration**.

3. Click **Site**.

4. Highlight an existing site, click the **Edit** button, and select **Show Details**.

5. Select a **Bandwidth policy** from the selection box.

6. Click **Commit**.

7. Repeat these steps to associate each site with a bandwidth policy profile. Figure 18.7 shows a sample bandwidth policy based on a 5 Mb WAN link.

Alternatively, to use the Lync Server Management Shell to associate a bandwidth policy profile with a site, use the following:

```
Set-CSNetworkSite -Identity <Network Site Name> -BWPolicyProfileID <Bandwidth
policy profile ID>
```

18

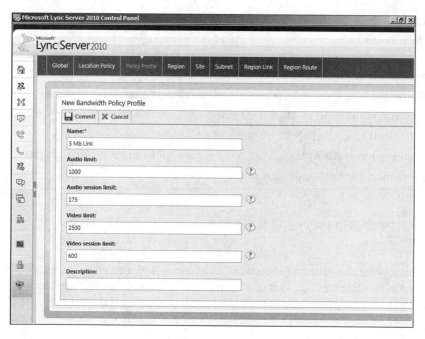

FIGURE 18.7 Bandwidth Policy Profile

Network Region Links

Network region links in Lync Server represent a bandwidth constraint between two network regions or central sites. Because network regions are generally geographically large, these links apply to a number of sites when communicating across regions. For example, a region link might be defined between North America and Europe for an organization. Region links must be created between two regions and might have a bandwidth policy profile associated. The bandwidth policy can be an existing policy or an administrator can create a new policy specifically for the region link.

To create a new network region link, use the following steps:

1. Open the **Lync Server 2010 Control Panel**.
2. Click **Network Configuration**.
3. Click **Region Link**.
4. Click the **New** button.
5. Enter a **Name** for the link.
6. Choose a **Network region #1** from the selection menu.
7. Choose a **Network region #2** from the selection menu.
8. Choose a **Bandwidth policy**.
9. Click **Commit**.

Alternatively, to use the Lync Server Management Shell to create a network region link, use the following:

```
New-CSNetworkRegionLink -Identity <Region Link Name> -NetworkRegionID1
<Region 1 ID> -NetworkRegionID2 <Region 2 ID> -BWPolicyProfileID <Bandwidth
policy profile ID>
```

Network Region Routes

A network region route object represents the network path between two regions. This might sound similar to a network region link. However, whereas a region link defines bandwidth on a direct link, a route defines the network path between regions.

In many cases such as a direct connection, there is a 1:1 ratio between region links and region routes, but this might differ when direct links between regions do not exist. For example, consider a scenario where North America and Europe have direct connectivity and Europe and Asia have direct connectivity each with network region links defined.

Those two region routes are straightforward, but a region route between North America and Asia needs to exist, and because calls traverse both region links, it must include each in the definition. In simple terms, a region route is a list of the region links traversed when communicating between two regions. When a call traverses multiple region links, the bandwidth policy of each link is applied.

To create a new network region route, use the following steps:

1. Open the **Lync Server 2010 Control Panel**.
2. Click **Network Configuration**.
3. Click **Region Route**.
4. Click the **New** button.
5. Enter a **Name** for the route.
6. Choose a **Network region #1** from the selection menu.
7. Choose a **Network region #2** from the selection menu.
8. Click the **Add** button, select a region link, and click **OK**.
9. Repeat for any additional region links that will be traversed by this path.
10. Click **Commit**.

Alternatively, to use the Lync Server Management Shell to create a network region route, use the following:

```
New-CSNetworkRegionRoute -Identity <Region Route Name> -NetworkRegionID1
<Region 1 ID> -NetworkRegionID2 <Region 2 ID> -NetworkRegionLinkIDs <Comma
separated list of network region link IDs>
```

18

Network Intersite Policies

Network intersite policies are used to define a bandwidth policy between two sites in the same region that have a direct link. Similar to a region link, two sites are defined and a bandwidth policy profile is associated with the link. Intersite policies are generally created when two sites have constrained bandwidth to the central site in a region, but also have a direct link between each other without traversing the central site. Network intersite policies can be created only using the Lync Server Management Shell.

For each intersite policy required, use the following syntax:

```
New-CSNetworkInterSitePolicy -InterNetworkSitePolicyID <Inter-Site Policy
Name> -NetworkSiteID1 <Network Site 1 ID> -NetworkSiteID2 <Network Site 2
ID> -BWPolicyProfileID <Bandwidth Policy Profile ID>
```

Enable Call Admission Control

After configuring all the required objects and links, the final step in the process is to actually enable Call Admission Control.

To enable the feature, use the following steps:

1. Open the **Lync Server 2010 Control Panel**.
2. Click **Network Configuration**.
3. Click **Global**.
4. Highlight the global policy, click **Edit**, and then select **Show Details**.
5. Check the box **Enable call admission control**.
6. Click **Commit**.

Alternatively, to use the Lync Server Management Shell to create a network region route, use the following:

```
Set-CSNetworkConfiguration -EnableBandwidthPolicyCheck 1
```

Media Bypass

For Media Bypass to function, the following requirements must be met:

▶ A Mediation Server role is deployed either as a standalone server or collocated on a Front End Server.

▶ Media Bypass must be enabled on a SIP trunk. The centralized media processing option must also be enabled on the trunk.

▶ Media Bypass must be enabled at a global level.

Enable Media Bypass

Media Bypass must be enabled at a global level before clients attempt to use the bypass features. When enabling Media Bypass in the Lync Server infrastructure, an administrator has two options:

▶ **Always bypass**—This choice instructs clients to always bypass the Mediation Server role. This option works only if a trunk configuration also has the enable media bypass option selected. All Lync clients must have good network connectivity to the other end of every single SIP trunk for this option to be effective. This option may make sense in very small deployments.

▶ **Use sites and region configuration**—This choice is a better option when Lync end-points might not have good network connectivity to each SIP trunk and enables the network region and site configuration to limit when Media Bypass is actually used. **Enable bypass for non-mapped sites** can be selected only if **Use sites and region configuration** is selected first. This allows for sites and subnets not explicitly configured to use Media Bypass.

> **NOTE**
>
> If Call Admission Control is also enabled, the only available option for Media Bypass is to use the network site and region configuration.

To select a choice in enabling Media Bypass, use the following steps:

1. Open the **Lync Server 2010 Control Panel**.
2. Click **Network Configuration.**
3. Click **Global**.
4. Highlight the global policy, click **Edit**, and then select **Show Details**.
5. Check the box **Enable media bypass**.
6. Select either **Always bypass** or **Use sites and region configuration**.
7. If selecting the **Use sites and region configuration**, optionally check the box **Enable bypass for non-mapped sites**.
8. Click **Commit**.

Site Configuration

For Media Bypass to function properly when sites are bandwidth-constrained, the appropriate network region and bandwidth policy profiles must be created. Media Bypass does not use the actual bandwidth values, but does compare links with a bandwidth value set to ones without a value. In other words, sites with any bandwidth policy applied do not use Media Bypass across the link, but sites without a policy applied attempt to use Media Bypass.

18

Call Admission Control and Media Bypass

Keep in mind that although Call Admission Control and Media Bypass use the same network configuration objects, there are some situations in which they behave slightly differently. For instance, calls that use Media Bypass do not have bandwidth policy profiles applied to restrict the bandwidth used. In other words, calls using Media Bypass do not count toward the cumulative audio limit or restricted by the audio session limit. It is assumed in scenarios where Media Bypass is used that no bandwidth constraint exists.

Enhanced 911

Enhanced 911 is a feature that was not possible in earlier product versions of Lync Server. Enhanced 911 provides the caller's telephone number and street address to a dispatcher automatically. This is an advantage over traditional 911 service that requires the caller to provide an address where assistance is required.

Lync Server 2010 can maintain a location database for an organization that associates specific gateways, subnets, and wireless SSIDs with physical location addresses. Lync Server 2010 supports E-911 with support from a certified emergency services provider. Emergency calls are routed through a SIP trunk to the emergency services provider.

Configuring Site Locations

Lync Server 2010 enables clients to detect their locations on a network automatically, but a database of locations in the organization must be defined in advance for this automation to work correctly. Lync can match clients to a street address location based on the following network objects:

- ▶ **Wireless Access Point**—Matches a wireless access point based on the Basic Service Set Identifier (BSSID) of the device that is the MAC address.

- ▶ **Subnet**—Matches a location based on the subnet of the Lync endpoint it connects from.

- ▶ **Port**—Matches a unique port on a switch based on the switch's MAC address and the port ID. The port ID can be an interface alias, name, or just locally assigned port number.

- ▶ **Switch**—Matches a switch based on the chassis ID MAC address.

When defining each of these objects, they can be associated with an address. The address parameters configurable are listed here:

- ▶ **City**—The location city. For example, San Francisco.

- ▶ **Company Name**—The name of the company at this location. For example, Company ABC.

- ▶ **Country**—The two-character location country. For example, US.

- ▶ **HouseNumber**—The location address number. For example, 123.

- **HouseNumberSuffix**—Additional information after the address number. For example, B.

- **Location**—A more detailed location after the street number, such as a suite or specific floor. For example, Suite 456.

- **PostalCode**—The location postal code. For example, 12345.

- **PostDirectional**—Any directional information after the street address. For example, NE.

- **PreDirectional**—Any directional information before the street address. For example, SW.

- **State**—The location state. For example, CA.

- **StreetName**—The location street name. For example, Market.

- **StreetSuffix**—The location street suffix. For example, Street or Avenue.

All the location information must be entered through the Lync Server Management Shell. Creating each object is done through the Set-<LIS Object Type> cmdlets:

- Set-CsLisWirelessAccessPoint

- Set-CsLisSubnet

- Set-CsLisPort

- Set-CsLisSwitch

For example, to create a new subnet and location definition:

```
Set-CsLisSubnet -Subnet 192.168.22.0 -Description "Client Subnet"
-CompanyName "Company ABC"-HouseNumber 123 -Location "Suite 456"-StreetName
"Fake" -StreetSuffix "Avenue" -City "San Francisco" -State CA -PostalCode
12345 -Country US
```

Because importing every single wireless access point, subnet, port, or switch manually would be a tedious effort, defining all the required objects in advance through a CSV file can help speed up the process of building the database. The CSV file can then be used for a bulk-import process.

After creating all the Location Information Service objects, the configuration must be published. The objects are not recognized by Lync clients until this step is performed. To publish the location database, run the following cmdlet from the Lync Server Management Shell:

```
Publish-CsLisConfiguration
```

18

Validate Addresses

Lync Server 2010 cannot route emergency calls with location information directly by itself and instead relies on an E-911 Network Routing Provider to route the calls appropriately. Lync transmits the location information it knows about to the routing provider, which delivers it to the emergency service.

To configure a routing provider, use the following:

```
Set-CsLisServiceProvider –ServiceProviderName <Name> -ValidationServiceUrl
<URL from Provider> -CertFileName <Certificate path and filename issued by
provider> -Password <Password issued by provider>
```

After a provider has been provisioned, each address in the location database should be validated with the provider. To run a test against all existing addresses, use the following cmdlet:

```
Get-CsLisCivicAddress ¦ Test-CsLisCivicAddress -UpdateValidationStatus
```

The UpdateValidationStatus also stamps each address with an attribute indicating it has been verified successfully.

Create Location Policy

For Lync to support location information objects, users must be associated with a Location Policy that allows these features. Location policies can exist at the global, site, or user level so that not all users or sites must be enforced the same way. When creating a location policy, an administrator has the following options:

- ▶ **Enable enhanced emergency services**—This setting enables the client for E-911. When registering with a Lync registrar service, the client acquires location information.

- ▶ **Location**—This setting takes effect only if emergency services are enabled, and it is used when a Lync client cannot determine a location automatically. Setting this value to no means the user is not prompted for a location. A value of yes means the user sees a visible red error in the location field, so he enters the information. Disclaimer means the user is prompted for location and cannot dismiss the prompt until a location is entered. Users cannot place any calls except to emergency services unless entering a location with this setting.

- ▶ **Use location for emergency services only**—Location information gathered from Lync clients can also be shared with team members. Selecting this option prevents Lync from sharing location information between users.

- ▶ **PSTN Usage**—This is the PSTN usage associated with placing emergency calls. This determines what voice route is used for callers associated with the location policy. This usage must already exist, so be sure to define a new Emergency Services usage prior to configuring a location policy.

▶ **Emergency dial number**—This is the number dialed by a client that signifies an emergency call is being made, so location and callback information is automatically included.

▶ **Emergency dial mask**—A list of dial strings that users might use to dial emergency services; it is separated by semicolons. For example, emergency dial strings from other countries can be used here which will then be mapped to the actual emergency dial number.

▶ **Notification URI**—SIP URI that receives an instant message notification when an emergency call is placed. Should contain the sip: prefix.

▶ **Conference URI**—SIP URI that should be conferenced into the call when an emergency call is placed. Should contain the SIP prefix and can also be a phone number.

▶ **Conference Mode**—Specifies whether the conference URI contact can be included in the call using one-way or two-way communication. One-way means the conference URI can listen only to the call as it occurs and two-way means the contact can participate.

To create a new location policy, use the following steps:

1. Open the **Lync Server 2010 Control Panel**.
2. Click **Network Configuration.**
3. Click **Location Policy.**
4. Click **New** and select either **Site policy** or **User policy**.
5. Check the box **Enable enhanced emergency services** to enable the feature.
6. Select a **Location** specification requirement policy.
7. Select whether to **Use location for emergency services only**.
8. Enter an **Emergency dial number**.
9. Enter any **Emergency dial masks**, separated by semicolons.
10. Enter a **Notification URI**, if necessary.
11. Enter a **Conference URI**, if necessary.
12. Select a **Conference mode**.
13. Click **Commit**.

Alternatively, the Lync Server Management Shell can be used to create a location policy:

```
New-CsLocationPolicy -Identity <Name> -ConferenceMode <Oneway ¦ Twoway>
-ConferenceUri <SIP URI to conference in to calls> -EmergencyDialMask <Dial
Masks, semi-colon separated> -EmergencyDialString <Dial String for Emergency
Services> -EnhancedEmergencyServicesEnabled <$True ¦ $False>
-LocationRequired <No ¦ Yes ¦ Disclaimer> -NotificationUri <SIP URI to
notify> -PstnUsage <PSTN Usage for Routing> -UseLocationForE911Only <$True ¦
$False>
```

18

> **NOTE**
>
> An emergency voice route must be created in Lync and an applicable PSTN associated with users to successfully send emergency calls using E-911.

Remote Site Survivability

Another welcome feature new to Lync Server 2010 is the capability for branch sites to continue PSTN call access in the event of a WAN failure, making the Front End pool unavailable to the location.

> ▶ More details about remote site surviviability can be found in Chapter 28. However, remote surviviability is primarily accomplished through the use of PSTN gateways in each branch office.

A special type of gateway called a survivable branch appliance also serves as a registrar for users in the branch locations so that when a WAN connection goes out, the users stay logged in to their Lync client. For larger branch sites, a Lync Front End pool can be created and paired with a PSTN gateway or Internet Telephony Service Provider SIP trunk to provide resiliency.

Defining Branch Sites

The first step, whether deploying a survivable branch appliance or a survivable branch server, is to define each branch site within the Lync Server topology.

1. Open the **Lync Server Topology Builder** and import the current topology.
2. Right-click **Branch Office Sites** and select **New Branch Site**.
3. Enter a **Name** for the site and, optionally, a **Description**.
4. Click **Next**.
5. Enter the **City** where the site is located.
6. Enter a **State/Region** where the site is located.
7. Enter a two-digit **Country Code** where the site is located.
8. Click **Next**.
9. Clear the check box **Open the New Survivable Wizard when this wizard closes**, and then click **Finish**. A survivable branch appliance or server can be added to the site later.

Defining Survivable Branch Appliances and Servers

After defining each of the branch sites, the survivable branch appliances or servers must be added to the topology.

1. Ensure the **Lync Server Topology Builder** is still open and a branch site has been defined.

2. Expand the branch site and, right-click **Survivable Branch Servers,** and then select **New Survivable Branch Server**.

3. Click **FQDN**, enter the fully qualified name of the survivable branch appliance or server, and then click **Next**.

4. Click **Front-End pool** and select the Front End pool associated with the branch site.

5. Click **Edge server** and select the Edge Server pool associated with the branch site.

6. Click **Gateway FQDN or IP Address** and enter the name or IP address of the gateway used for routing inbound and outbound calls with the branch site.

7. Click **Listening Port** and enter the correct port.

8. Click **SIP Transport Protocol** and select the protocol used to communicate with the gateway.

9. After all branch sites and survivable branch appliances have been defined, be sure to publish the topology. Figure 18.8 shows a sample branch site configuration. Notice that in this case the survivable branch appliance and Mediation server names are the same. This is because they are the same device. The PSTN gateway entered may even be the same hardware device, but will always have a separate IP address.

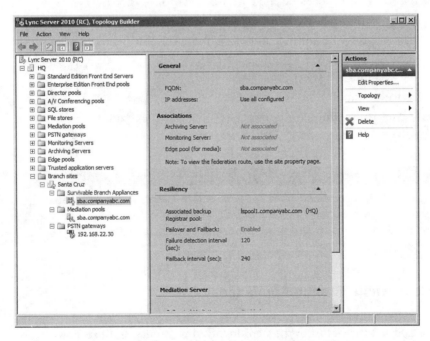

FIGURE 18.8   Survivable Branch Appliance in Topology Builder

Add the Survivable Branch Appliance to Active Directory

Each survivable branch appliance deployed needs to have a computer account in Active Directory defined prior to being placed in operation. Because survivable branch servers are already domain-joined computers, these steps are not necessary.

Use the following steps when deploying only a survivable branch appliance.

1. Log on to a computer with the Active Directory Domain Services role administration tools installed.

2. Open **Active Directory Users and Computers.**

3. Right-click an organizational unit, click **New,** and select **Computer.**

4. Enter a **Computer name** for the survivable branch appliance. This is just the host-name, not the fully qualified domain name.

5. Under **User or group,** click the **Change** button.

6. Enter **RTCUniversalSBATechnicians,** and then click **OK.**

7. Click **OK.**

After staging a computer account for the survivable branch appliance, a service principal name (SPN) must be added to the computer account.

Use the following steps to add the SPN:

1. Open **ADSI Edit.**

2. Right-click the **ADSI Edit** root node and click **Connect to.**

3. Leave the default options selected and click **OK.**

4. Expand the **Default naming context** and locate the survivable branch appliance computer account.

5. Right-click the **account** and select **Properties.**

6. Highlight **servicePrincipalName** and click **Edit.**

7. Enter **HOST/<Survivable Branch Appliance FQDN>** and click **Add.**

8. Click **OK** twice.

> **NOTE**
>
> Normally, using the SETSPN command is the preferred way to manage SPNs associated with domain accounts. Because the survivable branch appliance has not joined the domain yet, the SETSPN commands do not work properly. Instead, use ADSI Edit to configure the appropriate SPN.

Deploying a Survivable Branch Appliance

Installation and configuration is going to vary widely depending on the survivable branch appliance vendor and software. Most of the steps involved are similar to the following:

1. Physically cable the survivable branch appliance.

2. Configure an IP address.

3. Join the domain.

4. Enable replica of configuration.

5. Request and assign certificates.

6. Start services.

7. Test connectivity.

8. Move user accounts.

> **NOTE**
>
> The user account used to join the survivable branch appliance to the domain must be a member of the RTCUniversalSBATechnicians group. This is the group selected to join the computer to the domain when the computer account is created in Active Directory.

Deploying a Survivable Branch Server

Installation and configuration of a survivable branch server is identical to configuring a new Front End pool with Mediation Server functionality.

- ▶ Use the steps discussed in Chapter 5, "Microsoft Lync Server 2010 Front End," to create a new Front End pool with voice services. The pool should be enabled for Enterprise Voice and an IP/PSTN gateway needs to be associated.

Move Branch Users to a New Pool

After implementing the required infrastructure for remote site survivability, the last step is to move branch users to the new pool for their registrar service. Through associating the branch site with a Front End pool, the users' conferencing data is still associated with a main Front End pool and moves only the registrar for each user.

Response Groups

Response Groups are a feature first introduced in Office Communications Server 2007 R2 that has been enhanced in Lync Server 2010. A Response Group is a method to route calls to a specific queue or set of agents. Some consider Response Groups to be on a similar level as hunt groups from traditional telephony, but an administrator typically has much greater control over a Response Group than a PBX hunt group. Many PBXs call this feature Automatic Call Distribution (ACD).

Response Groups are comprised of the following components:

- ▶ **Agent Groups**—Agent groups contain a specified set of user accounts that belong to a Response Group. How calls are routed in the group and what options a member has are configured at the agent group level.

- ▶ **Queues**—A *queue* is an object that holds callers as they dial in to the Response Group. A queue can contain multiple agent groups or sometimes just a single agent group is included. Settings such as timeouts and call capacity are configured at the queue level.

- ▶ **Workflows**—Workflows are the glue that ties together the agent groups and queues. The workflow settings determine how a caller reaches a specific queue depending on question responses, time of day, or holidays.

The following sections explain each of these components in more detail and discuss how to configure a complete Response Group.

Agent Groups

Agent groups are a collection of users who include a number of user accounts. Distribution groups or individual user accounts might be added to an agent group. After group membership has been defined, administrators can select how calls are routed within the agent group, such as round robin or in parallel. The last option administrators can define is whether users are automatically signed in to the agent group when signed in to Lync or whether they can manually participate or leave the group. The following options are available when creating an agent group:

▸ **Participation Policy**—Determines whether agents need to sign in or out of the group manually. Selecting formal here means users have to manually enter and leave the agent group. Informal means the agents are automatically included in the group as long as they are signed in to Lync.

▸ **Alert Time**—The number of seconds a call rings an agent before attempting to ring the next agent.

▸ **Routing Method**—How the calls are routed among agents in the group.

▸ **Agents**—User accounts or a distribution group used for the agent group membership. Keep in mind that distribution groups do not recognize nested groups and that only one distribution group can be specified.

> **NOTE**
>
> Response group agents must be an Enterprise Voice user. Users enabled for Lync services but not Enterprise Voice cannot be selected to participate in an agent group.

The routing methods are a key part of defining how agents take calls. These options are separated here for some additional clarity on behavior.

▸ **Longest idle**—The call is routed to the agent who has had a presence status of Available the longest without taking a call. For example, if three agents are part of the agent group and one agent is Busy while two are Available, the call is routed to the user with the Available presence the longest.

▸ **Parallel**—Rings all agents at the same time. The agent who accepts the call first is placed in a conversation with the caller.

▸ **Round Robin**—Call requests are evenly sent to agents. Assuming three agents exist, the first call goes to Agent A, the second to Agent B, and the third to Agent C. The fourth call rings Agent A again.

▸ **Serial**—Calls are sent to agents in the order defined in the agent list. Assuming three agents exist, the first call goes to Agent A. The next call again attempts to ring Agent

A, and if Agent A is unavailable, the call then goes to Agent B. The difference from round robin distribution is that the next call will follow the same order, starting with Agent A again.

▸ **Attendant**—Calls are routed to all agents just as in parallel fashion, but includes agents who are busy or currently in a call. Calls are not routed to agents with a status of Do Not Disturb.

To create a new agent group, use the following steps:

1. Open the **Lync Server 2010 Control Panel**.
2. Click **Response Groups.**
3. Click **Group**.
4. Click **New**.
5. Select an application server and click **OK**. This is typically just a Front End pool.
6. Enter a **Name** for the group.
7. Enter a **Description** for the group.
8. Select a **Participation policy** for the agents.
9. Specify the **Alert time** in seconds for how long a call will ring an agent.
10. Select a **Routing method** for the group.
11. If using a distribution list for the agent list, select **Use an existing email distribution list** and then enter the SMTP address of the list.
12. If manually adding agents to the group, click the **Select** button.
13. Enter a search for users and click **Find**.
14. Highlight the selected user and click **OK**.
15. Click **Commit** after all agents have been added.

Alternatively, the Lync Server Management Shell can be used to create a new agent group:

```
New-CsRgsAgentGroup -Parent ApplicationServer:<Application Server ID> -Name
<Agent Group Name> -AgentAlertTime <Seconds a call will ring agents>
-AgentsByUri <Comma separated SIP URIs to add as agents including sip:
prefix> -Description <Agent Group Description> -DistributionGroupAddress
<Distribution Group SMTP Address> -ParticipationPolicy <Informal ¦ Format>
-RoutingMethod <LongestIdle ¦ RoundRobin ¦ Serial ¦ Parallel ¦ Attendant>
```

After completing the agent group configuration, continue the Response Group setup process by creating queues.

Queues

A Response Group queue is used to hold calls while waiting for an agent to answer. A queue can contain a single agent group, or administrators might add multiple agent groups to a queue. The following options are available when creating a queue:

18

▶ **Enable queue timeout**—Determines whether a time limit is enforced when callers wait for an agent.

▶ **Time-out period**—The number of seconds a caller can remain in the queue before timing out.

▶ **Call Target**—The action taken when a call reaches the time-out period. The options for call targets are discussed in greater detail later in this section.

▶ **Maximum number of calls**—The number of calls that can be in the queue at any given time.

▶ **Forward the call**—Determines whether the call is forwarded when the queue reaches a maximum number of calls. Administrators can choose to forward either the oldest call in the queue or the newest call.

In a situation where either the time period elapses or the maximum number of calls is reached, an administrator has a number of choices for how to route the call:

▶ **Disconnect**—Drops the call.

▶ **Forward to voice mail**—Forwards the call to a voicemail address, which must be a SIP URI.

▶ **Forward to telephone number**—Forwards the call to a telephone number in the sip:number@domain format.

▶ **Forward to SIP address**—Forwards the call to another user account in the sip:user-name@domain format.

▶ **Forward to another queue**—Forwards the call to another queue defined previously.

To create a new queue, use the following steps:

1. Open the **Lync Server 2010 Control Panel**.
2. Click **Response Groups**.
3. Click **Queue**.
4. Click **New**.
5. Select an application server and click **OK**. This is typically just a Front End pool.
6. Enter a **Name** for the queue.
7. Enter a **Description** for the queue.
8. Click **Select** to choose existing agent groups that belong to the queue.
9. Highlight any groups to add and click **OK**.
10. Check the box for **Enable queue time-out** if required.
11. After selecting **queue time-out**, enter a **Time-out period**.
12. After selecting **queue time-out**, select a **Call action** and enter an appropriate SIP URI if required.
13. Check the box for **Enable queue overflow** if required.

14. After selecting **queue overflow**, enter a **Maximum number of calls**.

15. After selecting **queue overflow**, click **Forward the call** and select an option.

16. After selecting **queue overflow**, select a **Call action** and enter an appropriate SIP URI if required.

17. Click **Commit** when completed.

Alternatively, the Lync Server Management Shell can be used to create a new queue:

```
New-CsRgsAgentGroup –Parent ApplicationServer:<Application Server ID> -Name
<Queue Name> -AgentGroupIDList <Collection of Agent Groups belonging to the
queue> -Description <Queue description> -OverflowAction <Overflow Action>
–OverflowCandidate <NewestCall ¦ OldestCall> -OverFlowThreshold <Number of
simultaneous calls in the queue> –TimeoutThreshold <Number of seconds a call
can be in queue before timing out> -TimeoutAction <Timeout Action>
```

Setting the OverflowAction and TimeoutAction parameters involves an extra step. Save the action into a variable, and then pass that variable to the appropriate action parameter:

```
$Action = New-CsRgsCallAction –Action <Terminate ¦ TransferToQueue ¦
TransferToQuestion ¦ TransferToUri ¦ TransferToVoiceMailUri ¦
TransferToPSTN> -Uri <SIP URI>
```

After completing the queue configuration, continue the response group setup process by creating workflows.

Workflows

The Response Group workflow is what ties together the agent groups and workflows along with how calls should be routed. There are two different types of workflows that can be created:

▶ **Hunt Group**—A simple workflow that routes callers to queues based on time of day and agent availability.

▶ **Interactive**—Allows the user to be prompted with questions and is then routed to queues based on the responses.

The two types of workflows both share many configuration options, which are discussed in detail in the following:

▶ **Activate the workflow**—If selected, the workflow immediately begins to accept calls. This parameter can be changed later if the workflow should not immediately be active.

▶ **Enable for federation**—The workflow can be contacted by federated contacts if this option is selected.

▶ **Agent Anonymity**—Selecting this option hides the identity of the agent after the call is established. There are some feature limitations imposed if this is enabled. For

18

example, conferencing, application and desktop sharing, file transfer, and call recording are not available.

▶ **Group Address**—The SIP URI assigned to the workflow. This should be a unique URI in the organization.

▶ **Display name**—The name visible to clients when calling the workflow.

▶ **Telephone number**—The line URI for the workflow.

▶ **Display number**—The number visible to clients when calling the workflow. This can be in any format.

▶ **Description**—A description for the workflow.

▶ **Language**—The language used for speech recognition or text-to-speech conversion.

▶ **Welcome message**—A configurable audio message can be played to callers as they enter the workflow. This can either be accomplished through text-to-speech, or by uploading an existing audio recording.

▶ **Time Zone**—The time zone that the opening and closing times are based around.

▶ **Business Hours Schedule**—The schedule for the workflow can be based on an existing schedule created separately or it can be a custom schedule defined directly within the workflow.

▶ **Outside business hours message**—A configurable audio message can be played to callers if they dial the workflow outside of the defined business hours. This can be done through text-to-speech or by uploading an existing audio recording.

▶ **Outside business hours action**—If callers reach the workflow outside of the defined open hours, the call can either be disconnected, forwarded to a voicemail box, forwarded to another SIP URI, or forwarded to a telephone number. This action occurs after playing the message, if it is defined.

▶ **Holiday lists**—A collection of days that are defined as holidays. A separate action can be taken on these days.

▶ **Holidays message**—A configurable audio message can be played to callers if they dial the workflow on a defined holiday. This can be done through text-to-speech or by uploading an existing audio recording.

▶ **Holidays action**—If callers reach the workflow during a defined holiday, the call can either be disconnected, forwarded to a voicemail box, forwarded to another SIP URI, or forwarded to a telephone number. This action occurs after playing the message, if it is defined.

▶ **Queue**—The queue selected here receives calls for this workflow.

▶ **Music on Hold**—The default music on hold can be selected or administrators can configure a custom music on hold file.

To create a new queue, use the following steps:

1. Open the **Lync Server 2010 Control Panel**.
2. Click **Response Groups**.
3. Click **Workflow**.
4. Click **Create or edit a workflow**.
5. Select an application server and click **OK**. This is typically just a Front End pool.

The Response Group Configuration Tool opens in a web browser. Unlike the rest of the Response Group setup, workflow creation is done using an interface separate from the Lync Server Control Panel. What type of workflow is created depends on the administrator. Steps for creating each type of workflow can be found in the next section.

Hunt Group Workflow

To create a new hunt group workflow, use the following steps after launching the Response Group Configuration Tool:

1. Under Hunt Group, click the **Create** button.
2. Select whether to **Activate the workflow**.
3. Select an option for **Enable for federation**.
4. Select an option for **Enable agent anonymity**.
5. Enter a **SIP address** for the workflow. The sip: prefix is automatically prepended.
6. Enter a **Display name** for the workflow.
7. Enter a **Telephone number** to associate with the workflow. The tel: prefix is automatically included, so just the E.164 format is required with the plus prefix.
8. Enter a **Display number** for the telephone number.
9. Enter a **Description** for the workflow.
10. Select a **Language**.
11. Choose whether to **Play a welcome message** and select the message type.
12. Specify the **Time zone**.
13. Select a **Business hours schedule** by **Use a preset schedule** or by **Use a custom schedule** and defining the schedule.
14. Select whether to **Play a message when the Response Group is outside of business hours** and select a message type.
15. Select an action to take when **Outside of business hours, process call as follows**.
16. Select a **Standard holiday list** if one has been created.
17. Select whether to **Play a message during holidays**, and then select a message type.
18. Select an action to take **During holidays, process call as follows**.
19. **Configure a queue** to receive the calls.
20. Select an option to **Configure music on hold**.
21. Click **Deploy** to complete the workflow creation.

18

Interactive Workflow

To create an interactive workflow, use the following steps after launching the Response Group Configuration Tool:

1. Under Hunt Group, click the **Create** button.
2. Select whether to **Activate the workflow**.
3. Select an option for **Enable for federation**.
4. Select an option for **Enable agent anonymity**.
5. Enter a **SIP address** for the workflow. The sip: prefix is automatically prepended.
6. Enter a **Display name** for the workflow.
7. Enter a **Telephone number** to associate with the workflow. The tel: prefix is automatically included, so just the E.164 format is required with the plus prefix.
8. Enter a **Display number** for the telephone number.
9. Enter a **Description** for the workflow.
10. Select a **Language**.
11. Choose whether to **Play a welcome message** and select the message type.
12. Specify the **Time zone**.
13. Select a **Business hours schedule** by **Use a preset schedule** or by **Use a custom schedule**, and then define the schedule.
14. Select whether to **Play a message when the response group is outside of business hours** and select a message type.
15. Select an action to take when **Outside of business hours, process call as follows**.
16. Select a **Standard holiday list** if one has been created.
17. Select whether to **Play a message during holidays** and select a message type.
18. Select an action to take **During holidays, process call as follows**.
19. **Configure a queue** to receive the calls.
20. Select an option to **Configure music on hold**.
21. Select whether to **Use text-to-speech** or **Select a recording** to use for the first interactive question.
22. **Enter a voice response** text phrase and select a digit to **Assign keypad response**.
23. **Select a queue** the caller is placed in when matching the voice or keypad response.
24. Repeat the previous steps for any additional valid responses or questions that should be asked.
25. Click **Deploy** to complete the workflow creation.

Business Hour Collections

Business hour schedules for a workflow can actually be created in advance of a workflow. This is useful for when multiple workflows are created that use the same schedule, so instead of defining the same schedule each time, the business hours collection can be assigned instead. If the hours change, the only item that needs to be updated is the business hours collection instead of each individual workflow.

Defining business hour collections is a task that can be performed only by using the Lync Server Management Shell. The first step is to define a time range, which simply consists of a name, an open time, and a close time. These ranges can be reused for situations such as where the open and close times are the same each weekday. Use the following command to create a new time range, and store it in a variable that can be passed to a business hours collection object later. Times should be defined using a 24-hour format.

```
$Weekdays = New-CsRgsTimeRange –Name <Name of Time Range> -OpenTime <Time
when business hours start> -CloseTime <Time when business hours end>
```

After creating a unique variable for each different set of hours, the business hours collection object can be created. This cmdlet accepts two values for each day of the week. If the business hours stay open with no break, only the first day hours need to be specified. If the business hours include a break, such as from 12:00 to 13:00, the first day hours parameter should be from business open to 12:00, and the second day hours parameter be from 13:00 to business close. The first day hours parameter is simply titled the day of the week followed by a 1, with the second parameter using a 2 instead of the 1.

Use the following command to create a new business hours collection where no breaks occur during the day:

```
New-CsRgsHoursOfBusiness –Parent ApplicationServer:<Front-End Pool FQDN>
-Name <Business Hours Collection Name> -MondayHours1 <Time Range Object>
-TuesdayHours1 <Time Range Object>-WednesdayHours1 <Time Range Object>
-ThursdayHours1 <Time Range Object>-FridayHours1 <Time Range Object>
-SaturdayHours1 <Time Range Object>-SundayHours1 <Time Range Object>
```

> **TIP**
>
> After creating the business hours collection, it can be used when configuring a workflow.

18

Holiday Sets

Similar to business hour collections, Lync administrators can create a holiday set to define the appropriate holiday schedule for a business. Also, like the business hour collections, a holiday set can be created only using the Lync Server Management Shell.

The first step in defining a holiday set is to create a unique variable for each holiday, which defines a name, a start date, and an end date. After all the holidays are stored in a variable, they can be added to a holiday set.

To create a holiday and store it in a variable, use the following syntax:

```
$Christmas = New-CsRgsHoliday –Name <Holiday Name> -StartDate <Date
formatted as dd/mm/yyyy> -EndDate <Date formatted as dd/mm/yyyy>
```

After repeating the previous step to create each of the holiday objects, use the following syntax to create the holiday object. Naming the object based on the year usually makes the most sense because some holidays might fall on different days depending on the year. To configure a new holiday set, use the following cmdlet:

```
New-CsRgsHolidaySet –Parent ApplicationServer:<Front-End Pool FQDN> -Name
<Holiday Set Name> -HolidayList (<Comma separated list of each variable
representing a holiday>)
```

> **TIP**
>
> After the holiday set is created, it should be available for use when creating or modifying a workflow.

Audio Files

Instead of using text-to-speech abilities for welcome, business, or holiday greetings, an organization can elect to use prerecorded custom audio files for a Response Group workflow. Although the text-to-speech abilities of Lync are excellent, custom audio files generally deliver a more personal touch to callers. Custom files can also be used to play music-on-hold to a caller. The audio files used for any of these scenarios can either be in the .WAV or .WMA format.

If using a .WAV format, the file must meet the following requirements:

▶ An 8- or 16-bit file

▶ Linear Pulse Code Modulation (LPCM), a-Law, or μ-Law format

▶ Mono or stereo

▶ 4 MB or smaller

> **TIP**
>
> The recommended audio format is a 16-bit, 16 kHz mono wave file.

If using a Windows Media Audio file, the Windows Media Encoder 9 Series tool should be used to convert the source audio to a compatible format. The recommended audio format for WMA files is 16-bit, 44 kHz, mono constant bit rate (CBR) at 32 kbps.

Importing custom audio files is done using the Import-CsRgsAudioFile cmdlet. Audio files are stored only in memory and must be assigned to a workflow after being imported or they are lost. The easiest approach is to store the imported audio file as a variable temporarily, and then pass the variable when creating a workflow.

```
$AudioFile = Import-CsRgsAudioFile –Identity
service:ApplicationServer:<Front-End Pool FQDN> -FileName <File name of file
being imported without the path> -Content (Get-Content <File path and name
of file> -Encoding byte –ReadCount 0)
```

At this point, the audio file is stored in the $AudioFile variable and can be passed along to a workflow prompt.

Workflows Using the Management Shell

Creating a Response Group workflow entirely in the Management Shell gives some added flexibility to configuration. Specifically, interactive workflows have no limit to the number of questions or responses, unlike the Response Group Configuration Tool, which limits both items.

TIP

Take care to not make interactive workflows with too many menu levels because callers can quickly become frustrated and end the call if they have to navigate through too many levels.

NOTE

Much of the Response Group configuration done using the Management Shell relies heavily on storing objects as variables. Being descriptive with variable names can reduce the complexity involved when trying to tie all the pieces together.

A basic hunt group workflow can be created easily. All workflows need a default action defined, so the first step in creating a workflow within the Management Shell is to store a default action in a variable. The New-CsRgsCallAction cmdlet creates an action stored in memory that can be used in another command:

```
New-CsRgsCallAction –Action <Terminate ¦ TransferToQueue ¦
TransferToQuestion ¦ TransferToUri ¦ TransferToVoiceMailUri ¦
TransferToPSTN> -Prompt <Response Group Prompt> -Question <Response Group
Question> -QueueID <Response Group Queue ID> -Uri <Transfer URI>
```

A simple example that stores the action and sends calls to a specific queue is displayed here:

```
$TransferToCustomerServiceQueue = New-CsRgsCallAction –Action
TransferToQueue –QueueID CustomerService
```

After creating an action, a workflow object can be created. The actual workflow setup is flexible and can become extremely complicated. The full list of parameters is displayed here:

```
New-CsRgsWorkflow –Name <Workflow name> -Parent
service:ApplicationServer:<Front-End Pool FQDN> -PrimaryUri <SIP address for
workflow> -Active <$True ¦ $False> -Anonymous <$True ¦ $False>
```

18

```
-BusinessHoursID <Business Hours Collection ID> -CustomMusicOnHoldFile
<Response Group Audio File> -DefaultAction <Response Group Call Action>
-Description <Workflow Description> -DisplayNumber <Telephone Display Number>
-EnabledForFederation <$True ¦ $False> - HolidayAction < Response Group Call
Action > -HolidaySetIdList <Holiday Set ID> -Language <4 character language
code in language-Localization format> -LineURI tel:<Line URI>
-NonBusinessHoursAction <Response Group Call Action> -TimeZone <Text string
of time zone>
```

Building off the previous example and stored $TransferToCustomerService variable, a simple hunt group workflow example is presented as follows:

```
New-CsRgsWorkflow –Name MyWorkflow -Parent
service:ApplicationServer:lyncpool.companyabc.com -PrimaryUri
CustomerService@companyabc.com -DefaultAction
$TransferToCustomerServiceQueue -Description "Routes callers dialing
customer support" -DisplayNumber "+1 (234) 456-7890" -LineURI
"tel:+1234567890"
```

> **NOTE**
>
> An interactive workflow requires more upfront preparation and object configuration prior to creating the workflow object. Each prompt, question, and answer object must be defined.

To get started, a new prompt must be created and saved using the New-CsRgsPrompt cmdlet. The New-CsRgsPrompt cmdlet accepts an audio file as input if one has been stored in a separate variable, as discussed previously in this section; the alternative is to enter a text string that reads as text-to-speech. To get started, create a prompt using the following syntax:

```
New-CsRgsPrompt –AudioFilePrompt <Audio Prompt Variable> ¦ -TextToSpeechPrompt
<Text to be read to callers>
```

For example, to store the prompt in a variable using an audio file saved earlier as $MyAudioFile, use the following:

```
$PromptDoYouNeedHelp= New-CsRgsPrompt –AudioFilePrompt $MyAudioFile
```

After creating a prompt to be played to calls, a question must be posed in an interactive workflow. What might seem a little backward is that an answer list must be formed before a question can be created when using the shell. The New-CsRgsAnswer syntax is as follows:

```
New-CsRgsAnswer –Action <Response Group Call Action> -DtmfResponse <Keypad
mapping of answer> -VoiceResponseList <Voice strings to match the prompt,
separated by commas>
```

For example, to store an answer option if the caller says "Yes," "Maybe," or presses 1 on the keypad, use

```
$AnswerYesMaybe = New-CsRgsAnswer -Action $TransferToCustomerServiceQueue
-DtmfResponse 1 -VoiceResponseList "Yes","Maybe"
```

Because there is more than one option, assume another Response Group Answer object exists called $AnswerNo and it disconnects the call if the user says "No" or presses 2 on the keypad.

After all the possible answers have been defined, a Response Group Question object can be created. The syntax for the New-CsRgsQuestion cmdlet is as follows:

```
New-CsRgsQuestion -Prompt <Response Group Prompt> -AnswerList <List of
possible answers> -Name <Text string of question> -NoAnswerPrompt < Response
Group Prompt if no answer is received>
```

Continuing the previous example, assume the custom prompt asks the caller if she actually needs help. So far, responses for "Yes" and "Maybe" have an action that transfers the caller to the Customer Service queue. If the user says "No," the call ends. The following example ties the two responses into a question and stores it to yet another variable.

```
$DoesCustomerNeedHelpQuestion = New-CsRgsQuestion -Prompt $DoYouNeedHelp
-AnswerList $YesMaybe,$No -Name "Do you need help" -NoAnswerPrompt
$AreYouStillThere
```

This example shows creating just one question with only two responses. Be sure to thoroughly plan a workflow before continuing with the setup because it does require quite a bit of scripting. Repeat the previous steps for any additional prompts, questions, and answers that will be part of the workflow.

Before the workflow can be created, the initial prompt must be assigned to a default action object.

```
$AskIfHelpNeeded = New-CsRgsCallAction -Action TransferToQuestion -Question
$DoesCustomerNeedHelpQuestion
```

Now that a question and call action have been created, an entire interactive workflow can be initiated. To finish the example, the following commands create the workflow that asks the caller whether he needs help.

```
New-CsRgsWorkflow -Name "Customer Service Workflow" -Parent
service:ApplicationServer:lyncpool.companyabc.com -PrimaryUri
CustomerService@companyabc.com - -DefaultAction $AskIfHelpNeeded
-Description "Asks user if they need help and routes to Customer Service if
yes" -DisplayNumber "+1 (234) 456-7890 -LineURI "tel:+1234567890"
```

18

Best Practices

The following are best practices from this chapter:

- ▶ Collocate Mediation Servers with a Front End server when possible to reduce the hardware required for each deployment.

- ▶ Use a unique dial plan for each location that has different dialing habits.

- ▶ Use translation rules on a trunk configuration only if the opposite end of the trunk is not manipulating digits.

- ▶ Configure the required network objects before attempting Call Admission Control, Media Bypass, or Enhanced 911 setup.

- ▶ Use test cases to verify an Enterprise Voice configuration before publishing changes.

- ▶ Use a survivable branch appliance or survivable branch server in each remote office without a resilient WAN connection to the central site.

- ▶ Plan a Response Group workflow with diagram tools before attempting to create the workflow.

- ▶ Do not use too many levels or questions in Response Group workflows. Callers might become frustrated and hang up.

Summary

The improvements to Enterprise Voice and the Mediation role in Lync Server become apparent during the configuration phase. It is easy to see just how much flexibility an administrator has with the deployment and why the product feels so much more mature. On top of the flexibility, new features such as Call Admission Control and Media Bypass help ensure network stability and a strong end-user experience for Enterprise Voice users.

The emergency services improvements with E-911 enable organizations to meet certain regulations or goals not possible with earlier versions of Communications Server. The survivable branch appliances from third-party partners ease the mind of administrators everywhere by helping ensure branch offices still get dial tone access when their connection to a main site goes out. The flexible Response Group configuration enables organizations to build an entire interactive voice response workflow in a manner that meets business requirements. The bottom line is the Lync Server 2010 Enterprise Voice feature set meets or exceeds the capabilities of many other IP-PBXs available today.

CHAPTER 19

Audio Conferencing

In addition to providing compelling telephony features related to Enterprise Voice users, Lync Server 2010 has expanded the dial-in conferencing support first introduced in Office Communications Server (OCS) 2007 R2.

This chapter covers the steps involved in deploying dial-in conferencing on top of an existing Lync voice infrastructure where IP/PSTN gateways are in place and functional. Dial plan and conferencing regions are examined along with how to assign a dial-in access number to a particular region. Customization of the dual-tone multi-frequency (DTMF) commands and conferencing announcement behavior is also covered in this chapter.

Finally, enablement and management of users for dial-in conferencing is covered. This involves assigning dial plans, conferencing policies, and managing PINs for users.

Dial-In Conferencing Overview

The dial-in conferencing features of Lync Server 2010 can certainly be considered part of the voice enhancements, but the key differentiator with dial-in conferencing is that an organization can continue to leverage its existing phone handsets and PBX while still using the rich dial-in conferencing meeting and scheduling experience. This enables organizations that already use Lync for instant messaging and presence to begin using the audio conferencing service without a significant investment or change to user behavior. Users can continue to use their current handsets, but gain the capability to schedule and join meetings using a Lync client.

When joining audio conferences, Lync can even dial the user's work number automatically when entering the meeting. This removes the need for users to manually dial the access number and enter an extension and PIN to authenticate because they are already authenticated to Active Directory through the Lync client. Figure 19.1 depicts how a user can select to have Lync dial their work or mobile number automatically when joining a meeting.

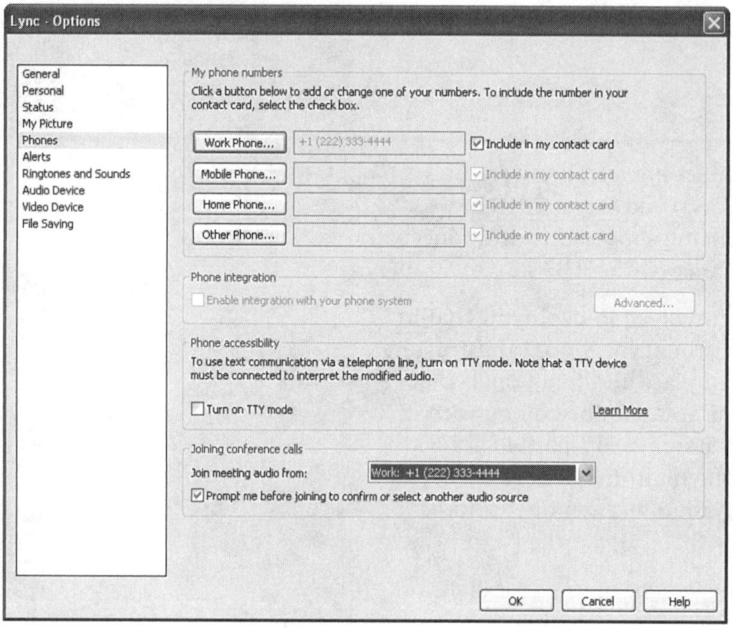

FIGURE 19.1   Join Meeting Preferences

> **NOTE**
>
> There is no feature that enables Lync Server to dial attendees when the meeting time starts. Attendees must either click a join meeting link before the server places an outbound call or dial the access number manually.

Most of the configuration required for dial-in conferencing builds on the steps used to provision Enterprise Voice services. For instance, the infrastructure for a Front End pool, Mediation Server role, and an IP/PSTN gateway must already be in place before configuring dial-in conferencing.

Depending on the PBX integration in place for voice services, it might be necessary to create a separate trunk configuration for dial-in conferencing. This is typical if an Internet Telephony Service Provider provides SIP trunks for the dial-in conferencing. If the trunk configuration differs for the provider, an additional Mediation pool might be required with the trunk configuration scoped to the new pool.

Dial-In Conferencing Configuration

Leveraging the Lync Server 2010 dial-in conferencing features depends greatly on a successful voice routing and trunk configuration that's in place. The actual steps for adding dial-in conferencing to a functional voice infrastructure are not difficult and can be provisioned quickly. This section covers the different aspects of the configuration process.

Prerequisites

Before deploying dial-in conferencing, several prerequisites should be in place. The rest of this configuration section assumes these items have been configured and focuses only on the additional steps required for the conferencing configuration.

- ▶ Deploy a Front End pool
- ▶ Either collocate the Mediation Server role with the Front End pool, or deploy a standalone Mediation pool
- ▶ Deploy an IP/PSTN Gateway to interoperate with the Mediation Server role

Dial Plan

A dial plan object is required for dial-in conferencing to normalize numbers entered by users. The normalization rules are used with conferencing to convert extensions entered by users to E.164-formatted numbers that are then matched to a user account. This enables users to enter only their extension instead of full phone number when dialing in to a conference from a phone.

To create a new dial plan to be assigned to dial-in conferencing users, perform the following steps:

1. Open the **Lync Server 2010 Control Panel**.
2. Click **Voice Routing**.
3. Click **Dial Plan**.
4. A dial plan can be scoped to apply at the site level, to a specific pool, or even just to a specific set of users. Click **New** and then select either **Site dial plan**, **Pool dial plan** or **User dial plan**.
5. Enter a **Simple name** for the dial plan to uniquely identify it within the topology.
6. Enter a **Description** for the dial plan.
7. If the dial plan is associated with a **Dial-in Conferencing Region**, enter the name of that region.
8. If users need to use any kind of prefix to dial external numbers, enter these digits in the **External access prefix** field.

19

Normalization Rules

Normalization rules are what dial plans use to take a user's extension and translate it to a full E.164 format that can be matched to a user account. Continuing from the dial plan creation screen, perform the following steps to create a normalization rule:

1. On the Edit Dial Plan screen, click the **New** button in the Associated Normalization Rules section.

2. Provide a **Name** for the rule and **Description** for the rule.

> **NOTE**
>
> This example uses the Normalization Rule tool. For more advanced pattern matching, click the **Edit** button at the bottom of the screen to manually enter the matching pattern and translation rule using regular expressions.

3. In the **Starting digits** field, enter the beginning digits of the string to be matched.

4. Specify a **Length** of the string to be matched. Options include matching at least a specific number of digits, exactly a certain number of digits, or any number of digits.

5. Specify a number of **Digits to remove** after a string matches the starting digits and length.

6. Specify **Digits to add** after the selected number of digits are removed.

7. If the pattern matches numbers that are internal to the organization, check the **Internal extension box**.

8. Click **OK** to save the translation rule, and then click **OK** again to save the trunk configuration.

For example, assume an organization uses four-digit dialing from a specific site. All direct inward dial (DID) numbers within that site start with 234–567, followed by the four-digit extension. In this scenario, the pattern and translation rule are configured as in the following:

```
Pattern to match: ^(\d{4})$
Translation rule: +1234567$1
```

This takes a four-digit extension and prepends +1234567 in front of the four digits. Assuming a user has the 1234 extension and a user account was assigned a Tel URI of tel:+12345671234, the conferencing service matches the user account based on this rule.

> **CAUTION**
>
> It might be necessary to include a number of normalization rules in the dial plan in case blocks of DID numbers are noncontiguous. In a worst-case scenario, the DIDs do not follow a repeatable pattern when matched to extensions and many rules might need to be created.

When creating multiple rules, be sure to order them in a top-to-bottom format because Lync uses the first rule that it matches. Keep this in mind when troubleshooting why a normalization rule is not translating correctly.

One way to mitigate these kinds of errors is to test the pattern immediately. When creating a new rule, simply enter a dial string in the **Phone number to test** field and a success or failure will be returned immediately. If the test succeeds, be sure the normalized number is correct because the test only indicates a failure or success at matching the original pattern.

NOTE

One common question organizations have is how to enable dial-in conferencing for users without a DID. In these cases, use a main office or front desk number as the Tel URI, but append an ;ext=xxxx string to the end of the Tel URI. Using the previous example, assume the user's extension is still 1234, but the main office number is 234-567-8000. The user's Tel URI would be tel:+1234567890;ext=1234.

Regions

Each dial plan created can be associated with a dial-in conferencing region, which is how a dial-in conferencing access number determines what normalization rules to apply. Despite the same terminology, regions are not actually tied to the network region definitions used for the Call Admission Control and Media Bypass features. Dial-in conferencing regions can be defined and created only through a dial plan object.

NOTE

There is no specific configuration required for dial-in conferencing regions; however, at least one must be specified on a dial plan to use the dial-in conferencing features.

Dial-In Access Numbers

Dial-in access numbers are the phone numbers users dial to reach the audio conferencing service. For each access number, a SIP-enabled contact object is created within Active Directory. These objects should not be modified with regular tools and should only be managed using the Lync management tools.

Dial-in access numbers have a region associated that ties them to a particular dial plan. This association is how a dial-in access contact knows which normalization rules to apply when callers enter extensions or attempt to dial out.

The following options are available when creating a dial-in access number:

▶ **Display number**—The text format of the number as it is displayed to callers who dial the number from a Lync client. PSTN dial-in users do not see this format because they do not have a screen, but the format entered here is also used when online meeting invitations are sent from an Outlook client.

▶ **Display name**—The name displayed in meeting invitations and on the dial-in conferencing settings page. This is the name of the Active Directory contact created for the access number. Use a name here that is recognizable to callers.

▶ **Line URI**—The actual phone number users dial. This should be specified in E.164 format with the tel: prefix.

▶ **SIP URI**—The SIP URI assigned to the contact object. It must be unique within the organization and use a sip: prefix.

▶ **Pool**—The pool where the contact object is homed.

▶ **Primary language**—The primary language used to make conferencing announcements.

▶ **Secondary languages**—Any secondary language choices for conferencing announcements. Up to four secondary languages can be specified.

▶ **Associated regions**—Dial plan regions that are associated with the dial-in access number.

Perform the following steps to create a new dial-in access number:

1. Open the **Lync Server 2010 Control Panel**.
2. Click **Conferencing**.
3. Click **Dial-In Access Number**.
4. Click **New**.
5. Enter a **Display number** for the contact.
6. Enter a **Display name** for the contact.
7. Enter a **Line URI** in E.164 format using a tel: prefix.
8. Enter a **SIP URI** using a sip: prefix and select a SIP domain internal to the organization.
9. Select a **Pool** where the object will be homed.
10. Select a **Primary language** for the conference announcements.
11. Press the **Add** button and select up to four **Secondary languages**.
12. Click the **Add** button and select **Associated regions** for the dial-in access number. Figure 19.2 shows a sample dial-in access number.

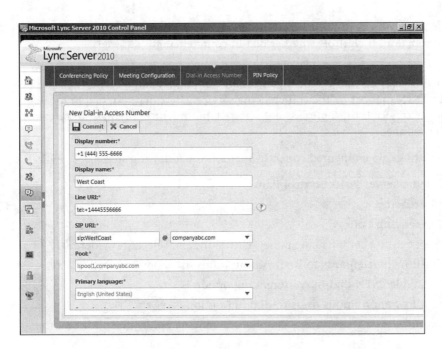

FIGURE 19.2   Creating a Dial-In Access Number

To use the Lync Server Management Shell to create the dial-in access number, use the following syntax:

```
New-CsDialInConferencingAccessNumber –PrimaryURI <SIP URI including sip: prefix>
-DisplayNumber <String as displayed to users> -LineUri <Line URI including tel:
➥prefix> -
Regions <Comma separated list of regions> -Pool <Fully-qualified name of pool>
-PrimaryLanguage <Language code> -DisplayName <Contact display name>
➥-SecondaryLanguages
<Comma separated list of language codes>
```

Conferencing Policy

Part of enabling user accounts for dial-in conferencing is assigning a conferencing policy the enables the PSTN dial-in capability. Conferencing settings apply to more than only dial-in conferencing. However, the settings required to use PSTN dial-in conferencing are controlled through a conferencing policy. These settings are the following:

▶ **Allow participants to invite anonymous users**—Controls whether anonymous, unauthenticated users from outside the organization can participate in conferences. Although this setting is not required to be enabled, if it is not selected, it limits the use of audio conferencing to only users inside the organization.

19

▶ **Enable PSTN dial-in conferencing**—This setting must be enabled for dial-in conferencing to function. It controls whether dial-in conferencing is allowed.

▶ **Allow anonymous participants to dial out**—Controls whether anonymous, unauthenticated users from outside the organization can join an audio conference and be called at a PSTN number by the conferencing service. Users may still dial in to the conferencing service if this option is not selected, but might not request to be called at another number.

To verify these settings are configured correctly, perform the following steps:

1. Open the **Lync Server 2010 Control Panel**.
2. Click **Conferencing**.
3. Click **Conferencing Policy**.
4. Highlight an existing conferencing policy, click **Edit**, and select **Show details**.
5. Verify the **Allow participants to invite anonymous users** option is set.
6. Verify the **Enable PSTN dial-in conferencing** option is set.
7. Verify the **Allow anonymous users to dial out** option is set.
8. Click **Commit**. Figure 19.3 shows a sample conferencing policy that allows all these features.

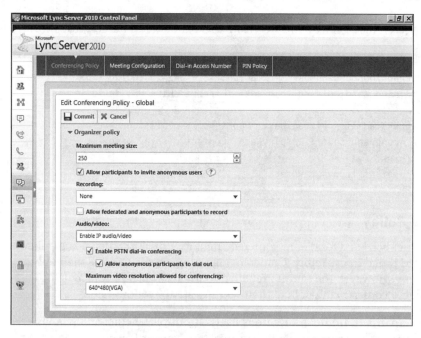

FIGURE 19.3   Conferencing Policy Allowing Dial-In Conferencing

▶ The Lync Server Management Shell can also be used to configure these settings. The example here modifies the Global setting for conferencing:

```
Set-CsConferencingPolicy Global –EnableDialInConferencing <$True ¦ $False>
-AllowAnonymousUsersToDialOut <$True ¦ $False> -AllowAnonymousParticipantsInMeetings
<$True ¦ $False>
```

PIN Policies

Lync Server 2010 enables users to join audio conferences either through a Lync client or by simply dialing in from a phone. When dialing from a phone, the users are unauthenticated until entering an extension and matching PIN. This is required because when joining conferences from a Lync client, users are already authenticated after passing Active Directory credentials to log in to Lync. When dialing in from a phone, the PIN and extension provide a method for Lync to still validate the user as internal to the organization. Administrators can define PIN policies that apply globally to all users, only to a specific site, or to assigned user accounts.

CAUTION

The PIN policy discussed here is separate from an organization's PIN for Exchange Unified Messaging. The PINs between the two systems are not synchronized in any way, and users must maintain them separately. For that reason, strong end-user communication is encouraged so the users understand the difference and the need to change PINs in both locations. Future versions of Lync Server and Exchange Server might introduce synchronization of PINs and PIN policies.

When configuring a PIN policy, administrators have the following options:

▶ **Minimum PIN length**—The minimum number of digits a user may use for a PIN. Only a minimum value can specified, so users may choose any number of digits for their PIN equal to or more than this value.

▶ **Maximum logon attempts**—The number of times a user may attempt to authenticate with a PIN before the PIN is locked out and must be reset by an administrator. If a user successfully authenticates with a PIN, this counter is reset to zero.

▶ **PIN Expiration**—Determines whether a PIN will expire. The PIN expiration value is set in days. Using a value of 0 for PIN expiration means the user PINs will never expire.

▶ **Allow common patterns**—Determines whether commonly used patterns are allowed for a PIN. Examples of common patterns are repeating digits, four consecutive digits, or PINs that match a user's phone number or extension.

▶ **PIN History Count**—The number of PINs the system remembers before a user is allowed to reuse a PIN. This parameter is only available through the Lync Server Management Shell.

To create a new PIN policy, perform the following steps:

1. Open the **Lync Server 2010 Control Panel**.

2. Click **Conferencing**.

3. Click **PIN Policy**.

4. Click **New** and select either **Site policy** or **User policy**.

5. Select a **Minimum PIN length**.

6. Select whether to **Specify maximum logon attempts** and enter a maximum number of attempts.

7. Select whether to enable **PIN Expiration** and enter a number of days.

8. Select whether to enable **Allow common patterns**.

9. Click **Commit** when complete. Figure 19.4 shows a sample PIN policy where the PIN never expires.

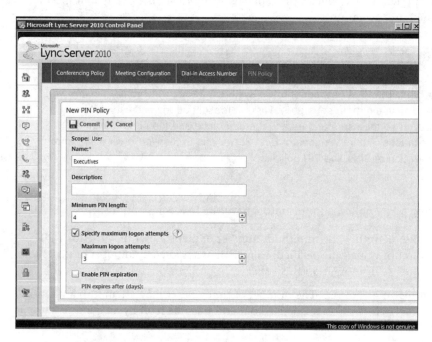

FIGURE 19.4   Creating a PIN Policy

To create a new PIN policy using the Lync Server Management Shell, use the following syntax:

```
New-CsPinPolicy –Identity <PIN Policy Name> –AllowCommonParameters <$True ¦ $False>
-MaximumLogonAttempts <Number of attempts> -MinPasswordLength <Minimum number of PIN
digits> -PinHistoryCount <Number of PINs remember> -PinLifetime <Number of days a PIN
is valid>
```

NOTE

Be sure to assign the PIN policy to user accounts if a user PIN policy is created. Site policies are applied automatically, but user policies must be manually assigned to end users.

Meeting Configuration

The meeting configuration commands in Lync Server 2010 are provided to enable organizations more control over what types of meetings are allowed to occur. Meeting configuration settings control items such as what types of meetings can happen and how the lobby is used for users dialing in from the PSTN. Meeting configurations can be created at the global, site, or pool level.

When modifying a meeting configuration, the following options are available:

▸ **PSTN callers bypass lobby**—Controls whether users who dial in to the conference from a PSTN phone are automatically entered into the meeting. If this option is not enabled, a presenter must admit all users in the lobby before they can participate in the conference. This generally is not an obstacle when the presenter is using Lync and can visibly see users are waiting in a lobby, but consider a scenario where presenters dial in from a PSTN number and do not have this visual clue. Presenters can use DTMF controls to admit users in the lobby, but not all users know this feature.

▸ **Designate as presenter**—Controls which users can be promoted as presenters throughout the meeting. This can be set to no one, people from inside the organization, or everyone.

▸ **Assigned conference type by default**—Controls whether meetings are created with unique meeting IDs. If set to true, each meeting has the same ID by default. If set to false, each meeting generates a unique ID. Using a unique ID can be helpful so that if a user has back-to-back meetings, attendees from the second meeting do not accidentally join the first meeting.

▸ **Admit anonymous users by default**—Controls whether anonymous, unauthenticated users are admitted into meetings by default.

EnableAssignedConferenceType Parameter

One additional parameter, EnableAssignedConferenceType, is configured only through the Lync Server Management Shell. This setting controls whether scheduling public meetings is allowed at all. A public meeting to Lync means the conference ID and URL do not change. This is very similar to the "Assigned conference type by default" option, but controls whether public meetings are allowed at all instead of assigning a default. To modify a meeting configuration, perform the following steps:

1. Open the **Lync Server 2010 Control Panel**.
2. Click **Conferencing**.
3. Click **Meeting Configuration**.
4. Click **New**.

19

5. Select either **Site configuration** or **Pool configuration.**

6. Select a site or pool service.

7. Select an option for **PSTN callers bypass lobby.**

8. Select an option for **Designate as presenter.**

9. Select an option for **Assigned conference type by default.**

10. Select an option for **Admit anonymous users by default.**

11. Press **Commit.**

To use the Lync Server Management Shell to create a meeting configuration, use the following syntax:

```
New-CsMeetingConfiguration -Identity <Identity> -AdmitAnonymousUsersByDefault
➥<$True ¦$False> -AssignedConferenceTypeByDefault <$True ¦ $False> -
DesignateAsPresenter
➥<None ¦Company ¦ Everyone> -EnableAssignedConferenceType <$True ¦ $False>
-PstnCallersBypassLobby <$True ¦ $False>
```

Conference Announcements

Conference announcements settings in Lync control what occurs when participants join or leave a meeting. These settings can be configured at a global level or assigned to a specific site.

NOTE

Enabling or disabling the announcements is a default setting that can be passed to users. However, users may change this default as they see fit.

When configuring conferencing announcements, the following options are available:

▶ **Enable Name Recording**—Controls whether users are prompted to record their name prior to joining the conference. Internal users are not prompted to record a name, and their name is played through the text-to-speech engine instead.

▶ **Entry and Exit Announcements Type**—Defines the type of announcement played when attendees join or leave the meeting. The options are to use the person's name or to simply play a tone.

▶ **Entry and Exit Announcements Enabled by Default**—Controls whether announcements are enabled or disabled by default for new Lync user accounts. This is simply a default setting passed to users that they might change.

The conference announcement settings can be configured only through the Lync Server Management Shell using the following syntax:

```
Set-CsDialInConferencingConfiguration –Identity <Identity> –EnableNameRecording
➥<$True ¦$False> -EntryExitAnnouncementsEnabledByDefault <$True ¦ $False>
-EntryExitAnnouncementsType <UseNames ¦ ToneOnly >
```

Creating a configuration that applies to a specific site is, unfortunately, not intuitive. To create a new sample configuration that applies to the SF site, the command looks like the following:

```
Set-CsDialInConferencingConfiguration –Identity site:SF –EnableNameRecording $True
-EntryExitAnnouncementsEnabledByDefault True –EntryExitAnnouncementsType UseNames
```

DTMF Commands

Lync Server 2010 enables attendees to use DTMF commands when in a conference to control certain features normally visible within a Lync client. For example, users can send DTMF tones that might mute their microphone, play an attendee roll call, or lock the conference. Usually these features can be accessed through a Lync client, but without a visible user interface, DTMF tones must be used. By default, a global configuration of the key mappings is assigned to all users. If required, administrators can modify the global configuration or modify the key mappings on a per-site basis.

> **NOTE**
>
> There is no method to assign different DTMF key mappings directly to users within the same site, so key mappings are either global or site specific. In addition, the DTMF configuration can be modified only by using the Lync Server Management Shell.

The following DTMF commands are available to assign to phone keys:

▶ **AdmitAll**—Enables users waiting in the lobby to join the meeting. This key is not enabled by default. Assign a value to enable this feature.

▶ **AudienceMuteCommand**—Mutes all microphones except the presenter. This key is 4 by default.

▶ **CommandCharacter**—The key pressed before entering any other DTMF command digits. This key is * by default.

▶ **EnableDisableAnnouncementsCommand**—Toggles whether entry and exit announcements are played during the meeting. This key is 9 by default.

▶ **HelpCommand**—Plays a summary of the DTMF commands available to a user. This key is 1 by default.

19

▶ **LockUnlockConferenceCommand**—Toggles whether the audio conference is locked or unlocked to allow new participants to join. This key is 7 by default.

▶ **MuteUnmuteCommand**—Toggles whether the participant's audio microphone is muted or unmuted. This key is 6 by default.

▶ **PrivateRollCallCommand**—Plays a roll call of participants only to the user issuing the command. This key is 3 by default.

TIP

If any of these DTMF commands needs to be disabled, assign a $Null value to the parameter.

To set the values, an administrator must use the following Lync Server Management Shell syntax:

```
Set-CsDialInConferencingDtmfConfiguration -Identity <Global or site:<Site Name>>
-AdmitAll <Digit> -AudienceMuteCommand <Digit> -CommandCharacter <Digit>
-EnableDisableAnnouncementsCommand <Digit> -HelpCommand <Digit>
-LockUnlockConferenceCommand <Digit> -MuteUnmuteCommand <Digit>
➥-PrivateRollCallCommand<Digit>
```

Test Dial-In Conferencing

Validating the dial-in conferencing configuration should be performed after the initial setup is completed, but before users are using the new features in production. Testing can be performed either through manually dialing each of the access numbers or by leveraging the synthetic transactions in Lync Server 2010. If using the manual route, simply dial each of the access numbers assigned and verify that the conferencing attendant is heard. Also be sure to verify that DTMF tones can be passed and successfully control the command features.

To use the Lync synthetic transactions, the Lync Server Management Shell must be used. Open a new session and use the following commands:

1. Invoke a credentials prompt and enter credentials of a user authorized for PSTN dial-in conferencing:

   ```
   $TestCredentials = Get-Credential
   ```

2. Run the Test-CsDialInConferencing cmdlet:

   ```
   Test-CsDialInConferencing -UserSipAddress <SIP address of user with sip:
   ➥prefix>
   -UserCredential $TestCredentials -TargetFQDN <Pool Name>
   ```

3. Verify that the test reports a success.

NOTE

Lync synthetic transactions are internal to the system and can only validate the Lync Server configuration. Be sure to manually dial the access numbers to verify that IP/PSTN gateways and SIP trunks successfully pass the calls to Lync.

Configure Users for Dial-In Conferencing

After all the required infrastructure is in place and is fully tested, the dial-in conferencing features can be extended to users. This involves assigning a Tel URI to user accounts and a conferencing policy that permits PSTN conferencing.

Enable Users

Enabling the user account consists of just assigning a Tel URI to the user account. Perform the following steps to assign a Tel URI:

1. Open the **Lync Server 2010 Control Panel**.
2. Click **Users**.
3. Enter a username to enable and click **Find**.
4. Highlight the user, click the **Edit** button, and click **Show details**.
5. In the **Line URI** field, enter an E.164 number with a tel: prefix.
6. Click **Commit**.

TIP

If a conferencing policy that permits dial-in conferencing does not exist at the global or site level, it will not be automatically applied and must be assigned to users. The same goes for if a PIN policy targeted to users has been created.

On the same screen where the Tel URI is entered, perform the following steps to modify the conferencing or PIN policy:

1. Under **Conferencing policy**, select a policy that enables PSTN dial-in conferencing.
2. Under **PIN policy**, select an appropriate policy for the user.
3. Click **Commit**.

The same tasks can be performed using the Lync Server Management Shell for situations where these tasks might be completed for many users at once. To assign a Tel URI, use the following syntax:

```
Set-CsUser –Identity <User Name> -LineURI <Line URI with tel: prefix>
```

19

Assigning a conferencing or PIN policy must be done through separate cmdlets. Assign a conferencing policy with the following syntax:

```
Grant-CsConferencingPolicy -Identity <User Name> -PolicyName <Conferencing Policy
➥Name>
```

Assign a PIN policy with the following syntax:

```
Grant-CsPinPolicy -Identity <User Name> -PolicyName <PIN Policy Name>
```

Send Welcome PIN

After enabling users for dial-in conferencing, Lync Server provides the capability for administrators to send users an e-mail message welcoming them to the service. This initial e-mail can also set and display the PIN for each user account. The welcome message can only be generated through a Lync Server Management Shell command. The actual message is based on an HTML file that can be modified to accommodate any organization. This cmdlet is included as an additional script file found in C:\Program Files\Common Files\Microsoft Lync Server 2010\Modules\Lync.

TIP

You might need to include additional information in the welcome e-mail about how to use the system. You can also include links to a Help recording so that users can become comfortable with the new conferencing system.

When generating a welcome message, the following parameters are available:

- ▶ **UserUri**—The URI of the message recipient.
- ▶ **From**—The email address of the user sending the message.
- ▶ **Subject**—The subject of the email message.
- ▶ **Cc**—Any recipients who should be carbon copied when sending the welcome message.
- ▶ **Bcc**—Any recipients who should be blind carbon copied when sending the welcome message.
- ▶ **TemplatePath**—The file path to the template used for generating the welcome message.
- ▶ **SmtpServer**—The SMTP server to use when sending the message. If recipients are internal to the organization, relay capability should not be required.
- ▶ **BodyAsPlainText**—Specifies whether the message should be sent in plain text as opposed to HTML.

▶ **UseSsl**—Specifies whether SSL should be used when sending the message through the SMTP server.

▶ **Pin**—The PIN that should be set for the user's account.

> **NOTE**
>
> The Set-CsPinSendCAWelcomeEmail cmdlet sets a user PIN only if it has not been set previously. The PIN can be forced to change the parameter specified in the cmdlet if the Force parameter is included with the command.

To send a welcome message, use the following syntax with the Lync Server Management Shell:

```
Set-CsPinSendCAWelcomeMail.ps1 –UserUri <SIP URI of user to set> -From <Email
↪address of
sender> -Subject <Message subject> -Cc <Comma separated list of email addresses to be
carbon copied> -Bcc <Comma separated list of email addresses to be blind carbon
↪copied>
-TemplatePath <File path to HTML template> -SmtpServer <Mail server address>
-BodyAsPlainText <$True ¦ $False> -UseSsl <$True ¦ $False> -PIN <PIN String>
```

Generating Bulk Welcome Messages

In reality, many users are most likely enabled for dial-in conferencing at the same time. To send this message in bulk, first create a CSV file called DialInUsers.csv with the following format:

```
SipUri,Pin
"sip:user1@companyabc.com",12345
"sip:user2@companyabc.com",67890
```

Then import the CSV and use a loop to generate a message for each user:

```
Import-CSV DialInUsers.csv ¦ ForEach-Object {Set-CsPinSendCAWelcomeMail.ps1 –UserUri
$_.SipUri –From "helpdesk@companyabc.com" -Subject "Welcome to Conferencing"
–SmtpServer
"mail.companyabc.com" –Pin $_.Pin}
```

Managing PINs

Throughout the lifetime of the conferencing system, there will be users who find a way to lock themselves out with a PIN or need a PIN reset because it has been forgotten. Lync Server provides several ways for administrators to manage dial-in conferencing PINs, such

19

as viewing the status of a current PIN or assigning a new PIN. This section covers the various operations an administrator can use with PINs.

Viewing PIN Status

Viewing the PIN status enables an administrator to verify whether a PIN has been set or whether the user is locked out. To view the PIN status, perform the following steps:

1. Open the **Lync Server 2010 Control Panel**.
2. Click **Users.**
3. Enter a username to enable and click **Find.**
4. Highlight the user and click the **Action** button.
5. Click **View PIN Status**. Figure 19.5 shows how an administrator can view the status of a user's PIN.

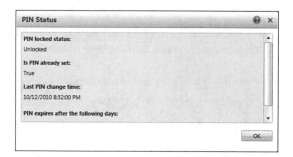

FIGURE 19.5   Sample PIN Status

Viewing PIN status can also be performed using the Lync Server Management Shell:

```
Get-CsClientPinInfo -Identity <User Name>
```

Setting a PIN

Administrators can set a user account to a specific PIN or it can be randomly generated. To set a PIN, perform the following steps:

1. Open the **Lync Server 2010 Control Panel**.
2. Click **Users.**
3. Enter a username to enable and click **Find.**
4. Highlight the user and click the **Action** button.
5. Click **Set PIN.**
6. Select **Automatically generate a valid PIN** or **Manually enter a specific PIN.**
7. If a PIN was automatically generated, click the **Show PIN** box and notify the user of the new PIN.

> **NOTE**
>
> Unlike Exchange Unified Messaging, randomly generating a PIN does not automatically
> e-mail the user with the new PIN. The new PIN must be manually communicated to the
> end user or it will need to be reset again.

Generating a new PIN can also be performed using the Lync Server Management Shell:

```
Set-CsClientPin -Identity <User name > -PIN <New PIN. Leave blank to automatically
generate one>
```

Locking a PIN

Administrators can manually lock a PIN, which prevents a user from authenticating to the
system from a PSTN phone. Users cannot use a PIN to authenticate until the PIN is
unlocked. PINs might also be locked automatically if a user exceeds the number of
authentication attempts allowed.

To lock a PIN, perform the following steps:

1. Open the **Lync Server 2010 Control Panel**.
2. Click **Users.**
3. Enter a username to enable and click **Find.**
4. Highlight the user and click the **Action** button.
5. Click **Lock PIN.**
6. A visible lock icon displays next to the user's account. Figure 19.6 shows a sample
   user that has had his PIN locked by a Lync Server administrator.

Locking a user PIN can also be performed using the Lync Server Management Shell:

```
Lock-CsClientPin -Identity <User Name>
```

Unlocking a PIN

If a user's PIN is locked manually or because of too many failed authentication attempts,
an administrator can unlock the PIN.

To unlock a PIN, perform the following steps:

1. Open the **Lync Server 2010 Control Panel**.
2. Click **Users.**
3. Enter a username to enable and click **Find.**
4. Highlight the user and click the **Action** button.
5. Click **Unlock PIN.**

19

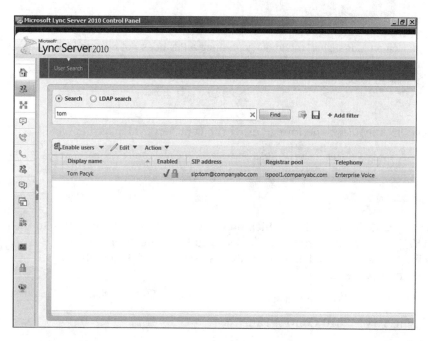

FIGURE 19.6   User Account with Locked PIN

Unlocking a user PIN can also be performed using the Lync Server Management Shell:

```
Unlock-CsClientPin –Identity <User Name>
```

Best Practices

The following are best practices from this chapter:

▶ Configure and test a Front End pool with voice service before deploying dial-in conferencing. If basic voice services are nonfunctional, it might be difficult to troubleshoot whether the dial-in conferencing configuration is at fault.

▶ Plan for voice redundancy when deploying dial-in conferencing. This is usually considered a critical service and any outage can have a large impact. Each component of the Lync infrastructure should be designed for high availability to prevent this situation.

▶ Define at least one dial-in conferencing region within a dial plan.

▶ Test the dial plan and ensure that extensions are correctly normalized to user SIP URIs.

▶ Plan a PIN policy and communicate this policy to end users.

- ▶ Define at least one access number for each dial-in conferencing region.
- ▶ Fully test the dial-in conferencing system prior to enabling user accounts and sending welcome messages.

Summary

It should be readily apparent that Lync Server has made significant improvements to the dial-in conferencing experience for end users.

Conferencing and PIN policies provide a degree of flexibility for users to grant different levels of capabilities to user groups. For example, executives might be allowed a PIN policy that never expires, whereas the rest of the staff might be required to change a PIN every 90 days. The new DTMF commands and conference announcements enable users to choose how they want to conduct conferences, all through a few simple clicks in an application they are already using.

Dial-in conferencing can be provisioned through an existing PBX if capacity allows, or organizations might choose to leverage an Internet Telephony Service Provider and SIP trunks for additional telephony capacity. In either case, organizations that are deploying Lync for other functions should spend some time reviewing the potential cost savings in moving to Lync dial-in conferencing over a hosted, subscription service.

19

PART VII

Integration with Other Applications

IN THIS PART

CHAPTER 20

Exchange 2010 and SharePoint 2010 Integration

Overview

Lync Server 2010 spreads its UC power to other platforms in the Microsoft stack as well. This chapter reviews how Lync Server integrates with and empowers Microsoft Exchange 2010 and SharePoint 2010. Lync Server's integration with SharePoint occurs mostly through built-in functions in Active Directory. In contrast, Lync Server integration with Exchange 2010 is complex and requires significant configuration to both platforms.

Exchange 2010 Unified Messaging

Exchange Server 2010 unified messaging (UM) delivers voice messaging, fax, and email into a unified inbox. These messages can be accessed from a telephone or a computer. Exchange Server 2010 unified messaging integrates with the telephony systems, operating fundamentally as a voicemail server using the Exchange Information Store as a repository for the messages.

Exchange Server 2010 extends the UM features first introduced in Exchange 2007. Unified messaging seamlessly integrates voice messaging, faxing, and electronic mail into a single inbox. This frees up the user from having to manage separate accounts and inboxes for these three types of messages. With the new role, there are a number of new features.

Telephony Integration

With unified messaging, Exchange is integrated into the telephony world. This integration takes place between the Exchange Unified Messaging (UM) Server and gateways or private branch exchanges (PBXs).

In a classic set of telephony and electronic mail systems, there are two separate networks that deliver voice messages and electronic messages (email). In the telephony system, there are separate components for the PBX, voicemail, external lines, and phones. Calls from the Public Switched Telephone Network (PSTN) come into a PBX device. Typically, an incoming call is routed by the PBX to the telephone. If the phone does not answer or is busy, the call is routed to the voicemail system. Similarly, email from the Internet arrives at the Exchange messaging server (see Figure 20.1).

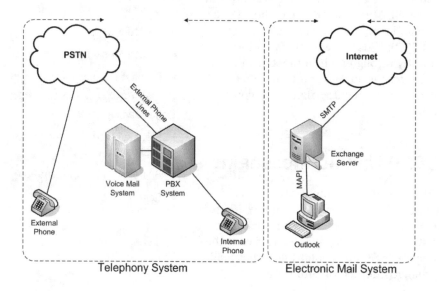

FIGURE 20.1   Classic Telephone and Electronic Mail Systems

NOTE

In the classic system, there is no integration or connectivity between the telephony and email systems.

With Exchange Server 2010 and unified messaging, these two disparate systems are integrated, as shown in Figure 20.2. Although the UM Server does not connect directly with a traditional PBX, it does integrate with PBXs through gateways. The combination of the PBX and the Internet Protocol (IP) gateway can also be replaced by an IP-PBX, which provides both sets of functionality.

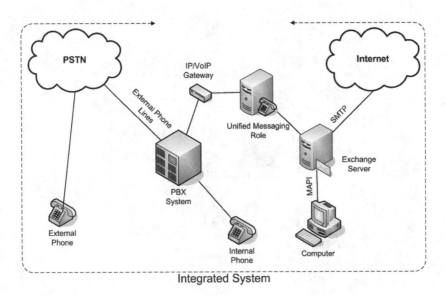

FIGURE 20.2   New Integrated System

One such IP-PBX option is Microsoft Lync Server 2010. Integrating these two Microsoft platforms provides a powerful enterprise voice solution that can replace most modern PBXs at a fraction of the cost.

Notice that, in effect, the Unified Messaging server has replaced the voicemail server in the classic system. The new Microsoft Exchange Server 2010 Unified Messaging server is a voicemail server.

The more detailed view with all the Exchange 2010 server roles is shown in Figure 20.3, which includes the various ways that a user can interact with the integrated system.

Figure 20.3 is discussed in more detail in later sections of this chapter.

Single Inbox

The Unified Messaging server enables the true unification of email messages, voicemail messages, and fax messages into a single inbox. Messages from all these disparate sources are stored in the user's inbox and are accessible through a wide variety of interfaces, such as Outlook, a telephone, a web browser, or even a mobile PDA.

The inbox can be managed just like a traditional email inbox, with folders, inbox rules, message retention, and so on. Exchange administrators can back up and restore inboxes with all the forms of data just as they do with email data. This reduces the complexity and ease of use for both users and administrators.

Call Answering

Call answering picks up incoming calls for a user who does not answer the phone. It plays the personal greeting, records voice messages, and converts the voice messages to an email message to be submitted to the user's Exchange mailbox.

20

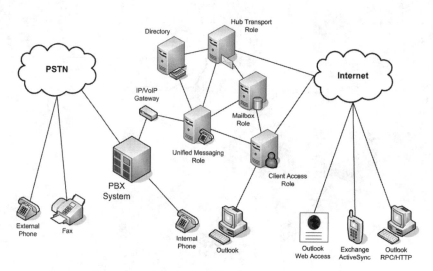

FIGURE 20.3   Detailed Architecture Diagram

Fax Receiving

The Exchange 2010 Unified Messaging role has limited functionality for fax support. Instead, Exchange 2010 leverages solutions from partners to provide fax support. This is a departure from previous versions of Exchange, which included a full fax solution.

Subscriber Access

The subscriber access feature enables a user to access the Exchange mailbox using a phone. This access mechanism is called *Outlook Voice Access*.

Outlook Voice Access Features

With Outlook Voice Access, a user can access the Exchange mailbox using the telephone to perform the following functions:

- ▶ Listen to and forward voicemail messages
- ▶ Listen to, forward, and reply to email messages
- ▶ Listen to calendar information
- ▶ Access or dial contacts
- ▶ Accept or cancel meeting requests
- ▶ Notify attendees that the user will be late
- ▶ Set a voicemail Out-of-Office message
- ▶ Set user security preferences and personal options

This, in effect, gives the user working access to the Exchange mailbox while out in the field with only a telephone.

The system not only recognizes dual tone multiple frequency (DTMF) key presses from the phone, but also understands voice commands. The system guides the user through the prompts responding to voice commands, which gives the user complete hands-free operation.

For example, a user might be on the freeway running late for a lunch meeting. Not remembering the exact time, the user calls into the subscriber access and says, "Today's Calendar." The unified messaging system speaks the summary of the next meeting, which is at 12 p.m. Recognizing that the traffic will force him to be 20 minutes late, the user says, "I'll be 20 minutes late for this appointment." The unified messaging system confirms and then sends a message to all the attendees.

The speech recognition is remarkably effective and able to recognize commands even over cell phones with background noise.

Outlook Play on Phone

The Exchange 2010 Outlook Web App client and Outlook 2007 or better clients both support a feature called Play on Phone. This feature enables users to play voicemail on a phone rather than through the computer. The user opens the voicemail message, selects the Play on Phone option, enters the number to play the message, and clicks the Dial button, as shown in Figure 20.4. For this example, the phone at the extension 102 will ring.

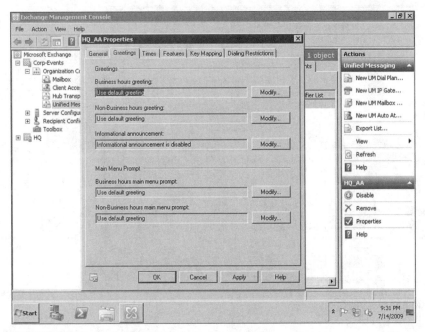

FIGURE 20.4   Exchange 2010 Auto Attendant Menu

20

This feature enables the user to send the audio stream of the voicemail message to a phone for more privacy or to allow a third party to hear the message. The system also provides prompts over the phone following the playback with message-handling options.

Outlook Voicemail Preview

Outlook voicemail preview is a new feature to Exchange 2010 unified messaging. In Exchange 2007 UM, you see caller information and message priority. Exchange 2010 kicks it up a notch with speech-to-text functionality. Before the voicemail message arrives in your inbox, Exchange UM transcribes the voicemail and puts the text in the body of the email.

TIP

Although Voice Preview is not perfect, it's pretty accurate. This is especially helpful for spam voicemail with anonymous caller information. Using this function, a user can save time, and frustration, by deleting unwanted messages without listening to them with no fear of deleting a legitimate message.

Call Answering Rules

New to Exchange 2010 is the concept of call answering rules. A user can configure basic call workflows using Outlook Web App. By default, no call answering rules are configured. However, users can browse to the phone tab, and then select voice mail in the OWA options menu. See an example in Figure 20.5.

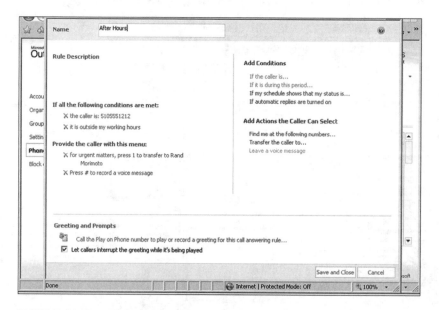

FIGURE 20.5   Call Answering Rules

For example, let's say you want your kids to be able to reach you anytime but you don't want coworkers to reach you after 5 p.m. You can set a rule to allow calls from your children's phone numbers to come through to the Lync client and also ring your mobile phone or another phone.

You can also set a rule to force calls from a business associate or coworker to be forwarded directly to voicemail after 5 p.m. The interface is reminiscent of Outlook Web App email rules and should be familiar to most users. Even after rules are created, they may be disabled or enabled through the Outlook Web App Voice Mail menu. Rules, by default, are created as enabled.

Intelligent call routing, a more generic term for Microsoft's call answering rules, was a frequently noted omission in Exchange 2007. Its inclusion in Exchange 2010 and Exchange 2010 UM's tight integration with Lync Server 2010 offers a rich voice platform capable of being a full PBX replacement.

Auto Attendant

The Exchange 2010 auto attendant is like a secretary, providing voice prompts to guide an external or internal caller through the voicemail system. The system can respond to either telephone keypad presses or voice commands.

The auto attendant features include the following:

- A customizable set of menus for external users

- Greetings for business hours and nonbusiness hours

- Hours of operation and holiday schedules

- Access to the organization's directory

- Access for external users to the operator

The voice prompts that provide the preceding information can be customized to suit the organization.

Exchange 2010 Unified Messaging Architecture

The Exchange 2010 UM features and telephony integration bring a new set of concepts, terminology, and architectural elements to the Exchange platform. This section explores these different components: objects, protocols, and services.

Unified Messaging Components

The central repository for all the UM components is Active Directory. The schema extensions that are installed as part of the Exchange 2010 prerequisites add a variety of objects and attributes that support the UM functionality. These objects are as follows:

- Dial plan objects

- IP gateway objects

- ▶ Hunt group objects

- ▶ Mailbox policy objects

- ▶ Auto attendant objects

- ▶ Unified messaging server objects

The objects and their relationships are illustrated in the example shown in Figure 20.6. The example consists of two locations, San Francisco (SFO) and Paris (PAR), with an integrated Exchange 2010 unified messaging infrastructure. The unified messaging objects are shown with a dotted line around them to separate them from the telephony objects.

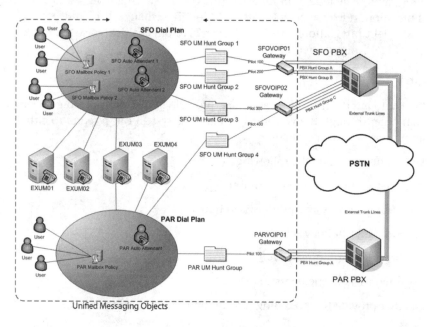

FIGURE 20.6   Unified Messaging Objects and Relationships

When a UM hunt group is created manually, not only do the associated UM IP gateway and the associated UM dial plan get specified, but a pilot identifier is also specified.

This diagram is referenced in the subsequent sections describing the various unified messaging objects and components.

Dial Plan Objects

Dial plans are the central component of the Exchange 2010 unified messaging architecture. A UM dial plan logically corresponds to PBX or subsets of extensions within a PBX. The UM dial plan objects can be found in the Exchange Management Console on the UM Dial Plan tab of the Organization, Unified Messaging container.

Different PBXs with an organization, such as between SFO and PAR in Figure 20.6, can have overlapping extensions. For example, a user in San Francisco might have extension

150 and a user in Paris might also have extension 150. Because the two users are on different PBXs, there is no inherent conflict. However, when Exchange 2010 unified messaging is deployed and the telephony infrastructure is unified in Active Directory, there will be a conflict.

Dial plans ensure that all extensions are unique within the architecture by mapping a dial plan to a PBX. Extensions within a dial plan must be unique. However, extensions between different dial plans do not have to be unique. A user can only belong to a single dial plan and will have an extension number that uniquely identifies him within the dial plan.

In Figure 20.6, there is one dial plan for each location. In the example, San Francisco is the large office with more users and Paris is smaller. There can be multiple dial plans per location.

Dial plans also provide a way to set up common settings among a set of users, such as the following:

- ▸ Number of digits in an extension
- ▸ Capability to receive faxes
- ▸ Subscriber greetings
- ▸ Caller contacts within the dial plan
- ▸ Users' call restrictions (international calls)
- ▸ Languages supported

These settings should not be confused with UM mailbox policies, which are covered in the "Mailbox Policy Objects" section later in this chapter.

NOTE

When a new UM dial plan object is created, a default UM mailbox policy object is also created and associated with the dial plan.

The dial plan also associates the extension for the subscriber access to Outlook Voice Access.

There can be multiple dial plans within an architecture and even associated with the same PBX.

UM IP Gateway Objects

The UM IP gateway object is the logical representation of the next hop in the VoIP chain. It can be either a media gateway device connected to the PSTN or a PBX such as Lync Server 2010. The UM IP gateway object is a critical component because it specifies the connection between the UM dial plan and the physical IP/VoIP gateway. The major configuration of the UM IP gateway object is the IP address of the IP/VoIP gateway device it represents and the associated dial plan. The UM IP gateway objects can be found in the Exchange Management Console on the UM IP Gateway tab of the Organization, Unified Messaging container.

20

The UM IP gateway is created as enabled. The gateway can be disabled, either immediately (which disconnects any current calls) or by specifying to disable after completing calls. The latter mode disables the gateway for any new calls but does not disconnect any current calls.

If a UM IP gateway object is not created or is deleted, the Unified Messaging servers in the dial plan will not be able to accept, process, or place calls.

Within the same Active Directory, there can only be one UM IP gateway object for each physical IP/VoIP gateway, and it is enforced through the IP addresses. However, multiple UM IP gateway objects can be defined within the Exchange Management Console for redundancy or advanced call routing.

UM IP gateway objects can be associated with multiple dial plans. This is accomplished by creating multiple hunt groups, as discussed in the following section.

Hunt Group Objects

In the telephony world, *hunt groups* are collections of lines that a PBX uses to organize extensions. The hunt group collections enable the system to treat the extensions as a logical group. Hunt groups are used for incoming lines, for outgoing lines, and to route calls to groups of users such as the Sales department. The UM hunt group objects can be found in the Exchange Management Console on the UM IP Gateway tab of the Organization, Unified Messaging container. They are listed under each of the UM IP gateways.

Calls with a hunt group can be routed using different methods or algorithms, such as the following:

- ▶ **Rollover**—The PBX starts with the lowest numbered line each time and increments until it finds a free line.

- ▶ **Round-robin**—The PBX rotates equally among all the lines when starting and then rolls over from the starting point. This ensures that the calls are distributed evenly within the hunt group.

- ▶ **Utilization**—The PBX tracks extension utilization and routes the call to the least utilized line first, and then rolls over to the next least busy line.

These algorithms basically encode what the organization deems the appropriate behavior for the routing.

Each hunt group has an associate pilot number, which is the extension that is dialed to access the hunt group. This is frequently the lowest numbered extension in the set of extensions because the most common implementation of a hunt group is rollover.

Within Exchange 2010, the UM hunt group object performs a different function. Essentially, the UM hunt group object maps the IP/VoIP gateway and an extension to a UM dial plan.

> **NOTE**
>
> If a default hunt group is created when the UM IP gateway object is created, that UM hunt group will not have a pilot extension associated with it. This creates call routing problems if you create additional hunt groups, so it is best to remove the default hunt group. When a new UM hunt group is created after that, the pilot identifier must be specified.

Additional UM hunt groups can be created to route different incoming extensions to different UM dial plans. There is no limit to the number of UM hunt group objects that can be created. There must be at least one hunt group per UM IP gateway object for calls to be routed to a dial plan.

Mailbox Policy Objects

Mailbox policy objects control unified messaging settings and security for users. The UM mailbox policy objects can be found in the Exchange Management Console on the UM Mailbox Policies tab of the Organization, Unified Messaging container.

These settings include the following:

▶ Maximum greeting duration

▶ Message text for UM-generated messages to users

▶ PIN policies

▶ Dialing restrictions

Mailbox policies are created to control security and provide customized messages to users. For example, in Figure 20.6, the SFO Mailbox Policy 1 is a general user policy with default PIN settings that require a minimum of six characters. The second policy, SFO Mailbox Policy 2, is for executives with higher security requirements and more secure PIN settings that require a minimum of 10 characters.

The UM mailbox policy is associated with one UM dial plan, but dial plans can be associated with multiple mailbox policies. This enables the dial plan to be associated to the users associated with the mailbox policy. Each user is associated with one UM mailbox policy object, but many users can be associated with a single mailbox policy object.

Auto Attendant Objects

The auto attendant provides an automated phone-answering function, essentially replicating a human secretary. The auto attendant answers the incoming calls, provides helpful prompts, and directs the caller to the appropriate services. The UM auto attendant objects can be found in the Exchange Management Console on the UM Auto Attendant tab of the Organization, Unified Messaging container.

20

The auto attendant supports both phone key press (DTMF) and voice commands. This sophisticated voice recognition technology enables the caller to navigate the menus and prompts with only her voice.

The auto attendant objects support the following configurable features:

▶ Customized greetings and menus for business hours and nonbusiness hours

▶ Predefined and custom schedules for business hours and time zones

▶ Holiday schedules for exceptions to business hours

▶ Operator extension and transfers to operator during business and nonbusiness hours

▶ Key mapping to enable the transfer of callers to specific extensions or other auto attendants based on hard-coded key presses or voice commands

NOTE

Everyone has felt the frustration of moving through an automated call system and not being able to reach an operator or a live person. With unified messaging, the Exchange administrator now has control over that behavior.

The auto attendant can allow or disallow transfer to the operator by specifically allowing or disallowing transfer to the operator during business and nonbusiness hours.

We recommend transferring to the operator at least during business hours to reduce caller frustration.

Each auto attendant can be mapped to specific extensions to provide a customized set of prompts. For example, an organization can set up one auto attendant to support the sales organization calls with specific prompts for handling calls to sales. The organization can then set up a second auto attendant to support the service organization with specific prompts for technical support and help. These can service different pilot numbers, depending on the number that the caller used.

A front-end menu can be created with key mapping and an auto attendant with customized prompts. This enables the organization in the previous example to create a top-level auto attendant that can prompt callers to "Press or say 1 for Sales or 2 for Service" and then perform the appropriate transfer. Figure 20.7 shows the key mapping configuration, which can be accompanied by customized prompts.

The initial greeting can be customized as well. In fact, there are two default greetings: one for business hours and a second for off-hours. By default, the system says, "Welcome to Microsoft Exchange..." In most implementations, you want to customize this to your company name and include other relevant information. Customized greetings must be saved as PCM/16-bit/8 kHz/mono .WAV files. Each auto attendant may have a unique set of customized greetings and prompts.

There is no limit to the number of auto attendants that can be created in Active Directory. An auto attendant can be associated with only a single dial plan, although a dial plan can be associated with multiple auto attendants.

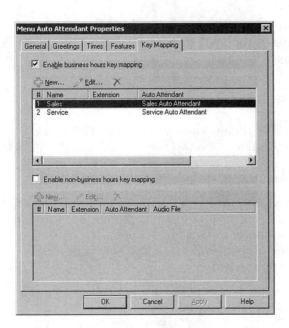

FIGURE 20.7   Key Mapping Example

Unified Messaging Server Objects

In Active Directory, the Unified Messaging server object is a logical representation of the physical Exchange 2010 Unified Messaging Server. The UM server objects can be found in the Exchange Management Console in the Server Configuration, Unified Messaging container.

The Microsoft Exchange Unified Messaging service (`umservice.exe`) is the service that instantiates the unified messaging functionality that runs under the Local System account. It is dependent on the Microsoft Exchange Active Directory Topology service.

The major configuration task for the Unified Messaging server object is to specify the associated dial plans, of which there can be more than one as in Figure 20.7. The Unified Messaging server must be associated with a dial plan to function. The other configurable parameters for the service are the maximum concurrent calls (default is 100) and maximum concurrent faxes (default is 100).

The Unified Messaging server checks for changes when the service is started and every 10 minutes thereafter. Changes take effect as soon as they are detected by the server.

After determining the dial plans for which it is associated, the server then locates and establishes communications with the appropriate IP/VoIP gateways.

Much like the UM IP gateway, the Unified Messaging server is created as enabled. The server can be disabled through the Exchange Management Console or through the Exchange Management Shell for graceful shutdown or maintenance. This can be executed

20

either immediately (which disconnects any current calls) or when specifying to disable after completing calls. The latter mode disables the server for any new calls but does not disconnect current calls. Any current calls are allowed to complete.

Unified Messaging Users

There is actually not an Active Directory object for unified messaging users. Rather, the unified messaging properties are stored in the Active Directory user account and the Exchange 2010 mailbox. Voicemail messages and fax mail messages are stored in the user's mailbox.

These properties can be found in the Exchange Management Console in the properties of the user's account in the Recipient Configuration, Mailbox folder. Within the user account properties, the unified messaging settings are under the Mailbox Features tab in the properties of the Unified Messaging feature. After navigating to the Unified Messaging feature, click the properties button to access the feature properties.

When enabling a user for unified messaging, the associated UM mailbox policy and extension must be specified. The link to the mailbox policy provides a one-to-one link to the UM dial plan.

The user's mailbox quotas apply to both voicemail messages and fax messages. If the user's quota settings prevent the user from receiving email (for example, the user's mailbox is full), unified messaging functionality will be affected. Callers attempting to leave a message will not be allowed to do so and will be informed that the user's mailbox is full.

> **NOTE**
>
> Interestingly, if a user's mailbox is almost full, a caller will be allowed to leave a message for the user even if that message will cause the mailbox to exceed its quota. For example, consider a user who only has 25 KB before exceeding the quota and is prevented from receiving messages. A caller can leave a minute long 100 KB voice message. However, the next caller would not be able to leave a message for the user.

Exchange 2010 unified messaging includes several features to control the size of voicemail messages to help control the storage impacts.

UM Web Services

A component that is not represented in Active Directory is the UM Web Services. This is a web service that is installed on Exchange 2010 servers that have the Client Access role.

The service is used for the following:

▶ Play on Phone feature for both Outlook 2010 and Exchange 2010 Outlook Web App

▶ PIN Reset feature in Exchange 2010 Outlook Web App

This service requires that at least one Exchange 2010 server run the Client Access, Hub Transport, and Mailbox Server roles in addition to the Unified Messaging role.

Audio Codecs and Voice Message Sizes

Codec is a contraction of *coding* and *decoding* digital data. This is the format in which the audio stream is stored. It includes both the number of bit rate (bits/sec) and compression that is used.

One of the following codecs is used by the Unified Messaging server to encode the messages:

- ▶ **Windows Media Audio (WMA)**—16-bit compressed

- ▶ **GSM 06.10 (GSM)**—8-bit compressed

- ▶ **G.711 PCM Linear (G711)**—16-bit uncompressed

- ▶ **Mpeg Audio Layer 3 (MP3)**—16-bit compressed

The Exchange 2010 unified messaging default is MP3. This is a change from Exchange 2007 where the default was WMA. Although using WMA results in slightly smaller file sizes, most people prefer the universal nature of MP3. This enables a much larger number of mobile devices to play voicemail messages. The Audio Codec setting is configured on the UM dial plan on the Settings tab.

NOTE

A dirty little secret is that the digital compression results in loss of data. When the data is compressed and decompressed, information is almost always lost. That is, bits of the conversation or message can be lost. This is a trade-off that the codec makes to save space. This is why the G.711 codec is available, which doesn't compress data and doesn't lose data but at a heavy cost in storage.

These are stored in the message as attachments using the following formats:

- ▶ **Windows Media Audio (.wma)**—For the WMA codec

- ▶ **RIFF/WAV (.wav)**—For GSM or G.711 codecs

- ▶ **Mpeg Audio Layer 3 (.mp3)**—For the MP3 codec

The choice of the audio codec affects the audio quality and the size of the attached file. Table 20.1 shows the approximate size of data in the file attachment for each codec.

TABLE 20.1   Audio Size for Codec Options

Codec Setting	Approximate Size of 10-Second Audio
WMA	11,000 bytes
G.711	160,000 bytes
GSM	16,000 bytes
MP3	19,500 bytes

The G.711 audio codec setting results in a greater than 10:1 storage penalty when compared to the WMA audio codec setting. Although the GSM audio codec setting results in approximately the same storage as the WMA codec setting, this comes at a cost of a 50% reduction in audio quality. MP3 provides similar audio quality to WMA at an acceptable file size. The ubiquitous nature of the MP3 codec makes it the preferred choice for Exchange 2010.

> **NOTE**
>
> The .wma file format has a larger header (about 7 KB) than the .wav format (about 0.1 KB). For small messages, GSM files are smaller. However, after messages exceed 15 seconds, WMA files are smaller than the GSM files.

Operating System Requirements

This section discusses the recommended minimum hardware requirements for Exchange 2010 servers.

Exchange 2010 unified messaging supports the following processors:

- x64 architecture-based Intel Xeon or Intel Pentium family processor that supports Intel Extended Memory 64 technology
- x64 architecture-based computer with AMD Opteron or AMD Athlon 64-bit processor that supports AMD64 platform

The Exchange 2010 unified messaging memory requirements are as follows:

- 2 GB of RAM minimum
- 4 GB of RAM recommended

The Exchange 2010 unified messaging disk space requirements are as follows:

- A minimum of 1.2 GB of available disk space
- Plus 500 MB of available disk space for each unified messaging language pack
- 200 MB of available disk space on the system drive
- DVD drive

As features and complexity of the applications such as Exchange 2010 have grown, the installation code bases have grown proportionally. Luckily, so have the hardware specifications of the average new system, which now typically includes a DVD drive.

Exchange 2010 unified messaging supports the following operating system and Windows components:

- Windows Server 2008, x64 Standard Edition
- Windows Server 2008, x64 Enterprise Edition

- ▶ Windows Server 2008 R2, x64 Standard Edition

- ▶ Windows Server 2008 R2, x64 Enterprise Edition

Exchange 2010 unified messaging requires the following components to be installed:

- ▶ Microsoft .NET Framework Version 3.5

- ▶ Windows PowerShell 2.0

- ▶ Microsoft Management Console (MMC) 3.0

Out of the box, an Exchange 2010 Unified Messaging server is configured for a maximum of 100 concurrent calls. This is enough to support potentially thousands of users, given that the number of calls and voice messages per day is a fraction of the number of users and is spread out throughout the day.

Supported IP/VoIP Hardware

Exchange Server 2010 unified messaging relies on the capability of the IP/VoIP gateway to translate time-division multiplexing (TDM) or telephony circuit-switched based protocols, such as Integrated Services Digital Network (ISDN) or QSIG, from a PBX to protocols based on voice over IP (VoIP) or IP, such as Session Initiation Protocol (SIP), Real-Time Transport Protocol (RTP), or T.38 for real-time facsimile transport.

Although there are many types and manufacturers of PBXs, IP/VoIP gateways, and IP/PBXs, there are essentially two types of IP/VoIP gateway component configurations:

- ▶ **IP/VoIP Gateway**—A legacy PBX and an IP/VoIP gateway provisioned as two separate devices. The Unified Messaging server communicates with the IP/VoIP gateway.

- ▶ **IP/PBX**—A modern IP-based or hybrid PBX such as a Cisco CallManager. The Unified Messaging server communicates directly with the PBX.

Table 20.2 lists the currently supported IP/VoIP gateways.

TABLE 20.2   Supported IP/VoIP Gateways for Exchange 2010 UM

Manufacturer	Model	Supported Protocols
AudioCodes	MediaPack 114, MediaPack 118	Analog with In-Band or SMDI
AudioCodes	Mediant 1000/2000	-T1/ or E1 with CAS—In-Band or SMDI, T1/E1 with Primary Rate Interface (PRI) and Q.SIG or Analog PSTN
Dialogic	1000/2000	-T1/ or E1 with CAS—In-Band or SMDI, T1/E1 with Primary Rate Interface (PRI) and Q.SIG or Analog PSTN
Ferrari AG	OfficeMaster 3.2	PSTN Analog

20

TABLE 20.2   Supported IP/VoIP Gateways for Exchange 2010 UM

Manufacturer	Model	Supported Protocols
Net	VX1200	-T1/ or E1 with CAS—In-Band or SMDI, T1/E1 with Primary Rate Interface (PRI) and Q.SIG or
Nortel	CS1000	Direct SIP
Quintum	Tenor-series	Analog PSTN

To support Exchange Server 2010 unified messaging, one or both types of IP/VoIP device configurations are used when connecting a telephony network infrastructure to a data network infrastructure.

All these solutions must communicate with the unified messenger through SIP over TCP (TLS encrypted) and SRTP.

Unified Messaging Protocols

The Exchange 2010 Unified Messaging servers use several telephony-related protocols to integrate and communicate with telephony devices. These protocols are listed and discussed in the following list:

▶ **Session Initiation Protocol (SIP)**—This is the signaling protocol that is used to set up and tear down VoIP calls. These calls include voice, video, instant messaging, and a variety of other services. The SIP protocol is specified in RFC 3261 produced by the Internet Engineering Task Force (IETF) SIP Working Group. SIP is only a signaling protocol and does not transmit data. After the call is set up, the actual communications take place using the RTP for voice and video or T.38 for faxes.

> **NOTE**
>
> Exchange 2010 only supports SIP over TCP. SIP, in general, can be configured to run over User Datagram Protocol (UDP) or Transmission Control Protocol (TCP). UDP is connectionless and does not provide reliability guarantees over the network. TCP is connection-oriented and provides reliability guarantees for its packets. Exchange 2010 UM supports either SIP over TCP, SIP over TLS, or Dual where both are supported simultaneously.

▶ **Real-Time Transport Protocol (RTP)**—This protocol sends the voice and video data over the TCP/IP network. The protocol relies on other protocols, such as SIP or H.323, to perform call setup and teardown. It was developed by the IETF Audio-Video Transport Working Group and is specified in RFC 3550. There is not a defined port for the RTP protocol, but it is normally configured to use ports 16384–32767. The protocol uses a dynamic port range, so it is not ideally suited to traversing firewalls.

▶ **Real-Time Facsimile Transport (T.38)**—This protocol is an International Telecommunication Union (ITU) standard for transmitting faxes over TCP/IP. The protocol is described in RFC 3362. Although it can support call setup and teardown, it is normally used in conjunction with a signaling protocol such as SIP.

It is important to note that the Exchange 2010 Unified Messaging server is also a Windows server, a web server, and a member of the Active Directory domain. There are a myriad of protocols, including domain name system (DNS), Hypertext Transfer Protocol (HTTP), Lightweight Directory Access Protocol (LDAP), remote procedure calls (RPCs), and Simple Mail Transfer Protocol (SMTP), among others, that the server uses to communicate with other servers in addition to the telephony communications.

Unified Messaging Port Assignments

Table 20.3 shows the IP ports that unified messaging uses for each protocol. The table also shows whether the ports can be changed and where.

TABLE 20.3   Ports Used for Unified Messaging Protocols

Protocol	TCP Port	UDP Port	Can Ports Be Changed?
SIP-UM Service	5060		Ports are hard-coded.
SIP-Worker Process	5061 and 5062		Ports are set by using the Extensible Markup Language (XML) configuration file.
RTP		Port range above 1024	The range of ports can be changed in the Registry.
T.38		Dynamic port above 1024	Ports are defined by the system.
UM Web Service	Dynamic port above 1024		Ports are defined by the system.

Unified Messaging Installation

The installation of Exchange 2010 is surprisingly easy, although the configuration can be tricky. This section covers the installation and configuration of a basic system to illustrate the concepts.

Installation of the Unified Messaging server role modifies the base installation of Exchange 2010 and is done in Maintenance mode. The procedures in this section step through the build of a basic Exchange 2010 unified messaging system and are shown in Figure 20.8.

20

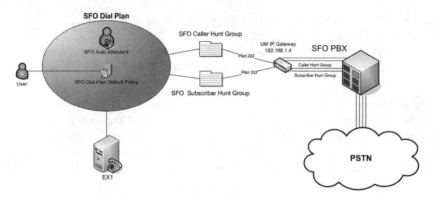

FIGURE 20.8   Sample Exchange 2010 UM System

Installation Prerequisites

Before starting the installation, it is important that the users' mailboxes, which will be serviced by the Unified Messaging server, are on Exchange 2010 servers. In other words, Exchange 2010 UM cannot service users with mailboxes on an Exchange 2007 or earlier mailbox server. Of course, the requirements (such as PowerShell) for any Exchange 2010 server role apply to the Unified Messaging server.

Telephony Prerequisites

Because the Exchange 2010 Unified Messaging server is essentially a voicemail system, all the other components must be in place and operational before introducing it. This includes the following:

▶ **PBX**—The existing PBX must be configured with the appropriate hunt groups to route calls correctly.

▶ **Hunt groups**—The hunt groups and pilot numbers should be provisioned in the PBX. The auto attendant pilot numbers and the subscriber access pilot numbers should be part of a rollover group so that if one number is busy, the call will roll over to the next line.

NOTE

Set up separate hunt groups and pilot access numbers on the PBX for the auto attendant and the subscriber access lines.

▶ **IP/VoIP gateway**—The IP gateway must be configured to route calls from the pilot extensions to the Exchange 2010 UM server IP address. The gateway must also be configured to use SIP over TCP, rather than SIP over UDP. Some gateways attempt UDP first and then try TCP, resulting in strange connection behavior such as delays in initiating calls.

▶ **Phones**—The phones must be provisioned and assigned to users. At least two test phones should be available.

▶ **External lines**—External lines must be provisioned within the PBX.

▶ **Early Media**—This setting is not supported in Exchange 2010 Unified messaging.

See the manufacturer's documentation for specific details of the configuration for each of the telephony components.

Installing the Unified Messaging Role

The first step is to install the Unified Messaging role. This procedure assumes that the Exchange 2010 server has already been installed. To add the Unified Messaging server role, complete the following steps:

1. In Control Panel, select **Add or Remove Programs**.

2. Select **Microsoft Exchange Server 2010**.

3. Click the **Change** button to enter Exchange Maintenance mode.

4. Click **Next**.

5. Select the **Unified Messaging Role** check box, as shown in Figure 20.9, and click **Next**.

6. After the installer conducts readiness checks, click the **Install** button to install the Unified Messaging server role.

7. After the installation has successfully completed, click **Finish**.

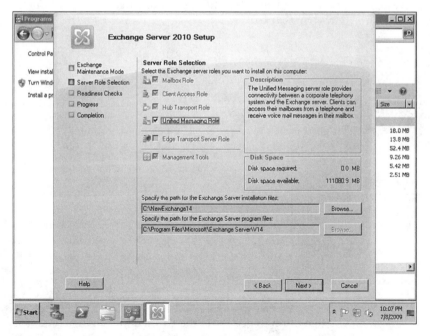

FIGURE 20.9   Choosing the Unified Messaging Role from the Setup Screen

The basic software has been installed, but the UM server needs to be configured post-installation to function properly.

Postinstall Configuration

After the server has the Unified Messaging server role installed, complete several postinstall configuration tasks for a basic installation:

- ► Create a UM dial plan
- ► Associate subscriber access numbers
- ► Create a UM IP gateway
- ► Associate the UM server with the dial plan
- ► Create a UM auto attendant
- ► Create the hunt groups
- ► Enable mailboxes for UM
- ► Test functionality

Following these tasks results in a functioning Exchange 2010 Unified Messaging system. The remainder of this section details the installation steps for each task.

Creating a UM Dial Plan

The first task is to create the central organizing element of the Exchange 2010 UM infrastructure—the dial plan shown in Figure 20.10.

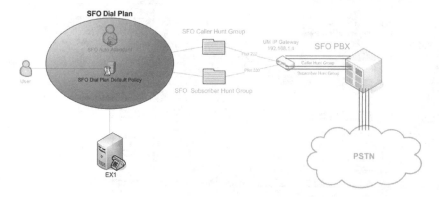

FIGURE 20.10   Creating the Dial Plan

To create a dial plan, execute the following steps:

1. Launch the Exchange Management Console.
2. Under the Organization Configuration folder, select the **Unified Messaging** container.
3. Select the **UM Dial Plan** tab.

4. In the Action menu, select **New UM Dial Plan**.

5. Enter the dial plan name, such as **SFO Dial Plan**.

6. Enter the number of digits in the PBX extensions, such as **3**.

7. Click **New** to create the UM dial plan.

8. Click **Finish** to close the wizard.

The newly created dial plan displays in the results pane. Notice in Figure 20.10 that the default mailbox policy (SFO Dial Plan Default Policy) was automatically created at the same time.

Associating Subscriber Access Numbers

For subscribers to access their mailbox, one or more subscriber access numbers must be specified in the dial plan. This should be the pilot number for the PBX hunt group that the subscribers will use.

To associate a subscriber access extension to the dial plan, execute the following steps:

1. Launch the Exchange Management Console.

2. Under the Organization Configuration folder, select the **Unified Messaging** container.

3. Select the **UM Dial Plan** tab.

4. Select the dial plan in the results pane, such as **SFO Dial Plan**.

5. In the Action menu, select **Properties**.

6. Select the **Subscriber Access** tab.

7. Enter the extension that subscribers will use to access their mailboxes, such as **333**.

8. Click **Add**.

9. Click **OK** to close the window.

The UM server now recognizes that subscribers will use the extension to access their mailboxes.

Creating a UM IP Gateway

The next task is to create a UM IP gateway to link the dial plan with the IP/VoIP gateway and the PBX (see Figure 20.11).

To create the UM IP gateway, execute the following steps:

1. Launch the Exchange Management Console.

2. Under the Organization Configuration folder, select the **Unified Messaging** container.

3. Select the **UM IP Gateway** tab.

4. In the Action pane, click **New UM IP Gateway**.

5. Enter the IP gateway name, such as SFO IP **Gateway**.

6. Enter the IP address for the IP gateway, such as **192.168.1.4** shown in Figure 20.12.

7. Click **Browse**.

8. Select a dial plan with which to associate the IP gateway, such as the **SFO Dial Plan**.

20

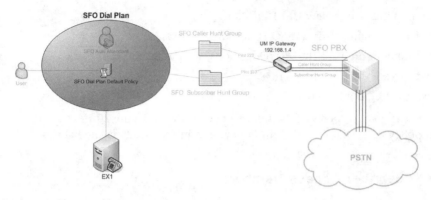

FIGURE 20.11   Creating an IP Gateway

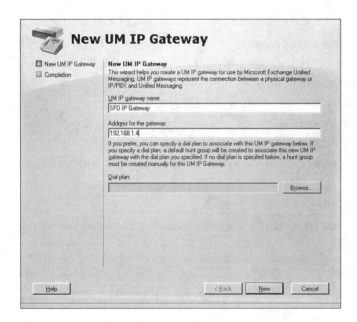

FIGURE 20.12   New UM IP Gateway

9. This also creates a default hunt group (which will be deleted later).

10. Click **OK**.

11. Click **New** to create the UM IP gateway.

12. Click **Finish** to close the wizard.

The newly created UM IP gateway displays in the results pane. The default hunt group is removed and a new one is created in a later task.

Associating the UM Server with the Dial Plan

The dial plan needs to be associated with the UM server that was installed in the first task. This eventually causes the UM server to register with the IP/VoIP gateway to receive calls.

To associate the UM server with the new dial plan, execute the following steps:

1. Launch the Exchange Management Console.
2. Under the Server Configuration folder, select the **Unified Messaging** container.
3. Select the Unified Messaging server.
4. In the actions pane, click **Properties**.
5. Select the **UM Settings** tab.
6. Click **Add**.
7. Select the dial plan to associate, such as the **SFO Dial Plan**.
8. Click **OK**.
9. Click **OK** to close the Properties dialog box.

The pilot number is now associated to the dial plan for subscriber access.

Create a Unified Messaging Auto Attendant

For the UM server to answer callers, a UM auto attendant must be created and associated with a dial plan. This enables incoming calls to be answered and directed to the appropriate voice mailbox.

To create an auto attendant and associate it with a dial plan, execute the following tasks.

1. Launch the Exchange Management Console.
2. Under the Organization Configuration folder, select the **Unified Messaging** container.
3. Select the **UM Auto Attendant** tab.
4. In the actions pane, click **New UM Auto Attendant**.
5. Enter the name of the auto attendant, such as **SFO Auto Attendant**.
6. Click **Browse**.
7. Select a dial plan, such as the **SFO Dial Plan**.
8. Click **OK**.
9. Enter the pilot extension number, such as **222**, and click **Add**.
10. Select the **Create Auto Attendant as Enabled** check box.
11. Select the **Create Auto Attendant as Speech-Enabled** check box, shown in Figure 20.13, to have the auto attendant accept voice commands.
12. Click **New**.
13. Click **Finish** to close the wizard.

The newly created auto attendant displays in the results pane.

FIGURE 20.13 Creating an Auto Attendant

If the auto attendant is created as speech-enabled, a secondary fallback auto attendant that is not speech-enabled should be created on the primary auto attendant. If a
user cannot use voice commands, he can use DTMF commands on the secondary
auto attendant. Although the speech-enabled auto attendant accepts DTMF commands, the user is not notified this is possible unless a DTMF fallback auto attendant
is configured.

Creating the Hunt Groups

The default hunt group that is created with the UM IP gateway does not contain a pilot
number. To have the system handle incoming calls correctly, the default hunt group
should be deleted and new ones created for the caller and subscriber hunt groups.

To create hunt groups, execute the following steps:

1. Launch the Exchange Management Console.
2. Under the Organization Configuration folder, select the **Unified Messaging** container.
3. Select the **UM IP Gateway** tab.
4. Select **DefaultHuntGroup** in the results pane.
5. In the actions pane, click **Remove**.

6. At the prompt, click **Yes**.

7. Select the UM IP gateway, such as **SFO IP Gateway**.

8. In the actions pane, click **New UM Hunt Group**.

9. Enter the caller hunt group name, such as **SFO Caller Hunt Group**.

10. Click **Browse**.

11. Select the dial plan to associate, such as **SFO Dial Plan**.

12. Click **OK**.

13. Enter the hunt group pilot number, such as **222**.

14. Click **New**.

15. Click **Finish**.

16. Repeat steps 7 through 14, using **SFO Subscriber Hunt Group** as the name and **333** as the hunt group pilot.

The result of the configuration is shown in Figure 20.14, including the new hunt groups.

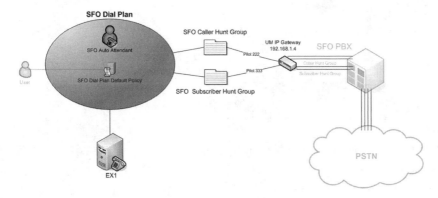

FIGURE 20.14   Creation of Hunt Groups

The system is now configured and ready for the final configuration step in the basic configuration—enabling a user for unified messaging.

Enabling Mailboxes for UM

The final task is to enable a user's mailbox. This associates the user with a mailbox policy and, therefore, to the rest of the unified messaging infrastructure.

To enable a user, execute the following steps:

1. Launch the Exchange Management Console.

2. Under the Recipient Configuration folder, select the **Mailbox** folder.

3. In the results pane, select the user to be enabled.

4. In the actions pane, select **Enable Unified Messaging**.

5. Click **Browse**.

6. Select the UM policy, such as the **SFO Dial Plan Default Policy**.

7. Click **OK**.

8. Enter the extension, such as **102**, shown in Figure 20.15.

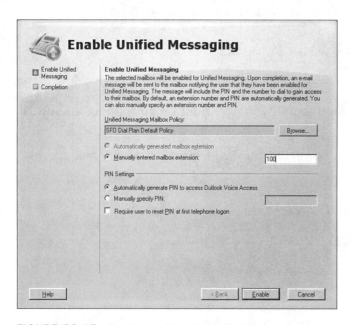

FIGURE 20.15   Enabling a User for Unified Messaging

9. Click **Enable**.

10. Click **Finish** to close the wizard.

A simple welcome email message with the extension and the confidential PIN automatically sends to the Exchange mailbox.

Testing Functionality

The final step is to make sure that it works. This can be the most difficult testing tasks for an average Exchange administrator who is not familiar with the telephony elements of the infrastructure.

Make sure that the following critical functions are tested:

▶ The UM server is operating.

▶ The UM server can connect to the gateway and PBX.

▶ The UM server can be reached from an internal phone.

▶ The UM server can be reached from an external phone.

Figure 20.16 shows the paths of the critical tests.

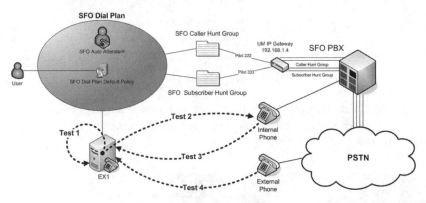

FIGURE 20.16   Testing the UM Server

The specific commands and steps for testing are discussed in the following sections.

Testing Unified Messaging Server Operation

The Unified Messaging server operations test needs to run on the local UM server in the Exchange Management Shell. The shell command is

```
Test-UMConnectivity
```

This command attempts a diagnostic SIP call and reports back on the success. Figure 20.17 shows the result of a successful test. Specifically, the value of EntireOperationSuccess is True.

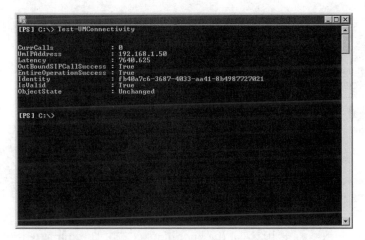

FIGURE 20.17   Testing the UM Server

Testing Unified Messaging Server Connectivity

This test shows whether the UM server can communicate with the PBX and access a phone. Specifically, it causes the internal phone to ring.

The following command needs to be run from the Exchange Management Shell:

```
Test-UMConnectivity –IPGateway "IP Gateway Name" –Phone extension
```

For example, the command might be

```
Test-UMConnectivity –IPGateway "SFO IP Gateway" –Phone 102
```

The results for a successful test are shown in Figure 20.18. The phone at the extension should ring. If the test is successful, it shows that "The call was disconnected by the other party" at the end of the test.

FIGURE 20.18 Connectivity Success

To show the results of an unsuccessful test, enter the following command:

```
Test-UMConnectivity –IPGateway "SFO IP Gateway" –Phone 104
```

This command specifies a nonexistent extension. It shows that the requested operation failed (see Figure 20.19).

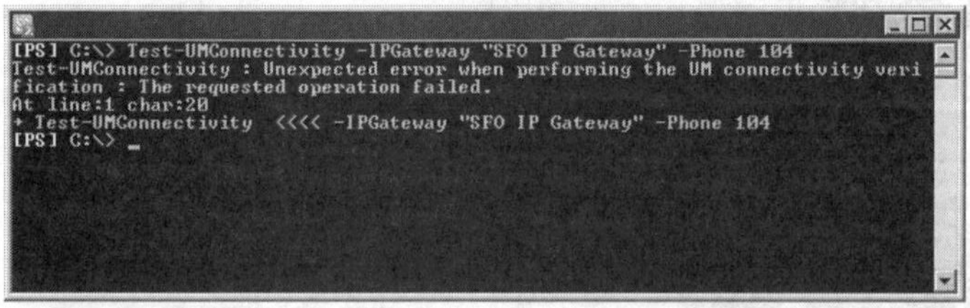

FIGURE 20.19 Connectivity Failure

Testing Unified Messaging Server with an Internal Phone

To test the Unified Messaging server from a phone, pick up a phone from within the dial plan and dial the pilot number.

For example, from the phone at extension 102, dial the pilot number 222. The auto attendant should pick up and prompt the caller.

Leave a message for a test user and then hang up.

Dial the pilot number for subscriber access (for example, extension 333) and check the message. Alternatively, check the message using Outlook or Outlook Web App.

Testing Unified Messaging Server with an External Phone

Use an outside line to call the company number that the PBX routes to the caller hunt group. Say the user's name. Press # and leave a message for the user.

To verify that the message was received, dial the external number for subscriber access and check the message. Alternatively, check the message using Outlook or Outlook Web App.

Data Storage in Unified Messaging

Unified messaging stores data in a variety of locations and formats. The different types of data include custom audio prompts, incoming calls, configuration, and setup.

It is important to understand where the data is stored, the relative importance of backing it up, and the method of restoring the data. Tables 20.4, 20.5, 20.6, and 20.7 list the relevant data storage information for each type of data.

TABLE 20.4   Custom Audio Prompt Data

Data Type	Custom audio files (.wav) for UM dial plans and UM auto attendants
	Custom audio files (.wav) for telephone user interface (TUI) and Outlook Voice Access
Storage	File system in \UnifiedMessaging\Prompts
Backup	File-level backup is only needed on the prompt publishing server
Restore	File-level restore is only needed on the prompt publishing server
Data Type	Custom audio files (.wav) for UM dial plans and UM auto attendants
	Custom audio files (.wav) for telephone user interface (TUI) and Outlook Voice Access
Storage	File system in \UnifiedMessaging\Prompts

TABLE 20.5   Incoming Call Data

Critical Data	Incoming calls: .eml and .wma files for each voicemail
Storage	File system \UnifiedMessaging\temp
Backup	None
Restore	None

20

TABLE 20.6   Server Configuration Data

Critical Data	Server configuration data, including all objects and settings
Storage	Active Directory configuration container
Backup	Backup method is domain controller replication or Active Directory backup
Restore	This data is reapplied to the server during a setup /m:recoverserver restore

TABLE 20.7   Setup Data

Critical Data	Limited information is stored in the Registry by Setup that is not essential to server restore
Storage	HKLM\SOFTWARE\Microsoft\Exchange
	HKLM\SYSTEM\currentcontrolset\Services
Backup	Backup method is System State backup or Registry export
Restore	Restore method is System State restore or Registry import

Exchange 2010 Outlook Web Application

Lync Server 2010 empowers the Exchange 2010 Outlook Web Application (OWA) with presence and IM chat. Although Outlook users are familiar with presence, this integration enables Outlook Web App users the same functionality. Of course, users must be both mailbox enabled on Exchange 2010 and Lync enabled for Lync Server 2010 to use this cool new feature.

Here is how to enable the Lync Server functionality in Exchange 2010 OWA:

1. First download the following files from Microsoft.com:

   CWAOWA Web Service Provider (previously known as the OCS 2007 R2 Web Service Provider), CWAOWASSPMAIN.msi

   Hotfix for Lync Web Service provider found in KB 981256

   Unified Communications Managed API (UCMA) hotfix found in KB 2282949

   Unified Communications Managed API (UCMA) update found in KB 968802. The filename is UCMARedist.msp.

2. On the Exchange 2010 CAS server, install the following packages in the order listed:

   vcredist_x64.exe

   dotnetfx35setup.exe

   ucmaredist.msp

   ucmaredistHottfix2282949.msp

   ucmaredistHotfix968802.mssp

CWAWebserviceProvider.msi

CWAWebServProviderHotfix981256.msi

3. Open the Exchange Management Shell and enter the **Get-ExchangeCertificate |fl Services,Thumbprint**.

4. Record the thumbprint of the certificate assigned to IIS.

5. Run the following command to configure the CAS server as a Lync presence endpoint:

```
Get-OWAVirtualDirectory | Set-OWAVirtualDirectory –InstantMessagingType OCS
–InstantMessagingEnabled:$true –InstantMessagingCertificateThumbprint <IIS
Certificate thumbprint> -InstantMessagingServerName <FQDN of Lync Pool/Server>
```

6. Run **IISReset** to complete the process on the Exchange side.

7. Open a console or remote desktop session to your Lync Front End Server.

8. Open the **Topology Builder** tool and download the current topology.

9. Expand the pool and find the **Trusted Application Servers** item.

10. Click **Create a new trusted application pool**.

11. Enter the FQDN of your Exchange CAS server, or the FQDN of the CAS array if applicable, and select **Single Computer Pool**.

12. Select the current pool and site as the **Next Hop Pool**. Note that if you only have one pool, only one option will be present here.

13. Click **Finish** and then publish the topology again.

14. Create a new trusted application and associate it with trusted application pool you just created.

15. Decide on a TCP port that is currently unused using **netstat –a**. We recommend 5059 because it is in close proximity to the standard Lync Server ports, but not in use by default.

16. Use the **New-CsTrustedApplication** cmdlet. The following is an example:

```
New-CsTrustedApplication –ApplicationID ExchangeOWA –TrustedApplicationFQDN
<FQDN of CAS server or CAS Array> -port <choose an unused port on the Lync
Server such as 5059>
```

17. Run the **Enable-CsTopology** to apply the configuration changes. Check the log files to ensure the process is successful.

With the configuration complete, log in to the Outlook Web Application to ensure the presence functionality is working.

SharePoint 2010 Integration

SharePoint 2010 is the platform for creating business solutions based on a web front end, an application layer, and a database back end. As such, SharePoint 2010 was designed to be integrated with other applications to extend their functionality and to make their content available through SharePoint 2010. Lync Server 2010 is no exception to the "better together" rule of Microsoft. That is to say, Lync Server 2010 offers several functions that integrate into SharePoint 2010 to enable data to be shared by each platform.

Simplifying Tasks through SharePoint 2010

An excellent example of using SharePoint 2010 to improve a task in Lync Server 2010 is in the area of managing photographs for contacts. Lync Server 2010 leverages the thumbnailPhoto attribute in Active Directory to store and access photos for contacts, yet it doesn't offer any interface to import photos into this attribute. This is where SharePoint 2010 comes in. Users of SharePoint 2010 can upload their photo to their "My Site" and the administrator can configure profile synchronization in SharePoint 2010 to synchronize the photo to the thumbnailPhoto attribute in Active Directory.

Configuring profile synchronization involves several steps, which can be found on the Microsoft website at http://technet.microsoft.com/en-us/library/ee721049.aspx.

The following five key phases, each with several substeps, describe the process at a high level:

Phase 1: Configuring the Farm
- ▶ Verify account permissions
- ▶ Create a Web application to host My Sites
- ▶ Create a managed path for My Sites
- ▶ Create a My Site Host site collection
- ▶ Create a User Profile service application
- ▶ Start the User Profile service

Phase 2: Start the User Profile Synchronization service
- ▶ Start the User Profile Synchronization service
- ▶ Remove unnecessary permissions
- ▶ Reset IIS

Phase 3: Configure connections and import data from directory services
- ▶ Create a synchronization connection to s directory service
- ▶ Define exclusion filters for a synchronization connection
- ▶ Map user profile properties
- ▶ Start profile synchronization

Phase 4: Configure connections and import data from business systems

▶ Create external content types

▶ Give the User Profile service application permission to use the external content type

▶ Configure a Business Data Connectivity synchronization connection

▶ Add or edit user profile properties

▶ Import data

Phase 5: Configure connections and export data to directory services

▶ Grant Replicate Directory Changes permissions on the domain

▶ Grant Replicate Directory Changes permissions on the Configuration container

▶ Grant Create Child Objects and Write permissions

> **NOTE**
>
> Although this might seem like a complicated process, once done there are several places where this configuration can be leveraged to place information into Active Directory.

Integrated Presence with SharePoint 2010

Like with most Microsoft applications, SharePoint 2010 is able to take advantage of presence information from Lync Server 2010. This is most noticeable when browsing documents in a SharePoint document store. When looking at documents, the name of the person who posted the document is displayed in SharePoint. With Lync integration present, users are able to see presence information associated with the name displayed. This can make it easy to send an IM with a question about a document to the person who posted it because users will immediately know whether that person is available. Much like the integration with Outlook, this enables users to send an IM, initiate a call, or even create a conference that enables them to collaborate on the document.

Skills Search with SharePoint 2010

One of the more impressive integrations between Lync Server 2010 and SharePoint 2010 is the capability to search skills, expertise, and organizational information from a SharePoint 2010 My Site. If users populate these fields in their My Site, Lync users will be able to search for users based on these fields. Imaging being able to search for a contact with "powershell skills" and getting back a list of corporate contacts who have flagged themselves are experts in PowerShell. No longer do users have to already know who to contact for specific questions. Users can build a dynamic searchable database of skills and organizational information that make it infinitely easier for users to find the right people with whom to collaborate.

To enable skills search, users must have SharePoint 2010 (or 2007) with maintained My Sites. SharePoint search center URL is provisioned through in-band settings and SharePoint must be published to the Internet. It also requires a full version of SharePoint; Windows SharePoint Services is not compatible with skills search.

20

First, a client policy must be configured and applied to configure the Lync clients to point to the correct SharePoint URLs. The policy sets both SPSearchInternalURL and SPSearchExternalURL.

Through the Lync Server Management Shell, issue the following two commands:

```
Set-CSClientPolicy –SPSearchInternalURL http://<server>/_vti_bin/search.asmx
Set-CSClientPolicy –SPSearchExternalURL http://<server>/_vti_bin/search.asmx
```

To also display the Search Center URL at the bottom of the search results, run the following two commands from the Lync Server Management Shell:

```
Set-CSClientPolicy –SPSearchCenterInternalURL
http://<server>/SearchCenter/Pages/PeopleResults.aspx
Set-CSClientPolicy –SPSearchCenterExternalURL
http://<server>/SearchCenter/Pages/PeopleResults.aspx
```

After the commandlets run, restart the Lync client for the policy to take effect. There are two ways to tell whether it is applied. When performing a search, there are two options: Name and Skill (see Figure 20.20).

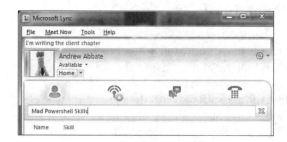

FIGURE 20.20 Searching by Name or Skill

The other way to tell whether is applied is to Control-right-click the Lync icon in the taskbar and select the Configuration Information table. There are two new entries, as shown in Figure 20.21.

| Skill Search URL | http://lync2010.companyabc.com/_vti_bin/search.asmx |
| SharePoint Search Center URL | http://lync2010.companyabc.com/SearchCenter/Pages/PeopleResults.aspx |

FIGURE 20.21 Viewing the Configuration Information

- ▶ Skill Search URL
- ▶ SharePoint Search Center URL

If results are found in this manner, there will be an option to View results in SharePoint at the bottom of the client. This links to the full SharePoint interface to display more detailed information about the results.

Best Practices

The following are best practices from this chapter:

- ▶ Enable transfers to the operator at least during business hours to reduce caller frustration.

- ▶ Be careful when implementing mailbox quotas because it can affect the capability of users to receive voicemail.

- ▶ Create a secondary auto attendant that is not speech-enabled and configure the primary auto attendant to fall back to it.

- ▶ Enable Outlook Web App with Lync presence and chat. It's amazing how many people use it.

- ▶ The voicemail preview function requires one CPU core per concurrent voicemail. Be sure to plan your infrastructure and number of UM servers accordingly.

- ▶ For most organizations, 10% of the total user population is a good estimate of the number of concurrent UM connections to plan for when building your architecture.

- ▶ Integrate the skills search function between Lync and SharePoint for greatly enhanced search features that go beyond names and allow for searching for a skill type.

- ▶ Although both SharePoint 2007 and SharePoint 2010 are supported, use SharePoint 2010 for the enhanced feature set it provides when integrating Lync with SharePoint.

- ▶ If you have SharePoint in your environment, integrate it with Active Directory through profile synchronization to make additional information available to Lync Server 2010.

Overview

When it comes to extensibility, there is so much that Lync
can do that at first it can be overwhelming to consider all
the possibilities. Imagine being able to enable your whole
enterprise for VoIP. Think of the savings you can get by
replacing all the telephony hardware with a software solution. The capability to have instant communications with
employees, vendors, and customers worldwide using a
single Lync client is powerful. Think of the travel expenses
you can save by using the same client instead of having
to gather your far-flung team together in one city for
meetings.

Think about your company help desk and your customer
support individuals being able to share desktops to resolve
problems. What could be done to decrease the time it takes
to deal with support issues? What would it do for employee
morale or for customer satisfaction? All this functionality is
available right out of the box.

But there comes a time when the "wow" starts to wear off
and you begin asking the what-if questions. What if Lync
could do this? Or what if it could do that? How can Lync
help me conduct my business better? After using Lync for a
while, you begin to see not limitations in Lync but rather
possibilities. You start seeing areas of your business that
could benefit from the features of Lync. You begin to see
how it can integrate and become an integral part of your
business processes.

At this point, you might ask how Lync can do the things you need. Microsoft has thought of you and provided application programming interfaces (APIs) that enable you to tap into the power and functionality of Lync. In the rest of this chapter, we look at these APIs and how you can leverage them to enhance your business.

Server APIs

The server-side API is UCMA 3.0, which is a managed code API for building communications solutions that run against Lync Server—though in some cases the applications run under the UCMA Runtime without Communications Server. This API is highly scalable, very extensible, and is made up of multiple modalities (for example, Core, UCMA Runtime, and so on).

It allows for application provisioning and management as well as handling publishing of endpoints and subscribing to events. It enables you to create endpoints for audio, video, and messaging and can even serve as a back-to-back user agent. So, what kind of applications can you create with UCMA 3.0?

It can be used in a help desk or contact center/call center environment for enabling supervisors to monitor IM chats or voice calls, whisper instructions to an agent, or enable the supervisor to take over the conversation if needed.

One popular use is for Interactive Voice Response (IVR) or personal virtual assistants. Think what it would be like if your customers started a voice call or an IM chat with an application that prompted the user for information and provided the caller with needed information or directed the call/chat to the correct agent to handle the customer's request. You can even enable your customers to do all this from your website without requiring the Lync client to be installed on its local PC.

Have you ever received automated phone calls around election time or had an automated call from your doctor's office or the kid's school? UCMA 3.0 can do these tasks, too. Imagine what it would do for your business if you called your customers telling them about a new product in your line.

There are two basic modalities that you can use to achieve all this functionality. The Core API enables you full access to Lync Server and lets you get down and dirty by wiring up your event handlers to respond and add functionality to audio, video, and IM streams.

My favorite modality, and the one that most people start out with, is the UCMA 3.0 Workflow API. The Workflow API abstracts a subset of the functionality found in the UCMA 3.0 SDK. You can call the UCMA 3.0 SDK code directly from your Workflow activities. It is also built on top of Microsoft Speech, which means it gives you text-to-speech (TTS), speech recognition, and speech synthesis capabilities. It leverages the communications features of the UCMA SDK, but does so using an easy-to-read visual development model.

Client APIs

On the client side, the Lync Server API enables you to add Lync client functionality and features to your own line-of-business applications. Imagine being able to view and display presence in your custom inventory control software. What if, while running your custom inventory application, you could open an IM chat window and chat with the supply room clerk to verify that you have enough inventories or start a chat with your counterpart at another store to ask a question about a product? And pass your current context to the remote party so that they will know exactly what you want to chat about?

The Communicator API enables you to do all these things. You can use it to automate the Lync client or build custom Lync clients (imagine what a round version of the Lync client would look like). You get to define what the UI of your application looks like. The API does this by reusing the Lync client connection, which means that you need the Lync client running on your client PC. Sometimes, as in the case of a lobby kiosk, you might not want the user to know that the Lync client is running. You can hide it so that your application is all the user sees.

API Objects and Methods

Let's look at some of these features starting with an overview of some of the objects and methods that make up the API.

The UIAutomation object starts conversations (IM and voice) as well as enabling you to join a conference or add contacts. The UIAutomation class enables you to start instant messaging or audio conversations, share the desktop, or transfer a file. In other words, it enables you to automate the Lync client and is used for common UI scenarios.

The UCClient object represents the instance of the Lync client belonging to the currently logged-in Lync user. This object gives you full access to the object model and lets you create your own UI in your applications. You have access to Lync contacts lists, contact presence, and contact card info.

PowerShell

For Lync, Microsoft has changed the way that Lync is administered. There is a new browser-based management interface called the Lync Server Control Panel (LCSP) that you can use for all your administration tasks. If you are an administrator type that prefers a command line–type interface, there is something for you, too. Microsoft has also included the Lync Server Management Shell. Both these administration tools have one big thing in common: They both run on PowerShell. This means that anything you can do from the browser-based LSCP, you can do from the command prompt.

There are more than 500 new Lync PowerShell cmdlets to enable users for Lync, set up SIP domains, set up routing, and a host of other tasks.

TIP

Although it might seem daunting to figure out which Lync cmdlet to use, it isn't that difficult. Microsoft has created an excellent blog at http://blogs.technet.com/b/csps/ to introduce you to Lync PowerShell programming. It even has a blog post on UI mapping that shows the relationship between the LSCP and the Lync Management Shell so that you know which Lync cmdlet to use and how the cmdlet parameters relate to the fields you see in the browser. We won't try to duplicate that here, but we show how you can get help to determine which cmdlet you need.

Let's start with the basics. To get started, go to the Windows Start menu, expand the **Microsoft Lync Server 2010** menu item, and then click **Lync Server management Shell**. This starts a PowerShell session and loads the Lync Server module.

Now that you have the management shell running, let's make the assumption that you want to do something with a user such as enable a user for Lync. Well, how do you go about finding which cmdlet to use? You can use the **Get-Command** to get a list of Lync-related commands by typing the following command:

```
Get-Command *CS* ¦ More
```

This command gives some extraneous information, but it includes all the Lync cmdlets and you will see that they follow the normal PowerShell methodology of verb-noun. Quickly skimming through the list, notice some cmdlets with CsUser in the name columns so that you can modify your command to look for just the user-related cmdlets. Figure 21.1 shows the results of running the command looking for CsUser-related cmdlets.

FIGURE 21.1   Results of Running Get-Command *CS*

Notice that we now have a list of the Lync cmdlets that deal with Lync users, and you can quickly determine that **Enable-CsUser** is probably the one that you need. But, to be sure, you can use the **Get-Help** to check that assumption. Figure 21.2 shows the results of that command.

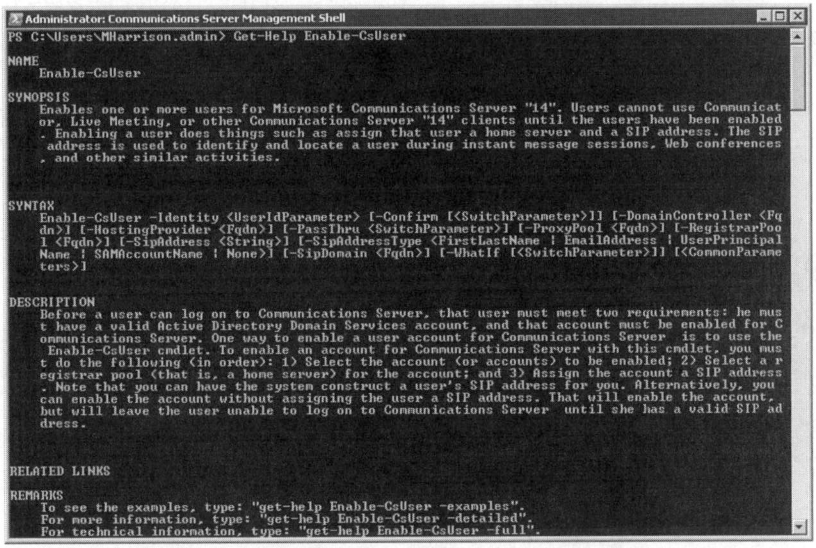

```
Administrator: Communications Server Management Shell
PS C:\Users\MHarrison.admin> Get-Help Enable-CsUser

NAME
    Enable-CsUser

SYNOPSIS
    Enables one or more users for Microsoft Communications Server "14". Users cannot use Communicat
    or, Live Meeting, or other Communications Server "14" clients until the users have been enabled
    . Enabling a user does things such as assign that user a home server and a SIP address. The SIP
    address is used to identify and locate a user during instant message sessions, Web conferences
    , and other similar activities.

SYNTAX
    Enable-CsUser -Identity <UserIdParameter> [-Confirm [<SwitchParameter>]] [-DomainController <Fq
    dn>] [-HostingProvider <Fqdn>] [-PassThru [<SwitchParameter>]] [-ProxyPool <Fqdn>] [-RegistrarPoo
    l <Fqdn>] [-SipAddress <String>] [-SipAddressType <FirstLastName | EmailAddress | UserPrincipal
    Name | SAMAccountName | None>] [-SipDomain <Fqdn>] [-WhatIf [<SwitchParameter>]] [<CommonParame
    ters>]

DESCRIPTION
    Before a user can log on to Communications Server, that user must meet two requirements: he mus
    t have a valid Active Directory Domain Services account, and that account must be enabled for C
    ommunications Server. One way to enable a user account for Communications Server  is to use the
    Enable-CsUser cmdlet. To enable an account for Communications Server with this cmdlet, you mus
    t do the following (in order): 1) Select the account (or accounts) to be enabled; 2) Select a r
    egistrar pool (that is, a home server) for the account; and 3) Assign the account a SIP address
    . Note that you can have the system construct a user's SIP address for you. Alternatively, you
    can enable the account without assigning the user a SIP address. That will enable the account,
    but will leave the user unable to log on to Communications Server  until she has a valid SIP ad
    dress.

RELATED LINKS

REMARKS
    To see the examples, type: "get-help Enable-CsUser -examples".
    For more information, type: "get-help Enable-CsUser -detailed".
    For technical information, type: "get-help Enable-CsUser -full".
```

FIGURE 21.2   Using the Get-Help Command

We now have all the information we need to enable a user for Lync. The following command enables the user for Lync:

```
Enable-CsUser –Identity "alex@companyabc.com" –RegistrarPool
"Lyncfe2.companyabc.com" –SipAddress "sip:alex@companyabc.com"
```

As you can see, you need to tell the cmdlet what user to enable, which pool to register the user with, and what the SIP address of the user will be. That is all there is to it. If you were to look at the users in the Lync Server Control Panel, you would see that the user is now enabled for Lync.

TIP

There are more steps, such as enabling the user for enterprise voice (Set-CsUser) and setting up the user for voicemail (Set-CsUser again), but you get the idea. As mentioned previously, the Lync PowerShell blog on Microsoft TechNet is an excellent start for learning more about administering Lync using the PowerShell command-line interface.

Installing UCMA 3.0

After downloading the UCMA 3.0 SDK from Microsoft, you should end up with a file called UcmaSdkSetup.exe. When you double-click the application, you get a screen similar to Figure 21.3. Simply follow the prompts.

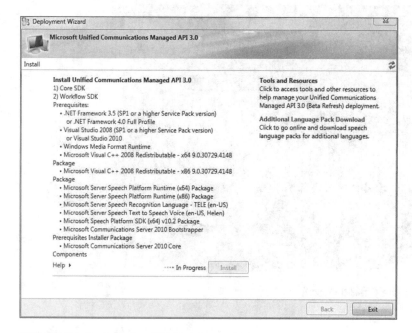

FIGURE 21.3   Installing UCMA 3.0

The installation creates a UCMA 3.0 directory in your Program Files directory such as what is shown in Figure 21.4. Note the subdirectories for the different APIs along with the runtime and documentation. If you look closely, you can also see a couple of Sample Applications directories.

Walkthrough of the UCMA 3.0 Components

After the UCMA SDK is installed, look at the UCMA components in Visual Studio 2010. After opening VS 2010, clicking **File**, **New**, **Project** gives you the New Project Wizard, as shown in Figure 21.5. To start a UCMA 3.0 project, expand the **Visual C#** tree and select **Communications Workflow**. At first you might be surprised to find that there are no templates showing under Communications Workflow. If nothing is shown, select **.NET Framework 3.5** in the drop-down at the top of the wizard.

NOTE

Currently, UCMA 3.0 does not support .NET Framework 4.0.

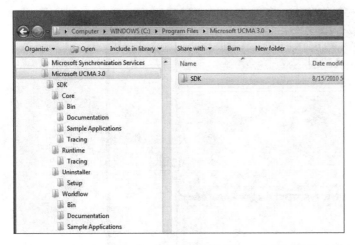

FIGURE 21.4   UCMA Installation Location

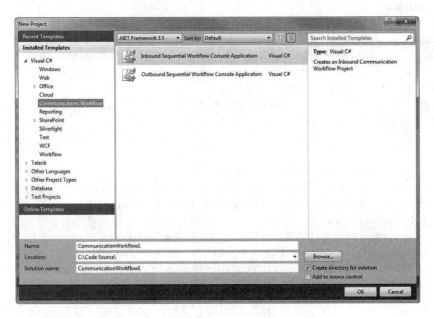

FIGURE 21.5   New Project Wizard

Next, select the **Inbound Sequential Workflow Console Application**. In the bottom half of the wizard, name your application and select a location for the application. Click **OK** and Visual Studio asks you to select a language for your project. The language options available depend on what languages you have installed on your computer. After selecting the correct language for your project, Visual Studio creates your application and presents you with a screen that looks like the one shown in Figure 21.6.

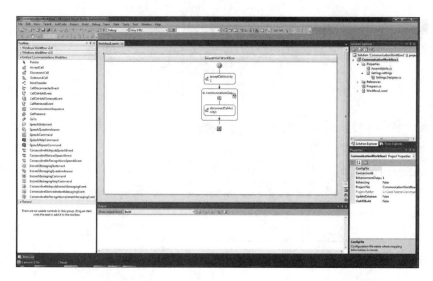

FIGURE 21.6   Workflow Design

NOTE

At first glance, the Visual Studio interface looks similar to any other project that you have created in the past. In a typical Visual Studio layout, notice your workflow in the center along with the Solution Explorer showing the files in your application. You also see the toolbox showing the various components of the UCMA Workflow.

First, let's look at the default Workflow. Notice that the first component is an acceptCallActivity. This component does exactly what its name implies: It accepts a call. But you need to be aware that in the case of a UCMA Workflow application the call can be either a voice call or an IM request. Yes, this component can handle both and that means you can design your application so that it can handle both types of calls by branching in your code based on the call type. The next component is a communications SequenceActivity. This component executes a series of activities in order and is necessary to control the call.

In the Solution Explorer, notice that the project consists of a WPF piece that controls the markup for your Workflow (along with the accompanying C# code behind) as well as a Program.cs file. The logic part of your application is split between these two files, with the Program.cs file running when your application starts. It handles the setting up of the endpoints for the call as well as the trust relationship (using certificates) between the application and the Lync machine. It is also responsible for the initialization of the Workflow and setting up the collaboration with Lync. It is the setting up of the endpoints that enable Lync to direct calls to your application (for example, the endpoint).

After the console application runs and the endpoints are established, the application simply waits for calls to get directed to it. When the application receives a call, it fires up the Workflow piece of your application, which is where your call flow resides. It is this part of the application that interacts with the caller receiving input from the caller and providing feedback to the caller. Figure 21.7 shows a visual description of the Workflow.

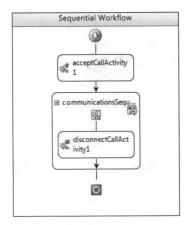

FIGURE 21.7   Workflow Detail

Toolbox Components

Now let's look at the components on the Toolbox that you use in the course of your application development. First, there are a couple of warnings. On your Toolbox, you might see tabs for Windows Workflow 3.5 or even a Windows Workflow 3.0 tab.

> **CAUTION**
>
> Avoid using most of these components because they will not work properly with the UCMA components. The UCMA components are built on top of and extend the older Windows Workflow v3.0 and v3.5 components, and can handle the call control logic to keep your application endpoint from dropping the call.

However, there are a few exceptions. You can (and will) use the Windows Workflow v3.0 Code and IfElse activities to add branching logic and the capability to add code blocks your workflow. The IfElse activity gives you the capability to make decisions and send your calls down different logic branches. When the Code activity is dropped into your application, you can attach code behind to do such things as query a database and handle other programming tasks in your application.

A quick look at the Toolbox, which is shown in Figure 21.8, shows that the activities are grouped logically in three or four groups.

FIGURE 21.8   Toolbox

The first group of activities handles call control. In this group, you find activities for accepting a call (AcceptCall), transferring a call (BlindTransfer), making outbound calls (OutboundCall), and hanging up a call (DisconnectCall). This group of activities enables you to control how your application handles a call. For example, after accepting a call, you might want to prompt the user with a menu of phone extensions that he can select to get information about your business or products. After selecting from the menu prompt, send the call to the correct department using the blindTransferActivity.

You also see activities for handling call events such as CallDisconnectEvent or the CallOnHoldEvent. This group of activities enables you to control how your application responds to typical events that occur in a phone call or IM, such as the caller hanging up or closing the IM chat window. You can also use these activities to log the caller information or update a SQL database with the results of the call.

Next you see the CommunicationsSequence activity, which is the basic container in which you put all the other activities that make up the application call flow. This activity knows and understands the concept of a call and is necessary to keep the call alive.

Following that you see a GetPresence activity along with a Goto activity. The former enables you to get the presence status of a user and comes in handy for deciding how to deal with a caller. For example, the party you want to transfer the call to might have her presence showing as Busy, so you can send the caller to the target's voicemail rather than opening an IM chat with the caller.

The gotoActivity gives you an easy way to divert your call flow to some other place in your Workflow logic. Although you can almost always use nested IfElse activities to control your logic, this can cause your Workflow to get quite large and hard to understand. Use of the gotoActivity simplifies your Workflow, making it easier to read and maintain.

The next two groups are similar in functionality. The first group handles voice calls and the second group duplicates the same functionality for IM chats. With the right branching logic, you can have your application handle both.

> **NOTE**
>
> We discuss only the speech-related activities because the Instant Message activities are the same.

Notice two activities that interact with the user. The first SpeechStatement enables you to play a message to the caller. Think of this as a greeting or providing instructions. The application plays its prompt and simply moves on without expecting user input.

If you want to ask the caller something or give the caller choices, use the SpeechQuestionAnswer activity. This activity does exactly what its name implies: It asks the caller a question and receives the caller's answer. You can use this activity to find information, such as what type of pizza the caller wants or the caller's account number. After you drop this control into your Workflow, set the prompt (your question) and then attach a grammar that controls the acceptable inputs nine answers. *Grammars* are XML files that list the allowed user input and assign the values the speech recognition engine will return to your application. For example, if you ask the caller what type of pizza she wants, your grammar would have choices, such as "cheese," "pepperoni," "meat lovers," or "deluxe."

The different command activities, such as SpeechHelpCommand and SpeechRepeatCommand, are activities that handle global commands and are normally scoped to the whole Workflow. However, when you nest CommunicationsSequence activities, they can be scoped to individual CommunicationsSequence activities to change the behavior for the container. They enable the user to say "Help" or "Repeat," and you can use the SpeechCommand activity to create your own command such as one that responds to the user, saying "Operator."

The command activities are active anytime there is speech recognition taking place. For example, if you ask the user what type of pizza he wants to order and during recognition the caller says, "Operator," your application can respond accordingly and direct the caller to a live person. Using commands like this keeps you from needing to add "Help," "Repeat," or "Operator" to all your grammars.

Error Condition Components

The next set of components handle error conditions such as the user remaining silent (ConsecutiveSilencesSpeechEvent) or saying something that isn't valid for the question asked and isn't in the grammar—for example, ConsecutiveNoRecognitionsSpeechEvent. The default logic for a SpeechQuestionAnswer activity is to simply loop and repeat the question, but these activities enable you to have more control. For example, you might determine that after three wrong replies that you want to send the caller to an operator. You can do this by using a ConsecutiveNoRecognitionsSpeechEvent activity and setting its MaximumNoRecognitions property to three. After the user has three wrong replies, ConsecutiveNoRecognitionsSpeechEvent fires and you can the transfer the call to the operator.

The ConsecutiveNoInputsSpeechEvent is a special case. It works the same as the other two Event handlers, but it doesn't matter whether the events were caused by silence or no recognition. After you reach the value of its MaximumNoInputs, it fires. Note that it does so on any combination of silence or no recognition events. It is kind of a catch all and you will probably find yourself using it in most cases.

TIP

If you try to drop one of the event-handling components into your Workflow, you will find it cannot be done. To use the event handlers, right-click the communincationsSequence Activity (see Figure 21.9) and then click View CommunicationsEvents. This also applies to speech commands and fault handlers.

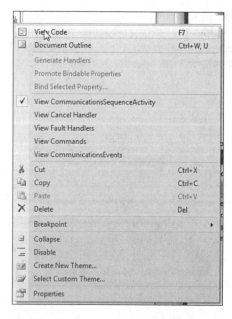

FIGURE 21.9   Event Handlers

After completing these steps, your designer looks something like the one shown in Figure 21.10. Now, simply drag and drop the appropriate Speech event into the box between the blue arrows.

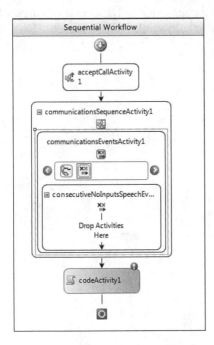

FIGURE 21.10   Designer Workflow

Next, set the properties for the event such as the name and MaximumNoInputs properties. Then drag and drop components into the canvas to control your call flow. For example, you might want to add a SpeechStatement to tell the user to stay on the line for an operator and drop a BlindTransfer activity into the Workflow to transfer the caller.

Summary

In this chapter, we looked at how Lync can be enhanced using the various APIs from Microsoft. We saw examples of how UCMA 3.0 and the Workflow APIs can be used server side to automate processes or to provide IVR type applications that can respond to voice calls of instant message type inquiries from your customers. We also saw how to extend the Lync client to add context-sensitive content and how to add Lync client functionality to your own applications.

So, the fact that the Wow Factor for Lync has worn off is not a bad thing. It is replaced by an infinite Wow Factor wrapped around what you can do with the programming tools that Microsoft provides. The Wow Factor never goes away. It just keeps changing and growing.

The next group of components is the Instant Messaging components. They are duplicates of the Speech components we just covered, and you use them similar to the Speech components.

PART VIII
Clients

IN THIS PART

Microsoft Communicator Client for Macintosh

Although Lync Server 2010 is an impressive application by itself, most users will experience Lync Server 2010 only through one of its many clients. Microsoft has gone out of its way to provide clients for most of the larger platforms. Microsoft Communicator is the Mac-based client that enables users to access the client-side functionality of Lync Server 2010. This includes the following functions:

▸ Instant messaging

▸ Presence

▸ PC-to-PC calls

▸ Enterprise Voice functions

▸ Video conferencing

▸ Web conferencing

▸ Desktop and sharing

As such, this chapter covers the more commonly used functions of the Microsoft Communicator client and should act as the basis of end-user training that most administrators want to provide to their user community to ensure successful adoption of Lync Server 2010.

One feature that most users appreciate when using the Microsoft Communicator client for Macintosh is that Microsoft has placed all the functionality into a single client. In older versions of Office Communications Server (OCS), there were multiple clients for performing IM, web conferences, group chat, or acting as a software-based phone. Microsoft Communicator combines all these features into a single client to make it even more seamless for users to participate in multiple types of collaborative communications.

It's important to point out that the Microsoft Communicator client isn't the same as the Microsoft Messenger client that installs as part of Office 2011. Microsoft Messenger can't connect to Lync and is meant for the pubic IM services provided by Microsoft. Microsoft Communicator is an add-on to Office 2011 that allows for connectivity to Lync 2010 and offers the additional integration into Office 2011 applications.

Installing the Client

Although the Microsoft Communicator client for Macintosh integrates into the Office 2011 suite, it is actually a separate install. Given that most clients want to integrate the functions, we start with the steps for installing Office 2011 itself and then the Communicator client. To install Office 2011, perform the following steps:

1. Download the Microsoft Office 2011 installer. This is likely in the form of a .DMG file.

2. Double-click the **.DMG** file.

3. Double-click the **Office Installer** icon as shown in Figure 22.1.

FIGURE 22.1   Running the Office Installer

4. The installer offers to guide you through the install. Click **Continue**.

5. Read the licensing agreement and click **Continue**.

6. Click **Agree** to accept the license agreement.

7. The installer tells you which hard drive will be used for the installation. Click **Change Install Location** if you want to change installation locations or click **Install** to accept the recommended location.

8. When prompted, enter your password to authorize the installation. Click **OK**.

9. The installation prepares and a scrolling candy cane appears. Packages are validated and the installation commences.

10. When the installation completes successfully, click **Close**.

After the installation completes, the user is prompted to choose the licensing method: Either purchase a key online, enter a product key, or select a 30-day trial. Pick the option that is appropriate for your environment.

To install the Microsoft Communicator client, perform the following steps:

1. Download the Microsoft Communicator for Mac installer.

2. Double-click the **.DMG** file.

3. Double-click the **Communicator Installer** icon, as shown in Figure 22.2.

FIGURE 22.2   Running the Communicator Installer

4. The installer offers to guide you through the install. Click **Continue**.

5. Read the licensing agreement and click **Continue**.

6. Click **Agree** to accept the license agreement.

7. The installer tells you which hard drive will be used for the installation. Click **Change Install Location** if you want to change installation locations or click **Install** to accept the recommended location.

8. When prompted, enter your password to authorize the installation. Click **OK**.

9. The installation prepares and a scrolling candy cane appears. Packages are validated and the installation commences.

10. When the installation complete successfully, click **Close**.

There is now a big blue C icon in the chooser. Click it to launch Communicator.

When the Microsoft Communicator client launches, you will be asked to once again accept the license agreement. Click **Accept**. Communicator offers to make itself the default application for the following functions:

▶ Presence

▶ Telephone calls

▶ Conferences

For each offer, check the box marked **Do not show this message again**, and click **Use Communicator**.

After the offers process, Communicator launches. At the prompt, click **Sign In** and you are prompted to enter your Kerberos identity. Enter your logon name for Active Directory and click **Continue**. If this fails to find a Kerberos realm, click **Cancel** and you will instead be asked for the following information:

▶ E-mail address

▶ User ID

▶ Password

Although the wording is for E-mail address, if you are using a SIP address that doesn't match your e-mail address, enter the SIP address instead.

If the DNS records are configured correctly to support Lync Server 2010, connect at this point to see the screen shown in Figure 22.3.

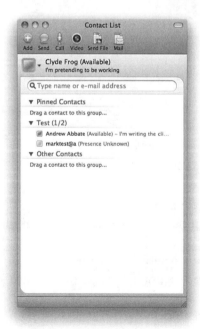

FIGURE 22.3   Connecting to Lync Server 2010

If the necessary SRV records are not present, the Communicator client has options to manually configure the connection; however, using the correct SRV records is the preferred method and it makes the client more transparent to the end user. To create the record in DNS, perform the steps:

1. From a Windows DNS server, click **Start**, **Administrative Tools**, **DNS**.
2. Expand the DNS server and expand **Forward Lookup Zones**.
3. In the zone that holds Lync Server 2010, right-click the zone and select **Other New Records**.
4. Choose a resource record type of SRV (Service Location) and click **Create Record**.
5. For Service, enter **_sipinternaltls**.
6. For Protocol, enter **_tcp**.
7. For Port Number, enter **5061**.
8. For Host offering this service, enter the FQDN of the Lync Server 2010 Front End pool.
9. Leave Priority and Weight at the default values of 0 and click **OK**.

After the record propagates through DNS, Communicator clients should be able to connect correctly.

Dealing with Certificates

Unlike PCs, Macintoshes don't automatically trust certificate authorities that are tied to Active Directory. If you have deployed Lync Server with internally generated certificates, they will need to import them into a Keychain on the Macintosh. This is a relatively simple process and can be completed with the following steps:

1. Open **Finder**.
2. Expand **Applications** and then **Utilities**.
3. Drag the **Root Certificate Authority** certificate to **Keychain**.
4. Select the **System Keychain** and click **Add**.
5. When prompted, type a name and password with local administrator rights and click **OK**.

Features and Improvements

The new Communicator for Mac 2011 replaces the previous Messenger for Mac 7 client. Although there is a Messenger for Mac 8, it no longer connects to a corporate communications system such as Lync Server 2010. Messenger 8 is used only for external IM services. Communicator improves on many previous features and introduces some new ones as well, as shown in Table 22.1.

TABLE 22.1   Improvements in Communicator for Mac 2011

Feature	Messenger 7	Communicator
Outbound/inbound audio calls from PSTN callers	Not Available	Available
Quick access to conferences in Communicator for Mac 2011 by clicking conf: URL in a meeting request	Not Available	Available
Calendar-based presence status, such as In a Meeting	Not Available	Available
Presence status integrated with Office for Mac 2011	Partial	Available
Access to the Conversation History from the conversation window	Partial	Available
Instant messaging (IM)	Available	Available
Basic presence	Available	Available
Computer-to-computer audio calls with Communicator for Mac 2011 and Office Communicator for Windows users	Available	Available
Computer-to-computer video calls with Communicator for Mac 2011 and Office Communicator for Windows users	Available	Available
Access to external federated users	Available	Available
Public IM connectivity	Available	Available
File transfer with Communicator for Mac 2011 clients	Available	Available
Global Address List (GAL) search	Available	Available
Integration for presence states between Communicator for Mac 2011 and Office Communicator for Windows	Available	Available

Getting Around in the Client

Now that the client is installed and attached to the Lync 2010 Server, it's time to become familiar with the client. On the initial screen, you can see the current status and presence information. Presence status can be altered by clicking the downward-facing arrow next to the large presence jellybean. Status can be altered by clicking the text and retyping a new status. Below this area, you can see contacts, which can be organized. In the top of the client, you find the following six buttons:

▶ Add

▶ Send

▶ Call

▶ Video

- ▶ Send file

- ▶ Mail

These buttons and their functions are explained in the following sections.

Configuring Basic Options

In the Communicator client, many options can be configured. For administrators not familiar with Macintosh operating systems, options that are normally found in the client interface on a PC are typically moved to the menus at the top of the screen. Although there is a main GUI that looks like the PC client, there are also context-based menus that appear at the top of the screen depending on which application is currently the focus. In the case of Communicator, these options across the top of the application include the following:

- ▶ Communicator

- ▶ File

- ▶ Edit

- ▶ View

- ▶ Network

- ▶ Contact

- ▶ Window

- ▶ Help

Clicking Communicator at the top of the menu offers several other options, including a link to information about the specific version of Communicator, an option to hide Communicator, an option to quit Communicator, and most importantly the capability to modify application preferences.

Clicking Preferences within the Communicator menu offers up the following six icons:

- ▶ **Appearance**—This area is where the user can alter IM font choices.

- ▶ **General**—This area enables you to control the status behavior, to define the Presence Service, Communications Service for Telephone, and Conference, and to define where received files will go. You can also enable troubleshooting logging from here.

- ▶ **Alerts**—This area is where users can enable or disable alerts for various actions that will occur within the Communicator client.

- ▶ **Account**—From this area, you can change your logon information, manually configure the Lync 2010 Server, and choose to enable or disable integration with Exchange.

- ▶ **History**—This area is where you can save conversations and alter the behavior of when the system will prompt you to save a conversation.

▶ **Privacy**—This area is where you can choose to block or allow various contacts. You can also enable a notification when another user adds you as a contact through these menu options. You can even get a consolidated view of who added you as a contact.

Clicking File at the top of the menu gives access to the capability to save contact lists or to import contacts from a saved list.

Clicking Edit gives access to the usual copy, cut, and paste but also enables you to access special characters and to set spelling options.

Clicking View enables you to quickly move to the Contact List or to the Conversation History. You can also modify the Toolbar from here and enable or disable Search.

Clicking Network enables you to sign out, change the status, and view recent alerts.

Clicking Contact gives the following options:

▶ Sort Contacts by:

▶ Group Offline Contacts Together

▶ Send Instant Message

▶ Call a Contact

▶ Start a Video Call

▶ Send File

▶ Send Mail

▶ Block

▶ Add a Contact

▶ Delete a Contact

▶ View Profile

▶ Add Group

▶ Delete Group

▶ Rename Group

▶ Privacy

Clicking Window gives you the option to minimize, zoom, or bring the Communicator window to the forefront.

Clicking Help gives quick access to Search and offers links ranging from checking for updates to visiting the product website.

Managing Contacts

Most people have grown accustomed to the behaviors in Outlook where you can quickly look up a user in the contacts or by starting to type the person's name. Microsoft

Communicator client follows this model by organizing contacts by groups and by allowing you to quickly search for contacts by typing the person's name.

For example, on the search line (indicated by a magnifying glass), if you type a name, the client will suggest names based on the contacts. From here, click and drag the contact to add the contact to a contact group. When this occurs, the person you added will receive a notification that you added him and have the option to add you as well. Once added, the contacts appear in the group you selected and you are able to see the presence information at any time.

After a contact is added, he can be moved from one contact group to another by clicking and dragging the contact from one group to another. By holding the mouse over the name of the contact, you can see the notes he has set in his client as well as his picture, as shown in Figure 22.4.

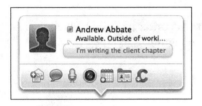

FIGURE 22.4   Viewing Contact Information

Managing Groups

The Microsoft Communicator client enables users to organize their contacts by placing them inside groups. By default, the group is Other Contacts.

On the Contact menu at the top of the screen, you can click Add a Group. When this is clicked, a new group called New Group displays. This can be renamed to anything of the user's choosing.

These groups show a status of how many contacts there are in that group and how many are currently online. For example, you might see Other Contacts (4/5) to indicate that four of the five contacts in that group are online. You can expand the group by clicking the hollow triangle to the left of the name to populate the full list of contacts.

From the Contact menu, you can also choose to automatically group offline contacts together. This results in the creation of a group called Not Online. Contacts automatically move to this container when they are offline. Contacts can be dragged back and forth between groups, but can exist in only one group at a time. Groups can be deleted or renamed with the Contacts menu functions.

A convenient use of groups is to organize members of a project or department. By right-clicking the group name, you can choose to launch a conference call that will invite all members of that group. Similar functionality can be achieved by selecting multiple contacts by control-clicking them and then right-clicking to choose Start a Conference Call. This call can use Lync's PC-to-PC call features or through the phone system.

IM Features

For most environments, the most commonly used feature in the Microsoft Communicator client is Instant Messaging. This function enables users to stop cluttering mailboxes with "where do you want to go for lunch?"-type messages and enables users to limit their messages to only people who are likely to respond quickly. This also is where accurate presence information comes in handy.

Starting an IM conversation is as simple as double-clicking a contact. Doing so launches the IM window, which defaults to the IM tab, as shown in Figure 22.5.

FIGURE 22.5   Launching the IM Interface

The IM client works like any other IM client. You can see the status information for the person to which you are communicating, and there are two areas in the window: one to type in and one to display the conversation. Users have access to the usual features such as altering the font, color, and size of the text as well as a menu of emoticons.

22

CAUTION

Remember that you can access emoticons with the usual combinations of characters. Although this is useful, be aware that sometimes messages you send will inadvertently turn into emoticons. This is especially common when using an IM client to troubleshoot programming code with a coworker.

Archiving IM Conversations

IM conversations can be archived in two ways. One way is for an administrator to implement an archiving policy on an archiving server.

To review the coverage on implementing an archiving policy, review this information in Chapter 8, "Microsoft Lync Server 2010 Archiving."

The other way to archive messages is to choose the option to save a conversation when closing the IM window. When it's closed, there will be a pop-up request offering to save the conversation. Clicking Save saves conversations that can later be viewed through the Conversation History. This is a useful way to access old conversations, and this folder's contents are indexed for easy searches.

NOTE

Unlike most IM systems, if you try to send an IM to a user that is offline, it won't queue up and wait for his or her next logon. You simply receive a message that "This person is not online right now. Do you want to send him or her mail?" with a yes or no option.

The IM interface enables one person to send a file to the other participant of the IM conversation. In the main set of icons is an option to Send File. Clicking this icon opens a file-browsing session to enable the user to identify a file to send to the other user. Files can be sent only one at a time because trying to control-click multiple files results in simply changing the file, not adding them to a list. Click Open after the file is selected. The person set to receive the file receives a notification and gets the option to Accept, Save As, or Decline the file. Accepting the file triggers a warning window to warn the user that the file might contain harmful malware and to accept files only from known sources. Once accepted, it downloads and a link appears to access the file. The sender of the file receives a notification that the transfer was successful.

Audio/Video Calls and Conferencing

One of the more interesting features in the Microsoft Communicator Client is the capability to participate in audio or video conferences with other users of the Lync Server 2010 environment. Prior to the first participation in either an audio or video conference, users should configure their audio and video devices as described in the "Configuring Basic Options" section of "Getting Around in the Client" at the beginning of this chapter. After these devices are configured, a user is ready to start the first conference.

For purposes of this section, view a call and a conference as essentially the same event with the only difference being the number of parties involved. If there are two parties involved, it's a call. If there are more than two parties involved, it's a conference. Generally the steps are identical for initiating and managing both. In cases where the steps vary, they will be called out as such.

Making an Audio Call

Initiating an audio call is as simple as clicking Call and then choosing a contact. After this is done, the contact receives a pop-up and an audio notification and has the option to answer, decline, or redirect. Answer and decline are obvious in what they do. Redirect gives the option to reply through IM or to set one's status to Do Not Disturb. Accepting the call updates both users' status to In a call.

When the call connects, a new window appears that looks similar to the IM window. In fact, it is the same window, but with some additional buttons and status items, as shown in Figure 22.6.

FIGURE 22.6   The Call Window

The call window offers several buttons, including the following:

▶ Hang Up

▶ Put call on hold

▶ Mute microphone

▶ Adjust volume or mute speakers

▶ Network Quality

▶ Time in the call

Muting the microphone alters the icon on the client that muted the microphone. No indication of this action is given to other participants of the call or conference. Sliding the blue ball on the speaker range raises or lowers the speaker volume. The hold button places the call on hold, which notifies other participants on the call. Clicking resume returns the call to an active status. Both "on hold" and the call itself display the amount of time the call has been at a particular status.

One of the other icons visible in the window is a Network Connectivity status. This indicates the quality of the network connection and is useful in troubleshooting issues with voice quality on a call. At the upper-left corner of the window is an icon of a red phone that is used to end the call.

Although calls are archived into the Conversation History folder on the local system, they contain only IM conversations from the Macintosh client. Call information is not recorded nor stored here.

NOTE

As one might guess based on the fact that the IM interface and call interface are merely different views within the same window, an IM conversation can be escalated to an audio call by simply clicking Call from the existing IM window.

Making a Video Call

Initiating a video call is as simple as clicking Video and then picking a contact. Much as with the audio call, the recipient has the option to accept, decline, or redirect. Redirect gives the option to reply with an IM or to mark the recipient as Do Not Disturb.

When the call is accepted, the usual client window opens in the Video view. The recipient initially sees the caller but the caller won't see the recipient until she clicks Start My Video in the window. By default, each participant in a two-way call sees herself in a picture-in-picture window inside the main video window. The picture-in-picture can be moved anywhere within the video window and will not block access to the following buttons. The picture-in-picture, also called the *preview*, can be modified by right-clicking it. This gives the options to hide or resize the preview.

Inside the video window are several buttons, including the following:

▶ End video call

▶ Put video call on hold

▶ Enter full screen

▶ Mute microphone

▶ Adjust volume or mute speakers

▶ Network Quality

▶ Time in the call

Enter full screen expands the video windows to encompass the entire screen. The option at the upper-right corner becomes Exit full screen.

Clicking End video call ends the call and downgrades to a simple IM conversation.

At the default window sizes, video conferences across a LAN connection are quite good. Factors such as latency and bandwidth might affect video conferencing across a WAN connection.

TIP

If you expect widespread adoption of video conferencing and calls in your environment, don't skimp on the video cameras. Modern webcams can have nice lenses and modern processors can easily keep up with the loads of high definition video conferencing.

Web Conferencing

Probably the biggest driving force behind companies implementing Lync Server 2010 is replacing outsourced web conferencing services. Many companies spend tens of thousands of dollars a month on services such as Webex or GoToMeeting. Although there might be situations where a company running Lync Server 2010 needs to create a conference so large that its infrastructure isn't sufficient, the other 95% of the time it can use a platform it owns rather than paying an external company for the services. In many environments, OCS 2007 R2 implementations paid for themselves in 6 to 12 months for this reason. Lync Server 2010 looks to offer similar return on investment for companies in need of web conferencing.

Web conferences are not supported on the Macintosh Communicator client. There is no option to create one and trying to invite a contact using the Macintosh Communicator client through a PC client results in a notification that "Sharing is not supported with this contact." The only way to get into a web conference from a Macintosh is from the Silverlight client.

CAUTION

Be aware that having multiple participants of the same conference in the same room can result in a fair amount of feedback through the clients. The client will actually detect this and recommend that one or more participants mute the microphone. In a video conference with more than two participants, the view switches to whoever is the active speaker.

Joining a Conference

Most invitations to a web conference arrive through e-mail. This is to say that in most corporate environments, invites to web conferences are part of an Exchange meeting invite. It appears as a web link inside the meeting invite, as shown in Figure 22.7.

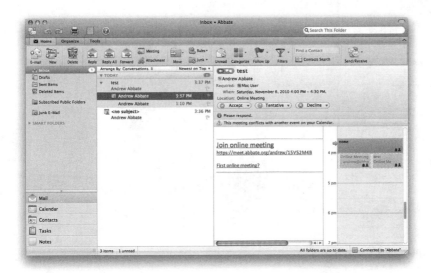

FIGURE 22.7   Viewing a Meeting URL

Clicking the web link results in the default web browser launching. If pop-up blockers are turned on, the Lync Server warns the user. He can opt to either disable the pop-up blocker for this site and refresh or he can click a link to "Join with pop-up blocker turned on" although that might interfere with screen sharing. It is recommended to disable the pop-up blocker and refresh the connection.

> **NOTE**
>
> In Safari, the pop-up blocker can be disabled by clicking Safari at the top context menu and unchecking Block Pop-Up Windows.

With the pop-up blocker disabled, the main web page notifies the user that the meeting has started in a separate browser window and that the main window can be closed. Meanwhile, a second window pops up and is identified as the Lync Web App, as shown in Figure 22.8.

FIGURE 22.8   Launching the Web App

The Lync Web App window offers the user two options:

- Join as a guest
- Join using your corporate credentials

When a meeting is organized, the organizer can choose which participants can join automatically and which participants can request to share information or request to control a session. Typically these rights are not given out to guest users. Similarly, guest users are typically placed into a lobby before they are added to the meeting by the organizer.

The Lync Web App window enables you to choose the preferred language in the Language drop-down. Similarly, you can click the gear in the upper-right corner to access the following two options:

- Forget me on this computer
- Enable logging

Checking the box to Forget me on this computer ensures that all personal information entered from the current session is cleared when the user signs out. Enabling logging enables you to choose a location for saving support logs that can be used by Lync support to help troubleshoot any issues that might arise during the conference.

Choosing Join as a guest prompts the user to pick a display name. This name can be anything and shouldn't be considered a valid form of identification for a guest user. This is to say that a guest user isn't prevented from using names that might be valid within the organization, so always keep that in mind when allowing guests to join a meeting. Users are offered an option to Remember me on this computer, which results in the display name being persistent should they join future meetings as a guest. Clicking the Join Meeting button connects to the meeting. Users receive a notification that they have successfully joined the meeting.

In the meeting, the user has the ability to share a whiteboard and can show the Stage. The stage is the area that shows shared items. If the organizer of the meeting shares a whiteboard, the state automatically appears on the Silverlight client for the Macintosh user who connected to the meeting. Alternatively, the Macintosh Silverlight client user can share a whiteboard, if allowed by meeting options, and it appears for other users. Unfortunately the Macintosh Silverlight client cannot view a shared application, only a shared whiteboard. This is a different behavior than the Windows-based Silverlight client because the additional plug-in for application sharing doesn't yet exist for the Macintosh.

Should one choose to Join using your corporate credentials, the client prompts for the domain\user name for logon as well as the password. Entering these and clicking Join Meeting connects the user to the meeting as an authenticated user. This means that the identity can be trusted and that the user will be considered "People from the organizer's company" when applying Meeting Access rights or Presenter rights.

Sharing Information in a Meeting

Due to the limitations within the Macintosh Silverlight Client for Lync Server, the only type of sharing that it can participate in is whiteboard sharing. You can click Share and then New Whiteboard to create a new whiteboard. If one has been previously used and the Stage is shown, you can use the drop-down menu called Content List in the upper right to select a previously populated whiteboard. This is especially useful if a meeting is broken up into several parts and participants want to quickly pick up where they left off. The whiteboard interface includes the following buttons:

- Laser Pointer
- Select and Type
- Line
- Color
- Pen
- Arrow Stamp

- ▶ Insert Image
- ▶ Additional Tools
- ▶ Save with Annotations
- ▶ Full Screen

The Laser Pointer function enables the person who currently controls the meeting to create and move a pointer. By clicking in the whiteboard and moving the pointer around with the mouse or a touch pen, you can point to objects in the whiteboard while speaking to call attention to them. This is meant to mimic the use of a traditional laser pointer in a presentation where you can point to an object to call attention to it.

The option of Select and Type, which includes a submenu for font and font size, enables the user to create a text box and type text into it. This is meant to mimic the most common use of a physical whiteboard, which is to write notes onto it.

The Line button enables the user to create lines, arrows, ovals, and rectangles. These are often used to either enclose information on a whiteboard or can serve as the basis for basic sketches or diagrams within a conference session. For the creation of shapes, select a shape, click into the whiteboard, drag the mouse to the end of the shape, and release it.

The Color button enables you to alter the color of objects. For example, you can make a line in the default black and then decide to change the color for subsequent lines to show that they are different things. This mimics the multiple colors of whiteboard pens often used when whiteboarding.

The Pen enables you to draw freehand with the mouse. Clicking into the submenu of Pen, you can select different colors of pens or define the pen as a highlighter. Using a high-lighter pen results in not overwriting existing lines. This can be helpful when calling attention to text because it won't obscure the original text.

The Arrow Stamp button, which also enables you to choose a Check stamp or an X stamp, enables you to place an arrow onto the whiteboard. The easiest way is to click into the whiteboard, drag the mouse to where you want to place the object, and then release the mouse.

The Insert Image button enables you to search the system for image files to paste into the whiteboard.

The Additional Tools button includes the typical undo/redo functions, allows for cut/copy/paste functionality, and enables you to delete selected annotations or all annotations.

The Save with Annotations button enables the user to save the whiteboard as a Portable Network Graphics (PNG) image. You are prompted to choose a location to save the image.

The Full Screen button expands the whiteboard to fill the entire screen. During this full-screen mode, you are not able to see the normal interface for Lync, text that is typed into the conversation pane, nor the status change for other participants. To exit full-screen mode, either click the left bar's arrow labeled Show Conversation or press the escape key (ESC).

Client Integrations with Other Applications

As is typical with many Microsoft back office applications, one of its key value propositions is its integration with other Microsoft applications. Microsoft always touts its concept of "better together" when selling its products and Lync Server 2010 is no different. After the client is installed, there are hooks into several other Microsoft applications, which are discussed in the following sections.

Integration with Outlook

One of the strongest areas of integration for the Communicator client is with Outlook. When the Communicator client is installed, it adds hooks into the Outlook view that integrate into contact information. For example, when an e-mail is received in Outlook, you can immediately see Presence information for any Lync Server users that are listed in any of the To, CC, or From fields. This immediately tells the recipient whether these people are available. By placing the mouse over a name with Presence information, you receive information about the users and are presented an interface that contains many of the Communicator buttons, as shown in Figure 22.9.

FIGURE 22.9 Viewing Extended Options

Visible in the initial pop-up is the display name of the user, the current status, calendar information, and the status message. The available options include the following:

- Send mail
- Send an instant message
- Call contact
- Start a video call
- Schedule a meeting
- Open Outlook contact
- Add contact to instant messenger contact list

Focusing on the options that are specific to the Communicator client integration, clicking Send an instant message spawns the typical IM window from within Communicator. Sending an IM results in the contact getting a pop-up that the other person is requesting an IM conversation. This pop-up can be either responded to or ignored. This process is effectively identical to finding the contact in the Communicator client and launching an IM conversation, but with the added convenience of having done it directly from Outlook. In this manner, you get additional choices in terms of how you will interact with another user. Rather than being forced to reply to an e-mail through e-mail, you can choose to communicate through instant messages.

Clicking Call contact results in the contact getting a pop-up that the other person is requesting an audio call. Accepting the call connects the two users through an audio conference that is hosted by Lync Server. This is a useful option to avoid a lengthy e-mail reply or if a conversation is of a sensitive nature and shouldn't be stored in e-mail.

Clicking Start a video call results in the contact getting a pop-up that the other person is requesting a video connection. Assuming the user has a camera, she is able to join a video call with the other person. As with any video call, the person who receives the call needs to start the video if she has a camera and wants the other person to see her. Similarly, video calls include audio so that the two are able to easily communicate with each other.

Clicking Add contact to instant messenger contact list adds contacts that don't yet exist in the Communicator contact list. Using this interface effectively invokes the normal interface for adding contacts, but it prepopulates the e-mail address of the contact you want to add. Just click Next and Finish to add the user. Optionally, you can type a message to personalize the invitation.

The Communicator client also accesses your calendar if you are hosted on Exchange. From this connection, it is able to see calendar availability and can automatically change your status based on the calendar. For example, if you are in a meeting, your status automatically changes to Busy (In a meeting).

Integration with Office

Communicator offers some integration with Microsoft Office that can make it easier to collaborate with other users. For example, in the Review tab in Microsoft Word, you can choose to share a document through an instant message. This offers contacts from Communicator or enables the user to choose Other. Clicking Other gives access to the full contact list from Communicator or enables you to type an e-mail address to which to send the document. Selecting an IM contact invites the contact to a conversation and offers the contact a file transfer with the document in it. This is a quick and handy way to have a coworker perform a document review for you. Somewhat oddly, Excel 2011 and PowerPoint 2011 don't offer the IM option in review.

Tuning Hardware for Communicator Client

The Communicator client for Macintosh enables users to communicate with each other through both audio and video. As such, it's a good idea to tune the audio and video subsystems of the Macintosh that is running the client in order to optimize the experience for the user.

For those that might not be familiar with the Macintosh operating system, items such as audio and video are managed through System Preferences. This can be accessed either through the Dock (the icons displayed on the bottom of the screen) or by clicking the Apple logo at the top left corner of the screen and choosing System Preferences. When looking for System Preferences in the Dock, look for a grey square with a large gear and two smaller gears.

Tuning the Display

The System Preferences interface is broken up into five rows including Personal, Hardware, Internet & Wireless, System, and Other. Clicking the Displays icon, located in the Hardware row, opens a new menu. From this menu, you can select screen resolutions. In general, for the best visual results, pick the native resolution of the screen. This is especially important when using an LCD or liquid crystal display. Although displays can generally run in multiple resolutions, they are optimized for one particular resolution. As Wikipedia describes it, "While CRT monitors can usually display images at various resolutions, an LCD monitor has to rely on interpolation (scaling of the image), which causes a loss of image quality. An LCD has to scale up a smaller image to fit into the area of the native resolution. This is the same principle as taking a smaller image in an image editing program and enlarging it; the smaller image loses its sharpness when it is expanded." Thus when using an external LCD or the built-in LCD display on a Macintosh laptop, it is important to ensure that it's running at its native resolution. Typically, a monitor can inform a computer of its native resolution through extended display identification data (EDID). If a monitor doesn't support this standard, search online for the native resolution. If it can't be found, experiment with various resolutions. Generally, it is obvious when you select the native resolution because the text will look crisper.

Another feature that is available on the Macintosh laptops is support for automatically adjusting brightness as ambient light changes. This enables the laptop screen to adjust to the conditions of the room and is helpful when users move their laptop back and forth between well-lit and poorly lit locations.

Clicking the Color button offers additional options for managing the display profiles. Picking a profile that matches the output monitor can result in a more accurate representation of colors, which means people will look more natural when in a video call.

Tuning the Audio

In the Hardware row of the System Preferences page is an icon for sound. Clicking this icon opens a screen with three tabs, which include Sound Effects, Output, and Input. Sound effects are used by various notifications within the Communicator client and their relative volume can be managed here.

Clicking the Output tab enables you to control overall volume of the output and gives you control over basic audio features such as left/right balance.

Clicking Input enables you to modify the sensitivity of the microphone. This is probably the most critical step in optimizing the experience in audio calls. If the microphone is too sensitive, it can clip or send a distorted signal. If sensitivity is too low, other users will have a difficult time hearing the person speaking into the microphone. One excellent feature offered on the Macintosh is native noise reduction. By checking the box labeled Use ambient noise reduction, there will be less distracting background noise sent over the microphone and this will benefit anyone in the audio conference.

Troubleshooting

The Communicator client is stable and easy to configure, but there are a few things that might go wrong in a large deployment.

▶ If the client doesn't connect, try setting the client to a manual configuration and list the pool name. If this results in the client connecting, your service records in DNS are not configured properly.

▶ If a manual connection still doesn't work, try pinging the pool name. If it fails to resolve, there might be an issue with DNS. Try pinging the DNS server as well; it's possible you're having other network issues.

▶ If you're getting audio feedback when conferencing, your sound card might not support noise cancelation. Having a good sound card results in a better overall experience. Another possible fix is to run the configuration utilities for your sound card. This enables you to correctly set levels for the speakers and the microphone. This can prevent clipping of the signal that can result in a distorted voice.

▶ If you aren't getting presence information or if the client complains about Outlook integration, it's possible that you activated an account for Lync Server 2010 and created a SIP name for the user that doesn't match the e-mail address. These need to match for everything to work perfectly.

▶ If you are using certificates from your own CA and external users are having issues connecting, they might not trust your root CA. The public certificate from the Root CA needs to be imported into the Trusted Root store in Keychain. If external systems trust the Root CA but aren't able to reach the Certificate Revocation List for the CA, they will fail to connect.

▶ If you are having problems connecting through the Silverlight client, double-check the security zone settings. If you aren't able to run JavaScript or if pop-ups are blocked, you will have problems connecting.

▶ If you're having issues with the Lync client, check the Application event log.

An excellent way to check on network connection to Lync Server 2010 is the netstat command. If a connection on TCP 5061 is in a Syn_sent state, it means the Lync Server is unavailable. If the connection is sitting at Time_Wait, odds are the application is having issues. It means that the connection was acknowledged, but that the application isn't sending data.

Best Practices

By following a few best practices, you can optimize the Microsoft Communicator experience for your users. Little tricks to ensure that things work the first time and configure automatically simplifies the deployment of the Microsoft Communicator client.

▶ Whenever possible, use a certificate from a public CA to ensure that clients will automatically trust the CA and that the CRL will be readily available.

▶ If you plan to do video conferencing, spend a couple of bucks and get a nice webcam. Pan and tilt support is a great feature for keeping people well centered in the view.

▶ When doing large conferences with video presentation or application sharing, consider setting up the conference to use a PSTN dial-in for audio to conserve bandwidth for video.

▶ Always properly calibrate cameras and microphones to give users the best possible experience with the Microsoft Communicator client.

▶ Always be sure to configure the Lync client to use the microphone you want. It's common for webcams to have a built-in microphone and Lync might default to this, even though the user is playing sound through the headset. This typically manifests itself in the person's voice being faint. Or, in some cases, distorted because the user might have turned up the sensitivity all the way thinking the problem was with the headset microphone.

▶ Be sure to end your meetings when they are over. Otherwise, you needlessly tie up resources on the back-end servers.

▶ Although this is a good idea for any type of meeting, avoid having side conversations during a conference. Not only does it cause background noise that can distract others, you potentially take focus from the presenter if it is a video conference.

▶ Make sure you don't have anything non-business-related on your screen if you are doing a full desktop share. The potential here for embarrassment is noticeable.

▶ If you are inviting meeting attendees from outside your company, set the meeting options to first place these guests into the waiting room so that you can verify their identity before allowing them into the meeting.

▶ Finish your meetings with the Remove everyone and end the meeting function from the People menu.

▶ Configure Microsoft Communicator to use Transport Layer Security (TLS). This provides encrypted communications from the client to the server. This prevents possible interception of communications by an attacker who can read an unencrypted transmission.

▶ Always scan files received in Communicator with an anti-virus program before opening them.

▶ Consider using Managed Preferences to block specific features or functions of the Communicator client.

CHAPTER 23

Windows, Browser, and Silverlight Clients

Although Lync Server 2010 is an impressive application by itself, most users experience Lync Server 2010 only through one of its many clients. The most common client is likely Lync 2010 in most environments. Lync 2010 is the Windows-based client that enables users to access the client-side functionality of Lync Server 2010. This includes functions such as the following:

▶ Instant Messaging

▶ Presence

▶ PC-to-PC calls

▶ Enterprise voice functions

▶ Video conferencing

▶ Web conferencing

▶ Desktop and application sharing

This chapter covers the more commonly used functions of the Lync 2010 client and should act as the basis of end-user training that most administrators want to provide to their user community to ensure successful adoption of Lync Server 2010.

> **NOTE**
>
> One of the biggest improvements Microsoft has made with the new Lync client is that it has placed all the functionality into a single client.

In older versions of OCS, there were multiple clients for performing IM, web conferences, group chat, or acting as a software-based phone. Lync 2010 combines all these features into a single client to make it even more seamless for users to participate in multiple types of collaborative communications.

Installing the Client

The Lync 2010 client for Windows comes in two installer flavors: 32-bit and 64-bit. The functionality is identical, so simply choose the version that matches the operating system you are running. To install the client, follow these steps:

1. Double-click **LyncSetup.exe**.

2. When prompted by User Account Control, click **Yes**.

3. Browse to the location where you want to install the Lync client and choose whether to share information with Microsoft. Click **Install**, which will launch the installer as shown in Figure 23.1.

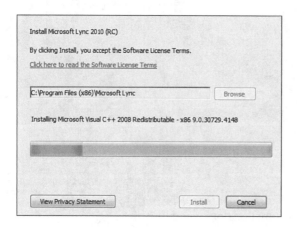

FIGURE 23.1   Installing the Lync 2010 Client

At this step, you might notice two items that seem slightly odd. First, the default installation path for the 64-bit installer is c:\Program Files (x86). Second, if the 32-bit version of Visual C++ redistributable isn't already installed, it is installed as part of the Lync client installation. Although the installer is 64-bit, the client is actually 32-bit. Attempting to install through the 32-bit installer on a 64-bit operating system generates an error telling you it is the incorrect version.

4. When the installation is finished, click **Close**. If the box is checked, Lync begins.

When the Lync 2010 client launches, it will be at the sign-in prompt. Enter the SIP address of the user you want to log on as and click **Sign In**, as shown in Figure 23.2.

FIGURE 23.2   Signing in with Lync 2010 Client

If the DNS records are configured correctly to support Lync Server 2010, you are prompted for Active Director credentials. If the necessary SVR records are not present, manually override the logon setting with these steps:

1. Click the downward-pointing arrow located to the right of the gear icon in the upper right of the client.
2. Choose **Tools** and then choose **Options**.
3. Next to the Sign-in address, click **Advanced**.
4. Choose **Manual** configuration and enter the name of the Lync 2010 Server.
5. Click **OK**, and then click **OK** again.
6. Click **Sign In**.

At this point, you should see the Lync client logged in successfully, as shown in Figure 23.3.

Navigating in the Client

Now that the client is installed and attached to the Lync 2010 Server, it's time to become familiar with the client. On the initial screen, you can see the current status and location. Both of these can be changed by simply clicking the drop-down arrows next to the respective items. The majority of the basic settings can be viewed and modified by clicking the gear icon, which opens Options.

FIGURE 23.3 The Lync 2010 Client

Configuring Basic Options

In the Options windows, the options are broken up into multiple categories. These categories are organized in the left pane for easy access and include the following:

▶ **General**—This is where users can turn on or off emoticons, modify background colors for messages, determine the language Lync will use, turn logging on or off, and determine notification behaviors.

▶ **Personal**—This is where users can alter their logon information, determine Lync's startup behavior, opt to integrate presence information with Exchange or Outlook, configure Lync conversation archiving to Outlook, and opt to show photos for contacts.

▶ **Status**—This section contains options for how one's status will be managed.

▶ **My Picture**—This is where a user can determine whether she will present a photo with her contact information and if so, what that photo will be.

▶ **Phones**—This is where a user can modify his phone number information as well as opt to integrate Lync client with the phone system, enable functions such as TTY, or configure his behavior for joining conference calls.

▶ **Alerts**—This is where the user can choose to be notified whether someone else adds her to the contact list or to configure the behavior of her Do Not Disturb status.

▶ **Ringtones and Sounds**—This is where the user can choose the incoming call ringtone or configure sounds on specific events.

▶ **Audio Device**—This is where the user can choose which audio devices will be used by the Lync client. He can also change the volume associated with the speakers and ringer as well as modify the microphone sensitivity. These settings are useful for optimizing the user experience. When adjusting the microphone, simply slide the bar all the way to the right and then speak into the microphone a bit louder than normal. If the resulting signal is deemed too high, the slider will automatically move left after you finish speaking.

▶ **Video Device**—This is where the user can choose the video source (see Figure 23.4) and access that device's settings. These settings include Exposure, Focus, Brightness, Contrast, Hue, Sharpness, Gamma, and Backlight compensation. The user can also access advanced and extended settings to include zoom, white balance, and even face tracking, if the device supports it.

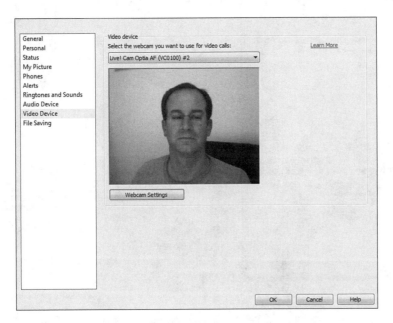

FIGURE 23.4   Testing the Video Device

▶ **File Saving**—This is where the user determines where file transfers and Lync recordings will be saved.

Managing Contacts

Most people are accustomed to the behaviors in Outlook where you can quickly look up a user in the contacts or by starting to type that person's name. The Lync 2010 client follows this model by organizing contacts by groups and by enabling users to quickly search for contacts by simply typing the person's name.

For example, on the **Find a contact** line, if you type a name, the client suggests names based on the contacts. From here, simply click **Add** to add the contact to a contact group as shown in Figure 23.5. When this occurs, the person you added receives a notification of the addition and has the option to add you as well. Once added, the contacts appear in the group you selected and you are able to see their presence information at any time.

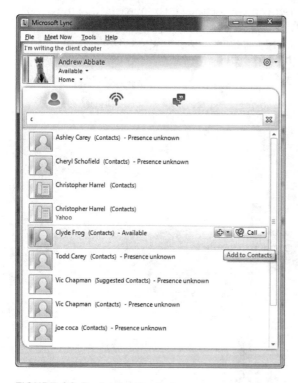

FIGURE 23.5   Adding Contacts

After a contact is added, he can be moved from one contact group to another by simply left-clicking and dragging the contact from one group to another. By holding the mouse over the name of the contact, you can see any notes he has set in the client as well as his picture.

Managing Groups

The Lync 2010 client enables users to organize their contacts by placing them inside groups. By default, the groups are

- Frequent Contacts
- All Contacts

Frequent Contacts is automatically populated by the client based on how often particular contacts are used. The All Contacts group becomes the Other Contacts group as soon as a user creates the first custom group. Groups can be deleted or renamed using the right-click function.

> **CAUTION**
>
> Contacts can be dragged back and forth between groups but can exist only in one "real" group at a time. This is to say that any contacts that appear in Frequent Contacts must also exist in some other group because Frequent Contacts isn't a true group.

A convenient use of groups is to organize members of a project or department. By right-clicking the group name, you can choose to launch a conference call that invites all members of that group. Similar functionality can be achieved by selecting multiple contacts by Ctrl-clicking them and then right-clicking to choose Start a Conference Call. This call can use Lync's PC-to-PC call features or the phone system.

Groups can be organized within the client by either using the right-click–accessed Move Group Up or Move Group Down functions or by simply dragging them from one position to another.

Status View

The second view supported in the client is the status view. This arranges your contacts based on their current status. In this view, their group membership is irrelevant and only their current status affects where their contact appears. Statuses include

- Online
- Away
- Unknown
- Unavailable

The status view is a quick and easy way to determine which of your contacts are available.

Relationship View

The third view available in the Lync 2010 client is the relationship view. This view is a bit more interesting because the relationships actually enforce behaviors on the contacts that are members of them. The relationships include the following:

▶ **Friends and Family**—Contacts in this relationship can view all your contact information except meeting details.

▶ **Workgroup**—Contacts in this relationship can view all your contact information except Home and Other phone; they can interrupt Do Not Disturb status.

▶ **Colleagues**—Contacts in this relationship can view all your contact information except Home, Other and Mobile phone, and meeting details.

▶ **External Contacts**—Contacts in this relationship can view only your name, title, email address, company, and picture.

▶ **Blocked Contacts**—Contacts in this relationship can view only you name, e-mail address, office, and picture; they can't reach you through Lync.

Beyond these permissions, the Relationship view operates the same way as the other two views in terms of initiating IMs with contacts.

IM Features

For most environments, the most commonly used feature in the Lync 2010 client is Instant Messaging. This function enables users to stop cluttering mailboxes with messages such as "Where do you want to go for lunch," and enables users to limit their messages to only people who are likely to respond quickly. This is where accurate presence information really comes in handy.

Starting an IM conversation is as simple as double-clicking a contact. Doing so launches the IM window that defaults to the IM tab, as shown in Figure 23.6.

The IM client works like any other IM client. You can see the status information for the person to which you are communicating, and there are two areas in the window: one to type in and one to display the conversation. Users have access to the usual features such as altering the font, color, and size of the text as well as a menu of emoticons. You can access emoticons with the usual combinations of characters.

CAUTION

Although this feature is useful, be aware that sometimes messages you send inadvertently turn into emoticons. This is especially common when using an IM client to troubleshoot programming code with a coworker. This behavior can be disabled in Settings.

FIGURE 23.6   The IM Window

Archiving IM Conversations

IM conversations can be archived in two ways. One way is for an administrator to implement an archiving policy on an archiving server. The other way to archive messages is into Outlook.

▶   For a review on implementing archiving policies on an archiving server, refer to Chapter 8, "Microsoft Lync Server 2010 Archiving."

In the Options area, under the Personal tab, is the option to Save instant message conversations in my email Conversation History folder. If this option is checked, each conversation is saved into this e-mail folder at the time the IM window is closed. This is a useful way to access old conversations and this folder's contents are indexed for easy searches.

> **TIP**
>
> Note that unlike most IM systems, if you send an IM to a user that is offline, it won't queue up and wait for the user's next logon. You simply receive a message saying, "This message was not delivered to [target name] because this person is unavailable or offline."

The IM interface enables one person to send a file to the other participant of the IM conversation. On the far right side of the toolbar is a paperclip icon. Clicking this icon opens a file-browsing session to enable the user to identify a file to send to the other user. Files can only be sent one at a time. Trying to Ctrl-click multiple files results in simply changing the file, not adding users to a list. Click Open after the file is selected. The person set to receive the file receives a notification and has the option to Accept, Save As, or Decline the file. Accepting the file triggers a warning window to warn the user that the file might contain harmful malware and that she should accept files from only someone she knows. After it is accepted, it downloads and a link displays to access the file. The sender of the file receives a notification that the transfer was successful.

Audio Calls, Video Calls, and Conferencing

One of the most interesting features in the Lync 2010 client is the capability to participate in audio or video conferences with other users in the Lync Server 2010 environment. Prior to their first participation in either an audio or video conference, users should configure their audio and video devices as described in the "Configuring Basic Options" section earlier in this chapter. After these devices are configured, users are ready to start their first conference.

For purposes of this section, view a call and a conference as essentially the same event with the only difference being the number of parties involved. If there are two parties involved, it's a call. If there are more than two parties involved, it's a conference. Generally the steps are identical for initiating and managing both. In cases where the steps vary, they will be called out as such.

> **NOTE**
>
> As you might guess, based on the fact that the IM interface and Call interface are merely different tabs on the same window, an IM conversation can be escalated to an audio call by simply clicking Call from the existing IM window.

Making Audio Calls

Initiating an audio call is as simple as right-clicking a contact, choosing Call, and specifying that it should be a Lync call. Then, the contact receives a pop-up and an audio notification and has the option to answer, decline, or redirect. Answer and decline should be fairly obvious in what they do. Redirect gives the option to reply through IM or to set one's status to Do Not Disturb. Accepting the call updates both users' status to In a call.

When the call connects, a new window displays that looks similar to the IM window. In fact, it is the same window, but now it's on the Call tab, as shown in Figure 23.7.

FIGURE 23.7   The Call Window

The Call window offers several buttons, including

▶ Mute microphone

▶ Adjust volume or mute speakers

▶ Display dial pad

▶ Hold

Muting the microphone alters the icon on the client that muted his microphone. Clicking the adjust volume or mute speakers button presents a sliding volume level that can be modified.

Similarly, there is a speaker icon below the sliding volume that can be clicked to mute or unmute the speakers. Clicking Display dial pad presents a clickable dial pad that can be used for key-driven events on the phone system. Typically this is used to navigate phone trees and the like. The hold button places the call on hold, which notifies other participants on the call.

Clicking Resume returns the call to an active status. Both on hold and the call itself display the amount of time the call has been at a particular status.

Network Connectivity Icon

One of the other icons visible in the window is a Network Connectivity status. This indicates the quality of the network connection and is useful in troubleshooting issues with voice quality on a call. In the upper-right corner of the windows is a phone icon with a red x. This button is used to end the call.

> **NOTE**
>
> Although calls are archived into the Conversation History folder in Outlook, they contain only the list of participants and the duration of the call. The call itself is neither recorded nor stored here.

Making Video Calls

Initiating a video call is as simple as right-clicking a contact and choosing Start a Video Call. Much as with the audio call, the recipient has the option to accept, decline, or redirect. Redirect gives the option to reply with an IM or to mark the recipient as Do Not Disturb.

When the call is accepted, the usual client window opens and is located on the Video tab. The recipient initially sees the caller, but the caller won't see the recipient until after clicking Start My Video in the window.

Inside the video window are several buttons, including

- Mute microphone

- Adjust volume or mute speakers

- Display dial pad

- Hold

In addition, inside the video area itself, if the mouse enters this area, several additional buttons become available, including

- **Pause My Video**—Turns off the webcam on the system of the user that clicked it. At this point, the option changes to Start My Video, which turns the webcam back on.

- **Pop Out Video**—Disconnects the video window from the rest of the Lync client window so that it can be repositioned elsewhere. In this configuration, as well as in the initial configuration, the video window can be resized by simply dragging a corner.

- **View Full Screen**—Expands the video windows to encompass the entire screen. The option at the upper-right corner becomes Exit full screen.

- **End Video**—Click to downgrade the video call to an audio call.

Additionally, the name of the other participant appears in the lower-left section of the video window.

At the default window sizes, video conferences across a LAN connection are quite good. Factors such as latency and bandwidth might affect video conferencing across a WAN connection.

Web Conferencing

Probably the biggest driving force behind companies implementing Lync Server 2010 is replacing outsourced web conferencing services. Many companies spend tens of thousands of dollars a month on services, such as Webex or GoToMeeting. Although there might be situations in which a company running Lync Server 2010 needs to create a conference so large that its infrastructure isn't sufficient, the other 95% of the time it can use a platform it owns rather than pay an external company for these services. In many environments, OCS 2007 R2 implementations pay for themselves in 6–12 months for this reason. Lync Server 2010 looks to offer similar ROI for companies in need of web conferencing.

> **CAUTION**
>
> Be aware that having multiple participants of the same conference in the same room can result in a fair amount of feedback through the clients. The client can actually detect this and recommend that one or more participants mute their microphones. In a video conference with more than two participants, the view switches to whomever the active speaker is.

Starting a Conference

Web conferences can be initiated either through the direct sharing of a monitor or by scheduling a meeting and including a web conference. However, the simplest way to initiate a conference is through the Meet Now option.

In the top menu of the Lync client, when you click Meet Now, the following three options for joining an Audio meeting are offered:

▶ Do not join audio

▶ Use Lync (integrated audio and video)

▶ Call me at:

This creates a conference with only the initiating user in it. From here, use the People menu to perform the following tasks:

▶ Invite by Name or Phone Number

▶ Invite by Email

▶ Mute Audience

▶ Make Everyone an Attendee

▶ Play Entry and exit Announcements

▶ Remove Everyone and End Meeting

When inviting by name or phone number, Lync displays the existing contacts to simplify adding an attendee who is already known to the meeting organizer. Highlighting the contact and clicking OK sends an invite to the contact. The person is notified by a pop-up box and can opt to either join the conference or set her status to Do Not Disturb. From this point, the normal IM, audio, video, and application sharing functions are available. If authorized to do so, attendees can also send invitations to the conference.

Adding a Web Conference to a Meeting

Most commonly, people add web conferences through Lync Server 2010 to meeting invitations. You can either initiate this through the Lync client, by right-clicking a contact and choosing Schedule a Meeting, or by creating a normal meeting invite through Outlook and clicking the Online Meeting button. Clicking this button adds a link to the invite to allow recipients to join the online meeting as shown in Figure 23.8.

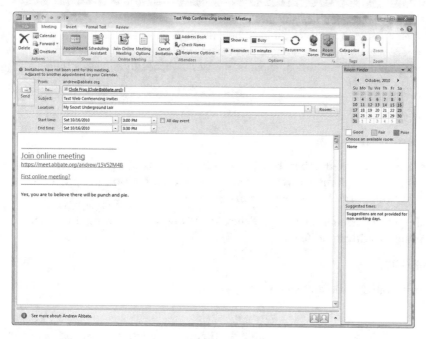

FIGURE 23.8   The Call Window

Clicking the Meeting Options button enables you to configure behaviors for dealing with meeting access and identifying who can be a presenter, as shown in Figure 23.9.

After it is sent, the meeting request appears in the recipient's mailbox where it can be accepted. Opening the calendar item, the user is able to click the web link for the meeting.

> **NOTE**
>
> Note that the link received points to Meet.domain.com/sender/meetingID. This means that if you haven't created an A record or a CNAME for "meet" yet, your link does not work.

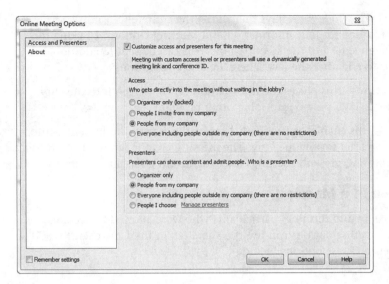

FIGURE 23.9   Access and Presenters

When the link is clicked, the client is presented with options for how to join the audio conference:

- ▶ Do not join audio
- ▶ Use Lync (integrated audio and video)
- ▶ Call me at:

Although any of the options are valid, for this example, select **Use Lync** and click **OK** as shown in Figure 23.10.

FIGURE 23.10   Choosing Audio and Video

From here, the familiar Lync window displays that shows the conference call is starting. In the top of the window is a link for Join Information and Meeting Options. Clicking this link identifies the Conference ID and the Meeting link. This can be sent to additional attendees that you want to add after the fact. There are also two buttons:

▶ **Copy All Information**—This places the information on the screen into the clipboard where it can be later pasted into some other program.

▶ **Meeting Options**—This enables participants to view the Access and Presenter information that was set easier for the meeting. The meeting creator can use this button to modify the access and presenter settings after the meeting has already started.

Sharing Information in a Meeting

With the web conference up and running, participants who were allowed to become presenters based on the meeting options can use the Share tab in the Lync client to add resources to the conference. These options include

▶ Main Monitor

▶ Secondary Monitor

▶ All Monitors

▶ Program

▶ PowerPoint Presentation

▶ New Whiteboard

▶ New Poll

When a presenter chooses to share something, the stage displays for all users. If your client doesn't list Main, Secondary, and All monitors, it's likely because you have only one monitor, in which case these options are replaced with Desktop.

Sharing something, such as the Whiteboard, enables participants to type into text boxes as well as to draw or to place images into the Whiteboard, as shown in Figure 23.11.

Sharing monitors or applications enables participants to follow along with what the presenter views. This makes it easy for participants to see what you are talking about on the audio portion of the conference. Choosing to share a program gives presenters a view into which programs are currently running on their system. When they choose a program to share, they receive a warning making sure they know that everyone else is about to see what they are sharing. This warning helps ensure that you've picked the correct application.

FIGURE 23.11   Using the Whiteboard

Client Integrations with Other Applications

As is typical with many Microsoft back office applications, one of its key value propositions is integration with other Microsoft applications. Microsoft touts its concept of "better together" when selling its products, and Lync Server 2010 is no different. After the client is installed, there are hooks into several other Microsoft applications, which are discussed in this section.

Integration with Outlook

One of the strongest areas of integration for the Lync client is with Outlook. When the Lync client is installed, it adds several buttons to the Respond area of the Outlook toolbar. This gives the following options:

- Meeting
- IM Reply
- IM Reply to All
- Call
- Call All

Instead of being locked into responding to an e-mail with another e-mail, you can choose to start up an IM conversation, initiate a voice call, or initiate a web conference. This offers tremendous flexibility in how to collaborate with coworkers.

23

This integration extends to the contacts managed by Outlook. By looking at an e-mail received from a coworker and double-clicking that person's name, you see the integrated Lync functionality on the contact card. Figure 23.12 shows how you can trigger an IM, a call, or immediately start a shared desktop conference with the other user. You can also see the presence information for the other user, which often influences how you respond.

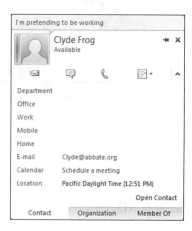

FIGURE 23.12   Contact Cards in Outlook

Integration with Calendar View

Another integration between Lync Client and Outlook is in the Calendar view. You will quickly notice a New Online Meeting button in the main bar containing the Lync logo. Clicking this button launches the traditional meeting interface where you can invite attendees and attach agenda information. Additionally, it embeds a link that enables invitees to join an online conference. In the invite pane, there are two more Lync buttons:

- ▶ Join Online Meeting
- ▶ Meeting Options

Join Online Meeting accomplishes the same thing as clicking the embedded link and joins the conference. The Meeting Options button enables the meeting creator to define access behaviors and to define who can and cannot act as a presenter. In the meeting link is a second link that leads to online help information for answering common questions for first-time meeting organizers.

Integration of Presence Information

The last area of integration is presence information. When looking at e-mail messages from other Lync Server 2010 users, you can see their current status. Administrators who are familiar with older versions of OCS notice that the presence circle is now a rounded square. Hovering the mouse over the presence icon gives additional information and exposes the menus to immediately send an IM, place an audio or video call, schedule a meeting, or start sharing resources.

Integration with Office

Lync offers some integration with Microsoft Office that can make it easier to collaborate with other users. For example, in Microsoft Word, you can go into the File area of the ribbon and look at the info page. The name of the person who authored the file and the name of the person who last edited the file are located on the far right. Notice that the presence jellybean is shown next to each of the names with accurate presence information. If you have a question about the last set of edits made to a document, simply hover over the "last modified by" name to get the option to IM or call that person through Lync. This level of integration makes collaborative communications easy, and they quickly become second nature for most users.

Lync integration with Office also adds two share options in the Review ribbon. You can send the document to a contact through the Send by IM button or you can click Share Now and choose a contact to open a screen-sharing session with that user. This enables two people to share the document and make changes to it collaboratively.

Useful Lync Client Shortcuts

Microsoft has gone out of its way to improve functionality and accessibility in the Lync client, and one of the ways is to create hotkeys for commonly used tasks. This sort of information makes a great cheat sheet for new users of the Lync client because it not only simplifies accessing certain functions, it also serves to highlight what functions are available. Some of those commonly used tasks are highlighted in Table 23.1:

TABLE 23.1   Global Hotkeys

Shortcut Key	Description
Windows Key + Q	Bring Lync main window to foreground
Windows Key + A	Accept an incoming toast invitation
Windows Key + X	Decline toast invitation and change your status to "Do not disturb"
Windows Key + Esc	Decline toast invitation
Ctrl + Shift + Space	Set focus on the application sharing toolbar
Ctrl + Alt + Space	Take back control when sharing your screen
Ctrl + Shift + S	Stop sharing your screen

TABLE 23.2　Main Window Shortcuts

Shortcut Key	Description
Ctrl + 1	Go to the Contact List tab
Ctrl + 2	Go to the Activity Feeds tab
Ctrl + 3	Go to the Conversation List tab
Ctrl + 4	Go to the Phone tab
Alt + A	View all conversations when in Conversation List tab
Alt + D	View missed conversations when in Conversation List tab
Alt + C	View missed calls when in Conversation List tab

TABLE 23.3　Conversation Window Shortcuts

Shortcut Key	Description
Ctrl + W	Show/hide IM area
Ctrl + R	Show/hide participant list
Ctrl + Shift + Y	Show/hide left region when sharing stage is visible
Alt + I	Invite a contact to an existing conversation
Ctrl + F	Send a file
Alt + P	Open a file received
Alt + C, Alt + D	Accept or decline an invitation to share audio or video modalities
Ctrl + Shift + Enter	Start or end phone call
Ctrl + Shift + H	Hold/resume an ongoing audio conversation
Ctrl + M	Pause/resume video (only if already in progress)
Alt + R	Rejoin audio in a conference
Escape	Exit full screen view if present or, closes the conversation window only if it has no audio, video, or sharing
Ctrl + Shift + <, Ctrl + Shift + >	Increase/decrease selected text font size in IM input
Ctrl +], Ctrl + [	Zoom in/zoom out the text in IM input and history

Lync Silverlight Client

Lync Server 2010 offers a web-based client that is based on Microsoft's Silverlight technology. It's capable of running from any operating system and browser that runs Silverlight.

By simply pointing a web browser at the URL sent in a meeting invite with a Lync meeting attached, users are able to connect.

When initially connecting, the browser might warn users that JavaScript is not enabled. If they have an installed "full" client, they can click a link to use that instead. Otherwise, they'll need to have JavaScript enabled. Often this is as simple as placing the Lync Server URL into the Trusted Sites or altering the security settings in the browser.

If the browser doesn't have version 4.0 or higher of Silverlight, the user will be notified and presented a link to download and install Microsoft Silverlight. After successfully connected, ensure that the site (meet.domain.com) allows pop-ups.

TIP

If pop-ups remain blocked, users can still join a meeting but they won't be able to share their screen or view online Help information. If the pop-up is allowed, the meeting starts in a new browser window, as shown in Figure 23.13.

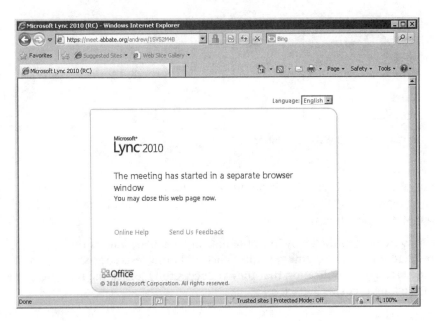

FIGURE 23.13   Launching the Meeting

The Silverlight client gives users the option to either join as a guest or to authenticate with their credentials. If users have an account in the system, they should click Join using the corporate credentials. If they join a meeting outside their company, they should choose to join as a guest. Users have the ability to choose their language for the client.

Access Options

Clicking the gear icon at the upper right of the client gives access to two options:

▶ Forget me

▶ Enable logging

Using the Forget me option ensures that all personal information from the upcoming session will be cleared out when the user logs out. Enabling logging enables the user to choose a location where logs will be saved that can later be used for support. These can be configured as shown in Figure 23.14.

FIGURE 23.14   Setting the Lync Web App Options

Joining as a guest, as shown in Figure 23.15, prompts users for a display name and gives them the option to remember their settings on that particular computer. From there, they need to click Join Meeting to enter the meeting.

At this point, guests are held in the lobby until the meeting organizer admits them, as shown in Figure 23.16. After the meeting organizer clicks Admit, guests successfully join the meeting. Guests receive a notification that they've successfully joined the meeting. Once confirmed, Silverlight clients are active.

Silverlight Functions

The Silverlight client looks similar to the full client, although there are a few functions that are not available (for example, audio or video features). When Silverlight users click the Phone menu, they are prompted to enter their own number, and Lync Server 2010 calls them when they click Call Me, as shown in Figure 23.17.

FIGURE 23.15   Joining as a Guest

FIGURE 23.16   Lobbying Users

Users who join a conference through the Silverlight client see the same IM information as the full client. They also are able to participate in screen sharing and application sharing. If the user joined as a guest, the meeting organizer needs to update the Meeting Option to allow everyone to act as a presenter in order for the guest user to be able to initiate sharing.

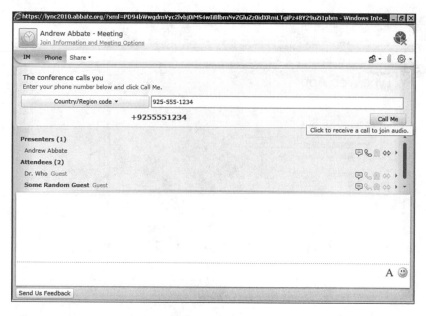

FIGURE 23.17 Using the Call Me Option

By clicking Share from the Silverlight client, users receive several items from which to choose:

▶ Desktop

▶ Program

▶ New Whiteboard

▶ New Poll

▶ Show Stage

NOTE

Sharing the desktop or a program for the first time triggers a download of a plug-in for the Silverlight client. When prompted, the user should click **Install**. Assuming the Lync Server is in a browser zone that enables downloads, the user is prompted to either run or save the LWAPluginInstaller.exe (or LWAPluginInstaller64.exe, if the client is running a 64-bit operating system). Clicking **Run** installs the plug-in. If users receive an error stating that administrative policy prevents them from running the plug-in, they should save the file and then use the UAC features of Windows to run as administrator. This should enable the plug-in to install on a Windows system.

Sharing the desktop gives Silverlight clients an indication that their desktop is shared. This triggers the Show Stage function on other participants so that they can see what Silverlight users are sharing.

Choosing to share a program shows a preview of the applications that are currently running on Silverlight users' systems, and they can select one of these programs, as shown in Figure 23.18, and click Start Sharing.

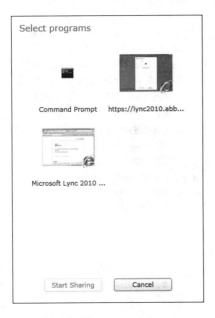

FIGURE 23.18   Sharing Programs

This action causes the application to appear on the stage of other participants who see the sharer's screen with near real-time updates. Some visual lag might occur and will be affected by latency, bandwidth, and the complexity of the images that change in the shared application. This is to say that something like a Word document will appear to update very quickly but something like a PowerPoint presentation will take a little longer to update from the point of view of the participants following along.

Effective Ways to Use Silverlight

Having access to this type of functionality can be exceptionally useful for presentations to customers because they can quickly and easily connect to a visual presentation, have the central system call them to include them in the audio features, and simply have them follow along during the presentation. The necessary software is platform independent and can be removed after the presentation if necessary. The user is prompted with easy-to-follow choices the whole way through and the organizer of the meeting has full control over who enters the meeting and exactly when they enter. They can assume complete control over the presentation or they can hand the mouse and keyboard over to someone else to drive the presentation. Considering how many companies rely on third-party applications to do this, the potential for long-term savings is huge.

Another great use for this technology is in the area of troubleshooting. You can use the Lync client to send an IM to the corporate help desk to ask questions. If the questions become complicated, you can be escalated to a voice call. If the technician needs to perform an action on the remote system, you can share the desktop and give control to the help desk technician. Now you can watch the support person fix the system so that there is little concern about what the support person was doing. It can even be limited to a specific application. Imagine that a user needs to be walked through the process of performing a mail merge in Word. He can search the address book for someone who listed Word mail merge as a skill, determine whether the person is available, IM a question, turn it into a call, and potentially share Word with that person to walk him through the process while explaining it. This type of collaboration between users or between users and support is easily extended outside the immediate office by giving experts access to the Silverlight-based client so that they can quickly and easily participate. Obviously, this has some security implications that should be reviewed by the security group, but the system offers plenty of options for centrally controlling behaviors to mitigate possible risks.

Troubleshooting

The Lync client is stable and easy to configure, but there are a few things that might go wrong in a large deployment.

▶ If the client doesn't connect, try setting the client to a manual configuration and listing the pool name. If this results in the client connecting, your service records in DNS are not configured properly.

▶ If a manual connection still doesn't work, try pinging the pool name. If it fails to resolve, there might be an issue with DNS. Try pinging the DNS server as well; it's possible you're having other network issues.

▶ If you're getting audio feedback when conferencing, your sound card might not support noise cancelation. Having a good sound card results in a better overall experience. Another possible fix is to run the configuration utilities for your sound card. This enables you to correctly set levels for the speakers and the microphone. This can prevent clipping of the signal that results in a distorted voice.

▶ If you aren't getting presence information or if the client complains about Outlook integration, it's possible that you activated an account for Lync Server 2010 and created a SIP name for the user that doesn't match the e-mail address. These need to match for everything to work perfectly.

▶ If you are using certificates from your own CA and external users are having issues connecting, they might not trust your root CA. The public certificate from the Root CA needs to be imported into the Trusted Root store. If external systems trust the Root CA but aren't able to reach the Certificate Revocation List for the CA, they will fail to connect.

▶ If you are having problems connecting through the Silverlight client, double-check the security zone settings. If you aren't able to run JavaScript or if the plug-ins aren't allowed to download, you will have problems connecting.

▶ If you're having issues with the Lync client, check the Application event log.

▶ If the client isn't connecting, an excellent way to check on network connections to Lync Server 2010 is the netstat command. If a connection on TCP 5061 is in a Syn_sent state, it means the Lync Server is unavailable. If the connection is sitting at Time_Wait, odds are that the application is having issues. It means that the connection was acknowledged, but that the application isn't sending data.

Best Practices

By following a few best practices, you can optimize the Lync 2010 experience for your users. Little tricks to ensure that things work the first time and configure automatically will greatly simplify the deployment of Lync 2010 client.

▶ Whenever possible, use a certificate from a public CA to ensure that clients automatically trust the CA and that the CRL is readily available.

▶ If you plan to do video conferencing, spend a couple of bucks and get a nice webcam. Pan and tilt support is a great feature for keeping people well centered in the view.

▶ When doing large conferences with video presentation or application sharing, consider setting up the conference to use a PSTN dial in for audio to conserve bandwidth for video.

▶ Always properly calibrate cameras and microphones to give users the best possible experience with the Lync 2010 client.

▶ Always be sure to configure the Lync client to use the microphone you want. It's common for webcams to have a built-in microphone and Lync might default to this, even though the user is playing sound through her headset. This typically manifests itself in the person's voice being faint. Or, in some cases, her voice might be distorted because she might have turned up the sensitivity all the way thinking the problem was with the headset microphone.

▶ Be sure to end your meetings when they are over. Otherwise, you needlessly tie up resources on the back-end servers.

▶ Although this is a good idea for any type of meeting, try to avoid having side conversations during a conference. Not only does it cause background noise that can distract others, you potentially take focus from the presenter if it is a video conference.

▶ Make sure you don't have anything non-business related on your screen if you are doing a full desktop share. The potential here for embarrassment is noticeable.

▶ If you are inviting meeting attendees from outside your company, set the meeting options to first place the guests into the waiting room so that you can verify their identity before allowing them into the meeting.

▶ Finish your meetings with the Remove everyone option and end the meeting function from the People menu.

Summary

In this chapter we've covered the primary clients for Windows users to connect to Microsoft Lync Server 2010. We've seen what features are available in terms of IM, audio/video conferencing, and application sharing. As users become more and more familiar with the application, this chapter will serve as a guide for how users access various functions within the system and should help ease the transition to this application.

Administrators should take advantage of the troubleshooting and best practices offered in this chapter to try to provide for the best end user experience possible. Ultimately, the success of a Microsoft Lync Server 2010 deployment will be measured by the end users and taking advantage of the information in this chapter will help increase the odds of having happy end users.

It is useful for administrators to understand the limitations of the various clients so that when users ask "How do I do this with the Silverlight client," they'll know whether it's supported and if it is, how to enable it. This can be especially useful when dealing with external users who attach via the web-based clients.

By knowing when to use various client options, administrators and help desk staff can guide users toward the best decisions on how to meet their needs.

CHAPTER 24

UC Endpoints

Overview

Although many administrators might gloss over this chapter
in the book, it is likely one of the most important. The
concept of user experience is often an overlooked idea and
yet vital to a successful unified communications (UC)
deployment. Although IT success is often measured by
metrics and numbers, they rarely tell the whole story. UC
adoption can be viral, but only if the right tools are in place
and end users have a quality experience. The back end infrastructure is certainly important; however, end users never
see any of it. What they use everyday is a UC endpoint.

UC endpoints encompass a wide range of devices. Although
some argue that PCs should be included, others suggest that
they provide a poor experience and a dedicated, purpose-
built device such as a headset or IP/USB phone should be
used for an optimal experience. For that reason, we leave
laptops and PCs out of the discussion for this chapter.

Microsoft ensures that specific devices meet set user experience quality levels through a third-party test and evaluation
process. These devices are labeled "Optimized for Microsoft
Lync." Without getting into a sales pitch over what's the
best, the key point is to recognize that devices certified to
work with Lync are sure to provide a quality end user experience. In addition, the Lync client will always prefer
Optimized for Microsoft Lync devices over standard devices.
At launch, Microsoft announced more than 60 optimized
devices ranging from wired and wireless headsets to
webcams to IP phones to conference devices. Lync
Optimized devices are literally plug and play. The Lync
Communicator client will find them automatically as soon
as they are plugged in and start using the device.

This chapter covers a wide range of devices including the following:

- Standalone IP phones

- USB headsets, speakerphones, and handsets

- Webcams

- Conferencing devices

Finally, the chapter concludes with best practices for choosing and deploying UC endpoints for a variety of scenarios.

Standalone IP Phones

There are two types of standalone IP phones for Microsoft Lync: fully featured phones, which require a user to be signed in all the time, and basic or common area phones, which can be used without a user credential in public areas or for hot desking with basic functions when a user logs in.

The fully featured phones include the following models and provide a premium experience for users requiring a handset:

- Polycom CX700

- Polycom CX600

- Aastra 6725ip

These phones enable a user to sign in and, if desired, connect the phone to a PC through USB to be used as a USB audio device for the Lync client. They offer a full-color LCD screen and some models include a touch screen.

> **NOTE**
>
> Per the Microsoft reference design, all phones in this category must also have a speakerphone and support wideband audio or a supported variant of HD voice. They also offer integration features such as calendar view from the on-phone screen.

For common areas or hot desking, there is a different class of phones, named Aries. This type of phone is new for Lync Server 2010 and fills a much-needed gap from previous versions of the product. These phones are generally lower cost and offer functions similar to most standard corporate desk phones available today. Models include the following:

- Polycom CX500

- Aastra 6721ip

Although these phones don't have some of the advanced features of fully featured standalone IP phones such as the Polycom CX600, they offer the capability to be used in common areas and not tied to an actual user. They also have a lower price point that is comparable to traditional PBX phones.

USB Headsets, Speakerphones, and Handsets

USB headsets, and their bulkier counterparts—handsets—are the most common UC endpoints available with USB speakerphones having a niche market. The Lync Communicator client functions as a softphone, eliminating the need for a dedicated desk phone for most users.

Headsets

Headsets are portable and they provide a superior experience to a traditional handset in nearly every way. However, they take a little bit of getting used to. There is a wide variety of headsets available from several manufacturers. In fact, there are too many individual headset models to discuss all of them here, so we highlight a handful of devices—at least one from each category: wired and wireless.

A good example of a USB-wired headset is the Plantronics Blackwire 420 (see Figure 24.1). This is an affordable solution for desktop users or even mobile users because it folds flat to be stored in a laptop bag. It provides binaural audio with an adjustable boom microphone.

FIGURE 24.1   Plantronics Blackwire 420

Other solutions include monaural audio, which might be better for some environments where workers still need to hear the environment around them.

Wireless headsets have a dongle plugged into the user's PC but require no other connections. The headset enables the user to roam freely up to 300 feet from the PC. Many headsets also have controls for redial, answer, hang up, and volume control. An great example is the Plantronics Voyager Pro UC shown in Figure 24.2.

FIGURE 24.2   Plantronics Voyager Pro UC

TIP

Most wireless solutions have docking stations used for recharging, whereas others come with just a USB charging cable. The latter are better for users who travel often or might not have a permanent office.

Speakerphones

Although there is only a niche market for USB speakerphones, they still play an important role in the UC endpoint ecosystem. These devices are designed for impromptu meetings or group conversations in locations without a dedicated conferencing device. The Plantronics Calisto 825 in particular has a remote microphone, as shown in Figure 24.3. The remote microphone makes this speakerphone perfect for leading meetings in an auditorium or across the room from the device.

FIGURE 24.3   Plantronics Calisto 825

USB Handsets

Sometimes there's no need for a deskphone, but a user insists on having a handset form factor. These devices connect to a user's PC through a USB but provide the familiar user interface and look and feel of a traditional phone handset. From the PC's perspective, the handset is just another audio device for Lync Communicator. However, for the user, the handset is a familiar tool that works the same way as the legacy phone. This can be a great tool to begin the process of empowering nontechnical users with UC. The Plantronics Calisto 540 shown in Figure 24.4 shows off a caller ID screen and powerful speakerphone.

Webcams

It's difficult to say that anything is more revolutionary than desktop video. Even better is high-definition desktop video. Add in integration with popular video conferencing solutions from Tandberg and Polycom and you have a complete solution. Adding video to a conversation has a profound impact. Although most newer laptops are equipped with webcams, USB-connected webcams are ideal for users with desktop systems or external monitors.

Users with a webcam can share video with one or multiple users at the same time. The receiving user will see a request bar asking to share video for the current conversation. The Microsoft RT Video codec constantly adapts to network conditions, providing the best quality for the conditions available.

FIGURE 24.4   Plantronics Calisto 540

Conferencing Devices

New to Lync Server 2010 are conferencing devices. Well, that's not entirely true... Microsoft released the Roundtable device with five cameras for a conference room. It didn't sell well and was licensed to Polycom as the CX5000. It was expensive and simply too much and too complicated for most scenarios. It also required connecting to a PC.

The new Polycom CX3000 conference phone is a true conference room solution. It offers a 3.5-inch QVGA screen with all the Lync integration functions users expect. Most importantly, it's a standalone device. It just needs power (AC or PoE) and an Ethernet cable—no PC required! It also allows for Outlook contacts search and one-click-to-join Lync conference calls.

NOTE

Lync Server also offers tight integration with the Polycom HDX room video conferencing platform when video is a requirement.

Best Practices

▶ Although some users demand desk phones, in general headsets provide a better and more mobile overall solution.

▶ Replace legacy conferencing devices with Lync-enabled devices such as the Polycom CX3000.

▶ Wherever possible, deploy webcams to users. The addition of video adds a lot of value to communication and collaboration.

▶ Deploy headsets to new employees as part of their laptop/desktop system and teach them to use the unified communications solution during orientation. Training is key, especially for nontechnical users.

▶ Encourage use by letting users choose from a variety of devices depending on their situation.

24

PART IX

Planning for Deployment

IN THIS PART

CHAPTER 25

Virtualization

Many organizations today are moving to take advantage of the cost savings and flexibility of server virtualization. Live Communications Server had no official support policy and Office Communications Server 2007 R2 had a limited set of features that were supported in a virtual environment. With Lync Server 2010, Microsoft has finally introduced support for virtualizing every single workload from IM and presence to A/V conferencing to telephony integration with virtualized Mediation Servers. This change is going to allow many companies to reduce hardware costs and virtualize the Lync Server 2010 deployment.

This chapter begins with a basic overview of what virtualization is and what benefits a company can realize by leveraging virtualization. It also discusses some of the common features and the different names for it as it is used in competing products such as Microsoft Hyper-V and VMware vSphere.

Although virtualization of each role is now possible, there are some strict requirements for what is supported and what is not supported when using virtual Lync Servers. This chapter covers what those support boundaries are and what some of the surprise restrictions might be. Sample topologies of a few different deployment models are also included.

Lastly, this chapter covers requirements and best practices for the host servers and for the virtual machine guest servers that run Lync Server 2010 roles. This includes processor, memory, disk, and network considerations for each type of server.

Virtualization Overview

Virtualization is a technology that has been around for a long time now, but has made a significant impact over the last decade. Most organizations already leverage the technology for new flexibility and cost savings. This section covers some of the basic concepts for those unfamiliar with virtualization so that the remainder of the chapter can be understood.

What Is Virtualization?

Virtualization has the capability for a physical piece of hardware to run multiple virtual instances of an operating system. In a traditional sense, every server deployed was associated with physical hardware, had a single operating system installed, and the server performed a specific function. When it was time to add a new server to the environment, companies purchased a new piece of hardware, installed the operating system, and then configured any applications or services. With virtualization, companies no longer require new hardware for every single new server because virtual machines can share a common set of physical resources.

In virtualization, the physical hardware with the resources, such as processing power, memory, and disk space, is referred to as the *host*, whereas any virtual instance of a server running on the host is considered a *virtual machine guest*. Because a single physical machine can support running multiple virtual machines, companies can now use a single piece of hardware to support running multiple servers and each virtual machine running on a host shares the resources physically installed on the host. For example, if a host machine has 16 GB of RAM, only 16 GB of RAM is available to be allocated to the virtual machine guests running on that host.

> **NOTE**
>
> Many products offer the capability to do some form of dynamic memory management so that over-allocating or dynamically moving physical memory between guests is possible, but the bottom line here is that guest machines use the resources installed in the host.

Hypervisor Types

The key to virtualization is the concept of a *hypervisor*, which is a layer that sits between the host physical hardware and the guest virtual machines. The hypervisor facilitates access for the virtual machines to the physical hardware resources.

Virtualization hypervisors come in two distinct flavors. The first, Type 1, allows virtualization to occur directly in an existing operating system. Good examples of a Type 1 hypervisor are the Microsoft Virtual PC or VMware Workstation products. These are applications that run in an existing operating system on a workstation or server, and they allow the user to run virtual machines in the operating system. The hypervisor in these instances runs on top of the host operating system, as depicted in Figure 25.1.

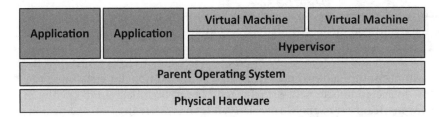

FIGURE 25.1   Type 1 Hypervisor

The second type of hypervisor, Type 2, is far more efficient than Type 1 because it actually operates at a level directly above the physical hardware, as shown in Figure 25.2. This is the type of hypervisor product is used in Microsoft Hyper-V or VMware vSphere products. Type 2 hypervisors are more efficient because there is no need to have the hypervisor first pass through the host operating system before addressing resources for the virtual machine guests.

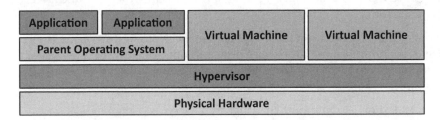

FIGURE 25.2   Type 2 Hypervisor

> **NOTE**
>
> It may be confusing to think of Hyper-V as a Type 2 hypervisor for a Windows Server 2008 full installation because an operating system is installed on the physical host, but the reality is that the hypervisor layer is loaded prior to the host operating system. It is completely abstracted from the Hyper-V management console, but the host operating system is essentially a virtual machine that runs on top of the hypervisor.

Benefits of Virtualization

It should be apparent from the previous few pages that virtualization offers companies a new level of flexibility in server deployment and management not possible with using only physical hardware. This section covers some of the benefits that organizations can realize from hardware virtualization, including the following:

▶ **Fewer physical servers**—By virtualizing servers, an organization requires fewer physical servers. Because new servers now support nearly 100 GB of RAM at an affordable price point, companies can increase their consolidation ratios by placing more and more virtual machines on the same physical hardware.

▶ **Infrastructure flexibility**—As physical servers begin to demand additional hardware upgrades, the traditional model required organizations to purchase more memory or processing power. In a virtual environment, administrators can easily shut down a virtual machine and add more memory or processors. Some products even allow this to happen without shutting down the virtual machine. Additionally, expanding the infrastructure to accommodate new virtual machines can become a simple matter of adding a new physical host to the cluster. This adds an entirely new level of flexibility to managing server resources.

▶ **Increased availability**—In physical environments, servers were often built to be as redundant as possible with multiple hard drives and power supplies. These additional expenses are still useful for a host server, but do not apply to virtual machines. As long as a virtual machine is made highly available, it can be easily restarted on a different host if a physical host fails. It is still best practice to design the hosts to be fault tolerant, but the additional expense of designing every single server for hardware redundancy becomes unnecessary. Organizations can achieve a higher level of service and availability for servers by abstracting the hardware layer through virtualization.

▶ **Reduced operating expenses**—By reducing the number of physical servers in the environment, organizations can also realize decreased operating expenses associated with physical servers. Fees for rack space, cooling, and power are reduced when fewer physical servers are used.

▶ **Application isolation**—A significant challenge in the days of using physical servers for everything was that each new server required its own physical hardware. Typically, this was difficult because of the additional expense involved to purchase and install a new server. To work around budget issues, administrators began to collocate different applications on the same physical server, but because application vendors usually test and expect their application to have its own dedicated environment, this caused performance or configuration issues that were difficult to troubleshoot. With virtualization, each application can have its own dedicated server due to how easy it is to create virtual machines.

▶ **Legacy application support**—An unfortunate reality for many organizations is a need to support legacy applications that run on only legacy operating systems. As the hardware these systems run on begins to fail or needs replacement, organizations must either deploy these applications on new hardware or operating systems not certified for the product. Using virtualization, companies can create a new virtual machine running a legacy operating system very easily. They can also perform a physical-to-virtual (P2V) migration of the existing physical server to transform it as-is to a virtual machine.

Virtualization Vendors

There are various vendors around who produce virtualization technologies today. Some of the most commonly used products are Microsoft Hyper-V, VMware vSphere, and Citrix XenServer. All these vendors offer a fairly similar base feature set and each expands into its own different target markets. In relation to Lync Server 2010, Microsoft certifies particular hypervisor products for use in order to be supported. Today, only the Microsoft Hyper-V that runs on Windows Server 2008 R2 and VMware vSphere 4.0 is certified for use with Lync Server 2010. Additional vendors can work with Microsoft at a later time to achieve certification.

> **NOTE**
>
> The reason that Windows Server 2008 R2 Hyper-V is required is because the original Hyper-V release in Windows Server 2008 lacks some media support required for Lync Server virtualization.

The Microsoft Hyper-V management console is shown in Figure 25.3. This chapter focuses on the Microsoft and VMware products because they are the only two supported platforms at this time.

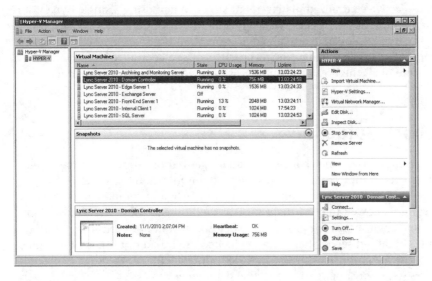

FIGURE 25.3   Microsoft Hyper-V Management Console

Advanced Features

As these enterprise-class virtualization products have grown, more features have been added, enabling them to cluster physical host machines, move virtual machines seamlessly between hosts while still online, and manage virtual machines from a single point of view. Most of these features are identical between the two products, but have different names. This section covers those naming differences and describes the different features because they are referenced later and have a direct effect on support in Lync Server 2010.

▶ **Failover Clustering / High-Availability**—Refers to the capability to join multiple physical hosts into a cluster where shared storage from a storage area network (SAN) is provisioned. When running on a clustered set of physical hosts, a virtual machine can be made highly available. If a physical host fails or restarts at some point, the highly available virtual machines running on that host can be automatically restarted on a different host. The virtual machine is also restarted during this process similarly to if the power was turned off and then back on.

▶ **Live Migration / vMotion**—This provides the capability to move virtual machines between different hosts in a cluster without any disruption of service or perceived downtime. For example, a virtual machine that is online and running can be migrated to another host while users remain connected to the virtual machine. This is accomplished by the host machines transferring the memory state of the guest over the network and then simultaneously bringing the machine online on the new host while the previous host removes its copy. Both host machines must remain online during this process, and the virtual machine remains online as well.

▶ **Virtual Machine Manager / vCenter**—These two products are Microsoft and VMware's respective centralized management suites. When using a single hypervisor, management of the host and guest virtual machines can be done individually, but as more hosts and guests are added to an environment, managing each host separately can become tedious. These management products offer a centralized view and configuration store of all the hosts and guests within the virtualization environment.

Lync Support Guidelines

Lync Server 2010 brings a welcome change for many organizations in terms of the support policy offered for virtualization. In Microsoft Office Communications Server 2007 R2, only a few workloads were certified for virtualization. In a nutshell, any component that used a type of media was not allowed to be virtualized. This didn't mean those features wouldn't function in a virtual environment; it just meant Microsoft would not officially support a deployment with virtualized servers handling media because it had not tested or designed the product for those scenarios. This meant that web conferencing, A/V conferencing, and telephony features were not supported in a virtual deployment in OCS.

With Lync Server 2010, nearly all scenarios can be virtualized with only a few exceptions. The most welcome change is that the web conferencing, A/V conferencing, and telephony integration features are now supported. This means that Front-End Servers handling media and Mediation Servers handling SIP trunks or media gateway integration can now be deployed in a virtual machine. The roles and features supported for Lync Server 2010 virtualization are listed here:

▶ **Standard Edition Front-End Server**—Supported for presence, IM, Enterprise Voice, A/V, and conferencing

- **Enterprise Edition Front-End Server**—Supported for presence, IM, Enterprise Voice, and A/V

- **A/V Conferencing Server**—Supported for A/V conferencing

- **Enterprise Edition Back-End Server**—Supported for SQL Server store and file share server

- **Edge Server**—Supported for remote access, federation, public IM connectivity, presence, IM, Enterprise Voice, and A/V

- **Director**—Supported for authentication and routing

- **Monitoring Server**—Supported for the monitoring service and collocated SQL Server store

- **Archiving Server**—Supported for the archiving service and collocated SQL server store

> **NOTE**
>
> If archiving or monitoring communications from a virtualized Standard Edition Front-End server, the archiving and monitoring roles must be deployed on a physical server to fall within the support boundaries. Microsoft has not provided an explanation for this anomaly, but it is explicitly called out.

The only roles that cannot be virtualized for use in Lync Server 2010 are the IP-PSTN gateways or the survivable branch appliances. Considering most of these appliances would require a physical telephony connection that would be impossible in a virtual environment, this should not be an issue for most organizations.

This support shift should open the option for many organizations to fully virtualize Lync deployments. However, there are still some significant support boundaries as listed here:

- **Hyper-V 2008 R2 or VMware vSphere 4 Only**—The only supported virtualization platforms at this time are Windows Server 2008 R2 Hyper-V or VMware vSphere 4.0 products. This should include the Hyper-V 2008 R2 standalone free product and both the ESX and ESXi products from VMware. This means that older versions such as Microsoft Virtual Sever 2005, Microsoft Windows Server 2008 Hyper-V, and VMware ESX 3.5 are not supported for use with Lync Server 2010.

- **No Live Migration**—Live migration or vMotion of Lync virtual servers is not a supported feature. Because media traffic heavily depends on low latency and CPU processing, moving a Lync VM between hosts can lead to a poor experience for users by either degrading or completely disconnecting a media stream.

▶ **Cannot mix physical and virtual machines within the same pool**—There are some additional guidelines when mixing physical and virtual servers for Lync, but the most basic one is that a pool cannot contain a mix of physical and virtual servers. All servers in a single Front-End, Edge, Director, or Mediation pool must either be physical or virtual to be supported.

▶ **Virtual Front-End pool required**—To virtualize roles such as the Director, Edge Server, or A/V Conferencing Server, the associated Enterprise or Standard Edition Front-End Server must also be virtualized. This means that if an organization deploys the Front-End Servers on physical machines, the Director or Edge Server cannot be virtualized. This negates a common scenario where it might make sense to use physical hardware for a front-end pool, yet virtualize a less intensive role such as a Director. The opposite case is perfectly valid. Organizations can virtualize the front-end pool, but use physical hardware for a Director or Edge Server.

Lync Server Virtual Topologies

Microsoft has released some documentation so far that discusses a few different sample virtualization topologies. One example covers a Standard Edition deployment and the other covers an Enterprise Edition deployment. For up to 2,000 users, the Standard Edition virtual topology should be sufficient and for any larger deployments, the Enterprise Edition virtual topology should be used.

The issue with these two topologies is many organizations require a deployment that sits somewhere between these two situations. The Enterprise Edition deployment is scaled to a point much higher than most organizations are going to require, and the Standard Edition deployment might be too small and lack the availability desired.

This section summarizes the different topologies tested by Microsoft and offers some additional sample topologies. These additional topologies are not officially supported or recommended by Microsoft support, but organizations can use them as suggested guidance when implementing Lync Server 2010.

> **TIP**
>
> Proper performance and load testing should be completed with any scenario prior to placing the deployment in production.

Standard Edition Example

The first topology tested by Microsoft is based on a Standard Edition Front-End Server deployment and supports up to 2,000 users in the example. This topology is primarily geared toward smaller deployments with no need for redundancy or proof-of-concept scenarios where rapid deployment is a priority. This example also scaled to allow approximately 100 users concurrently connected to a single A/V conference before performance began to degrade. The Standard Edition virtual topology layout is depicted in Figure 25.4.

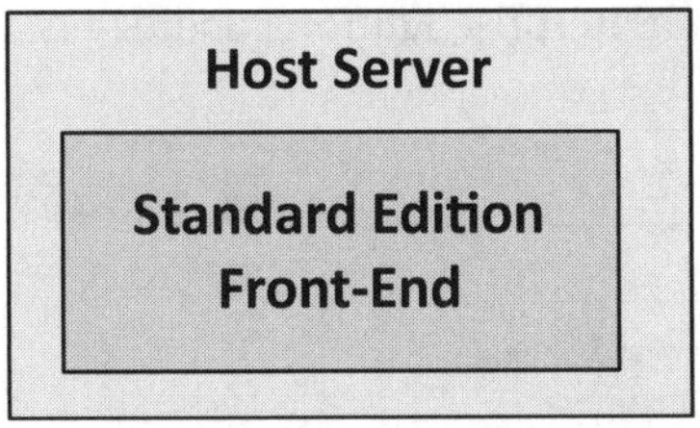

FIGURE 25.4   Standard Edition Virtual Topology

The host machine running Windows Server 2008 R2 had the following hardware configuration using a single virtual host:

▶ 2.26 GHz or higher CPU with four processor cores

▶ 16 GB RAM

▶ 500 GB SAS disk (RAID 0)

▶ Two network adapters

The virtual machine running the Standard Edition Front-End role used the following configuration:

▶ Four virtual CPUs

▶ 15 GB RAM

▶ One network adapter

An important note here is that Microsoft recommends using a single host for any Standard Edition Front-End Server. If more Standard Edition Front-End Servers are used, each should have its own dedicated host server.

NOTE

When using this topology, Microsoft also recommends limiting the bandwidth used for application sharing to 150 Mbps. Allowing values past this point created excessive CPU usage. Use the Set-CsConferencingConfiguration –Identity Global –MaxBandwidthPerAppSharingServiceMb 150 command to set this value.

Enterprise Edition Example

The other topology Microsoft tested is an expanded Enterprise Edition deployment designed for very large organizations. This topology is scaled to support 40,000 users and used seven different virtual hosts. The logical layout of the Enterprise Edition topology is displayed in Figure 25.5.

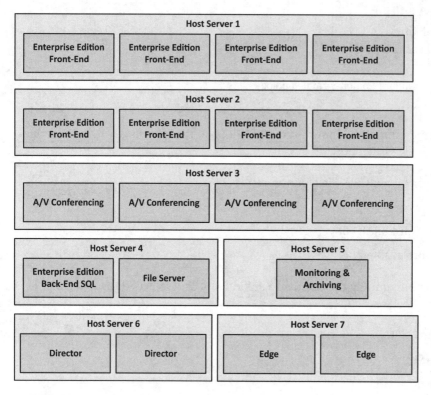

FIGURE 25.5   Enterprise Edition Virtual Topology

Front-End Hosts and VMs

Two hosts were dedicated to run eight Enterprise Edition Front-End Servers with a machine running Windows Server 2008 R2 and the following hardware configuration:

- ▶ 2.26 GHz or higher CPU with 16 processor cores
- ▶ 64 GB RAM
- ▶ 500 GB SAS disk (RAID 0)
- ▶ Four or more network adapters

Each virtual machine running the Enterprise Edition Front-End Server role used the following configuration:

- ▶ Four virtual CPUs
- ▶ 15 GB RAM
- ▶ One network adapter

A/V Conferencing Host and VM

The third virtual host server ran four different A/V Conferencing Server virtual machines. This offloaded A/V conferencing from the Front-End Servers to provide greater scalability. As with a physical deployment, for every 10,000 users, a dedicated A/V Conferencing Server should be deployed. The host had the following hardware configuration:

- 2.26 GHz or higher CPU with 16 processor cores

- 64 GB RAM

- 500 GB SAS disk (RAID 0)

- Four or more network adapters

Each A/V conferencing server virtual machine used the following configuration:

- Four virtual CPUs

- 15 GB RAM

- One network adapter

Back-End Host and VMs

The fourth host server was dedicated to the Back-End SQL Server and Back-End File Server. It had the following hardware configuration:

- 2.26 GHz or higher CPU with 8 processor cores

- 32 GB RAM

- 500 GB SAS disk (RAID 1+0)

- Two or more network adapters

Each virtual machine running the Back-End SQL Server or File Server role used the following configuration:

- Four virtual CPUs

- 15 GB RAM

- One network adapter

Monitoring and Archiving Host and VM

The fifth host server was dedicated to running a single virtual machine providing the Monitoring and Archiving roles with a collocated SQL Server database. The host had the following hardware configuration:

- 2.26 GHz or higher CPU with four processor cores

- 16 GB RAM

- 500 GB SAS disk (RAID 1+0)

- Two or more network adapters

25

The single virtual machine running the Monitoring and Archiving roles with a collocated SQL instance used the following configuration:

▶ Four virtual CPUs

▶ 15 GB RAM

▶ One network adapter

Director Host and VMs

The sixth virtual host server was dedicated to running two virtual machines with the Director role installed. The host had the following hardware configuration:

▶ 2.26 GHz or higher CPU with eight processor cores

▶ 32 GB RAM

▶ 500 GB SAS disk (RAID 0)

▶ Two or more network adapters

Each virtual machine serving as a Director used the following configuration:

▶ Four virtual CPUs

▶ 15 GB RAM

▶ One network adapter

Edge Server Host and VMs

The final virtual host server was dedicated to running two virtualized Lync Edge Servers. These were intentionally placed on a separate host for security reasons because the Edge Servers communicate with external hosts. The host had the following hardware configuration:

▶ 2.26 GHz or higher CPU with eight processor cores

▶ 32 GB RAM

▶ 500 GB SAS disk (RAID 0)

▶ More than four network adapters

Each virtual machine serving as a Director used the following configuration:

▶ Four virtual CPUs

▶ 15 GB RAM

▶ Two network adapters

Sample Topology Considerations

These topologies provide some general guidance, but organizations ultimately need to design a virtualized solution that works best for them. These topologies provide a starting point, but should be taken with consideration and adjusted to meet the needs of each organization instead of simply reusing the sample topologies. There are a few key issues with the sample topology; these are discussed in this section.

Guest Placement

With the published example, Microsoft has dedicated particular virtual hosts for specific Lync Server roles such as only Front-End Servers, only A/V Conferencing Servers, or only Directors. The obvious issue with this type of deployment is that if a single host server fails, it will bring down all the virtual machines running on that server. With many of these roles, each host becomes a single point of failure. So, although mixing roles across different host servers might make performance testing or troubleshooting slightly more difficult, it does remove one piece of hardware from being a single point of failure.

Disk Layout

The examples provided by Microsoft also use RAID 0 disk configurations for the host servers in most cases. Although this provides a performance benefit over other RAID configurations, the reality is that most organizations prefer to offer some form of redundancy at the physical disk level. If a single disk in a RAID 0 array fails, the entire array is lost, and all virtual machine disks on that array are unavailable. Using a redundant disk configuration such as RAID 5 or RAID 1+0 for most host servers offers some redundancy with slightly reduced performance.

Edge Virtual Machine Collocation

One security concern the Microsoft design addresses is the fact that the Edge Server should not be located on the same host machine as any other server roles. This is because the Edge Server is designed to sit in a perimeter network surrounded by firewalls on both sides.

> **CAUTION**
>
> Placing Edge Servers on a host machine within the internal network is a bit of a security concern, which is why Microsoft recommends separating these virtual machines.

In reality, many organizations will probably deploy Edge Servers on the same host as other virtual machines. With the ability to tag individual virtual machine adapters with a specific VLAN, the perimeter network traffic can be directed to only the adapters assigned to Edge Servers. Of course this means the perimeter network traffic passes through the host hypervisor at some level, but this seems to be a security issue less important for organizations because of the flexibility gained with VLAN tagging. Of course, the proper firewall rules should be in place to protect both the host and guest operating systems. If nothing else, it might make sense to use perimeter network hosts to also deploy virtual reverse proxy servers such as Microsoft Forefront Threat Management Gateway, which also is typically placed in a perimeter network.

Reverse Proxy

An often overlooked component of a deployment can be the requirement for a reverse proxy server when enabling remote access. The sample topology does not account for these servers, but organizations should plan for these additional virtual machines when deploying Lync Server. The requirements for each server are not nearly as high as for a Lync Server role, but do consume some resources on a host. Because these servers are typically placed in a perimeter network, the same concerns exist as when virtualizing an Edge Server deployment.

Additional Topologies

This section builds on the guidance suggested by Microsoft and offers some additional sample topologies. These have not been performance tested by Microsoft and are only a suggested starting point. Each topology should be thoroughly tested for performance by an organization before being placed into production.

Small Business

Small businesses looking to take advantage of virtualizing Lync Server 2010 on-premises will likely be looking to leverage the core feature set with remote access and possibly telephony integration. The priority in this configuration is to deploy as many features as possible with the least amount of hardware. High availability and failover are not requirements in this scenario, but the downside here is that a host or guest VM failure causes a complete loss in service. The small business topology is shown in Figure 25.6.

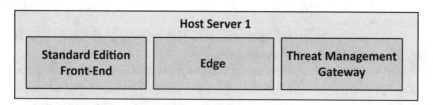

FIGURE 25.6   Sample Small Business Virtual Topology

A single virtual host can be used with the following hardware configuration:

- ▶ 2.26 GHz or higher CPU with 12 processor cores
- ▶ 48 GB RAM
- ▶ 500 GB SAS Disk (RAID 1+0)
- ▶ Six network adapters

Three virtual machines will be created: one Standard Edition Front-End Server with the Mediation Server collocated, one Edge Server, and one reverse proxy server running Microsoft Forefront Threat Management Gateway.

The Standard Edition Front-End Server would have the following configuration:

- ▶ Four virtual CPUs
- ▶ 16 GB RAM
- ▶ One network adapter

The Edge Server would have the following configuration:

▶ Four virtual CPUs

▶ 16 GB RAM

▶ Two network adapters

The Threat Management Gateway would have the following configuration:

▶ Two virtual CPUs

▶ 4 GB RAM

▶ Two network adapters

Medium-Sized Business

For those businesses that require a higher level of availability in Lync deployments, it becomes necessary to use more host server hardware and create additional virtual machines. This sample builds on the deployment for a small business, but provides redundancy at each role while adding monitoring and archiving abilities. Shared storage through an iSCSI SAN is a requirement for providing database clustering capabilities. This is only an example and can be modified to meet the needs of a business. The sample medium-sized business topology is depicted in Figure 25.7.

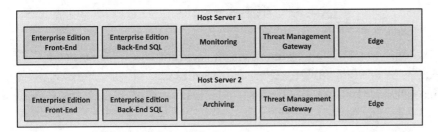

FIGURE 25.7   Sample Medium-Sized Business Virtual Topology

Two virtual hosts can be used with the following hardware configuration:

▶ 2.26 GHz or higher CPU with 16 processor cores

▶ 72 GB RAM

▶ 500 GB SAS Disk (RAID 1+0)

▶ 10 network adapters

Each host will run one virtual machine with the Enterprise Edition Front-End Server role in the following configuration:

▶ Four virtual CPUs

▶ 16 GB RAM

▶ One network adapter

25

Each host will run one virtual machine with the Back-End Server role in the following configuration. The two Back-End Servers can use SQL Server Failover Clustering to provide high-availability across hosts:

▶ Four virtual CPUs

▶ 16 GB RAM

▶ Four network adapters

NOTE

The additional network adapters here are for SQL Server Failover Clustering. In addition to the regular adapter, a private heartbeat network should be used. Also, because SQL clustering requires a shared disk, network adapters for iSCSI access to a SAN are required. Two are used here to allow iSCSI multipathing for redundancy.

Each host will run one virtual machine with the Edge Server role in the following configuration:

▶ Four virtual CPUs

▶ 16 GB RAM

▶ Two network adapters

Each host will run one virtual machine with Microsoft Forefront Threat Management Gateway in the following configuration:

▶ Two virtual CPUs

▶ 4 GB RAM

▶ Two network adapters

One host will run a Monitoring Server virtual machine and the other will run the Archiving Server virtual machine. Both will use the following configuration:

▶ Four virtual CPUs

▶ 16 GB RAM

▶ One network adapter

Host Server Configuration

When planning to virtualize Lync Servers, the virtual host server hardware and configuration have a direct effect on how well the virtual machine guests can perform. This section summarizes some of the support requirements and performance recommendations to follow when building a host server. Most of these requirements are based around treating each Lync virtual machine as if it were a physical server with its own dedicated processor, memory, disk, and network adapter.

Processor Requirements

Any host used for Lync virtual machines should have a modern processor, which is 2.26 GHz or faster. This means that the CPU used should be manufactured at least from January of 2009 or later to achieve the required performance. From a planning perspective, the number of logical cores on the processor determines the maximum number of virtual machines that can run on the host. To fall within the Lync support boundaries, each virtual machine must have four dedicated CPU cores. This means that for a server that has eight cores, only two Lync virtual machines can run on the host, whereas a server with 16 cores can support up to four Lync virtual machines.

> **NOTE**
>
> The host server is not going to consume many CPU cycles, so for planning purposes it is acceptable to ignore trying to dedicate a core to the host. If cores for the host were included, everyone would wind up with an odd number of CPU cores.

The number of cores is the important value here, not the number of physical processors. For example, two quad-core processors are equivalent to four dual-core processors. Both yield eight physical cores that can be used by virtual machines.

Memory Requirements

To meet the support requirements, each Lync Server virtual machine must be allocated a minimum of 15 GB of RAM. This memory should be allocated exclusively for each virtual machine. Hyper-V Service Pack 1 has a new feature called Dynamic Memory that allows defining startup and maximum RAM values for a virtual machine. This feature should not be used with Lync Server 2010, or if it is, the startup RAM for each VM should be at least 15 GB to guarantee that amount is always available.

Likewise, virtual machines that run on VMware should not be overcommitted on memory. VMware allows administrators to collectively assign more memory to virtual machines than is actually physically installed in the host server. This feature cannot be used with Lync and will have a negative impact on performance.

> **NOTE**
>
> When planning for memory allocation, it is important to reserve some memory for the host operating system. This amount varies based on the hypervisor and can be anywhere from 512 MB to 2 GB. It seems the Lync Server team is already planning for this by defining a minimum of 15 GB for virtual machines where the physical counterparts require at least 16 GB. The extra 1 GB leaves some memory for the host. As more virtual machines are placed on the host, more memory can be made available to the host server.

Disk Requirements

The only support requirement dictated by Microsoft around disk space is that each host must support at least 500 GB of free space. The actual space consumed by Lync virtual machines varies by role and by business requirements for monitoring or archiving data. Using fixed or dynamically expanding disks also has a big effect on how much space is required. Generally, allocating 40 to 50 GB of disk space per virtual machine for the operating system is sufficient. Lync Back-End database Servers or Monitoring and Archiving Servers with a collocated SQL database are going to consume much more space than a Front-End or Edge Server.

Both direct attached storage (DAS) and SAN disks are supported to hold Lync virtual machines. Which option is used depends greatly on the infrastructure that an organization already has in place. SAN provisioning is generally more flexible, but there is a significant upfront cost to these types of systems. DAS storage can be more affordable and yield acceptable performance for virtual machines.

Another consideration for organizations is whether to use a single RAID volume for all virtual machines or to separate each virtual machine disk on to its own physical hard disk. There is no requirement for separate disk spindles, but the best performance is realized if each virtual machine disk can be placed on a dedicated hard disk spindle. The downside to dedicated disks is that unless the disk count is doubled, there is no redundancy at the physical disk level. Many organizations find that placing virtual hard disks on a RAID 1+0 or RAID 5 volume meets the disk requirements of most virtual machines.

> **NOTE**
>
> Separating the disks used for the host system shows a performance benefit both for the host and guest VMs. A common configuration for host machines is to use two hard disks in a RAID 1 mirror set for redundancy, and then provision the remaining number of disks in a RAID 1+0 or RAID 5 configuration for virtual machine storage. This way, the host reads and writes do not compete with the virtual machine hard disk activity.

Networking Requirements

A fairy strict suggestion from Microsoft around network adapters is that a dedicated network adapter should be used for each Lync virtual machine. In a traditional virtualization environment, most virtual machines share traffic through a single or teamed set of physical network adapters. Virtual machines compete for network bandwidth resources through the same physical links and can be subject to delays or queues when other virtual machines have heavy bursts of traffic.

> **CAUTION**
>
> To avoid Lync Servers being affected by these contention issues, Microsoft recommends providing a dedicated physical adapter for each Lync virtual machine. This ensures that each Lync Server has a direct connection to a switch that can help eliminate jitter or delay problems encountered when sharing adapters.

Operating System Requirements

As indicated previously, the only supported hypervisors today are Microsoft Windows Server 2008 R2 Hyper-V and VMware vSphere 4. More hypervisor support might become available at a later time as vendors certify a platform with Microsoft. For Microsoft, either the full or core installation of Windows Server 2008 R2 can be used. The standalone, free product Microsoft Hyper-V R2 can also be used to virtualize Lync Servers. On the VMware side, both the ESX and ESXi platforms can be used.

Software Recommendations

In addition to the support requirements, there are some general recommendations that can help improve the performance of the Lync virtual servers. The first is to use host servers only for virtualization. Do not run additional applications or services on servers that host virtual machines. These applications or services have processing, memory, and network requirements that might have an adverse effect on virtual machines.

The second recommendation is to properly configure any anti-virus application because anti-virus applications that run on a host server can have a serious performance effect on virtual machines. Any locations with a virtual disk file should be excluded from virus scans to avoid performance issues. Anti-virus applications are not aware of how to scan a virtual disk file, so they treat it as any other file. Because virtual disk files are quite large, this can cause performance issues while the anti-virus application attempts to scan the file.

Virtual Machine Server Configuration

When designing a virtualized Lync Server 2010 deployment, there are a number of considerations to keep in mind. What might be difficult is separating what statements are provided for support reasons versus what are provided simply as recommendations. This section aims to detail some of the different recommendations Microsoft makes and to explain the pros and cons of each choice.

Processor Requirements

All virtual machines that run a Lync Server 2010 role must have four virtual processors assigned. This is because processing media requires many CPU cycles, so Microsoft recommends dedicating logical cores to each virtual machine.

Memory Requirements

Each virtual machine that runs a Lync Server 2010 role must have at least 15 GB of memory allocated. This value might increase over time, or it might be necessary to allocate more memory immediately for a large Back-End database server. 15 GB is the supported minimum tested by Microsoft, but services can operate with less memory for smaller environments at the risk of falling outside the support boundary.

Disk Requirements

There are no specific disk requirements for virtual machine disks used with Lync Server 2010. The only consideration is to allocate enough space for the operating system installation and Lync application installation. For Back-End database servers, the same planning figures apply for database sizing. This also applies to the Monitoring and Archiving database size planning figures.

Disk Types

When creating a virtual machine, options exist to create a hard disk for the VM as a fixed size or dynamically expanding. In VMware, the dynamically expanding disk is referred to as *thin provisioning*. The difference is that with a fixed-size disk, the space allocated to a virtual machine is immediately accounted for on the host operating system disk volume. For instance, if the host has 500 GB of free disk space and a 100 GB fixed size disk is created, the host will reflect 400 GB of free space. Dynamically expanding disks differ in that a maximum size is specified that the disk can grow to, but the space is not immediately consumed. Continuing the previous example, the virtual machine still believes it has a 100 GB hard disk, but space on the host physical disk is consumed only as the virtual machine begins to write data to the disk. The virtual disk is negligible at first, but it might consume 10 GB of space after an operating system is installed, and more when applications and data are added.

> **CAUTION**
>
> The advantage, and danger, to dynamically expanding disks is that disk space can be over-allocated. Virtual machines appear to have more disk space available to them than might be actually present on the disk, but this allows organizations to provision more virtual machines because they might not require that much space.

A third type of option in disk configuration for virtual machines is to use pass-through disks. Pass-through disks present a physical hard disk directly to a virtual machine. This configuration is not as typical for small environments, but where performance must be guaranteed, and resources not shared with other virtual machines, pass-through disks are an attractive option.

In earlier versions of virtualization products, the rule of thumb was that fixed-size disks yielded significantly greater performance for a virtual machine. With the most recent releases from both Microsoft and VMware, this notion has shifted quite a bit and dynamically expanding disks are now nearly equal in performance after they have been initially expanded. This means that the first time an application writes to a virtual disk, a fixed-size disk will be quicker because a dynamically expanding disk has to first grow the disk before writing the data. At the point where the dynamically expanding disk no longer is growing in size though, the performance is nearly equal.

For SQL Servers, the Microsoft SQL Server team recommends using either fixed-size disks or pass-through disks, so it might make sense to use these types for a Back-End Server.

For the other roles in Lync Server, it becomes a business or policy decision to use dynamically expanding disks. Initial performance might not be as good, but when the disks reach a growth plateau, the performance is on par with fixed-size disks and uses significantly less disk space.

Networking Requirements

Each virtual machine running a Lync Server 2010 role should have at least one virtual network adapter added. Edge Servers require at least two adapters just as with a physical installation.

Synthetic Device Drivers

Both the Hyper-V and VMware virtualization products contain emulated and synthetic device drivers. Emulated drivers were the original approach to virtualization where each hard disk or network adapter assigned to a virtual machine is emulated in software. The advantage to emulated drivers is that almost all operating systems contain support for these drivers because it emulates a baseline set of abilities. Synthetic drivers are used to provide an additional level of performance and abilities within a virtual machine such as jumbo frames or TCP offloading features.

In general, synthetic device drivers cannot be used in a virtual machine until special software is installed in the guest operating system to provide these drivers. In Microsoft Hyper-V, these are called the integration components, whereas in VMware these are referred to as the VMware tools. In Microsoft Hyper-V, adding a legacy network adapter device to a virtual machine uses an emulated device driver, but when adding one of the default network adapters to a virtual machine, the synthetic device driver is used. For VMware, the VMXNET network adapter types provide the best performance. With Lync Server 2010, deployments always use a synthetic network adapter to achieve the best possible performance.

Virtual Machine Queue

Virtual Machine Queue (VMQ) is a new network adapter feature that provides some performance benefit in a virtualized environment. VMQ allows the physical network adapter to provide virtual queues for each virtual machine running on the host. This allows the hypervisor to pass external traffic directly to each virtual machine without routing through the management operating system first. This feature should not be confused with Virtual Machine Chimney, which is a separate function that provides TCP offloading features from the guest virtual CPU to the physical network adapter.

Early versions of driver software that supported VMQ automatically disabled VMQ if an adapter used for virtual machines was placed in a network team. If you run an older version of the driver, be sure to update to the latest release to allow both teaming and VMQ to function. Support for Hyper-V network adapter teaming is up to the adapter vendors, so also verify that the hardware installed is supported by the manufacturer.

If the adapters used on a host machine allow this feature, it should be enabled for optimal performance in Lync Server 2010. Because media traffic is extremely sensitive to latency or delays, any optimizations at the network layer can lead to increased virtual machine performance. Adapters do not support an unlimited amount of virtual machine queues, so VMQ should be enabled only for virtual machines that receive a heavy amount of traffic. VMware includes a feature called *VMDirectPath*, which gives a virtual machine direct access to the physical adapters.

> **TIP**
>
> If a physical adapter can be provided for each virtual machine, this feature can be leveraged for increased performance.

Send/Receive Buffers

Microsoft recommends adjusting the send and receive buffers on any network adapter dedicated to virtual machines to be a value of at least 1024. This helps to improve network performance and reduces the number of dropped packets.

Operating System Requirements

When virtualizing Lync Server 2010, the only supported guest operating system is Windows Server 2008 R2. Although the original release of Windows Server 2008 x64 is supported for physical deployments, it is not supported when deployed within a virtual machine.

Software Recommendations

As with a physical host server, the Lync virtual machines should not run any additional applications or services. Additionally, any anti-virus applications should be configured to exclude both the Lync Server 2010 binary files location and the Lync services running.

Infrastructure and Application Virtualization

The topics in this section do not fit within any other section of the chapter, but are worth discussing. Organizations look to virtualize all servers and take advantage of desktop virtualization with Lync, but both scenarios still have some issues today.

Infrastructure Virtualization

Companies looking to completely virtualize the infrastructure can get a head start now with Lync Server 2010, but one consideration to be aware of is that the Microsoft Exchange Unified Messaging role still does not have any virtualization support. So, although organizations can virtualize their conferencing and telephony infrastructure, the voice mail component must remain on a physical server.

Another option for organizations looking to remove the dependencies on physical servers is to leverage the Exchange online hosted service from Microsoft for unified messaging. On-premises Lync Servers can communicate with hosted Exchange Unified Messaging Servers, which removes the need for locally hosted Exchange servers.

Application Virtualization

A popular shift in desktop deployment has been the concept of virtual desktops or using host servers to provide virtual machines for desktop users, which are accessed through some kind of thin client.

The issue with many of these deployments is a lack of media support. Because Lync clients operate as a softphone, there is a dependency on local speakers, microphones, and video cameras to use many of the media conferencing features. Even if thin clients have these hardware items installed, most desktop virtualization software does not support mapping to them or passing these devices through to a virtual machine running in a datacenter. These thin clients are also typically not high-end hardware, so the performance of these devices can suffer, especially when trying to process real-time media from a thin client to a virtual desktop.

25

CAUTION

These features might become available and improve at some point, but the current stance on virtualization for Lync endpoints is that they are supported only for non-media traffic. IM and presence can be used from within a terminal or virtual desktop session, but web conferencing, application sharing, and A/V conferencing are not supported features.

Best Practices

The following are best practices from this chapter:

- ▶ Use a supported hypervisor for Lync Server 2010 virtual machines such as Windows Server 2008 R2 Hyper-V or VMware vSphere 4.0.

- ▶ Use Windows Server 2008 R2 as the guest operating system for any Lync Server 2010 virtual machine.

- ▶ Allocate at least four virtual CPUs, 15 GB RAM, and one physical network adapter for each Lync Server virtual machine.

- ▶ Stress-test the virtual environment and monitor the Lync performance counters prior to placing the system in production.

▶ Do not use Live Migration or vMotion for Lync Server virtual machines.

▶ Use the Standard Edition virtual topology for fewer than 2,000 users and the Enterprise Edition virtual topology for larger deployments.

▶ Use the virtual machine queue (VMQ) feature if possible.

Summary

The new support for Lync Server 2010 virtualization will most likely lead to many organizations using a virtual deployment as opposed to physical servers. Some companies even mandate all new servers must be deployed virtually, which put administrators in a tough position when Microsoft would not support earlier versions for media traffic. The cost savings and flexibility in infrastructure not possible before will drive organizations in this direction.

However, there are some strict requirements that might deter organizations from using virtual servers. Requirements such as dedicated logical processors and network adapters are not typical in virtual environments, so companies might find themselves having to deploy new hardware specifically for Lync Server 2010 virtual infrastructure. Live Migration and vMotion are features many administrators have come to rely on and might be frustrated when they are unable to use them.

Although there are some restrictions, using the information in this chapter should allow an organization to effectively plan for and deploy Lync Server 2010 in a virtualized topology. This new flexibility in deployment support allows companies to take advantage of Lync Server 2010 in an easier and possibly more cost-effective manner.

CHAPTER 26

Planning for Internal Non-Voice Deployment

When deploying a potentially complex application like Microsoft's Lync Server 2010, it is critical to plan the deployment prior to the build in order to optimize the chances for a successful deployment. By planning the features to deploy and by determining the capacity needed and what hardware and software are necessary to support that capacity, you can avoid the pitfalls of deploying off the cuff and potentially having to make major changes to the architecture midway through a build or, wor se yet, midway through a deployment to the users.

Prior to this chapter, you should be familiar with the various roles and tools involved with Lync Server 2010. You should understand the basics of Lync Server topologies, sites, and server pools. If you are not yet familiar with these items, review those sections of this book before proceding with the upcoming planning chapters.

Determining the Scope of the Deployment

Lync Server 2010 contains such a wealth of features that planning a deployment, even one limited to internal non-voice features, can seem quite daunting at first. This section provides some guidance that can assist with the process and assist adminstrators in creating a well-thought-out and structured implementation plan.

Rather than forging ahead with no plan or goals and simply building new servers, loading application software, and inserting them into an existing network environment, a more organized process will control the risks involved and define in detail what the end state will look like.

The first steps involve getting a better sense of the scope of the project; in essence, writing the executive summary of the design document. The scope should define from a high level what the project consists of and why the organization is devoting time, energy, and resources to its completion.

Creating this scope of work requires an understanding of the different goals of the organization, as well as the pieces of the puzzle that need to fit together to meet the company's stated goals for the project. For Lync Server 2010, this means understanding how the various parts of the business will use the new functionality to improve collaboration and real-time communication. Different groups will focus on different aspects, such as IM with federated partners, or on leveraging video conferencing for departmental meetings. Understanding the needs of the various groups is key to a successful deployment.

Identifying the Business Goals and Objectives to Implement Lync Server 2010

It is important to establish a thorough understanding of the goals and objectives of a company that guide and direct the efforts of the different components of the organization, to help ensure the success of the Lync Server 2010 project.

> **NOTE**
>
> It might seem counterintuitive to start at this very high level and keep away from the bits- and bytes-level details, but time spent in this area will clarify the purposes of the project and start to generate productive discussions.

As an example of the value of setting high-level business goals and objectives, an organization can identify the desire for zero downtime on IM and conferencing services. Starting with the broad goals and objectives creates an outline for a technical solution that will meet all the organization's criteria, at a lower cost and with an easier-managed solution.

In every organization, a variety of goals and objectives need to be identified and met for a project to be considered successful. These goals and objectives represent a snapshot of the end state that the company or organization is seeking to create. For a smaller company, this process might be completed in a few brainstorming sessions, whereas larger companies might require more extensive discussions and assistance from external resources or firms.

High-Level Business Goals

To start the organizational process, it is helpful to break up business goals and objectives into different levels, or vantage points. Most organizations have high-level business goals, often referred to as the *vision* of the company, which is typically shaped by the key decision makers in the organization (such as the CEO, CFO, CIO, and so on); these goals are commonly called the 50,000-foot view. Business unit or departmental goals, or the

10,000-foot view, are typically shaped by the key executives and managers in the organization (such as the VP of sales, Director of Human Resources, site facilities manager, and so on). Most organizations also have well-defined 1,000-foot view goals that are typically tactical in nature and implemented by IT staff and technical specialists.

It is well worth the time to perform research and ask the right questions to help ensure that the Lync Server 2010 implementation will be successful. To get specific information and clarification of the objectives of the different business units, make sure the goals of a technology implementation or upgrade are in line with the business goals.

Although most organizations have stated company visions and goals, and a quick visit to the company's website or intranet can provide this information, it is worth taking the time to gather more information on what the key stakeholders feel to be their primary objectives. Often, this task starts with asking the right questions of the right people and then opening discussion groups on the topic. Of course, it also matters who asks the questions because the answers will vary accordingly, and employees might be more forthcoming when speaking with external consultants as opposed to coworkers. Often, the publicly stated vision and goals are the tip of the iceberg and might even be in contrast to internal company goals, ambitions, or initiatives.

High-level business goals and visions can vary greatly among different organizations, but generally they bracket and guide the goals of the units that make up the company. For example, a corporation might be interested in offering the best product in its class, and this requires corresponding goals for the sales, engineering, marketing, finance, and manufacturing departments. Additional concepts include whether the highest-level goals embrace change and new ideas and processes, or want to refine the existing practices and methods.

High-level business goals of a company can also change rapidly, whether in response to changing economic conditions or as affected by a new key stakeholder or leader in the company. So, it is also important to get a sense of the timeline involved for meeting these high-level goals.

NOTE

Examples of some high-level business goals include a desire to have no downtime, access to the communications infrastructure from any of the organization's offices around the world, and secured communications when users access the network from home or a remote location.

Business Unit or Departmental Goals

When the vision or 50,000-foot view is defined, additional discussions should reveal the goals of the different departments and the executives who run them. Theoretically, they should add up to the highest-level goals, but the findings might be surprising. Whatever the case turns out to be, the results will start to reveal the complexity of the organization and the primary concerns of the different stakeholders.

The high-level goals of the organization also paint the picture of which departments carry the most weight in the organization, and will most likely get budgets approved, which will assist in the design process. Logically, the goals of the IT department play an important role in a Lync Server 2010 deployment project, but the other key departments shouldn't be forgotten.

> **NOTE**
>
> As an example of the business unit or departmental goals for an organization, an HR department might typically influence the decision for right-to-privacy access to core personnel records. Or a legal department might typically influence security access on information storage rights and storage retention. These groups will prove invaluable when discussing topics such as archiving and whether to allow integration with public IM infrastructures.
>
> If the department's goals are not aligned with the overall vision of the company, or don't take into account the needs of the key stakeholders, the result of the project might not be appreciated. Technology for technology's sake does not always fulfill the needs of the organization and in the long run is viewed as a wasteful expenditure of organizational funds.

In the process of clarifying the goals, the features of the collaboration system and network applications that are most important to the different departments and executives should be apparent. It is safe to assume that access to collaboration and presentation tools as well as the ability to raplidly communicate with one another will affect the company's ability to meet its various business goals.

The sales department most likely has goals that require a specific type of communication to be supported and will likely push hard for an optimal conferencing experience. The IT department has its key technologies that support the applications in use, store and maintain the company's data, and manage key servers and network devices, and these need to be taken into consideration to ensure that Lync Server 2010 follows similar practices to those of existing systems.

It is also worth looking for the holes in the goals and objectives presented. Some of the less-glamorous objectives, such as a stable network, data-recovery capabilities, and protection from the hostile outside world, are often neglected.

A by-product of these discussions will ideally be a sense of excitement over the possibilities presented by the new technologies that will be introduced, and will convey to the executives and key stakeholders that they are involved in helping to define and craft a solution that takes into account the varied needs of the company. Many executives look for this high-level strategy, thinking, and discussions to reveal the maturity of the planning and implementation process in action.

NOTE

Examples of some departmental goals include a desire to have an integrated address book that enables them to quickly add contacts for partner companies, the capability to add web-based conferencing to meeting requests, or the capability to participate in video conferences from home.

Determining Your Infrastructure Needs

To build a successful Lync Server 2010 infrastructure to support basic functions such as instant messaging, web conferencing, and group chat, these services need to be built on a stable infrastructure. That is to say, the services outside of Lync Server 2010 need to be healthy, available, and of sufficient performance to take on the added load of Lync Server 2010. It is also important to plan the hardware that will be used to support Lync Server 2010 and ensure that it is capable of supporting the new environment.

Planning for Hardware and Software

Although many implementations of Lync Server 2010 for non-voice deployments will be virtualized, both physical and virtual servers used for Lync Server 2010 must meet a few standards. Keep these in mind when planning a Lync Server 2010 deployment:

▶ Lync Server 2010 only runs as a 64-bit application and must have 64-bit hardware.

▶ Lync Server 2010 does not support Intel Itanium processors.

From an operating perspective, plan to use one of the following operating systems to support Lync Server 2010:

▶ Windows Server 2008 R2 Standard operating system

▶ Windows Server 2008 R2 Enterprise operating system

▶ Windows Server 2008 R2 Datacenter operating system

▶ Windows Server 2008 x64 Standard operating system with Service Pack 2 (SP2)

▶ Windows Server 2008 x64 Enterprise operating system with SP2

▶ Windows Server 2008 x64 Datacenter operating system with SP2

WARNING

Installation of any Lync Server 2010 role on a computer running Windows Server 2008 x64 Datacenter or Windows Server 2008 R2 Datacenter that has multiple processor groups configured is not supported. This is due to an incompatibility with SQL Server 2008 Express and multiple processor groups.

Although the Lync Server 2010 roles are limited to the previous operating systems, the Planning Tool can be run on any of the following operating systems:

▶ The 32-bit version of Windows 7 operating system

▶ The 64-bit version of Windows 7 operating system using the WOW64 x86 emulator

▶ The 32-bit edition of Windows Vista with SP2 operating system

▶ The 64-bit edition of Windows Vista with SP2 operating system using the WOW64 x86 emulator

▶ The 32-bit edition of Windows XP with SP3 operating system

▶ The 64-bit edition of Windows XP with SP3 operating system using WOW64 x86

▶ The 32-bit edition of Windows Server 2008 operating system

▶ The 64-bit edition of Windows Server 2008 operating system using WOW64 x86

▶ The 32-bit edition of Windows Server 2008 R2 operating system

▶ The 64-bit edition of Windows Server 2008 R2 operating system using WOW64 x86

Also, plan for a somewhat standardized build for the operating system for Lync Server 2010 systems. By planning what software and features will and won't be present on the system, it is easier to understand the security implication of the systems and they become easier to support as their configuration is well known to the group supporting them.

▶ The individual role chapters in this book, which are Chapters 5 through 9, go into detail on which roles need which features and services, and these should be accounted for in the planning of the deployment.

Planning for Network Infrastructure Requirements

When planning a non-voice Lync Server 2010 deployment, don't forget to take into account the needs you will have of the network. Each Lync Server 2010 server should have at least one network interface rated for 1Gb per second of throughput. It should be connected to a low-latency, high-speed local area network (LAN).

Take into consideration plans for how servers will be logically deployed when planning for their physical deployment. For example, if multiple Front End Servers are load balanced for redundancy, consider placing them into different physical racks and connecting them to independent power circuits.

CAUTION

Placing all the load-balanced systems into a single rack only increases the possibility of a single event taking out all the systems, thus negating the benefits of load balancing for redundancy.

When planning the requirements for the LAN or WAN (wide area network), there might be some deviation between predicted loads and actual observed loads. Take this under consideration when evaluating whether existing network connections will handle the added load of Lync Server 2010.

Use the following rules of thumb for Lync Server 2010 when planning network usage:

- ▶ Plan for 65 Kbps per audio stream and 500 Kbps per video stream as peak values.

- ▶ Bidirectional audio and video sessions count as two streams.

- ▶ Lync Server media endpoints can adapt to varying network conditions and can usually handle oversubscriptions of up to 3 times. Although an audio stream peaks its usage at 65 Kbps, you can typically run three audio streams in the same 65 Kbps without users noticing a drop in quality.

- ▶ If a site lacks the capacity to comfortably run video streams, consider disabling video for that site.

- ▶ Expect degraded audio and video performance between endpoints separated by more than 150 ms of latency.

Planning for Active Directory Dependencies

Like most Microsoft applications, Lync Server 2010 depends heavily on Active Directory to authenticate users, find server pools, and generally keep data flowing. As such, it is critical to account for this when planning a Lync Server 2010 deployment of any kind. Plan to upgrade legacy domain controllers and be aware that Windows Server 2003 mixed mode is not supported by Lync Server 2010.

One of the best things you can do prior to a large deployment into Active Directory is to perform an Active Directory health check. This involves reviewing event logs, running tools such as DCDiag and NetDiag, and checking replication health to ensure that the directory itself is healthy and operating correctly.

> **CAUTION**
>
> Failure to realize that the directory itself is unstable or unhealthy greatly increases the chances of running into problems during a deployment of an application such as Lync Server 2010.

- ▶ Although performing an Active Directory health check is beyond the scope of this chapter, there are many references available on the Internet. In addition, Sams offers an e-book on this topic, *Performing an Active Directory Health Check* (ISBN 0768668425).

Planning for Certificates

One of the more difficult decisions when using Public Key Infrastructure (PKI)-enabled applications, such as Lync Server 2010, is the decision to use internal or public certificates. In this context, *internal* is defined as coming from a Certificate Authority that is not automatically trusted by the operating system, whereas *public* means one coming from a Certificate Authority that is already present in the trusted root store of operating systems.

Lync Server 2010 uses certificates for the following purposes:

▶ External or remote user access to audio/video sessions as well as conferencing and application sharing

▶ Remote user access for instant messaging

▶ Federation using automatic DNS discovery of partners

▶ Mutual Transport Layer Security (MTLS) connections between servers

▶ Transport Layer Security (TLS) connections between client and server

Regardless of whether internal or public certificates are used, the following requirements must be met:

▶ All server certificates must support server authentication (Server EKU [1.3.6.1.5.5.7.3.1])

▶ All server certificates must contain a valid and reachable Certificate Revocation List (CRL) Distribution Point (CDP)

▶ Key lengths must be either 1024, 2048, or 4096

▶ All server certificates must use one of the following hashes:

    ▶ ECDH_P256

    ▶ ECDH_P384

    ▶ ECDH_P512

    ▶ RSA

Various Lync Server 2010 roles have specific needs around the names contained in the certificates. Luckily for administrators, the Certificate Wizard builds the certificate request automatically and accounts for pool names, fully qualified domain names of hosts, as well as simple URLs such as meet or dialin that are created as a result of roles and features. The Lync Server 2010 administrator should ensure that the Certificate Authority to be used, whether internal or public, supports subject alternate names.

> **NOTE**
>
> In general, subject alternate name or SAN certificates are more expensive than traditional single-name certificates. Many public certificate providers charge the same price per name as they do a normal single-name certificate. Other providers offer a flat rate for a SAN certificate and allow the purchaser to insert as many names as will fit into the SAN certificate because there is a fixed amount of space available to fit names. The shorter the names, the more will fit. Some providers place arbitrary limits on the number of SAN entries that go into the certificate.

Planning for Capacity

One of the challenges that faces the new Lync Server 2010 administrator is the eternal question of "How big do I build it?" Luckily, Microsoft offers some guidance, in the following sections, around sizing servers to provide sufficient capacity for various types of deployments.

General Sizing

Microsoft provides some general sizing guidelines, which are summarized in Table 26.1.

TABLE 26.1   General Sizing of Servers

Server Role	Maximum Number of Users Supported
One Standard Edition server	5,000
Front End pool with eight Front End Servers and one Back End Server	80,000 unique users, plus 50% multiple point of presence (MPOP) for a total of 120,000 endpoints
One A/V Conferencing Server	20,000
One Edge Server	15,000 remote users
One Director	15,000 remote users
One Monitoring Server	250,000 users, if not collocated with Archiving Server; 100,000, if collocated
One Archiving Server	500,000 users, if not collocated with Monitoring Server; 100,000, if collocated

A dual 2.0 GHz, 16 GB supports 10,000 users as a Front End Server, whereas a dual 2.0 GHz, 32 GB supports up to 80,000 users as a Back End Server. That said, it is generally a good idea to account for an n+1 design when populating Front End Servers. If you were to plan for 30,000 users, take that number and divide it by the 10,000 users per Front End Server and add 1 for a total of 4 Front End Servers. This places a normal load of 7,500 users per server with the capability to redistribute to 10,000 users per server should a Front End Server suffer a failure or should it need to be brought down for maintenance.

If a site has fewer than 10,000 users and a typical audio/video conferencing load, it is generally recommended to collocate the A/V Conferencing Server role with the Front End Server role. Sites with a larger number of users should deploy a dedicated A/V Conferencing Server. In general, an A/V Conferencing Server can support around 1,000 concurrent A/V conference users. So, if your users are particularly fond of A/V conferences, you might need to deploy more A/V Conferencing Servers.

For non-voice deployments that support external users, the typical rule of thumb is one Edge Server for every 15,000 remote users. It is recommended to always deploy at least two Edge Servers to provide for redundancy.

Capacity Planning for Collaboration and Application Sharing

One of the more common uses for Lync Server 2010 conferences is to present a common document or application to multiple users. Sometimes this is a one-sided presentation and other times it might be a collaborative back and forth where users share control and modify a single document or presentation. As such, it's useful to understand bandwidth and disk usage for application sharing and conferencing collaboration. Microsoft offers the information included in Tables 26.2 through 26.5 to help plan for the impact of this feature.

TABLE 26.2   Application Sharing Capacity Planning

Modality	Average Bandwidth (Kbps)	Maximum Bandwidth (Kbps)
Application sharing using Remote Desktop Protocol (RDP)	434Kbps sent per sharer	938Kbps sent per sharer
Application sharing using compatibility conferencing server	713Kbps sent per sharer 552Kbps received per viewer	566Kbps sent per sharer 730Kbps sent per sharer

TABLE 26.3   Application Sharing Capacity Planning for Persistent Shared Object Model (PSOM) Applications

Application Sharing Usage	Sent and Received (Kbps)	Processor Time	Average Bandwidth Usage per User (Kbps)
15 conferences, 90 users	Received: 1,370 (2,728 peak) Sent: 6,370 (12,315 peak)	Average: 8.5 Peak: 24.4	Sent per sharer: 713.57 Received per viewer: 552.92

TABLE 26.4   Content Collaboration Capacity Planning

Content Type	Average Size	Number of Instances per Conference
PowerPoint	40MB	4
Handouts	10MB	3
Total default share per meeting	250MB	n/a

TABLE 26.5   Content Collaboration Upload and Download Rate

Category	Peak Usage in Bytes per Read and Write, 10,000 Provisioned Users	Average Usage in Bytes per Read and Write, 10,000 Provisioned Users
Data Conferencing Server content upload and download	Received: 17,803,480 bytes/read Sent: 19,668,079 bytes/write	Received: 706,655 bytes/read Sent: 860,224

These values serve as a starting point for administrators and can be scaled up or down if the profile isn't a good match for a specific environment.

Planning for the Address Book

One area that is often overlooked when planning a Lync Server 2010 deployment is the impact of the Address Book on the network. Depending on how well populated the Address Book is and whether all users have pictures in the Address Book, it has the potential to become quite large. Because each user will download the Address Book in its entirety when he first attaches to Lync Server 2010, a widescale deployment of clients can have a large impact on bandwidth usage. Microsoft offers the information in Tables 26.6 through 26.8 to estimate space and bandwidth around Address Book planning.

TABLE 26.6   Address Book Bandwidth

Modality	Number of Users	Average Bandwidth (Kbps)	Maximum Bandwidth (Kbps)
Initial Address Book Server download	80,000	99,000	332,000 (fresh deployment with 2,000 users on-boarding every hour)
Overall Address Book Web Query service	80,000	40,000	60,000
Bandwidth utilization per query	1	160	240

26

TABLE 26.7   Storage Rate for Address Book Server Download

Storage	Size for One Day	Size for 30 Days
File share size for Address Book Server, per user	1GB	26GB

TABLE 26.8   Database Storage Rate for Address Book Server and Address Book Web Query Service

Storage	Database Size
Address Book Server database size	3GB

These numbers are based on a large 80,000 user rollout and can be scaled appropriately for smaller deployments.

Planning for IM

Although instant messaging (IM) is one of the simplest features offered by Lync Server 2010, it is nonetheless important to plan for the implications of supporting this feature. Decisions around remote users, public users, and federated users influence how the environment is architected and deployed.

Considerations for Internal Users

When planning a deployment including IM, there are a few items to take into consideration when there will be internal users on the system. Although things such as server capacity are accounted for with the capacity planning of the Front End Server, it is important to consider the following impacts:

▶ Compliance and regulatory requirements

▶ Impacts on supporting systems

▶ End-user training

▶ Appropriate usage policies

When planning a deployment, always be aware of laws and regulations that might affect your users and your implementation. For example, find out whether there are requirements around archiving IM traffic for particular departments such as legal, finance, or executives. If there are, be sure to account for the Archive role in the deployment and determine how much space is required to archive the data for the period specified by company policy or specific applicable regulations.

For general users, determine whether there will be integration between the Lync client and applications such as Outlook. By default, Lync wants to store conversations in Exchange so that they can be recalled later by the user. If this will be enabled, account for the added storage usage in Exchange. If storage quotas are already enforced in Exchange, this might not be an issue, but users should be made aware that their usage within Exchange might increase and that they might end up with a shorter window of messages in their mailbox in order to stay within their quota.

> **TIP**
>
> Consider creating archive rules within Outlook to manage the Conversation History folder.

One area often missed by deployments of enterprisewide applications, such as Lync Server 2010, is the creation of appropriate end-user training. Although administrators spend a lot of their time researching and learning technologies, most end users do not. As such, it is the responsibility of the team deploying the application to develop training for end users. This typically should consist of cheat sheets explaining how to perform basic tasks and when possible, include screenshots to make it clear to users where to click and what to do.

> ▶ Chapters 22, 23, and 24, which cover the Windows, Macintosh and End Point clients, are an excellent place to start when developing end-user training.

The last thing to consider when planning a non-voice deployment of Lync Server 2010 is the creation of an appropriate use policy. This is where you can set the rules around the usage of IM and define behaviors that are to be avoided. For example, although it might seem common sense to some, set a policy stating that instant messaging is not to be used to send sensitive materials outside the company.

> **TIP**
>
> By setting guidelines ahead of time, you greatly reduce the chances of the new tool being used to circumvent other protective measures that have already been put in place in the enterprise. The main point is to make sure that IM is seen as another potential source for data leak.

Consideration for Remote Users

One of the big strengths of Lync Server 2010 is the capability to communicate with users that are outside the corporate environment. This might include partner companies or it might include random users on the Internet who need to participate in the occasional conversation and usually includes internal users who are in remote locations. When planning for Lync Server 2010, be mindful of which scenarios need to be supported. Typically, account for the following three major groups of external users:

▶ Remote users

▶ Federated users

▶ Public users

A *remote user* in this context refers to one who belongs to the organization but needs to connect from outside the organization. This might include situations in which the user travels or otherwise connects to Lync Server 2010 without the benefit of a virtual private network (VPN) connection into the network.

The primary consideration for remote users include planning for availability of the Edge Server role to ensure that they can always get a connection into the Lync Server 2010 environment and to plan for integration of certificates for Secure Sockets Layer (SSL) connections.

▶ For more detailed coverage of Edge services, refer to Chapter 27, "Planning for Deploying External Services."

If the Lync Server 2010 deployment uses public certificates, this will likely not be a problem because the major public certificate authorities are already trusted by the operating systems supported by the Lync client and the Communicator client. If, on the other hand, you plan to use an internal Certificate Authority, plan for not only the deployment of the root certificate into the certificate trust store of the clients, but also ensure that the Certificate Revocation List of the Certificate Authorities involved are reachable by users when they are connecting remotely.

Because most Lync Server 2010 deployments using internal PKI use Active Directory–integrated certificate authorities, typically you can depend on the directory to present the CRL to clients. Because domain controllers are almost never exposed to a demilaritized zone (DMZ) or the Internet, you must depend on the HTTP publishing of the CRL. Because this needs to be reached by remote clients who aren't connected to the internal LAN, the CRL path in the CRL distribution point should reference a web server that is reachable through the Internet. This ensures that systems can access a valid CRL to ensure that the certificates are good and thus enable successful connections over SSL.

The other value of an HTTP published CRL is for the support of clients that aren't bound to Active Directory. In many environments, Macintosh computers, which can run the Communicator client to connect to Lync Server 2010, aren't bound to Active Directory. As such, they can't access the CRL through the LDAP path, so they'll end up using the HTTP path for CRL checking.

Federated users refer to those from companies that also run Lync Server 2010 or older versions of Office Communications Server, such as OCS 2007 or OCS 2007 R2. *Federating* is the creation of a formal relationship between the two environments that give each the capability to share contact lists and presence information with one another. The primary items to plan for are the creation of an external access policy and the establishment of a list of federated domains. Both of these items are configured through the Lync Server 2010 Control Panel in the External User Access pane.

Planning for public users means making a determination of whether or not the Lync Server 2010 system will integrate with existing public IM services such as Yahoo!, AOL, or MSN. This gives the capability to consolidate all IM traffic into a single client because users would no longer need a secondary client to talk to their public contacts. This can be especially useful in environments that archive IM traffic for regulatory or compliance reasons. It also enables users to potentially use an existing public IM identity through Lync to maintain their original identity in the eyes of Internet public IM users.

Some additional public services can be integrated by using an XMPP gateway. This allows integration with Google Talk as well as Jabber.

> **NOTE**
>
> Public IM connectivity with MSN, AOL, and Yahoo! requires a separate license. If you plan to offer public IM connectivity, don't forget to purchase the license and account for the fact that it might take several weeks for these providers to process the SIP routes.

Planning for Conferencing

Conferencing in Lync Server 2010 describes any type of audio or video communication that involves three or more people. Although this chapter focuses on non-voice deployments of Lync Server 2010, this really refers to Voice over IP and as such, this section also takes into consideration PC-to-PC conferences as part of an audio conference. Because both scheduled conferences and ad hoc conferences can be initiated by users, it is important to take both into account.

> **TIP**
>
> Don't underestimate the popularity of conferencing. After users know it's available, it will become extremely popular. Management will love the potential of reducing costs around external conferencing services, too.

Defining Your Requirements

The first big step in planning a deployment is determining what features you plan to support. This greatly influences the overall design, has a big impact on server roles that are deployed, and affects infrastructure services such as the LAN and the WAN.

If you plan to enable web conferencing, which includes both document and application sharing, account for the following:

▶ Enable conferencing for the Front End pool in the Topology Builder.

▶ Account for increased network usage for application sharing. The default throttling is 1.5 KB/sec for each session and can be modified as needed.

▶ Build custom meeting policies if there is a need to enable either application sharing or document collaboration but a desire to prevent the other.

To enable audio and video conferencing, which in this type of deployment includes PC-to-PC calls but not PBX integration, plan for the following tasks:

▶ Enable conferencing for the Front End pool in the Topology Builder

▶ Account for increased network usage, typically 50 Kbps for audio and 350 Kbps for video

If requirements include supporting external users connecting to internally hosted conferences, consider the following tasks:

▶ Deploy Edge Servers in the topology.

▶ Properly protect access to the Edge Servers.

▶ Properly resolve the meeting URLs externally.

▶ Be sure users trust the certificates used on the Edge Servers to establish SSL connections.

▶ Decide whether federation will be supported.

Another decision, which must be accounted for, is whether it is necessary to support legacy clients on Lync Server 2010. Each time a client connects, its version is checked and compared against policies to determine whether it can be used. Web-based connections attempt to detect a local client and always offer the option of the web-based client. This is an important decision because there are compatibility limitations between various clients and back ends:

▶ Lync 2010 clients can neither schedule Live Meeting online conferences nor modify or migrate meetings of this type.

▶ Lync 2010 clients who need to attend Live Meeting online conferences hosted on OCS 2007 R2 servers must also have the Live Meeting client installed in order to participate.

Planning Your Conferencing Topology

Conferencing can be deployed in either the Standard Edition of Lync Server 2010 or in the Enterprise Edition. Topologies are simple in the Standard Edition because, by definition, all roles are placed on a single server. This is easy to plan because there are no options. Deploying on Enterprise Edition, on the other hand, opens up several options that must be considered.

Typically, you deploy on Enterprise Edition of Lync Server 2010 to gain redundancy by running a given role on more than one server and load balancing them to gain redundancy. Usually the decision on deployment is on whether to collocate the A/V Conferencing Server role with the Front End role. The decision point is usually on user load. Typically for deployments of fewer than 10,000 users, it is recommended to collocate the A/V Conferencing Server role with the Front End role. For more than 10,000, it is recommended to separate the roles (see Figure 26.1). Additionally, in a noncollocated topology, an A/V Conferencing Server can support up to 35,000 users. Going beyond this number requires additional A/V Conferencing Servers. Also keep in mind that if the reason for deploying on Enterprise Edition was to achieve redundancy, strongly consider deploying an n+1 architecture so that loads can be maintained if a server fails.

N+1 configuration with combined A/V
Conferencing and Front End Pool
Recommended for under 10,000 users

N+1 configuration with seperated A/V
Conferencing and Front End Pool
Recommended with loads exceed 10,000 users

FIGURE 26.1   Configuration for AV Topology

When planning hardware for conferencing, install servers to handle the load. Although Microsoft's recommendations typically call for a collocated A/V Conferencing and Front End Server to support 10,000 users, that is based on the following hardware:

▶ Eight processor cores (dual quad-core or quad dual-core)

▶ 16 GB RAM

▶ Multiple 10,000 RPM disks or solid state hard drives

▶ Dual Gigabit Ethernet adapters

Regardless of whether the A/V Conferencing and Front End roles are collocated, the configuration can run on Standard Edition of either Windows 2008 x64 or Windows 2008 R2.

Planning for Clients and Devices

There are several clients for Lync Server 2010 in which to plan. Administrators have the ability to limit which clients can connect so that users can only use a client that is currently supported. This simplifies troubleshooting because it's possible to prevent unexpected clients from connecting. The current list of clients includes

▶ **Lync 2010**—The primary Windows client

▶ **Lync 2010 Attendee**—The web-based plug-in for clients that don't have a full client

▶ **Lync Web App**—The web-based client that provides the primary features

▶ **Lync Server 2010 Attendant**—The integrated call management application, typically used by a receptionist for managing multiple lines and for routing calls

▶ **Lync 2010 Mobile**—The client for smart phones

▶ **Lync 2010 Phone Edition**—The client running on traditional handsets

▶ **Online Meeting Add-in for Lync 2010**—The client that provides integration with Outlook for meeting management

Another item to plan for on the topic of clients is the deployment of clients to end users. The two supported methods are to either deploy the .exe version of the client, or to extract the .msi from the executable and deploy this through Group Policy. It's typically preferred to deploy the executable version through some other application deployment method because the .exe version performs the following tasks that the .msi doesn't:

▶ Automatically performs prerequisite checks

▶ Installs Visual C++ components and Silverlight if missing

▶ Uninstalls Lync 2010 Attendee

▶ Notifies the user about Media Player 11 requirements

▶ Uninstalls legacy OCS clients

Planning for Archiving

When planning a non-voice deployment of Lync Server 2010, determine whether archiving is required in the environment. Archiving, from the perspective of Lync Server 2010, is the behavior of capturing IM conversations and conference attachments and storing them in a dedicated database for long-term storage. This gives administrators the ability to review IM conversations and to see attachments that were part of conferences. Specifically, the following types of contact are archived by the Archive server:

▶ Peer-to-peer instant messages

▶ Multiparty IMs

▶ Uploaded conference content

▶ Conference events, such as joining, leaving, uploading, and so on

The following types of content are not archived by the Archive server:

▶ Peer-to-peer file transfers

▶ Audio or video for peer-to-peer IMs and conferences

► Application sharing for peer-to-peer IMs and conferences

► Conferencing annotations and pools

The primary driver behind archiving in Lync Server 2010 is regulatory compliance. Some industries must archive all communications between users and potentially between internal users and external parties. Lync Server 2010 allows for flexible archiving policies to be deployed addressing these needs.

Defining Your Archiving Requirements

The first step in planning for archiving in a Lync Server 2010 deployment is determining the requirements. Start by answering the following questions about the environment:

► Which sites and users in the organization require archiving support?

► Will archiving be needed for internal communications, external communications, or both?

► Should archiving include IM, conferencing, or both?

► Is archiving critical enough that IMs and conferences shouldn't be allowed to occur if archiving is unavailable?

► How long should archived materials be retained?

Answering these questions enables you to determine how the archiving policies should be created.

Archiving policies are used by Lync Server 2010 to make decisions around what content should be archived, for whom it should be archived, and for how long it should remain in the archive. When planning the archiving policies, keep in mind that there are three types of archiving policies, each with a different intended purpose:

► **Global archiving policy**—This default policy applies to all users and sites in the deployment. The available options include the archiving of internal communications, external communications, or both. This policy cannot be deleted.

► **Site archiving policy**—This policy enables or disables archiving for a specific site within Lync Server 2010. Typically when deploying site archiving policies, disable archiving in the global policy; otherwise, all sites effectively process the global policy.

► **User archiving policy**—This policy enables or disables archiving for a specific user within Lync Server 2010, regardless of the sites in which the user is associated. This type of policy is typically used in environments where only a specific class of users requires archiving.

In each of the archiving policies, you can choose to archive IM only, conferences only, or both. If both site and user policies are implemented, user policies will override site policies.

The other decision that must be made when planning archiving policies is whether to implement critical mode archiving. Critical mode enforces a behavior such that if archiving isn't available, the system will prevent IM and conferencing from occurring. Critical mode is configured in the Archiving Configuration tab within the Lync Server 2010 Control Panel.

Finally, when planning the archiving requirements, determine how long archived data should remain in the archive. By default, purging archives is not enabled. The purge period can be set to as low as 1 day or as high as 2,562 days (just over 7 years). You can also choose to only purge exported archiving data. This option purges records that have been exported and marked as safe to delete by the session export tool.

Planning Your Archiving Topology

In Lync Server 2010, archiving consists of three components:

- ▶ **Archiving agents**—These agents are automatically installed on every Front End pool and Standard Edition server. The agent captures messages for archiving and sends them to the destination queue on the Archiving Server. Although the agent is always present, it only acts when an archiving policy is enabled.

- ▶ **Archiving Server**—This is the server role that reads the messages sent by the archiving agents and writes these messages to the Archiving back end database.

- ▶ **Archiving Server back end database**—This is the SQL server that stores the archived messages. This database can be collocated on the same computer as the Archiving Server or can be on a dedicated system if scalability is an issue.

There are three typical topologies for deploying archiving, as shown in Figure 26.2.

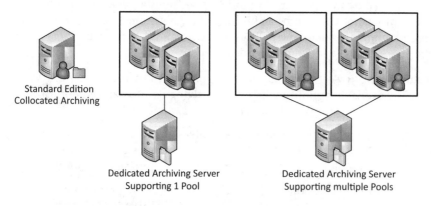

Standard Edition
Collocated Archiving

Dedicated Archiving Server
Supporting 1 Pool

Dedicated Archiving Server
Supporting multiple Pools

FIGURE 26.2   Typical Topologies for Deploying Archiving

The Archiving Server can be collocated with a Monitoring Server, with a SQL store of a Front End pool, or with a file store of a Front End pool. The Archiving database can also be collocated on the same computer that runs Archiving Server or the computer that runs Monitoring Server.

Regardless of which topology is chosen, there are some common requirements that should be planned. In addition to the normal requirements for Lync Server 2010 in terms of supported versions of Windows, also ensure that a valid version of SQL is used. The Archiving Server is compatible with the following versions of SQL:

▶ Microsoft SQL Server 2008 SP1 Enterprise Edition

▶ Microsoft SQL Server 2008 SP1 Standard Edition (x64)

▶ Microsoft SQL Server 2005 SP3 Enterprise Edition

▶ Microsoft SQL Server 2005 SP3 Standard Edition (x64)

▶ Microsoft SQL Server 2008 Express (x64) only when used on Standard Edition Lync Server 2010

In addition, the Archiving Server needs Message Queuing installed with Active Directory Integration enabled. This requirement is applicable to any Front End or Standard Edition Lync Server 2010 systems that host users who have archiving enabled.

From a scaling perspective, support as many as 500,000 users on a single dedicated Archiving Server. For environments with fewer than 500,000 users and multiple Front End pools, deploy a centralized Archiving Server unless unusual network constraints exist. It is also recommended to validate a topology with the legal department to ensure that there are no issues with holding archived communications from one country to another. Some localized privacy laws might affect the capability to deploy a centralized Archiving Server.

To optimize performance on the Archiving Server, plan to deploy three physical disk groups to hold the following information:

▶ System files and Message Queuing files

▶ Archiving Server database data file

▶ Archiving Server database log file

Based on the typical Lync Server 2010 user model, anticipate around 49 KB of data per day per user. Based on this, database sizing can be approximated as the following:

DB size = (DB growth per day per user) * (number of users) * (number of days)

For example, with a deployment to 10,000 users that will archive data for 60 days, anticipated database size is the following for a DB size of 28 GB:

DB size = (49 KB) * (10,000) * (60)

If an organization varies significantly from the average Lync user model, adjust the growth estimate accordingly.

Planning for Virtualization

Many modern datacenters are moving toward virtualizing their workload as much as possible. Lync Server 2010 supports virtualizing all its roles, although it is supported with a lower-rated capacity when virtualization is involved. This isn't to suggest that virtualization adds overhead, but should be taken as a statement from Microsoft that although it supports Lync Server 2010 on virtualized systems, it would rather see them run on physical hardware and, as such, lower their capacity ratings for virtualized roles. Microsoft even goes as far as to state that if the virtual host is given dedicated resources equivalent to a physical host, it will support the same number of users as the physical host. Its conservative stance is based on the resources that are typically allocated to a given virtual guest.

For example, when using virtualized servers, Microsoft suggests a maximum load of 2,000 users per virtual Standard Edition server and a maximum of 5,000 users per virtual Enterprise Edition Front End Server. Compare these values to the 5,000 users per Standard Edition and 10,000 per Enterprise Front End Server when used with physical hardware.

NOTE

Microsoft officially supports only Windows Server 2008 R2 for the guest operating systems when used for Lync Server 2010. On the host side, both VMWare and Hyper-V virtualization platforms are supported.

Given that typically virtualized environments are shared across a variety of applications and usually connected to some form of shared storage, pay careful attention to the amount of disk I/O available to various Lync Server 2010 roles.

CAUTION

Don't automatically assume that because a virtualization environment is attached to a high performance SAN that there's automatically enough I/O to keep a new application happy. Always evaluate current loads on the infrastructure, both the virtualization farm and the back end storage, to ensure that the new loads imposed on the environment won't degrade the performance of all applications running on the farm.

Another area to plan for is the networking aspect of the virtualization platform. To optimize performance for Lync Server 2010, it is recommended that each virtualized host be bound to a dedicated Ethernet port on the host system. For large deployments, this can mean a large number of Ethernet ports. Strongly consider deploying multiport network interface cards (NICs) into virtualization hosts.

Another technology to consider, especially when virtualizing Lync Server 2010, is the use of NICs that support Virtual Machine Queue (VMQ). VMQ is a virtualization technology that allows for the efficient transfer of network traffic to a virtualized operating system. VMQ enables virtual machines to filter their queue of packets within the NIC to improve the efficiency of network traffic. If the NICs support it, VMQ can be enabled for individual virtual machines from within the hypervisor's management console.

It is also recommended to increase the transmit and receive buffers on NICs dedicated to virtual machines to at least 1,024 to avoid packet loss. Not all NICs support a buffer of this size, so take this into account when planning where to deploy the virtual machines for Lync Server 2010 or when planning what hardware to purchase to support a virtualized Lync Server 2010 deployment.

▶ For more detailed information on how virtualization works with Lync Server 2010, refer to Chapter 25, "Virtualization."

Planning for Management

Lync Server 2010 follows the currently popular model of role based access control (RBAC). The concept is that one defines a role, typically based around common tasks, and then delegates the capability to perform these tasks to the role group. Existing security groups or individuals are then populated into that role group to grant them the necessary rights to perform the tasks.

Lync Server 2010 predefines nine RBAC groups that cover most of the commonly delegated tasks within Lync Server 2010. These groups and their allowed tasks are as follows:

▶ **CsAdministrator**—This group can perform all administrative tasks and modify all settings within Lync Server 2010. This includes creating and assigning roles, and modification or creation of new sites, pools, and services.

▶ **CsUserAdministrator**—This group can enable or disable users for Lync Server 2010. They can also move users and assign existing policies to users. They can neither create new policies nor modify existing policies.

▶ **CsVoiceAdministrator**—This group can manage, monitor, and troubleshoot servers and services. They can prevent new connections to servers, apply software updates, as well as start and stop services. They cannot, however, make changes that affect global configuration.

▶ **CsViewOnlyAdministrator**—This group can view the deployment, including server and user information, in order to monitor deployment health.

▶ **CsHelpDesk**—This group can view the deployment, including user's properties and policies. They can also run specific troubleshooting tasks. They can neither change user properties or policies nor server configuration or services.

▶ **CsArchivingAdministrator**—This group can modify archiving configuration and policies.

▶ **CsResponseGroupAdministrator**—This group can manage the configuration of the Response Group application within a site.

▶ **CsLocationAdministrator**—This group offers the lowest level of rights for Enhanced 911 (E911) management. This includes creating E911 locations and network identifiers and network identifiers and enables associating these with each other. This role is assigned with a global scope as opposed to a site-specific scope.

26

To comply with RBAC best practices, do not assign users to roles with global scopes if they are supposed to administer only a limited set of servers or users. This means creating additional role-based groups with similar rights to previous groups, but applied to a more limited scope because all default role groups in Lync Server 2010 have a global scope. That is to say, the rights apply to all users and to servers in all sites.

These scoped role groups can be created through the PowerShell commandlets provided with Lync Server 2010 by using an existing global group as a template and by assigning the rights to a precreated group in Active Directory. For example:

```
New-CsAdminRole -Identity "Site01 Server Administrators" -Template
CsServerAdministrator -ConfigScopes "site:Site01"
```

This commandlet gives the Site01 Server Administrators group the same rights as the predefined CsServerAdministrator role, but rather than giving the rights globally, the rights apply only to servers in Site01.

A similar process can be used to create a role that is scoped based on users rather than on sites:

```
New-CsAdminRole -Identity "Finance Users Administrators" -Template
CsUserAdministrator -UserScopes "OU:OU=Finance, OU=Corporate Users,
DC=CompanyABC, DC=com"
```

This grants a group called Finance Users Administrators rights similar to the predefined CsUserAdministrator group but rather than getting the rights across all user objects, they will be limited to user objects in the Finance OU as defined in the commandlet.

After the necessary role groups have been defined, simply add users or other groups to the role groups through Active Directory Users and Computers.

> **NOTE**
>
> When users are placed into either a new security group or into a role group, they need to log out and then log on for the Kerberos ticket to be updated with the new group membership. Without this process, they will not be able to use the new rights that they are granted.

For users who are given any level of administrative rights within Lync Server 2010, carefully consider which tasks they need to perform and then assign them to the roles with the least privilege and scope necessary to perform the tasks.

For administrators interested in what rights are available to each of the predefined groups, Microsoft has published a fairly exhaustive list at the following URL: http://technet. microsoft.com/en-us/library/gg425917.aspx.

Documenting the Plan

After all the various requirements have been determined and the options thought out and decided on, put these decisions and requirements into a design document. The complexity of the project affects the size of the document and the effort required to create it. The intention is that this design document summarizes the goals and objectives that were gathered in the initial discovery phase and describes how the project's result will meet them. It should represent a detailed picture of the end state when the new technologies and clients are implemented. The amount of detail can vary, but it should include key design decisions made in the discovery process and collaboration sessions.

The following is a sample table of contents and brief description of the design document:

- ▶ **Executive Summary**—Provides a brief discussion of the scope of the Lync Server 2010 implementation (the pieces of the puzzle).

- ▶ **Goals and Objectives**—Includes the 50,000-foot view business objectives, down to the 1,000-foot view staff level tasks that will be met by the project.

- ▶ **Background**—Provides a high-level summary of the current state of the network, focusing on problem areas, as clarified in the discovery process, as well as summary decisions made in the collaboration sessions.

- ▶ **Approach**—Outlines the high-level phases and tasks required to implement the solution (the details of each task are determined in the migration document).

- ▶ **End State**—Defines the details of the new technology configurations. For example, this section describes the number, placement, and functions of Lync Server 2010.

- ▶ **Budget Estimate**—Provides an estimate of basic costs involved in the project. Whereas a detailed cost estimate requires the creation of the migration document, experienced estimators can provide order of magnitude numbers at this point. Also, it should be clear what software and hardware are needed, so budgetary numbers can be provided.

When developing the document further, one will want to add additional detail in various sections to lay out the costs and benefits as well as providing a long-term vision to the project. Consider including these details in the various sections of the document:

- ▶ **Executive Summary**—The executive summary should set the stage and prepare the audience for what the document will contain, and it should be concise. It should outline, at the highest level, what the scope of the work is. Ideally, the executive summary also positions the document in the decision-making process and clarifies that approvals of the design are required to move forward.

- ▶ **Goals and Objectives**—The goals and objectives section should cover the high-level goals of the project and include the pertinent departmental goals. It's easy to go too far in the goals and objectives sections and get down to the 1,000-foot view level, but this can end up becoming confusing, so this information might be better to record in the migration document and the detailed project plan for the project.

26

▶ **Background**—The background section should summarize the results of the discovery process and the collaboration sessions, and can list specific design decisions that were made during the collaboration sessions. Additionally, decisions made about what technologies or features not to include can be summarized here. This information should stay at a relatively high level as well, and more details can be provided in the end state section of the design document. This information is useful as a reference later in the project when the infamous question "Who made that decision?" comes up.

▶ **Approach**—The approach section should document the implementation strategy agreed upon to this point, and should also serve to record decisions made in the discovery and design process about the timeline (end to end and for each phase) and the team members participating in the different phases. This section should avoid going into too much detail because in many cases the end design might not yet be approved and might change after review. Also, the migration document should provide the details of the process that will be followed.

▶ **End State**—In the end state section, the specifics of the Lync Server 2010 implementation should be spelled out in detail and the high-level decisions that were summarized in the background section should be fleshed out. Essentially, the software to be installed on each server and the roles that will be installed on each server are spelled out here, along with the future roles of existing legacy servers. Information on the clients that will be supported, policies that will be enforced, and so on should be in this section. Diagrams and tables can help explain the new concepts and show what the solution will look like, where the key systems will be located, and how the overall topology of the implementation will look. Often, besides a standard physical diagram of what goes where, a logical diagram illustrating how devices communicate is needed.

▶ **Budget Estimate**—The budget section is not exact but should provide order of magnitude prices for the different phases of the project. If an outside consulting firm is assisting with this document, it can draw from experience with similar projects of like-sized companies. Because no two projects are ever the same, there needs to be some flexibility in these estimates. Typically, ranges for each phase should be provided. The goal is for the audience of the document to understand what the project will cost and what they are getting for that money. This is also a great place to point out anticipated returns on investment (ROI) because these often act as the primary justification for a Lync Server 2010 implementation.

Best Practices

There are several items recommended in this chapter that should be taken into account when planning a non-voice deployment of Lync Server 2010. By following these recommendations, you can be better prepared for the deployment and can avoid the common pitfalls associated with planning a topology and deployment of a complex technology. The following is a summary of recommended best practices from this chapter.

▶ Start the deployment planning with a comprehensive design document. This ensures that decisions have been made, and it gives an excellent opportunity to shop the design around to other groups to get buy-in and to ensure that other groups know how they'll be affected by the upcoming deployment.

▶ Treat your deployment like a formal project. Produce a project plan that includes anticipated tasks and anticipated durations, and calls out the required resources. This makes it easier to get support from management to dedicate the appropriate resources and time to the deployment.

▶ Make sure that any constraints are understood prior to the completion of the design. Things such as regulator compliances have a major impact on decisions made in the design.

▶ Make sure the deployment can handle the anticipated load. Use the Microsoft sizing guidelines to ensure that the design can support the load you expect to place on it.

▶ Start the deployment with a pilot. This gives an excellent opportunity to validate the impact of users on the system and gives administrators an opportunity to get familiar with the infrastructure while supporting only a limited number of users.

▶ Involve the networking group when designing a non-voice deployment. The new features offered by Lync Server 2010 will greatly impact a WAN and the networking group will have bandwidth and latency information that might affect the design.

▶ Make decisions about how external users will be supported early in the process. Designs for internal only versus external support will be significantly different. These decisions affect several other decisions, so the earlier this can be decided, the less impact it has on the overall effort.

▶ If possible, use public certificates that use subject alternate names. This greatly reduces the impact on end users and on external users because the certificates will already be trusted by the operating system.

▶ Use modern hardware. Current-generation processors can provide a much larger capacity than processors from only one generation ago. The Microsoft sizing guides are based on current generation processors. Deviating from that practice renders the sizing guides inaccurate and puts the project at risk of being underpowered. This results in a poor user experience when loads increase.

▶ Train the end users on how to use the new system. Ensure that the users understand the limitations of various clients because they do not all provide the same features. Consider an online FAQ (Frequently Asked Questions) for users to refer to.

▶ Define an acceptable use policy for the Lync Server 2010 system. This reduces the exposure of the end users because they will know what behaviors can potentially put them at risk. It also enables administrators to more easily block risky behaviors because there will be a written policy to back up the configuration.

▶ Make sure the archive is designed with enough storage to hold the anticipated volume of data.

▶ Regularly test the recovery of data from the archive. This helps ensure that the data will be available and readable when the time comes that it's needed for something important. Consider a monthly test.

▶ Plan carefully when using virtualization and understand what other services are provided by the virtualization farm. Most virtualizations farms are oversubscribed because virtualization is a popular form of consolidation for servers. Be aware that not having dedicated resources reduces the potential capacity of the systems.

▶ Whenever possible, use a system of role based access control. Roles should be well defined and administrators should be given only the minimum of rights needed to perform their jobs. If their jobs change, their role-based group memberships should change. Don't forget that this goes both ways: Add them to new groups when they need additional rights, but don't forget to remove them from groups if there are tasks they longer perform.

▶ Don't forget to monitor the Lync Server 2010 environment with an application, such as SCOM or Nagios or SiteScope, to ensure that the systems are available. Leverage the monitoring software to trend the loads on the system to be able to predict when extra capacity will need to be added to maintain an acceptable load on each server.

By following these best practices, administrators can maximize their chances for a successful Lync Server 2010 deployment and can keep their end users happy and productive.

Summary

As we've seen in this chapter, there's a lot more to preparing for a deployment than merely gathering up the software and installing it. Many of the most important steps are the so-called "soft decisions" and the proper presentation of the project to the decision makers. This includes not only those who make the technical decisions but those who make the financial decisions as well. It's critical to understand the needs of the business and to determine how Lync Server 2010 can address those needs in the best manner. By aligning the technology solutions with the business drivers, one can greatly increase the chances of getting the project approved and of implementing it successfully.

The goal in the preparation phase should be to build an architecture as simple as possible that still meets all the requirements of the environment. By the time the installation occurs, all questions should have already been answered and be accepted by all the project stakeholders. In this manner, there won't be any surprises because everyone will already know exactly what to expect from the project.

Always take the opportunity to look beyond the design and implementation and to ask questions such as "Who is going to manage this environment?" or "How will we make sure the Help Desk can do their jobs without giving them the ability to break the application?" and plan for those events. By accounting for them in the preparation phase, it's easier to avoid situations where one has to make suboptimal decisions at the last minute. With Lync Server 2010, it's especially true that an ounce of prevention is worth a pound of cure.

26

Planning for Deploying External Services

The Edge Server role is a key part of why Lync Server is such a compelling solution for businesses, but along with that power and flexibility comes a good deal of configuration work and upfront planning. Networking, firewalls, certificates, and load balancing mean the Edge Server touches practically every part of the network and consequently, almost every team from server administrators to network engineers.

The Edge role has traditionally been the most difficult to configure and Microsoft has made significant improvements to that process in the latest version. Configuration changes are now pushed out to Edge Servers from a central location instead of individually configuring servers, which cuts down on the chance for human error and ensures consistency among server pool members.

This chapter discusses what details to consider when planning for an Edge Server and how to properly prepare an Edge Server's network adapters. It also details the firewall requirements and different topologies that can be used to support an Edge Server. Certificate requirements and planning guidance for the reverse proxy are also discussed. Lastly, some sample scenarios are presented for various deployment sizes with a full diagram, list of certificate requirements, and public DNS entries.

Edge Server Considerations

The first step in planning for Edge services is to determine what the business requirements are, which features need to be deployed, and what kind of topology to use. For instance, a small business that wants to communicate with public IM networks might deploy a single server running the Access Edge Server role, whereas a larger business that wants to replace a hosted virtual conferencing solution might deploy multiple, load-balanced Edge Servers with full support for A/V conferencing. This section discusses the different forms of remote access and considerations for each feature.

Remote Access

When planning for Edge services it is important to realize that the remote access features touch many different facets of Lync Server. The remote access features allows endpoints to sign in to Lync Server across the Internet. Keep in mind that to support any of the web conferencing or A/V features across the Internet, remote access must be configured.

Remote access policies can be used to control which users, groups, or locations are permitted to sign in remotely. Identify what user sets should be configured for remote access, and then create access policies to assign to these groups.

> **TIP**
>
> If everyone in the organization should be enabled for remote access, it makes sense to leverage the Global remote access policy. If different groups of users receive various levels of functionality, it might be necessary to create site-level or more specific policies.

Anonymous Access

Whether an organization supports anonymous access to Lync Server is a decision the business must make when considering an Edge Server deployment. Allowing anonymous access provides the ability for internal users to invite participants from outside to the organization to web or A/V conferencing sessions. This ability can often replace hosted or subscription-based conferencing services for most users, providing immediate cost savings. For extremely large conferences, it might still make sense to use a hosted service, but the majority of ad-hoc or smaller conferences can easily be handled by Lync Server.

Another option is that only specific users, groups, or locations can be given the ability to communicate with anonymous users through the use of conferencing policies. This allows administrators the flexibility of allowing all authenticated users to use web conferencing, but maybe only a select few are allowed to host conferences with anonymous participants.

Federation

When deploying Edge Servers, make a decision about whether users are allowed to federate with other organizations that run Lync Server. Making a decision about whether federation is enabled is the first step, but the second is to determine what type of federation is allowed.

In Lync Server, organizations can use open federation, where federation to all domains is allowed, or direct federation, where users might federate only with organizations explicitly approved by an administrator. There are advantages to both approaches, but there is an increasing trend to allowing open federation because of how easily it extends the reach of a Lync Server deployment.

A good analogy here when considering whether to use open or closed federation is to think of federation in terms of e-mail. Imagine if e-mail operated like direct federation where users in different domains cannot send mail to each other without an administrator on both sides first approving the partner domain. If that were the case, e-mail probably would not have become the universal communication modality that it is today. Instead, any user can generally send mail to any domain without administrators making server configuration changes. Open federation is the Lync Server equivalent of that ability; users have full access to presence, instant messaging, web conferencing, and A/V conferencing with any other user across the world without any additional configuration. Federation has a leg up on e-mail because it allows for much richer communication methods between partners.

Direct Federation

There might be times when open federations simply are not an option because of security or policies. In those cases, it might be necessary to use direct federation and manually configure the Edge Servers to federate with only specific domains. If using closed federation, be sure to coordinate with an administrator at any partner domains to check whether they also use closed federation. If so, the administrator for the partner also needs to make a change to the system to allow the federation so it works in both directions. These extra steps are another reason open federation is an attractive option.

There is no dependency on both sides of a federated relationship to use the same type of federation. One organization might use direct federation and allow only one specific partner, but that partner might have open federation enabled, allowing users to communicate with any federated domain.

Either way, upfront planning is necessary to determine whether to allow federation and what type of federation will be enabled. After making that decision, identify any domains that should be specifically allowed or blocked.

The next step in deploying federation is to identify the users who should be allowed to use federation. Even if federation is provisioned for an Access Edge Server configuration, the ability to use federation can still be controlled on a global, site, or per-user basis with remote access policies.

Public IM Connectivity

Lync Server Public IM Connectivity (PIC) enables users to communicate with public instant messaging (IM) networks such as MSN, AOL, and Yahoo!. It operates in a similar fashion to federation in that it uses the same ports and topology, but has a slightly different set of steps to configure. The main difference is that Public IM Connectivity must be configured through the organization's licensing site with Microsoft. The public IM providers do not use the SRV record for open federation and instead require these manual steps to provision the initial connectivity.

27

Administrators can choose to allow only specific SIP domains to communicate with the public IM providers. Each SIP domain supported for Public IM Connectivity must be provisioned through the licensing site. After provisioning the Public IM Connectivity, it can take up to 30 days before each provider activates the change, and because each provider is independent, they can come online at different times.

Public IM connections have a more limited feature set than federation does. The Public IM providers do not support any kind of multiparty IM or conferencing, so all conversations are limited to two participants. Public IM providers also do not support any kind of web conferencing or A/V features, even on a two-party basis. The only exceptions to this are the MSN and Windows Live services that actually do allow two-party A/V conversations with Lync Server users.

Capacity Planning

Plan for enough Edge Servers to meet capacity requirements of the environment. An Edge Server that meets the recommended specifications is capable of supporting up to 15,000 simultaneous IM and presence users. For redundancy, or to support more than 15,000 external users, and then simply use additional Edge Servers in the pool.

Edge Placement

Edge Server placement is critical in a deployment to optimize media paths. The SIP signaling used for presence and IM is more tolerant of slight delays, but web conferencing and A/V traffic are sensitive to latency, so it is important to properly plan Edge Server placement.

> **TIP**
>
> As a rule of thumb, Edge Servers are generally deployed in any location with a Front-End pool that supports remote conferencing or A/V features.

For example, consider a small deployment for Company ABC, as shown in Figure 27.1 where a single Front-End Server in San Francisco exists. In this deployment, only a single Edge Server is necessary to support all the remote features. Media paths are all local to San Francisco.

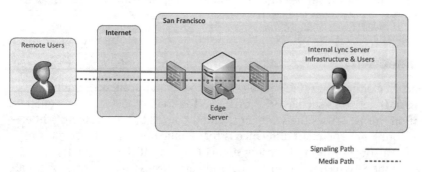

FIGURE 27.1   Single Edge Server

Imagine Company ABC expands with a new office in London with a WAN link back to San Francisco and adds a new Front-End pool for the London users. The London users have been assigned policies that allow remote access, but no conferencing or A/V traffic. In this case, the single Edge Server in San Francisco can still support the London Front-End pool. The SIP signaling enters the San Francisco Edge Server, uses the San Francisco Front-End as next hop, and then communicates with the London Front-End Server. London users have full remote access presence and IM capabilities.

Now consider that Company ABC wants to allow London users to conduct conferences with A/V remotely. There is the potential for users in London who must use the San Francisco A/V Edge Server to relay media traffic. This is inefficient and can result in a poor experience for the remote London users because of the latency involved with each packet traversing to San Francisco and back. There can be a London user on the Internet trying to do an A/V call with another London user who is internal, but the media traffic flows all the way back to the San Francisco Edge Server just to reach the internal London user. Figure 27.2 shows how inefficient this media path can be.

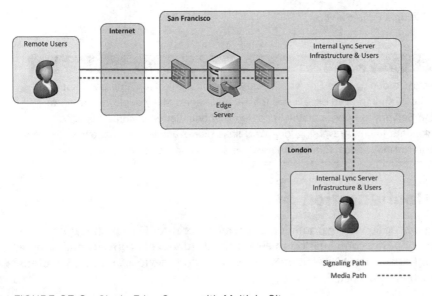

FIGURE 27.2   Single Edge Server with Multiple Sites

The solution in this scenario is to also deploy an Edge Server in London so that users there have a local point to relay media when remote. The SIP signaling still travels through the San Francisco Access Edge Server, but media traffic is much improved. If Company ABC deploys an Edge Server in London, the traffic flow shown in Figure 27.2 changes to the traffic flow shown in Figure 27.3. In this case, the remote users can exchange media traffic with London users directly across the Internet.

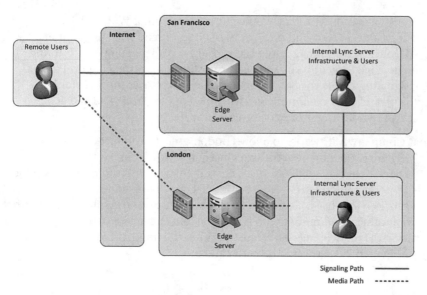

FIGURE 27.3   Multiple Edge Servers

TIP

It isn't necessary to deploy Edge Servers in every location with a Front-End pool, but it generally results in an improved experience for the end users. Many deployments try to distribute Edge Servers to service distinct geographical boundaries such as opposite coasts or continents to limit traversing long WAN links. For example, using separate Edge servers in North America, Europe, and Asia is a common deployment model.

Firewall Configuration

When planning a Lync Server environment, any remote access or federation features require significant firewall configuration to ensure the features work correctly and to properly secure the infrastructure. Many different firewall vendors, devices, and configurations can be used to achieve the goal.

The key points to keep in mind are as follows:

- ▶ The Edge Server has two network adapters to account for, and two different sets of rules must be created.

- ▶ The Edge Server requires at least two network adapters. One is internal facing and communicates with the internal Front-End Servers, Directors, and clients, and the second adapter communicates with the external traffic from the Internet.

Organizations might have a dedicated network security team that is different from the team responsible for implementing and managing Lync Server. Because the deployment planning typically crosses different teams, it is important for all parties to meet early in the planning stages to discuss the deployment requirements. Much of the work and troubleshooting with Edge Server firewall configuration is a collaborative effort between multiple teams to ensure each component is configured correctly.

The following section discusses the different firewall topologies that can be used for Lync Server and key considerations for each design.

> **TIP**
>
> It is highly recommended you place Edge Servers in a perimeter or DMZ network where they can be secured both from the Internet and internal network. This design allows the Edge Server to operate as designed—in a secure manner with limited exposure externally and a limited ability to impact internal operations.

Back-to-Back Firewalls

The ideal approach to any perimeter network or DMZ is to utilize two different security devices where one provides a layer of defense from the Internet to the perimeter network and the second provides another layer of defense by filtering traffic between the perimeter network and internal network. The Lync Server Edge Servers are situated between the two firewalls in the perimeter network. This approach is illustrated in Figure 27.4.

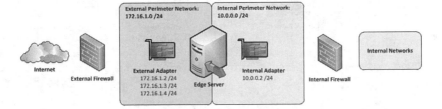

FIGURE 27.4   Back-to-Back Firewalls

> **TIP**
>
> This configuration is generally considered the most secure because even if an attack compromises the external firewall, the internal firewall still isolates traffic from the attacker. Organizations might even use different firewall vendors for the two firewalls. This ensures that if an exploit exists for one firewall, it is unlikely the same exploit can be used against the secondary firewall, keeping malicious attacks contained to the perimeter network.

In this configuration, the Edge Server has the external-facing adapter connected to the more external perimeter network and the internal adapter residing in the internal or more trusted perimeter network.

Three-Legged Firewall

A three-legged firewall approach can be used when it is not feasible to have two physically separate firewall devices separating traffic from the different network segments. Typically, a smaller organization does not have or want a back-to-back firewall, so a single device is used instead to logically construct the same functionality as a back-to-back firewall provides. This single firewall device is generally at least three physical network interfaces or "legs" that are all connected to different networks: one to the public Internet, one to the perimeter network, and one to the internal network. In this scenario, the Edge Server has all network adapters connected to the same network segment. Figure 27.5 shows the logical layout of a three-legged firewall design.

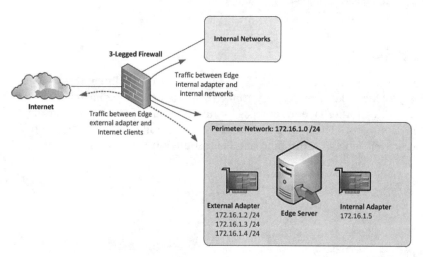

FIGURE 27.5   Three-Legged Firewall

Firewall rules can still be used to control the flow of traffic between each segment like in a back-to-back scenario, but the primary difference here is that all traffic is run through the same physical device. Whether it is external traffic destined for the perimeter network or perimeter traffic destined for the internal network, it all flows through the same device.

The primary advantage of a three-legged firewall is that it is generally less expensive because only a single device is required. The disadvantage is that although a three-legged firewall can be used to simulate a back-to-back configuration, setting up the rules can be more difficult to configure, manage, and troubleshoot. It can be easy to mistakenly associate a rule with the wrong source or destination interface.

Another downside compared to a back-to-back firewall design is that if an attacker compromises the firewall, access to all network segments is achieved. Instead of having to infiltrate both firewall devices, simply using one exploit grants access to all networks. That said, a three-legged firewall design is popular for small- and medium-sized businesses.

No Perimeter Network

If there is no perimeter network, a last-resort option is to leave both Edge Server adapters as part of the internal network. In this configuration, both Edge Server interfaces are part of the internal network, and NAT can be used to expose the required Edge services.

> **WARNING**
>
> This approach is not recommended at all and should be avoided if possible. Instead, take the time to plan for a perimeter network if one does not exist prior to the Lync Server deployment. This topology is included here only as an example of how *not* to deploy Lync Edge Servers.

Although this approach can work, from a technical perspective it is not ideal for the following reasons, as shown in Figure 27.6:

▶ The only firewall exception for the Edge Server's interface to reach back to internal network Front-End or Directors should be TCP 5061 for MTLS SIP communication.

▶ If the internal adapter is instead part of the internal network, there is no filtering or restrictions for other ports.

▶ If an Edge Server is compromised by an attacker, an attack to any internal server and port can be attempted without restriction. Instead, if the internal interface is properly secured, an attacker is able to use only TCP 5061 to reach a Front-End or Director.

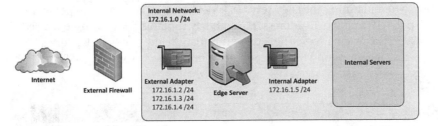

FIGURE 27.6   No Perimeter Network

Straddling the Internal Firewall

Another firewall that, unfortunately, is used too often is where the internal interface of the Edge Server does not pass through any firewall. Instead, it straddles the firewall by being connected directly to the internal network. Administrators still secure the external adapter in this scenario. However, instead of creating the appropriate rules for the internal adapter, they just place it on the internal network.

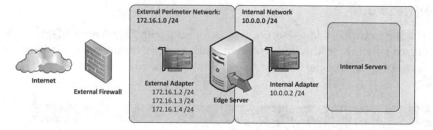

FIGURE 27.7   Lync Server Firewall Straddling

There is not much benefit to straddling a firewall with the internal adapter because, just like the previous scenario, several risks are associated with placing the internal adapter directly on the internal network. Furthermore, if the time has been taken to properly secure the external adapter, much of the hard work has already been completed.

Typically, routing has been planned and validated, so creating the few remaining rules should be fairly easy. Spend the extra time to properly secure the internal adapter to protect the rest of the Lync Server infrastructure.

TIP

Microsoft has designed the Edge Server to be secured properly on both the internal- and external-facing interfaces. Therefore, always avoid placing the internal adapter directly on the internal network whenever possible.

Publicly Routable Perimeter Network

One consideration when planning for Edge services is determining whether the perimeter network contains publicly routable IP addresses. A publicly routable address space is a set of public IP addresses that reach a server directly without any kind of network address translation (NAT). This means public IP addresses are bound directly to the Edge Server network interfaces.

CAUTION

Typically, this suggestion is met with a negative reaction from network security teams that are accustomed to using NAT to allow external access to any service. It is important to note that NAT is not a method of security. Instead, it is designed to accommodate a shortage of IPv4 addresses and although it might mask a server's internal IP address as long as the external ports are available, NAT does not provide any extra security.

The reason for the publicly routable network requirement is because of how the A/V Edge role uses Interactive Connectivity Establishment (ICE), Session Traversal Utilities for NAT (STUN) and Traversal using Relay NAT (TURN) to facilitate media traffic between endpoints that might be masked by NAT, such as two users at home behind their own routers.

Without delving into too many of the technical details, this requirement comes from the fact that to make the media path work where clients cannot contact each other directly, they must have some middle ground where they can both send to. That middle ground is the public IP address space. Without following the publicly routable address requirements, the environment is susceptible to situations where media transfer follows a nonoptimal path or completely fails if clients cannot contact each other directly.

NOTE

It is also important to realize that placing Lync Server Edge Servers in a publicly routable address is *not* considered a security issue. This placement does not mean that firewall rules are bypassed or that the server becomes more of a risk. The appropriate rules should still be put in place to allow only the required protocols and services to each interface. The only difference is that the IP addressing used is part of the public address space instead of a privately addressable space.

When Office Communications Server 2007 was released, it was a requirement to have a publicly routable address space for the external A/V Edge Server interface. In Office Communications Server 2007 R2, support was added for using NAT on the A/V Edge Server interface, but NAT could be used only in a scenario with a single A/V Edge Server. If high availability for redundancy was required, using a publicly routable address space was again required.

Lync Edge Servers have the same limitation as Office Communications Server 2007 R2. If a single Edge Server is used, the A/V Edge Server can use an IP address translated by NAT, but if multiple Edge Servers are hardware load-balanced, each A/V Edge Server requires a publicly routable IP address bound to its interface. The only exception to this rule is if DNS load-balancing is used, NAT can be used for all external interfaces.

The Access Edge and Web Conferencing Edge Server roles have never required a public IP address bound directly to their interfaces, but following the same approach selected for the A/V Edge generally makes the deployment simpler. In other words, use private IP addresses and NAT if using NAT for the A/V Edge interface, but if using public IP addresses for the A/V Edge interface, do the same for the Access Edge and Web Conferencing Edge interfaces.

NOTE

When discussing NAT, the conversation usually centers around the external IP addresses of an Edge Server. Keep in mind that the internal-facing adapter on the Edge must be *routable* from the internal network. Unlike the external interfaces, it cannot be translated by NAT through a firewall under *any* circumstance. It can be a private address, but must be completely routable from all server and client subnets without address translation.

Firewall Rules

This section provides a comprehensive list of the firewall rules involved in Edge Server deployments and what features require each of the ports. It also discusses which direction the connections take so that the appropriate ports can be opened inbound or outbound. In some scenarios, the Edge Server initiates the outbound connection to external destinations.

Access Edge Server

The Access Edge Server is the core of any remote access. At a minimum, remote user access must be allowed to the Access Edge Server to support any kind of web conferencing or A/V traffic. Table 27.1 displays the firewall requirements for traffic between the Internet and the Access Edge Server IP addresses.

TABLE 27.1   Access Edge Firewall Rules

Source	Destination	Destination Port	Function
Internet	Access Edge	TCP 443	Remote user access
Internet	Access Edge	TCP 5061	Federation Public IM Connectivity
Access Edge	Internet	TCP 5061	Federation Public IM Connectivity

Web Conferencing Edge Server

The Web Conferencing Edge Server requires only a single port to be allowed inbound. Additionally, TCP 443 to the Access Edge must already be allowed to support authentication to the web conferences. Table 27.2 displays the firewall requirements for traffic between the Internet and Web Conferencing Edge Server IP addresses.

TABLE 27.2   Web Conferencing Edge Firewall Rules

Source	Destination	Destination Port	Function
Internet	Web Conferencing Edge	TCP 443	Remote web conferencing

A/V Edge Server

The A/V Edge Server has the trickiest set of rules because it varies depending on business requirements. Minimally, to support audio and video traffic with external authenticated users, TCP 443 and UDP 3478 must be allowed inbound to the A/V Edge IP address.

If an organization wants to support A/V federation, the A/V Edge IP address must be allowed to initiate outbound connections to the partner organization. The destination port used by the A/V Edge for outbound federation connections is always within the TCP 50,000–59,999 range. This range is required only for outbound and not required to be opened inbound to support federation with Lync Server or Office Communications Server 2007 R2 organizations.

To support A/V federation to organizations running the original release of Office Communications Server 2007, there are some additional requirements. Both TCP and UDP ranges of 50,000–59,999 must be opened to and from the A/V Edge IP address. Table 27.3 displays the firewall requirements for traffic between the Internet and A/V Edge Server IP addresses.

TABLE 27.3 A/V Edge Firewall Rules

Source	Destination	Destination Port	Function
Internet	A/V Edge	TCP 443 UDP 3478	Remote user A/V
A/V Edge	Internet	TCP 50,000–59,999 UDP 3478	Federation A/V Legacy Federation A/V
Internet	A/V Edge	TCP 50,000–59,999 UDP 50,000–59,999	Legacy Federation A/V
A/V Edge	Internet	UDP 50,000–59,999	Legacy Federation A/V

> **NOTE**
>
> This large inbound port gave many network security and firewall administrators heart attacks when Office Communications Server 2007 R2 was first released. The Microsoft document "Designing Your Perimeter Network for Office Communications Server 2007 R2" addresses these concerns in detail and should be read before supporting legacy A/V federation. The executive summary version of the security details is that the ports are not actively open on an Edge Server until a user has authenticated and retrieved a media encryption key over an SSL channel. The ports are randomly chosen and opened only during a call. After reviewing the technical details, many organizations allowed the port range.

27

Internal Edge Interface

The last set of firewall rules to account for are the ports used by the internal adapter of the Edge Server. TCP 5061 should be allowed from the Edge to the next-hop address to support remote access, federation, and public IM connectivity.

> **TIP**
>
> If a Director pool is used as the next hop, it should be used in the rule. If not, each Front-End pool should be configured to reach the internal Edge IP address.

The ports used for signaling are easy to understand, but one detail that might cause confusion is the source IP address to support web conferencing and A/V traffic: It must be allowed from *any* internal IP address, not just a specific server. Internal endpoints and users contact these ports on the internal Edge Server adapter directly. The server with the

Central Management Store should also be allowed to reach the internal Edge adapter on TCP 4443 to push any configuration updates. Wherever referenced in Table 27.4, Edge Server refers to the internal-facing adapter of the Edge Server.

TABLE 27.4   Internal Edge Interface Firewall Rules

Source	Destination	Destination Port	Function
Edge Server	Front-End Pool/Servers Director Pool/Servers	TCP 5061	Remote access Federation Public IM Connectivity
Front-End Pool/Server Director Pool/Servers	Edge Server	TCP 5061	Remote access Federation Public IM Connectivity
Any internal IP address	Edge Server	TCP 8057	Web conferencing
Any internal IP address	Edge Server	TCP 5062 TCP 443 UDP 3478	A/V authentication STUN STUN
Front-End Pool/Server	Edge Server	TCP 4443	CMS configuration

Figure 27.8 summarizes all of the rules discussed in the section.

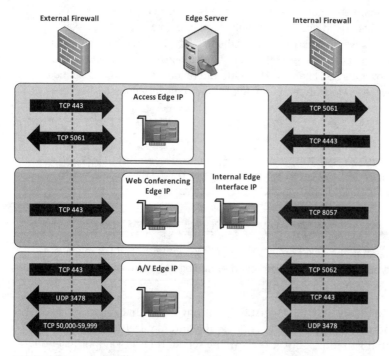

FIGURE 27.8   Edge Server Firewall Rules

High Availability

When adding high availability to a Lync Server Edge Server deployment, an organization must make a decision about how it will provide load-balancing features. The only options available for load-balancing Edge Servers are to use DNS-based load-balancing or to leverage a hardware load-balancing solution.

> **NOTE**
>
> Windows Network Load Balancing (NLB) is not supported for load balancing any of the Lync Server roles, including Edge Server features.

DNS load balancing seems like an attractive feature at first, but does have some limitations. Organizations should review these limitations and then make a decision about whether a hardware load balancer is required. The main limitation of DNS load balancing is that it does not work with some features or legacy endpoints, including

Endpoints running previous versions of the Communicator client

Federated organizations running previous versions of Communications Server

▶ Public IM connectivity

▶ XMPP Gateway

▶ Exchange Server 2007 and 2010 RTM Unified Messaging Signaling and Audio

▶ Exchange Server 2010 SP1 Unified Messaging for Audio

Not all organizations are affected by these limitations and might still be able to deploy DNS load balancing for their Lync Server infrastructure.

Hardware Load Balancer

Using a hardware load balancer comes at a greater cost than DNS load balancing, but adds some flexibility and backward compatibility that an organization might require. Configuring the hardware load balancer is typically the most difficult part of an Edge Server deployment simply because of how flexible the load-balancing software generally is.

Some basic guidelines must be followed when using a hardware load balancer for Edge services:

▶ Each external-facing Edge service needs a publicly routable virtual IP address.

▶ Each Edge Server needs three publicly routable IP addresses assigned.

To summarize the requirements, if an organization deploys two Edge Servers with a hardware load balancer, it needs nine publicly routable IP addresses: three for the virtual IP addresses and three for each Edge Server. That logical configuration is depicted in Figure 27.9.

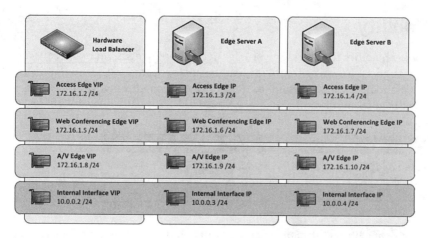

FIGURE 27.9   Hardware Load Balancer VIPs and Edge Server Real IP Addresses

In addition to the public IP addressing requirements, there are some stipulations about what type of Network Address Translation (NAT) must be configured on the load balancer. For traffic from the Internet to the server, the hardware load balancer must use Destination Network Address Translation (DNAT).

This means that as a packet is received from the Internet to the virtual IP address, the hardware load balancer rewrites the packet to change the destination IP address to one of the IP addresses actually assigned to an Edge Server network adapter.

> **NOTE**
>
> The fact that the term *NAT* is used here does not imply that the Edge Server uses private IP addresses. Even though the Edge Server has a public IP address, the load balancer must still translate requests to the virtual IP address to an IP address actually assigned to an Edge Server.

For traffic from the server to the Internet, the load balancer must be configured for Source Network Address Translation (SNAT). This means that packets sent outbound from the Edge Servers are translated by the load balancer back to the virtual IP address that the external Internet clients expect to communicate with.

Hardware Load Balancer Configuration

This section discusses the hardware load balancer configuration for an Edge Server. There are two perspectives to look at for load balancing Edge Servers because the external-facing adapter and internal-facing adapter have their own requirements. An Edge Server must be load balanced on both sides to function properly, but each side has slightly different requirements.

> **WARNING**
>
> Many load balancers have the option to balance "All Ports" for a given pool. Avoid this configuration, no matter how tempting and easy it seems. Instead, load balance only the ports found in the tables that follow.

Starting with the external interfaces, the load balancer should have three publicly routable virtual IP (VIP) addresses: one for the Access Edge, one for the Web Conferencing Edge, and one for the A/V Edge. These three virtual IP addresses map to the three public IP addresses configured on each Edge Server. So, the VIP used for Access Edge maps to the real IP addresses for each Edge Server's Access Edge service, and the same goes for the Web Conferencing Edge and A/V Edge services. Depending on the load balancer configuration, this usually requires three separate pool objects, as depicted in Figure 27.10.

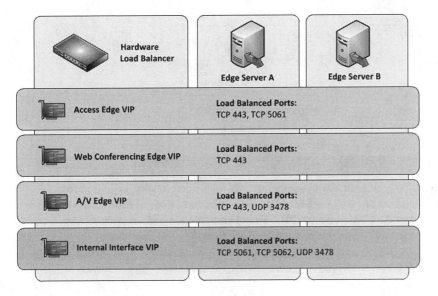

FIGURE 27.10   Edge Server Load-Balanced Ports

Table 27.5 outlines what ports must be load balanced to each virtual IP address.

TABLE 27.5   External Edge Interface Load Balancing

Virtual IP Address	Port	Function
Access Edge	TCP 443	Remote access
Access Edge	TCP 5061	Federation and Public IM
Web Conferencing Edge	TCP 443	Remote web conferencing

TABLE 27.5   External Edge Interface Load Balancing

Virtual IP Address	Port	Function
A/V Edge	TCP 443	STUN
A/V Edge	UDP 3478	STUN

After configuring the external interface load balancing, the internal adapter configuration must be completed. Unlike the external adapter that uses three virtual IP addresses, only a single virtual IP address is required for the internal adapter because each Edge Server has only a single IP address for its internal adapter.

Table 27.6 outlines what ports must be load balanced to each virtual IP address.

TABLE 27.6   Internal Edge Interface Load Balancing

Virtual IP Address	Port	Function
Edge Internal Interface	TCP 5061	Signaling
Edge Internal Interface	TCP 5062	A/V Authentication
Edge Internal Interface	TCP 443	STUN
Edge Internal Interface	UDP 3478	STUN

NOTE

There is no entry here for load balancing the internal Web Conferencing Edge interface. That is not an omission or error; port 8057 on the internal interface should *not* be load balanced by the hardware load balancer. The Front-End pools automatically distribute requests to multiple Web Conferencing Edge Servers if configured. Don't forget to include TCP 8057 in the firewall rules, though, because even though it's not load balanced, the Front-End servers need to be able to reach that port on Edge Servers.

DNS Load Balancing

If the limitations of DNS load balancing described earlier don't pose any issues to an organization's Lync Server deployment, the organization can proceed with that method instead of purchasing a hardware load balancer. There are actually some advantages to using DNS load balancing, mainly the simplicity involved in configuring the load balancing that just involves using multiple A records for the same name in public DNS. Table 27.7 shows the DNS records required to achieve DNS load balancing.

TABLE 27.7   DNS Load-Balancing Entries

Host Record	IP Address
sip.companyabc.com	Access Edge Server A IP address
sip.companyabc.com	Access Edge Server B IP address
webconf.companyabc.com	Web Conferencing Edge Server A IP address
webconf.companyabc.com	Web Conferencing Edge Server B IP address
av.companyabc.com	A/V Edge Server A IP address
av.companyabc.com	A/V Edge Server B IP address

When using DNS load balancing, the Edge Server can use private IP addresses that are translated by NAT for all three roles including A/V Edge. This is a big advantage for organizations that might not have many public IP addresses available because when using DNS load balancing, there is no virtual IP address requirement.

In other words, DNS-based load balancing requires three fewer IP addresses than a hardware load-balancing solution. Each Edge Server IP still needs to be mapped to a unique public IP address if it is being translated by NAT, but there is no idea of a virtual IP address in this type of solution. In fact, when using DNS load balancing, Microsoft recommends using NAT for the IP addresses bound to the Edge Server network adapters.

Another advantage of DNS load balancing is that the native server-draining feature in Lync Server is available. This enables administrators to prepare a server by maintenance through the Lync Server Control Panel the same way as the other roles.

In some organizations, the team responsible for Lync Server might not be the same team that manages the network and hardware load balancers, which can make it difficult to coordinate preparing a server for maintenance. Instead of the Lync Server administrators quickly draining a server's connections, they might need to submit a request to have the network team drain the load balancer connections for a particular node and then check back later to determine whether the connections have cleared.

Sometimes this separation of teams can be just as efficient as one person having complete control, but often times it slows down the maintenance process.

> **NOTE**
>
> Although DNS load balancing is available for Edge Servers, keep in mind that the reverse proxy for web component services is a critical piece of remote access. Load balancing for a reverse proxy must be addressed separately and can either be done with a hardware load balancer or possibly through Windows Network Load Balancing (NLB) for Microsoft Forefront Threat Management Gateway or Unified Access Gateway.

Edge Server Preparation

A good deal of preparation work goes into making an Edge Server ready for deployment, and the actual installation of Lync Server is probably one of the easiest parts after a server is correctly configured. This section discusses some of the configuration requirements and considerations an organization must make when preparing an Edge Server.

Domain Membership

There are pros and cons to joining an Edge Server to an internal Active Directory domain. From a security perspective, it is undesirable because an Edge Server behaves identically whether it is joined to a domain or not. By not joining the Edge Server to the domain, the attack exposure is limited and there is no way a compromised Edge Server has any Active Directory information.

From a management perspective, though, having an Edge Server or multiple Edge Servers in a workgroup configuration creates some additional issues, such as security policy enforcement and patching. Administrators must manually account for patching these servers, changing local security policies instead of using Group Policy and Windows Server Update Services (WSUS). By not being part of the domain, these servers can potentially be left unpatched with security vulnerabilities.

There are workarounds to these issues, such as using registry keys to point servers at an internal WSUS server or allowing Edge Servers to automatically update patches. However, organizations might block the ports required for WSUS to a perimeter network or not want servers to apply patches without being tested first.

TIP

Generally, it is recommended to not join an Edge Server to the domain. However, if that creates more of a problem for managing the servers, it is acceptable to join the servers to the domain. Alternatively, if an organization has deployed a separate forest within the perimeter network specifically for management purposes, an Edge Server can be joined to that domain instead of the internal domain.

If the Edge Server is part of a workgroup configuration, be sure to define a primary DNS suffix for the machine and use that fully qualified domain name in the Topology Builder and for any certificates using the internal server name.

NOTE

If the Edge Server is a workgroup member, it most likely is not able to register its own name to the internal DNS servers. Be sure to manually create the Edge Server host records so that internal servers can resolve the names.

Network Adapter Configuration

Setting up IP addresses, DNS servers, and gateways on the Edge Server adapters can be a point of confusion in a deployment because of the requirement for dual network adapters. To begin with, an Edge Server must have a minimum of two separate network adapters: one that is internal facing and one that is external or public facing. The internal adapter should have a single IP address and the external adapter should have three separate IP address associated—one for each Edge service.

Organizations can also choose to use a separate network adapter for each public-facing IP address, which requires four network adapters. Both are valid choices and these two configurations are detailed in Figures 27.11 and 27.12.

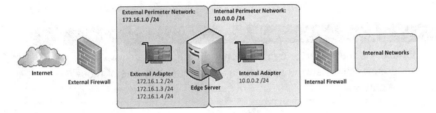

FIGURE 27.11   Edge Server Dual Network Adapters

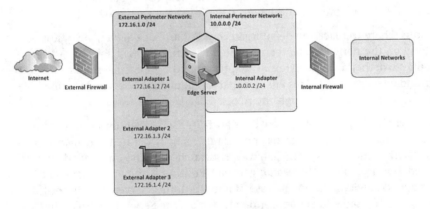

FIGURE 27.12   Edge Server Quad Network Adapters

> **NOTE**
>
> In most cases, two adapters are sufficient unless an organization requires separation of the traffic.

Keep in mind that saturating a gigabit NIC exceeds the recommended capacity planning and that using two adapters simplifies the Edge Server configuration. If using a dedicated adapter for each external IP address, be sure to read the strong host model section later in this chapter. Also, it always helps to name the network connections descriptively instead of leaving the "Local Area Connection <Connection Number>" name on the adapter. Naming the interfaces "Internal" and "External" makes a clear distinction about what function each adapter serves.

> **TIP**
>
> Using the first entered or primary IP address for the network adapter as the Access Edge service IP address helps ensure reliable routing.

Default Gateways and Routing

Another point of confusion when configuring the network adapters is where to place the default gateway.

> **TIP**
>
> A rule of thumb to follow is that a server can have only one default gateway. This means that no matter how many network adapters a server has, only one of those should have a default gateway.

Many administrators try to place gateways on both network adapters, which causes extremely unreliable traffic flows. It does not matter if the adapters are all on the same or different subnets; only one adapter should have a default gateway assigned.

The next decision is where to place the default gateway. For an Edge Server, always place the default gateway on the network adapter associated with the Access Edge Server IP address. This applies whether a single external adapter is used for all three roles or whether multiple adapters are used. This ensures that all requests the server does not know how to route are passed out through the Access Edge IP address.

A question that inevitably comes up is, "How does an Edge Server communicate with the internal network through an adapter that has no default gateway defined?" The answer to that question is, "With static routes." The gateway associated with the internal adapter's IP address is still used, but it won't be the *default* gateway. Routing is something generally associated with network devices, but in the case of a multi-homed server, an administrator must configure the routing table to act appropriately. For a Lync Server Edge role, the administrator must manually enter route statements to use that internal adapter for internal subnets. Figure 27.13 shows how the external adapter has a default gateway associated, but routing statements for internal networks make use of the internal adapter.

> **NOTE**
>
> Remember that any internal client or server must be able to route directly to the internal network adapter of the Edge Server. To be able to respond to the request, the Edge Server must have a route statement for that subnet telling it to use the internal-facing network adapter. If not, the request is routed out the interface associated with the default gateway and either not routed or dropped by the server.

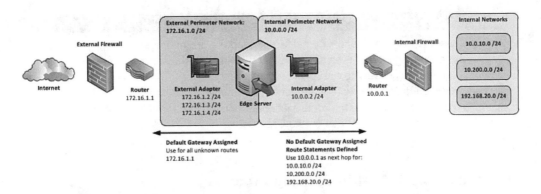

FIGURE 27.13   Edge Server Gateways and Routing

Adding Static Routes

Static routes can be added via a command prompt either through the older route command or with the newer netsh command set.

First, identify the internal-facing network adapter's name. If it was named descriptively, such as "Internal," this information is already known. Open a command prompt with elevated administrative privileges and type each route statement with the following syntax:

```
netsh interface ipv4 add route <IP address /mask> <Interface Name> <Gateway>
```

As an example, assume there are three internal subnets—10.0.1.x, 10.0.2.x, and 10.0.3.x—that are all /24 subnets where servers and clients exist. The internal-facing adapter of the Edge Server is named Internal, the adapter's IP address is 172.16.0.20, and the gateway for that subnet is 172.16.0.1.

The following commands should be entered on the Edge Server to tell the server to use the internal-facing adapter and gateway to reach those subnets:

```
netsh interface ipv4 add route 10.0.1.0 /24 "Internal" 172.16.0.1
netsh interface ipv4 add route 10.0.2.0 /24 "Internal" 172.16.0.1
netsh interface ipv4 add route 10.0.3.0 /24 "Internal" 172.16.0.1
```

Alternatively, if an organization uses all 10.x.x.x IP addressing for internal subnets, those statements can be reduced to a single line that accounts for all three subnets listed and possibly any new subnets added later.

The following example uses a /8 bitmask to route any traffic destined for a 10.x.x.x address through the internal adapter:

```
netsh interface ipv4 add route 10.0.0.0 /8 "Internal" 172.16.0.1
```

To recap the procedure, first identify the internal subnets where clients and servers are located. Next, try to summarize those subnets to minimize the amount of route statements required. Finally, enter the route statements on the Edge Server.

NOTE

In some cases, the internal- and external-facing adapters are on the same subnet in a perimeter network and might even still have to route through the same gateway IP address. It is still necessary to assign only the default gateway to the external-facing adapter and then define the route statements for the internal adapter. Even though the same gateway might be used, the route statement ensures the traffic originates from the correct adapter and IP address on the Edge Server.

DNS and Network Adapter Binding Order

Being able to resolve DNS queries correctly is absolutely critical to making an Edge Server functional. At a minimum, an Edge Server must be able to resolve the names of internal pools and servers, so be sure to enter an internal DNS server IP address on the internal adapter's network configuration.

It's also important that an Edge Server resolve external DNS queries for federation or public IM scenarios. These queries can be answered by internal DNS servers, or an Edge Server can use a public DNS server to resolve queries if entered on the network adapter configuration. In a single Edge Server deployment where the A/V Edge is behind NAT, the service must be able to resolve its own publicly addressable name and IP address.

The binding order of the network adapters is not critical to an Edge Server operation, but can have an effect on how an Edge Server resolves DNS queries. Servers use the DNS servers entered on an adapter starting with the adapter listed first in the binding order.

The impact is if a split-DNS namespace is in place where internal and external queries can return the same name with different IP addresses, the Edge Server might resolve names incorrectly. For example, if the external adapter is listed first in the binding order, the Edge Server might be unable to resolve the name of an internal pool correctly because that name is not registered in the public DNS.

TIP

To avoid this issue, enter the IP addresses of the internal DNS servers on the internal adapter, and then place the internal adapter highest in the binding order. If internal DNS lookups are not allowed, a host file can be used.

If this configuration still does not make DNS lookups succeed and resolve correctly, it might be necessary to use a host file for resolving internal names. Usually only a few internal pool and server names need to be entered, so it is fairly quick to configure, but be aware, this option exists when troubleshooting name resolution issues.

> **NOTE**
>
> Disable all unused network adapters and move them lowest in the binding order priority list. This ensures active adapters are always accessed first. Plus, if a cable is ever plugged in to a disabled adapter, it can't affect the server without being enabled by an administrator.

Strong Host Model

A possible Edge Server option discussed earlier uses a dedicated network adapter for each external Edge service.

> **NOTE**
>
> Just like with a two-adapter configuration, name the different network interfaces descriptively, such as "Access Edge," "Web Conferencing Edge," and "AV Edge."

Something to be aware of with this option is that both Windows Server 2008 and Server 2008 R2 utilize the strong host model for the network adapters, which means that traffic sent outbound from a source IP address must always be sent from the network adapter associated with that IP address. Now that might seem like common sense, but Windows Server 2003 and earlier allowed outbound traffic to be sent from any network adapter regardless of which adapter had the source IP address assigned.

To provide the relation to Lync Server, this meant that when the Web Conferencing Edge or A/V Edge service needed to respond to a request, it used the Access Edge service adapter and default gateway to respond. This doesn't happen by default in Windows Server 2008 or Windows Server 2008 R2 where each adapter must use its own gateway or route configuration. Figure 27.14 shows the weak host model where outbound Web Conferencing and A/V traffic was able to be initiated through the Access Edge adapter.

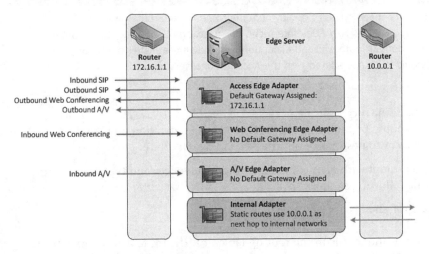

FIGURE 27.14   Weak Host Model

27

With the Strong Host Model, the Web Conferencing Edge and A/V Edge adapters need a static route to respond to unknown networks such as Internet clients. Figure 27.15 shows how the outbound Web Conferencing and A/V traffic now is initiated from the dedicated adapter.

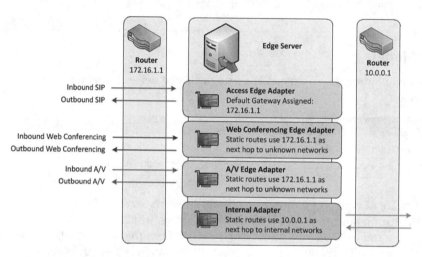

FIGURE 27.15   Strong Host Model

The impact of this change to an Edge Server deployment is that if the Access Edge interface has the default gateway assigned, the Web Conferencing Edge and A/V Edge technically don't know of a default gateway because there is not one associated with their interfaces. This ends up causing Web Conferencing Edge and A/V Edge traffic to fail because the server cannot respond to external clients without knowing where to send that traffic.

TIP

The best solution for these types of deployments is to add static routes for both the Web Conferencing Edge and A/V Edge interfaces to the external gateway. These routes are identical to a default route with the exception that they are a higher metric or priority than the default route associated with the Access Edge service.

To do this, first check the metric of the Access Edge default gateway. The metric for the other two services should be higher or less preferred, so all federation and Public IM Connectivity traffic continues to flow out the Access Edge interface.

Open a command prompt with elevated administrative privileges and type each route statement with the following syntax:

```
netsh interface ipv4 show route
```

Find the default route and metric in the routing table. It is the route with prefix 0.0.0.0 and should point at the Access Edge adapter's default gateway already.

```
Publish  Type   Met  Prefix     Idx  Gateway/Interface
No       Manual 256  0.0.0.0/0  12   192.168.1.1
```

Now add a route statement for the Web Conferencing Edge and A/V Edge with metrics both higher than the Access Edge.

```
netsh interface ipv4 add route 0.0.0.0/0 "Web Conferencing Edge" 192.168.1.1
metric=258
netsh interface ipv4 add route 0.0.0.0/0 "AV Edge" 192.168.1.1metric=260
```

When viewing the routing table again, all three routes should be visible. The index value differentiates the interfaces.

```
Publish  Type   Met  Prefix     Idx  Gateway/Interface
No       Manual 256  0.0.0.0/0  12   192.168.1.1
No       Manual 258  0.0.0.0/0  14   192.168.1.1
No       Manual 260  0.0.0.0/0  16   192.168.1.1
```

This issue doesn't exist when a single adapter is used for external services because all three IP addresses are associated with the same physical adapter that already has the default gateway. As you can see, using two adapters is a significantly simpler configuration. With gigabit speed network adapters, the need for separating the adapters for bandwidth purposes diminishes, and a better solution for the extra adapters is to team the interfaces for failover redundancy only and not throughput.

Certificates

Provisioning certificates for Edge Servers was another sore subject in prior versions of Lync Server. This has been greatly simplified by the new certificate wizard, which automatically populates the required names and attributes based on the published topology. This section discusses the certificate requirements and considerations for organizations deciding between public certificates and privately issued certificates.

An Edge Server requires certificates for four different services:

- ▶ Internal Edge Service
- ▶ Access Edge Service
- ▶ Web Conferencing Edge Service
- ▶ A/V Edge Authentication Service

A common misconception is that all of these certificates should be purchased from a public certificate authority, which is only partly true. Only the Access Edge and Web Conferencing Edge certificates are presented to external clients, so those are the only services which require a certificate that should be purchased from a public certificate authority. Both the Edge Server internal certificate and A/V Edge Authentication Service certificate can be issued from an internal, private certificate authority that is trusted by internal clients.

NOTE

Probably the most confusing part of previous version Edge Server deployments was centered around the A/V Edge and A/V Authentication Edge services. The A/V Edge service actually doesn't use a certificate, even though port 443 is involved. The A/V Authentication service, however, does require a certificate. Because the A/V Authentication service runs on the internal-facing adapter, this certificate can actually be issued by a private certificate authority. This split is a bit more hidden in Lync Server 2010 because the A/V authentication certificate automatically uses the certificate assigned to the internal Edge service.

Another common misconception is that subject alternative name (SAN) certificates are an absolute requirement, but there are only a few cases where a subject alternative name is required. First, only the Access Edge certificate needs a subject alternative name. Every other certificate can use a standard, single name SSL certificate. Furthermore, a subject alternative name certificate is required only when an organization is using multiple SIP domains or if the public name of the Access Edge service does not match the primary SIP domain.

The specific requirements for subject names and subject alternative names for Edge Servers are outlined in the following:

- ▶ **Access Edge**—The subject name should match the published name of the Access Service in public DNS. If a hardware load balancer is used, this is the name clients resolve to the virtual IP address. The subject alternative name field should contain any supported SIP domains in the sip.<SIP Domain> format.

- ▶ **Web Conferencing Edge**—The subject name should match the published name of the Web Conferencing Edge in public DNS. If a hardware load balancer is used, this is the name clients resolve to the virtual IP address. No subject alternative names are required.

- ▶ **A/V Edge**—This service has no certificate associated, but is included here to provide the distinction from the A/V Edge Authentication service.

- ▶ **A/V Edge Authentication**—The subject name has no specific name requirement, but generally matches the internal Edge Server interface name. No subject alternative names are required.

- ▶ **Internal Edge**—The subject name should match the published name of the Edge Server internal pool. If a hardware load balancer is used, this is the name that resolves to the internal virtual IP address. No subject alternative names are required.

The last certificate required is not actually bound to the Edge Servers and is required for the reverse proxy.

▶ **Reverse Proxy**—The subject name should match the published name of the external web services. The subject alternative name should contain any simple URLs for dial-in and hosted meetings.

TIP

Many times, administrators think of subject alternative names as the "in addition to" field to the certificate subject name. As a best practice, follow an "either, or" mentality, meaning clients read either the subject name or the subject alternative name field, but not both. To accommodate this, always include the subject name as one of the subject alternative names and usually as the first entry.

As an example, assume Company ABC deploys a single Edge Server, the only supported SIP domain is companyabc.com, and sip.companyabc.com is the Access Edge Server public name. In this case, only a single name SSL certificate with the subject name sip.companyabc.com is required for the Access Edge service. Company ABC also needs to purchase a second single name certificate for the Web Conferencing Edge service. In this scenario, only two publicly issued certificates are required: both with only a single name.

If Company ABC also supports another domain such as companyxyz.com, a subject alternative name certificate is required for the Access Edge Service. The subject name would be sip.companyabc.com, and the subject alternative names would be sip.companyabc.com and sip.companyxyz.com. Company ABC would not need to purchase a second single name certificate for the Web Conferencing Edge service. In this scenario, only two publicly issued certificates are required: one with subject alternative names and one without.

Table 27.8 outlines what type of certificate is recommended for each service on an Edge Server.

TABLE 27.8   External Access Server Certificates

Service	Certificate Authority	Subject Alternative Names
Access Edge	Public	Additional SIP domains
Web Conferencing Edge	Public	No
A/V Edge	None	No
A/V Edge Authentication	Private	No
Internal Edge	Private	No
Reverse Proxy	Public	Simple URLs

When using multiple Edge Servers, the certificates must be installed on each Edge Server that is being load-balanced together. Depending on the certificate, vendor certificates can be licensed for one or more severs, but generally the same public certificate can be placed on each of the Edge Servers in the pool.

NOTE

If Public IM Connectivity to AOL is used, the certificate for the Access Edge Service must have Client Enhanced Key Usage (EKU) enabled.

Organizations should decide on a certificate vendor prior to the Lync Server deployment. Microsoft has partnered with a few certificate vendors to ensure that the X.509 certificates work with Lync Server. Those vendors are listed here:

▶ Entrust

▶ Comodo

▶ Digicert

▶ GoDaddy

Certificates from other vendors also work if all clients trust the certificate, but Microsoft has not verified those vendors. The vendors listed previously have the best compatibility between different server, desktop, and device platforms.

TIP

Be sure to use the same advice here when planning for a reverse proxy server and install any internal certificate chains on the reverse proxy. To complete an SSL bridging scenario, the reverse proxy needs to trust the certificates presented by the internal pool member servers.

Using Single Subject Alternative Name Certificates

A newly supported scenario in Lync Server is the capability to use a single certificate that contains many subject alternative names. This certificate can then be exported and used on both Edge Servers and reverse proxy servers. Although this simplifies the number of certificates required, it might not actually be any less expensive than using a few single name certificates. This may vary depending on the number of SIP domains and simple URLs configured. The advantage to this approach is names for the simple URLs for meetings or dial-in conferencing can be added to the same certificate and used on the reverse proxy server.

Following is an example of what a certificate like this looks like that would then be placed on each Edge Server and reverse proxy server. Each Edge Server still requires a separate, internally issued certificate for the internal-facing interface. In this scenario, a single subject alternative name certificate can be placed on all Edge Servers and reverse proxy servers.

Subject name: sip.companyabc.com

Subject alternative names: sip.companyabc.com, webconf.companyabc.com, av. companyabc.com, lyncpoolweb.companyabc.com, dialin.companyabc.com, and meet.companyabc.com

Wildcard Certificates

Wildcard certificates in the format of *.<domain> have become increasingly popular because they provide a way to secure a large number of websites at a low cost by using only a single certificate. Unfortunately, many functions in Lync Server simply don't work well or at all if a wildcard certificate is used. Even if it does appear to work for some clients or features, it can produce some odd behavior which makes troubleshooting very difficult. At this time, the recommendation is to avoid using a wildcard certificate for any Lync Server roles.

CAUTION

Because the reverse proxy functionality is basic, it is acceptable to use a wildcard certificate for the external web services or meeting pages. Just avoid using it on an Edge Server.

Reverse Proxy

A critical piece in planning for Edge services is the reverse proxy. Unfortunately, this tends to be overlooked or considered a secondary task, even though it provides some important functionality to a deployment. Without a reverse proxy, the following features will not work:

- ▶ Address book download
- ▶ Distribution group expansion
- ▶ Web conferencing content such as whiteboards, uploaded presentations, and document sharing.
- ▶ Device updates
- ▶ Dial-in conferencing page
- ▶ Simple meet conferencing pages

As you can see, almost every deployment with Edge services has some feature in the previous list. If a reverse proxy does not exist today in the organization, one should be deployed with Lync Server if external access is provisioned.

The concept of a reverse proxy is simple to understand when considering it as an extra hop or barrier between external clients and an internal resource. What a reverse proxy offers is the capability to inspect the traffic a client sends for any malicious requests, or possibly even pre-authenticates the user before being allowed to reach an internal client. In the overall scheme of external services, the reverse proxy fits in as depicted in Figure 27.16.

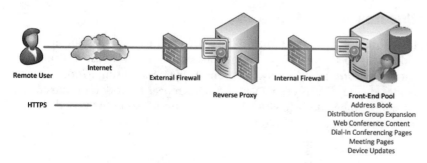

FIGURE 27.16   Reverse Proxy for Web Services

SSL Pass Through, Offloading, Termination, and Bridging

After understanding the functionality of a reverse proxy, it's important to comprehend the different methods a reverse proxy can use to publish internal services. Three main methods are used and not all of them are available depending on the reverse proxy used. Starting with Microsoft Internet Security and Acceleration Server (ISA) 2006 or higher, which includes the Microsoft Forefront Threat Management Gateway and Microsoft Forefront Unified Access Gateway, any of the methodologies can be used. The preferred method for publishing Lync Server is to use SSL Bridging, which encrypts the traffic from end to end.

The easiest way to understand the differences is through diagrams. The most basic method is SSL pass through. This means that the traffic from Internet clients runs through the reverse proxy and can be inspected, but the SSL connection exists from the client all the way to the internal resource like shown in Figure 27.17.

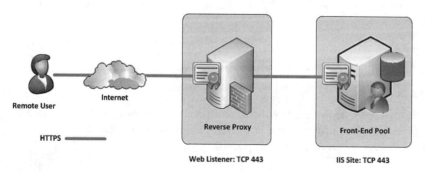

FIGURE 27.17   SSL Pass Through

SSL Offloading

The next most common methodology in reverse proxy scenarios is to use SSL offloading. In this scenario, the client's SSL tunnel terminates at the reverse proxy, which then initiates a clear-text, HTTP request to the internal resource. Many hardware load balancers offer this functionality and advertise it can improve performance of servers by "offloading" the SSL encryption and decryption duties from the internal server.

This is a valuable feature when a server is CPU-constrained, but with modern hardware, this is rarely necessary. Any hardware used for Lync Server probably far exceeds the CPU capabilities of most load-balancing devices. Furthermore, Lync Server is designed to operate in a secure manner end-to-end and does not actually support SSL offloading. Figure 27.18 shows how the SSL tunnel is terminated at the reverse proxy which then communicates over port 80 to the Front-End pool.

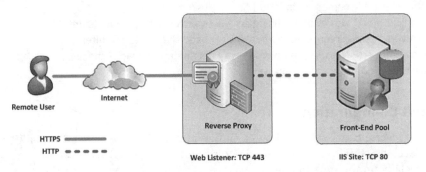

FIGURE 27.18   SSL Offloading or Termination

27

SSL Bridging

The final methodology, which is the preferred scenario, is to use SSL Bridging. In this case, the client's SSL tunnels at the reverse proxy like in an offloading scenario, but the reverse proxy then opens a second HTTPS connection back to the internal resource. This ensures the entire transmission is encrypted from end to end.

There is also some added flexibility in this case where a reverse proxy can redirect that second connection to a port other than 443 back on the internal resource without the client knowing. As far as the client knows, it still has a connection on port 443 to the internal resource, even though the reverse proxy might bridge this connection to port 4443 on the internal Front-End pool. Figure 27.19 shows where the reverse proxy bridges a port 443 connection from the client to port 4443 on the Front-End pool, but still secures the traffic.

So, to summarize the options, the preferred method for Lync Server is SSL Bridging to ensure an end-to-end encryption of the traffic with the most flexibility. SSL offloading is not supported, so if bridging is not an option, the reverse proxy deployment should use SSL pass through.

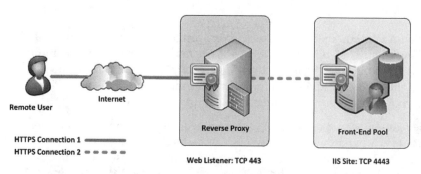

Remote User

Internet

HTTPS Connection 1 ━━━━━

HTTPS Connection 2 ▬ ▬ ▬ ▬

Reverse Proxy

Front-End Pool

Web Listener: TCP 443

IIS Site: TCP 4443

FIGURE 27.19   SSL Bridging

CAUTION

The question that inevitably comes up is, "Do I have to use a reverse proxy?" The answer is, "Technically, no." However, not using a reverse proxy is a serious security risk. Without a reverse proxy, internal resources are exposed directly to the Internet and unauthenticated users. Not using a reverse proxy also means public certificates may need to be placed on the Front End servers.

Placement and Configuration

Where to place the reverse proxy server follows a similar idea as the Edge Server. It usually makes sense to place one close to any Front-End pools that have external access allowed. This becomes especially important when users leverage web conferencing because the display of content comes through the reverse proxy. So, like the Edge Server, optimizing that traffic path results in a better user experience.

Setting up the reverse proxy is similar to an Edge Server. Generally the reverse proxy is placed in a perimeter network and has two network adapters: one internal facing and one external facing. To reach internal server subnets, route statements must also be configured.

The reverse proxy server does not have to be a part of the domain, but can be joined for the same reasons as an Edge Server. Additionally, if a reverse proxy such as Microsoft Forefront Threat Management Gateway is domain-joined, it can easily pre-authenticate user requests, which is a feature discussed in more detail later in the "Pre-Authentication" section later in this chapter.

Another valid configuration for reverse proxy scenarios with Forefront Threat Management Gateway is to use a single network adapter. Most modern hardware has plenty of adapters by default, but using only a single network adapter can simplify the deployment.

NOTE

Microsoft Forefront Unified Access Gateway 2010 can also be used, but it requires at least two network adapters.

Reverse Proxy Load Balancing

As far as load balancing the reverse proxy goes, there are a few options, which might vary depending on which reverse product is used. With Microsoft Forefront Threat Management Gateway or Microsoft Forefront Unified Access Gateway, a hardware load balancer or Windows Network Load Balancing (NLB) can be used. Windows Network Load Balancing comes at no additional cost, so it might be more attractive for organizations without a hardware load balancer and those that want to leverage DNS load balancing.

The only port required for load balancing the reverse proxy is TCP 443. Organizations might also want to load balance TCP 80, but only so that the reverse proxy can redirect that traffic automatically to TCP 443 instead.

Pre-Authentication

Pre-authentication of network clients is a feature found in both Microsoft Forefront Threat Management Gateway and Microsoft Forefront Unified Access Gateway, which lets the reverse proxy authenticate a user before completing the SSL bridge back to an internal server. This way, unauthenticated traffic is not allowed to communicate with internal services, which makes the deployment more secure. Without pre-authentication, the SSL traffic is authenticated by the internal pool server. It is still inspected and filtered for malicious code by the reverse proxy, but pass-through authentication requires the internal servers to handle authentication of the requests.

Not all features of Lync Server support pre-authentication and whether pre-authentication can be leveraged depends greatly on business requirements. Specifically, if anonymous remote access is required for web conferences or dial-in conferencing, there must be some form of anonymous access allowed through the reverse proxy without authentication. In those situations, simple URLs can be used to split the traffic so pre-authentication can be used for all traffic, except the traffic destined for the meeting and dial-in conferencing URLs. Figure 27.20 shows how a separate web listener and IP address can present different authentication options depending on the service.

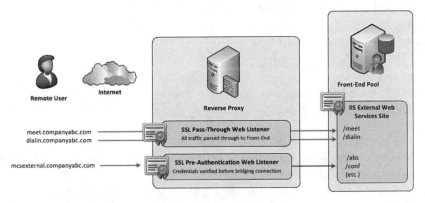

FIGURE 27.20   Pre-authentication with Unique Simple URLs

The reason why subdomains are required is because reverse proxy rules are generally configured based on a destination URL. As an example, consider the external web services URL being https://lyncexternal.companyabc.com/ and the simple URL for meetings being https://lyncexternal.companyabc.com/meet. Microsoft Forefront Threat Management Gateway pre-authentication is configured at the web listener level and web listeners are bound to a specific IP address.

Although it is possible to specify unique paths on each rule, such as /meet or /*, those URLs share the same base URL, so they must share a listener. Because the listener can have only one authentication method, a choice must be made between pass-through or pre-authentication. Conversely, using the simple URL https://meet.companyabc.com enables resolving that name to a separate IP address, web listener, and pre-authentication setting.

As discussed previously, using subdomain simple URLs grants some additional flexibility, but comes at additional cost because more subject alternative names are required. Instead of having a certificate just with lyncexternal.companyabc.com, an additional name, meet.companyabc.com, must be secured either with a subject alternative name entry or another certificate.

Sample Scenarios

This section outlines some sample scenarios. By no means are these intended to be an end-to-end deployment sample, but they should provide additional clarity and examples of what is possible. In each of these examples, assume an internal infrastructure already exists and Edge services are being added.

Single Edge Server

Company ABC is a small company of about 200 people located in San Francisco, uses sip.companyabc.com as its only SIP domain, and the internal Active Directory domain companyabc.local. The single Edge Server is named mcsedge and has a DNS suffix defined to match the internal domain. Company ABC plans to use a single subject alternative certificate for all external functionality. Figure 27.21 displays what the overall topology would look like. There are no high-availability requirements, and the external URLs are defined as follows:

- ▶ Access Edge Service: sip.companyabc.com
- ▶ Web Conferencing Edge Service: webconf.companyabc.com
- ▶ A/V Edge Service: av.companyabc.com
- ▶ External Web Services URL: lyncexternal.companyabc.com
- ▶ Simple Meet URL: lyncexternal.companyabc.com/meet
- ▶ Simple Dial-In URL: lyncexternal.companyabc.com/dialin

Table 27.9 displays the public and private certificate requirements while Table 27.10 indicates the DNS record requirements.

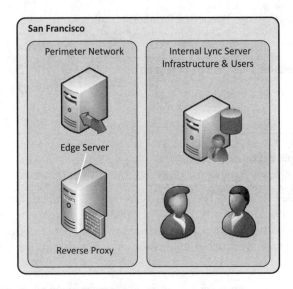
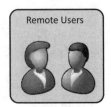

FIGURE 27.21   Single Edge and Reverse Proxy

TABLE 27.9   Single Edge External Access Server Certificates

Placement	Type	Names
Access Edge	Public	SN: sip.companyabc.com
Web Conferencing Edge		SAN: sip.companyabc.com
Reverse Proxy		SAN: webconf.companyabc.com
		SAN: lyncexternal.companyabc.com
A/V Edge Authentication	Private	SN: lyncedge.companyabc.local
Internal Edge	Private	SN: lyncedge.companyabc.local

TABLE 27.10   Single Edge Required External DNS Entries

Type	Name	Value
Host	sip.companyabc.com	10.0.0.2
Host	webconf.companyabc.com	10.0.0.3
Host	av.companyabc.com	10.0.0.4
Host	lyncexternal.companyabc.com	10.0.0.5
SRV	_sip._tls.companyabc.com	Host: sip.companyabc.com Weight: 5 Priority: 5 Port: 443

27

TABLE 27.10   Single Edge Required External DNS Entries

Type	Name	Value
SRV	_sipfederationtls._tcp.companyabc.com	Host: sip.companyabc.com Weight: 5 Priority: 5 Port: 5061

Scaled Single Site

Company ABC is a large company of about 5,000 people with a single office located in San Francisco, uses sip.companyabc.com as its only SIP domain, and the internal Active Directory domain is companyabc.local. The Edge Servers are named lyncedge1 and lyncedge2 and both have DNS suffixes defined to match the internal domain. The internal Edge pool name is lyncedge.companyabc.com. The overall topology is displayed in Figure 27.22.

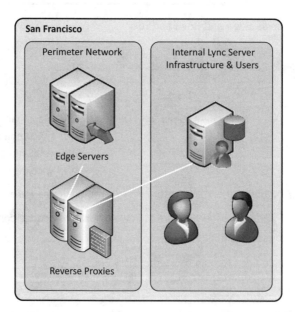

FIGURE 27.22   Single-Scaled Site with DNS and Windows Network Load Balancing

To save costs, DNS load balancing is used because Company ABC does not require Public IM Connectivity or down-level federation. Company ABC uses individual certificates where required. Two Forefront Threat Management Gateway reverse proxy servers are configured with Windows Network Load Balancing. The external URLs are defined as follows:

▶ Access Edge Service: sip.companyabc.com

▶ Web Conferencing Edge Service: webconf.companyabc.com

- ► A/V Edge Service: av.companyabc.com

- ► External Web Services URL: lyncexternal.companyabc.com

- ► Simple Meet URL: lyncexternal.companyabc.com/meet

- ► Simple Dial-In URL: lyncexternal.companyabc.com/dialin

Table 27.11 displays the public and private certificate requirements, whereas Table 27.12 indicates the DNS record requirements.

TABLE 27.11   Scaled Single Site External Access Server Certificates

Placement	Type	Names
Access Edge	Public	SN: sip.companyabc.com
Web Conferencing Edge	Public	SN: webconf.companyabc.com
Reverse Proxy	Public	SN: lyncexternal.companyabc.com
A/V Edge Authentication	Private	SN: lyncedge.companyabc.local
Internal Edge	Private	SN: lyncedge.companyabc.local

TABLE 27.12   Scaled Single Site Required External DNS Entries

Type	Name	Value
Host	sip.companyabc.com	10.0.0.2
Host	sip.companyabc.com	10.0.0.3
Host	webconf.companyabc.com	10.0.0.4
Host	webconf.companyabc.com	10.0.0.5
Host	av.companyabc.com	10.0.0.6
Host	av.companyabc.com	10.0.0.7
Host	lyncexternal.companyabc.com	10.0.0.10
SRV	_sip._tls.companyabc.com	Host: sip.companyabc.com Weight: 5 Priority: 5 Port: 443
SRV	_sipfederationtls._tcp.companyabc.com	Host: sip.companyabc.com Weight: 5 Priority: 5 Port: 5061

27

Scaled Multiple Sites

Company ABC is a growing company of about 7,500 people split between two offices in San Francisco and New York. Each office has a Front-End pool hosting users. It uses sip.companyabc.com as its only SIP domain, and the internal Active Directory domain is companyabc.local.

The Edge Servers in San Francisco are named sfoedge1 and sfoedge2 and they belong to the Edge pool sfoedge.companyabc.local, whereas the New York Edge Servers are named nyedge1 and nyedge2 belonging to the Edge pool nyedge.companyabc.local. All have DNS suffixes defined to match the internal domain.

Company ABC uses hardware load balancers in both locations to support Public IM Connectivity and down-level federation. Company ABC uses individual certificates where required. Two Forefront Threat Management Gateway reverse proxy servers are configured in each location and also use hardware load balancing. Figure 27.23 displays the overall topology and the external URLs are defined as follows:

▶ SFO Access Edge Service: sip.companyabc.com

▶ SFO Web Conferencing Edge Service: webconf.companyabc.com

▶ SFO A/V Edge Service: av.companyabc.com

▶ SFO External Web Services URL: sfo.companyabc.com

▶ SFO Simple Meet URL: meetsfo.companyabc.com

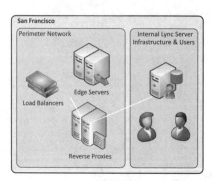

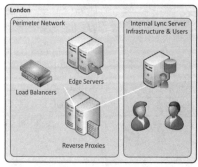

FIGURE 27.23   Multiple Sites with Hardware Load Balancers

- ▸ NY Access Edge Service: nysip.companyabc.com

- ▸ NY Web Conferencing Edge Service: nywebconf.companyabc.com

- ▸ NY A/V Edge Service: nyav.companyabc.com

- ▸ NY External Web Services URL: ny.companyabc.com

- ▸ NY Simple Meet URL: meetny.companyabc.com

- ▸ Simple Dial-In URL: dialin.companyabc.com

TABLE 27.13   Multiple Sites External Access Server Certificates

Placement	Type	Names
SFO Access Edge	Public	SN: sip.companyabc.com
SFO Web Conferencing Edge	Public	SN: webconf.companyabc.com
SFO Reverse Proxy	Public	SN:sfo.companyabc.com SN:meetsfo.companyabc.com SN:dialin.companyabc.com
SFO A/V Edge Authentication	Private	SN: sfoedge.companyabc.local
SFO Internal Edge	Private	SN: sfoedge.companyabc.local
NY Access Edge	Private	SN:nysip.companyabc.com SN: nysip.companyabc.com SAN: sip.companyabc.com
NY Web Conferencing Edge	Public	SN: nywebconf.companyabc.com
NY Reverse Proxy	Public	SN:ny.companyabc.com SN:meetny.companyabc.com
NY A/V Edge Authentication	Private	SN: nyedge.companyabc.local
NY Internal Edge	Private	SN: nyedge.companyabc.local

TABLE 27.14   Multiple Sites Required External DNS Entries

Type	Name	Value
Host	sip.companyabc.com	10.0.0.4
Host	webconf.companyabc.com	10.0.0.7
Host	av.companyabc.com	10.0.0.10
Host	sfo.companyabc.com	10.0.0.13
Host	nysip.companyabc.com	10.20.0.24

TABLE 27.14   Multiple Sites Required External DNS Entries

Type	Name	Value
Host	nywebconf.companyabc.com	10.20.0.27
Host	nyav.companyabc.com	10.20.0.30
Host	ny.companyabc.com	10.20.0.33
SRV	_sip._tls.companyabc.com	Host: sip.companyabc.com Weight: 5 Priority: 5 Port: 443
SRV	_sipfederationtls._tcp.companyabc.com	Host: sip.companyabc.com Weight: 5 Priority: 5 Port: 5061

NOTE

10.x.x.x addresses are used here as an example. However, publicly routable IP addresses must be used when leveraging a hardware load balancer. Both the VIPs and IPs on the servers must be publicly routable.

Summary

Spending a good deal of time planning for Edge services makes any deployment much easier. Admittedly, there are so many moving pieces to an Edge Server deployment that it is easy to miss something, but Microsoft has made great strides to improve the installation and configuration process with Lync Server. Planning the Edge names, IP addressing, routing, and firewall configuration in advance of any installation streamlines the deployment process.

CHAPTER 28

Planning for Voice Deployment

The voice services improvements in Lync Server 2010 play a large part in why organizations are looking to migrate more and more users to Microsoft's Enterprise Voice. This chapter covers how to plan for deploying Enterprise Voice and all the features included for end users. This includes dial plan, normalization rules, voice policies, PSTN usages, routes, and trunk configuration.

This chapter also covers the following topics:

▶ Different strategies used to provide voice resilience to end users, including features available to users based on the failover scenario.

▶ The new, advanced Enterprise Voice features such as Call Admission Control, Media Bypass, and Enhanced 911 along with the planning and preparation required before placing each service into production.

▶ Device considerations for users and analog devices and planning steps for Response Group workflows.

This chapter is a starting point for any organization looking to implement Enterprise Voice services.

Dial Plan

When beginning a Lync Server 2010 voice deployment, one of the first steps is to determine the dial plan. The dial plan defines how users will contact other users in the organization and includes how many digits are used in each site, whether site prefixes are used, and any number translations required from site to site. Dial plan objects in Lync Server 2010 contain a collection of normalization rules that are associated with a site, pool, or directly assigned to user accounts.

In a migration scenario from a legacy PBX, an organization has the option to maintain as much of the existing dial plan as possible or to begin developing a new dial plan for Lync Server 210. Which option is selected varies based on the tolerance of the organization and end users to accommodate changes. However, in many cases some changes are necessary to facilitate a period of coexistence.

Assigning Telephone URIs

When deploying Lync Server 2010 voice services, an organization assigns telephone URIs to each user account enabled for Enterprise Voice. These URIs can either be direct inward dial (DID) numbers, which are unique both internally and across the PSTN. Alternatively, the URIs can be based on extensions that are unique only to the organization or within a site.

When assigning URIs to end users, keep in mind that all URIs within the organization must be unique. Typically, organizations with multiple sites have different or multiple DID ranges per office, or extensions that are unique only within a specific site. To accommodate these scenarios, multiple dial plans and normalization rules can be created to accommodate the expectations of end users.

Direct Inward Dialing

The simplest dial plan possible within Lync Server 2010 is when each user in the organization has a direct DID number. DIDs are unique across the PSTN, and therefore, unique with the Lync Server deployment. A PSTN caller or an internal user can use the same dial string to reach another user when DIDs are assigned to each user in the organization.

The downside of DIDs is that they are longer dial strings than an extension, which means that they require a user to enter more digits to reach a user. The Lync client is primarily based on click-to-dial functionality, so a dial string becomes less of an issue. However, for users manually dialing using keypads, this can be frustrating.

DIDs also typically map to a user's internal extension. For example, at Company ABC's San Francisco office, Alice has a DID of +1 (415) 333-3234, but internal users can simply dial a four-digit extension, 3234, to reach Alice. This gives the flexibility of numbers being unique across the site, but with the capability for PSTN callers to reach users directly. Internal users also have a short dial string to remember in order to reach Alice.

On the Lync Server 2010 configuration side, Alice's telephone URI field should be entered as tel:+14153333234 in order to uniquely identify her in the organization. A normalization rule within the San Francisco dial plan converts a four-digit extension starting with 3 into the full E.164 URI for users. That rule resembles the following:

Dial Plan: San Francisco

Name: Four digits beginning with 3 to San Francisco

Starting Digits: 3

Length: Exactly four digits

Digits to Remove: None

Digits to Add: +1415333

This rule accommodates the dialing habits of San Francisco users, but consider a scenario where Company ABC also has a San Jose office where users have DIDs starting with +1 (408) 444-4xxx. Because all the San Jose extensions start with a 4, any four-digit extension beginning with a 4 can be translated to include the San Jose DID prefix. San Jose users should have a telephone URI assigned resembling tel:+14084444xxx.

Dial Plan: San Francisco

Name: 4 digits beginning with 4 to San Jose

Starting Digits: 4

Length: Exactly four digits

Digits to Remove: None

Digits to Add: +1408444

After this rule is added to the dial plan, San Francisco users can dial by entering just four digits on a keypad or within the Lync client and correctly route to a user in either San Francisco or San Jose.

Internal Extensions Only

Many times organizations will not offer DID numbers to users, or might assign DIDs to only some users. In this case, the remaining users only have an internal extension defined. This is a completely acceptable deployment option with Lync Server 2010, but there can be some confusion as to how the telephone URI should be assigned to user accounts.

The most common method is to identify a main office, or automated attendant phone number, that external users can dial and be transferred to in order to reach users with an internal extension. This type of attendant does not have to exist, but it usually makes sense to leverage this number in the telephone URI. After this number is identified, it should be used as the telephone URI with an ;ext=xxx suffix. The number of digits in the extension field can vary depending on the organization or even the site.

For example, let's say that Company ABC's San Francisco office does not offer DIDs to users and uses internal extensions only. The main office number is +1 (415) 333-3000 and Alice has extension 234. In this case, Alice's telephone URI field should be tel:+14153333000;ext=234, which uniquely identifies her within the organization.

This kind of scenario must also be accounted for within a dial plan. The dial plan within San Francisco must include a normalization rule that takes a three-digit dial into this URI, such as the following rule:

> Dial Plan: San Francisco
>
> Name: 3 digits to San Francisco
>
> Starting Digits: Blank
>
> Length: Exactly three digits
>
> Digits to Remove: 0
>
> Digits to Add: +14153333000;ext=

NOTE

The Normalization Rule Wizard cannot be used to create this type of rule because the ;ext= component is not a valid number. Instead, define the regular expression matching pattern and translation rule manually. In this example, the matching pattern is ^(\d{3}) and the translation rule is +14153333000;ext=$1.

Site Prefixes

A common scenario with an organization spread across multiple sites is that extensions are not unique within the organization. Typically, a PBX exists in each site and the same extensions are used across sites. When this occurs, users can either use a DID to reach users in another site or a site prefix might be assigned.

For example, consider a scenario where Company ABC has offices in San Francisco and San Jose. Alice and Bob both work in the San Francisco office where Alice has extension 234 and Bob has extension 456. When Bob wants to dial Alice, he can simply dial 234 and be connected immediately. Now assume Joe works in the San Jose office where a different PBX exists, also with extension 234. Bob cannot dial Joe using 234 because he will connect to Alice instead.

What happens as a workaround is a site prefix code is assigned to Bob's dial plan so that he can dial San Jose extensions by prepending an extra digit. In this scenario, assume 6 is the site prefix for San Jose from San Francisco. This means Bob can dial 6234 and be connected to Joe, but still dial 234 to reach Alice directly.

The same kind of site prefix is used in this scenario for San Jose users to dial San Francisco users directly. In Company ABC's case, San Jose users must use 7 as a prefix to dial San Francisco. Although Joe and Alice have the same three-digit extension, Joe can contact Alice by dialing 7234.

NOTE

San Jose users can potentially use 6 as a site prefix to dial San Francisco, but a separate digit was used here for clarity. There is no requirement to use the same site prefix between two sites.

TIP

The number of digits required for site prefixes depends on how many sites with overlapping extensions exist within an organization. If there are only a few sites with overlapping extensions, a single digit may be used to identify each site. If there are many sites with overlapping extensions, it might be necessary to use two or even three digits as a site prefix.

Site prefixes can be potentially confusing for end users because it requires them to remember to dial extra digits for different sites. Oftentimes, they have to consult a list of site prefixes or look up a contact phone number when dialing a different location.

Remembering site prefixes is mitigated by Lync Server 2010 endpoints because most of the dialing can be done by simply clicking a contact. As opposed to traditional telephony, users will become more and more reliant on click-to-dial features instead of remembering extensions. Despite the ease of the user experience, administrators will still be tasked with correctly assigning site prefixes to telephone URIs and creating appropriate normalization rules. This can become a complex voice routing and dial plan configuration in the end.

TIP

If at all possible, consider using a dial plan with unique extensions across the organization. This might not be possible in all cases, but will greatly simplify the voice deployment.

How Site Prefixes Affect Normalization Rules

Site prefix scenarios directly affect Lync Server telephone URIs and dial plan normalization rules. In Lync Server 2010, a telephone URI must be unique across the organization for it to be routed correctly. This means that Alice and Joe cannot both have a telephone URI of tel:+234 assigned because this is not unique.

TIP

Organizations can include a site prefix in the telephone URIs. However, the best practice is to use a full E.164-formatted number.

28

For example, assume San Francisco users have DID numbers all using the +1 (415) 333-3xxx format. Alice's telephone URI should be assigned as tel:+14153333234. Joe's office has DIDs as well with a +1 (408) 444-4xxxx format, and his telephone URI can be assigned as tel:+14154444234.

Now the URIs are unique, but this does not account for the expected user behavior of how to dial three digits in each location to reach local users. For example, users in San Francisco and San Jose both expect to use three-digit dialing, but depending on which office the call originates from, it should route to a different user. This must be handled by using separate dial plans and normalization rules.

For each unique site, administrators must create a separate dial plan to be assigned to users. These dial plans also contain different normalization rules depending on the site prefixes assigned.

Continuing the previous example, a San Francisco dial plan is assigned to Alice and Bob, which accommodates three-digit dialing rules that resolve to the local users. A separate rule needs to exist for dialing San Jose extensions with a 6 as the site prefix, but still be routed to Joe's URI.

Continuing this scenario, the San Francisco dial plan should contain rules such as the following:

> Dial Plan: San Francisco
>
> Name: 3 digits to San Francisco
>
> Starting Digits: Blank
>
> Length: Exactly three digits
>
> Digits to Remove: None
>
> Digits to Add: +14153333

This rule takes three digits and converts it to +14153333xxx so that San Francisco users can use three digits to reach a local user. In addition to this rule, the San Francisco dial plan needs another rule to accommodate dialing a site prefix to San Jose users:

> Dial Plan: San Francisco
>
> Name: 4 digits to San Jose
>
> Starting Digits: 6
>
> Length: Exactly four digits
>
> Digits to Remove: 1
>
> Digits to Add: +14084444

This rule matches a four-digit string starting with 6, the San Jose site prefix, removes the 6, and then prepends +14084444 to the remaining three digits. Once assigned to the San Francisco site, pool, or users accounts, Bob can dial 234, which translates to

+14153333234 and matches Alice's account. Bob can also dial 6234, which translates to +14084444234 that matches Joe's account in San Jose.

> **NOTE**
>
> In reality, Bob will most likely just click contacts within the Lync contact list to dial each contact. However, the dial plan normalization rules are still required to handle the behind-the-scenes routing.

On the opposite site, the San Jose dial plan contains at least two rules to facilitate local three-digit dialing to San Jose users and uses a site prefix of 7 to reach San Francisco users.

> Dial Plan: San Jose
>
> Name: 3 digits to San Jose
>
> Starting Digits: Blank
>
> Length: Exactly three digits
>
> Digits to Remove: None
>
> Digits to Add: +14084444

> Dial Plan: San Jose
>
> Name: 4 digits to San Francisco
>
> Starting Digits: 7
>
> Length: Exactly four digits
>
> Digits to Remove: 1
>
> Digits to Add: +14153333

It is easy to see how complex a dial plan can become when multiple overlapping sites are involved. This example only uses two sites, but for an organization with many sites, some significant planning should be performed in advance of the Lync Server 2010 voice deployment.

To simplify the dial plan, use the following guidance:

▶ Assign unique extensions to users whenever possible.

▶ Assign E.164-formatted telephone URIs to user accounts.

▶ Create and use the test cases in the voice routing configuration to validate a dial plan.

Voice Routing

Voice routing in Lync Server 2010 is composed of a few different components, including the dial plan discussed previously. It is difficult to discuss the remaining components separately because how they are connected directly affects voice routing.

This section discusses the voice policies, PSTN usages, routes, and trunk configuration that make up the rest of the voice routing components in Lync Server 2010.

Voice Policies

Voice policies in Lync Server 2010 define what features users might leverage with their Enterprise Voice service. This includes options such as simultaneous ringing, team call, or call forwarding. The other main component of voice policies is that PSTN usages are associated with a policy.

From a planning perspective, examine the various options of a voice policy and make a decision on whether multiple policies are required. Policies can be global, assigned to a site, or directly assigned to user accounts.

PSTN usages are the key component of voice policies from a dialing perspective because they control what routes a user account might use. For example, a route might exist that matches a dial string considered as long distance by the organization and a PSTN usage of Long Distance is associated with that route. For a user to successfully dial the number, he must be assigned a voice policy that includes the PSTN usage.

> **NOTE**
>
> Voice policies in Lync Server 2010 not only control what features users can use, but also control what numbers they are allowed to dial because PSTN usages are associated with a policy.

For example, assume Company ABC's San Francisco office is allowed to dial local numbers beginning only with the 415 area code. A route for the dial string pattern beginning with +1415 exists and is associated with the PSTN usage Local, and the PSTN usage Local is included in the Global voice policy for Company ABC. Now a group of executives must be able to dial long distance numbers to Chicago's 312 area code, but because they have no PSTN usage that allows this route, their calls will fail. The rest of the office should also not be allowed to dial this area code.

To accommodate the executives, a new policy, route, and PSTN usage must be created. First, create a route that begins with +1312 and is associated with a PSTN usage of Long Distance. Next, a voice policy called Executives should be created, which includes both the Local and Long Distance PSTN usages. Finally, the new voice policy should be assigned to the executive user accounts who require this capability.

Because they now have a voice policy that includes a PSTN usage matching the route, only their Enterprise Voice accounts are able to place calls to the 312 area code. The rest of the San Francisco office will still not be able to make those calls even when the route exists because their voice policy does not include the PSTN usage associated with the route.

> **NOTE**
>
> Instead of using special dial codes to accommodate long distance or international calling abilities, like many PBXs, Lync Server 2010 relies on voice policies to enforce dialing restrictions. Voice policies can also be assigned to analog or lobby phones to control outbound calling.

PSTN Usages

The PSTN usage object in Lync Server often seems confusing because it has no settings or configuration options other than a name. There are no user options or policies configured on a usage and it cannot even be created by itself. Instead, PSTN usages can only be created through a voice policy. Usages are also not even associated directly with users. They are associated with routes and voice policies so that they can be considered the glue that ties a route to a voice policy associated with a user.

PSTN usages are typically identified by different classes of services. For example, usages such as Emergency, Information, Local, Long Distance, or International might be created. An organization might choose to create more specific usages if necessary. PSTN usages can also be ordered within a voice policy and are processed from top to bottom. When placing a call, the routes that include the user's first PSTN usage are returned and a match for the dial string is attempted. If no match occurs, or if all the gateways are unavailable, the second PSTN usage in the voice policy is compared against the available routes. The first PSTN usage that matches an available route is used.

Routes

Routes in Lync Server 2010 are a definition of where to send calls that match a specific dial string. Administrators define a matching pattern and a gateway or gateways associated with the pattern to send a call. Each route is also associated with PSTN usages to define what type of call this might be.

The PSTN usage defined varies depending on the gateway associated with the route. For example, a route matching the +1312 area code associated with an IP/PSTN gateway in Chicago might be considered a PSTN usage of Local, but when associated with an IP/PSTN gateway in San Francisco, it necessitates a PSTN usage of Long Distance.

Route Resilience

Resiliency for routes is done by providing multiple gateways in a single route, or by creating a redundant route that uses a gateway in a different location. Routes are processed in from a top-to-bottom order so that the priority for a route can specified by adjusting the route placement within the list. For example, a route matching the +1312 area code using an IP/PSTN gateway in Chicago should be placed higher in the list than a route matching the same string using an IP/PSTN gateway in San Francisco because it is considered a local call to the Chicago gateways.

28

There are two aspects to consider when planning for route resilience in Lync Server 2010: high availability in the primary site and resilience in a failover scenario. High availability is typically achieved by associating multiple gateways within the same location with the route and PSTN usage. In this example, Lync Server 2010 round-robins requests across the two IP/PSTN gateways in Chicago when operating at full capacity. If one of the gateways fails, calls are sent only to the gateway still available.

If both of these gateways fail, an organization might want to still route calls to the destination number, but accept potential long distance charges and route calls out at the gateway in another physical site. This is accomplished by creating a second route with the same dial string, different gateway, and different PSTN usage.

CAUTION

This additional, backup PSTN usage associated with the backup route should be associated only with voice policies allowed to use this secondary route. For user accounts with a voice policy not including this usage, the calls would fail when both primary IP/PSTN gateways are unavailable.

Continuing the example, assume Company ABC also has an IP/PSTN gateway in San Francisco and a secondary route for the +1312 area code using this gateway. The primary route for +1312 should use the Chicago IP/PSTN gateway. Additionally, a PSTN usage of Chicago Backup Long Distance is associated with the secondary route. A voice policy including the Local and Chicago Backup Long Distance PSTN usages is created and assigned to San Francisco users. This ensures that in the event of both Chicago IP/PSTN gateways becoming unavailable, calls are routed out the San Francisco IP/PSTN gateway. This scenario is shown in Figure 28.1. The reason the San Francisco gateway is not associated with the same route as the Chicago gateways is that Lync Server will distribute outbound calls to each gateway equally. To use San Francisco only as a backup route, it needs to have a unique route and PSTN usage associated.

Trunks

Trunk configuration in Lync Server 2010 is an object that administrators can use to define the connection between Lync Mediation servers and IP/PSTN gateways within the infrastructure. One important feature is that a trunk configuration can control how dial strings are passed to a specific IP/PSTN gateway.

In Office Communications Server 2007 R2, any outbound dialing rules had to be performed by the IP/PSTN gateway itself, which required organizations to maintain dialing rules in multiple locations. With Lync Server 2010, dial strings can be manipulated before being sent to an IP/PSTN gateway so that digits can be removed, added, or translated.

A common example is where an IP/PSTN gateway does not support the + prefix in E.164 and needs to be removed before being sent. In other cases, the PBX might require special

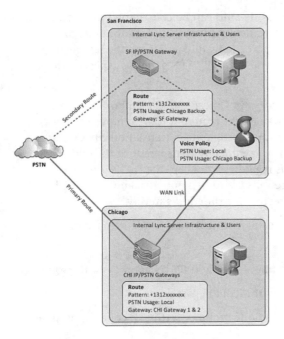

FIGURE 28.1   Route Resilience Example

prefixes for local, long distance, or international calls and these digits can be appended through the trunk configuration.

> **NOTE**
>
> When configuring a trunk, be sure to set up the translation rules on only one side or the other. Ideally, handle the translation rules within Lync Server and have the opposite IP/PSTN gateway perform no modification of the dial strings. If both sides are manipulating digits, it might become difficult to troubleshoot the calls.

Trunk configuration is also where Media Bypass features can be enabled or disabled. Media Bypass is a new feature that enables a Lync endpoint to bypass the Mediation server transcoding of RTAudio to G.711 and simply send G.711 directly to the IP/PSTN gateway. This removes the need for additional processing resources on the Mediation server and is the main reason support for collocating the Mediation server with the Front End is available in Lync Server 2010.

In addition to translation rules and Media Bypass features, the trunk configuration controls whether media encryption is required and whether a separate media termination point exists.

Trunk configuration exists at a global level by default, can be constrained to a site, or can be defined on a specific IP/PSTN gateway. This flexibility enables organizations to use Media Bypass on IP/PSTN gateways that support the feature and leave the feature disabled on others. It also accommodates situations where the IP/PSTN gateway expects different dial strings in different locations.

For example, Company ABC's IP/PSTN gateways in Chicago might support a + in the dial string, but the San Francisco IP/PSTN gateway might require it to be removed before passing a call successfully. Because all the trunk configuration translation rules occur only after a number is normalized and routed, it is completely transparent to the end user and she can continue dialing the same patterns regardless of where the call is sent. This is especially useful in a failure scenario where calls are routed out a backup location, but the users have no idea that their calls are redirected to a different gateway.

Use the following steps when planning for trunk configuration to identify whether any changes should be made:

▶ Identify the appropriate dial string format for each IP/PSTN gateway in the topology.

▶ Identify which IP/PSTN gateways support Media Bypass.

▶ Create a trunk configuration for each unique group of settings, scoped appropriately to a site or IP/PSTN gateway.

Tying It All Together

Now that voice policies, PSTN usages, routes, and trunk configuration have been defined, an important step is determining how all these components interact. Figure 28.2 shows a sample configuration where two different voice policies exist, each with a different set of PSTN usages assigned. Office workers can only make calls considered local, but executives can place local, long distance, and international calls. Company ABC has voice gateways in both San Francisco and Chicago, so even if a San Francisco user dials a Chicago area code such as 312, the call can still be considered local if going out the Chicago voice gateway.

Executives can place calls which begin with the dial strings +1415, +44, +1312, or +1765 because each of these routes is associated with a PSTN usage included in their voice policy. Because office workers only have the Local PSTN usage in their policy, they can place calls only to numbers beginning with +1415 or +1312. Calls placed to a dial string beginning with +44 or +1765 will be unsuccessful for office workers. After a call matches a route, it will pass through the trunk configuration associated with the gateway. In this case, the San Francisco and Chicago voice gateways have different trunk configurations that manipulate digits before being sent to the gateway.

Sizing

How to correctly size an IP/PSTN gateway or SIP trunk for Lync Server 2010 voice services is a common question and, unfortunately, is going to vary greatly depending on the users in each location. Sizing for an IP/PSTN gateway depends on the user's dialing habits as well as whether any simultaneous ringing is configured.

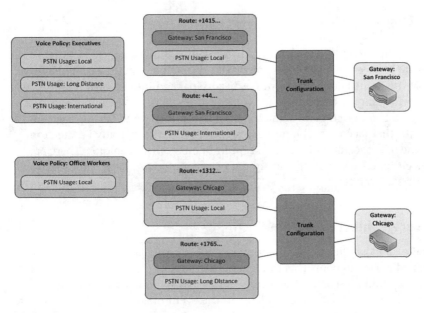

FIGURE 28.2   Voice Routing

Simultaneous ringing of a work and mobile number is a common scenario for users because it grants them the flexibility to answer calls in either location. For an organization, however, this can potentially occupy an extra port on an IP/PSTN gateway or SIP trunk. If a call originates from the PSTN and then rings the user's work number, simultaneous ring settings might allow for another call to be placed out to the user's mobile number. This consumes an extra port, so consider this scenario when planning for gateways. Simultaneous ringing abilities can be limited to specific users through voice policies.

Microsoft offers some planning numbers that can be used to perform a rough analysis. If at all possible, retrieve reporting data from the existing PBX to determine the expected usage requirements for each site. Table 28.1 offers a suggestion on how many PSTN ports to allocate to a site depending on the usage level. For example, in a branch office with 25 users with light usage, only two PSTN ports are suggested.

TABLE 28.1   Voice Port Planning Figures

Usage Level	PSTN Calls per Hour	Users per PSTN Port
Light	1	15
Medium	2	10
Heavy	3 or More	5

Voice Resilience

Voice resiliency in Lync Server 2010 is achieved by providing endpoints with a primary and backup registrar service. The registrar service existed in Office Communications Server 2007 R2 as part of the Front End Service, but has been separated into its own role in Lync Server 2010 to provide failover capabilities for voice features. When Lync endpoints sign in, they are informed through in-band signaling of both a primary and backup registrar pool associated with their account. The primary registrar pool will typically be the Front End pool where the user account is homed, except in branch office scenarios. There are two different voice resilience scenarios that should be accounted for: datacenter survivability and branch site survivability.

Datacenter Survivability

To provide the failover capability when the primary pool is unavailable, each Front End pool can be assigned a backup pool. This can be another pool in the same site, or more commonly will be a pool in a separate datacenter across a WAN link. Using a separate datacenter ensures the voice services are available in the event of a primary datacenter site failure. When assigned, as clients sign in, they will receive information about which pool is the primary and which pool is the backup. Figure 28.3 shows what happens in a datacenter failover scenario.

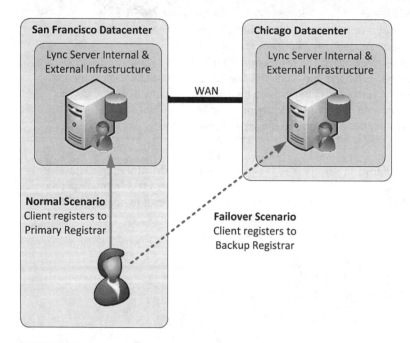

FIGURE 28.3   Datacenter Resilience

> **NOTE**
>
> Under normal operating circumstances, endpoints use the registrar service located on the primary pool. In the event the endpoint cannot contact the primary pool, it will attempt to contact the backup. If the backup pool determines the endpoint's primary pool is indeed unavailable, it will accept the registration for the user.

As indicated previously, the backup pool maintains a monitor to check whether the primary pool is available at all times. This monitoring is accomplished through the use of heartbeat messages exchanged between the two pools across a WAN link. Only after the backup pool stops receiving heartbeat messages from the primary will it mark the pool as offline and begin accepting user registrations. The default timeout interval for the heartbeat messages is 300ms, but it can be modified by an administrator if a longer or shorter timeout period is required.

Pools in different sites can serve as backup registrars for each other. For example, Company ABC can have Lync Server 2010 Front End pools in both San Francisco and Chicago. Each pool can serve as a backup registrar for the other so that users will still have voice services through the opposite registrar in the event of a pool failure.

When clients are using a backup registrar service, not all features are available. Features that are available in a failover scenario include

- ▶ **PSTN Calls**—Outbound calls should have no issues, but inbound call availability is dependent on the PSTN carrier service delivering inbound calls to the backup location. The capability for this feature varies depending on location and carrier.

- ▶ **Internal Calls**—Internal voice calls are possible between users in the same site and to additional sites.

- ▶ **Call Control**—Users are able to use basic call features such as hold and transfer. Advanced features such as call forwarding, simultaneous ringing, and team call are also available in a failover scenario.

- ▶ **Instant Messaging**—Instant messaging service is available, but only between two parties. No instant messaging conferencing services are available.

- ▶ **Audio/Video Calls**—Audio and video calls are between two parties only. Audio/video conferencing services are unavailable.

- ▶ **Call Detail Records**—As long as the backup pool is associated with a CDR, collector data is still added.

Features that are unavailable to users in a failover scenario include

- ▶ **Conferencing Auto Attendant**—The dial-in conferencing attendant service and all scheduled meetings with the conference bridge are unavailable.

- ▶ **Conferencing**—Any type of conferencing is unavailable. This applies to instant message, meeting, and audio/video conferences involving more than two parties.

28

▶ **Presence-Based Routing**—Because presence data is unavailable, calls to users homed on the failed pool do not have calls routed around this presence. For example, if a user sets the status to Do Not Disturb, instant message and phone calls are still delivered.

▶ **Call Park**—The ability to park calls is unavailable to users homed on the failed pool.

▶ **Response Group Service**—Any workflows and queues associated with the failed pool are unavailable. Agents will be unable to sign in.

▶ **Call Forwarding Settings**—Although call forwarding capabilities remain in effect during a failover, users are unable to update or change their call forwarding settings.

▶ **Voicemail Delivery**—Assuming the users' Exchange servers were part of a site failure, new voicemail messages cannot be delivered.

▶ **Voicemail Retrieval**—Again, assuming the users' Exchange servers were part of a site failure, voicemail messages cannot be accessed.

TIP

If resilient voice services are required, organizations should plan to designate a backup registrar pool in the event of a primary pool outage. The WAN link between the two pools should be sufficient to support the additional voice traffic and ideally be resilient.

Branch Site Survivability

Very similar to how voice resiliency can be achieved between multiple datacenters, branch office survivability depends heavily on using a separate registrar service. The size of the branch site plays a large factor in determining how the resiliency is achieved.

For branch sites of more than 5,000 users, it makes sense to deploy an entire Lync Server 2010 Front End pool in a highly available configuration to where user accounts are homed. Just as in a datacenter, failover scenario user accounts use the local pool as a primary registrar and a pool across the WAN link as a backup registrar. Figure 28.4 shows how the primary and backup registrars operate for a branch office user.

Medium-sized sites of 1,000 to 5,000 users can deploy a survivable branch server, which is really a Front End pool with a collocated Mediation Server role. User accounts are homed to the survivable branch server, but still receive the majority of services from an associated Front End pool in a central site. The survivable branch server is designated as the primary registrar for the users so that when they sign in, they will register to a local server. Conferencing services and web component services are still always accessed across a WAN link to the pool associated with the branch site. The survivable branch server is typically paired with a local IP/PSTN gateway to provide branch users with a local route the PSTN for inbound and outbound calls.

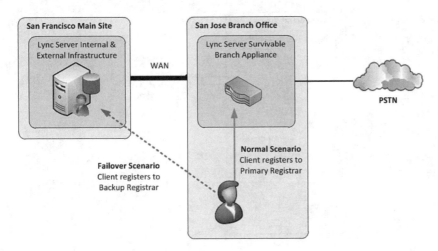

FIGURE 28.4   Branch Site Resilience

For branch office deployments of 25 to 1,000 users, dedicated hardware devices called *survivable branch appliances* are created by third-party Microsoft partners. These survivable branch appliances are similar to a survivable branch server, but include a registrar service, Mediation server, and IP/PSTN gateway all in one hardware device. These devices are typically more economical than deploying a separate server and IP/PSTN gateway, so it makes sense to leverage these devices in small branch offices. Like the survivable branch server, users in the branch office use the survivable branch appliance as the primary registrar service.

In the event of a WAN outage, users in branch sites will have continued voice services through the use of a survivable branch server or appliance because the primary registrar service is local to the site. Not all features are available to users when the WAN link is unavailable. Figure 28.5 shows how a branch office user remains connected to their local registrar service when a WAN link is unavailable.

The features available during a WAN outage include

▶ **PSTN Calls**—Inbound and outbound calls are possible because the local IP/PSTN gateway is available and not dependent on the WAN link.

▶ **Internal Calls**—Internal voice calls between users within the branch site have no issues. Calls to users in another site must leverage PSTN rerouting to be completed.

▶ **Call Control**—Users are able to use basic call features such as hold and transfer. Advanced features such as call forwarding, simultaneous ringing, and team call are also available in a failover scenario.

▶ **Instant Messaging**—Instant messaging services are available, but only between two parties within the branch site. No instant messaging conferencing services are available.

28

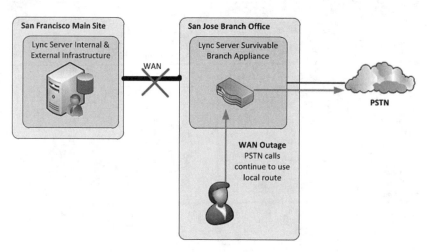

FIGURE 28.5   Branch Site WAN Outage

▸ **Audio/Video Calls**—Audio and video calls are between two parties only within the branch site. Audio/video conferencing services are unavailable.

▸ **Call Detail Records**—Call detail records continue to queue on the primary registrar and are delivered after the WAN link is restored.

▸ **Audio Conferencing**—Audio conferencing attendants can be used, but only by dialing the PSTN access numbers so that calls are routed through the local PSTN gateway to their associated datacenter site.

▸ **Voicemail Retrieval**—Assuming the Exchange infrastructure exists in a primary datacenter, users can still dial the PSTN number for Outlook Voice Access to retrieve voicemail.

▸ **Voicemail Deposit**—Assuming the Exchange infrastructure exists in a primary datacenter, survivable branch servers and appliances can reroute voicemail delivery across the PSTN. This is an Exchange Unified Messaging directory auto attendant that only accepts voicemail and does not allow transfer to users.

Features that are unavailable to users in a failover scenario include

▸ **Cross-Site Communication**—Any form of communication to other sites is unavailable.

▸ **Conferencing**—Any type of conferencing is unavailable. This applies to instant message, meeting, and audio/video conferences involving more than two parties because the multipoint control units (MCUs) exist at the datacenter pool where user accounts are homed.

▸ **Presence Based Routing**—Because presence data is unavailable, calls to users homed on the inaccessible pool across the WAN link will not have calls routed around this presence. For example, if a user sets the status to Do Not Disturb, instant message and phone calls will still be delivered.

- ► **Call Park**—Parking calls are unavailable to users homed on the pool, which is inaccessible across the WAN link.

- ► **Response Group Service**—Any workflows and queues associated with the pool across the WAN link are unavailable.

- ► **Call Forwarding Settings**—Although call forwarding capabilities remain in effect during a failover, users are unable to update or change their call forwarding settings.

In the event of the pool, survivable branch server, or survivable branch appliance in the branch site becoming unavailable, users will begin to use the backup registrar service located across the WAN link. In this scenario, users will not experience any loss in functionality. There might be additional bandwidth used on the WAN link, but clients can still access the PSTN through IP/PSTN gateways located in the backup site.

Network Configuration

Planning the network configuration first is key when beginning to plan for Call Admission Control, Media Bypass, or Enhanced 911 services in Lync Server 2010. Each of these components relies on network regions, sites, and links to be configured correctly before they can be enabled. The definition of each region, sites, and subnets might seem overwhelming at first, but it offers quite a bit of flexibility and control over call routing.

There are a few basic components that must first be understood when planning for these services:

- ► **Regions**—Network regions are the backbone of a network. Each network region must be associated with a Lync Server central site defined within the topology. This is a site where Lync Front End Servers are deployed and users are homed. Network regions are typically a hub where many other network sites are connected. Examples of regions are North America and Europe, or even on a smaller scale such as West Coast and East Coast.

- ► **Sites**—Each network region consists of at least one site and possibly many more. *Sites* are offices or locations that are associated with the major network region. In other words, all the offices or locations that have users homed in the central site for the region should be created as sites. This site definition should not be confused with the central site to which the network region was associated. In fact, a network site object should also be created for the central site if users or voice gateways are physically located there. This might seem redundant, but is required for appropriate routing.

- ► **Subnets**—Each site defined should contain at least one subnet definition. Each subnet used at a site should be entered and associated with the correct site. Lync endpoints are associated with a site and region by matching to a subnet defined

28

here. The Call Admission Control and Media Bypass features rely on matching the subnet of the IP/PSTN gateway to callers, so be sure to include the subnets used for voice hardware.

▶ **Bandwidth Policy Profiles**—Bandwidth policy profiles define a network link speed and the available bandwidth for audio or video calls. Both the individual session limit (two-way) can be specified as well as the total amount of bandwidth used for audio and video traffic. Bandwidth policy profiles are associated with a site or region link. Sites do not require a bandwidth policy profile to be assigned. In fact, if sites within a region are not bandwidth constrained, no profile should be assigned. Assign bandwidth policy profiles only to sites that should have their audio and video WAN usage limited.

▶ **Region Links**—When multiple regions exist, and by definition a region is multiple Front End pools with different central sites, region links should be defined that identify the amount of bandwidth available between regions. When defining a region link two regions are required as well as a bandwidth policy profile to apply between the two regions.

▶ **Region Route**—A region route specifies how two regions should be connected. In many cases, a region route mimics a region link and can just be between two different regions. In other cases where two regions are not directly linked, but share a link to a common region, a region route defines how these regions must traverse the common region to communicate. In that case, two different region links must be crossed, which might each have a different bandwidth policy profile.

▶ **Site Link**—The final component of the network configuration is a site link. In most cases, sites are connected to a network region directly, which acts as a hub for the users. There might be instances where in addition to a connection to the network region central site, sites have a direct connection to each other that bypasses the central site. Site links are used to create these objects that can then have a bandwidth policy profile associated.

Figure 28.6 depicts a sample configuration. The definition of each component will vary based on the organization.

Call Admission Control

Planning to deploy call admission control features in Lync Server 2010 is going to depend greatly on the network configuration discussed in the previous section. The basis for this is because this feature relies heavily on locating an endpoint based on subnet and then applying policies appropriately. Call Admission Control in Lync Server 2010 applies to both audio and video traffic, but organizations can specify different limits for each type of traffic. Both a session limit (two-way traffic) and a total limit for all sessions can be specified.

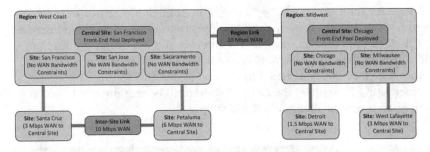

FIGURE 28.6   Network Configuration Example

The key to successful Call Admission Control deployment is to correctly define and associate the bandwidth policy profiles to sites and links by completing the following steps:

1. Identify the connection speed of each WAN link to sites that are bandwidth constrained.

2. Define the maximum audio and video session and total bandwidth limits to be used by Lync endpoints associated with site and policy. These limits vary based on the desired traffic type and the different audio codecs used.

3. Evaluate the site and make some estimates on the type of audio codecs used to create an appropriate limit. For example, if users make several Lync-to-Lync calls, RTAudio is predominantly used. If most calls are conferences, Siren might be more prevalent.

Bandwidth Estimates

Table 28.2 defines the various bandwidth estimates for each protocol. Usually the typical bandwidth usage values can be used for planning purposes. Forward error correction (FEC) is enabled when Lync clients detect poor network connectivity and attempts to provide a more resilient voice connection to combat network jitter or latency.

TABLE 28.2   Bandwidth Codec Estimates

Codec	Planning Value	Maximum Bandwidth without FEC	Maximum Bandwidth with FEC
RTAudio (Narrowband)	26 kbps	40 kbps	52 kbps
RTAudio (Wideband)	35 kbps	57 kbps	86 kbps
Siren	22 kbps	52 kbps	68 kbps
G.711	60 kbps	92 kbps	156 kbps
RTVideo (CIF)	203 kbps	250 kbps	N/A
RTVideo (VGA)	492 kbps	600 kbps	N/A

28

When a bandwidth policy limit is exceeded by a user, Call Admission Control kicks in with an attempt to reroute the call. First, the call attempts to be directed over the Internet. Instead of using the WAN link, the call traverses the Internet and Edge infrastructure. If that is not possible or fails, the call can reroute across the PSTN. Whether this is allowed depends on whether the voice policy assigned to the user allows this feature. If neither Internet nor PSTN rerouting is possible, the call will attempt to be sent directly to voicemail. Lastly, if voicemail is unavailable, the call will simply fail.

> **NOTE**
>
> Whether PSTN rerouting or bandwidth policy override is allowed for a call depends on the voice policy of the user *receiving* the call. Enable these features carefully because they can have a significant effect on how calls are routed. If limiting the WAN bandwidth with a policy is in effect, be sure the local IP/PSTN gateway can support the number of calls expected to be rerouted when enabling PSTN rerouting.

It is also important to note that Call Admission Control only applies to Lync Server endpoints traversing a WAN link. Other applications transmitting data on the same WAN link are not affected by Lync Call Admission Control policies. Organizations can define a bandwidth limit for Lync traffic and still see that WAN link become saturated due to other applications. In this scenario, it makes sense to enforce QoS policies on the WAN link to ensure Lync endpoints can always place calls.

The bandwidth override policy is enforced by the receiving endpoint and not the sender. When a call is placed, the receiving endpoint leverages its subnet information and checks whether the call will exceed the bandwidth policy limit. If not, the call will be allowed.

The only clients that actually respect Call Admission Control policies are Lync 2010 endpoints. Earlier clients, such as Office Communicator 2007 R2, are not able to perform a bandwidth check when a Lync client calls. However, media calls from Office Communicator 2007 R2 to a Lync endpoint enforce Call Admission Control policies.

Media Bypass

Planning for Media Bypass is not too complicated because it only encompasses identifying which IP/PSTN gateways in the organization support the feature and then configuring the trunks appropriately to enable the support. The majority of the configuration typically involves defining the network topology correctly. Media bypass enables a Lync endpoint to communicate directly with an IP/PSTN gateway, bypassing the Mediation server role. Figure 28.7 displays how a user's signaling traffic continues to flow through the server to the IP/PSTN gateway, but the actual audio stream is sent from the user directly to the IP/PSTN gateway.

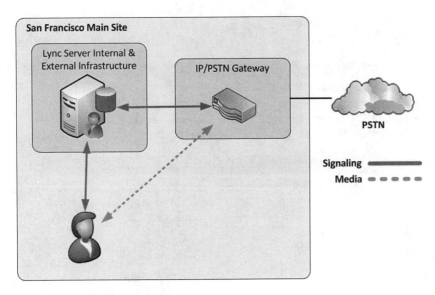

FIGURE 28.7   Media Bypass

Media Bypass is especially useful in branch office scenarios where no Mediation server is present, but a local IP/PSTN gateway exists. Without Media Bypass, calls are sent across a WAN link to a Mediation server at the central site, transcoded to G.711, and then sent back across the WAN link to the IP/PSTN gateway. With media bypass, endpoints can send the G.711 audio directly to the IP/PSTN gateway without traversing the WAN.

> **NOTE**
>
> Signaling traffic still flows across the WAN link in a Media Bypass scenario, but the audio media stream, which accounts for the majority of the bandwidth, does not.

Bypass IDs

Media Bypass works by assigning a unique Bypass ID to each location, and each subnet associated with that location automatically inherits the same Bypass ID. When a Lync endpoint attempts a call, the subnet of the endpoint is examined. If the Bypass ID of the subnet matches the Bypass ID of the subnet where the IP/PSTN gateway resides, Media Bypass will be leveraged.

The same concept applies for inbound calls from the PSTN. When the IP/PSTN gateway receives a call and sees an endpoint with a matching Bypass ID, the audio flows directly to the Lync client. Using the network configuration example in Figure 28.8, the San Francisco, San Jose, and Sacramento sites share a Bypass ID because they are not band-width constrained. The Santa Cruz and Petaluma sites each receive a unique ID because they have WAN bandwidth limitations.

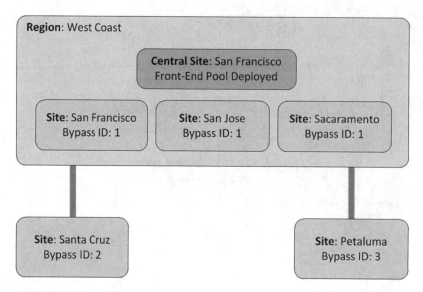

FIGURE 28.8   Media Bypass IDs

The terminology location used here is intentional. A unique Bypass ID does not necessarily get assigned to each network region or site. Any network region with sites that
have no bandwidth policy profile assigned share the same Bypass ID. This is because
without a policy applied, it is assumed all subnets have sufficient bandwidth between
each other and Bypass can be used from any endpoint to any IP/PSTN gateway.

If a site does have a bandwidth policy profile assigned because WAN bandwidth is limited,
a new Bypass ID is generated for the site. Users placing calls from within the bandwidth-
constrained site are allowed to use Media Bypass to a local IP/PSTN gateway. When users
attempt a call from a subnet with a different Bypass ID, Media Bypass is not allowed and
the audio flows through a Mediation server. Figure 28.9 shows how a user can leverage
Media Bypass in a local office, but be forced to send media through a Mediation server in
the Santa Cruz office across a constrained WAN link. This is because the bypass ID of the
user's endpoint does not match the Bypass ID of the gateway in the Santa Cruz site.

Lync Server 2010 assigns Bypass IDs automatically. These do not need to be created
or managed by an administrator.

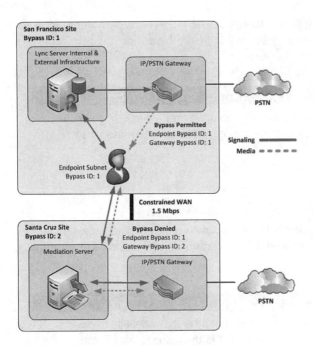

FIGURE 28.9   Media Bypass Example

Enabling Media Bypass

After the network components are in place, an organization has two choices when enabling Media Bypass support:

▶ **Always Bypass**—This setting indicates endpoints should attempt to use Media Bypass with IP/PSTN gateways at all times. This configuration is useful for simple, small deployments where control over when Bypass use is not required. When a call is routed to a trunk with the Enable Media Bypass option selected, Lync endpoints bypass the Mediation server role. All sites and subnets are mapped to a single Bypass ID with this setting. This option cannot be selected if Call Admission Control is also used. This is because bandwidth policy profiles are not applied when bypassing a Mediation server. Media Bypass should only be used in scenarios where WAN bandwidth is not an issue, so it is assumed there is no need to check for available bandwidth.

▶ **Use Site and Region Information**—This setting enables Media Bypass based on scenarios defined in the network configuration. The actual values in the bandwidth policy profiles are not important with this option, but the profiles are used to determine when Bypass should be used. If there is any bandwidth policy profile assigned to a site or link, it will be assigned a unique Bypass ID. Subnets within the site have a matching Bypass ID so that only endpoints within the site are allowed to use Media Bypass with the IP/PSTN gateways in that location.

The final step in configuring Media Bypass is to ensure the IP/PSTN gateways used in each location supports Media Bypass. Also be sure to enable Media Bypass on the trunk configuration used with each IP/PSTN gateway.

> **NOTE**
>
> Many Internet Telephony Service Providers accept calls from only a single IP address. For this reason, it is important to verify that the provider will support Bypass when using SIP trunking.

Enhanced 911

Lync Server 2010 has the capability to provide location information to an Emergency Services Service Provider through the network configuration objects and a location information database.

> **CAUTION**
>
> It is important to clarify that Lync Server 2010 does not have the capability to contact a Public Safety Access Point (PSAP) directly. Instead, it is the responsibility of the Emergency Services Service Provider to route the emergency calls to the correct PSAP.

Lync Server 2010 provides an endpoint's location to the Emergency Services Service Provider that can then use that location information to route the call correctly. Figure 28.10 displays the process that occurs when an emergency call is placed from a Lync endpoint.

Lync identifies an endpoint's physical location by examining the network subnet, switch, and wireless access point the client uses. This database of network objects must be populated by administrators and each object associated with a physical location in advance of enabling E911.

Location Policies

When planning for Enhanced 911 services, an organization must first identify where E911 will be deployed. This might only be within a primary site, multiple sites, or extended to branch sites. When planning E911 for branch sites, be sure to consider scenarios where a WAN link is unavailable. It is possible that branch or remote sites will not be able to provide location information or even contact an Emergency Services Service Provider without a resilient WAN link.

Location policies should be created for each set of unique requirements. If not all users are enabled for E911, a separate site or user policy should be created and assigned. Location policies also control whether an internal security desk is notified or conferenced in when an emergency services call is placed.

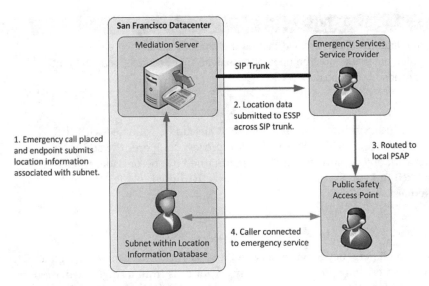

FIGURE 28.10 Enhanced 911

TIP

Expanding E911 support to remote users can also be a tricky subject because Internet users can connect from any physical location. If Enhanced 911 service is a legal or corporation requirement, organizations should adjust the location policy for users to require a disclaimer when selecting a location. Using a disclaimer requires users to enter a physical address for their location before they can place calls.

Location Information Database

After identifying the location policies, the next step in deploying E911 is to populate the location information database. This database can be populated manually or can be linked to a secondary location information database if one already exists. For Lync Server 2010 to use a secondary location information database, the service must adhere to the Lync Server 2010 Request/Response schema.

If manually populating the location database, start by identifying each of the network access points, switches, and subnets within the organization and the physical location associated with each object. This identification is, unfortunately, separate from the objects defined in the network configuration and relates only to the location information database. When determining an endpoint's location, Lync Server 2010 first uses the wireless access point, and then the switch ID, and lastly a subnet to determine location. This is because each of these items can potentially span multiple rooms or floors in a building, so none is an exact location.

28

NOTE

After creating the database, keep in mind that as the network expands or changes, the location information database must be updated to ensure that accurate location information can be provided by endpoints.

After populating the location information database, it should be validated with the Emergency Services Service Provider. This validation process compares the addresses associated to each network object with the database maintained by the provider to ensure each location entered in Lync Server 2010 can be correctly routed to a PSAP, which can respond to the request.

SIP Trunk

The connection to the Emergency Services Service Provider is accomplished through a dedicated SIP trunk. Emergency providers can only accept calls from a single Mediation server, so if a pool of Mediation servers exists already, an additional, standalone Mediation server must be deployed to support E911 to the Emergency Services Service Provider.

To provide resiliency for E911, an additional SIP trunk to a different Mediation server must be provisioned. This ensures that if the primary SIP trunk or Mediation server is unavailable, E911 calls can still be delivered correctly. This additional trunk can be in the same location or, ideally, in a different site, to ensure site survivability. When provisioning the SIP trunk, a VPN tunnel to the Emergency Services Service Provider is created using an existing Internet connection, or a dedicated connection can be provisioned to separate and isolate the emergency calls.

The final consideration with the SIP trunk is to recognize it does not bypass Call Admission Control policies. If a bandwidth policy is exceeded by an emergency call, the call will not succeed. When planning for E911, be sure to consider the effects of Call Admission Control on where SIP trunks to an Emergency Services Service Provider are placed. For example, in a site where WAN bandwidth is constrained, it makes sense to deploy a local Mediation server and SIP trunk to a provider to ensure Call Admission Controls never prevent an emergency call across the WAN link.

Devices

After planning the necessary infrastructure components in a Lync Server 2010 deployment, remember that end users in the environment invest some time planning what the experience will be for them. The devices deployed alongside the Lync Server 2010 infrastructure have a big impact on how the project is accepted and viewed by an organization.

Analog

Lync Server 2010 has introduced support for analog devices, which was a feature lacking from Office Communications Server 2007 R2. There are many scenarios where it is simply not possible to remove the requirement for analog devices such as with fax machines, PA systems, or elevator phones. These devices are all analog based and there is no equivalent in Lync Server 2010 to replace them.

TIP

Analog devices are not intended to be deployed to user accounts for Enterprise Voice. Therefore, organizations should invest in a handset or headset for Enterprise Voice users.

To support these devices, an Analog Telephone Adapter (ATA) is required. Analog devices can be connected to an IP/PSTN gateway or survivable branch appliance that supports analog ports. On the server side, a SIP-enabled contact object is created to represent the analog device. Just like with a user account, a voice policy consisting of allowed PSTN usages can be assigned to the contact object and control the features that each analog device is allowed to use. Figure 28.11 demonstrates how analog devices are integrated with a Lync deployment through physical ports on an IP/PSTN gateway.

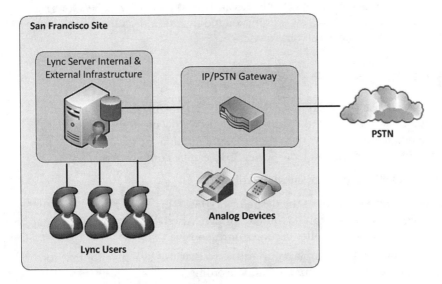

FIGURE 28.11   Analog Device Support

Because analog devices do not register to a Lync Front End pool, the IP/PSTN gateway or survivable branch appliance provides an interface to associate each analog port with a specified Line URI. Outbound calls from the port use the assigned Line URI, and inbound calls to the Line URI are routed to the associated port.

Handsets and Headsets

Each user enabled for Enterprise Voice services with Lync Server 2010 require an optimized audio device to ensure a good end-user experience. Enabling Enterprise Voice for users enables them to begin placing and receiving calls using the built-in speakers and microphone. However, these calls do not sound good for either party involved.

Using an optimized device enhances the user experience by ensuring that echo and background noise are reduced to a minimum. Many headset and handset options exist for an organization and it is likely that many different devices will be selected. Organizations might standardize on a few specific models, but different levels of users might require different feature sets. For example, users primarily in the office and not making many calls generally prefer a stationary handset, whereas customer service representatives on the phone all day might prefer a hands-free headset. Remote or mobile workers also tend to prefer headset devices, which are more portable and enable them to use a high-quality device regardless of location.

After distributing optimized audio devices to end users, it is important to provide end-user training for how to use these devices effectively. Because most users new to Enterprise Voice are not familiar with these devices, training should include a discussion of the functionality and flexibility available with voice services.

Response Groups

Before configuring Response Groups in Lync Server 2010, an organization should run through a number of planning steps to ensure that the workflow creation is as easy as possible. When a completed workflow diagram and configuration are created in advance, the actual creation of the workflow in Lync Server 2010 can be completed quickly.

The following steps ease the process of creating workflows:

1. Begin by developing a diagram of the desired workflow. This should include all the possible call flows that a user can be routed through. Also be sure to include scenarios for what happens when a caller becomes unresponsive.

2. Document the exact text that is played to callers so that it is available for text-to-speech translation or to be read for an audio recording.

3. If using audio files, identify a user who is responsible for the recording or hire a professional agency to create the recording.

4. Identify the queues required within the workflow. The queue planning phase should include specifying how many concurrent calls can exist within a queue and what action should be taken when the queue reaches capacity. If sending calls to a

voicemail box, be sure that the mailbox is monitored in some way so that callers leaving a message receive a response.

5. Identify the different agent groups that will belong to the queues and the individual agents. Ensure agents are aware they belong to an agent group and are trained on how to handle calls. If using formal groups, make sure agents understand how to log in and out of the group to take calls.

6. Identify what business hours and holiday schedules will affect the workflow.

7. After collecting all the required information, proceed with creating the agent groups, queues, and workflow objects.

8. Thoroughly test the Response Group workflow. This should involve traversing every possible option within the workflow to ensure callers are routed correctly and never unexpectedly disconnected.

9. Perform any adjustments necessary to the workflow before placing it in production and allowing external callers to reach the workflow.

Planning Tool

Microsoft offers a free official Lync Server 2010 Planning Tool application, which can be used to suggest the required server infrastructure based on a number of questions. This tool does not take every scenario into account, but does provide a great starting point when planning a new deployment. Questions regarding user count, expected PSTN usage, and bandwidth estimates are asked along with questions about WAN connections and what kind of PSTN connectivity will exist.

At the end of the question section, a suggested topology displays for each site. Administrators can also enter IP address information and receive a detailed firewall requirements document. The entire topology can even be exported directly to Microsoft Visio or to the Lync Server 2010 Topology Builder to begin a deployment.

Best Practices

The following are best practices from this chapter:

▶ Create a dial plan in advance. Identify all required normalization rules and user dialing habits.

▶ Plan the voice policies, PSTN usages, and routes to match the different levels of service required to each user.

▶ Use existing data to analyze PSTN usage in order to estimate IP/PSTN port requirements.

▶ Assign a backup registrar to pools where voice resiliency is required.

▶ Deploy survivable branch servers or survivable branch appliances in branch offices without resilient WAN links.

▶ Complete the network configuration before attempting to enable Call Admission Control, Media Bypass, or Enhanced 911.

▶ Apply appropriate bandwidth policy limits to sites where WAN bandwidth is constrained.

▶ Use Media Bypass whenever possible to reduce the processing requirements on the Mediation Server role.

▶ Validate all addresses in the location information database before deploying Enhanced 911.

▶ Train users on the new devices and features they will experience with Enterprise Voice.

▶ Outline Response Group workflows, queues, and agent groups before attempting to create the objects in Lync Server 2010.

▶ Leverage the Lync Server 2010 Planning Tool prior to beginning a deployment in order to create a base configuration.

Summary

As with any major deployment, a good deal of advance planning and analysis before building a system always makes the implementation a bit smoother. Correctly identifying all the components required and how each component should function within the system directly maps to how the Lync Server 2010 topology should be configured.

When planning for coexistence or migration from an existing PBX, spend time developing a dial plan that works between the two systems. Ensure the dial plan contains all normalization rules required for users and that voice routing is configured to meet the needs of the organization. If voice resilience is required, make a decision on what type of resilience is offered and communicate what features are actually available in a failover scenario.

The advanced voice features such as Call Admission Control, Media Bypass, and Enhanced 911 offer some significant features, but do require some up-front planning and preparation before they can be enabled or expected to work correctly. This planning likely involves network teams to determine existing WAN links, bandwidth capacity, and traffic usage.

Planning for Lync Server 2010 voice services is a major exercise because voice is so critical to every organization. As long as organizations spend the appropriate time planning and developing a migration strategy, the project should be a success.

Index

Numbers

A

How can we make this index more useful? Email us at indexes@samspublishing.com

How can we make this index more useful? Email us at indexes@samspublishing.com

J–K

L

M

O

P

How can we make this index more useful? Email us at indexes@samspublishing.com

UNLEASHED

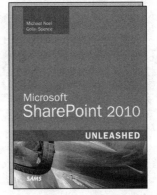

Microsoft SharePoint 2010 Unleashed
ISBN-13: 9780672333255

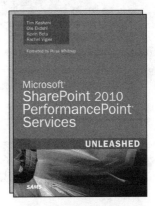

Microsoft SharePoint 2010 PerformancePoint Services Unleashed
ISBN-13: 9780672330940

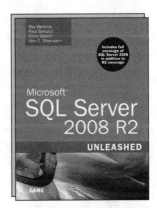

Microsoft SQL Server 2008 R2 Unleashed
ISBN-13: 9780672330568

SAMS

informit.com/sams

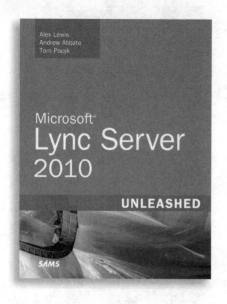

FREE Online Edition

Your purchase of **Microsoft® Lync Server 2010 Unleashed** includes access to a free online edition for 45 days through the Safari Books Online subscription service. Nearly every Sams book is available online through Safari Books Online, along with more than 5,000 other technical books and videos from publishers such as Addison-Wesley Professional, Cisco Press, Exam Cram, IBM Press, O'Reilly, Prentice Hall, and Que.

SAFARI BOOKS ONLINE allows you to search for a specific answer, cut and paste code, download chapters, and stay current with emerging technologies.

Activate your FREE Online Edition at
www.informit.com/safarifree

> **STEP 1:** Enter the coupon code: FZSSREH.

> **STEP 2:** New Safari users, complete the brief registration form.
> Safari subscribers, just log in.

Addison Wesley   Adobe Press   ALPHA   Cisco Press   FT Press   IBM Press   lynda.com   Microsoft Press   New Riders

O'REILLY   Peachpit Press   Que   Redbooks   SAMS   SAS Publishing   Sun microsystems   Wharton School Publishing   WILEY